# 2016/17
# FACTS & FIGURES

### TABLES FOR THE CALCULATION OF DAMAGES

# 2016/17 FACTS & FIGURES

## TABLES FOR THE CALCULATION OF DAMAGES

Compiled and Edited by:

**Members of the
Professional Negligence Bar Association**

**General Editor: Robin de Wilde QC**

Editors:

Chris Daykin CB FIA
Peter Jennings
Simon Levene
Tejina Mangat
Harry Trusted
and
Maurice Faull FCA MAE
(Forensic Accountant)

SWEET & MAXWELL

Published in 2016 by Thomson Reuters (Professional) UK Limited
trading as Sweet & Maxwell, Friars House, 160 Blackfriars Road, London, SE1 8EZ
(Registered in England & Wales, Company No 1679046.
Registered Office and address for service:
2nd floor, Aldgate House, 33 Aldgate High Street, London EC3N 1DL)

Designed and typeset by Wright & Round Ltd, Gloucestershire
Printed and bound in Great Britain by Ashford Colour Press, Gosport, Hants

No natural forests were destroyed to make this product; only farmed timber was used and re-planted.

ISBN 978-0-414-05980-1

A CIP catalogue record for this book is available from the British Library.

All rights reserved. Crown Copyright material is reproduced with the permission of the Controller of HMSO and the Queen's Printer for Scotland.

No part of this publication may be reproduced or transmitted in any form or by any means, or stored in any retrieval system of any nature without prior written permission, except for permitted fair dealing under the Copyright, Designs and Patents Act 1988, or in accordance with the terms of a licence issued by the Copyright Licensing Agency in respect of photocopying and/or reprographic reproduction. Application for permission for other use of copyright material including permissions to reproduce extracts in other published works shall be made to the publishers. Full acknowledgement of author, publisher and source must be given.

Material is contained in this publication for which publishing permission has been sought, and for which copyright is acknowledged. Permission to reproduce such material cannot be granted by the publishers and application must be made to the copyright holder.

© Professional Negligence Bar Association 2016

# ACKNOWLEDGMENTS

We are very grateful to the following contributors:

- Adrian Gallop of the Government Actuary's Department for his assistance in preparing *Section A: Ogden Tables & Related Material.*

- Maurice Faull's team at Hilton Sharp & Clarke Forensic Accountants, who have helped with the meticulous preparation and updating of annually changing tables at *C1–C5, D1–D3, E1–E2, F1–F3, F5–F6, F8, G1–G5, H1–H3* and *L2*, and for preparing and/or checking the calculations at *A1, A2* and *A4*.

- Dr Victoria Wass of Cardiff Business School for updating *Section B6: Step-by-step guide to finding the annual estimates for hourly pay in ASHE SOC 2000 6115* and for providing the guide to the ASHE earnings tables at *F7: Average Earning Statistics* and her input into *F4*.

- Rodney Nelson Jones of Field Fisher Waterhouse and Lexis Nexis for allowing us to use and to develop his table for the calculation of special damages interest in *C4: Special and General Damages Interest.*

- Lynn Bourne of Keith Carter & Associates for the research undertaken for the preparation of the tables F4 and F7 in *Section F: Earnings.*

- Melissa Chapman and the Family Law Bar Association for their permission to use table *I1 & I2: Social Security Benefits* and *I5: Foster Care Allowances* taken from At A Glance.

- Lynne Bradey and Austin Thornton of Wrigleys for preparing *I3: Personal Injury Trusts.*

- Hugh Jones of Hugh Jones Solicitors for *J1: Note on the Court of Protection.*

- Adrian Mundell of Ashton KCJ, for *J2: The Incidence of Deputyship Costs* over a Claimant's Life and *J3: Deputyship Costs.*

- Alison Somek of Somek & Associates Ltd and James Rowley QC of Byrom Street Chambers, for their work on *K1: Care and Attendance.*

- Nicholas Leviseur for preparing the notes for *L3: Motability Scheme.*

- Margaret McDonald, specialist costs counsel of Kenworthy's Chambers, for permission to reproduce her table of *Senior Court Costs Office Guideline Rates for Summary Assessment* at *M1*.

We are very grateful to the following organisations for kindly granting us permission to use their material:

- The HMSO for their permission to use *Table A3: Life Tables, Table A8: The Ogden Tables, Table C2: Real and Nominal Interest Rates and Price Inflation, Table F5: Average Weekly Earnings Index, Table F6: Average Weekly Earnings, Table F7: Average Earnings Statistics* and the material from the NHS leaflet HC12, NHS charges. Crown Copyright is reproduced with the permission of HMSO.

Acknowledgments

- HM Revenue & Customs and HMSO for their permission to use the material in *Table L2: Taxation of Car and Fuel Benefits*.

- Sweet & Maxwell for their permission to use the tables from *Kemp & Kemp: The Quantum of Damages* at *C3: Special Investment Account Rates*, *C8: Judgment Debt Interest Rates*, *E1: Retail Prices Index* and *E2: Inflation Table*.

- W. Green for their permission to use *Table C9: Judicial Rates of Interest*.

- FTSE Russell for their permission to use the FTSE 100 Index at *Table D1: Share Price Index*.

- Halifax for providing the up-to-date material for *Table E3: House Price Indices* and *Table E4: Average semi-detached house prices by region*.

- Intuition Communication Ltd for their permission to reproduce figures from their website *www.privatehealth.co.uk* at *K4: Hospital self-pay (uninsured) charges*.

- Bodily Injury Claims Management Association for their permission to produce the Code of Best Practice on Rehabilitation at *K6: The 2007 Rehabilitation Code* and *K7*.

- APIL for their permission to reproduce the APIL Serious Injury Guide at *K8: APIL Serious Injury Guide*.

- The Automobile Association for their permission to use the AA figures in *Table L1: Motoring Costs*.

- The RAC Motoring Services in conjunction with Emmerson Hill Associates who compiled the illustrative motorcycle running costs at *L1: Motoring Costs*.

- Bauer Media, publishers of Parker's Car Price Guide upon whose figures the calculations in *Table L4: Calculations Involving Cars* are based.

- Collins Debden Australia for their permission to reproduce the perpetual calendar, as featured in the International Management Diary, at *Table M3: Perpetual Calendar*.

# FOREWORD TO THE FIRST EDITION

### by the Hon. Mr Justice Bell

The assessment of damages for personal injuries and consequential losses has become a matter of increasingly intricate calculation. Detailed schedules of damages and counter-schedules are vital to the proper portrayal of claim and defence to claim but they are arduous and time consuming to compile. Much the same building blocks of information and aids to calculation are required over and over again. This volume has gathered many of the most frequently used building blocks and aids together in a readily accessible form and those who prepare, argue and settle such cases should be grateful for it. Robin de Wilde and his committee have put a lot of work into what is in fact a manual of very practical assistance and they are to be congratulated on a new venture which should mature year by year with the help of your own suggestions.

May 1996

# INTRODUCTION TO THE TWENTY-FIRST EDITION

> "Then turned to me and noting one that brings
> With careless step a mist of shadowy things:
> Laughter and memories, and a few regrets,
> Some honour, and a quantity of debts,
> A doubt or two of sorts, a trust in God,
> And (what will seem to you extremely odd)
> His father's granfer's father's father's name,
> Unspoilt, untitled, even spelt the same:"
>
> Hilaire Belloc, "To Dives"

**Who we are**

We are the same people who set out on this voyage in 1996, save for the one retirement/replacement a few years ago. This year I am delighted to welcome Christopher Daykin, CB, FIA, some time Government Actuary. He is the second longest person serving in that office. He now works as an independent Consultant Actuary. He has, as a professional expert witness, laid several fruitful eggs that have hatched and come to glory in the Law Reports. He will ensure that we miss no significant Tables, particularly the Mortality Tables, as produced by the Office of National Statistics.

Doubtless his presence will add other benefits, not immediately appreciated, but which will be discovered during the course of each year, as we attempt to keep up with the changing face of the calculation of damages, whether in the field of personal injuries or elsewhere. I have received a number of indications that in the calculation of damages other practitioners in different fields have also found advantage in the use of these Tables.

I have not received any correspondence this year, which is either a good sign, such that it suggests that we have not had any serious or fundamental mistakes discovered, or it may be that no one has actually missed such mistakes as have appeared, which is a far more likely explanation.

It becomes crucially important in a book of this style, that everyone should know from whence we derive the information contained in it, so that it can be looked up and checked.

**The purpose**

This continues to be intended as a handy book of reference, which may be carried by the practitioner to some obscure County Court (if there are any left) to be cited to a District or County Court Judge, whose experience prior to appointment was entirely based on his or her skill in Rating Cases.

**The Schedule of Damages**

This is still as important, as it ever was, and should set out all the heads of claim, whatever they may be, together with the calculations based on the evidence which may or may not exist, to support those claims. Evidence is usually in writing, but it can clearly be anything that you can feel, see or touch, and when it comes to human behaviour, that is often made manifest either in the Witness Statements or what the judge may perceive from the view that he or she has of a witness giving evidence in court.

Introduction to the Twenty-First Edition

The importance of careful gathering of such evidence is still crucial, and depends on the instructing solicitor and his/her awareness and subtlety in preparing such evidence for presentation to the court. When counsel is used, then the skill and thought behind the preparation of the evidence should be a joint effort, so that the best may be made of any case that it is wished to present. This process is not only a legal skill but may even be the human ability to appreciate that the claimant is no longer the person that he or she once was.

Often, to demonstrate the change in personality or behaviour is something that can be measured, as we continue to learn how human behaviour and conduct is often determined by what takes place in the brain. The neurologists, neuro-psychiatrist, and neuro-psychologist can be of great value in that difficult and troublesome area. A member of the family may say: "he hasn't been the same since the accident . . . ", but it can now be measured and understood, and scans may even show which areas of the brain have been affected. Up until about 1990, days, sometimes weeks, would be spent by experts giving evidence to a court in attempting to determine when a baby was brain damaged; but, as a result of scanning, a neuro-radiologist is now able to identify exactly when, in the birth process, the damage had occurred. More is being learned every year!

To that end, I commend a book, recently published in paperback, entitled *It's All in Your Head*, subtitled "True Stories of Imaginary Illness", by Dr Suzanne O'Sullivan, a consultant neurologist at Queen Square, specialising in clinical neuro-psychology, who concentrates on "psychogenic disorders". It won the Wellcome Prize for the best medical book of 2016. It is in paperback through Vantage Books. On reflection, I have had three or four cases over the years that may have fallen into that category, where there was no other reasonable explanation as to what had happened to the lay client, which confused and astonished all the other experts who were concerned with the case.

We all need to know what is being discovered, not only from what is seen on television or the computer, but from asking the right experts to interpret what is now capable of being discovered and, sometimes, measured. Otherwise, we are nothing more than blind people wandering the streets when they are shrouded in fog.

**Causation**

Causation is difficult. Anyone who suggests otherwise is mad. However, the decision of the Privy Council in *Williams v The Bermuda Hospital Board*[1], the sole judgment by Lord Toulson, has made the almost scriptural subtleties of this area of law a little plainer. The facts are simple enough. The claimant was admitted to hospital with abdominal pain. He was suffering from acute appendicitis. He had an appendectomy but there were complications. He was seriously unwell for a period of weeks. His argument was that he had suffered complications from sepsis because of the delay in his treatment. That was found as a fact by the trial Judge, but he was persuaded to distinguish between a "guilty cause" and a "non-guilty cause". He failed to do so, as the Bermuda Court of Appeal found.

The trial judge found that there had been negligence but the claimant had failed to prove that the culpable delay caused the complications and damage complained of. The Bermuda Court of Appeal disagreed, reversing the trial judge's decision on both fact and causation. It was from that decision that the Hospital Board appealed to the Privy Council. The judge who gave the leading judgment, Lord Toulson, examined a number of old friends in this area from *Bonnington Castings Ltd v Wardlaw*[2], which was said to be the defendants' central point, where it was held that causation was insufficiently proved until it was found established, unless it came from two sources, one of them being noxious and the other non-causative. This was followed by an apposite quotation from the textbook by Professor Sarah Green where she is quoted as saying: "It is equally trite that, where a defendant has been found

---

[1] [2016] UKPC 4.
[2] [1956] AC 613.

to have caused or contributed to an indivisible injury, she will be held fully liable for it, even though there may well have been other contributing causes . . . ". Such a definition simplifies the whole murky issue of causation.

I think that Lord Toulson has made it clear that the apparent distinction between "guilty" and "non-guilty" cause or dust can no longer be permitted; however, once there is "some clear causal damage", depending on the trial judge's finding, then the answer will be final even if some equivalent of 'non-guilty cause (or dust)' is present. If my interpretation of this is correct, then there is one less feature to prevent sleepless nights in the course of satisfying the test for causation in the progress of a trial. Law is easy!

## The Ogden Tables return

In *Knauer v Ministry of Justice*[3], the Supreme Court sorted out a problem that had existed too long, when they decided that the point at issue in *Cookson v Knowles*[4] and *Graham v Dodd*[5] as to the proper approach of calculating the financial losses should be calculated from the date of death or the date of trial. The Law Commission in their report on *Claims for Wrongful Death*[6] had recommended the calculation of the multiplier from the date of trial, as such a method which was both fairer and more accurate. To do so, the argument being accepted that all the earlier decisions were wrong and to correct this the Supreme Court used the *1966 Practice Statement*. I have written about this particular issue before; it had gone on for too long, but the reality is that a "right facts" case is needed to invoke the process and though all the arguments were rehearsed for doing nothing, both parties, through their counsel, accepted that this was the way to sort out a long standing problem as to the correct method of discovering the proper multiplier.

All that is presently needed is some funding to update the Ogden Tables, which are now out of date, particularly in respect of the Life Expectation Tables.

## Dame Caroline Swift

It is with regret that I report that Dame Caroline Swift has retired from the Bench of the Queen's Bench Division after 10 years. At the Bar she had a stellar career and, having been Dame Janet Smith's pupil, continued to practise predominantly in the field of personal injury work and clinical negligence. She was the leading counsel to the Shipman Inquiry, which, for those who have lived in ignorance, was an inquiry into the activities of the late Dr Harold Shipman, the most prolific mass murderer so far known to have operated in Britain. It is thought that his final tally could have amounted to more than 250 deaths, but no one will ever know. That inquiry lasted more than four years.

After that inquiry she did not return to practice at the Bar, but was appointed to the Queen's Bench Division, where she added some notable decided cases to the body of learning on personal injury practice. One of her significant decisions was *Thompstone v Tameside*[7] the landmark decision on PPOs, linking care damages to ASHE 6115, which was appealed in many respects and the Court of Appeal upheld her on every point. Another noted case was the complex quantum case of *Whiten v St Georges Healthcare NHS Trust*[8]—the enormous quantum judgment touching life expectancy, numerous issues on care, and particularly issues on accommodation where she explained why parents should not be charged rent by their injured offspring when they bought a property and came down against a

---

[3] [2016] UKSC 9.
[4] [1979] AC 556.
[5] [1983] 1 WLR 808.
[6] (1999) (Law Comm No. 263).
[7] [2006] EWHC 2904.
[8] [2011] EWHC 2066.

hydro pool at home on the facts. It is thought that the care and attention to the complex detail of the case deterred the defendants from appealing further from her judgment. Another case which was complex was in *Jones v Secretary of State for Energy and Climate Change*[9]—the Phurmacite Litigation—333 pages of complete clarity in the judgment, especially the causation sections which have influenced later courts. Neither side felt they could successfully appeal.

At all times, she was regarded as being in control of what she did, and was always fair minded. On the Bench, her great skills were fairness, courtesy and thoroughness. Everyone knew they had received a fair trial—win or lose; she heard approval hearings with sensitivity and sympathy. There have been many other judges of whom the above could not be said! I know little of her private life; but, adapting what a philosopher once said, "may she enjoy cultivating her garden".

**Harvey McGregor QC**

His passing was noted in the obituary columns of many newspapers, quite rightly so. However, he had become a great friend of mine, and someone whom I consulted when I had a problem which I could not easily sort out. He was clever, literate, witty, irreverent and seriously musical. He did not take himself or anyone else seriously. He was a magnificent Warden of New College and those there during his period of office must have been stimulated by his presence. I have two strong memories. In his lodgings at New College, there were a pair of grand pianos facing each other. On the piano stools of each was a large teddy bear, and both were dressed with enormous scarlet bow ties.

The second recollection was following a meeting with a Government Actuary, who was being recalcitrant. After the meeting, we returned to have lunch together at the Bencher's Table of the Inner Temple. Another Bencher asked him why he was not wearing one of his splendid bow ties. His answer was simple but indicated how much he thought about the trivia as well as the big picture. He said: "Where Robin and I have been, it would not have been appropriate!" He twinkled at me and I laughed.

**How the other half lives**

It was reported in the press that the cost of the Wendy House belonging to two-year old Sophia Ecclestone, daughter of Formula One heiress Tamara, was £10,000. It is modelled on the family's 57-room, £70 million house in Kensington: it is double-fronted, made of red brick and has a large wooden door.

It was reported in the Sunday Times "Rich List" of 24 April 2016 that Bernie Ecclestone's estimated wealth has fallen by £460 million since last year. The "Formula One Boss", as the newspapers describe him, who is now believed to be worth £2.48 billion, has fallen nine places to 42nd in the annual index of the richest people in Britain. It is the largest drop in his wealth since his 2009 divorce settlement after splitting from his second wife, Slavica, whose wealth is now valued at £740m.

His position does not compare with the highest award in the personal injury world that I have been able to find in the United Kingdom, in respect of a case which occurred in 2012, when a settlement was agreed for £23 million for a grievously injured girl, Agnes Collier, 17, on 23 November 2012. She was left paralysed in all four limbs after the family Audi she was travelling in was forced into the path of a lorry after a BMW pulled out of a side road. Her mother Karen Hood was killed in the accident and Agnes, who was 13 at the time, sustained devastating spinal injuries. Despite the tragedy, Agnes was able to return to her school, Cheltenham Ladies' College, and passed her AS-level exams with flying colours. The teenager hoped to go on to university. Mr Justice Macduff approved her award of

---

[9] [2012] EWHC 2936.

a £7.25 million lump sum. She also received index-linked, tax-free payments of £270,000 a year to cover the costs of her care for the rest of her life. Outside court her solicitor said that, given a normal life expectancy, the total award is expected to reach £23 million.

I emphasise the contrast between Mr Ecclestone's wealth and that award, merely to draw attention to the disparity.

**New material**

We have been asked to include a new document, which we are only too happy to do—see Table K8, which relates to an agreement reached between APIL and FOIL which is entitled "A Guide to the Conduct of Cases involving Serious Injury". That there is agreement as to form and structure of handling serious cases is plainly a good thing. However, I confess to a small concern about the "cowboy firms" on both sides of the divide. Will it become a tool to make people behave properly?

That did not happen in the recently reported case of *Gavin Edmondson Solicitors Limited v Haven Insurance Company Ltd*[10] which indicated the sort of behaviour deprecated by the Court of Appeal. The insurance company sought to avoid paying the claimants' solicitors' costs on the ground that they had settled privately with each claimant, knowing that each claimant had signed a CFA with their solicitors. Equitable restitution was the answer!

**Appointment of a Lord Chancellor**

It is bizarre that we have now had three Lord Chancellors in a row without any previous history of legal qualifications whatsoever. It is a constitutional office of significance. The Lord Chancellor sat in the Cabinet. He was there to assist the Cabinet with the legality of their conduct, as well as preventing them from doing anything unlawful or unconstitutional. He was also required to maintain the independence of the judges and the court system. He was the Sovereign's conscience. This function derived from before the Bill of Rights of 1685 and was strengthened by subsequent practice. The system of justice was always intended to be and was independent of the government of the day and was to protect the courts and judges from any government interference.

The judges, the court system and those who operated it were to be seen and intended to be totally independent of the government. He appointed and protected the judges and the courts. That independence was maintained by the Courts Act of 1971, which was a part of the Lord Chancellor's Department, as was Legal Aid, from the passing of the Criminal Legal Aid Act of 1949 and subsequently the Civil Legal Aid of 1956.

The Law Officers of the Crown, that is the Attorney-General and the Solicitor-General, carry out the government's legal business, which includes prosecuting serious cases, both in civil and criminal matters and organising the prosecuting authorities, in serious cases, having the powers to stop prosecutions in the public interest. Effectively, they were there to see that the system, whether civil or criminal, was properly used. They also gave the government legal advice, though as we learn from Chilcot, not always followed or understood.

**Conclusion**

I try and deal with such correspondence and enquiries as appear, whether it be criticism or helpful suggestions.

---

[10] [2015] EWCA Civ 1230.

Introduction to the Twenty-First Edition

As always, I am grateful to everyone involved in assisting the core team and the publication in any way. We try to list everyone involved and their work is appreciated and recorded in the previous Acknowledgments page.

Robin de Wilde QC

218 Strand Chambers
Third Floor,
218 Strand
London WC2R 1AT

1 August 2016
rdewilde@clerksroom.com
T: 0845 083 3000
M: 07889 161 604

# INTRODUCTION TO THE FIRST EDITION

Schedules of Damages have become more complex. These tables are intended as an assistance to those who have to check the details which support a Schedule. The Tables themselves come from a variety of primary sources. In one volume they should be easier to use.

The task of compiling this volume has proved more onerous than any of the members of the Committee assigned to the task would have imagined. The discussions as to what should be included or excluded became intense. When dealing with comparative and comparable earnings, should not Mr Bernie Ecclestone of Formula One Promotions and International Sports World receive a mention? He was paid in 1993 the sum of £30,750,109 and became easily the highest paid director by £8,000,000 or so. He is not included in the Table of Comparable Earnings.

We are also conscious that the application of each Table may or may not be easy depending on the contents. We do not intend to triple the size of the volume by setting out worked examples, but would refer the reader to the appropriate text books. It is intended as a source book, easily to hand, so that the practitioner may find what is needed quickly and easily in a single volume.

As this is our first foray into the world of tables, we appreciate that some matters will have been omitted that should be included and some of that which is included should not be present. We rely on our readers to tell us what is wanted and needed, so that the next annual update can be improved. The intention is that each edition is published in late January or early February of each year, incorporating the declarations announced in the Budget in November the previous year.

We have plundered shamelessly from a variety of sources. The final stimulus has been the Family Law Bar Association's "At A Glance" annual publication, but it is designed for practitioners in a different world, facing other demands and needs.

We are also grateful to Mr Justice Bell, who attended the final Advisory Committee Meeting and agreed to write a Foreword to this venture.

We conclude with the thought expressed by the historian Edward Gibbon in *The Decline and Fall of the Roman Empire*, when he states in a footnote about one Emperor that:

> "Twenty-two acknowledged concubines and a library of sixty-two thousand volumes, attested the variety of his inclinations; and from the productions which he left behind him, it appears that the former as well as the latter were designed for use rather than ostentation."

These Tables, too, are designed for use rather than ostentation.

199 Strand  
London WC2R 1DR  
May 1996

Robin de Wilde, QC

# CONTENTS

**Group A—Ogden Tables and Related Materials**
A1  2.5 per cent discount tables "at a glance" .................................................................. 3
A2  Nil discount tables "at a glance" .............................................................................. 10
A3  Life tables and projected life tables ......................................................................... 17
A4  Loss of earnings multipliers adjusted for education, disability and employment status ...... 22
A5  Multipliers for fixed periods and at intervals ............................................................ 36
A6  Tables of deferred loss ............................................................................................ 42
A7  Table of adjustments to multiplier for Fatal Accidents Acts dependency .................... 46
A8  The Ogden Tables ................................................................................................... 48
A9  The Lord Chancellor's statement, 27 July 2001 ....................................................... 125

**Group B—Damages**
B1  General damages table following *Heil v Rankin* and *Simmons v Castle* ..................... 133
B2  Bereavement damages ............................................................................................ 137
B3  *Auty v National Coal Board* (pension claims) .......................................................... 138
B4  *Roberts v Johnstone* (accommodation claims) ......................................................... 139
B5  Periodical payments ................................................................................................ 140
B6  Step-by-step guide to finding the annual estimates for hourly pay in ASHE SOC 2000 6115 .. 142

**Group C—Interest Rates**
C1  Interest base rates .................................................................................................. 147
C2  Real and nominal interest rates and price inflation .................................................. 149
C3  Special investment account rates ............................................................................ 151
C4  Special and general damages interest ..................................................................... 152
C5  Base rate + 10 per cent .......................................................................................... 154
C6  Number of days between two dates ....................................................................... 156
C7  Decimal years ......................................................................................................... 157
C8  Judgment debt interest rates (England and Wales) .................................................. 158
C9  Judicial rates of interest (Scotland) .......................................................................... 158

**Group D—Investment**
D1  Share price index (FTSE 100) ................................................................................. 161
D2  Graph of share price index ..................................................................................... 162
D3  Index-linked stock .................................................................................................. 163

**Group E—Prices**
E1  Retail Prices Index .................................................................................................. 169
E2  Inflation table ......................................................................................................... 171
E3  House price indices ................................................................................................ 172
E4  Average semi-detached house prices by region ....................................................... 174
E5  How prices have changed over 12 years ................................................................. 174

**Group F—Earnings**
F1  Earnings losses in personal injury and fatal accident cases ....................................... 177
F2  Payroll documents .................................................................................................. 181

| | | |
|---|---|---|
| F3 | National minimum wage | 183 |
| F4 | Regional unemployment statistics | 185 |
| F5 | Average weekly earnings index | 191 |
| F6 | Average weekly earnings | 192 |
| F7 | Average earnings statistics | 193 |
| F8 | Public sector comparable earnings | 215 |

### Group G—Tax and National Insurance
| | | |
|---|---|---|
| G1 | Net equivalents to a range of gross annual income figures | 219 |
| G2 | Illustrative net earnings calculations | 230 |
| G3 | Income tax reliefs and rates | 231 |
| G4 | National Insurance contributions | 234 |
| G5 | VAT registration thresholds and rates | 238 |

### Group H—Pension
| | | |
|---|---|---|
| H1 | Net equivalents to a range of gross annual pension figures | 241 |
| H2 | Illustrative net pension calculations | 243 |
| H3 | Note on pension losses | 245 |
| H4 | State pension age timetables | 249 |

### Group I—Benefits, Allowances, Charges
| | | |
|---|---|---|
| I1 | Social security benefits (non-means-tested) | 255 |
| I2 | Social security benefits and tax credits (means-tested) | 258 |
| I3 | Personal injury trusts | 261 |
| I4 | Claims for loss of earnings and maintenance at public expense | 271 |
| I5 | Foster care allowances | 271 |

### Group J—Court of Protection
| | | |
|---|---|---|
| J1 | Note on the Court of Protection | 275 |
| J2 | The incidence of Deputyship costs over a claimant's life | 284 |
| J3 | Deputyship costs | 288 |

### Group K—Carer Rates and Rehabilitation
| | | |
|---|---|---|
| K1 | Care and attendance | 293 |
| K2 | Nannies, cleaners and school fees | 310 |
| K3 | DIY, gardening and housekeeping | 311 |
| K4 | Hospital self-pay (uninsured) charges | 313 |
| K5 | NHS charges | 314 |
| K6 | The 2007 Rehabilitation Code | 315 |
| K7 | Rehabilitation: a practitioner's guide | 319 |
| K8 | APIL Serious Injury Guide | 333 |

### Group L—Motoring and Allied Material
| | | |
|---|---|---|
| L1 | Motoring costs | 343 |
| L2 | Taxation of car and fuel benefits | 349 |
| L3 | The Motability Scheme | 351 |
| L4 | The costs of buying and replacing cars | 352 |
| L5 | Time, speed and distance | 360 |

### Group M—Other Information
| | | |
|---|---|---|
| M1 | Senior Court Costs Office Guideline Rates for Summary Assessment | 365 |

| | | |
|---|---|---|
| M2 | Conversion formulae | 368 |
| M3 | Perpetual calendar | 371 |
| M4 | Religious festivals | 374 |
| M5 | Medical reference intervals and scales | 375 |
| M6 | Websites | 380 |
| M7 | Useful organisations | 382 |

# Group A
*Ogden Tables and Related Materials*

A1: **2.5 per cent discount tables "at a glance"**

A2: **Nil discount tables "at a glance"**

A3: **Life tables and projected life tables**

A4: **Loss of earnings multipliers adjusted for education, disability and employment status**

A5: **Multipliers for fixed periods and at intervals**

A6: **Combination tables**

A7: **Table of adjustments to multiplier for Fatal Accidents Acts dependency**

A8: **The Ogden Tables**

A9: **The Lord Chancellor's statement, 27 July 2001**

# A1: 2.5 per cent discount tables "at a glance"

The following tables comprise the 2.5 per cent columns from Ogden Tables 1–26. However, we now include columns for loss of earnings to, and loss of pension from, ages 66, 67, 68 and 69, which have been obtained by interpolation.

The method of interpolation for the multiplier for loss of earnings to pension age is as recommended in paragraph 13 of the Explanatory Notes to the 7th Edition of the Ogden Tables (see table A8).

The Ogden Tables for loss of earnings are not extended below age 16. The appropriate starting figure for loss of earnings where an equivalent age below age 16 is required has been calculated as the difference between the multiplier for life and the multiplier from the equivalent retirement age.

Readers are reminded that the figures for loss of earnings must be adjusted in accordance with Section B of the Explanatory Notes to the Ogden Tables (Contingencies other than mortality) reproduced in Table A8. Multipliers already adjusted for these contingencies are set out in Table A4.

The multiplier for loss of pension commencing at ages 66 to 69 is calculated as the difference between the multiplier for life, as set out in tables 1 and 2 of the Ogden Tables, and the calculated multiplier to pension age.

---

Multipliers for loss of earnings/loss of pension to and from ages 66 to 69 are shown at the back of Table A1 for a 2.5 per cent discount rate and at the back of Table A2 for a Nil discount rate.

A1: 2.5 per cent discount tables "at a glance"

## 2.5 per cent discount tables "at a glance"—MALE

| | Table 1 Pecuniary loss for life | Table 3 Loss of earnings to age 50 | Table 5 Loss of earnings to age 55 | Table 7 Loss of earnings to age 60 | Table 9 Loss of earnings to age 65 | Table 11 Loss of earnings to age 70 | Table 13 Loss of earnings to age 75 | Table 15 Loss of pension from age 50 | Table 17 Loss of pension from age 55 | Table 19 Loss of pension from age 60 | Table 21 Loss of pension from age 65 | Table 23 Loss of pension from age 70 | Table 25 Loss of pension from age 75 |
|---|---|---|---|---|---|---|---|---|---|---|---|---|---|
| 0 | 35.41 | | | | | | | 7.00 | 5.69 | 4.54 | 3.54 | 2.69 | 1.97 |
| 1 | 35.46 | | | | | | | 7.20 | 5.85 | 4.66 | 3.64 | 2.76 | 2.02 |
| 2 | 35.33 | | | | | | | 7.37 | 5.98 | 4.77 | 3.72 | 2.82 | 2.06 |
| 3 | 35.19 | | | | | | | 7.54 | 6.12 | 4.88 | 3.80 | 2.88 | 2.10 |
| 4 | 35.05 | | | | | | | 7.72 | 6.26 | 4.98 | 3.88 | 2.94 | 2.14 |
| 5 | 34.90 | | | | | | | 7.89 | 6.40 | 5.10 | 3.97 | 3.00 | 2.19 |
| 6 | 34.75 | | | | | | | 8.08 | 6.54 | 5.21 | 4.05 | 3.06 | 2.23 |
| 7 | 34.59 | | | | | | | 8.26 | 6.69 | 5.32 | 4.14 | 3.13 | 2.27 |
| 8 | 34.42 | | | | | | | 8.45 | 6.84 | 5.44 | 4.23 | 3.19 | 2.32 |
| 9 | 34.25 | | | | | | | 8.65 | 7.00 | 5.56 | 4.32 | 3.26 | 2.36 |
| 10 | 34.08 | | | | | | | 8.84 | 7.15 | 5.68 | 4.41 | 3.33 | 2.41 |
| 11 | 33.90 | | | | | | | 9.05 | 7.32 | 5.81 | 4.51 | 3.39 | 2.46 |
| 12 | 33.72 | | | | | | | 9.26 | 7.48 | 5.94 | 4.60 | 3.46 | 2.50 |
| 13 | 33.53 | | | | | | | 9.47 | 7.65 | 6.07 | 4.70 | 3.54 | 2.55 |
| 14 | 33.34 | | | | | | | 9.69 | 7.82 | 6.20 | 4.80 | 3.61 | 2.60 |
| 15 | 33.14 | | | | | | | 9.91 | 8.00 | 6.34 | 4.91 | 3.68 | 2.65 |
| 16 | 32.94 | 22.80 | 24.76 | 26.46 | 27.92 | 29.18 | 30.23 | 10.14 | 8.18 | 6.48 | 5.01 | 3.76 | 2.71 |
| 17 | 32.73 | 22.36 | 24.37 | 26.11 | 27.61 | 28.89 | 29.97 | 10.37 | 8.37 | 6.62 | 5.12 | 3.84 | 2.76 |
| 18 | 32.52 | 21.91 | 23.97 | 25.75 | 27.29 | 28.61 | 29.71 | 10.61 | 8.56 | 6.77 | 5.23 | 3.92 | 2.81 |
| 19 | 32.31 | 21.45 | 23.56 | 25.39 | 26.97 | 28.31 | 29.44 | 10.86 | 8.75 | 6.92 | 5.34 | 4.00 | 2.87 |
| 20 | 32.10 | 20.99 | 23.14 | 25.02 | 26.64 | 28.01 | 29.17 | 11.11 | 8.95 | 7.08 | 5.46 | 4.08 | 2.92 |
| 21 | 31.87 | 20.50 | 22.72 | 24.64 | 26.30 | 27.71 | 28.89 | 11.37 | 9.16 | 7.23 | 5.58 | 4.17 | 2.98 |
| 22 | 31.64 | 20.01 | 22.28 | 24.25 | 25.95 | 27.39 | 28.61 | 11.63 | 9.37 | 7.40 | 5.70 | 4.25 | 3.04 |
| 23 | 31.41 | 19.51 | 21.83 | 23.85 | 25.59 | 27.07 | 28.31 | 11.90 | 9.58 | 7.56 | 5.82 | 4.34 | 3.10 |
| 24 | 31.17 | 18.99 | 21.37 | 23.44 | 25.22 | 26.74 | 28.01 | 12.18 | 9.80 | 7.73 | 5.95 | 4.43 | 3.16 |
| 25 | 30.92 | 18.46 | 20.90 | 23.02 | 24.85 | 26.40 | 27.70 | 12.46 | 10.02 | 7.90 | 6.08 | 4.52 | 3.22 |
| 26 | 30.67 | 17.92 | 20.42 | 22.59 | 24.47 | 26.06 | 27.39 | 12.76 | 10.25 | 8.08 | 6.21 | 4.62 | 3.29 |
| 27 | 30.42 | 17.36 | 19.93 | 22.16 | 24.07 | 25.70 | 27.07 | 13.06 | 10.49 | 8.26 | 6.34 | 4.71 | 3.35 |
| 28 | 30.15 | 16.79 | 19.42 | 21.71 | 23.67 | 25.34 | 26.74 | 13.36 | 10.73 | 8.45 | 6.48 | 4.81 | 3.42 |
| 29 | 29.88 | 16.21 | 18.91 | 21.25 | 23.26 | 24.97 | 26.40 | 13.67 | 10.97 | 8.63 | 6.62 | 4.91 | 3.48 |
| 30 | 29.60 | 15.61 | 18.38 | 20.78 | 22.84 | 24.59 | 26.05 | 13.99 | 11.23 | 8.83 | 6.76 | 5.01 | 3.55 |
| 31 | 29.32 | 15.00 | 17.83 | 20.29 | 22.41 | 24.20 | 25.70 | 14.33 | 11.49 | 9.03 | 6.91 | 5.12 | 3.62 |
| 32 | 29.04 | 14.37 | 17.28 | 19.80 | 21.97 | 23.81 | 25.35 | 14.67 | 11.76 | 9.23 | 7.07 | 5.23 | 3.69 |
| 33 | 28.75 | 13.73 | 16.72 | 19.30 | 21.53 | 23.41 | 24.98 | 15.02 | 12.03 | 9.45 | 7.22 | 5.34 | 3.77 |
| 34 | 28.46 | 13.08 | 16.14 | 18.79 | 21.07 | 23.00 | 24.61 | 15.38 | 12.32 | 9.66 | 7.38 | 5.45 | 3.84 |
| 35 | 28.15 | 12.41 | 15.55 | 18.27 | 20.60 | 22.58 | 24.23 | 15.75 | 12.61 | 9.89 | 7.55 | 5.57 | 3.92 |
| 36 | 27.84 | 11.72 | 14.94 | 17.73 | 20.13 | 22.15 | 23.84 | 16.13 | 12.90 | 10.11 | 7.72 | 5.69 | 4.00 |
| 37 | 27.53 | 11.01 | 14.32 | 17.18 | 19.64 | 21.72 | 23.45 | 16.51 | 13.21 | 10.35 | 7.89 | 5.81 | 4.08 |
| 38 | 27.20 | 10.29 | 13.68 | 16.61 | 19.13 | 21.27 | 23.04 | 16.91 | 13.52 | 10.58 | 8.07 | 5.93 | 4.16 |
| 39 | 26.86 | 9.54 | 13.02 | 16.04 | 18.62 | 20.80 | 22.62 | 17.32 | 13.84 | 10.83 | 8.24 | 6.06 | 4.24 |
| 40 | 26.52 | 8.78 | 12.35 | 15.44 | 18.09 | 20.33 | 22.19 | 17.74 | 14.17 | 11.08 | 8.43 | 6.19 | 4.33 |
| 41 | 26.17 | 8.00 | 11.67 | 14.84 | 17.55 | 19.85 | 21.75 | 18.17 | 14.50 | 11.33 | 8.62 | 6.32 | 4.42 |
| 42 | 25.81 | 7.20 | 10.96 | 14.21 | 17.00 | 19.36 | 21.31 | 18.61 | 14.85 | 11.60 | 8.81 | 6.46 | 4.51 |
| 43 | 25.45 | 6.38 | 10.24 | 13.58 | 16.44 | 18.85 | 20.85 | 19.07 | 15.21 | 11.87 | 9.01 | 6.60 | 4.60 |
| 44 | 25.08 | 5.54 | 9.50 | 12.93 | 15.86 | 18.34 | 20.39 | 19.54 | 15.57 | 12.15 | 9.21 | 6.74 | 4.69 |
| 45 | 24.70 | 4.68 | 8.74 | 12.26 | 15.27 | 17.81 | 19.91 | 20.02 | 15.95 | 12.44 | 9.43 | 6.89 | 4.79 |
| 46 | 24.31 | 3.79 | 7.97 | 11.58 | 14.67 | 17.27 | 19.42 | 20.52 | 16.34 | 12.73 | 9.64 | 7.04 | 4.88 |
| 47 | 23.91 | 2.88 | 7.17 | 10.88 | 14.05 | 16.72 | 18.93 | 21.03 | 16.74 | 13.03 | 9.86 | 7.19 | 4.99 |
| 48 | 23.51 | 1.95 | 6.35 | 10.16 | 13.42 | 16.16 | 18.42 | 21.56 | 17.15 | 13.35 | 10.09 | 7.35 | 5.09 |
| 49 | 23.10 | 0.99 | 5.52 | 9.43 | 12.77 | 15.58 | 17.90 | 22.11 | 17.58 | 13.67 | 10.33 | 7.52 | 5.20 |
| 50 | 22.69 | | 4.66 | 8.68 | 12.11 | 15.00 | 17.38 | 22.69 | 18.03 | 14.01 | 10.58 | 7.69 | 5.31 |
| 51 | 22.27 | | 3.78 | 7.91 | 11.44 | 14.40 | 16.85 | | 18.49 | 14.36 | 10.83 | 7.87 | 5.42 |
| 52 | 21.85 | | 2.87 | 7.12 | 10.75 | 13.80 | 16.31 | | 18.98 | 14.72 | 11.10 | 8.05 | 5.54 |
| 53 | 21.42 | | 1.94 | 6.32 | 10.05 | 13.18 | 15.76 | | 19.48 | 15.11 | 11.37 | 8.24 | 5.67 |
| 54 | 20.99 | | 0.99 | 5.49 | 9.33 | 12.55 | 15.20 | | 20.01 | 15.50 | 11.66 | 8.44 | 5.80 |

## 2.5 per cent discount tables "at a glance"—MALE *continued*

| Age | Table 1 Pecuniary loss for life | Table 3 Loss of earnings to age 50 | Table 5 Loss of earnings to age 55 | Table 7 Loss of earnings to age 60 | Table 9 Loss of earnings to age 65 | Table 11 Loss of earnings to age 70 | Table 13 Loss of earnings to age 75 | Table 15 Loss of pension from age 50 | Table 17 Loss of pension from age 55 | Table 19 Loss of pension from age 60 | Table 21 Loss of pension from age 65 | Table 23 Loss of pension from age 70 | Table 25 Loss of pension from age 75 |
|---|---|---|---|---|---|---|---|---|---|---|---|---|---|
| 55 | 20.56 | | | 4.64 | 8.59 | 11.90 | 14.63 | | 20.56 | 15.92 | 11.97 | 8.65 | 5.93 |
| 56 | 20.12 | | | 3.76 | 7.84 | 11.25 | 14.05 | | | 16.36 | 12.29 | 8.88 | 6.08 |
| 57 | 19.68 | | | 2.86 | 7.06 | 10.57 | 13.46 | | | 16.82 | 12.62 | 9.11 | 6.23 |
| 58 | 19.23 | | | 1.94 | 6.26 | 9.88 | 12.85 | | | 17.29 | 12.97 | 9.35 | 6.38 |
| 59 | 18.77 | | | 0.98 | 5.45 | 9.18 | 12.23 | | | 17.79 | 13.32 | 9.59 | 6.54 |
| 60 | 18.30 | | | | 4.60 | 8.45 | 11.60 | | | 18.30 | 13.69 | 9.85 | 6.70 |
| 61 | 17.81 | | | | 3.74 | 7.71 | 10.95 | | | | 14.08 | 10.11 | 6.87 |
| 62 | 17.33 | | | | 2.85 | 6.94 | 10.28 | | | | 14.48 | 10.38 | 7.04 |
| 63 | 16.84 | | | | 1.93 | 6.16 | 9.61 | | | | 14.91 | 10.67 | 7.23 |
| 64 | 16.35 | | | | 0.98 | 5.36 | 8.93 | | | | 15.37 | 10.98 | 7.42 |
| 65 | 15.86 | | | | | 4.54 | 8.23 | | | | 15.86 | 11.32 | 7.63 |
| 66 | 15.38 | | | | | 3.70 | 7.52 | | | | | 11.68 | 7.86 |
| 67 | 14.90 | | | | | 2.82 | 6.79 | | | | | 12.07 | 8.11 |
| 68 | 14.42 | | | | | 1.92 | 6.04 | | | | | 12.50 | 8.38 |
| 69 | 13.93 | | | | | 0.98 | 5.27 | | | | | 12.96 | 8.67 |
| 70 | 13.44 | | | | | | 4.47 | | | | | 13.44 | 8.97 |
| 71 | 12.94 | | | | | | 3.65 | | | | | | 9.30 |
| 72 | 12.43 | | | | | | 2.79 | | | | | | 9.64 |
| 73 | 11.90 | | | | | | 1.90 | | | | | | 10.00 |
| 74 | 11.36 | | | | | | 0.97 | | | | | | 10.39 |
| 75 | 10.81 | | | | | | | | | | | | 10.81 |
| 76 | 10.25 | | | | | | | | | | | | |
| 77 | 9.69 | | | | | | | | | | | | |
| 78 | 9.15 | | | | | | | | | | | | |
| 79 | 8.61 | | | | | | | | | | | | |
| 80 | 8.09 | | | | | | | | | | | | |
| 81 | 7.60 | | | | | | | | | | | | |
| 82 | 7.13 | | | | | | | | | | | | |
| 83 | 6.69 | | | | | | | | | | | | |
| 84 | 6.28 | | | | | | | | | | | | |
| 85 | 5.88 | | | | | | | | | | | | |
| 86 | 5.50 | | | | | | | | | | | | |
| 87 | 5.14 | | | | | | | | | | | | |
| 88 | 4.78 | | | | | | | | | | | | |
| 89 | 4.43 | | | | | | | | | | | | |
| 90 | 4.10 | | | | | | | | | | | | |
| 91 | 3.79 | | | | | | | | | | | | |
| 92 | 3.49 | | | | | | | | | | | | |
| 93 | 3.21 | | | | | | | | | | | | |
| 94 | 2.96 | | | | | | | | | | | | |
| 95 | 2.74 | | | | | | | | | | | | |
| 96 | 2.54 | | | | | | | | | | | | |
| 97 | 2.37 | | | | | | | | | | | | |
| 98 | 2.22 | | | | | | | | | | | | |
| 99 | 2.08 | | | | | | | | | | | | |
| 100 | 1.95 | | | | | | | | | | | | |

A1: 2.5 per cent discount tables "at a glance"

## 2.5 per cent discount tables "at a glance"—FEMALE

| | Table 2<br>Pecuniary<br>loss for<br>life | Table 4<br>Loss of<br>earnings<br>to age 50 | Table 6<br>Loss of<br>earnings<br>to age 55 | Table 8<br>Loss of<br>earnings<br>to age 60 | Table 10<br>Loss of<br>earnings<br>to age 65 | Table 12<br>Loss of<br>earnings<br>to age 70 | Table 14<br>Loss of<br>earnings<br>to age 75 | Table 16<br>Loss of<br>pension<br>from age<br>50 | Table 18<br>Loss of<br>pension<br>from age<br>55 | Table 20<br>Loss of<br>pension<br>from age<br>60 | Table 22<br>Loss of<br>pension<br>from age<br>65 | Table 24<br>Loss of<br>pension<br>from age<br>70 | Table 26<br>Loss of<br>pension<br>from age<br>75 |
|---|---|---|---|---|---|---|---|---|---|---|---|---|---|
| 0 | 35.94 | | | | | | | 7.43 | 6.09 | 4.92 | 3.90 | 3.01 | 2.25 |
| 1 | 35.97 | | | | | | | 7.64 | 6.26 | 5.06 | 4.00 | 3.09 | 2.31 |
| 2 | 35.86 | | | | | | | 7.82 | 6.41 | 5.17 | 4.09 | 3.16 | 2.36 |
| 3 | 35.73 | | | | | | | 8.00 | 6.56 | 5.29 | 4.19 | 3.23 | 2.41 |
| 4 | 35.60 | | | | | | | 8.19 | 6.71 | 5.41 | 4.28 | 3.30 | 2.46 |
| 5 | 35.47 | | | | | | | 8.39 | 6.87 | 5.54 | 4.38 | 3.37 | 2.51 |
| 6 | 35.34 | | | | | | | 8.58 | 7.03 | 5.66 | 4.47 | 3.44 | 2.56 |
| 7 | 35.19 | | | | | | | 8.78 | 7.19 | 5.79 | 4.57 | 3.52 | 2.61 |
| 8 | 35.05 | | | | | | | 8.99 | 7.36 | 5.92 | 4.68 | 3.59 | 2.67 |
| 9 | 34.90 | | | | | | | 9.20 | 7.53 | 6.06 | 4.78 | 3.67 | 2.72 |
| 10 | 34.75 | | | | | | | 9.42 | 7.70 | 6.20 | 4.89 | 3.75 | 2.78 |
| 11 | 34.59 | | | | | | | 9.64 | 7.88 | 6.34 | 4.99 | 3.83 | 2.84 |
| 12 | 34.42 | | | | | | | 9.86 | 8.06 | 6.48 | 5.11 | 3.92 | 2.90 |
| 13 | 34.26 | | | | | | | 10.09 | 8.25 | 6.63 | 5.22 | 4.00 | 2.96 |
| 14 | 34.09 | | | | | | | 10.33 | 8.44 | 6.78 | 5.33 | 4.09 | 3.02 |
| 15 | 33.91 | | | | | | | 10.57 | 8.63 | 6.93 | 5.45 | 4.17 | 3.08 |
| 16 | 33.73 | 22.91 | 24.90 | 26.64 | 28.16 | 29.47 | 30.59 | 10.82 | 8.83 | 7.09 | 5.57 | 4.26 | 3.14 |
| 17 | 33.55 | 22.47 | 24.51 | 26.29 | 27.85 | 29.19 | 30.34 | 11.07 | 9.03 | 7.25 | 5.70 | 4.36 | 3.21 |
| 18 | 33.36 | 22.02 | 24.11 | 25.94 | 27.53 | 28.91 | 30.08 | 11.33 | 9.24 | 7.42 | 5.82 | 4.45 | 3.27 |
| 19 | 33.16 | 21.56 | 23.71 | 25.58 | 27.21 | 28.62 | 29.82 | 11.60 | 9.46 | 7.58 | 5.95 | 4.55 | 3.34 |
| 20 | 32.97 | 21.09 | 23.29 | 25.21 | 26.88 | 28.32 | 29.56 | 11.87 | 9.68 | 7.76 | 6.09 | 4.64 | 3.41 |
| 21 | 32.76 | 20.61 | 22.86 | 24.83 | 26.54 | 28.02 | 29.28 | 12.15 | 9.90 | 7.93 | 6.22 | 4.74 | 3.48 |
| 22 | 32.56 | 20.12 | 22.42 | 24.44 | 26.20 | 27.71 | 29.00 | 12.44 | 10.13 | 8.12 | 6.36 | 4.85 | 3.55 |
| 23 | 32.34 | 19.61 | 21.97 | 24.04 | 25.84 | 27.39 | 28.71 | 12.73 | 10.37 | 8.30 | 6.50 | 4.95 | 3.63 |
| 24 | 32.12 | 19.09 | 21.51 | 23.63 | 25.47 | 27.06 | 28.42 | 13.03 | 10.61 | 8.49 | 6.65 | 5.06 | 3.70 |
| 25 | 31.89 | 18.56 | 21.04 | 23.21 | 25.10 | 26.73 | 28.12 | 13.33 | 10.85 | 8.68 | 6.79 | 5.16 | 3.78 |
| 26 | 31.66 | 18.01 | 20.56 | 22.78 | 24.72 | 26.39 | 27.81 | 13.65 | 11.10 | 8.88 | 6.94 | 5.28 | 3.85 |
| 27 | 31.42 | 17.45 | 20.06 | 22.34 | 24.33 | 26.03 | 27.49 | 13.97 | 11.36 | 9.08 | 7.10 | 5.39 | 3.93 |
| 28 | 31.18 | 16.88 | 19.56 | 21.89 | 23.93 | 25.68 | 27.17 | 14.30 | 11.62 | 9.29 | 7.26 | 5.50 | 4.01 |
| 29 | 30.93 | 16.30 | 19.04 | 21.43 | 23.51 | 25.31 | 26.84 | 14.64 | 11.89 | 9.50 | 7.42 | 5.62 | 4.10 |
| 30 | 30.68 | 15.70 | 18.51 | 20.96 | 23.09 | 24.93 | 26.50 | 14.98 | 12.17 | 9.71 | 7.58 | 5.74 | 4.18 |
| 31 | 30.41 | 15.08 | 17.96 | 20.48 | 22.66 | 24.55 | 26.15 | 15.33 | 12.45 | 9.94 | 7.75 | 5.87 | 4.27 |
| 32 | 30.15 | 14.45 | 17.40 | 19.98 | 22.22 | 24.15 | 25.79 | 15.70 | 12.74 | 10.16 | 7.92 | 6.00 | 4.35 |
| 33 | 29.87 | 13.80 | 16.83 | 19.48 | 21.77 | 23.75 | 25.43 | 16.07 | 13.04 | 10.40 | 8.10 | 6.13 | 4.44 |
| 34 | 29.59 | 13.14 | 16.25 | 18.96 | 21.31 | 23.34 | 25.06 | 16.45 | 13.35 | 10.64 | 8.28 | 6.26 | 4.54 |
| 35 | 29.31 | 12.46 | 15.65 | 18.43 | 20.84 | 22.91 | 24.68 | 16.84 | 13.66 | 10.88 | 8.47 | 6.39 | 4.63 |
| 36 | 29.01 | 11.77 | 15.03 | 17.88 | 20.35 | 22.48 | 24.29 | 17.24 | 13.98 | 11.13 | 8.66 | 6.53 | 4.73 |
| 37 | 28.71 | 11.06 | 14.40 | 17.32 | 19.86 | 22.04 | 23.89 | 17.65 | 14.30 | 11.38 | 8.85 | 6.67 | 4.82 |
| 38 | 28.40 | 10.33 | 13.76 | 16.75 | 19.35 | 21.58 | 23.48 | 18.07 | 14.64 | 11.65 | 9.05 | 6.82 | 4.92 |
| 39 | 28.09 | 9.58 | 13.10 | 16.17 | 18.83 | 21.12 | 23.06 | 18.50 | 14.98 | 11.92 | 9.25 | 6.97 | 5.02 |
| 40 | 27.76 | 8.82 | 12.42 | 15.57 | 18.30 | 20.65 | 22.63 | 18.95 | 15.34 | 12.19 | 9.46 | 7.12 | 5.13 |
| 41 | 27.43 | 8.03 | 11.73 | 14.96 | 17.76 | 20.16 | 22.20 | 19.40 | 15.70 | 12.47 | 9.67 | 7.27 | 5.23 |
| 42 | 27.09 | 7.22 | 11.02 | 14.33 | 17.20 | 19.66 | 21.75 | 19.87 | 16.07 | 12.76 | 9.89 | 7.43 | 5.34 |
| 43 | 26.75 | 6.40 | 10.29 | 13.69 | 16.63 | 19.15 | 21.29 | 20.35 | 16.45 | 13.06 | 10.12 | 7.59 | 5.45 |
| 44 | 26.39 | 5.55 | 9.55 | 13.03 | 16.05 | 18.63 | 20.82 | 20.84 | 16.84 | 13.36 | 10.35 | 7.76 | 5.57 |
| 45 | 26.03 | 4.69 | 8.79 | 12.36 | 15.45 | 18.10 | 20.35 | 21.35 | 17.25 | 13.68 | 10.58 | 7.93 | 5.69 |
| 46 | 25.67 | 3.80 | 8.00 | 11.67 | 14.84 | 17.56 | 19.86 | 21.87 | 17.66 | 14.00 | 10.83 | 8.11 | 5.81 |
| 47 | 25.29 | 2.88 | 7.20 | 10.96 | 14.22 | 17.01 | 19.36 | 22.41 | 18.09 | 14.33 | 11.08 | 8.29 | 5.93 |
| 48 | 24.91 | 1.95 | 6.38 | 10.24 | 13.58 | 16.44 | 18.86 | 22.97 | 18.53 | 14.67 | 11.33 | 8.47 | 6.06 |
| 49 | 24.53 | 0.99 | 5.54 | 9.50 | 12.93 | 15.86 | 18.34 | 23.54 | 18.99 | 15.03 | 11.60 | 8.67 | 6.19 |
| 50 | 24.14 | | 4.68 | 8.74 | 12.26 | 15.27 | 17.82 | 24.14 | 19.46 | 15.39 | 11.88 | 8.86 | 6.32 |
| 51 | 23.74 | | 3.79 | 7.97 | 11.58 | 14.67 | 17.28 | | 19.95 | 15.77 | 12.16 | 9.07 | 6.46 |
| 52 | 23.33 | | 2.88 | 7.17 | 10.88 | 14.05 | 16.73 | | 20.45 | 16.16 | 12.45 | 9.28 | 6.60 |
| 53 | 22.92 | | 1.95 | 6.36 | 10.17 | 13.42 | 16.17 | | 20.97 | 16.56 | 12.75 | 9.49 | 6.75 |
| 54 | 22.50 | | 0.99 | 5.52 | 9.43 | 12.78 | 15.60 | | 21.51 | 16.98 | 13.06 | 9.72 | 6.90 |

## 2.5 per cent discount tables "at a glance"—FEMALE *continued*

| | Table 2 Pecuniary loss for life | Table 4 Loss of earnings to age 50 | Table 6 Loss of earnings to age 55 | Table 8 Loss of earnings to age 60 | Table 10 Loss of earnings to age 65 | Table 12 Loss of earnings to age 70 | Table 14 Loss of earnings to age 75 | Table 16 Loss of pension from age 50 | Table 18 Loss of pension from age 55 | Table 20 Loss of pension from age 60 | Table 22 Loss of pension from age 65 | Table 24 Loss of pension from age 70 | Table 26 Loss of pension from age 75 |
|---|---|---|---|---|---|---|---|---|---|---|---|---|---|
| 55 | 22.07 | | | 4.66 | 8.68 | 12.12 | 15.02 | | 22.07 | 17.41 | 13.39 | 9.95 | 7.06 |
| 56 | 21.64 | | | 3.78 | 7.92 | 11.45 | 14.42 | | | 17.86 | 13.73 | 10.19 | 7.22 |
| 57 | 21.21 | | | 2.87 | 7.13 | 10.76 | 13.81 | | | 18.33 | 14.08 | 10.44 | 7.39 |
| 58 | 20.76 | | | 1.94 | 6.32 | 10.05 | 13.19 | | | 18.81 | 14.44 | 10.70 | 7.56 |
| 59 | 20.30 | | | 0.99 | 5.49 | 9.33 | 12.56 | | | 19.31 | 14.81 | 10.97 | 7.74 |
| 60 | 19.83 | | | | 4.64 | 8.59 | 11.91 | | | 19.83 | 15.19 | 11.24 | 7.92 |
| 61 | 19.35 | | | | 3.76 | 7.83 | 11.24 | | | | 15.59 | 11.52 | 8.11 |
| 62 | 18.86 | | | | 2.86 | 7.05 | 10.56 | | | | 16.00 | 11.81 | 8.30 |
| 63 | 18.37 | | | | 1.94 | 6.25 | 9.86 | | | | 16.43 | 12.11 | 8.50 |
| 64 | 17.87 | | | | 0.98 | 5.44 | 9.16 | | | | 16.89 | 12.43 | 8.71 |
| 65 | 17.38 | | | | | 4.60 | 8.43 | | | | 17.38 | 12.78 | 8.94 |
| 66 | 16.88 | | | | | 3.74 | 7.70 | | | | | 13.15 | 9.19 |
| 67 | 16.39 | | | | | 2.85 | 6.94 | | | | | 13.54 | 9.45 |
| 68 | 15.89 | | | | | 1.93 | 6.17 | | | | | 13.96 | 9.72 |
| 69 | 15.39 | | | | | 0.98 | 5.37 | | | | | 14.40 | 10.02 |
| 70 | 14.87 | | | | | | 4.55 | | | | | 14.87 | 10.33 |
| 71 | 14.35 | | | | | | 3.70 | | | | | | 10.65 |
| 72 | 13.80 | | | | | | 2.82 | | | | | | 10.98 |
| 73 | 13.24 | | | | | | 1.92 | | | | | | 11.32 |
| 74 | 12.66 | | | | | | 0.98 | | | | | | 11.68 |
| 75 | 12.06 | | | | | | | | | | | | 12.06 |
| 76 | 11.45 | | | | | | | | | | | | |
| 77 | 10.84 | | | | | | | | | | | | |
| 78 | 10.24 | | | | | | | | | | | | |
| 79 | 9.64 | | | | | | | | | | | | |
| 80 | 9.07 | | | | | | | | | | | | |
| 81 | 8.51 | | | | | | | | | | | | |
| 82 | 7.99 | | | | | | | | | | | | |
| 83 | 7.49 | | | | | | | | | | | | |
| 84 | 7.01 | | | | | | | | | | | | |
| 85 | 6.55 | | | | | | | | | | | | |
| 86 | 6.11 | | | | | | | | | | | | |
| 87 | 5.68 | | | | | | | | | | | | |
| 88 | 5.26 | | | | | | | | | | | | |
| 89 | 4.86 | | | | | | | | | | | | |
| 90 | 4.47 | | | | | | | | | | | | |
| 91 | 4.11 | | | | | | | | | | | | |
| 92 | 3.77 | | | | | | | | | | | | |
| 93 | 3.46 | | | | | | | | | | | | |
| 94 | 3.18 | | | | | | | | | | | | |
| 95 | 2.94 | | | | | | | | | | | | |
| 96 | 2.74 | | | | | | | | | | | | |
| 97 | 2.56 | | | | | | | | | | | | |
| 98 | 2.39 | | | | | | | | | | | | |
| 99 | 2.23 | | | | | | | | | | | | |
| 100 | 2.08 | | | | | | | | | | | | |

## A1: 2.5 per cent discount tables "at a glance"

### A1: 2.5 per cent discount tables for retirement ages 66 to 69 – MALE

| | Loss of earnings to age 66 | Loss of earnings to age 67 | Loss of earnings to age 68 | Loss of earnings to age 69 | | Loss of pension from age 66 | Loss of pension from age 67 | Loss of pension from age 68 | Loss of pension from age 69 |
|---|---|---|---|---|---|---|---|---|---|
| 16 | 28.19 | 28.45 | 28.70 | 28.94 | 16 | 4.75 | 4.49 | 4.24 | 4.00 |
| 17 | 27.88 | 28.14 | 28.40 | 28.65 | 17 | 4.85 | 4.59 | 4.33 | 4.08 |
| 18 | 27.57 | 27.84 | 28.10 | 28.36 | 18 | 4.95 | 4.68 | 4.42 | 4.16 |
| 19 | 27.25 | 27.52 | 27.79 | 28.05 | 19 | 5.06 | 4.79 | 4.52 | 4.26 |
| 20 | 26.92 | 27.20 | 27.48 | 27.75 | 20 | 5.18 | 4.90 | 4.62 | 4.35 |
| 21 | 26.59 | 26.88 | 27.16 | 27.43 | 21 | 5.28 | 4.99 | 4.71 | 4.44 |
| 22 | 26.25 | 26.54 | 26.83 | 27.11 | 22 | 5.39 | 5.10 | 4.81 | 4.53 |
| 23 | 25.90 | 26.20 | 26.50 | 26.79 | 23 | 5.51 | 5.21 | 4.91 | 4.62 |
| 24 | 25.54 | 25.85 | 26.16 | 26.45 | 24 | 5.63 | 5.32 | 5.01 | 4.72 |
| 25 | 25.17 | 25.49 | 25.80 | 26.11 | 25 | 5.75 | 5.43 | 5.12 | 4.81 |
| 26 | 24.80 | 25.12 | 25.44 | 25.75 | 26 | 5.87 | 5.55 | 5.23 | 4.92 |
| 27 | 24.42 | 24.75 | 25.07 | 25.39 | 27 | 6.00 | 5.67 | 5.35 | 5.03 |
| 28 | 24.02 | 24.36 | 24.69 | 25.02 | 28 | 6.13 | 5.79 | 5.46 | 5.13 |
| 29 | 23.62 | 23.97 | 24.31 | 24.64 | 29 | 6.26 | 5.91 | 5.57 | 5.24 |
| 30 | 23.21 | 23.57 | 23.91 | 24.25 | 30 | 6.39 | 6.03 | 5.69 | 5.35 |
| 31 | 22.79 | 23.16 | 23.51 | 23.86 | 31 | 6.53 | 6.16 | 5.81 | 5.46 |
| 32 | 22.36 | 22.74 | 23.10 | 23.46 | 32 | 6.68 | 6.30 | 5.94 | 5.58 |
| 33 | 21.92 | 22.31 | 22.68 | 23.05 | 33 | 6.83 | 6.44 | 6.07 | 5.70 |
| 34 | 21.48 | 21.87 | 22.25 | 22.63 | 34 | 6.98 | 6.59 | 6.21 | 5.83 |
| 35 | 21.02 | 21.43 | 21.82 | 22.20 | 35 | 7.13 | 6.72 | 6.33 | 5.95 |
| 36 | 20.55 | 20.96 | 21.37 | 21.77 | 36 | 7.29 | 6.88 | 6.47 | 6.07 |
| 37 | 20.07 | 20.49 | 20.91 | 21.32 | 37 | 7.46 | 7.04 | 6.62 | 6.21 |
| 38 | 19.58 | 20.02 | 20.44 | 20.85 | 38 | 7.62 | 7.18 | 6.76 | 6.35 |
| 39 | 19.07 | 19.53 | 19.96 | 20.38 | 39 | 7.79 | 7.33 | 6.90 | 6.48 |
| 40 | 18.56 | 19.02 | 19.47 | 19.91 | 40 | 7.96 | 7.50 | 7.05 | 6.61 |
| 41 | 18.03 | 18.51 | 18.96 | 19.42 | 41 | 8.14 | 7.66 | 7.21 | 6.75 |
| 42 | 17.49 | 17.98 | 18.45 | 18.91 | 42 | 8.32 | 7.83 | 7.36 | 6.90 |
| 43 | 16.94 | 17.44 | 17.92 | 18.40 | 43 | 8.51 | 8.01 | 7.53 | 7.05 |
| 44 | 16.38 | 16.89 | 17.38 | 17.87 | 44 | 8.70 | 8.19 | 7.70 | 7.21 |
| 45 | 15.80 | 16.33 | 16.83 | 17.33 | 45 | 8.90 | 8.37 | 7.87 | 7.37 |
| 46 | 15.22 | 15.75 | 16.27 | 16.78 | 46 | 9.09 | 8.56 | 8.04 | 7.53 |
| 47 | 14.62 | 15.16 | 15.69 | 16.22 | 47 | 9.29 | 8.75 | 8.22 | 7.69 |
| 48 | 14.00 | 14.56 | 15.11 | 15.64 | 48 | 9.51 | 8.95 | 8.40 | 7.87 |
| 49 | 13.37 | 13.95 | 14.51 | 15.05 | 49 | 9.73 | 9.15 | 8.59 | 8.05 |
| 50 | 12.73 | 13.32 | 13.90 | 14.45 | 50 | 9.96 | 9.37 | 8.79 | 8.24 |
| 51 | 12.07 | 12.68 | 13.28 | 13.85 | 51 | 10.20 | 9.59 | 8.99 | 8.42 |
| 52 | 11.40 | 12.03 | 12.64 | 13.23 | 52 | 10.45 | 9.82 | 9.21 | 8.62 |
| 53 | 10.71 | 11.36 | 11.98 | 12.59 | 53 | 10.71 | 10.06 | 9.44 | 8.83 |
| 54 | 10.02 | 10.68 | 11.33 | 11.94 | 54 | 10.97 | 10.31 | 9.66 | 9.05 |
| 55 | 9.30 | 9.98 | 10.64 | 11.29 | 55 | 11.26 | 10.58 | 9.92 | 9.27 |
| 56 | 8.56 | 9.27 | 9.95 | 10.61 | 56 | 11.56 | 10.85 | 10.17 | 9.51 |
| 57 | 7.81 | 8.53 | 9.24 | 9.91 | 57 | 11.87 | 11.15 | 10.44 | 9.77 |
| 58 | 7.04 | 7.79 | 8.51 | 9.21 | 58 | 12.19 | 11.44 | 10.72 | 10.02 |
| 59 | 6.24 | 7.01 | 7.76 | 8.48 | 59 | 12.53 | 11.76 | 11.01 | 10.29 |
| 60 | 5.43 | 6.22 | 6.99 | 7.74 | 60 | 12.87 | 12.08 | 11.31 | 10.56 |
| 61 | 4.59 | 5.41 | 6.20 | 6.96 | 61 | 13.22 | 12.40 | 11.61 | 10.85 |
| 62 | 3.73 | 4.58 | 5.40 | 6.18 | 62 | 13.60 | 12.75 | 11.93 | 11.15 |
| 63 | 2.84 | 3.72 | 4.56 | 5.38 | 63 | 14.00 | 13.12 | 12.28 | 11.46 |
| 64 | 1.93 | 2.84 | 3.72 | 4.55 | 64 | 14.42 | 13.51 | 12.63 | 11.80 |
| 65 | 0.98 | 1.93 | 2.83 | 3.71 | 65 | 14.88 | 13.93 | 13.03 | 12.15 |
| 66 | | 0.98 | 1.92 | 2.83 | 66 | 15.38 | 14.40 | 13.46 | 12.55 |
| 67 | | | 0.98 | 1.92 | 67 | | 14.90 | 13.92 | 12.98 |
| 68 | | | | 0.98 | 68 | | | 14.42 | 13.44 |
| 69 | | | | | 69 | | | | 13.93 |

See notes at the start of section A1 for details of methodology

### A1: 2.5 per cent discount tables for retirement ages 66 to 69 – FEMALE

| | Loss of earnings to age 66 | Loss of earnings to age 67 | Loss of earnings to age 68 | Loss of earnings to age 69 | | Loss of pension from age 66 | Loss of pension from age 67 | Loss of pension from age 68 | Loss of pension from age 69 |
|---|---|---|---|---|---|---|---|---|---|
| 16 | 28.43 | 28.70 | 28.96 | 29.21 | 16 | 5.30 | 5.03 | 4.77 | 4.52 |
| 17 | 28.13 | 28.40 | 28.68 | 28.94 | 17 | 5.42 | 5.15 | 4.87 | 4.61 |
| 18 | 27.82 | 28.10 | 28.38 | 28.65 | 18 | 5.54 | 5.26 | 4.98 | 4.71 |
| 19 | 27.50 | 27.79 | 28.08 | 28.35 | 19 | 5.66 | 5.37 | 5.08 | 4.81 |
| 20 | 27.18 | 27.47 | 27.77 | 28.05 | 20 | 5.79 | 5.50 | 5.20 | 4.92 |
| 21 | 26.85 | 27.15 | 27.45 | 27.74 | 21 | 5.91 | 5.61 | 5.31 | 5.02 |
| 22 | 26.51 | 26.82 | 27.12 | 27.42 | 22 | 6.05 | 5.74 | 5.44 | 5.14 |
| 23 | 26.17 | 26.48 | 26.79 | 27.09 | 23 | 6.17 | 5.86 | 5.55 | 5.25 |
| 24 | 25.81 | 26.13 | 26.45 | 26.76 | 24 | 6.31 | 5.99 | 5.67 | 5.36 |
| 25 | 25.44 | 25.78 | 26.10 | 26.42 | 25 | 6.45 | 6.11 | 5.79 | 5.47 |
| 26 | 25.07 | 25.41 | 25.74 | 26.06 | 26 | 6.59 | 6.25 | 5.92 | 5.60 |
| 27 | 24.69 | 25.03 | 25.37 | 25.71 | 27 | 6.73 | 6.39 | 6.05 | 5.71 |
| 28 | 24.29 | 24.65 | 25.00 | 25.34 | 28 | 6.89 | 6.53 | 6.18 | 5.84 |
| 29 | 23.89 | 24.26 | 24.62 | 24.96 | 29 | 7.04 | 6.67 | 6.31 | 5.97 |
| 30 | 23.48 | 23.86 | 24.22 | 24.58 | 30 | 7.20 | 6.82 | 6.46 | 6.10 |
| 31 | 23.05 | 23.44 | 23.82 | 24.19 | 31 | 7.36 | 6.97 | 6.59 | 6.22 |
| 32 | 22.62 | 23.02 | 23.41 | 23.79 | 32 | 7.53 | 7.13 | 6.74 | 6.36 |
| 33 | 22.18 | 22.59 | 22.98 | 23.37 | 33 | 7.69 | 7.28 | 6.89 | 6.50 |
| 34 | 21.73 | 22.15 | 22.55 | 22.95 | 34 | 7.86 | 7.44 | 7.04 | 6.64 |
| 35 | 21.27 | 21.69 | 22.11 | 22.52 | 35 | 8.04 | 7.62 | 7.20 | 6.79 |
| 36 | 20.80 | 21.23 | 21.66 | 22.08 | 36 | 8.21 | 7.78 | 7.35 | 6.93 |
| 37 | 20.31 | 20.76 | 21.20 | 21.62 | 37 | 8.40 | 7.95 | 7.51 | 7.09 |
| 38 | 19.82 | 20.27 | 20.73 | 21.16 | 38 | 8.58 | 8.13 | 7.67 | 7.24 |
| 39 | 19.31 | 19.78 | 20.24 | 20.69 | 39 | 8.78 | 8.31 | 7.85 | 7.40 |
| 40 | 18.79 | 19.27 | 19.74 | 20.20 | 40 | 8.97 | 8.49 | 8.02 | 7.56 |
| 41 | 18.26 | 18.75 | 19.23 | 19.70 | 41 | 9.17 | 8.68 | 8.20 | 7.73 |
| 42 | 17.72 | 18.22 | 18.71 | 19.19 | 42 | 9.37 | 8.87 | 8.38 | 7.90 |
| 43 | 17.16 | 17.68 | 18.18 | 18.67 | 43 | 9.59 | 9.07 | 8.57 | 8.08 |
| 44 | 16.59 | 17.12 | 17.64 | 18.14 | 44 | 9.80 | 9.27 | 8.75 | 8.25 |
| 45 | 16.01 | 16.55 | 17.09 | 17.60 | 45 | 10.02 | 9.48 | 8.94 | 8.43 |
| 46 | 15.41 | 15.97 | 16.52 | 17.05 | 46 | 10.26 | 9.70 | 9.15 | 8.62 |
| 47 | 14.81 | 15.38 | 15.94 | 16.48 | 47 | 10.48 | 9.91 | 9.35 | 8.81 |
| 48 | 14.19 | 14.77 | 15.34 | 15.90 | 48 | 10.72 | 10.14 | 9.57 | 9.01 |
| 49 | 13.55 | 14.15 | 14.74 | 15.31 | 49 | 10.98 | 10.38 | 9.79 | 9.22 |
| 50 | 12.90 | 13.52 | 14.12 | 14.70 | 50 | 11.24 | 10.62 | 10.02 | 9.44 |
| 51 | 12.23 | 12.87 | 13.48 | 14.08 | 51 | 11.51 | 10.87 | 10.26 | 9.66 |
| 52 | 11.55 | 12.20 | 12.84 | 13.45 | 52 | 11.78 | 11.13 | 10.49 | 9.88 |
| 53 | 10.86 | 11.53 | 12.18 | 12.81 | 53 | 12.06 | 11.39 | 10.74 | 10.11 |
| 54 | 10.15 | 10.83 | 11.50 | 12.15 | 54 | 12.35 | 11.67 | 11.00 | 10.35 |
| 55 | 9.41 | 10.12 | 10.81 | 11.48 | 55 | 12.66 | 11.95 | 11.26 | 10.59 |
| 56 | 8.66 | 9.39 | 10.10 | 10.78 | 56 | 12.98 | 12.25 | 11.54 | 10.86 |
| 57 | 7.90 | 8.64 | 9.37 | 10.07 | 57 | 13.31 | 12.57 | 11.84 | 11.14 |
| 58 | 7.11 | 7.88 | 8.63 | 9.35 | 58 | 13.65 | 12.88 | 12.13 | 11.41 |
| 59 | 6.31 | 7.10 | 7.87 | 8.61 | 59 | 13.99 | 13.20 | 12.43 | 11.69 |
| 60 | 5.48 | 6.29 | 7.08 | 7.85 | 60 | 14.35 | 13.54 | 12.75 | 11.98 |
| 61 | 4.63 | 5.47 | 6.28 | 7.07 | 61 | 14.72 | 13.88 | 13.07 | 12.28 |
| 62 | 3.76 | 4.62 | 5.46 | 6.26 | 62 | 15.10 | 14.24 | 13.40 | 12.60 |
| 63 | 2.86 | 3.75 | 4.62 | 5.45 | 63 | 15.51 | 14.62 | 13.75 | 12.92 |
| 64 | 1.94 | 2.86 | 3.75 | 4.61 | 64 | 15.93 | 15.01 | 14.12 | 13.26 |
| 65 | 0.98 | 1.94 | 2.85 | 3.74 | 65 | 16.40 | 15.44 | 14.53 | 13.64 |
| 66 | | 0.98 | 1.93 | 2.85 | 66 | 16.88 | 15.90 | 14.95 | 14.03 |
| 67 | | | 0.98 | 1.93 | 67 | | 16.39 | 15.41 | 14.46 |
| 68 | | | | 0.98 | 68 | | | 15.89 | 14.91 |
| 69 | | | | | 69 | | | | 15.39 |

See notes at the section A1 for details of methodology

# A2: Nil discount tables "at a glance"

## A1: 2.5 per cent discount tables for retirement ages 66 to 69 – FEMALE

| | Loss of earnings to age 66 | Loss of earnings to age 67 | Loss of earnings to age 68 | Loss of earnings to age 69 | | Loss of pension from age 66 | Loss of pension from age 67 | Loss of pension from age 68 | Loss of pension from age 69 |
|---|---|---|---|---|---|---|---|---|---|
| 16 | 28.43 | 28.70 | 28.96 | 29.21 | 16 | 5.30 | 5.03 | 4.77 | 4.52 |
| 17 | 28.13 | 28.40 | 28.68 | 28.94 | 17 | 5.42 | 5.15 | 4.87 | 4.61 |
| 18 | 27.82 | 28.10 | 28.38 | 28.65 | 18 | 5.54 | 5.26 | 4.98 | 4.71 |
| 19 | 27.50 | 27.79 | 28.08 | 28.35 | 19 | 5.66 | 5.37 | 5.08 | 4.81 |
| 20 | 27.18 | 27.47 | 27.77 | 28.05 | 20 | 5.79 | 5.50 | 5.20 | 4.92 |
| 21 | 26.85 | 27.15 | 27.45 | 27.74 | 21 | 5.91 | 5.61 | 5.31 | 5.02 |
| 22 | 26.51 | 26.82 | 27.12 | 27.42 | 22 | 6.05 | 5.74 | 5.44 | 5.14 |
| 23 | 26.17 | 26.48 | 26.79 | 27.09 | 23 | 6.17 | 5.86 | 5.55 | 5.25 |
| 24 | 25.81 | 26.13 | 26.45 | 26.76 | 24 | 6.31 | 5.99 | 5.67 | 5.36 |
| 25 | 25.44 | 25.78 | 26.10 | 26.42 | 25 | 6.45 | 6.11 | 5.79 | 5.47 |
| 26 | 25.07 | 25.41 | 25.74 | 26.06 | 26 | 6.59 | 6.25 | 5.92 | 5.60 |
| 27 | 24.69 | 25.03 | 25.37 | 25.71 | 27 | 6.73 | 6.39 | 6.05 | 5.71 |
| 28 | 24.29 | 24.65 | 25.00 | 25.34 | 28 | 6.89 | 6.53 | 6.18 | 5.84 |
| 29 | 23.89 | 24.26 | 24.62 | 24.96 | 29 | 7.04 | 6.67 | 6.31 | 5.97 |
| 30 | 23.48 | 23.86 | 24.22 | 24.58 | 30 | 7.20 | 6.82 | 6.46 | 6.10 |
| 31 | 23.05 | 23.44 | 23.82 | 24.19 | 31 | 7.36 | 6.97 | 6.59 | 6.22 |
| 32 | 22.62 | 23.02 | 23.41 | 23.79 | 32 | 7.53 | 7.13 | 6.74 | 6.36 |
| 33 | 22.18 | 22.59 | 22.98 | 23.37 | 33 | 7.69 | 7.28 | 6.89 | 6.50 |
| 34 | 21.73 | 22.15 | 22.55 | 22.95 | 34 | 7.86 | 7.44 | 7.04 | 6.64 |
| 35 | 21.27 | 21.69 | 22.11 | 22.52 | 35 | 8.04 | 7.62 | 7.20 | 6.79 |
| 36 | 20.80 | 21.23 | 21.66 | 22.08 | 36 | 8.21 | 7.78 | 7.35 | 6.93 |
| 37 | 20.31 | 20.76 | 21.20 | 21.62 | 37 | 8.40 | 7.95 | 7.51 | 7.09 |
| 38 | 19.82 | 20.27 | 20.73 | 21.16 | 38 | 8.58 | 8.13 | 7.67 | 7.24 |
| 39 | 19.31 | 19.78 | 20.24 | 20.69 | 39 | 8.78 | 8.31 | 7.85 | 7.40 |
| 40 | 18.79 | 19.27 | 19.74 | 20.20 | 40 | 8.97 | 8.49 | 8.02 | 7.56 |
| 41 | 18.26 | 18.75 | 19.23 | 19.70 | 41 | 9.17 | 8.68 | 8.20 | 7.73 |
| 42 | 17.72 | 18.22 | 18.71 | 19.19 | 42 | 9.37 | 8.87 | 8.38 | 7.90 |
| 43 | 17.16 | 17.68 | 18.18 | 18.67 | 43 | 9.59 | 9.07 | 8.57 | 8.08 |
| 44 | 16.59 | 17.12 | 17.64 | 18.14 | 44 | 9.80 | 9.27 | 8.75 | 8.25 |
| 45 | 16.01 | 16.55 | 17.09 | 17.60 | 45 | 10.02 | 9.48 | 8.94 | 8.43 |
| 46 | 15.41 | 15.97 | 16.52 | 17.05 | 46 | 10.26 | 9.70 | 9.15 | 8.62 |
| 47 | 14.81 | 15.38 | 15.94 | 16.48 | 47 | 10.48 | 9.91 | 9.35 | 8.81 |
| 48 | 14.19 | 14.77 | 15.34 | 15.90 | 48 | 10.72 | 10.14 | 9.57 | 9.01 |
| 49 | 13.55 | 14.15 | 14.74 | 15.31 | 49 | 10.98 | 10.38 | 9.79 | 9.22 |
| 50 | 12.90 | 13.52 | 14.12 | 14.70 | 50 | 11.24 | 10.62 | 10.02 | 9.44 |
| 51 | 12.23 | 12.87 | 13.48 | 14.08 | 51 | 11.51 | 10.87 | 10.26 | 9.66 |
| 52 | 11.55 | 12.20 | 12.84 | 13.45 | 52 | 11.78 | 11.13 | 10.49 | 9.88 |
| 53 | 10.86 | 11.53 | 12.18 | 12.81 | 53 | 12.06 | 11.39 | 10.74 | 10.11 |
| 54 | 10.15 | 10.83 | 11.50 | 12.15 | 54 | 12.35 | 11.67 | 11.00 | 10.35 |
| 55 | 9.41 | 10.12 | 10.81 | 11.48 | 55 | 12.66 | 11.95 | 11.26 | 10.59 |
| 56 | 8.66 | 9.39 | 10.10 | 10.78 | 56 | 12.98 | 12.25 | 11.54 | 10.86 |
| 57 | 7.90 | 8.64 | 9.37 | 10.07 | 57 | 13.31 | 12.57 | 11.84 | 11.14 |
| 58 | 7.11 | 7.88 | 8.63 | 9.35 | 58 | 13.65 | 12.88 | 12.13 | 11.41 |
| 59 | 6.31 | 7.10 | 7.87 | 8.61 | 59 | 13.99 | 13.20 | 12.43 | 11.69 |
| 60 | 5.48 | 6.29 | 7.08 | 7.85 | 60 | 14.35 | 13.54 | 12.75 | 11.98 |
| 61 | 4.63 | 5.47 | 6.28 | 7.07 | 61 | 14.72 | 13.88 | 13.07 | 12.28 |
| 62 | 3.76 | 4.62 | 5.46 | 6.26 | 62 | 15.10 | 14.24 | 13.40 | 12.60 |
| 63 | 2.86 | 3.75 | 4.62 | 5.45 | 63 | 15.51 | 14.62 | 13.75 | 12.92 |
| 64 | 1.94 | 2.86 | 3.75 | 4.61 | 64 | 15.93 | 15.01 | 14.12 | 13.26 |
| 65 | 0.98 | 1.94 | 2.85 | 3.74 | 65 | 16.40 | 15.44 | 14.53 | 13.64 |
| 66 | | 0.98 | 1.93 | 2.85 | 66 | 16.88 | 15.90 | 14.95 | 14.03 |
| 67 | | | 0.98 | 1.93 | 67 | | 16.39 | 15.41 | 14.46 |
| 68 | | | | 0.98 | 68 | | | 15.89 | 14.91 |
| 69 | | | | | 69 | | | | 15.39 |

See notes at the section A1 for details of methodology

# A2: Nil discount tables "at a glance"

## Tables at 0.0%

### MALE

| | Table 1 Pecuniary loss for life | Table 3 Loss of earnings to age 50 | Table 5 Loss of earnings to age 55 | Table 7 Loss of earnings to age 60 | Table 9 Loss of earnings to age 65 | Table 11 Loss of earnings to age 70 | Table 13 Loss of earnings to age 75 | Table 15 Loss of pension from age 50 | Table 17 Loss of pension from age 55 | Table 19 Loss of pension from age 60 | Table 21 Loss of pension from age 65 | Table 23 Loss of pension from age 70 | Table 25 Loss of pension from age 75 |
|---|---|---|---|---|---|---|---|---|---|---|---|---|---|
| 0 | 88.96 | | | | | | | 39.61 | 34.80 | 30.06 | 25.41 | 20.90 | 16.58 |
| 1 | 88.31 | | | | | | | 39.70 | 34.87 | 30.10 | 25.44 | 20.91 | 16.56 |
| 2 | 87.22 | | | | | | | 39.59 | 34.76 | 30.00 | 25.33 | 20.81 | 16.47 |
| 3 | 86.12 | | | | | | | 39.49 | 34.65 | 29.89 | 25.23 | 20.70 | 16.37 |
| 4 | 85.01 | | | | | | | 39.37 | 34.54 | 29.78 | 25.12 | 20.60 | 16.28 |
| 5 | 83.89 | | | | | | | 39.26 | 34.43 | 29.67 | 25.01 | 20.50 | 16.18 |
| 6 | 82.78 | | | | | | | 39.14 | 34.32 | 29.56 | 24.90 | 20.39 | 16.08 |
| 7 | 81.66 | | | | | | | 39.03 | 34.20 | 29.45 | 24.80 | 20.29 | 15.98 |
| 8 | 80.55 | | | | | | | 38.91 | 34.09 | 29.34 | 24.69 | 20.19 | 15.88 |
| 9 | 79.43 | | | | | | | 38.80 | 33.97 | 29.22 | 24.58 | 20.08 | 15.79 |
| 10 | 78.31 | | | | | | | 38.68 | 33.86 | 29.11 | 24.47 | 19.97 | 15.69 |
| 11 | 77.19 | | | | | | | 38.56 | 33.74 | 29.00 | 24.36 | 19.87 | 15.59 |
| 12 | 76.07 | | | | | | | 38.44 | 33.63 | 28.88 | 24.25 | 19.76 | 15.49 |
| 13 | 74.96 | | | | | | | 38.33 | 33.51 | 28.77 | 24.14 | 19.66 | 15.39 |
| 14 | 73.84 | | | | | | | 38.21 | 33.40 | 28.66 | 24.03 | 19.56 | 15.29 |
| 15 | 72.73 | | | | | | | 38.10 | 33.29 | 28.55 | 23.92 | 19.45 | 15.20 |
| 16 | 71.61 | 33.63 | 38.44 | 43.18 | 47.80 | 52.26 | 56.51 | 37.99 | 33.17 | 28.44 | 23.82 | 19.35 | 15.10 |
| 17 | 70.51 | 32.63 | 37.44 | 42.18 | 46.80 | 51.26 | 55.50 | 37.88 | 33.06 | 28.33 | 23.71 | 19.25 | 15.01 |
| 18 | 69.41 | 31.64 | 36.45 | 41.18 | 45.80 | 50.25 | 54.49 | 37.77 | 32.96 | 28.23 | 23.61 | 19.15 | 14.92 |
| 19 | 68.31 | 30.65 | 35.46 | 40.19 | 44.80 | 49.26 | 53.49 | 37.67 | 32.85 | 28.12 | 23.51 | 19.06 | 14.82 |
| 20 | 67.22 | 29.66 | 34.47 | 39.20 | 43.81 | 48.26 | 52.48 | 37.57 | 32.75 | 28.02 | 23.41 | 18.96 | 14.74 |
| 21 | 66.13 | 28.66 | 33.48 | 38.21 | 42.82 | 47.26 | 51.48 | 37.46 | 32.65 | 27.92 | 23.31 | 18.87 | 14.65 |
| 22 | 65.04 | 27.67 | 32.49 | 37.21 | 41.82 | 46.27 | 50.48 | 37.36 | 32.55 | 27.82 | 23.21 | 18.77 | 14.55 |
| 23 | 63.94 | 26.68 | 31.49 | 36.22 | 40.83 | 45.27 | 49.48 | 37.26 | 32.45 | 27.72 | 23.11 | 18.67 | 14.46 |
| 24 | 62.85 | 25.69 | 30.50 | 35.23 | 39.84 | 44.27 | 48.48 | 37.16 | 32.34 | 27.62 | 23.01 | 18.58 | 14.37 |
| 25 | 61.76 | 24.70 | 29.52 | 34.24 | 38.85 | 43.28 | 47.48 | 37.06 | 32.24 | 27.52 | 22.91 | 18.48 | 14.28 |
| 26 | 60.68 | 23.71 | 28.53 | 33.25 | 37.86 | 42.29 | 46.48 | 36.96 | 32.15 | 27.42 | 22.82 | 18.39 | 14.20 |
| 27 | 59.59 | 22.72 | 27.54 | 32.27 | 36.87 | 41.29 | 45.48 | 36.87 | 32.06 | 27.33 | 22.73 | 18.30 | 14.11 |
| 28 | 58.51 | 21.73 | 26.55 | 31.28 | 35.88 | 40.30 | 44.48 | 36.77 | 31.96 | 27.23 | 22.63 | 18.21 | 14.02 |
| 29 | 57.42 | 20.74 | 25.56 | 30.29 | 34.89 | 39.31 | 43.49 | 36.68 | 31.86 | 27.13 | 22.53 | 18.11 | 13.93 |
| 30 | 56.34 | 19.76 | 24.57 | 29.30 | 33.90 | 38.32 | 42.49 | 36.58 | 31.76 | 27.04 | 22.44 | 18.02 | 13.85 |
| 31 | 55.27 | 18.77 | 23.59 | 28.32 | 32.92 | 37.33 | 41.50 | 36.50 | 31.68 | 26.95 | 22.35 | 17.93 | 13.76 |
| 32 | 54.20 | 17.78 | 22.61 | 27.34 | 31.94 | 36.35 | 40.52 | 36.42 | 31.60 | 26.86 | 22.26 | 17.85 | 13.69 |
| 33 | 53.15 | 16.80 | 21.63 | 26.36 | 30.96 | 35.37 | 39.54 | 36.35 | 31.52 | 26.79 | 22.18 | 17.77 | 13.61 |
| 34 | 52.09 | 15.82 | 20.65 | 25.38 | 29.99 | 34.40 | 38.56 | 36.27 | 31.44 | 26.71 | 22.10 | 17.69 | 13.53 |
| 35 | 51.03 | 14.83 | 19.67 | 24.40 | 29.01 | 33.42 | 37.58 | 36.20 | 31.36 | 26.63 | 22.02 | 17.61 | 13.45 |
| 36 | 49.98 | 13.85 | 18.69 | 23.43 | 28.03 | 32.45 | 36.60 | 36.13 | 31.29 | 26.55 | 21.94 | 17.53 | 13.38 |
| 37 | 48.93 | 12.86 | 17.71 | 22.45 | 27.06 | 31.47 | 35.62 | 36.06 | 31.22 | 26.47 | 21.87 | 17.45 | 13.30 |
| 38 | 47.87 | 11.88 | 16.73 | 21.48 | 26.08 | 30.50 | 34.64 | 35.99 | 31.14 | 26.40 | 21.79 | 17.37 | 13.23 |
| 39 | 46.82 | 10.89 | 15.75 | 20.50 | 25.11 | 29.52 | 33.67 | 35.92 | 31.07 | 26.32 | 21.71 | 17.30 | 13.15 |
| 40 | 45.76 | 9.91 | 14.76 | 19.52 | 24.13 | 28.55 | 32.69 | 35.85 | 31.00 | 26.24 | 21.63 | 17.22 | 13.07 |
| 41 | 44.71 | 8.92 | 13.78 | 18.54 | 23.16 | 27.57 | 31.71 | 35.79 | 30.93 | 26.17 | 21.55 | 17.14 | 13.00 |
| 42 | 43.67 | 7.93 | 12.80 | 17.57 | 22.19 | 26.60 | 30.74 | 35.73 | 30.86 | 26.10 | 21.48 | 17.07 | 12.93 |
| 43 | 42.62 | 6.95 | 11.82 | 16.59 | 21.22 | 25.63 | 29.77 | 35.68 | 30.80 | 26.03 | 21.41 | 16.99 | 12.86 |
| 44 | 41.59 | 5.96 | 10.84 | 15.62 | 20.25 | 24.66 | 28.80 | 35.63 | 30.74 | 25.97 | 21.34 | 16.92 | 12.79 |
| 45 | 40.55 | 4.97 | 9.86 | 14.64 | 19.28 | 23.70 | 27.83 | 35.58 | 30.69 | 25.91 | 21.27 | 16.85 | 12.72 |
| 46 | 39.52 | 3.98 | 8.88 | 13.67 | 18.31 | 22.73 | 26.87 | 35.54 | 30.64 | 25.85 | 21.21 | 16.79 | 12.65 |
| 47 | 38.49 | 2.99 | 7.90 | 12.70 | 17.34 | 21.77 | 25.90 | 35.50 | 30.59 | 25.79 | 21.15 | 16.72 | 12.59 |
| 48 | 37.47 | 1.99 | 6.92 | 11.73 | 16.38 | 20.81 | 24.95 | 35.47 | 30.55 | 25.74 | 21.09 | 16.66 | 12.52 |
| 49 | 36.45 | 1.00 | 5.93 | 10.75 | 15.41 | 19.85 | 23.99 | 35.46 | 30.52 | 25.70 | 21.04 | 16.60 | 12.46 |
| 50 | 35.45 | | 4.95 | 9.78 | 14.46 | 18.90 | 23.04 | 35.45 | 30.50 | 25.66 | 20.99 | 16.55 | 12.41 |
| 51 | 34.45 | | 3.97 | 8.81 | 13.50 | 17.95 | 22.10 | | 30.49 | 25.64 | 20.96 | 16.51 | 12.36 |
| 52 | 33.47 | | 2.98 | 7.84 | 12.54 | 17.00 | 21.16 | | 30.49 | 25.62 | 20.93 | 16.47 | 12.31 |
| 53 | 32.49 | | 1.99 | 6.87 | 11.59 | 16.06 | 20.23 | | 30.50 | 25.62 | 20.91 | 16.43 | 12.27 |
| 54 | 31.53 | | 1.00 | 5.90 | 10.63 | 15.12 | 19.30 | | 30.53 | 25.63 | 20.90 | 16.41 | 12.23 |

A2: Nil discount tables "at a glance"

## Nil discount tables "at a glance"—MALE continued

| Age | Table 1 Pecuniary loss for life | Table 3 Loss of earnings to age 50 | Table 5 Loss of earnings to age 55 | Table 7 Loss of earnings to age 60 | Table 9 Loss of earnings to age 65 | Table 11 Loss of earnings to age 70 | Table 13 Loss of earnings to age 75 | Table 15 Loss of pension from age 50 | Table 17 Loss of pension from age 55 | Table 19 Loss of pension from age 60 | Table 21 Loss of pension from age 65 | Table 23 Loss of pension from age 70 | Table 25 Loss of pension from age 75 |
|---|---|---|---|---|---|---|---|---|---|---|---|---|---|
| 55 | 30.58 | | | 4.93 | 9.68 | 14.19 | 18.37 | | 30.58 | 25.65 | 20.90 | 16.39 | 12.20 |
| 56 | 29.64 | | | 3.95 | 8.73 | 13.25 | 17.46 | | | 25.69 | 20.91 | 16.39 | 12.18 |
| 57 | 28.71 | | | 2.97 | 7.77 | 12.32 | 16.54 | | | 25.74 | 20.94 | 16.39 | 12.17 |
| 58 | 27.78 | | | 1.99 | 6.82 | 11.39 | 15.63 | | | 25.80 | 20.97 | 16.40 | 12.16 |
| 59 | 26.85 | | | 1.00 | 5.85 | 10.45 | 14.71 | | | 25.86 | 21.00 | 16.40 | 12.15 |
| 60 | 25.92 | | | | 4.89 | 9.51 | 13.79 | | | 25.92 | 21.03 | 16.41 | 12.13 |
| 61 | 25.00 | | | | 3.92 | 8.58 | 12.87 | | | | 21.07 | 16.42 | 12.12 |
| 62 | 24.08 | | | | 2.95 | 7.64 | 11.96 | | | | 21.12 | 16.44 | 12.12 |
| 63 | 23.17 | | | | 1.98 | 6.70 | 11.05 | | | | 21.20 | 16.47 | 12.12 |
| 64 | 22.28 | | | | 0.99 | 5.77 | 10.15 | | | | 21.29 | 16.52 | 12.13 |
| 65 | 21.42 | | | | | 4.83 | 9.25 | | | | 21.42 | 16.59 | 12.16 |
| 66 | 20.57 | | | | | 3.88 | 8.36 | | | | | 16.69 | 12.21 |
| 67 | 19.74 | | | | | 2.93 | 7.46 | | | | | 16.81 | 12.28 |
| 68 | 18.93 | | | | | 1.97 | 6.56 | | | | | 16.96 | 12.37 |
| 69 | 18.12 | | | | | 0.99 | 5.66 | | | | | 17.13 | 12.47 |
| 70 | 17.32 | | | | | | 4.75 | | | | | 17.32 | 12.58 |
| 71 | 16.53 | | | | | | 3.83 | | | | | | 12.70 |
| 72 | 15.72 | | | | | | 2.89 | | | | | | 12.83 |
| 73 | 14.92 | | | | | | 1.95 | | | | | | 12.97 |
| 74 | 14.10 | | | | | | 0.99 | | | | | | 13.12 |
| 75 | 13.29 | | | | | | | | | | | | 13.29 |
| 76 | 12.48 | | | | | | | | | | | | |
| 77 | 11.70 | | | | | | | | | | | | |
| 78 | 10.93 | | | | | | | | | | | | |
| 79 | 10.19 | | | | | | | | | | | | |
| 80 | 9.49 | | | | | | | | | | | | |
| 81 | 8.83 | | | | | | | | | | | | |
| 82 | 8.22 | | | | | | | | | | | | |
| 83 | 7.65 | | | | | | | | | | | | |
| 84 | 7.13 | | | | | | | | | | | | |
| 85 | 6.63 | | | | | | | | | | | | |
| 86 | 6.16 | | | | | | | | | | | | |
| 87 | 5.71 | | | | | | | | | | | | |
| 88 | 5.27 | | | | | | | | | | | | |
| 89 | 4.86 | | | | | | | | | | | | |
| 90 | 4.47 | | | | | | | | | | | | |
| 91 | 4.10 | | | | | | | | | | | | |
| 92 | 3.76 | | | | | | | | | | | | |
| 93 | 3.44 | | | | | | | | | | | | |
| 94 | 3.16 | | | | | | | | | | | | |
| 95 | 2.91 | | | | | | | | | | | | |
| 96 | 2.69 | | | | | | | | | | | | |
| 97 | 2.50 | | | | | | | | | | | | |
| 98 | 2.34 | | | | | | | | | | | | |
| 99 | 2.18 | | | | | | | | | | | | |
| 100 | 2.04 | | | | | | | | | | | | |

## Nil discount tables "at a glance"—FEMALE

| | Table 2 Pecuniary loss for life | Table 4 Loss of earnings to age 50 | Table 6 Loss of earnings to age 55 | Table 8 Loss of earnings to age 60 | Table 10 Loss of earnings to age 65 | Table 12 Loss of earnings to age 70 | Table 14 Loss of earnings to age 75 | Table 16 Loss of pension from age 50 | Table 18 Loss of pension from age 55 | Table 20 Loss of pension from age 60 | Table 22 Loss of pension from age 65 | Table 24 Loss of pension from age 70 | Table 26 Loss of pension from age 75 |
|---|---|---|---|---|---|---|---|---|---|---|---|---|---|
| 0 | 92.57 | | | | | | | 42.98 | 38.10 | 33.26 | 28.47 | 23.78 | 19.22 |
| 1 | 91.86 | | | | | | | 43.07 | 38.16 | 33.30 | 28.50 | 23.79 | 19.21 |
| 2 | 90.77 | | | | | | | 42.97 | 38.06 | 33.20 | 28.40 | 23.69 | 19.12 |
| 3 | 89.68 | | | | | | | 42.87 | 37.96 | 33.10 | 28.30 | 23.60 | 19.02 |
| 4 | 88.58 | | | | | | | 42.77 | 37.86 | 33.00 | 28.21 | 23.50 | 18.93 |
| 5 | 87.49 | | | | | | | 42.67 | 37.76 | 32.90 | 28.11 | 23.41 | 18.84 |
| 6 | 86.38 | | | | | | | 42.56 | 37.66 | 32.80 | 28.01 | 23.31 | 18.75 |
| 7 | 85.28 | | | | | | | 42.46 | 37.56 | 32.70 | 27.91 | 23.21 | 18.65 |
| 8 | 84.18 | | | | | | | 42.36 | 37.45 | 32.60 | 27.81 | 23.11 | 18.56 |
| 9 | 83.07 | | | | | | | 42.25 | 37.35 | 32.49 | 27.70 | 23.01 | 18.46 |
| 10 | 81.97 | | | | | | | 42.15 | 37.24 | 32.39 | 27.60 | 22.92 | 18.37 |
| 11 | 80.86 | | | | | | | 42.04 | 37.14 | 32.29 | 27.50 | 22.82 | 18.28 |
| 12 | 79.76 | | | | | | | 41.94 | 37.04 | 32.18 | 27.40 | 22.72 | 18.18 |
| 13 | 78.65 | | | | | | | 41.83 | 36.93 | 32.08 | 27.30 | 22.62 | 18.09 |
| 14 | 77.55 | | | | | | | 41.73 | 36.83 | 31.98 | 27.20 | 22.53 | 18.00 |
| 15 | 76.44 | | | | | | | 41.62 | 36.72 | 31.88 | 27.10 | 22.43 | 17.91 |
| 16 | 75.34 | 33.82 | 38.72 | 43.57 | 48.34 | 53.01 | 57.53 | 41.52 | 36.62 | 31.78 | 27.00 | 22.33 | 17.81 |
| 17 | 74.24 | 32.82 | 37.72 | 42.57 | 47.34 | 52.01 | 56.52 | 41.42 | 36.52 | 31.67 | 26.90 | 22.24 | 17.72 |
| 18 | 73.14 | 31.83 | 36.72 | 41.57 | 46.34 | 51.00 | 55.51 | 41.32 | 36.42 | 31.58 | 26.80 | 22.14 | 17.63 |
| 19 | 72.05 | 30.83 | 35.73 | 40.57 | 45.34 | 50.00 | 54.51 | 41.22 | 36.32 | 31.48 | 26.71 | 22.05 | 17.54 |
| 20 | 70.96 | 29.83 | 34.73 | 39.57 | 44.34 | 49.00 | 53.50 | 41.12 | 36.23 | 31.38 | 26.61 | 21.96 | 17.45 |
| 21 | 69.86 | 28.84 | 33.73 | 38.58 | 43.34 | 48.00 | 52.50 | 41.03 | 36.13 | 31.29 | 26.52 | 21.86 | 17.36 |
| 22 | 68.77 | 27.84 | 32.74 | 37.58 | 42.34 | 47.00 | 51.49 | 40.93 | 36.03 | 31.19 | 26.42 | 21.77 | 17.27 |
| 23 | 67.67 | 26.85 | 31.74 | 36.58 | 41.35 | 46.00 | 50.49 | 40.82 | 35.93 | 31.09 | 26.32 | 21.67 | 17.18 |
| 24 | 66.57 | 25.85 | 30.74 | 35.58 | 40.35 | 44.99 | 49.48 | 40.72 | 35.83 | 30.99 | 26.23 | 21.58 | 17.09 |
| 25 | 65.48 | 24.85 | 29.75 | 34.59 | 39.35 | 43.99 | 48.48 | 40.62 | 35.73 | 30.89 | 26.13 | 21.48 | 17.00 |
| 26 | 64.38 | 23.86 | 28.75 | 33.59 | 38.35 | 42.99 | 47.47 | 40.53 | 35.63 | 30.79 | 26.03 | 21.39 | 16.91 |
| 27 | 63.29 | 22.86 | 27.76 | 32.59 | 37.35 | 41.99 | 46.47 | 40.43 | 35.54 | 30.70 | 25.94 | 21.30 | 16.82 |
| 28 | 62.20 | 21.87 | 26.76 | 31.60 | 36.36 | 40.99 | 45.46 | 40.33 | 35.44 | 30.60 | 25.84 | 21.21 | 16.74 |
| 29 | 61.11 | 20.87 | 25.77 | 30.60 | 35.36 | 39.99 | 44.46 | 40.24 | 35.34 | 30.51 | 25.75 | 21.11 | 16.65 |
| 30 | 60.02 | 19.88 | 24.77 | 29.61 | 34.36 | 39.00 | 43.46 | 40.15 | 35.25 | 30.41 | 25.66 | 21.03 | 16.56 |
| 31 | 58.94 | 18.88 | 23.78 | 28.62 | 33.37 | 38.00 | 42.46 | 40.06 | 35.16 | 30.32 | 25.57 | 20.94 | 16.48 |
| 32 | 57.86 | 17.89 | 22.79 | 27.62 | 32.38 | 37.01 | 41.46 | 39.97 | 35.07 | 30.23 | 25.48 | 20.85 | 16.39 |
| 33 | 56.77 | 16.89 | 21.79 | 26.63 | 31.38 | 36.01 | 40.46 | 39.88 | 34.98 | 30.14 | 25.39 | 20.76 | 16.31 |
| 34 | 55.69 | 15.90 | 20.80 | 25.64 | 30.39 | 35.02 | 39.47 | 39.79 | 34.89 | 30.05 | 25.30 | 20.68 | 16.23 |
| 35 | 54.61 | 14.91 | 19.81 | 24.65 | 29.40 | 34.02 | 38.47 | 39.70 | 34.80 | 29.96 | 25.21 | 20.59 | 16.14 |
| 36 | 53.53 | 13.92 | 18.82 | 23.66 | 28.41 | 33.03 | 37.47 | 39.62 | 34.72 | 29.88 | 25.13 | 20.50 | 16.06 |
| 37 | 52.46 | 12.92 | 17.83 | 22.67 | 27.42 | 32.04 | 36.48 | 39.54 | 34.63 | 29.79 | 25.04 | 20.42 | 15.98 |
| 38 | 51.38 | 11.93 | 16.84 | 21.68 | 26.43 | 31.05 | 35.49 | 39.45 | 34.55 | 29.71 | 24.95 | 20.33 | 15.90 |
| 39 | 50.31 | 10.94 | 15.85 | 20.69 | 25.44 | 30.06 | 34.49 | 39.37 | 34.46 | 29.62 | 24.87 | 20.25 | 15.82 |
| 40 | 49.24 | 9.95 | 14.86 | 19.70 | 24.45 | 29.07 | 33.50 | 39.29 | 34.38 | 29.54 | 24.79 | 20.17 | 15.73 |
| 41 | 48.17 | 8.95 | 13.87 | 18.71 | 23.47 | 28.08 | 32.51 | 39.22 | 34.30 | 29.46 | 24.70 | 20.08 | 15.66 |
| 42 | 47.10 | 7.96 | 12.88 | 17.73 | 22.48 | 27.10 | 31.53 | 39.14 | 34.23 | 29.38 | 24.62 | 20.00 | 15.58 |
| 43 | 46.04 | 6.97 | 11.89 | 16.74 | 21.50 | 26.11 | 30.54 | 39.07 | 34.15 | 29.30 | 24.54 | 19.93 | 15.50 |
| 44 | 44.98 | 5.97 | 10.90 | 15.75 | 20.51 | 25.13 | 29.55 | 39.01 | 34.08 | 29.23 | 24.47 | 19.85 | 15.43 |
| 45 | 43.93 | 4.98 | 9.91 | 14.77 | 19.53 | 24.15 | 28.57 | 38.94 | 34.02 | 29.16 | 24.40 | 19.78 | 15.35 |
| 46 | 42.87 | 3.99 | 8.92 | 13.79 | 18.55 | 23.17 | 27.59 | 38.89 | 33.95 | 29.09 | 24.32 | 19.70 | 15.28 |
| 47 | 41.83 | 2.99 | 7.93 | 12.80 | 17.57 | 22.19 | 26.62 | 38.83 | 33.89 | 29.02 | 24.26 | 19.63 | 15.21 |
| 48 | 40.79 | 2.00 | 6.95 | 11.82 | 16.59 | 21.22 | 25.64 | 38.79 | 33.84 | 28.97 | 24.19 | 19.57 | 15.14 |
| 49 | 39.76 | 1.00 | 5.96 | 10.84 | 15.62 | 20.25 | 24.67 | 38.76 | 33.80 | 28.92 | 24.14 | 19.51 | 15.08 |
| 50 | 38.73 | | 4.97 | 9.86 | 14.65 | 19.28 | 23.71 | 38.73 | 33.76 | 28.87 | 24.08 | 19.45 | 15.02 |
| 51 | 37.71 | | 3.98 | 8.88 | 13.67 | 18.31 | 22.75 | | 33.73 | 28.83 | 24.03 | 19.39 | 14.96 |
| 52 | 36.69 | | 2.99 | 7.90 | 12.70 | 17.35 | 21.78 | | 33.70 | 28.79 | 23.99 | 19.34 | 14.90 |
| 53 | 35.68 | | 1.99 | 6.92 | 11.73 | 16.39 | 20.83 | | 33.68 | 28.76 | 23.95 | 19.29 | 14.85 |
| 54 | 34.68 | | 1.00 | 5.94 | 10.76 | 15.43 | 19.87 | | 33.68 | 28.74 | 23.91 | 19.25 | 14.80 |

A2: Nil discount tables "at a glance"

## Nil discount tables "at a glance"—FEMALE *continued*

| | Table 2 Pecuniary loss for life | Table 4 Loss of earnings to age 50 | Table 6 Loss of earnings to age 55 | Table 8 Loss of earnings to age 60 | Table 10 Loss of earnings to age 65 | Table 12 Loss of earnings to age 70 | Table 14 Loss of earnings to age 75 | Table 16 Loss of pension from age 50 | Table 18 Loss of pension from age 55 | Table 20 Loss of pension from age 60 | Table 22 Loss of pension from age 65 | Table 24 Loss of pension from age 70 | Table 26 Loss of pension from age 75 |
|---|---|---|---|---|---|---|---|---|---|---|---|---|---|
| 55 | 33.68 | | | 4.95 | 9.79 | 14.47 | 18.92 | | 33.68 | 28.73 | 23.89 | 19.21 | 14.76 |
| 56 | 32.69 | | | 3.97 | 8.82 | 13.51 | 17.97 | | | 28.73 | 23.87 | 19.19 | 14.72 |
| 57 | 31.71 | | | 2.98 | 7.85 | 12.55 | 17.02 | | | 28.73 | 23.86 | 19.16 | 14.69 |
| 58 | 30.74 | | | 1.99 | 6.88 | 11.59 | 16.08 | | | 28.74 | 23.86 | 19.14 | 14.66 |
| 59 | 29.76 | | | 1.00 | 5.91 | 10.64 | 15.13 | | | 28.76 | 23.85 | 19.12 | 14.62 |
| 60 | 28.78 | | | | 4.93 | 9.68 | 14.19 | | | 28.78 | 23.85 | 19.10 | 14.59 |
| 61 | 27.80 | | | | 3.95 | 8.72 | 13.24 | | | | 23.85 | 19.08 | 14.55 |
| 62 | 26.83 | | | | 2.97 | 7.76 | 12.30 | | | | 23.86 | 19.06 | 14.52 |
| 63 | 25.86 | | | | 1.99 | 6.80 | 11.36 | | | | 23.88 | 19.06 | 14.50 |
| 64 | 24.91 | | | | 1.00 | 5.85 | 10.43 | | | | 23.92 | 19.07 | 14.48 |
| 65 | 23.98 | | | | | 4.89 | 9.50 | | | | 23.98 | 19.10 | 14.49 |
| 66 | 23.07 | | | | | 3.92 | 8.57 | | | | | 19.15 | 14.51 |
| 67 | 22.18 | | | | | 2.95 | 7.64 | | | | | 19.22 | 14.54 |
| 68 | 21.29 | | | | | 1.98 | 6.70 | | | | | 19.32 | 14.59 |
| 69 | 20.42 | | | | | 0.99 | 5.77 | | | | | 19.43 | 14.65 |
| 70 | 19.55 | | | | | | 4.83 | | | | | 19.55 | 14.72 |
| 71 | 18.67 | | | | | | 3.88 | | | | | | 14.79 |
| 72 | 17.79 | | | | | | 2.93 | | | | | | 14.86 |
| 73 | 16.89 | | | | | | 1.97 | | | | | | 14.93 |
| 74 | 15.99 | | | | | | 0.99 | | | | | | 15.00 |
| 75 | 15.08 | | | | | | | | | | | | 15.08 |
| 76 | 14.17 | | | | | | | | | | | | |
| 77 | 13.28 | | | | | | | | | | | | |
| 78 | 12.40 | | | | | | | | | | | | |
| 79 | 11.56 | | | | | | | | | | | | |
| 80 | 10.77 | | | | | | | | | | | | |
| 81 | 10.02 | | | | | | | | | | | | |
| 82 | 9.31 | | | | | | | | | | | | |
| 83 | 8.65 | | | | | | | | | | | | |
| 84 | 8.03 | | | | | | | | | | | | |
| 85 | 7.45 | | | | | | | | | | | | |
| 86 | 6.89 | | | | | | | | | | | | |
| 87 | 6.36 | | | | | | | | | | | | |
| 88 | 5.85 | | | | | | | | | | | | |
| 89 | 5.36 | | | | | | | | | | | | |
| 90 | 4.90 | | | | | | | | | | | | |
| 91 | 4.47 | | | | | | | | | | | | |
| 92 | 4.08 | | | | | | | | | | | | |
| 93 | 3.72 | | | | | | | | | | | | |
| 94 | 3.41 | | | | | | | | | | | | |
| 95 | 3.14 | | | | | | | | | | | | |
| 96 | 2.91 | | | | | | | | | | | | |
| 97 | 2.70 | | | | | | | | | | | | |
| 98 | 2.52 | | | | | | | | | | | | |
| 99 | 2.35 | | | | | | | | | | | | |
| 100 | 2.18 | | | | | | | | | | | | |

## A2: Nil discount tables for retirement ages 66 to 69 – MALE

| | Loss of earnings to age 66 | Loss of earnings to age 67 | Loss of earnings to age 68 | Loss of earnings to age 69 | | Loss of pension from age 66 | Loss of pension from age 67 | Loss of pension from age 68 | Loss of pension from age 69 |
|---|---|---|---|---|---|---|---|---|---|
| 16 | 48.70 | 49.59 | 50.48 | 51.37 | 16 | 22.91 | 22.02 | 21.13 | 20.24 |
| 17 | 47.69 | 48.59 | 49.48 | 50.36 | 17 | 22.82 | 21.92 | 21.03 | 20.15 |
| 18 | 46.69 | 47.58 | 48.48 | 49.37 | 18 | 22.72 | 21.83 | 20.93 | 20.04 |
| 19 | 45.69 | 46.59 | 47.48 | 48.37 | 19 | 22.62 | 21.72 | 20.83 | 19.94 |
| 20 | 44.69 | 45.59 | 46.48 | 47.37 | 20 | 22.53 | 21.63 | 20.74 | 19.85 |
| 21 | 43.70 | 44.59 | 45.48 | 46.38 | 21 | 22.43 | 21.54 | 20.65 | 19.75 |
| 22 | 42.71 | 43.60 | 44.48 | 45.38 | 22 | 22.33 | 21.44 | 20.56 | 19.66 |
| 23 | 41.71 | 42.61 | 43.49 | 44.38 | 23 | 22.23 | 21.33 | 20.45 | 19.56 |
| 24 | 40.72 | 41.61 | 42.50 | 43.39 | 24 | 22.13 | 21.24 | 20.35 | 19.46 |
| 25 | 39.73 | 40.62 | 41.50 | 42.40 | 25 | 22.03 | 21.14 | 20.26 | 19.36 |
| 26 | 38.74 | 39.63 | 40.51 | 41.40 | 26 | 21.94 | 21.05 | 20.17 | 19.28 |
| 27 | 37.75 | 38.64 | 39.52 | 40.41 | 27 | 21.84 | 20.95 | 20.07 | 19.18 |
| 28 | 36.77 | 37.65 | 38.53 | 39.42 | 28 | 21.74 | 20.86 | 19.98 | 19.09 |
| 29 | 35.78 | 36.66 | 37.54 | 38.43 | 29 | 21.64 | 20.76 | 19.88 | 18.99 |
| 30 | 34.79 | 35.68 | 36.56 | 37.44 | 30 | 21.55 | 20.66 | 19.78 | 18.90 |
| 31 | 33.80 | 34.69 | 35.57 | 36.45 | 31 | 21.47 | 20.58 | 19.70 | 18.82 |
| 32 | 32.83 | 33.71 | 34.60 | 35.47 | 32 | 21.37 | 20.49 | 19.60 | 18.73 |
| 33 | 31.85 | 32.73 | 33.61 | 34.50 | 33 | 21.30 | 20.42 | 19.54 | 18.65 |
| 34 | 30.87 | 31.75 | 32.64 | 33.52 | 34 | 21.22 | 20.34 | 19.45 | 18.57 |
| 35 | 29.90 | 30.78 | 31.66 | 32.54 | 35 | 21.13 | 20.25 | 19.37 | 18.49 |
| 36 | 28.92 | 29.80 | 30.68 | 31.56 | 36 | 21.06 | 20.18 | 19.30 | 18.42 |
| 37 | 27.94 | 28.83 | 29.71 | 30.59 | 37 | 20.99 | 20.10 | 19.22 | 18.34 |
| 38 | 26.97 | 27.85 | 28.73 | 29.61 | 38 | 20.90 | 20.02 | 19.14 | 18.26 |
| 39 | 25.99 | 26.88 | 27.75 | 28.64 | 39 | 20.83 | 19.94 | 19.07 | 18.18 |
| 40 | 25.02 | 25.90 | 26.78 | 27.66 | 40 | 20.74 | 19.86 | 18.98 | 18.10 |
| 41 | 24.04 | 24.93 | 25.81 | 26.69 | 41 | 20.67 | 19.78 | 18.90 | 18.02 |
| 42 | 23.07 | 23.96 | 24.84 | 25.72 | 42 | 20.60 | 19.71 | 18.83 | 17.95 |
| 43 | 22.11 | 22.99 | 23.87 | 24.75 | 43 | 20.51 | 19.63 | 18.75 | 17.87 |
| 44 | 21.14 | 22.02 | 22.90 | 23.79 | 44 | 20.45 | 19.57 | 18.69 | 17.80 |
| 45 | 20.17 | 21.06 | 21.94 | 22.82 | 45 | 20.38 | 19.49 | 18.61 | 17.73 |
| 46 | 19.20 | 20.09 | 20.97 | 21.85 | 46 | 20.32 | 19.43 | 18.55 | 17.67 |
| 47 | 18.24 | 19.13 | 20.01 | 20.89 | 47 | 20.25 | 19.36 | 18.48 | 17.60 |
| 48 | 17.27 | 18.17 | 19.05 | 19.93 | 48 | 20.20 | 19.30 | 18.42 | 17.54 |
| 49 | 16.32 | 17.20 | 18.09 | 18.98 | 49 | 20.13 | 19.25 | 18.36 | 17.47 |
| 50 | 15.35 | 16.25 | 17.14 | 18.02 | 50 | 20.10 | 19.20 | 18.31 | 17.43 |
| 51 | 14.41 | 15.29 | 16.19 | 17.07 | 51 | 20.04 | 19.16 | 18.26 | 17.38 |
| 52 | 13.45 | 14.35 | 15.24 | 16.12 | 52 | 20.02 | 19.12 | 18.23 | 17.35 |
| 53 | 12.50 | 13.40 | 14.30 | 15.18 | 53 | 19.99 | 19.09 | 18.19 | 17.31 |
| 54 | 11.55 | 12.45 | 13.35 | 14.24 | 54 | 19.98 | 19.08 | 18.18 | 17.29 |
| 55 | 10.59 | 11.51 | 12.41 | 13.30 | 55 | 19.99 | 19.07 | 18.17 | 17.28 |
| 56 | 9.65 | 10.56 | 11.47 | 12.36 | 56 | 19.99 | 19.08 | 18.17 | 17.28 |
| 57 | 8.70 | 9.61 | 10.52 | 11.43 | 57 | 20.01 | 19.10 | 18.19 | 17.28 |
| 58 | 7.74 | 8.67 | 9.58 | 10.49 | 58 | 20.04 | 19.11 | 18.20 | 17.29 |
| 59 | 6.80 | 7.72 | 8.64 | 9.54 | 59 | 20.05 | 19.13 | 18.21 | 17.31 |
| 60 | 5.83 | 6.77 | 7.69 | 8.61 | 60 | 20.09 | 19.15 | 18.23 | 17.31 |
| 61 | 4.88 | 5.82 | 6.75 | 7.67 | 61 | 20.12 | 19.18 | 18.25 | 17.33 |
| 62 | 3.91 | 4.87 | 5.80 | 6.72 | 62 | 20.17 | 19.21 | 18.28 | 17.36 |
| 63 | 2.95 | 3.90 | 4.85 | 5.79 | 63 | 20.22 | 19.27 | 18.32 | 17.38 |
| 64 | 1.98 | 2.94 | 3.90 | 4.84 | 64 | 20.30 | 19.34 | 18.38 | 17.44 |
| 65 | 0.99 | 1.98 | 2.94 | 3.89 | 65 | 20.43 | 19.44 | 18.48 | 17.53 |
| 66 | | 0.99 | 1.97 | 2.93 | 66 | 20.57 | 19.58 | 18.60 | 17.64 |
| 67 | | | 0.99 | 1.97 | 67 | | 19.74 | 18.75 | 17.77 |
| 68 | | | | 0.99 | 68 | | | 18.93 | 17.94 |
| 69 | | | | | 69 | | | | 18.12 |

See notes at the section A1 for details of methodology

A2: Nil discount tables "at a glance"

### A2: Nil discount tables for retirement ages 66 to 69 – FEMALE

| | Loss of earnings to age 66 | Loss of earnings to age 67 | Loss of earnings to age 68 | Loss of earnings to age 69 | | Loss of pension from age 66 | Loss of pension from age 67 | Loss of pension from age 68 | Loss of pension from age 69 |
|---|---|---|---|---|---|---|---|---|---|
| 16 | 49.27 | 50.21 | 51.14 | 52.08 | 16 | 26.07 | 25.13 | 24.20 | 23.26 |
| 17 | 48.27 | 49.20 | 50.14 | 51.07 | 17 | 25.97 | 25.04 | 24.10 | 23.17 |
| 18 | 47.27 | 48.20 | 49.14 | 50.07 | 18 | 25.87 | 24.94 | 24.00 | 23.07 |
| 19 | 46.27 | 47.20 | 48.14 | 49.07 | 19 | 25.78 | 24.85 | 23.91 | 22.98 |
| 20 | 45.27 | 46.20 | 47.14 | 48.07 | 20 | 25.69 | 24.76 | 23.82 | 22.89 |
| 21 | 44.27 | 45.20 | 46.14 | 47.07 | 21 | 25.59 | 24.66 | 23.72 | 22.79 |
| 22 | 43.27 | 44.20 | 45.13 | 46.07 | 22 | 25.50 | 24.57 | 23.64 | 22.70 |
| 23 | 42.27 | 43.20 | 44.13 | 45.06 | 23 | 25.40 | 24.47 | 23.54 | 22.61 |
| 24 | 41.28 | 42.20 | 43.13 | 44.06 | 24 | 25.29 | 24.37 | 23.44 | 22.51 |
| 25 | 40.28 | 41.21 | 42.13 | 43.06 | 25 | 25.20 | 24.27 | 23.35 | 22.42 |
| 26 | 39.28 | 40.21 | 41.13 | 42.06 | 26 | 25.10 | 24.17 | 23.25 | 22.32 |
| 27 | 38.28 | 39.21 | 40.13 | 41.06 | 27 | 25.01 | 24.08 | 23.16 | 22.23 |
| 28 | 37.28 | 38.21 | 39.14 | 40.06 | 28 | 24.92 | 23.99 | 23.06 | 22.14 |
| 29 | 36.29 | 37.21 | 38.14 | 39.07 | 29 | 24.82 | 23.90 | 22.97 | 22.04 |
| 30 | 35.29 | 36.22 | 37.15 | 38.07 | 30 | 24.73 | 23.80 | 22.87 | 21.95 |
| 31 | 34.29 | 35.22 | 36.15 | 37.08 | 31 | 24.65 | 23.72 | 22.79 | 21.86 |
| 32 | 33.30 | 34.22 | 35.16 | 36.08 | 32 | 24.56 | 23.64 | 22.70 | 21.78 |
| 33 | 32.31 | 33.23 | 34.16 | 35.09 | 33 | 24.46 | 23.54 | 22.61 | 21.68 |
| 34 | 31.31 | 32.24 | 33.17 | 34.09 | 34 | 24.38 | 23.45 | 22.52 | 21.60 |
| 35 | 30.32 | 31.25 | 32.18 | 33.10 | 35 | 24.29 | 23.36 | 22.43 | 21.51 |
| 36 | 29.33 | 30.26 | 31.18 | 32.11 | 36 | 24.20 | 23.27 | 22.35 | 21.42 |
| 37 | 28.34 | 29.27 | 30.19 | 31.12 | 37 | 24.12 | 23.19 | 22.27 | 21.34 |
| 38 | 27.36 | 28.28 | 29.20 | 30.13 | 38 | 24.02 | 23.10 | 22.18 | 21.25 |
| 39 | 26.37 | 27.29 | 28.21 | 29.14 | 39 | 23.94 | 23.02 | 22.10 | 21.17 |
| 40 | 25.38 | 26.30 | 27.23 | 28.15 | 40 | 23.86 | 22.94 | 22.01 | 21.09 |
| 41 | 24.39 | 25.32 | 26.24 | 27.16 | 41 | 23.78 | 22.85 | 21.93 | 21.01 |
| 42 | 23.41 | 24.33 | 25.25 | 26.17 | 42 | 23.69 | 22.77 | 21.85 | 20.93 |
| 43 | 22.42 | 23.35 | 24.27 | 25.19 | 43 | 23.62 | 22.69 | 21.77 | 20.85 |
| 44 | 21.44 | 22.36 | 23.29 | 24.21 | 44 | 23.54 | 22.62 | 21.69 | 20.77 |
| 45 | 20.46 | 21.39 | 22.31 | 23.23 | 45 | 23.47 | 22.54 | 21.62 | 20.70 |
| 46 | 19.48 | 20.41 | 21.33 | 22.25 | 46 | 23.39 | 22.46 | 21.54 | 20.62 |
| 47 | 18.50 | 19.43 | 20.35 | 21.28 | 47 | 23.33 | 22.40 | 21.48 | 20.55 |
| 48 | 17.53 | 18.45 | 19.38 | 20.30 | 48 | 23.26 | 22.34 | 21.41 | 20.49 |
| 49 | 16.55 | 17.48 | 18.41 | 19.33 | 49 | 23.21 | 22.28 | 21.35 | 20.43 |
| 50 | 15.58 | 16.51 | 17.44 | 18.36 | 50 | 23.15 | 22.22 | 21.29 | 20.37 |
| 51 | 14.61 | 15.54 | 16.47 | 17.39 | 51 | 23.10 | 22.17 | 21.24 | 20.32 |
| 52 | 13.64 | 14.58 | 15.51 | 16.43 | 52 | 23.05 | 22.11 | 21.18 | 20.26 |
| 53 | 12.67 | 13.61 | 14.54 | 15.47 | 53 | 23.01 | 22.07 | 21.14 | 20.21 |
| 54 | 11.70 | 12.64 | 13.57 | 14.51 | 54 | 22.98 | 22.04 | 21.11 | 20.17 |
| 55 | 10.74 | 11.67 | 12.61 | 13.54 | 55 | 22.94 | 22.01 | 21.07 | 20.14 |
| 56 | 9.77 | 10.71 | 11.65 | 12.58 | 56 | 22.92 | 21.98 | 21.04 | 20.11 |
| 57 | 8.80 | 9.75 | 10.69 | 11.62 | 57 | 22.91 | 21.96 | 21.02 | 20.09 |
| 58 | 7.83 | 8.78 | 9.72 | 10.66 | 58 | 22.91 | 21.96 | 21.02 | 20.08 |
| 59 | 6.86 | 7.81 | 8.76 | 9.70 | 59 | 22.90 | 21.95 | 21.00 | 20.06 |
| 60 | 5.90 | 6.85 | 7.80 | 8.74 | 60 | 22.88 | 21.93 | 20.98 | 20.04 |
| 61 | 4.92 | 5.89 | 6.83 | 7.78 | 61 | 22.88 | 21.91 | 20.97 | 20.02 |
| 62 | 3.94 | 4.91 | 5.87 | 6.82 | 62 | 22.89 | 21.92 | 20.96 | 20.01 |
| 63 | 2.97 | 3.94 | 4.91 | 5.86 | 63 | 22.89 | 21.92 | 20.95 | 20.00 |
| 64 | 1.99 | 2.96 | 3.93 | 4.90 | 64 | 22.92 | 21.95 | 20.98 | 20.01 |
| 65 | 1.00 | 1.99 | 2.96 | 3.93 | 65 | 22.98 | 21.99 | 21.02 | 20.05 |
| 66 | | 1.00 | 1.98 | 2.95 | 66 | 23.07 | 22.07 | 21.09 | 20.12 |
| 67 | | | 0.99 | 1.98 | 67 | | 22.18 | 21.19 | 20.20 |
| 68 | | | | 0.99 | 68 | | | 21.29 | 20.30 |
| 69 | | | | | 69 | | | | 20.42 |

See notes at the section A1 for details of methodology

# A3: Life tables and projected life tables

**National Life Tables, United Kingdom**

Period expectation of life
Based on data for the years 2012–2014

Office for National Statistics

| Age | Males | | | | | Females | | | | |
|---|---|---|---|---|---|---|---|---|---|---|
| $x$ | $m_x$ | $q_x$ | $l_x$ | $d_x$ | $e_x$ | $m_x$ | $q_x$ | $l_x$ | $d_x$ | $e_x$ |
| 0 | 0.004361 | 0.004352 | 100000.0 | 435.2 | 79.07 | 0.003577 | 0.003570 | 100000.0 | 357.0 | 82.81 |
| 1 | 0.000330 | 0.000330 | 99564.8 | 32.9 | 78.41 | 0.000257 | 0.000257 | 99643.0 | 25.6 | 82.10 |
| 2 | 0.000177 | 0.000177 | 99531.9 | 17.6 | 77.44 | 0.000130 | 0.000130 | 99617.4 | 13.0 | 81.12 |
| 3 | 0.000116 | 0.000116 | 99514.4 | 11.6 | 76.45 | 0.000114 | 0.000114 | 99604.4 | 11.4 | 80.13 |
| 4 | 0.000098 | 0.000098 | 99502.8 | 9.8 | 75.46 | 0.000087 | 0.000087 | 99593.0 | 8.6 | 79.14 |
| 5 | 0.000098 | 0.000098 | 99493.0 | 9.8 | 74.47 | 0.000087 | 0.000087 | 99584.4 | 8.6 | 78.15 |
| 6 | 0.000093 | 0.000093 | 99483.2 | 9.3 | 73.48 | 0.000081 | 0.000081 | 99575.7 | 8.1 | 77.16 |
| 7 | 0.000090 | 0.000090 | 99473.9 | 9.0 | 72.48 | 0.000079 | 0.000079 | 99567.7 | 7.9 | 76.16 |
| 8 | 0.000083 | 0.000083 | 99465.0 | 8.2 | 71.49 | 0.000069 | 0.000069 | 99559.8 | 6.9 | 75.17 |
| 9 | 0.000090 | 0.000090 | 99456.7 | 8.9 | 70.50 | 0.000066 | 0.000066 | 99552.9 | 6.6 | 74.17 |
| 10 | 0.000095 | 0.000095 | 99447.8 | 9.4 | 69.50 | 0.000075 | 0.000075 | 99546.3 | 7.4 | 73.18 |
| 11 | 0.000094 | 0.000094 | 99438.4 | 9.4 | 68.51 | 0.000065 | 0.000065 | 99538.9 | 6.5 | 72.18 |
| 12 | 0.000109 | 0.000109 | 99429.0 | 10.8 | 67.51 | 0.000066 | 0.000066 | 99532.4 | 6.6 | 71.19 |
| 13 | 0.000115 | 0.000115 | 99418.2 | 11.4 | 66.52 | 0.000093 | 0.000093 | 99525.8 | 9.3 | 70.19 |
| 14 | 0.000131 | 0.000131 | 99406.8 | 13.0 | 65.53 | 0.000106 | 0.000106 | 99516.5 | 10.5 | 69.20 |
| 15 | 0.000147 | 0.000147 | 99393.8 | 14.6 | 64.54 | 0.000128 | 0.000128 | 99506.0 | 12.7 | 68.21 |
| 16 | 0.000215 | 0.000215 | 99379.2 | 21.4 | 63.55 | 0.000143 | 0.000143 | 99493.3 | 14.2 | 67.22 |
| 17 | 0.000308 | 0.000308 | 99357.8 | 30.6 | 62.56 | 0.000160 | 0.000160 | 99479.1 | 15.9 | 66.23 |
| 18 | 0.000443 | 0.000443 | 99327.2 | 44.0 | 61.58 | 0.000183 | 0.000183 | 99463.2 | 18.2 | 65.24 |
| 19 | 0.000477 | 0.000477 | 99283.1 | 47.3 | 60.61 | 0.000198 | 0.000198 | 99445.0 | 19.7 | 64.25 |
| 20 | 0.000467 | 0.000467 | 99235.8 | 46.3 | 59.64 | 0.000202 | 0.000202 | 99425.3 | 20.1 | 63.26 |
| 21 | 0.000473 | 0.000473 | 99189.5 | 46.9 | 58.66 | 0.000207 | 0.000207 | 99405.2 | 20.6 | 62.27 |
| 22 | 0.000468 | 0.000468 | 99142.6 | 46.4 | 57.69 | 0.000214 | 0.000214 | 99384.6 | 21.2 | 61.29 |
| 23 | 0.000555 | 0.000555 | 99096.3 | 55.0 | 56.72 | 0.000232 | 0.000232 | 99363.4 | 23.1 | 60.30 |
| 24 | 0.000521 | 0.000521 | 99041.3 | 51.6 | 55.75 | 0.000227 | 0.000227 | 99340.3 | 22.6 | 59.31 |
| 25 | 0.000559 | 0.000559 | 98989.7 | 55.3 | 54.78 | 0.000255 | 0.000255 | 99317.7 | 25.4 | 58.33 |
| 26 | 0.000641 | 0.000641 | 98934.4 | 63.4 | 53.81 | 0.000259 | 0.000259 | 99292.4 | 25.7 | 57.34 |
| 27 | 0.000620 | 0.000620 | 98871.0 | 61.3 | 52.84 | 0.000274 | 0.000274 | 99266.7 | 27.2 | 56.36 |
| 28 | 0.000628 | 0.000627 | 98809.7 | 62.0 | 51.87 | 0.000343 | 0.000343 | 99239.5 | 34.1 | 55.37 |
| 29 | 0.000709 | 0.000709 | 98747.7 | 70.0 | 50.91 | 0.000321 | 0.000321 | 99205.4 | 31.8 | 54.39 |
| 30 | 0.000755 | 0.000755 | 98677.7 | 74.5 | 49.94 | 0.000370 | 0.000370 | 99173.6 | 36.7 | 53.41 |
| 31 | 0.000793 | 0.000793 | 98603.2 | 78.2 | 48.98 | 0.000423 | 0.000422 | 99136.9 | 41.9 | 52.43 |
| 32 | 0.000796 | 0.000796 | 98525.0 | 78.4 | 48.02 | 0.000424 | 0.000424 | 99095.0 | 42.0 | 51.45 |
| 33 | 0.000875 | 0.000875 | 98446.6 | 86.1 | 47.06 | 0.000469 | 0.000469 | 99053.0 | 46.5 | 50.47 |
| 34 | 0.000925 | 0.000924 | 98360.5 | 90.9 | 46.10 | 0.000538 | 0.000538 | 99006.5 | 53.3 | 49.49 |
| 35 | 0.001017 | 0.001016 | 98269.6 | 99.8 | 45.14 | 0.000564 | 0.000564 | 98953.2 | 55.8 | 48.52 |
| 36 | 0.001048 | 0.001047 | 98169.7 | 102.8 | 44.18 | 0.000600 | 0.000600 | 98897.4 | 59.3 | 47.55 |
| 37 | 0.001177 | 0.001176 | 98066.9 | 115.3 | 43.23 | 0.000635 | 0.000635 | 98838.1 | 62.8 | 46.58 |
| 38 | 0.001356 | 0.001355 | 97951.5 | 132.7 | 42.28 | 0.000732 | 0.000732 | 98775.3 | 72.3 | 45.61 |
| 39 | 0.001421 | 0.001420 | 97818.8 | 138.9 | 41.34 | 0.000823 | 0.000822 | 98703.0 | 81.2 | 44.64 |
| 40 | 0.001577 | 0.001576 | 97679.9 | 153.9 | 40.40 | 0.000883 | 0.000883 | 98621.9 | 87.0 | 43.67 |
| 41 | 0.001628 | 0.001626 | 97526.0 | 158.6 | 39.46 | 0.000958 | 0.000957 | 98534.8 | 94.3 | 42.71 |
| 42 | 0.001692 | 0.001690 | 97367.3 | 164.6 | 38.52 | 0.001058 | 0.001058 | 98440.5 | 104.1 | 41.75 |
| 43 | 0.001884 | 0.001882 | 97202.8 | 182.9 | 37.59 | 0.001157 | 0.001156 | 98336.3 | 113.7 | 40.80 |
| 44 | 0.002064 | 0.002062 | 97019.8 | 200.0 | 36.66 | 0.001271 | 0.001270 | 98222.7 | 124.8 | 39.84 |
| 45 | 0.002251 | 0.002248 | 96819.8 | 217.7 | 35.73 | 0.001383 | 0.001382 | 98097.9 | 135.6 | 38.89 |
| 46 | 0.002362 | 0.002360 | 96602.1 | 228.0 | 34.81 | 0.001447 | 0.001446 | 97962.3 | 141.7 | 37.95 |
| 47 | 0.002505 | 0.002502 | 96374.2 | 241.1 | 33.89 | 0.001623 | 0.001622 | 97820.6 | 158.6 | 37.00 |
| 48 | 0.002680 | 0.002677 | 96133.1 | 257.3 | 32.98 | 0.001711 | 0.001710 | 97662.0 | 167.0 | 36.06 |
| 49 | 0.002944 | 0.002940 | 95875.8 | 281.9 | 32.06 | 0.001926 | 0.001924 | 97495.0 | 187.6 | 35.12 |
| 50 | 0.003106 | 0.003101 | 95593.9 | 296.4 | 31.16 | 0.002159 | 0.002156 | 97307.4 | 209.8 | 34.19 |

A3: Life tables and projected life tables

**Period expectation of life**
**Based on data for the years 2012–2014**

| Age | Males | | | | | Females | | | | |
|---|---|---|---|---|---|---|---|---|---|---|
| $x$ | $m_x$ | $q_x$ | $l_x$ | $d_x$ | $e_x$ | $m_x$ | $q_x$ | $l_x$ | $d_x$ | $e_x$ |
| 51 | 0.003428 | 0.003423 | 95297.5 | 326.2 | 30.25 | 0.002347 | 0.002344 | 97097.6 | 227.6 | 33.26 |
| 52 | 0.003709 | 0.003702 | 94971.3 | 351.6 | 29.35 | 0.002561 | 0.002558 | 96870.0 | 247.8 | 32.34 |
| 53 | 0.004075 | 0.004067 | 94619.7 | 384.8 | 28.46 | 0.002784 | 0.002780 | 96622.2 | 268.6 | 31.42 |
| 54 | 0.004538 | 0.004528 | 94234.9 | 426.7 | 27.57 | 0.002981 | 0.002977 | 96353.6 | 286.8 | 30.51 |
| 55 | 0.004877 | 0.004865 | 93808.2 | 456.4 | 26.70 | 0.003408 | 0.003402 | 96066.8 | 326.8 | 29.60 |
| 56 | 0.005368 | 0.005353 | 93351.8 | 499.8 | 25.83 | 0.003681 | 0.003674 | 95740.0 | 351.7 | 28.69 |
| 57 | 0.005980 | 0.005962 | 92852.0 | 553.6 | 24.96 | 0.004042 | 0.004033 | 95388.2 | 384.7 | 27.80 |
| 58 | 0.006629 | 0.006607 | 92298.5 | 609.8 | 24.11 | 0.004394 | 0.004385 | 95003.5 | 416.6 | 26.91 |
| 59 | 0.007444 | 0.007416 | 91688.6 | 680.0 | 23.27 | 0.004783 | 0.004772 | 94586.9 | 451.3 | 26.03 |
| 60 | 0.008034 | 0.008002 | 91008.6 | 728.3 | 22.44 | 0.005239 | 0.005226 | 94135.6 | 491.9 | 25.15 |
| 61 | 0.008848 | 0.008809 | 90280.4 | 795.3 | 21.61 | 0.005825 | 0.005808 | 93643.7 | 543.9 | 24.28 |
| 62 | 0.009726 | 0.009679 | 89485.0 | 866.1 | 20.80 | 0.006303 | 0.006283 | 93099.8 | 585.0 | 23.42 |
| 63 | 0.010394 | 0.010340 | 88618.9 | 916.3 | 20.00 | 0.006778 | 0.006755 | 92514.8 | 625.0 | 22.56 |
| 64 | 0.011370 | 0.011306 | 87702.6 | 991.5 | 19.20 | 0.007383 | 0.007356 | 91889.8 | 675.9 | 21.71 |
| 65 | 0.012185 | 0.012111 | 86711.1 | 1050.2 | 18.42 | 0.007968 | 0.007936 | 91213.9 | 723.9 | 20.87 |
| 66 | 0.013279 | 0.013191 | 85660.9 | 1130.0 | 17.64 | 0.008616 | 0.008579 | 90490.1 | 776.3 | 20.03 |
| 67 | 0.014714 | 0.014606 | 84530.9 | 1234.7 | 16.87 | 0.009686 | 0.009639 | 89713.8 | 864.8 | 19.20 |
| 68 | 0.016263 | 0.016131 | 83296.2 | 1343.7 | 16.11 | 0.010806 | 0.010748 | 88849.0 | 955.0 | 18.38 |
| 69 | 0.018133 | 0.017970 | 81952.5 | 1472.7 | 15.36 | 0.011788 | 0.011719 | 87894.0 | 1030.0 | 17.58 |
| 70 | 0.019994 | 0.019796 | 80479.9 | 1593.2 | 14.64 | 0.013208 | 0.013122 | 86864.0 | 1139.8 | 16.78 |
| 71 | 0.022319 | 0.022073 | 78886.7 | 1741.2 | 13.92 | 0.014533 | 0.014429 | 85724.2 | 1236.9 | 16.00 |
| 72 | 0.025597 | 0.025273 | 77145.5 | 1949.7 | 13.22 | 0.016612 | 0.016475 | 84487.3 | 1391.9 | 15.22 |
| 73 | 0.027619 | 0.027243 | 75195.7 | 2048.5 | 12.55 | 0.018449 | 0.018281 | 83095.4 | 1519.0 | 14.47 |
| 74 | 0.030452 | 0.029995 | 73147.2 | 2194.1 | 11.89 | 0.020417 | 0.020211 | 81576.3 | 1648.7 | 13.73 |
| 75 | 0.033765 | 0.033205 | 70953.1 | 2356.0 | 11.24 | 0.022788 | 0.022532 | 79927.6 | 1800.9 | 13.00 |
| 76 | 0.037254 | 0.036573 | 68597.2 | 2508.8 | 10.61 | 0.025435 | 0.025116 | 78126.7 | 1962.2 | 12.29 |
| 77 | 0.041036 | 0.040211 | 66088.4 | 2657.5 | 10.00 | 0.028630 | 0.028226 | 76164.5 | 2149.8 | 11.59 |
| 78 | 0.046518 | 0.045461 | 63430.9 | 2883.6 | 9.39 | 0.031770 | 0.031273 | 74014.7 | 2314.7 | 10.92 |
| 79 | 0.050873 | 0.049611 | 60547.2 | 3003.8 | 8.82 | 0.036497 | 0.035843 | 71700.0 | 2569.9 | 10.25 |
| 80 | 0.057954 | 0.056322 | 57543.4 | 3240.9 | 8.25 | 0.041666 | 0.040816 | 69130.1 | 2821.6 | 9.61 |
| 81 | 0.065348 | 0.063280 | 54302.5 | 3436.3 | 7.72 | 0.046844 | 0.045772 | 66308.5 | 3035.1 | 9.00 |
| 82 | 0.074171 | 0.071519 | 50866.2 | 3637.9 | 7.20 | 0.053068 | 0.051697 | 63273.4 | 3271.0 | 8.41 |
| 83 | 0.083147 | 0.079828 | 47228.3 | 3770.1 | 6.72 | 0.060756 | 0.058965 | 60002.4 | 3538.1 | 7.84 |
| 84 | 0.093206 | 0.089056 | 43458.2 | 3870.2 | 6.26 | 0.070031 | 0.067661 | 56464.4 | 3820.5 | 7.30 |
| 85 | 0.105538 | 0.100248 | 39588.0 | 3968.6 | 5.82 | 0.079108 | 0.076098 | 52643.9 | 4006.1 | 6.80 |
| 86 | 0.118388 | 0.111772 | 35619.4 | 3981.2 | 5.41 | 0.089452 | 0.085623 | 48637.8 | 4164.5 | 6.31 |
| 87 | 0.132144 | 0.123954 | 31638.1 | 3921.7 | 5.03 | 0.101286 | 0.096404 | 44473.3 | 4287.4 | 5.86 |
| 88 | 0.147896 | 0.137712 | 27716.5 | 3816.9 | 4.67 | 0.113019 | 0.106974 | 40185.9 | 4298.8 | 5.43 |
| 89 | 0.165102 | 0.152512 | 23899.6 | 3645.0 | 4.34 | 0.129950 | 0.122022 | 35887.1 | 4379.0 | 5.02 |
| 90 | 0.181566 | 0.166455 | 20254.6 | 3371.5 | 4.03 | 0.146089 | 0.136144 | 31508.1 | 4289.6 | 4.65 |
| 91 | 0.201408 | 0.182981 | 16883.1 | 3089.3 | 3.74 | 0.163333 | 0.151001 | 27218.4 | 4110.0 | 4.30 |
| 92 | 0.232343 | 0.208161 | 13793.8 | 2871.3 | 3.46 | 0.187654 | 0.171558 | 23108.4 | 3964.4 | 3.98 |
| 93 | 0.250647 | 0.222733 | 10922.5 | 2432.8 | 3.24 | 0.204129 | 0.185224 | 19144.0 | 3545.9 | 3.70 |
| 94 | 0.262338 | 0.231918 | 8489.7 | 1968.9 | 3.03 | 0.225065 | 0.202300 | 15598.1 | 3155.5 | 3.43 |
| 95 | 0.297602 | 0.259055 | 6520.8 | 1689.2 | 2.79 | 0.246122 | 0.219153 | 12442.6 | 2726.8 | 3.17 |
| 96 | 0.333723 | 0.286001 | 4831.5 | 1381.8 | 2.59 | 0.287120 | 0.251076 | 9715.7 | 2439.4 | 2.92 |
| 97 | 0.364647 | 0.308416 | 3449.7 | 1063.9 | 2.43 | 0.308803 | 0.267500 | 7276.4 | 1946.4 | 2.73 |
| 98 | 0.396400 | 0.330830 | 2385.8 | 789.3 | 2.29 | 0.338692 | 0.289642 | 5329.9 | 1543.8 | 2.54 |
| 99 | 0.420893 | 0.347717 | 1596.5 | 555.1 | 2.18 | 0.374876 | 0.315701 | 3786.2 | 1195.3 | 2.38 |
| 100 | 0.432971 | 0.355920 | 1041.4 | 370.6 | 2.07 | 0.395028 | 0.329873 | 2590.9 | 854.7 | 2.24 |

Source: Office for National Statistics licensed under the Open Government licence V.I.O.

## A3: Life tables and projected life tables

### Expectations of life table

Expectations of life for age attained in 2016 allowing for projected changes in mortality assumed in the 2014-based population projections produced by the Office for National Statistics.

| United Kingdom | | | | | |
|---|---|---|---|---|---|
| Age | Males | Females | Age | Males | Females |
| 0 | 90.6 | 93.5 | 51 | 35.0 | 37.6 |
| 1 | 89.9 | 92.6 | 52 | 33.9 | 36.5 |
| 2 | 88.8 | 91.5 | 53 | 32.9 | 35.5 |
| 3 | 87.6 | 90.4 | 54 | 31.9 | 34.5 |
| 4 | 86.5 | 89.3 | 55 | 30.9 | 33.5 |
| 5 | 85.4 | 88.2 | 56 | 29.9 | 32.4 |
| 6 | 84.2 | 87.1 | 57 | 28.9 | 31.4 |
| 7 | 83.1 | 85.9 | 58 | 28.0 | 30.4 |
| 8 | 82.0 | 84.8 | 59 | 27.0 | 29.4 |
| 9 | 80.8 | 83.7 | 60 | 26.1 | 28.5 |
| 10 | 79.7 | 82.6 | 61 | 25.1 | 27.5 |
| 11 | 78.6 | 81.4 | 62 | 24.2 | 26.5 |
| 12 | 77.4 | 80.3 | 63 | 23.3 | 25.6 |
| 13 | 76.3 | 79.2 | 64 | 22.4 | 24.6 |
| 14 | 75.2 | 78.1 | 65 | 21.5 | 23.7 |
| 15 | 74.0 | 77.0 | 66 | 20.6 | 22.8 |
| 16 | 72.9 | 75.8 | 67 | 19.7 | 21.8 |
| 17 | 71.8 | 74.7 | 68 | 18.8 | 20.9 |
| 18 | 70.6 | 73.6 | 69 | 18.0 | 20.0 |
| 19 | 69.5 | 72.5 | 70 | 17.1 | 19.1 |
| 20 | 68.4 | 71.4 | 71 | 16.3 | 18.2 |
| 21 | 67.3 | 70.3 | 72 | 15.4 | 17.3 |
| 22 | 66.2 | 69.1 | 73 | 14.6 | 16.5 |
| 23 | 65.1 | 68.0 | 74 | 13.9 | 15.6 |
| 24 | 64.0 | 66.9 | 75 | 13.1 | 14.8 |
| 25 | 62.9 | 65.8 | 76 | 12.4 | 14.0 |
| 26 | 61.8 | 64.7 | 77 | 11.6 | 13.2 |
| 27 | 60.7 | 63.6 | 78 | 10.9 | 12.4 |
| 28 | 59.5 | 62.5 | 79 | 10.2 | 11.6 |
| 29 | 58.4 | 61.4 | 80 | 9.6 | 10.9 |
| 30 | 57.4 | 60.3 | 81 | 8.9 | 10.1 |
| 31 | 56.3 | 59.2 | 82 | 8.3 | 9.4 |
| 32 | 55.2 | 58.1 | 83 | 7.6 | 8.7 |
| 33 | 54.1 | 57.0 | 84 | 7.1 | 8.1 |
| 34 | 53.0 | 55.9 | 85 | 6.5 | 7.4 |
| 35 | 51.9 | 54.8 | 86 | 6.0 | 6.9 |
| 36 | 50.8 | 53.7 | 87 | 5.5 | 6.3 |
| 37 | 49.8 | 52.6 | 88 | 5.1 | 5.8 |
| 38 | 48.7 | 51.5 | 89 | 4.7 | 5.3 |
| 39 | 47.6 | 50.4 | 90 | 4.3 | 4.9 |
| 40 | 46.5 | 49.3 | 91 | 4.0 | 4.5 |
| 41 | 45.5 | 48.2 | 92 | 3.7 | 4.2 |
| 42 | 44.4 | 47.2 | 93 | 3.4 | 3.8 |
| 43 | 43.3 | 46.1 | 94 | 3.1 | 3.5 |
| 44 | 42.3 | 45.0 | 95 | 2.9 | 3.3 |
| 45 | 41.2 | 43.9 | 96 | 2.6 | 3.0 |
| 46 | 40.2 | 42.9 | 97 | 2.4 | 2.8 |
| 47 | 39.1 | 41.8 | 98 | 2.3 | 2.6 |
| 48 | 38.1 | 40.7 | 99 | 2.1 | 2.4 |
| 49 | 37.0 | 39.7 | 100 | 1.9 | 2.2 |
| 50 | 36.0 | 38.6 | | | |

Source: Office for National Statistics

A3: Life tables and projected life tables

**Notes:**

1. National life tables of various kinds and population projections have been produced for a considerable period, formerly by the Government Actuary's Department and, since February 2006, by the Office for National Statistics. The Decennial Life Tables for England and Wales combined and for Scotland are based on data for the three-year period around a Census. Between Censuses, life tables known as National Life Tables (formerly named Interim Life Tables) are produced which are based on data for the numbers in the population and the deaths by age and sex for the latest three-year period available. These National Life Tables are produced for the United Kingdom as a whole, Great Britain, England and Wales and also for each individual country of the United Kingdom. It is intended to update the life tables in *Facts and Figures* every year, using the latest data then available.

**The historical life tables**

2. The latest published Decennial Life Tables are the English Life Tables No.17 (ELT No.17). These are based on data on the numbers in the population and the numbers of deaths by age and sex for 2010–2012 (the three years around the 2011 Census). The latest published decennial life tables for Scotland are the Scottish Life Tables 2000–2002, based on data for the three years 2000 to 2002.

3. Data from the Decennial Life Table, ELT No.15, based on data for 1990–1992, formed the mortality assumptions underlying the calculations of the multipliers in Tables 1–18 of the 4th edition of the Ogden Tables. Tables of multipliers using mortality from the Decennial Life Tables are no longer reproduced in the Ogden Tables.

4. The tables reproduced on pages 17 and 18 are the latest available National Life Tables for the United Kingdom (based on data for 2012–2014). These life tables are based on historical data (and expectations of life which are calculated using these data), and effectively assume that the mortality rate for a given age and sex will remain constant in future years. They provide a measure of mortality for that particular period but are not a good indication of how long someone of a given age now is expected to live.

5. There have been large improvements in mortality rates over the last 100 years or so. For estimating how long someone of a given age is expected to live it is reasonable to assume that mortality rates will continue to improve in future

**Projected mortality**

6. The table reproduced on page 19 is the latest available official projection of expectations of life for the United Kingdom making allowance for expected future changes in mortality. This table allows for the projected changes in mortality assumed in the 2014-based population projections produced by the Office for National Statistics and published in October 2015. It should be noted that this is a more recent projection of mortality than that used to prepare the 7th edition of the Ogden Tables and the expectations of life are higher at most ages than the expectations of life shown in the 0.0% a year column of Tables 1 and 2 of the Ogden Tables (see Note 10).

7. At Appendix A to the Introduction to the 4th edition of the Ogden Tables there is an extract from ELT No.15, which shows graphs indicating rates of mortality expressed in percentages of the 1911

rates of mortality on a logarithmic scale. They demonstrate in stark fashion the improvement in longevity which has taken place since 1911.

8. The sole exception in some recent years has been small increases in the mortality of young males in their 30s due to increases in deaths caused by HIV infection and AIDS; suicide rates and alcohol-related mortality have also increased for men at young ages in some years. However, even if this slight worsening of mortality were to continue, the effects on the tables of multipliers (in the Ogden Tables) would not be significant.

9. The Office for National Statistics carries out official population projections for the United Kingdom and constituent countries, usually every two years. In particular, these projections include assumptions of improving mortality rates at most ages in the years following the base year of the projections.

10. Tables 1–26 of the 7th edition of the Ogden Tables give multipliers based on the projected mortality rates underlying the 2008-based principal population projections for the United Kingdom. These take as their base the estimated numbers in the population by sex and age in the constituent countries of the United Kingdom in mid-2008. The projections and the underlying assumptions are available on the website of the Office for National Statistics at: *http://www.ons.gov.uk/peoplepopulationandcommunity/populationandmigration/populationprojections/bulletins/nationalpopulationprojections/2015-10-29*.

11. Multipliers in earlier editions of the Ogden Tables were based on historical or projected mortality rates for the population of England and Wales combined. However, the Ogden Tables are used extensively in Scotland and Northern Ireland. Although it would be possible to produce separate Tables based on projected mortality rates for Scotland and for Northern Ireland, it was agreed for the 6th edition that rather than have three separate sets of tables there should be one set calculated using mortality rates from the population projections of the United Kingdom as a whole and this was continued in the 7th edition.

12. The Ogden Tables take account of the possibilities that a claimant may live for different periods, e.g. die soon or live to be very old. As mentioned above, the mortality assumptions for the 7th edition relate to the general population of the United Kingdom. Although comparable expectations of life are available for the constituent countries of the United Kingdom (and statistics are available which give a measure of variations in mortality between regions and areas), the Ogden Tables are recommended for use unadjusted regardless of location within the United Kingdom or for other potentially relevant factors such as earnings level, educational background, lifestyle or health status. Unless there is clear evidence in an individual case to support the view that the claimant concerned is "atypical" and can be expected to experience a significantly shorter or longer than average lifespan, no further increase or reduction should be made for mortality alone. Examples of an atypical claimant might be a lifelong heavy smoker, someone suffering from a head injury or epilepsy, an immobile patient or more likely a combination of adverse factors.

13. Where a claimant is thought to be atypical, medical or other relevant expert evidence should be sought on the possible impact of any condition on life expectancy. For large cases where it is thought appropriate to argue, on medical evidence or for other reasons, that the situation of the claimant is atypical, an actuary should be consulted on how an appropriate adjustment may be made to the Ogden Tables.

14. The mortality tables in this section and those underlying the Ogden Tables do not make any allowance for contingencies other than mortality. Appropriate adjustments for such contingencies are considered in section A4.

# A4: Loss of earnings multipliers adjusted for education, disability and employment status

The Ogden Tables dealing with loss of earnings (Ogden tables 3–14) are subject to adjustment for contingencies other than mortality (Ogden paras 26–44). The tables which follow incorporate those factors without the need for further calculation.

The contingencies are whether the claimant was in employment or not, whether he was disabled or not, and his educational or skill level. Earlier editions (1st–5th) of the Ogden Tables and of *Facts & Figures*, based on earlier research, made adjustments for the general state of the economy; the nature of the claimant's employment, whether clerical or manual; and for different geographical areas of the country. These are not used in the latest edition as more recent research has shown that when adjustments are made for education, disability and educational attainment the difference made by these other factors is small.

## Employment

Employed
Those who at the time of the accident are employed, self-employed or on a government training scheme.

Not employed
All others (including those temporarily out of work, full-time students and unpaid family workers).

## Disability

Disabled
A person is classified as being disabled if all three of the following conditions in relation to the ill-health or disability are met:

(i) he or she has either a progressive illness or an illness which has or is expected to last for over a year,

**and**

(ii) he or she satisfies the Equality Act definition that the impact of the disability substantially limits the person's ability to carry out normal day-to-day activities,

**and**

(iii) his or her condition affects either the kind **or** the amount of paid work they can do.

Not disabled.
All others.

Paragraph 35 of the Ogden notes (section A8 in this book) gives examples of the ways in which a disability may limit one's day-to-day activities.

**Educational attainment** means the highest level of education attained by the claimant. It is a shorthand for the level of skill and includes equivalent non-academic qualifications.

Degree or equivalent.

This includes professional qualifications, for example as a nurse.

GCSE grades A–C, O levels, or CSE grade 1, up to A-levels or equivalent.
In the tables which follow this is called "Good GCSE level education or equivalent".

Qualifications below GCSE grade C or CSE grade 1 or equivalent, or no qualifications.
In the tables which follow this is called "Education below good GCSE level".

There are 12 tables each for men and women arranged in the following order.

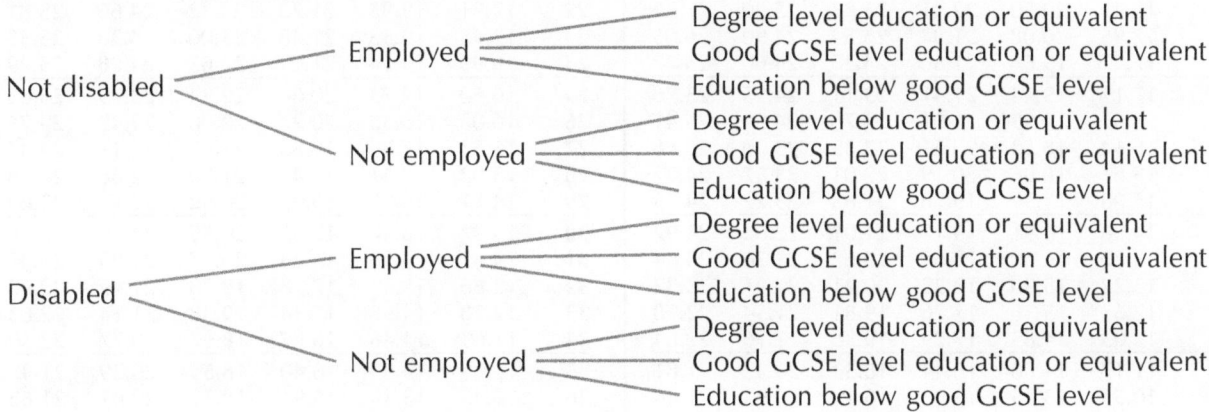

Thus if the claimant is a 32-year-old male solicitor, employed before the accident at a salary of £40,000, not disabled and proposing to retire at 60, the first table on the next page gives the multiplier for loss of earnings to age 60 as 18.22.

By using the tables for disabled claimants it is possible to obtain an estimate of the claimant's residual earning capacity, with an "inbuilt" allowance for employment risks which would otherwise require a separate *Smith v Manchester* award. Thus if the accident has seriously affected the solicitor's ability to work as a solicitor, and he is now employed at a salary of £25,000, the seventh table gives a multiplier of 11.68 for his new earning capacity to age 60. This approach will not always be suitable and there will be cases where a *Smith v Manchester* or *Blamire* award is still needed.

The 6th edition of the Ogden Tables had an adjustment factor for persons aged 16–19 with a degree level education. This caused difficulties. The 7th edition (para.41) recommends that in the case of someone who has not yet reached the age at which it is likely that he would start work, there should be an assessment of the level of education he would have attained, the age he would have started work, and whether he would have been employed or not. The multiplier appropriate to that age and those conditions should then be discounted for early receipt (for the period between the date of trial and the putative date of starting work).

The notes to the Ogden Tables do not provide specific adjustment factors for ages above 54 on the basis that, above that age, the likely course of someone's employment will depend on individual circumstances and the use of statistical averages may be inappropriate.

The adjustment factors as stated in the Ogden Tables are usually constant over a five year age range. This sometimes gives the appearance of anomalies or discontinuities in the figures—for example, in some tables a claimant of 18 or 19 has a smaller multiplier than one in his or her early 20s. The editors have been advised that this is the correct approach.

The tables assume a 2.5 per cent discount rate.

A4: Loss of earnings multipliers adjusted for education, etc.

**ND E Deg**

**Loss of earnings: not disabled; employed; degree level education or equivalent**

| Age | Male to retiring age | | | | | | Age | Female to retiring age | | | | | |
| --- | --- | --- | --- | --- | --- | --- | --- | --- | --- | --- | --- | --- | --- |
| | 50 | 55 | 60 | 65 | 70 | 75 | | 50 | 55 | 60 | 65 | 70 | 75 |
| 16 | | | | | | | 16 | | | | | | |
| 17 | | | See introductory notes | | | | 17 | | | See introductory notes | | | |
| 18 | | | | | | | 18 | | | | | | |
| 19 | | | | | | | 19 | | | | | | |
| 20 | 19.31 | 21.29 | 23.02 | 24.51 | 25.77 | 26.84 | 20 | 18.77 | 20.73 | 22.44 | 23.92 | 25.20 | 26.31 |
| 21 | 18.86 | 20.90 | 22.67 | 24.20 | 25.49 | 26.58 | 21 | 18.34 | 20.35 | 22.10 | 23.62 | 24.94 | 26.06 |
| 22 | 18.41 | 20.50 | 22.31 | 23.87 | 25.20 | 26.32 | 22 | 17.91 | 19.95 | 21.75 | 23.32 | 24.66 | 25.81 |
| 23 | 17.95 | 20.08 | 21.94 | 23.54 | 24.90 | 26.05 | 23 | 17.45 | 19.55 | 21.40 | 23.00 | 24.38 | 25.55 |
| 24 | 17.47 | 19.66 | 21.56 | 23.20 | 24.60 | 25.77 | 24 | 16.99 | 19.14 | 21.03 | 22.67 | 24.08 | 25.29 |
| 25 | 17.17 | 19.44 | 21.41 | 23.11 | 24.55 | 25.76 | 25 | 16.52 | 18.73 | 20.66 | 22.34 | 23.79 | 25.03 |
| 26 | 16.67 | 18.99 | 21.01 | 22.76 | 24.24 | 25.47 | 26 | 16.03 | 18.30 | 20.27 | 22.00 | 23.49 | 24.75 |
| 27 | 16.14 | 18.53 | 20.61 | 22.39 | 23.90 | 25.18 | 27 | 15.53 | 17.85 | 19.88 | 21.65 | 23.17 | 24.47 |
| 28 | 15.61 | 18.06 | 20.19 | 22.01 | 23.57 | 24.87 | 28 | 15.02 | 17.41 | 19.48 | 21.30 | 22.86 | 24.18 |
| 29 | 15.08 | 17.59 | 19.76 | 21.63 | 23.22 | 24.55 | 29 | 14.51 | 16.95 | 19.07 | 20.92 | 22.53 | 23.89 |
| 30 | 14.36 | 16.91 | 19.12 | 21.01 | 22.62 | 23.97 | 30 | 13.97 | 16.47 | 18.65 | 20.55 | 22.19 | 23.59 |
| 31 | 13.80 | 16.40 | 18.67 | 20.62 | 22.26 | 23.64 | 31 | 13.42 | 15.98 | 18.23 | 20.17 | 21.85 | 23.27 |
| 32 | 13.22 | 15.90 | 18.22 | 20.21 | 21.91 | 23.32 | 32 | 12.86 | 15.49 | 17.78 | 19.78 | 21.49 | 22.95 |
| 33 | 12.63 | 15.38 | 17.76 | 19.81 | 21.54 | 22.98 | 33 | 12.28 | 14.98 | 17.34 | 19.38 | 21.14 | 22.63 |
| 34 | 12.03 | 14.85 | 17.29 | 19.38 | 21.16 | 22.64 | 34 | 11.69 | 14.46 | 16.87 | 18.97 | 20.77 | 22.30 |
| 35 | 11.17 | 14.00 | 16.44 | 18.54 | 20.32 | 21.81 | 35 | 11.09 | 13.93 | 16.40 | 18.55 | 20.39 | 21.97 |
| 36 | 10.55 | 13.45 | 15.96 | 18.12 | 19.93 | 21.46 | 36 | 10.48 | 13.38 | 15.91 | 18.11 | 20.01 | 21.62 |
| 37 | 9.91 | 12.89 | 15.46 | 17.68 | 19.55 | 21.11 | 37 | 9.84 | 12.82 | 15.41 | 17.68 | 19.62 | 21.26 |
| 38 | 9.26 | 12.31 | 14.95 | 17.22 | 19.14 | 20.74 | 38 | 9.19 | 12.25 | 14.91 | 17.22 | 19.21 | 20.90 |
| 39 | 8.59 | 11.72 | 14.44 | 16.76 | 18.72 | 20.36 | 39 | 8.53 | 11.66 | 14.39 | 16.76 | 18.80 | 20.52 |
| 40 | 7.73 | 10.87 | 13.59 | 15.92 | 17.89 | 19.53 | 40 | 7.85 | 11.05 | 13.86 | 16.29 | 18.38 | 20.14 |
| 41 | 7.04 | 10.27 | 13.06 | 15.44 | 17.47 | 19.14 | 41 | 7.15 | 10.44 | 13.31 | 15.81 | 17.94 | 19.76 |
| 42 | 6.34 | 9.64 | 12.50 | 14.96 | 17.04 | 18.75 | 42 | 6.43 | 9.81 | 12.75 | 15.31 | 17.50 | 19.36 |
| 43 | 5.61 | 9.01 | 11.95 | 14.47 | 16.59 | 18.35 | 43 | 5.70 | 9.16 | 12.18 | 14.80 | 17.04 | 18.95 |
| 44 | 4.88 | 8.36 | 11.38 | 13.96 | 16.14 | 17.94 | 44 | 4.94 | 8.50 | 11.60 | 14.28 | 16.58 | 18.53 |
| 45 | 4.02 | 7.52 | 10.54 | 13.13 | 15.32 | 17.12 | 45 | 4.08 | 7.65 | 10.75 | 13.44 | 15.75 | 17.70 |
| 46 | 3.26 | 6.85 | 9.96 | 12.62 | 14.85 | 16.70 | 46 | 3.31 | 6.96 | 10.15 | 12.91 | 15.28 | 17.28 |
| 47 | 2.48 | 6.17 | 9.36 | 12.08 | 14.38 | 16.28 | 47 | 2.51 | 6.26 | 9.54 | 12.37 | 14.80 | 16.84 |
| 48 | 1.68 | 5.46 | 8.74 | 11.54 | 13.90 | 15.84 | 48 | 1.70 | 5.55 | 8.91 | 11.81 | 14.30 | 16.41 |
| 49 | 0.85 | 4.75 | 8.11 | 10.98 | 13.40 | 15.39 | 49 | 0.86 | 4.82 | 8.27 | 11.25 | 13.80 | 15.96 |
| 50 | | 3.87 | 7.20 | 10.05 | 12.45 | 14.43 | 50 | | 4.02 | 7.52 | 10.54 | 13.13 | 15.33 |
| 51 | | 3.10 | 6.49 | 9.38 | 11.81 | 13.82 | 51 | | 3.22 | 6.77 | 9.84 | 12.47 | 14.69 |
| 52 | | 2.32 | 5.77 | 8.71 | 11.18 | 13.21 | 52 | | 2.42 | 6.02 | 9.14 | 11.80 | 14.05 |
| 53 | | 1.55 | 5.06 | 8.04 | 10.54 | 12.61 | 53 | | 1.62 | 5.28 | 8.44 | 11.14 | 13.42 |
| 54 | | 0.78 | 4.34 | 7.37 | 9.91 | 12.01 | 54 | | 0.82 | 4.58 | 7.83 | 10.61 | 12.95 |

See introductory notes as regards claimants over 54 at date of trial

See introductory notes as regards claimants over 54 at date of trial

A4: Loss of earnings multipliers adjusted for education, etc.

**ND E GCSE**

**Loss of earnings: not disabled; employed; good GCSE level education or equivalent**

| Age | Male to retiring age | | | | | | Age | Female to retiring age | | | | | |
|---|---|---|---|---|---|---|---|---|---|---|---|---|---|
| | 50 | 55 | 60 | 65 | 70 | 75 | | 50 | 55 | 60 | 65 | 70 | 75 |
| 16 | 20.52 | 22.28 | 23.81 | 25.13 | 26.26 | 27.21 | 16 | 18.56 | 20.17 | 21.58 | 22.81 | 23.87 | 24.78 |
| 17 | 20.12 | 21.93 | 23.50 | 24.85 | 26.00 | 26.97 | 17 | 18.20 | 19.85 | 21.29 | 22.56 | 23.64 | 24.58 |
| 18 | 19.72 | 21.57 | 23.18 | 24.56 | 25.75 | 26.74 | 18 | 17.84 | 19.53 | 21.01 | 22.30 | 23.42 | 24.36 |
| 19 | 19.31 | 21.20 | 22.85 | 24.27 | 25.48 | 26.50 | 19 | 17.46 | 19.21 | 20.72 | 22.04 | 23.18 | 24.15 |
| 20 | 19.31 | 21.29 | 23.02 | 24.51 | 25.77 | 26.84 | 20 | 17.29 | 19.10 | 20.67 | 22.04 | 23.22 | 24.24 |
| 21 | 18.86 | 20.90 | 22.67 | 24.20 | 25.49 | 26.58 | 21 | 16.90 | 18.75 | 20.36 | 21.76 | 22.98 | 24.01 |
| 22 | 18.41 | 20.50 | 22.31 | 23.87 | 25.20 | 26.32 | 22 | 16.50 | 18.38 | 20.04 | 21.48 | 22.72 | 23.78 |
| 23 | 17.95 | 20.08 | 21.94 | 23.54 | 24.90 | 26.05 | 23 | 16.08 | 18.02 | 19.71 | 21.19 | 22.46 | 23.54 |
| 24 | 17.47 | 19.66 | 21.56 | 23.20 | 24.60 | 25.77 | 24 | 15.65 | 17.64 | 19.38 | 20.89 | 22.19 | 23.30 |
| 25 | 16.98 | 19.23 | 21.18 | 22.86 | 24.29 | 25.48 | 25 | 15.59 | 17.67 | 19.50 | 21.08 | 22.45 | 23.62 |
| 26 | 16.49 | 18.79 | 20.78 | 22.51 | 23.98 | 25.20 | 26 | 15.13 | 17.27 | 19.14 | 20.76 | 22.17 | 23.36 |
| 27 | 15.97 | 18.34 | 20.39 | 22.14 | 23.64 | 24.90 | 27 | 14.66 | 16.85 | 18.77 | 20.44 | 21.87 | 23.09 |
| 28 | 15.45 | 17.87 | 19.97 | 21.78 | 23.31 | 24.60 | 28 | 14.18 | 16.43 | 18.39 | 20.10 | 21.57 | 22.82 |
| 29 | 14.91 | 17.40 | 19.55 | 21.40 | 22.97 | 24.29 | 29 | 13.69 | 15.99 | 18.00 | 19.75 | 21.26 | 22.55 |
| 30 | 14.21 | 16.73 | 18.91 | 20.78 | 22.38 | 23.71 | 30 | 13.34 | 15.73 | 17.82 | 19.63 | 21.19 | 22.52 |
| 31 | 13.65 | 16.23 | 18.46 | 20.39 | 22.02 | 23.39 | 31 | 12.82 | 15.27 | 17.41 | 19.26 | 20.87 | 22.23 |
| 32 | 13.08 | 15.72 | 18.02 | 19.99 | 21.67 | 23.07 | 32 | 12.28 | 14.79 | 16.98 | 18.89 | 20.53 | 21.92 |
| 33 | 12.49 | 15.22 | 17.56 | 19.59 | 21.30 | 22.73 | 33 | 11.73 | 14.31 | 16.56 | 18.50 | 20.19 | 21.62 |
| 34 | 11.90 | 14.69 | 17.10 | 19.17 | 20.93 | 22.40 | 34 | 11.17 | 13.81 | 16.12 | 18.11 | 19.84 | 21.30 |
| 35 | 11.17 | 14.00 | 16.44 | 18.54 | 20.32 | 21.81 | 35 | 10.72 | 13.46 | 15.85 | 17.92 | 19.70 | 21.22 |
| 36 | 10.55 | 13.45 | 15.96 | 18.12 | 19.93 | 21.46 | 36 | 10.12 | 12.93 | 15.38 | 17.50 | 19.33 | 20.89 |
| 37 | 9.91 | 12.89 | 15.46 | 17.68 | 19.55 | 21.11 | 37 | 9.51 | 12.38 | 14.90 | 17.08 | 18.95 | 20.55 |
| 38 | 9.26 | 12.31 | 14.95 | 17.22 | 19.14 | 20.74 | 38 | 8.88 | 11.83 | 14.40 | 16.64 | 18.56 | 20.19 |
| 39 | 8.59 | 11.72 | 14.44 | 16.76 | 18.72 | 20.36 | 39 | 8.24 | 11.27 | 13.91 | 16.19 | 18.16 | 19.83 |
| 40 | 7.73 | 10.87 | 13.59 | 15.92 | 17.89 | 19.53 | 40 | 7.59 | 10.68 | 13.39 | 15.74 | 17.76 | 19.46 |
| 41 | 7.04 | 10.27 | 13.06 | 15.44 | 17.47 | 19.14 | 41 | 6.91 | 10.09 | 12.87 | 15.27 | 17.34 | 19.09 |
| 42 | 6.34 | 9.64 | 12.50 | 14.96 | 17.04 | 18.75 | 42 | 6.21 | 9.48 | 12.32 | 14.79 | 16.91 | 18.70 |
| 43 | 5.61 | 9.01 | 11.95 | 14.47 | 16.59 | 18.35 | 43 | 5.50 | 8.85 | 11.77 | 14.30 | 16.47 | 18.31 |
| 44 | 4.88 | 8.36 | 11.38 | 13.96 | 16.14 | 17.94 | 44 | 4.77 | 8.21 | 11.21 | 13.80 | 16.02 | 17.91 |
| 45 | 4.02 | 7.52 | 10.54 | 13.13 | 15.32 | 17.12 | 45 | 3.99 | 7.47 | 10.51 | 13.13 | 15.39 | 17.30 |
| 46 | 3.26 | 6.85 | 9.96 | 12.62 | 14.85 | 16.70 | 46 | 3.23 | 6.80 | 9.92 | 12.61 | 14.93 | 16.88 |
| 47 | 2.48 | 6.17 | 9.36 | 12.08 | 14.38 | 16.28 | 47 | 2.45 | 6.12 | 9.32 | 12.09 | 14.46 | 16.46 |
| 48 | 1.68 | 5.46 | 8.74 | 11.54 | 13.90 | 15.84 | 48 | 1.66 | 5.42 | 8.70 | 11.54 | 13.97 | 16.03 |
| 49 | 0.85 | 4.75 | 8.11 | 10.98 | 13.40 | 15.39 | 49 | 0.84 | 4.71 | 8.07 | 10.99 | 13.48 | 15.59 |
| 50 | | 3.87 | 7.20 | 10.05 | 12.45 | 14.43 | 50 | | 3.93 | 7.34 | 10.30 | 12.83 | 14.97 |
| 51 | | 3.10 | 6.49 | 9.38 | 11.81 | 13.82 | 51 | | 3.18 | 6.69 | 9.73 | 12.32 | 14.52 |
| 52 | | 2.32 | 5.77 | 8.71 | 11.18 | 13.21 | 52 | | 2.42 | 6.02 | 9.14 | 11.80 | 14.05 |
| 53 | | 1.55 | 5.06 | 8.04 | 10.54 | 12.61 | 53 | | 1.62 | 5.28 | 8.44 | 11.14 | 13.42 |
| 54 | | 0.78 | 4.34 | 7.37 | 9.91 | 12.01 | 54 | | 0.82 | 4.58 | 7.83 | 10.61 | 12.95 |

See introductory notes as regards claimants over 54 at date of trial

See introductory notes as regards claimants over 54 at date of trial

A4: Loss of earnings multipliers adjusted for education, etc.

**ND E <GCSE**

**Loss of earnings: not disabled; employed; education below good GCSE level**

| Age | Male to retiring age | | | | | | Age | Female to retiring age | | | | | |
|---|---|---|---|---|---|---|---|---|---|---|---|---|---|
| | 50 | 55 | 60 | 65 | 70 | 75 | | 50 | 55 | 60 | 65 | 70 | 75 |
| 16 | 19.38 | 21.05 | 22.49 | 23.73 | 24.80 | 25.70 | 16 | 14.66 | 15.94 | 17.05 | 18.02 | 18.86 | 19.58 |
| 17 | 19.01 | 20.71 | 22.19 | 23.47 | 24.56 | 25.47 | 17 | 14.38 | 15.69 | 16.83 | 17.82 | 18.68 | 19.42 |
| 18 | 18.62 | 20.37 | 21.89 | 23.20 | 24.32 | 25.25 | 18 | 14.09 | 15.43 | 16.60 | 17.62 | 18.50 | 19.25 |
| 19 | 18.23 | 20.03 | 21.58 | 22.92 | 24.06 | 25.02 | 19 | 13.80 | 15.17 | 16.37 | 17.41 | 18.32 | 19.08 |
| 20 | 18.26 | 20.13 | 21.77 | 23.18 | 24.37 | 25.38 | 20 | 14.34 | 15.84 | 17.14 | 18.28 | 19.26 | 20.10 |
| 21 | 17.84 | 19.77 | 21.44 | 22.88 | 24.11 | 25.13 | 21 | 14.01 | 15.54 | 16.88 | 18.05 | 19.05 | 19.91 |
| 22 | 17.41 | 19.38 | 21.10 | 22.58 | 23.83 | 24.89 | 22 | 13.68 | 15.25 | 16.62 | 17.82 | 18.84 | 19.72 |
| 23 | 16.97 | 18.99 | 20.75 | 22.26 | 23.55 | 24.63 | 23 | 13.33 | 14.94 | 16.35 | 17.57 | 18.63 | 19.52 |
| 24 | 16.52 | 18.59 | 20.39 | 21.94 | 23.26 | 24.37 | 24 | 12.98 | 14.63 | 16.07 | 17.32 | 18.40 | 19.33 |
| 25 | 16.43 | 18.60 | 20.49 | 22.12 | 23.50 | 24.65 | 25 | 13.36 | 15.15 | 16.71 | 18.07 | 19.25 | 20.25 |
| 26 | 15.95 | 18.17 | 20.11 | 21.78 | 23.19 | 24.38 | 26 | 12.97 | 14.80 | 16.40 | 17.80 | 19.00 | 20.02 |
| 27 | 15.45 | 17.74 | 19.72 | 21.42 | 22.87 | 24.09 | 27 | 12.56 | 14.44 | 16.08 | 17.52 | 18.74 | 19.79 |
| 28 | 14.94 | 17.28 | 19.32 | 21.07 | 22.55 | 23.80 | 28 | 12.15 | 14.08 | 15.76 | 17.23 | 18.49 | 19.56 |
| 29 | 14.43 | 16.83 | 18.91 | 20.70 | 22.22 | 23.50 | 29 | 11.74 | 13.71 | 15.43 | 16.93 | 18.22 | 19.32 |
| 30 | 13.89 | 16.36 | 18.49 | 20.33 | 21.89 | 23.18 | 30 | 11.77 | 13.88 | 15.72 | 17.32 | 18.70 | 19.88 |
| 31 | 13.35 | 15.87 | 18.06 | 19.94 | 21.54 | 22.87 | 31 | 11.31 | 13.47 | 15.36 | 17.00 | 18.41 | 19.61 |
| 32 | 12.79 | 15.38 | 17.62 | 19.55 | 21.19 | 22.56 | 32 | 10.84 | 13.05 | 14.98 | 16.66 | 18.11 | 19.34 |
| 33 | 12.22 | 14.88 | 17.18 | 19.16 | 20.83 | 22.23 | 33 | 10.35 | 12.62 | 14.61 | 16.33 | 17.81 | 19.07 |
| 34 | 11.64 | 14.36 | 16.72 | 18.75 | 20.47 | 21.90 | 34 | 9.86 | 12.19 | 14.22 | 15.98 | 17.50 | 18.79 |
| 35 | 11.04 | 13.84 | 16.26 | 18.33 | 20.10 | 21.56 | 35 | 9.72 | 12.21 | 14.38 | 16.26 | 17.87 | 19.25 |
| 36 | 10.43 | 13.30 | 15.78 | 17.92 | 19.71 | 21.22 | 36 | 9.18 | 11.72 | 13.95 | 15.87 | 17.53 | 18.95 |
| 37 | 9.80 | 12.74 | 15.29 | 17.48 | 19.33 | 20.87 | 37 | 8.63 | 11.23 | 13.51 | 15.49 | 17.19 | 18.63 |
| 38 | 9.16 | 12.18 | 14.78 | 17.03 | 18.93 | 20.51 | 38 | 8.06 | 10.73 | 13.07 | 15.09 | 16.83 | 18.31 |
| 39 | 8.49 | 11.59 | 14.28 | 16.57 | 18.51 | 20.13 | 39 | 7.47 | 10.22 | 12.61 | 14.69 | 16.47 | 17.99 |
| 40 | 7.73 | 10.87 | 13.59 | 15.92 | 17.89 | 19.53 | 40 | 7.06 | 9.94 | 12.46 | 14.64 | 16.52 | 18.10 |
| 41 | 7.04 | 10.27 | 13.06 | 15.44 | 17.47 | 19.14 | 41 | 6.42 | 9.38 | 11.97 | 14.21 | 16.13 | 17.76 |
| 42 | 6.34 | 9.64 | 12.50 | 14.96 | 17.04 | 18.75 | 42 | 5.78 | 8.82 | 11.46 | 13.76 | 15.73 | 17.40 |
| 43 | 5.61 | 9.01 | 11.95 | 14.47 | 16.59 | 18.35 | 43 | 5.12 | 8.23 | 10.95 | 13.30 | 15.32 | 17.03 |
| 44 | 4.88 | 8.36 | 11.38 | 13.96 | 16.14 | 17.94 | 44 | 4.44 | 7.64 | 10.42 | 12.84 | 14.90 | 16.66 |
| 45 | 4.02 | 7.52 | 10.54 | 13.13 | 15.32 | 17.12 | 45 | 3.80 | 7.12 | 10.01 | 12.51 | 14.66 | 16.48 |
| 46 | 3.26 | 6.85 | 9.96 | 12.62 | 14.85 | 16.70 | 46 | 3.08 | 6.48 | 9.45 | 12.02 | 14.22 | 16.09 |
| 47 | 2.48 | 6.17 | 9.36 | 12.08 | 14.38 | 16.28 | 47 | 2.33 | 5.83 | 8.88 | 11.52 | 13.78 | 15.68 |
| 48 | 1.68 | 5.46 | 8.74 | 11.54 | 13.90 | 15.84 | 48 | 1.58 | 5.17 | 8.29 | 11.00 | 13.32 | 15.28 |
| 49 | 0.85 | 4.75 | 8.11 | 10.98 | 13.40 | 15.39 | 49 | 0.80 | 4.49 | 7.70 | 10.47 | 12.85 | 14.86 |
| 50 | | 3.87 | 7.20 | 10.05 | 12.45 | 14.43 | 50 | | 3.79 | 7.08 | 9.93 | 12.37 | 14.43 |
| 51 | | 3.10 | 6.49 | 9.38 | 11.81 | 13.82 | 51 | | 3.07 | 6.46 | 9.38 | 11.88 | 14.00 |
| 52 | | 2.32 | 5.77 | 8.71 | 11.18 | 13.21 | 52 | | 2.33 | 5.81 | 8.81 | 11.38 | 13.55 |
| 53 | | 1.55 | 5.06 | 8.04 | 10.54 | 12.61 | 53 | | 1.58 | 5.15 | 8.24 | 10.87 | 13.10 |
| 54 | | 0.78 | 4.34 | 7.37 | 9.91 | 12.01 | 54 | | 0.81 | 4.53 | 7.73 | 10.48 | 12.79 |

See introductory notes as regards claimants over 54 at date of trial

A4: Loss of earnings multipliers adjusted for education, etc.

**ND NE Deg**

**Loss of earnings: not disabled; not employed; degree level education or equivalent**

| Age | Male to retiring age | | | | | | Age | Female to retiring age | | | | | |
|---|---|---|---|---|---|---|---|---|---|---|---|---|---|
| | 50 | 55 | 60 | 65 | 70 | 75 | | 50 | 55 | 60 | 65 | 70 | 75 |
| 16 | | | | | | | 16 | | | | | | |
| 17 | | | See introductory notes | | | | 17 | | | See introductory notes | | | |
| 18 | | | | | | | 18 | | | | | | |
| 19 | | | | | | | 19 | | | | | | |
| 20 | 18.68 | 20.59 | 22.27 | 23.71 | 24.93 | 25.96 | 20 | 17.72 | 19.56 | 21.18 | 22.58 | 23.79 | 24.83 |
| 21 | 18.25 | 20.22 | 21.93 | 23.41 | 24.66 | 25.71 | 21 | 17.31 | 19.20 | 20.86 | 22.29 | 23.54 | 24.60 |
| 22 | 17.81 | 19.83 | 21.58 | 23.10 | 24.38 | 25.46 | 22 | 16.90 | 18.83 | 20.53 | 22.01 | 23.28 | 24.36 |
| 23 | 17.36 | 19.43 | 21.23 | 22.78 | 24.09 | 25.20 | 23 | 16.47 | 18.45 | 20.19 | 21.71 | 23.01 | 24.12 |
| 24 | 16.90 | 19.02 | 20.86 | 22.45 | 23.80 | 24.93 | 24 | 16.04 | 18.07 | 19.85 | 21.39 | 22.73 | 23.87 |
| 25 | 16.43 | 18.60 | 20.49 | 22.12 | 23.50 | 24.65 | 25 | 15.40 | 17.46 | 19.26 | 20.83 | 22.19 | 23.34 |
| 26 | 15.95 | 18.17 | 20.11 | 21.78 | 23.19 | 24.38 | 26 | 14.95 | 17.06 | 18.91 | 20.52 | 21.90 | 23.08 |
| 27 | 15.45 | 17.74 | 19.72 | 21.42 | 22.87 | 24.09 | 27 | 14.48 | 16.65 | 18.54 | 20.19 | 21.60 | 22.82 |
| 28 | 14.94 | 17.28 | 19.32 | 21.07 | 22.55 | 23.80 | 28 | 14.01 | 16.23 | 18.17 | 19.86 | 21.31 | 22.55 |
| 29 | 14.43 | 16.83 | 18.91 | 20.70 | 22.22 | 23.50 | 29 | 13.53 | 15.80 | 17.79 | 19.51 | 21.01 | 22.28 |
| 30 | 13.58 | 15.99 | 18.08 | 19.87 | 21.39 | 22.66 | 30 | 12.72 | 14.99 | 16.98 | 18.70 | 20.19 | 21.47 |
| 31 | 13.05 | 15.51 | 17.65 | 19.50 | 21.05 | 22.36 | 31 | 12.21 | 14.55 | 16.59 | 18.35 | 19.89 | 21.18 |
| 32 | 12.50 | 15.03 | 17.23 | 19.11 | 20.71 | 22.05 | 32 | 11.70 | 14.09 | 16.18 | 18.00 | 19.56 | 20.89 |
| 33 | 11.95 | 14.55 | 16.79 | 18.73 | 20.37 | 21.73 | 33 | 11.18 | 13.63 | 15.78 | 17.63 | 19.24 | 20.60 |
| 34 | 11.38 | 14.04 | 16.35 | 18.33 | 20.01 | 21.41 | 34 | 10.64 | 13.16 | 15.36 | 17.26 | 18.91 | 20.30 |
| 35 | 10.55 | 13.22 | 15.53 | 17.51 | 19.19 | 20.60 | 35 | 9.97 | 12.52 | 14.74 | 16.67 | 18.33 | 19.74 |
| 36 | 9.96 | 12.70 | 15.07 | 17.11 | 18.83 | 20.26 | 36 | 9.42 | 12.02 | 14.30 | 16.28 | 17.98 | 19.43 |
| 37 | 9.36 | 12.17 | 14.60 | 16.69 | 18.46 | 19.93 | 37 | 8.85 | 11.52 | 13.86 | 15.89 | 17.63 | 19.11 |
| 38 | 8.75 | 11.63 | 14.12 | 16.26 | 18.08 | 19.58 | 38 | 8.26 | 11.01 | 13.40 | 15.48 | 17.26 | 18.78 |
| 39 | 8.11 | 11.07 | 13.63 | 15.83 | 17.68 | 19.23 | 39 | 7.66 | 10.48 | 12.94 | 15.06 | 16.90 | 18.45 |
| 40 | 7.20 | 10.13 | 12.66 | 14.83 | 16.67 | 18.20 | 40 | 6.88 | 9.69 | 12.14 | 14.27 | 16.11 | 17.65 |
| 41 | 6.56 | 9.57 | 12.17 | 14.39 | 16.28 | 17.83 | 41 | 6.26 | 9.15 | 11.67 | 13.85 | 15.72 | 17.32 |
| 42 | 5.90 | 8.99 | 11.65 | 13.94 | 15.88 | 17.47 | 42 | 5.63 | 8.60 | 11.18 | 13.42 | 15.33 | 16.97 |
| 43 | 5.23 | 8.40 | 11.14 | 13.48 | 15.46 | 17.10 | 43 | 4.99 | 8.03 | 10.68 | 12.97 | 14.94 | 16.61 |
| 44 | 4.54 | 7.79 | 10.60 | 13.01 | 15.04 | 16.72 | 44 | 4.33 | 7.45 | 10.16 | 12.52 | 14.53 | 16.24 |
| 45 | 3.60 | 6.73 | 9.44 | 11.76 | 13.71 | 15.33 | 45 | 3.38 | 6.33 | 8.90 | 11.12 | 13.03 | 14.65 |
| 46 | 2.92 | 6.14 | 8.92 | 11.30 | 13.30 | 14.95 | 46 | 2.74 | 5.76 | 8.40 | 10.68 | 12.64 | 14.30 |
| 47 | 2.22 | 5.52 | 8.38 | 10.82 | 12.87 | 14.58 | 47 | 2.07 | 5.18 | 7.89 | 10.24 | 12.25 | 13.94 |
| 48 | 1.50 | 4.89 | 7.82 | 10.33 | 12.44 | 14.18 | 48 | 1.40 | 4.59 | 7.37 | 9.78 | 11.84 | 13.58 |
| 49 | 0.76 | 4.25 | 7.26 | 9.83 | 12.00 | 13.78 | 49 | 0.71 | 3.99 | 6.84 | 9.31 | 11.42 | 13.20 |
| 50 | | 3.36 | 6.25 | 8.72 | 10.80 | 12.51 | 50 | | 3.00 | 5.59 | 7.85 | 9.77 | 11.40 |
| 51 | | 2.65 | 5.54 | 8.01 | 10.08 | 11.79 | 51 | | 2.27 | 4.78 | 6.95 | 8.80 | 10.37 |
| 52 | | 1.92 | 4.77 | 7.20 | 9.25 | 10.93 | 52 | | 1.61 | 4.02 | 6.09 | 7.87 | 9.37 |
| 53 | | 1.22 | 3.98 | 6.33 | 8.30 | 9.93 | 53 | | 0.98 | 3.18 | 5.09 | 6.71 | 8.09 |
| 54 | | 0.58 | 3.24 | 5.50 | 7.40 | 8.97 | 54 | | 0.44 | 2.43 | 4.15 | 5.62 | 6.86 |

See introductory notes as regards claimants over 54 at date of trial

See introductory notes as regards claimants over 54 at date of trial

A4: Loss of earnings multipliers adjusted for education, etc.

**ND NE GCSE**

**Loss of earnings: not disabled; not employed; good GCSE level education or equivalent**

| Age | Male to retiring age | | | | | | Age | Female to retiring age | | | | | |
|---|---|---|---|---|---|---|---|---|---|---|---|---|---|
| | 50 | 55 | 60 | 65 | 70 | 75 | | 50 | 55 | 60 | 65 | 70 | 75 |
| 16 | 19.38 | 21.05 | 22.49 | 23.73 | 24.80 | 25.70 | 16 | 17.64 | 19.17 | 20.51 | 21.68 | 22.69 | 23.55 |
| 17 | 19.01 | 20.71 | 22.19 | 23.47 | 24.56 | 25.47 | 17 | 17.30 | 18.87 | 20.24 | 21.44 | 22.48 | 23.36 |
| 18 | 18.62 | 20.37 | 21.89 | 23.20 | 24.32 | 25.25 | 18 | 16.96 | 18.56 | 19.97 | 21.20 | 22.26 | 23.16 |
| 19 | 18.23 | 20.03 | 21.58 | 22.92 | 24.06 | 25.02 | 19 | 16.60 | 18.26 | 19.70 | 20.95 | 22.04 | 22.96 |
| 20 | 18.47 | 20.36 | 22.02 | 23.44 | 24.65 | 25.67 | 20 | 16.03 | 17.70 | 19.16 | 20.43 | 21.52 | 22.47 |
| 21 | 18.04 | 19.99 | 21.68 | 23.14 | 24.38 | 25.42 | 21 | 15.66 | 17.37 | 18.87 | 20.17 | 21.30 | 22.25 |
| 22 | 17.61 | 19.61 | 21.34 | 22.84 | 24.10 | 25.18 | 22 | 15.29 | 17.04 | 18.57 | 19.91 | 21.06 | 22.04 |
| 23 | 17.17 | 19.21 | 20.99 | 22.52 | 23.82 | 24.91 | 23 | 14.90 | 16.70 | 18.27 | 19.64 | 20.82 | 21.82 |
| 24 | 16.71 | 18.81 | 20.63 | 22.19 | 23.53 | 24.65 | 24 | 14.51 | 16.35 | 17.96 | 19.36 | 20.57 | 21.60 |
| 25 | 16.24 | 18.39 | 20.26 | 21.87 | 23.23 | 24.38 | 25 | 13.92 | 15.78 | 17.41 | 18.83 | 20.05 | 21.09 |
| 26 | 15.77 | 17.97 | 19.88 | 21.53 | 22.93 | 24.10 | 26 | 13.51 | 15.42 | 17.09 | 18.54 | 19.79 | 20.86 |
| 27 | 15.28 | 17.54 | 19.50 | 21.18 | 22.62 | 23.82 | 27 | 13.09 | 15.04 | 16.75 | 18.25 | 19.52 | 20.62 |
| 28 | 14.78 | 17.09 | 19.10 | 20.83 | 22.30 | 23.53 | 28 | 12.66 | 14.67 | 16.42 | 17.95 | 19.26 | 20.38 |
| 29 | 14.26 | 16.64 | 18.70 | 20.47 | 21.97 | 23.23 | 29 | 12.23 | 14.28 | 16.07 | 17.63 | 18.98 | 20.13 |
| 30 | 13.42 | 15.81 | 17.87 | 19.64 | 21.15 | 22.40 | 30 | 11.77 | 13.88 | 15.72 | 17.32 | 18.70 | 19.88 |
| 31 | 12.90 | 15.33 | 17.45 | 19.27 | 20.81 | 22.10 | 31 | 11.31 | 13.47 | 15.36 | 17.00 | 18.41 | 19.61 |
| 32 | 12.36 | 14.86 | 17.03 | 18.89 | 20.48 | 21.80 | 32 | 10.84 | 13.05 | 14.98 | 16.66 | 18.11 | 19.34 |
| 33 | 11.81 | 14.38 | 16.60 | 18.52 | 20.13 | 21.48 | 33 | 10.35 | 12.62 | 14.61 | 16.33 | 17.81 | 19.07 |
| 34 | 11.25 | 13.88 | 16.16 | 18.12 | 19.78 | 21.16 | 34 | 9.86 | 12.19 | 14.22 | 15.98 | 17.50 | 18.79 |
| 35 | 10.42 | 13.06 | 15.35 | 17.30 | 18.97 | 20.35 | 35 | 9.22 | 11.58 | 13.64 | 15.42 | 16.95 | 18.26 |
| 36 | 9.84 | 12.55 | 14.89 | 16.91 | 18.61 | 20.03 | 36 | 8.71 | 11.12 | 13.23 | 15.06 | 16.64 | 17.97 |
| 37 | 9.25 | 12.03 | 14.43 | 16.50 | 18.24 | 19.70 | 37 | 8.18 | 10.66 | 12.82 | 14.70 | 16.31 | 17.68 |
| 38 | 8.64 | 11.49 | 13.95 | 16.07 | 17.87 | 19.35 | 38 | 7.64 | 10.18 | 12.39 | 14.32 | 15.97 | 17.38 |
| 39 | 8.01 | 10.94 | 13.47 | 15.64 | 17.47 | 19.00 | 39 | 7.09 | 9.69 | 11.97 | 13.93 | 15.63 | 17.06 |
| 40 | 7.11 | 10.00 | 12.51 | 14.65 | 16.47 | 17.97 | 40 | 6.35 | 8.94 | 11.21 | 13.18 | 14.87 | 16.29 |
| 41 | 6.48 | 9.45 | 12.02 | 14.22 | 16.08 | 17.62 | 41 | 5.78 | 8.45 | 10.77 | 12.79 | 14.52 | 15.98 |
| 42 | 5.83 | 8.88 | 11.51 | 13.77 | 15.68 | 17.26 | 42 | 5.20 | 7.93 | 10.32 | 12.38 | 14.16 | 15.66 |
| 43 | 5.17 | 8.29 | 11.00 | 13.32 | 15.27 | 16.89 | 43 | 4.61 | 7.41 | 9.86 | 11.97 | 13.79 | 15.33 |
| 44 | 4.49 | 7.70 | 10.47 | 12.85 | 14.86 | 16.52 | 44 | 4.00 | 6.88 | 9.38 | 11.56 | 13.41 | 14.99 |
| 45 | 3.60 | 6.73 | 9.44 | 11.76 | 13.71 | 15.33 | 45 | 3.00 | 5.63 | 7.91 | 9.89 | 11.58 | 13.02 |
| 46 | 2.92 | 6.14 | 8.92 | 11.30 | 13.30 | 14.95 | 46 | 2.43 | 5.12 | 7.47 | 9.50 | 11.24 | 12.71 |
| 47 | 2.22 | 5.52 | 8.38 | 10.82 | 12.87 | 14.58 | 47 | 1.84 | 4.61 | 7.01 | 9.10 | 10.89 | 12.39 |
| 48 | 1.50 | 4.89 | 7.82 | 10.33 | 12.44 | 14.18 | 48 | 1.25 | 4.08 | 6.55 | 8.69 | 10.52 | 12.07 |
| 49 | 0.76 | 4.25 | 7.26 | 9.83 | 12.00 | 13.78 | 49 | 0.63 | 3.55 | 6.08 | 8.28 | 10.15 | 11.74 |
| 50 | | 3.36 | 6.25 | 8.72 | 10.80 | 12.51 | 50 | | 2.57 | 4.81 | 6.74 | 8.40 | 9.80 |
| 51 | | 2.65 | 5.54 | 8.01 | 10.08 | 11.79 | 51 | | 1.93 | 4.06 | 5.91 | 7.48 | 8.81 |
| 52 | | 1.92 | 4.77 | 7.20 | 9.25 | 10.93 | 52 | | 1.32 | 3.30 | 5.00 | 6.46 | 7.70 |
| 53 | | 1.22 | 3.98 | 6.33 | 8.30 | 9.93 | 53 | | 0.80 | 2.61 | 4.17 | 5.50 | 6.63 |
| 54 | | 0.58 | 3.24 | 5.50 | 7.40 | 8.97 | 54 | | 0.35 | 1.93 | 3.30 | 4.47 | 5.46 |

See introductory notes as regards claimants over 54 at date of trial

See introductory notes as regards claimants over 54 at date of trial

A4: Loss of earnings multipliers adjusted for education, etc.

**ND NE <GCSE**

**Loss of earnings: not disabled; not employed; education below good GCSE level**

| Age | Male to retiring age | | | | | | Age | Female to retiring age | | | | | |
|---|---|---|---|---|---|---|---|---|---|---|---|---|---|
| | 50 | 55 | 60 | 65 | 70 | 75 | | 50 | 55 | 60 | 65 | 70 | 75 |
| 16 | 18.70 | 20.30 | 21.70 | 22.89 | 23.93 | 24.79 | 16 | 13.52 | 14.69 | 15.72 | 16.61 | 17.39 | 18.05 |
| 17 | 18.34 | 19.98 | 21.41 | 22.64 | 23.69 | 24.58 | 17 | 13.26 | 14.46 | 15.51 | 16.43 | 17.22 | 17.90 |
| 18 | 17.97 | 19.66 | 21.11 | 22.38 | 23.46 | 24.36 | 18 | 12.99 | 14.22 | 15.30 | 16.24 | 17.06 | 17.75 |
| 19 | 17.59 | 19.32 | 20.82 | 22.12 | 23.21 | 24.14 | 19 | 12.72 | 13.99 | 15.09 | 16.05 | 16.89 | 17.59 |
| 20 | 17.42 | 19.21 | 20.77 | 22.11 | 23.25 | 24.21 | 20 | 12.65 | 13.97 | 15.13 | 16.13 | 16.99 | 17.74 |
| 21 | 17.02 | 18.86 | 20.45 | 21.83 | 23.00 | 23.98 | 21 | 12.37 | 13.72 | 14.90 | 15.92 | 16.81 | 17.57 |
| 22 | 16.61 | 18.49 | 20.13 | 21.54 | 22.73 | 23.75 | 22 | 12.07 | 13.45 | 14.66 | 15.72 | 16.63 | 17.40 |
| 23 | 16.19 | 18.12 | 19.80 | 21.24 | 22.47 | 23.50 | 23 | 11.77 | 13.18 | 14.42 | 15.50 | 16.43 | 17.23 |
| 24 | 15.76 | 17.74 | 19.46 | 20.93 | 22.19 | 23.25 | 24 | 11.45 | 12.91 | 14.18 | 15.28 | 16.24 | 17.05 |
| 25 | 15.14 | 17.14 | 18.88 | 20.38 | 21.65 | 22.71 | 25 | 11.32 | 12.83 | 14.16 | 15.31 | 16.31 | 17.15 |
| 26 | 14.69 | 16.74 | 18.52 | 20.07 | 21.37 | 22.46 | 26 | 10.99 | 12.54 | 13.90 | 15.08 | 16.10 | 16.96 |
| 27 | 14.24 | 16.34 | 18.17 | 19.74 | 21.07 | 22.20 | 27 | 10.64 | 12.24 | 13.63 | 14.84 | 15.88 | 16.77 |
| 28 | 13.77 | 15.92 | 17.80 | 19.41 | 20.78 | 21.93 | 28 | 10.30 | 11.93 | 13.35 | 14.60 | 15.66 | 16.57 |
| 29 | 13.29 | 15.51 | 17.43 | 19.07 | 20.48 | 21.65 | 29 | 9.94 | 11.61 | 13.07 | 14.34 | 15.44 | 16.37 |
| 30 | 12.64 | 14.89 | 16.83 | 18.50 | 19.92 | 21.10 | 30 | 9.89 | 11.66 | 13.20 | 14.55 | 15.71 | 16.70 |
| 31 | 12.15 | 14.44 | 16.43 | 18.15 | 19.60 | 20.82 | 31 | 9.50 | 11.31 | 12.90 | 14.28 | 15.47 | 16.47 |
| 32 | 11.64 | 14.00 | 16.04 | 17.80 | 19.29 | 20.53 | 32 | 9.10 | 10.96 | 12.59 | 14.00 | 15.21 | 16.25 |
| 33 | 11.12 | 13.54 | 15.63 | 17.44 | 18.96 | 20.23 | 33 | 8.69 | 10.60 | 12.27 | 13.72 | 14.96 | 16.02 |
| 34 | 10.59 | 13.07 | 15.22 | 17.07 | 18.63 | 19.93 | 34 | 8.28 | 10.24 | 11.94 | 13.43 | 14.70 | 15.79 |
| 35 | 9.93 | 12.44 | 14.62 | 16.48 | 18.06 | 19.38 | 35 | 7.85 | 9.86 | 11.61 | 13.13 | 14.43 | 15.55 |
| 36 | 9.38 | 11.95 | 14.18 | 16.10 | 17.72 | 19.07 | 36 | 7.42 | 9.47 | 11.26 | 12.82 | 14.16 | 15.30 |
| 37 | 8.81 | 11.46 | 13.74 | 15.71 | 17.38 | 18.76 | 37 | 6.97 | 9.07 | 10.91 | 12.51 | 13.89 | 15.05 |
| 38 | 8.23 | 10.94 | 13.29 | 15.30 | 17.02 | 18.43 | 38 | 6.51 | 8.67 | 10.55 | 12.19 | 13.60 | 14.79 |
| 39 | 7.63 | 10.42 | 12.83 | 14.90 | 16.64 | 18.10 | 39 | 6.04 | 8.25 | 10.19 | 11.86 | 13.31 | 14.53 |
| 40 | 6.85 | 9.63 | 12.04 | 14.11 | 15.86 | 17.31 | 40 | 5.29 | 7.45 | 9.34 | 10.98 | 12.39 | 13.58 |
| 41 | 6.24 | 9.10 | 11.58 | 13.69 | 15.48 | 16.97 | 41 | 4.82 | 7.04 | 8.98 | 10.66 | 12.10 | 13.32 |
| 42 | 5.62 | 8.55 | 11.08 | 13.26 | 15.10 | 16.62 | 42 | 4.33 | 6.61 | 8.60 | 10.32 | 11.80 | 13.05 |
| 43 | 4.98 | 7.99 | 10.59 | 12.82 | 14.70 | 16.26 | 43 | 3.84 | 6.17 | 8.21 | 9.98 | 11.49 | 12.77 |
| 44 | 4.32 | 7.41 | 10.09 | 12.37 | 14.31 | 15.90 | 44 | 3.33 | 5.73 | 7.82 | 9.63 | 11.18 | 12.49 |
| 45 | 3.46 | 6.47 | 9.07 | 11.30 | 13.18 | 14.73 | 45 | 2.44 | 4.57 | 6.43 | 8.03 | 9.41 | 10.58 |
| 46 | 2.80 | 5.90 | 8.57 | 10.86 | 12.78 | 14.37 | 46 | 1.98 | 4.16 | 6.07 | 7.72 | 9.13 | 10.33 |
| 47 | 2.13 | 5.31 | 8.05 | 10.40 | 12.37 | 14.01 | 47 | 1.50 | 3.74 | 5.70 | 7.39 | 8.85 | 10.07 |
| 48 | 1.44 | 4.70 | 7.52 | 9.93 | 11.96 | 13.63 | 48 | 1.01 | 3.32 | 5.32 | 7.06 | 8.55 | 9.81 |
| 49 | 0.73 | 4.08 | 6.98 | 9.45 | 11.53 | 13.25 | 49 | 0.51 | 2.88 | 4.94 | 6.72 | 8.25 | 9.54 |
| 50 | | 3.26 | 6.08 | 8.48 | 10.50 | 12.17 | 50 | | 2.01 | 3.76 | 5.27 | 6.57 | 7.66 |
| 51 | | 2.57 | 5.38 | 7.78 | 9.79 | 11.46 | 51 | | 1.52 | 3.19 | 4.63 | 5.87 | 6.91 |
| 52 | | 1.89 | 4.70 | 7.10 | 9.11 | 10.76 | 52 | | 1.04 | 2.58 | 3.92 | 5.06 | 6.02 |
| 53 | | 1.22 | 3.98 | 6.33 | 8.30 | 9.93 | 53 | | 0.62 | 2.04 | 3.25 | 4.29 | 5.17 |
| 54 | | 0.58 | 3.24 | 5.50 | 7.40 | 8.97 | 54 | | 0.27 | 1.49 | 2.55 | 3.45 | 4.21 |

See introductory notes as regards claimants over 54 at date of trial

See introductory notes as regards claimants over 54 at date of trial

A4: Loss of earnings multipliers adjusted for education, etc.

**D E Deg**

**Loss of earnings: disabled; employed; degree level education or equivalent**

| Age | Male to retiring age | | | | | | Age | Female to retiring age | | | | | |
|---|---|---|---|---|---|---|---|---|---|---|---|---|---|
| | 50 | 55 | 60 | 65 | 70 | 75 | | 50 | 55 | 60 | 65 | 70 | 75 |
| 16 | | | | | | | 16 | | | | | | |
| 17 | | | See introductory notes | | | | 17 | | | See introductory notes | | | |
| 18 | | | | | | | 18 | | | | | | |
| 19 | | | | | | | 19 | | | | | | |
| 20 | 12.80 | 14.12 | 15.26 | 16.25 | 17.09 | 17.79 | 20 | 13.50 | 14.91 | 16.13 | 17.20 | 18.12 | 18.92 |
| 21 | 12.50 | 13.86 | 15.03 | 16.04 | 16.90 | 17.62 | 21 | 13.19 | 14.63 | 15.89 | 16.99 | 17.93 | 18.74 |
| 22 | 12.21 | 13.59 | 14.79 | 15.83 | 16.71 | 17.45 | 22 | 12.88 | 14.35 | 15.64 | 16.77 | 17.73 | 18.56 |
| 23 | 11.90 | 13.32 | 14.55 | 15.61 | 16.51 | 17.27 | 23 | 12.55 | 14.06 | 15.39 | 16.54 | 17.53 | 18.37 |
| 24 | 11.58 | 13.04 | 14.30 | 15.38 | 16.31 | 17.09 | 24 | 12.22 | 13.77 | 15.12 | 16.30 | 17.32 | 18.19 |
| 25 | 11.08 | 12.54 | 13.81 | 14.91 | 15.84 | 16.62 | 25 | 11.69 | 13.26 | 14.62 | 15.81 | 16.84 | 17.72 |
| 26 | 10.75 | 12.25 | 13.55 | 14.68 | 15.64 | 16.43 | 26 | 11.35 | 12.95 | 14.35 | 15.57 | 16.63 | 17.52 |
| 27 | 10.42 | 11.96 | 13.30 | 14.44 | 15.42 | 16.24 | 27 | 10.99 | 12.64 | 14.07 | 15.33 | 16.40 | 17.32 |
| 28 | 10.07 | 11.65 | 13.03 | 14.20 | 15.20 | 16.04 | 28 | 10.63 | 12.32 | 13.79 | 15.08 | 16.18 | 17.12 |
| 29 | 9.73 | 11.35 | 12.75 | 13.96 | 14.98 | 15.84 | 29 | 10.27 | 12.00 | 13.50 | 14.81 | 15.95 | 16.91 |
| 30 | 9.21 | 10.84 | 12.26 | 13.48 | 14.51 | 15.37 | 30 | 9.73 | 11.48 | 13.00 | 14.32 | 15.46 | 16.43 |
| 31 | 8.85 | 10.52 | 11.97 | 13.22 | 14.28 | 15.16 | 31 | 9.35 | 11.14 | 12.70 | 14.05 | 15.22 | 16.21 |
| 32 | 8.48 | 10.20 | 11.68 | 12.96 | 14.05 | 14.96 | 32 | 8.96 | 10.79 | 12.39 | 13.78 | 14.97 | 15.99 |
| 33 | 8.10 | 9.86 | 11.39 | 12.70 | 13.81 | 14.74 | 33 | 8.56 | 10.43 | 12.08 | 13.50 | 14.72 | 15.77 |
| 34 | 7.72 | 9.52 | 11.09 | 12.43 | 13.57 | 14.52 | 34 | 8.15 | 10.07 | 11.76 | 13.21 | 14.47 | 15.54 |
| 35 | 7.20 | 9.02 | 10.60 | 11.95 | 13.10 | 14.05 | 35 | 7.60 | 9.55 | 11.24 | 12.71 | 13.98 | 15.05 |
| 36 | 6.80 | 8.67 | 10.28 | 11.68 | 12.85 | 13.83 | 36 | 7.18 | 9.17 | 10.91 | 12.41 | 13.71 | 14.82 |
| 37 | 6.39 | 8.31 | 9.96 | 11.39 | 12.60 | 13.60 | 37 | 6.75 | 8.78 | 10.57 | 12.11 | 13.44 | 14.57 |
| 38 | 5.97 | 7.93 | 9.63 | 11.10 | 12.34 | 13.36 | 38 | 6.30 | 8.39 | 10.22 | 11.80 | 13.16 | 14.32 |
| 39 | 5.53 | 7.55 | 9.30 | 10.80 | 12.06 | 13.12 | 39 | 5.84 | 7.99 | 9.86 | 11.49 | 12.88 | 14.07 |
| 40 | 5.00 | 7.04 | 8.80 | 10.31 | 11.59 | 12.65 | 40 | 5.29 | 7.45 | 9.34 | 10.98 | 12.39 | 13.58 |
| 41 | 4.56 | 6.65 | 8.46 | 10.00 | 11.31 | 12.40 | 41 | 4.82 | 7.04 | 8.98 | 10.66 | 12.10 | 13.32 |
| 42 | 4.10 | 6.25 | 8.10 | 9.69 | 11.04 | 12.15 | 42 | 4.33 | 6.61 | 8.60 | 10.32 | 11.80 | 13.05 |
| 43 | 3.64 | 5.84 | 7.74 | 9.37 | 10.74 | 11.88 | 43 | 3.84 | 6.17 | 8.21 | 9.98 | 11.49 | 12.77 |
| 44 | 3.16 | 5.41 | 7.37 | 9.04 | 10.45 | 11.62 | 44 | 3.33 | 5.73 | 7.82 | 9.63 | 11.18 | 12.49 |
| 45 | 2.57 | 4.81 | 6.74 | 8.40 | 9.80 | 10.95 | 45 | 2.81 | 5.27 | 7.42 | 9.27 | 10.86 | 12.21 |
| 46 | 2.08 | 4.38 | 6.37 | 8.07 | 9.50 | 10.68 | 46 | 2.28 | 4.80 | 7.00 | 8.90 | 10.54 | 11.92 |
| 47 | 1.58 | 3.94 | 5.98 | 7.73 | 9.20 | 10.41 | 47 | 1.73 | 4.32 | 6.58 | 8.53 | 10.21 | 11.62 |
| 48 | 1.07 | 3.49 | 5.59 | 7.38 | 8.89 | 10.13 | 48 | 1.17 | 3.83 | 6.14 | 8.15 | 9.86 | 11.32 |
| 49 | 0.54 | 3.04 | 5.19 | 7.02 | 8.57 | 9.85 | 49 | 0.59 | 3.32 | 5.70 | 7.76 | 9.52 | 11.00 |
| 50 | | 2.47 | 4.60 | 6.42 | 7.95 | 9.21 | 50 | | 2.81 | 5.24 | 7.36 | 9.16 | 10.69 |
| 51 | | 2.00 | 4.19 | 6.06 | 7.63 | 8.93 | 51 | | 2.31 | 4.86 | 7.06 | 8.95 | 10.54 |
| 52 | | 1.55 | 3.84 | 5.81 | 7.45 | 8.81 | 52 | | 1.76 | 4.37 | 6.64 | 8.57 | 10.21 |
| 53 | | 1.05 | 3.41 | 5.43 | 7.12 | 8.51 | 53 | | 1.21 | 3.94 | 6.31 | 8.32 | 10.03 |
| 54 | | 0.53 | 2.96 | 5.04 | 6.78 | 8.21 | 54 | | 0.62 | 3.48 | 5.94 | 8.05 | 9.83 |

See introductory notes as regards claimants over 54 at date of trial

A4: Loss of earnings multipliers adjusted for education, etc.

**D E GCSE**

**Loss of earnings: disabled; employed; good GCSE level education or equivalent**

| Age | \multicolumn{6}{c|}{Male to retiring age} | Age | \multicolumn{6}{c}{Female to retiring age} |
| | 50 | 55 | 60 | 65 | 70 | 75 | | 50 | 55 | 60 | 65 | 70 | 75 |
| --- | --- | --- | --- | --- | --- | --- | --- | --- | --- | --- | --- | --- | --- |
| 16 | 12.54 | 13.62 | 14.55 | 15.36 | 16.05 | 16.63 | 16 | 9.85 | 10.71 | 11.46 | 12.11 | 12.67 | 13.15 |
| 17 | 12.30 | 13.40 | 14.36 | 15.19 | 15.89 | 16.48 | 17 | 9.66 | 10.54 | 11.30 | 11.98 | 12.55 | 13.05 |
| 18 | 12.05 | 13.18 | 14.16 | 15.01 | 15.74 | 16.34 | 18 | 9.47 | 10.37 | 11.15 | 11.84 | 12.43 | 12.93 |
| 19 | 11.80 | 12.96 | 13.96 | 14.83 | 15.57 | 16.19 | 19 | 9.27 | 10.20 | 11.00 | 11.70 | 12.31 | 12.82 |
| 20 | 11.54 | 12.73 | 13.76 | 14.65 | 15.41 | 16.04 | 20 | 9.28 | 10.25 | 11.09 | 11.83 | 12.46 | 13.01 |
| 21 | 11.28 | 12.50 | 13.55 | 14.47 | 15.24 | 15.89 | 21 | 9.07 | 10.06 | 10.93 | 11.68 | 12.33 | 12.88 |
| 22 | 11.01 | 12.25 | 13.34 | 14.27 | 15.06 | 15.74 | 22 | 8.85 | 9.86 | 10.75 | 11.53 | 12.19 | 12.76 |
| 23 | 10.73 | 12.01 | 13.12 | 14.07 | 14.89 | 15.57 | 23 | 8.63 | 9.67 | 10.58 | 11.37 | 12.05 | 12.63 |
| 24 | 10.44 | 11.75 | 12.89 | 13.87 | 14.71 | 15.41 | 24 | 8.40 | 9.46 | 10.40 | 11.21 | 11.91 | 12.50 |
| 25 | 9.97 | 11.29 | 12.43 | 13.42 | 14.26 | 14.96 | 25 | 8.35 | 9.47 | 10.44 | 11.30 | 12.03 | 12.65 |
| 26 | 9.68 | 11.03 | 12.20 | 13.21 | 14.07 | 14.79 | 26 | 8.10 | 9.25 | 10.25 | 11.12 | 11.88 | 12.51 |
| 27 | 9.37 | 10.76 | 11.97 | 13.00 | 13.88 | 14.62 | 27 | 7.85 | 9.03 | 10.05 | 10.95 | 11.71 | 12.37 |
| 28 | 9.07 | 10.49 | 11.72 | 12.78 | 13.68 | 14.44 | 28 | 7.60 | 8.80 | 9.85 | 10.77 | 11.56 | 12.23 |
| 29 | 8.75 | 10.21 | 11.48 | 12.56 | 13.48 | 14.26 | 29 | 7.34 | 8.57 | 9.64 | 10.58 | 11.39 | 12.08 |
| 30 | 8.12 | 9.56 | 10.81 | 11.88 | 12.79 | 13.55 | 30 | 7.22 | 8.51 | 9.64 | 10.62 | 11.47 | 12.19 |
| 31 | 7.80 | 9.27 | 10.55 | 11.65 | 12.58 | 13.36 | 31 | 6.94 | 8.26 | 9.42 | 10.42 | 11.29 | 12.03 |
| 32 | 7.47 | 8.99 | 10.30 | 11.42 | 12.38 | 13.18 | 32 | 6.65 | 8.00 | 9.19 | 10.22 | 11.11 | 11.86 |
| 33 | 7.14 | 8.69 | 10.04 | 11.20 | 12.17 | 12.99 | 33 | 6.35 | 7.74 | 8.96 | 10.01 | 10.93 | 11.70 |
| 34 | 6.80 | 8.39 | 9.77 | 10.96 | 11.96 | 12.80 | 34 | 6.04 | 7.48 | 8.72 | 9.80 | 10.74 | 11.53 |
| 35 | 5.96 | 7.46 | 8.77 | 9.89 | 10.84 | 11.63 | 35 | 5.98 | 7.51 | 8.85 | 10.00 | 11.00 | 11.85 |
| 36 | 5.63 | 7.17 | 8.51 | 9.66 | 10.63 | 11.44 | 36 | 5.65 | 7.21 | 8.58 | 9.77 | 10.79 | 11.66 |
| 37 | 5.28 | 6.87 | 8.25 | 9.43 | 10.43 | 11.26 | 37 | 5.31 | 6.91 | 8.31 | 9.53 | 10.58 | 11.47 |
| 38 | 4.94 | 6.57 | 7.97 | 9.18 | 10.21 | 11.06 | 38 | 4.96 | 6.60 | 8.04 | 9.29 | 10.36 | 11.27 |
| 39 | 4.58 | 6.25 | 7.70 | 8.94 | 9.98 | 10.86 | 39 | 4.60 | 6.29 | 7.76 | 9.04 | 10.14 | 11.07 |
| 40 | 4.21 | 5.93 | 7.41 | 8.68 | 9.76 | 10.65 | 40 | 4.50 | 6.33 | 7.94 | 9.33 | 10.53 | 11.54 |
| 41 | 3.84 | 5.60 | 7.12 | 8.42 | 9.53 | 10.44 | 41 | 4.10 | 5.98 | 7.63 | 9.06 | 10.28 | 11.32 |
| 42 | 3.46 | 5.26 | 6.82 | 8.16 | 9.29 | 10.23 | 42 | 3.68 | 5.62 | 7.31 | 8.77 | 10.03 | 11.09 |
| 43 | 3.06 | 4.92 | 6.52 | 7.89 | 9.05 | 10.01 | 43 | 3.26 | 5.25 | 6.98 | 8.48 | 9.77 | 10.86 |
| 44 | 2.66 | 4.56 | 6.21 | 7.61 | 8.80 | 9.79 | 44 | 2.83 | 4.87 | 6.65 | 8.19 | 9.50 | 10.62 |
| 45 | 2.25 | 4.20 | 5.88 | 7.33 | 8.55 | 9.56 | 45 | 2.53 | 4.75 | 6.67 | 8.34 | 9.77 | 10.99 |
| 46 | 1.82 | 3.83 | 5.56 | 7.04 | 8.29 | 9.32 | 46 | 2.05 | 4.32 | 6.30 | 8.01 | 9.48 | 10.72 |
| 47 | 1.38 | 3.44 | 5.22 | 6.74 | 8.03 | 9.09 | 47 | 1.56 | 3.89 | 5.92 | 7.68 | 9.19 | 10.45 |
| 48 | 0.94 | 3.05 | 4.88 | 6.44 | 7.76 | 8.84 | 48 | 1.05 | 3.45 | 5.53 | 7.33 | 8.88 | 10.18 |
| 49 | 0.48 | 2.65 | 4.53 | 6.13 | 7.48 | 8.59 | 49 | 0.53 | 2.99 | 5.13 | 6.98 | 8.56 | 9.90 |
| 50 |  | 2.28 | 4.25 | 5.93 | 7.35 | 8.52 | 50 |  | 2.62 | 4.89 | 6.87 | 8.55 | 9.98 |
| 51 |  | 1.85 | 3.88 | 5.61 | 7.06 | 8.26 | 51 |  | 2.20 | 4.62 | 6.72 | 8.51 | 10.02 |
| 52 |  | 1.41 | 3.49 | 5.27 | 6.76 | 7.99 | 52 |  | 1.73 | 4.30 | 6.53 | 8.43 | 10.04 |
| 53 |  | 0.95 | 3.10 | 4.92 | 6.46 | 7.72 | 53 |  | 1.21 | 3.94 | 6.31 | 8.32 | 10.03 |
| 54 |  | 0.50 | 2.75 | 4.67 | 6.28 | 7.60 | 54 |  | 0.65 | 3.64 | 6.22 | 8.43 | 10.30 |

See introductory notes as regards claimants over 54 at date of trial

See introductory notes as regards claimants over 54 at date of trial

A4: Loss of earnings multipliers adjusted for education, etc.

**D E <GCSE**

**Loss of earnings: disabled; employed; education below good GCSE level**

| Age | Male to retiring age | | | | | | Age | Female to retiring age | | | | | |
|---|---|---|---|---|---|---|---|---|---|---|---|---|---|
| | 50 | 55 | 60 | 65 | 70 | 75 | | 50 | 55 | 60 | 65 | 70 | 75 |
| 16 | 7.30 | 7.92 | 8.47 | 8.93 | 9.34 | 9.67 | 16 | 5.73 | 6.22 | 6.66 | 7.04 | 7.37 | 7.65 |
| 17 | 7.16 | 7.80 | 8.36 | 8.84 | 9.24 | 9.59 | 17 | 5.62 | 6.13 | 6.57 | 6.96 | 7.30 | 7.59 |
| 18 | 7.01 | 7.67 | 8.24 | 8.73 | 9.16 | 9.51 | 18 | 5.51 | 6.03 | 6.49 | 6.88 | 7.23 | 7.52 |
| 19 | 6.86 | 7.54 | 8.12 | 8.63 | 9.06 | 9.42 | 19 | 5.39 | 5.93 | 6.39 | 6.80 | 7.16 | 7.46 |
| 20 | 7.98 | 8.79 | 9.51 | 10.12 | 10.64 | 11.08 | 20 | 5.27 | 5.82 | 6.30 | 6.72 | 7.08 | 7.39 |
| 21 | 7.79 | 8.63 | 9.36 | 9.99 | 10.53 | 10.98 | 21 | 5.15 | 5.72 | 6.21 | 6.64 | 7.01 | 7.32 |
| 22 | 7.60 | 8.47 | 9.21 | 9.86 | 10.41 | 10.87 | 22 | 5.03 | 5.61 | 6.11 | 6.55 | 6.93 | 7.25 |
| 23 | 7.41 | 8.30 | 9.06 | 9.72 | 10.29 | 10.76 | 23 | 4.90 | 5.49 | 6.01 | 6.46 | 6.85 | 7.18 |
| 24 | 7.22 | 8.12 | 8.91 | 9.58 | 10.16 | 10.64 | 24 | 4.77 | 5.38 | 5.91 | 6.37 | 6.77 | 7.11 |
| 25 | 7.75 | 8.78 | 9.67 | 10.44 | 11.09 | 11.63 | 25 | 4.64 | 5.26 | 5.80 | 6.28 | 6.68 | 7.03 |
| 26 | 7.53 | 8.58 | 9.49 | 10.28 | 10.95 | 11.50 | 26 | 4.50 | 5.14 | 5.70 | 6.18 | 6.60 | 6.95 |
| 27 | 7.29 | 8.37 | 9.31 | 10.11 | 10.79 | 11.37 | 27 | 4.36 | 5.02 | 5.59 | 6.08 | 6.51 | 6.87 |
| 28 | 7.05 | 8.16 | 9.12 | 9.94 | 10.64 | 11.23 | 28 | 4.22 | 4.89 | 5.47 | 5.98 | 6.42 | 6.79 |
| 29 | 6.81 | 7.94 | 8.92 | 9.77 | 10.49 | 11.09 | 29 | 4.08 | 4.76 | 5.36 | 5.88 | 6.33 | 6.71 |
| 30 | 6.24 | 7.35 | 8.31 | 9.14 | 9.84 | 10.42 | 30 | 4.71 | 5.55 | 6.29 | 6.93 | 7.48 | 7.95 |
| 31 | 6.00 | 7.13 | 8.12 | 8.96 | 9.68 | 10.28 | 31 | 4.52 | 5.39 | 6.14 | 6.80 | 7.37 | 7.84 |
| 32 | 5.75 | 6.91 | 7.92 | 8.79 | 9.52 | 10.14 | 32 | 4.34 | 5.22 | 5.99 | 6.67 | 7.24 | 7.74 |
| 33 | 5.49 | 6.69 | 7.72 | 8.61 | 9.36 | 9.99 | 33 | 4.14 | 5.05 | 5.84 | 6.53 | 7.13 | 7.63 |
| 34 | 5.23 | 6.46 | 7.52 | 8.43 | 9.20 | 9.84 | 34 | 3.94 | 4.88 | 5.69 | 6.39 | 7.00 | 7.52 |
| 35 | 4.84 | 6.06 | 7.13 | 8.03 | 8.81 | 9.45 | 35 | 4.24 | 5.32 | 6.27 | 7.09 | 7.79 | 8.39 |
| 36 | 4.57 | 5.83 | 6.91 | 7.85 | 8.64 | 9.30 | 36 | 4.00 | 5.11 | 6.08 | 6.92 | 7.64 | 8.26 |
| 37 | 4.29 | 5.58 | 6.70 | 7.66 | 8.47 | 9.15 | 37 | 3.76 | 4.90 | 5.89 | 6.75 | 7.49 | 8.12 |
| 38 | 4.01 | 5.34 | 6.48 | 7.46 | 8.30 | 8.99 | 38 | 3.51 | 4.68 | 5.70 | 6.58 | 7.34 | 7.98 |
| 39 | 3.72 | 5.08 | 6.26 | 7.26 | 8.11 | 8.82 | 39 | 3.26 | 4.45 | 5.50 | 6.40 | 7.18 | 7.84 |
| 40 | 3.42 | 4.82 | 6.02 | 7.06 | 7.93 | 8.65 | 40 | 3.35 | 4.72 | 5.92 | 6.95 | 7.85 | 8.60 |
| 41 | 3.12 | 4.55 | 5.79 | 6.84 | 7.74 | 8.48 | 41 | 3.05 | 4.46 | 5.68 | 6.75 | 7.66 | 8.44 |
| 42 | 2.81 | 4.27 | 5.54 | 6.63 | 7.55 | 8.31 | 42 | 2.74 | 4.19 | 5.45 | 6.54 | 7.47 | 8.27 |
| 43 | 2.49 | 3.99 | 5.30 | 6.41 | 7.35 | 8.13 | 43 | 2.43 | 3.91 | 5.20 | 6.32 | 7.28 | 8.09 |
| 44 | 2.16 | 3.71 | 5.04 | 6.19 | 7.15 | 7.95 | 44 | 2.11 | 3.63 | 4.95 | 6.10 | 7.08 | 7.91 |
| 45 | 1.83 | 3.41 | 4.78 | 5.96 | 6.95 | 7.76 | 45 | 1.97 | 3.69 | 5.19 | 6.49 | 7.60 | 8.55 |
| 46 | 1.48 | 3.11 | 4.52 | 5.72 | 6.74 | 7.57 | 46 | 1.60 | 3.36 | 4.90 | 6.23 | 7.38 | 8.34 |
| 47 | 1.12 | 2.80 | 4.24 | 5.48 | 6.52 | 7.38 | 47 | 1.21 | 3.02 | 4.60 | 5.97 | 7.14 | 8.13 |
| 48 | 0.76 | 2.48 | 3.96 | 5.23 | 6.30 | 7.18 | 48 | 0.82 | 2.68 | 4.30 | 5.70 | 6.90 | 7.92 |
| 49 | 0.39 | 2.15 | 3.68 | 4.98 | 6.08 | 6.98 | 49 | 0.42 | 2.33 | 3.99 | 5.43 | 6.66 | 7.70 |
| 50 | | 1.86 | 3.47 | 4.84 | 6.00 | 6.95 | 50 | | 2.20 | 4.11 | 5.76 | 7.18 | 8.38 |
| 51 | | 1.55 | 3.24 | 4.69 | 5.90 | 6.91 | 51 | | 1.86 | 3.91 | 5.67 | 7.19 | 8.47 |
| 52 | | 1.18 | 2.92 | 4.41 | 5.66 | 6.69 | 52 | | 1.47 | 3.66 | 5.55 | 7.17 | 8.53 |
| 53 | | 0.81 | 2.65 | 4.22 | 5.54 | 6.62 | 53 | | 1.05 | 3.43 | 5.49 | 7.25 | 8.73 |
| 54 | | 0.43 | 2.36 | 4.01 | 5.40 | 6.54 | 54 | | 0.56 | 3.15 | 5.38 | 7.28 | 8.89 |

See introductory notes as regards claimants over 54 at date of trial

See introductory notes as regards claimants over 54 at date of trial

A4: Loss of earnings multipliers adjusted for education, etc.

**D NE Deg**

**Loss of earnings: disabled; not employed; degree level education or equivalent**

| Age | Male to retiring age | | | | | | Age | Female to retiring age | | | | | |
|---|---|---|---|---|---|---|---|---|---|---|---|---|---|
| | 50 | 55 | 60 | 65 | 70 | 75 | | 50 | 55 | 60 | 65 | 70 | 75 |
| 16 | | | | | | | 16 | | | | | | |
| 17 | | | See introductory notes | | | | 17 | | | See introductory notes | | | |
| 18 | | | | | | | 18 | | | | | | |
| 19 | | | | | | | 19 | | | | | | |
| 20 | 11.12 | 12.26 | 13.26 | 14.12 | 14.85 | 15.46 | 20 | 12.23 | 13.51 | 14.62 | 15.59 | 16.43 | 17.14 |
| 21 | 10.87 | 12.04 | 13.06 | 13.94 | 14.69 | 15.31 | 21 | 11.95 | 13.26 | 14.40 | 15.39 | 16.25 | 16.98 |
| 22 | 10.61 | 11.81 | 12.85 | 13.75 | 14.52 | 15.16 | 22 | 11.67 | 13.00 | 14.18 | 15.20 | 16.07 | 16.82 |
| 23 | 10.34 | 11.57 | 12.64 | 13.56 | 14.35 | 15.00 | 23 | 11.37 | 12.74 | 13.94 | 14.99 | 15.89 | 16.65 |
| 24 | 10.06 | 11.33 | 12.42 | 13.37 | 14.17 | 14.85 | 24 | 11.07 | 12.48 | 13.71 | 14.77 | 15.69 | 16.48 |
| 25 | 8.86 | 10.03 | 11.05 | 11.93 | 12.67 | 13.30 | 25 | 9.28 | 10.52 | 11.61 | 12.55 | 13.37 | 14.06 |
| 26 | 8.60 | 9.80 | 10.84 | 11.75 | 12.51 | 13.15 | 26 | 9.01 | 10.28 | 11.39 | 12.36 | 13.20 | 13.90 |
| 27 | 8.33 | 9.57 | 10.64 | 11.55 | 12.34 | 12.99 | 27 | 8.72 | 10.03 | 11.17 | 12.16 | 13.02 | 13.74 |
| 28 | 8.06 | 9.32 | 10.42 | 11.36 | 12.16 | 12.84 | 28 | 8.44 | 9.78 | 10.95 | 11.96 | 12.84 | 13.59 |
| 29 | 7.78 | 9.08 | 10.20 | 11.16 | 11.99 | 12.67 | 29 | 8.15 | 9.52 | 10.71 | 11.76 | 12.65 | 13.42 |
| 30 | 6.71 | 7.90 | 8.94 | 9.82 | 10.57 | 11.20 | 30 | 6.91 | 8.14 | 9.22 | 10.16 | 10.97 | 11.66 |
| 31 | 6.45 | 7.67 | 8.72 | 9.64 | 10.41 | 11.05 | 31 | 6.64 | 7.90 | 9.01 | 9.97 | 10.80 | 11.51 |
| 32 | 6.18 | 7.43 | 8.51 | 9.45 | 10.24 | 10.90 | 32 | 6.36 | 7.66 | 8.79 | 9.78 | 10.63 | 11.35 |
| 33 | 5.90 | 7.19 | 8.30 | 9.26 | 10.07 | 10.74 | 33 | 6.07 | 7.41 | 8.57 | 9.58 | 10.45 | 11.19 |
| 34 | 5.62 | 6.94 | 8.08 | 9.06 | 9.89 | 10.58 | 34 | 5.78 | 7.15 | 8.34 | 9.38 | 10.27 | 11.03 |
| 35 | 4.72 | 5.91 | 6.94 | 7.83 | 8.58 | 9.21 | 35 | 5.23 | 6.57 | 7.74 | 8.75 | 9.62 | 10.37 |
| 36 | 4.45 | 5.68 | 6.74 | 7.65 | 8.42 | 9.06 | 36 | 4.94 | 6.31 | 7.51 | 8.55 | 9.44 | 10.20 |
| 37 | 4.18 | 5.44 | 6.53 | 7.46 | 8.25 | 8.91 | 37 | 4.65 | 6.05 | 7.27 | 8.34 | 9.26 | 10.03 |
| 38 | 3.91 | 5.20 | 6.31 | 7.27 | 8.08 | 8.76 | 38 | 4.34 | 5.78 | 7.04 | 8.13 | 9.06 | 9.86 |
| 39 | 3.63 | 4.95 | 6.10 | 7.08 | 7.90 | 8.60 | 39 | 4.02 | 5.50 | 6.79 | 7.91 | 8.87 | 9.69 |
| 40 | 2.90 | 4.08 | 5.10 | 5.97 | 6.71 | 7.32 | 40 | 3.35 | 4.72 | 5.92 | 6.95 | 7.85 | 8.60 |
| 41 | 2.64 | 3.85 | 4.90 | 5.79 | 6.55 | 7.18 | 41 | 3.05 | 4.46 | 5.68 | 6.75 | 7.66 | 8.44 |
| 42 | 2.38 | 3.62 | 4.69 | 5.61 | 6.39 | 7.03 | 42 | 2.74 | 4.19 | 5.45 | 6.54 | 7.47 | 8.27 |
| 43 | 2.11 | 3.38 | 4.48 | 5.43 | 6.22 | 6.88 | 43 | 2.43 | 3.91 | 5.20 | 6.32 | 7.28 | 8.09 |
| 44 | 1.83 | 3.14 | 4.27 | 5.23 | 6.05 | 6.73 | 44 | 2.11 | 3.63 | 4.95 | 6.10 | 7.08 | 7.91 |
| 45 | 1.22 | 2.27 | 3.19 | 3.97 | 4.63 | 5.18 | 45 | 1.31 | 2.46 | 3.46 | 4.33 | 5.07 | 5.70 |
| 46 | 0.99 | 2.07 | 3.01 | 3.81 | 4.49 | 5.05 | 46 | 1.06 | 2.24 | 3.27 | 4.16 | 4.92 | 5.56 |
| 47 | 0.75 | 1.86 | 2.83 | 3.65 | 4.35 | 4.92 | 47 | 0.81 | 2.02 | 3.07 | 3.98 | 4.76 | 5.42 |
| 48 | 0.51 | 1.65 | 2.64 | 3.49 | 4.20 | 4.79 | 48 | 0.55 | 1.79 | 2.87 | 3.80 | 4.60 | 5.28 |
| 49 | 0.26 | 1.44 | 2.45 | 3.32 | 4.05 | 4.65 | 49 | 0.28 | 1.55 | 2.66 | 3.62 | 4.44 | 5.14 |
| 50 | | 1.12 | 2.08 | 2.91 | 3.60 | 4.17 | 50 | | 1.08 | 2.01 | 2.82 | 3.51 | 4.10 |
| 51 | | 0.87 | 1.82 | 2.63 | 3.31 | 3.88 | 51 | | 0.80 | 1.67 | 2.43 | 3.08 | 3.63 |
| 52 | | 0.63 | 1.57 | 2.37 | 3.04 | 3.59 | 52 | | 0.58 | 1.43 | 2.18 | 2.81 | 3.35 |
| 53 | | 0.41 | 1.33 | 2.11 | 2.77 | 3.31 | 53 | | 0.35 | 1.14 | 1.83 | 2.42 | 2.91 |
| 54 | | 0.20 | 1.10 | 1.87 | 2.51 | 3.04 | 54 | | 0.16 | 0.88 | 1.51 | 2.04 | 2.50 |

See introductory notes as regards claimants over 54 at date of trial

See introductory notes as regards claimants over 54 at date of trial

A4: Loss of earnings multipliers adjusted for education, etc.

**D NE GCSE**

**Loss of earnings: disabled; not employed; good GCSE level education or equivalent**

| Age | Male to retiring age | | | | | | Age | Female to retiring age | | | | | |
|---|---|---|---|---|---|---|---|---|---|---|---|---|---|
| | 50 | 55 | 60 | 65 | 70 | 75 | | 50 | 55 | 60 | 65 | 70 | 75 |
| 16 | 11.17 | 12.13 | 12.97 | 13.68 | 14.30 | 14.81 | 16 | 8.02 | 8.71 | 9.32 | 9.86 | 10.31 | 10.71 |
| 17 | 10.96 | 11.94 | 12.79 | 13.53 | 14.16 | 14.69 | 17 | 7.86 | 8.58 | 9.20 | 9.75 | 10.22 | 10.62 |
| 18 | 10.74 | 11.75 | 12.62 | 13.37 | 14.02 | 14.56 | 18 | 7.71 | 8.44 | 9.08 | 9.64 | 10.12 | 10.53 |
| 19 | 10.51 | 11.54 | 12.44 | 13.22 | 13.87 | 14.43 | 19 | 7.55 | 8.30 | 8.95 | 9.52 | 10.02 | 10.44 |
| 20 | 9.66 | 10.64 | 11.51 | 12.25 | 12.88 | 13.42 | 20 | 6.96 | 7.69 | 8.32 | 8.87 | 9.35 | 9.75 |
| 21 | 9.43 | 10.45 | 11.33 | 12.10 | 12.75 | 13.29 | 21 | 6.80 | 7.54 | 8.19 | 8.76 | 9.25 | 9.66 |
| 22 | 9.20 | 10.25 | 11.16 | 11.94 | 12.60 | 13.16 | 22 | 6.64 | 7.40 | 8.07 | 8.65 | 9.14 | 9.57 |
| 23 | 8.97 | 10.04 | 10.97 | 11.77 | 12.45 | 13.02 | 23 | 6.47 | 7.25 | 7.93 | 8.53 | 9.04 | 9.47 |
| 24 | 8.74 | 9.83 | 10.78 | 11.60 | 12.30 | 12.88 | 24 | 6.30 | 7.10 | 7.80 | 8.41 | 8.93 | 9.38 |
| 25 | 7.57 | 8.57 | 9.44 | 10.19 | 10.82 | 11.36 | 25 | 5.94 | 6.73 | 7.43 | 8.03 | 8.55 | 9.00 |
| 26 | 7.35 | 8.37 | 9.26 | 10.03 | 10.68 | 11.23 | 26 | 5.76 | 6.58 | 7.29 | 7.91 | 8.44 | 8.90 |
| 27 | 7.12 | 8.17 | 9.09 | 9.87 | 10.54 | 11.10 | 27 | 5.58 | 6.42 | 7.15 | 7.79 | 8.33 | 8.80 |
| 28 | 6.88 | 7.96 | 8.90 | 9.70 | 10.39 | 10.96 | 28 | 5.40 | 6.26 | 7.00 | 7.66 | 8.22 | 8.69 |
| 29 | 6.65 | 7.75 | 8.71 | 9.54 | 10.24 | 10.82 | 29 | 5.22 | 6.09 | 6.86 | 7.52 | 8.10 | 8.59 |
| 30 | 5.31 | 6.25 | 7.07 | 7.77 | 8.36 | 8.86 | 30 | 4.87 | 5.74 | 6.50 | 7.16 | 7.73 | 8.21 |
| 31 | 5.10 | 6.06 | 6.90 | 7.62 | 8.23 | 8.74 | 31 | 4.67 | 5.57 | 6.35 | 7.02 | 7.61 | 8.11 |
| 32 | 4.89 | 5.88 | 6.73 | 7.47 | 8.10 | 8.62 | 32 | 4.48 | 5.39 | 6.19 | 6.89 | 7.49 | 7.99 |
| 33 | 4.67 | 5.68 | 6.56 | 7.32 | 7.96 | 8.49 | 33 | 4.28 | 5.22 | 6.04 | 6.75 | 7.36 | 7.88 |
| 34 | 4.45 | 5.49 | 6.39 | 7.16 | 7.82 | 8.37 | 34 | 4.07 | 5.04 | 5.88 | 6.61 | 7.24 | 7.77 |
| 35 | 3.47 | 4.35 | 5.12 | 5.77 | 6.32 | 6.78 | 35 | 3.49 | 4.38 | 5.16 | 5.84 | 6.41 | 6.91 |
| 36 | 3.28 | 4.18 | 4.96 | 5.64 | 6.20 | 6.68 | 36 | 3.30 | 4.21 | 5.01 | 5.70 | 6.29 | 6.80 |
| 37 | 3.08 | 4.01 | 4.81 | 5.50 | 6.08 | 6.57 | 37 | 3.10 | 4.03 | 4.85 | 5.56 | 6.17 | 6.69 |
| 38 | 2.88 | 3.83 | 4.65 | 5.36 | 5.96 | 6.45 | 38 | 2.89 | 3.85 | 4.69 | 5.42 | 6.04 | 6.57 |
| 39 | 2.67 | 3.65 | 4.49 | 5.21 | 5.82 | 6.33 | 39 | 2.68 | 3.67 | 4.53 | 5.27 | 5.91 | 6.46 |
| 40 | 2.02 | 2.84 | 3.55 | 4.16 | 4.68 | 5.10 | 40 | 2.03 | 2.86 | 3.58 | 4.21 | 4.75 | 5.20 |
| 41 | 1.84 | 2.68 | 3.41 | 4.04 | 4.57 | 5.00 | 41 | 1.85 | 2.70 | 3.44 | 4.08 | 4.64 | 5.11 |
| 42 | 1.66 | 2.52 | 3.27 | 3.91 | 4.45 | 4.90 | 42 | 1.66 | 2.53 | 3.30 | 3.96 | 4.52 | 5.00 |
| 43 | 1.47 | 2.36 | 3.12 | 3.78 | 4.34 | 4.80 | 43 | 1.47 | 2.37 | 3.15 | 3.82 | 4.40 | 4.90 |
| 44 | 1.27 | 2.19 | 2.97 | 3.65 | 4.22 | 4.69 | 44 | 1.28 | 2.20 | 3.00 | 3.69 | 4.28 | 4.79 |
| 45 | 0.94 | 1.75 | 2.45 | 3.05 | 3.56 | 3.98 | 45 | 0.84 | 1.58 | 2.22 | 2.78 | 3.26 | 3.66 |
| 46 | 0.76 | 1.59 | 2.32 | 2.93 | 3.45 | 3.88 | 46 | 0.68 | 1.44 | 2.10 | 2.67 | 3.16 | 3.57 |
| 47 | 0.58 | 1.43 | 2.18 | 2.81 | 3.34 | 3.79 | 47 | 0.52 | 1.30 | 1.97 | 2.56 | 3.06 | 3.48 |
| 48 | 0.39 | 1.27 | 2.03 | 2.68 | 3.23 | 3.68 | 48 | 0.35 | 1.15 | 1.84 | 2.44 | 2.96 | 3.39 |
| 49 | 0.20 | 1.10 | 1.89 | 2.55 | 3.12 | 3.58 | 49 | 0.18 | 1.00 | 1.71 | 2.33 | 2.85 | 3.30 |
| 50 | | 0.84 | 1.56 | 2.18 | 2.70 | 3.13 | 50 | | 0.70 | 1.31 | 1.84 | 2.29 | 2.67 |
| 51 | | 0.64 | 1.34 | 1.94 | 2.45 | 2.86 | 51 | | 0.53 | 1.12 | 1.62 | 2.05 | 2.42 |
| 52 | | 0.46 | 1.14 | 1.72 | 2.21 | 2.61 | 52 | | 0.37 | 0.93 | 1.41 | 1.83 | 2.17 |
| 53 | | 0.29 | 0.95 | 1.51 | 1.98 | 2.36 | 53 | | 0.21 | 0.70 | 1.12 | 1.48 | 1.78 |
| 54 | | 0.14 | 0.77 | 1.31 | 1.76 | 2.13 | 54 | | 0.09 | 0.50 | 0.85 | 1.15 | 1.40 |

See introductory notes as regards claimants over 54 at date of trial

See introductory notes as regards claimants over 54 at date of trial

A4: Loss of earnings multipliers adjusted for education, etc.

**D NE Deg**

**Loss of earnings: disabled; not employed; degree level education or equivalent**

| Age | Male to retiring age | | | | | | Age | Female to retiring age | | | | | |
|---|---|---|---|---|---|---|---|---|---|---|---|---|---|
| | 50 | 55 | 60 | 65 | 70 | 75 | | 50 | 55 | 60 | 65 | 70 | 75 |
| 16 | | | | | | | 16 | | | | | | |
| 17 | | | See introductory notes | | | | 17 | | | See introductory notes | | | |
| 18 | | | | | | | 18 | | | | | | |
| 19 | | | | | | | 19 | | | | | | |
| 20 | 11.12 | 12.26 | 13.26 | 14.12 | 14.85 | 15.46 | 20 | 12.23 | 13.51 | 14.62 | 15.59 | 16.43 | 17.14 |
| 21 | 10.87 | 12.04 | 13.06 | 13.94 | 14.69 | 15.31 | 21 | 11.95 | 13.26 | 14.40 | 15.39 | 16.25 | 16.98 |
| 22 | 10.61 | 11.81 | 12.85 | 13.75 | 14.52 | 15.16 | 22 | 11.67 | 13.00 | 14.18 | 15.20 | 16.07 | 16.82 |
| 23 | 10.34 | 11.57 | 12.64 | 13.56 | 14.35 | 15.00 | 23 | 11.37 | 12.74 | 13.94 | 14.99 | 15.89 | 16.65 |
| 24 | 10.06 | 11.33 | 12.42 | 13.37 | 14.17 | 14.85 | 24 | 11.07 | 12.48 | 13.71 | 14.77 | 15.69 | 16.48 |
| 25 | 8.86 | 10.03 | 11.05 | 11.93 | 12.67 | 13.30 | 25 | 9.28 | 10.52 | 11.61 | 12.55 | 13.37 | 14.06 |
| 26 | 8.60 | 9.80 | 10.84 | 11.75 | 12.51 | 13.15 | 26 | 9.01 | 10.28 | 11.39 | 12.36 | 13.20 | 13.90 |
| 27 | 8.33 | 9.57 | 10.64 | 11.55 | 12.34 | 12.99 | 27 | 8.72 | 10.03 | 11.17 | 12.16 | 13.02 | 13.74 |
| 28 | 8.06 | 9.32 | 10.42 | 11.36 | 12.16 | 12.84 | 28 | 8.44 | 9.78 | 10.95 | 11.96 | 12.84 | 13.59 |
| 29 | 7.78 | 9.08 | 10.20 | 11.16 | 11.99 | 12.67 | 29 | 8.15 | 9.52 | 10.71 | 11.76 | 12.65 | 13.42 |
| 30 | 6.71 | 7.90 | 8.94 | 9.82 | 10.57 | 11.20 | 30 | 6.91 | 8.14 | 9.22 | 10.16 | 10.97 | 11.66 |
| 31 | 6.45 | 7.67 | 8.72 | 9.64 | 10.41 | 11.05 | 31 | 6.64 | 7.90 | 9.01 | 9.97 | 10.80 | 11.51 |
| 32 | 6.18 | 7.43 | 8.51 | 9.45 | 10.24 | 10.90 | 32 | 6.36 | 7.66 | 8.79 | 9.78 | 10.63 | 11.35 |
| 33 | 5.90 | 7.19 | 8.30 | 9.26 | 10.07 | 10.74 | 33 | 6.07 | 7.41 | 8.57 | 9.58 | 10.45 | 11.19 |
| 34 | 5.62 | 6.94 | 8.08 | 9.06 | 9.89 | 10.58 | 34 | 5.78 | 7.15 | 8.34 | 9.38 | 10.27 | 11.03 |
| 35 | 4.72 | 5.91 | 6.94 | 7.83 | 8.58 | 9.21 | 35 | 5.23 | 6.57 | 7.74 | 8.75 | 9.62 | 10.37 |
| 36 | 4.45 | 5.68 | 6.74 | 7.65 | 8.42 | 9.06 | 36 | 4.94 | 6.31 | 7.51 | 8.55 | 9.44 | 10.20 |
| 37 | 4.18 | 5.44 | 6.53 | 7.46 | 8.25 | 8.91 | 37 | 4.65 | 6.05 | 7.27 | 8.34 | 9.26 | 10.03 |
| 38 | 3.91 | 5.20 | 6.31 | 7.27 | 8.08 | 8.76 | 38 | 4.34 | 5.78 | 7.04 | 8.13 | 9.06 | 9.86 |
| 39 | 3.63 | 4.95 | 6.10 | 7.08 | 7.90 | 8.60 | 39 | 4.02 | 5.50 | 6.79 | 7.91 | 8.87 | 9.69 |
| 40 | 2.90 | 4.08 | 5.10 | 5.97 | 6.71 | 7.32 | 40 | 3.35 | 4.72 | 5.92 | 6.95 | 7.85 | 8.60 |
| 41 | 2.64 | 3.85 | 4.90 | 5.79 | 6.55 | 7.18 | 41 | 3.05 | 4.46 | 5.68 | 6.75 | 7.66 | 8.44 |
| 42 | 2.38 | 3.62 | 4.69 | 5.61 | 6.39 | 7.03 | 42 | 2.74 | 4.19 | 5.45 | 6.54 | 7.47 | 8.27 |
| 43 | 2.11 | 3.38 | 4.48 | 5.43 | 6.22 | 6.88 | 43 | 2.43 | 3.91 | 5.20 | 6.32 | 7.28 | 8.09 |
| 44 | 1.83 | 3.14 | 4.27 | 5.23 | 6.05 | 6.73 | 44 | 2.11 | 3.63 | 4.95 | 6.10 | 7.08 | 7.91 |
| 45 | 1.22 | 2.27 | 3.19 | 3.97 | 4.63 | 5.18 | 45 | 1.31 | 2.46 | 3.46 | 4.33 | 5.07 | 5.70 |
| 46 | 0.99 | 2.07 | 3.01 | 3.81 | 4.49 | 5.05 | 46 | 1.06 | 2.24 | 3.27 | 4.16 | 4.92 | 5.56 |
| 47 | 0.75 | 1.86 | 2.83 | 3.65 | 4.35 | 4.92 | 47 | 0.81 | 2.02 | 3.07 | 3.98 | 4.76 | 5.42 |
| 48 | 0.51 | 1.65 | 2.64 | 3.49 | 4.20 | 4.79 | 48 | 0.55 | 1.79 | 2.87 | 3.80 | 4.60 | 5.28 |
| 49 | 0.26 | 1.44 | 2.45 | 3.32 | 4.05 | 4.65 | 49 | 0.28 | 1.55 | 2.66 | 3.62 | 4.44 | 5.14 |
| 50 | | 1.12 | 2.08 | 2.91 | 3.60 | 4.17 | 50 | | 1.08 | 2.01 | 2.82 | 3.51 | 4.10 |
| 51 | | 0.87 | 1.82 | 2.63 | 3.31 | 3.88 | 51 | | 0.80 | 1.67 | 2.43 | 3.08 | 3.63 |
| 52 | | 0.63 | 1.57 | 2.37 | 3.04 | 3.59 | 52 | | 0.58 | 1.43 | 2.18 | 2.81 | 3.35 |
| 53 | | 0.41 | 1.33 | 2.11 | 2.77 | 3.31 | 53 | | 0.35 | 1.14 | 1.83 | 2.42 | 2.91 |
| 54 | | 0.20 | 1.10 | 1.87 | 2.51 | 3.04 | 54 | | 0.16 | 0.88 | 1.51 | 2.04 | 2.50 |

See introductory notes as regards claimants over 54 at date of trial

See introductory notes as regards claimants over 54 at date of trial

A4: Loss of earnings multipliers adjusted for education, etc.

**D NE GCSE**

**Loss of earnings: disabled; not employed; good GCSE level education or equivalent**

| Age | Male to retiring age | | | | | | Age | Female to retiring age | | | | | |
|---|---|---|---|---|---|---|---|---|---|---|---|---|---|
| | 50 | 55 | 60 | 65 | 70 | 75 | | 50 | 55 | 60 | 65 | 70 | 75 |
| 16 | 11.17 | 12.13 | 12.97 | 13.68 | 14.30 | 14.81 | 16 | 8.02 | 8.71 | 9.32 | 9.86 | 10.31 | 10.71 |
| 17 | 10.96 | 11.94 | 12.79 | 13.53 | 14.16 | 14.69 | 17 | 7.86 | 8.58 | 9.20 | 9.75 | 10.22 | 10.62 |
| 18 | 10.74 | 11.75 | 12.62 | 13.37 | 14.02 | 14.56 | 18 | 7.71 | 8.44 | 9.08 | 9.64 | 10.12 | 10.53 |
| 19 | 10.51 | 11.54 | 12.44 | 13.22 | 13.87 | 14.43 | 19 | 7.55 | 8.30 | 8.95 | 9.52 | 10.02 | 10.44 |
| 20 | 9.66 | 10.64 | 11.51 | 12.25 | 12.88 | 13.42 | 20 | 6.96 | 7.69 | 8.32 | 8.87 | 9.35 | 9.75 |
| 21 | 9.43 | 10.45 | 11.33 | 12.10 | 12.75 | 13.29 | 21 | 6.80 | 7.54 | 8.19 | 8.76 | 9.25 | 9.66 |
| 22 | 9.20 | 10.25 | 11.16 | 11.94 | 12.60 | 13.16 | 22 | 6.64 | 7.40 | 8.07 | 8.65 | 9.14 | 9.57 |
| 23 | 8.97 | 10.04 | 10.97 | 11.77 | 12.45 | 13.02 | 23 | 6.47 | 7.25 | 7.93 | 8.53 | 9.04 | 9.47 |
| 24 | 8.74 | 9.83 | 10.78 | 11.60 | 12.30 | 12.88 | 24 | 6.30 | 7.10 | 7.80 | 8.41 | 8.93 | 9.38 |
| 25 | 7.57 | 8.57 | 9.44 | 10.19 | 10.82 | 11.36 | 25 | 5.94 | 6.73 | 7.43 | 8.03 | 8.55 | 9.00 |
| 26 | 7.35 | 8.37 | 9.26 | 10.03 | 10.68 | 11.23 | 26 | 5.76 | 6.58 | 7.29 | 7.91 | 8.44 | 8.90 |
| 27 | 7.12 | 8.17 | 9.09 | 9.87 | 10.54 | 11.10 | 27 | 5.58 | 6.42 | 7.15 | 7.79 | 8.33 | 8.80 |
| 28 | 6.88 | 7.96 | 8.90 | 9.70 | 10.39 | 10.96 | 28 | 5.40 | 6.26 | 7.00 | 7.66 | 8.22 | 8.69 |
| 29 | 6.65 | 7.75 | 8.71 | 9.54 | 10.24 | 10.82 | 29 | 5.22 | 6.09 | 6.86 | 7.52 | 8.10 | 8.59 |
| 30 | 5.31 | 6.25 | 7.07 | 7.77 | 8.36 | 8.86 | 30 | 4.87 | 5.74 | 6.50 | 7.16 | 7.73 | 8.21 |
| 31 | 5.10 | 6.06 | 6.90 | 7.62 | 8.23 | 8.74 | 31 | 4.67 | 5.57 | 6.35 | 7.02 | 7.61 | 8.11 |
| 32 | 4.89 | 5.88 | 6.73 | 7.47 | 8.10 | 8.62 | 32 | 4.48 | 5.39 | 6.19 | 6.89 | 7.49 | 7.99 |
| 33 | 4.67 | 5.68 | 6.56 | 7.32 | 7.96 | 8.49 | 33 | 4.28 | 5.22 | 6.04 | 6.75 | 7.36 | 7.88 |
| 34 | 4.45 | 5.49 | 6.39 | 7.16 | 7.82 | 8.37 | 34 | 4.07 | 5.04 | 5.88 | 6.61 | 7.24 | 7.77 |
| 35 | 3.47 | 4.35 | 5.12 | 5.77 | 6.32 | 6.78 | 35 | 3.49 | 4.38 | 5.16 | 5.84 | 6.41 | 6.91 |
| 36 | 3.28 | 4.18 | 4.96 | 5.64 | 6.20 | 6.68 | 36 | 3.30 | 4.21 | 5.01 | 5.70 | 6.29 | 6.80 |
| 37 | 3.08 | 4.01 | 4.81 | 5.50 | 6.08 | 6.57 | 37 | 3.10 | 4.03 | 4.85 | 5.56 | 6.17 | 6.69 |
| 38 | 2.88 | 3.83 | 4.65 | 5.36 | 5.96 | 6.45 | 38 | 2.89 | 3.85 | 4.69 | 5.42 | 6.04 | 6.57 |
| 39 | 2.67 | 3.65 | 4.49 | 5.21 | 5.82 | 6.33 | 39 | 2.68 | 3.67 | 4.53 | 5.27 | 5.91 | 6.46 |
| 40 | 2.02 | 2.84 | 3.55 | 4.16 | 4.68 | 5.10 | 40 | 2.03 | 2.86 | 3.58 | 4.21 | 4.75 | 5.20 |
| 41 | 1.84 | 2.68 | 3.41 | 4.04 | 4.57 | 5.00 | 41 | 1.85 | 2.70 | 3.44 | 4.08 | 4.64 | 5.11 |
| 42 | 1.66 | 2.52 | 3.27 | 3.91 | 4.45 | 4.90 | 42 | 1.66 | 2.53 | 3.30 | 3.96 | 4.52 | 5.00 |
| 43 | 1.47 | 2.36 | 3.12 | 3.78 | 4.34 | 4.80 | 43 | 1.47 | 2.37 | 3.15 | 3.82 | 4.40 | 4.90 |
| 44 | 1.27 | 2.19 | 2.97 | 3.65 | 4.22 | 4.69 | 44 | 1.28 | 2.20 | 3.00 | 3.69 | 4.28 | 4.79 |
| 45 | 0.94 | 1.75 | 2.45 | 3.05 | 3.56 | 3.98 | 45 | 0.84 | 1.58 | 2.22 | 2.78 | 3.26 | 3.66 |
| 46 | 0.76 | 1.59 | 2.32 | 2.93 | 3.45 | 3.88 | 46 | 0.68 | 1.44 | 2.10 | 2.67 | 3.16 | 3.57 |
| 47 | 0.58 | 1.43 | 2.18 | 2.81 | 3.34 | 3.79 | 47 | 0.52 | 1.30 | 1.97 | 2.56 | 3.06 | 3.48 |
| 48 | 0.39 | 1.27 | 2.03 | 2.68 | 3.23 | 3.68 | 48 | 0.35 | 1.15 | 1.84 | 2.44 | 2.96 | 3.39 |
| 49 | 0.20 | 1.10 | 1.89 | 2.55 | 3.12 | 3.58 | 49 | 0.18 | 1.00 | 1.71 | 2.33 | 2.85 | 3.30 |
| 50 | | 0.84 | 1.56 | 2.18 | 2.70 | 3.13 | 50 | | 0.70 | 1.31 | 1.84 | 2.29 | 2.67 |
| 51 | | 0.64 | 1.34 | 1.94 | 2.45 | 2.86 | 51 | | 0.53 | 1.12 | 1.62 | 2.05 | 2.42 |
| 52 | | 0.46 | 1.14 | 1.72 | 2.21 | 2.61 | 52 | | 0.37 | 0.93 | 1.41 | 1.83 | 2.17 |
| 53 | | 0.29 | 0.95 | 1.51 | 1.98 | 2.36 | 53 | | 0.21 | 0.70 | 1.12 | 1.48 | 1.78 |
| 54 | | 0.14 | 0.77 | 1.31 | 1.76 | 2.13 | 54 | | 0.09 | 0.50 | 0.85 | 1.15 | 1.40 |

See introductory notes as regards claimants over 54 at date of trial

See introductory notes as regards claimants over 54 at date of trial

A4: Loss of earnings multipliers adjusted for education, etc.

**D NE <GCSE**

**Loss of earnings: disabled; not employed; education below good GCSE level**

| Age | Male to retiring age | | | | | | Age | Female to retiring age | | | | | |
|---|---|---|---|---|---|---|---|---|---|---|---|---|---|
|  | 50 | 55 | 60 | 65 | 70 | 75 |  | 50 | 55 | 60 | 65 | 70 | 75 |
| 16 | 5.70 | 6.19 | 6.62 | 6.98 | 7.30 | 7.56 | 16 | 4.35 | 4.73 | 5.06 | 5.35 | 5.60 | 5.81 |
| 17 | 5.59 | 6.09 | 6.53 | 6.90 | 7.22 | 7.49 | 17 | 4.27 | 4.66 | 5.00 | 5.29 | 5.55 | 5.76 |
| 18 | 5.48 | 5.99 | 6.44 | 6.82 | 7.15 | 7.43 | 18 | 4.18 | 4.58 | 4.93 | 5.23 | 5.49 | 5.72 |
| 19 | 5.36 | 5.89 | 6.35 | 6.74 | 7.08 | 7.36 | 19 | 4.10 | 4.50 | 4.86 | 5.17 | 5.44 | 5.67 |
| 20 | 5.04 | 5.55 | 6.00 | 6.39 | 6.72 | 7.00 | 20 | 3.59 | 3.96 | 4.29 | 4.57 | 4.81 | 5.03 |
| 21 | 4.92 | 5.45 | 5.91 | 6.31 | 6.65 | 6.93 | 21 | 3.50 | 3.89 | 4.22 | 4.51 | 4.76 | 4.98 |
| 22 | 4.80 | 5.35 | 5.82 | 6.23 | 6.57 | 6.87 | 22 | 3.42 | 3.81 | 4.15 | 4.45 | 4.71 | 4.93 |
| 23 | 4.68 | 5.24 | 5.72 | 6.14 | 6.50 | 6.79 | 23 | 3.33 | 3.73 | 4.09 | 4.39 | 4.66 | 4.88 |
| 24 | 4.56 | 5.13 | 5.63 | 6.05 | 6.42 | 6.72 | 24 | 3.25 | 3.66 | 4.02 | 4.33 | 4.60 | 4.83 |
| 25 | 4.43 | 5.02 | 5.52 | 5.96 | 6.34 | 6.65 | 25 | 2.97 | 3.37 | 3.71 | 4.02 | 4.28 | 4.50 |
| 26 | 4.30 | 4.90 | 5.42 | 5.87 | 6.25 | 6.57 | 26 | 2.88 | 3.29 | 3.64 | 3.96 | 4.22 | 4.45 |
| 27 | 4.17 | 4.78 | 5.32 | 5.78 | 6.17 | 6.50 | 27 | 2.79 | 3.21 | 3.57 | 3.89 | 4.16 | 4.40 |
| 28 | 4.03 | 4.66 | 5.21 | 5.68 | 6.08 | 6.42 | 28 | 2.70 | 3.13 | 3.50 | 3.83 | 4.11 | 4.35 |
| 29 | 3.89 | 4.54 | 5.10 | 5.58 | 5.99 | 6.34 | 29 | 2.61 | 3.05 | 3.43 | 3.76 | 4.05 | 4.29 |
| 30 | 3.59 | 4.23 | 4.78 | 5.25 | 5.66 | 5.99 | 30 | 2.36 | 2.78 | 3.14 | 3.46 | 3.74 | 3.97 |
| 31 | 3.45 | 4.10 | 4.67 | 5.15 | 5.57 | 5.91 | 31 | 2.26 | 2.69 | 3.07 | 3.40 | 3.68 | 3.92 |
| 32 | 3.31 | 3.97 | 4.55 | 5.05 | 5.48 | 5.83 | 32 | 2.17 | 2.61 | 3.00 | 3.33 | 3.62 | 3.87 |
| 33 | 3.16 | 3.85 | 4.44 | 4.95 | 5.38 | 5.75 | 33 | 2.07 | 2.52 | 2.92 | 3.27 | 3.56 | 3.81 |
| 34 | 3.01 | 3.71 | 4.32 | 4.85 | 5.29 | 5.66 | 34 | 1.97 | 2.44 | 2.84 | 3.20 | 3.50 | 3.76 |
| 35 | 2.48 | 3.11 | 3.65 | 4.12 | 4.52 | 4.85 | 35 | 1.74 | 2.19 | 2.58 | 2.92 | 3.21 | 3.46 |
| 36 | 2.34 | 2.99 | 3.55 | 4.03 | 4.43 | 4.77 | 36 | 1.65 | 2.10 | 2.50 | 2.85 | 3.15 | 3.40 |
| 37 | 2.20 | 2.86 | 3.44 | 3.93 | 4.34 | 4.69 | 37 | 1.55 | 2.02 | 2.42 | 2.78 | 3.09 | 3.34 |
| 38 | 2.06 | 2.74 | 3.32 | 3.83 | 4.25 | 4.61 | 38 | 1.45 | 1.93 | 2.35 | 2.71 | 3.02 | 3.29 |
| 39 | 1.91 | 2.60 | 3.21 | 3.72 | 4.16 | 4.52 | 39 | 1.34 | 1.83 | 2.26 | 2.64 | 2.96 | 3.23 |
| 40 | 1.32 | 1.85 | 2.32 | 2.71 | 3.05 | 3.33 | 40 | 1.15 | 1.61 | 2.02 | 2.38 | 2.68 | 2.94 |
| 41 | 1.20 | 1.75 | 2.23 | 2.63 | 2.98 | 3.26 | 41 | 1.04 | 1.52 | 1.94 | 2.31 | 2.62 | 2.89 |
| 42 | 1.08 | 1.64 | 2.13 | 2.55 | 2.90 | 3.20 | 42 | 0.94 | 1.43 | 1.86 | 2.24 | 2.56 | 2.83 |
| 43 | 0.96 | 1.54 | 2.04 | 2.47 | 2.83 | 3.13 | 43 | 0.83 | 1.34 | 1.78 | 2.16 | 2.49 | 2.77 |
| 44 | 0.83 | 1.43 | 1.94 | 2.38 | 2.75 | 3.06 | 44 | 0.72 | 1.24 | 1.69 | 2.09 | 2.42 | 2.71 |
| 45 | 0.51 | 0.96 | 1.35 | 1.68 | 1.96 | 2.19 | 45 | 0.52 | 0.97 | 1.36 | 1.70 | 1.99 | 2.24 |
| 46 | 0.42 | 0.88 | 1.27 | 1.61 | 1.90 | 2.14 | 46 | 0.42 | 0.88 | 1.28 | 1.63 | 1.93 | 2.18 |
| 47 | 0.32 | 0.79 | 1.20 | 1.55 | 1.84 | 2.08 | 47 | 0.32 | 0.79 | 1.21 | 1.56 | 1.87 | 2.13 |
| 48 | 0.21 | 0.70 | 1.12 | 1.48 | 1.78 | 2.03 | 48 | 0.21 | 0.70 | 1.13 | 1.49 | 1.81 | 2.07 |
| 49 | 0.11 | 0.61 | 1.04 | 1.40 | 1.71 | 1.97 | 49 | 0.11 | 0.61 | 1.04 | 1.42 | 1.74 | 2.02 |
| 50 |  | 0.47 | 0.87 | 1.21 | 1.50 | 1.74 | 50 |  | 0.47 | 0.87 | 1.23 | 1.53 | 1.78 |
| 51 |  | 0.34 | 0.71 | 1.03 | 1.30 | 1.52 | 51 |  | 0.34 | 0.72 | 1.04 | 1.32 | 1.56 |
| 52 |  | 0.23 | 0.57 | 0.86 | 1.10 | 1.30 | 52 |  | 0.23 | 0.57 | 0.87 | 1.12 | 1.34 |
| 53 |  | 0.14 | 0.44 | 0.70 | 0.92 | 1.10 | 53 |  | 0.14 | 0.45 | 0.71 | 0.94 | 1.13 |
| 54 |  | 0.06 | 0.33 | 0.56 | 0.75 | 0.91 | 54 |  | 0.06 | 0.33 | 0.57 | 0.77 | 0.94 |

See introductory notes as regards claimants over 54 at date of trial

See introductory notes as regards claimants over 54 at date of trial

# A5: Multipliers for fixed periods and at intervals

**Introductory notes**

1. The purpose of the table is to provide a means of calculating an appropriate multiplier which will produce the present day equivalent of a cost recurring, either continuously or at fixed intervals, over a given number of years. It does not allow for mortality or contingencies.

2. The table is based on a discount rate of 2.5 per cent per annum. The Lord Chancellor fixed the discount rate under the Damages Act 1996 (June 25, 2001) at 2.5 per cent, leaving open the possibility of a different rate in exceptional cases such as the effect of tax on large sums. In recent editions of this book, the range of discount rates was extended as a result of the decision in Helmot v Simon.[1] Readers requiring tables at -1.5 per cent or 1 per cent per annum should refer to the 2013/14 edition.

3. It is assumed that yearly loss is incurred at the *end* of each year in which the loss arises. (Continuous loss obviously accrues from day to day throughout the period. Weekly and monthly losses can in practice be treated as continuous.) For example:

    For expenditure assumed to recur every seven years the expenditure is shown as arising at the end of years seven, 14, and so on.

4. The table contains a number of columns: the number of years; the multiplier for a single payment in *n* years' time; that for a continuous loss over that period of *n* years; that for annual payments in the sense of a series of payments at intervals of one year; and those for payments at intervals of two, three, four and so on years.

5. The figures in the continuous column reproduce those in Table 28 of the Ogden Tables at a discount rate of 2.5 per cent, and hence make no allowance for mortality. For continuous loss for rest of life or up to a particular age, where due allowance should be made for mortality, the multiplier should be derived from Tables 1 to 14 of the Ogden Tables. In large and complex cases, where allowance for mortality could be material to the value of payments at fixed intervals, the advice of an actuary should be sought.

6. The multiplier for a single payment in *n* years' time (second column) is the same as the discount factor for deferment for the next *n* years.

7. The table shows a multiplier appropriate to each year in which expenditure is to be incurred, and also cumulative multipliers for expenditure up to the end of that year. For example, at 2.5 per cent discount:

    The multiplier for expenditure at the end of year 10 is 0.781. Thus the current lump sum required to provide £100 in 10 years' time is £78.10.

    And similarly:

    - £100 a year continuously over the next 10 years has a present value of £886;

    - £100 at the end of each of the next 10 years a present value of £875;

[1] [2010] GCA 31.

# A5: Multipliers for fixed periods and at intervals

- £100 at the end of two, four, six, eight and 10 years a present value of £432 (row 10, two-yearly column); and

- £100 at the end of three, six and nine years a present value of £259 (row 9, three-yearly column).

*The cumulative multipliers do not include an immediate payment: where one is needed in addition to the recurring payments add 1.00 to the multiplier.*

8. The multipliers have been rounded to two places of decimals. In order to use the table for valuing payments for life with a given periodicity, the value of *n* should be taken to be the highest value with an entry in the relevant column (from Table 1 or 2 of the Ogden Tables at 0.0% p.a. or as advised by an actuary or medical expert for an atypical case) which is no more than the expectation of life. Thus, as an example, for a 40 year old female, the Ogden Table 2 expectation of life is 49.24 (also available from the table on page 13). The value of payments every 4 years would be 6.69, for every 7 years would be 3.72 and for every 10 years would be 2.24.

## Multipliers where there is evidence of life expectancy

9. In some cases there is medical evidence of the particular claimant's life expectancy. As more distant losses have lower present value, the possibility of dying earlier than expected has more effect on the multiplier than that of dying later than expected. The multiplier for life of someone whose life expectancy is *n* years will therefore be lower than the multiplier for a fixed period of *n* years. The difference varies with sex and age. It is not large but at a discount rate of 2.5 per cent it is not negligible.

10. If the conditions set out in the cases of *Sarwar v Ali*[2] and *Burton v Kingsbury*[3] for the estimation of life expectancy are met, then it is appropriate to adopt term certain tables with no further reduction for mortality. In all other cases a reduction to the fixed term multipliers should be adopted for mortality.

## Reduction of fixed term multipliers for mortality

11. For the reasons discussed above in relation to cases where there is evidence of life expectancy, in all cases where the period of loss is dependent on someone's life the multiplier for a fixed period will be slightly higher than the true multiplier. In appropriate cases the fixed term multipliers can be reduced by the method discussed in paras 20–23 of the Ogden notes (Table A8 of this book), which calculates an equivalent age based on reduced life expectation.

12. For example:

The claimant is aged 53 and seven months. On the basis of evidence his life expectancy has been determined to be 30 years. For the first 12 years he will need care at £10,000 a year and incur expenditure on equipment of £5,000 at the end of every four years (i.e. after four, eight and 12 years). For the remaining 18 years he will need care at £20,000 a year and expenditure on equipment of £6,000 at the end of every three years (i.e. after 15, 18, 21, 24, 27 and 30 years).

[2] [2007] EWHC 2091 (QB).
[3] [2007] EWHC 2091 (QB).

## A5: Multipliers for fixed periods and at intervals

For a continuous loss of 30 years (eg required to value the future care expenditure) the multipliers—from Table A5 at 2.5 per cent—are:

|  | First 12 years: | Remaining 18 years[4] | 30 years |
|---|---|---|---|
| Care: | 10.39 | 10.80 | 21.19 |

The equivalent age to be adopted is calculated from interpolation of the 0% column in the life multipliers shown at Table 1 of the Ogden Tables, as follows:

55 year old multiplier for life at 0%      30.58
56 year old multiplier for life at 0%      29.64

$$\left(\frac{30.58 - 30.00}{30.58 - 29.64}\right) \times 56 + \left(\frac{30.00 - 29.64}{30.58 - 29.64}\right) \times 55 = 55.62$$

The life multiplier at a discount rate of 2.5 per cent for a male aged 55.62 is shown at Table 1 of the Ogden Tables to be 20.29. It is not 21.19 (the multiplier for a continuous loss), because the possibility of dying earlier than expected affects the multiplier more than the possibility of dying later. The fixed term multipliers for care are therefore too high and need to be reduced by a factor of 20.29/21.19 = 95.75 per cent.

Multipliers for care adjusted for mortality (that is multiplied by 95.75 per cent):

|  | First 12 years: | Remaining 18 years | 30 years |
|---|---|---|---|
| Care: | 9.95 | 10.34 | 20.29 |

For expenditure at fixed intervals (i.e. non-continuous) over a period of 30 years (i.e. required to value the future equipment expenditure) the multipliers—from Table A5 at 2.5 per cent—are:

|  | First 12 years: | Remaining 18 years[5] | 30 years |
|---|---|---|---|
| Equipment: | 2.47 | 3.47 | 20.93 |

It was shown above that the equivalent age multiplier is 20.29. Any future multiplier based on fixed interval tables must be reduced by 96.94 per cent (i.e. 20.29/20.93).

Multipliers for equipment adjusted for mortality (that is multiplied by 96.94 per cent):

|  | First 12 years: | Remaining 18 years | 30 years |
|---|---|---|---|
| Equipment: | 2.39 | 3.36 | 20.29 |

### Modifications

13. Multipliers for continuous loss for periods other than entire years can be obtained by interpolation:

---

[4] Calculated by subtraction—see point 13 below.
[5] Calculated by subtraction: 30 year multiplier for 3-yearly replacements 6.81 (Table A5) less 12 year multiplier for 3-yearly replacements 3.34 (Table A5)—see point 13 below.

## A5: Multipliers for fixed periods and at intervals

For continuous payments for 10 and 11 years the multipliers are 8.86 and 9.63. So, for weekly or monthly payments for 10 years 3 months (i.e. 10.25 years) the multiplier is:

$8.86 + (10.25 - 10.00) \times (9.63 - 8.86) = 8.86 + (0.25 \times 0.77) = 9.05$

14. Multipliers for payments beginning after a deferred period can be derived by subtraction or by multiplying by a factor from the single payment column:

    Multipliers for five-yearly payments for 15 and for 50 years are 2.36 and 5.40;

    So the multiplier for five-yearly payments from years 20 to 50 inclusive is $5.40 - 2.36 = 3.14$;

    Multiplier for one payment after 18 years is 0.641;

    So that for five-yearly payments from years 23–68 inclusive is $5.40 \times 0.641 = 3.46$.

15. Multipliers for irregular payments can be found by adding individual figures from the single payment column.

## A5: Multipliers for fixed periods and at intervals

## Multipliers at 2.5 per cent discount

| n | Single payment | Continuous loss | \multicolumn{13}{c}{Frequency of payments in years} |
|---|---|---|---|---|---|---|---|---|---|---|---|---|---|---|

| n | Single payment | Continuous loss | 1 | 2 | 3 | 4 | 5 | 6 | 7 | 8 | 10 | 12 | 15 | 20 |
|---|---|---|---|---|---|---|---|---|---|---|---|---|---|---|
| 1 | 0.976 | 0.99 | 0.98 | | | | | | | | | | | |
| 2 | 0.952 | 1.95 | 1.93 | 0.95 | | | | | | | | | | |
| 3 | 0.929 | 2.89 | 2.86 | | 0.93 | | | | | | | | | |
| 4 | 0.906 | 3.81 | 3.76 | 1.86 | | 0.91 | | | | | | | | |
| 5 | 0.884 | 4.70 | 4.65 | | | | 0.88 | | | | | | | |
| 6 | 0.862 | 5.58 | 5.51 | 2.72 | 1.79 | | | 0.86 | | | | | | |
| 7 | 0.841 | 6.43 | 6.35 | | | | | | 0.84 | | | | | |
| 8 | 0.821 | 7.26 | 7.17 | 3.54 | | 1.73 | | | | 0.82 | | | | |
| 9 | 0.801 | 8.07 | 7.97 | | 2.59 | | | | | | | | | |
| 10 | 0.781 | 8.86 | 8.75 | 4.32 | | | 1.67 | | | | 0.78 | | | |
| 11 | 0.762 | 9.63 | 9.51 | | | | | | | | | | | |
| 12 | 0.744 | 10.39 | 10.26 | 5.07 | 3.34 | 2.47 | | 1.61 | | | | 0.74 | | |
| 13 | 0.725 | 11.12 | 10.98 | | | | | | | | | | | |
| 14 | 0.708 | 11.84 | 11.69 | 5.77 | | | | | 1.55 | | | | | |
| 15 | 0.690 | 12.54 | 12.38 | | 4.03 | | 2.36 | | | | | | 0.69 | |
| 16 | 0.674 | 13.22 | 13.06 | 6.45 | | 3.14 | | | | 1.49 | | | | |
| 17 | 0.657 | 13.88 | 13.71 | | | | | | | | | | | |
| 18 | 0.641 | 14.53 | 14.35 | 7.09 | 4.67 | | | 2.25 | | | | | | |
| 19 | 0.626 | 15.17 | 14.98 | | | | | | | | | | | |
| 20 | 0.610 | 15.78 | 15.59 | 7.70 | | 3.75 | 2.97 | | | | 1.39 | | | 0.61 |
| 21 | 0.595 | 16.39 | 16.18 | | 5.26 | | | | 2.14 | | | | | |
| 22 | 0.581 | 16.97 | 16.77 | 8.28 | | | | | | | | | | |
| 23 | 0.567 | 17.55 | 17.33 | | | | | | | | | | | |
| 24 | 0.553 | 18.11 | 17.88 | 8.83 | 5.82 | 4.31 | | 2.80 | | 2.05 | | 1.30 | | |
| 25 | 0.539 | 18.65 | 18.42 | | | | 3.51 | | | | | | | |
| 26 | 0.526 | 19.19 | 18.95 | 9.36 | | | | | | | | | | |
| 27 | 0.513 | 19.71 | 19.46 | | 6.33 | | | | | | | | | |
| 28 | 0.501 | 20.21 | 19.96 | 9.86 | | 4.81 | | | | 2.65 | | | | |
| 29 | 0.489 | 20.71 | 20.45 | | | | | | | | | | | |
| 30 | 0.477 | 21.19 | 20.93 | 10.34 | 6.81 | | 3.98 | 3.28 | | | 1.87 | | 1.17 | |
| 31 | 0.465 | 21.66 | 21.40 | | | | | | | | | | | |
| 32 | 0.454 | 22.12 | 21.85 | 10.79 | | 5.26 | | | | 2.50 | | | | |
| 33 | 0.443 | 22.57 | 22.29 | | 7.25 | | | | | | | | | |
| 34 | 0.432 | 23.01 | 22.72 | 11.22 | | | | | | | | | | |
| 35 | 0.421 | 23.43 | 23.15 | | | | 4.40 | | 3.07 | | | | | |
| 36 | 0.411 | 23.85 | 23.56 | 11.63 | 7.66 | 5.67 | | 3.69 | | | | 1.71 | | |
| 37 | 0.401 | 24.26 | 23.96 | | | | | | | | | | | |
| 38 | 0.391 | 24.65 | 24.35 | 12.02 | | | | | | | | | | |
| 39 | 0.382 | 25.04 | 24.73 | | 8.04 | | | | | | | | | |
| 40 | 0.372 | 25.42 | 25.10 | 12.40 | | 6.05 | 4.78 | | | 2.87 | 2.24 | | | 0.98 |
| 41 | 0.363 | 25.78 | 25.47 | | | | | | | | | | | |
| 42 | 0.354 | 26.14 | 25.82 | 12.75 | 8.40 | | | 4.04 | 3.42 | | | | | |
| 43 | 0.346 | 26.49 | 26.17 | | | | | | | | | | | |
| 44 | 0.337 | 26.83 | 26.50 | 13.09 | | 6.38 | | | | | | | | |
| 45 | 0.329 | 27.17 | 26.83 | | 8.72 | | 5.10 | | | | | | 1.50 | |
| 46 | 0.321 | 27.49 | 27.15 | 13.41 | | | | | | | | | | |
| 47 | 0.313 | 27.81 | 27.47 | | | | | | | | | | | |
| 48 | 0.306 | 28.12 | 27.77 | 13.72 | 9.03 | 6.69 | | 4.35 | | 3.18 | | 2.01 | | |
| 49 | 0.298 | 28.42 | 28.07 | | | | | | 3.72 | | | | | |
| 50 | 0.291 | 28.72 | 28.36 | 14.01 | | | 5.40 | | | | 2.53 | | | |
| 51 | 0.284 | 29.00 | 28.65 | | 9.31 | | | | | | | | | |
| 52 | 0.277 | 29.28 | 28.92 | 14.28 | | 6.97 | | | | | | | | |
| 53 | 0.270 | 29.56 | 29.19 | | | | | | | | | | | |
| 54 | 0.264 | 29.82 | 29.46 | 14.55 | 9.58 | | | 4.61 | | | | | | |
| 55 | 0.257 | 30.08 | 29.71 | | | | 5.65 | | | | | | | |
| 56 | 0.251 | 30.34 | 29.96 | 14.80 | | 7.22 | | | | 3.97 | 3.43 | | | |
| 57 | 0.245 | 30.59 | 30.21 | | 9.82 | | | | | | | | | |
| 58 | 0.239 | 30.83 | 30.45 | 15.04 | | | | | | | | | | |
| 59 | 0.233 | 31.06 | 30.68 | | | | | | | | | | | |
| 60 | 0.227 | 31.29 | 30.91 | 15.26 | 10.05 | 7.44 | 5.88 | 4.84 | | | 2.76 | 2.24 | 1.72 | 1.21 |

## Multipliers at 2.5 per cent discount

| n | Single payment | Continuous loss | 1 | 2 | 3 | 4 | 5 | 6 | 7 | 8 | 10 | 12 | 15 | 20 |
|---|---|---|---|---|---|---|---|---|---|---|---|---|---|---|
| | | | \multicolumn{13}{c}{Frequency of payments in years} |
| 61 | 0.222 | 31.52 | 31.13 | | | | | | | | | | | |
| 62 | 0.216 | 31.74 | 31.35 | 15.48 | | | | | | | | | | |
| 63 | 0.211 | 31.95 | 31.56 | | 10.26 | | | | | 4.18 | | | | |
| 64 | 0.206 | 32.16 | 31.76 | 15.69 | | 7.65 | | | | | 3.64 | | | |
| 65 | 0.201 | 32.36 | 31.96 | | | | 6.08 | | | | | | | |
| 66 | 0.196 | 32.56 | 32.16 | 15.88 | 10.46 | | | | 5.03 | | | | | |
| 67 | 0.191 | 32.75 | 32.35 | | | | | | | | | | | |
| 68 | 0.187 | 32.94 | 32.54 | 16.07 | | 7.84 | | | | | | | | |
| 69 | 0.182 | 33.13 | 32.72 | | 10.64 | | | | | | | | | |
| 70 | 0.178 | 33.31 | 32.90 | 16.25 | | | 6.26 | | 4.36 | | 2.94 | | | |
| 71 | 0.173 | 33.48 | 33.07 | | | | | | | | | | | |
| 72 | 0.169 | 33.65 | 33.24 | 16.41 | 10.81 | 8.00 | | 5.20 | | 3.80 | | 2.41 | | |
| 73 | 0.165 | 33.82 | 33.40 | | | | | | | | | | | |
| 74 | 0.161 | 33.98 | 33.57 | 16.58 | | | | | | | | | | |
| 75 | 0.157 | 34.14 | 33.72 | | 10.96 | | 6.42 | | | | | | 1.88 | |
| 76 | 0.153 | 34.30 | 33.88 | 16.73 | | 8.16 | | | | | | | | |
| 77 | 0.149 | 34.45 | 34.03 | | | | | | 4.51 | | | | | |
| 78 | 0.146 | 34.60 | 34.17 | 16.87 | 11.11 | | | 5.35 | | | | | | |
| 79 | 0.142 | 34.74 | 34.31 | | | | | | | | | | | |
| 80 | 0.139 | 34.88 | 34.45 | 17.01 | | 8.30 | 6.55 | | | 3.94 | 3.08 | | | 1.35 |
| 81 | 0.135 | 35.02 | 34.59 | | 11.25 | | | | | | | | | |
| 82 | 0.132 | 35.15 | 34.72 | 17.15 | | | | | | | | | | |
| 83 | 0.129 | 35.28 | 34.85 | | | | | | | | | | | |
| 84 | 0.126 | 35.41 | 34.97 | 17.27 | 11.37 | 8.42 | | 5.48 | 4.63 | | | 2.54 | | |
| 85 | 0.123 | 35.53 | 35.10 | | | | 6.68 | | | | | | | |
| 86 | 0.120 | 35.65 | 35.22 | 17.39 | | | | | | | | | | |
| 87 | 0.117 | 35.77 | 35.33 | | 11.49 | | | | | | | | | |
| 88 | 0.114 | 35.89 | 35.45 | 17.50 | | 8.54 | | | | 4.06 | | | | |
| 89 | 0.111 | 36.00 | 35.56 | | | | | | | | | | | |
| 90 | 0.108 | 36.11 | 35.67 | 17.61 | 11.60 | | 6.79 | 5.58 | | | 3.18 | | 1.99 | |
| 91 | 0.106 | 36.22 | 35.77 | | | | | | 4.74 | | | | | |
| 92 | 0.103 | 36.32 | 35.87 | 17.72 | | 8.64 | | | | | | | | |
| 93 | 0.101 | 36.42 | 35.98 | | 11.70 | | | | | | | | | |
| 94 | 0.098 | 36.52 | 36.07 | 17.81 | | | | | | | | | | |
| 95 | 0.096 | 36.62 | 36.17 | | | | 6.88 | | | | | | | |
| 96 | 0.093 | 36.71 | 36.26 | 17.91 | 11.79 | 8.73 | | 5.68 | | 4.15 | | 2.63 | | |
| 97 | 0.091 | 36.81 | 36.35 | | | | | | | | | | | |
| 98 | 0.089 | 36.90 | 36.44 | 18.00 | | | | | 4.83 | | | | | |
| 99 | 0.087 | 36.98 | 36.53 | | 11.88 | | | | | | | | | |
| 100 | 0.085 | 37.07 | 36.61 | 18.08 | | 8.82 | 6.97 | | | | 3.27 | | | 1.43 |

1. The single payment column is the appropriate multiplier for one payment in *n* years' time.
2. The continuous loss column is for loss accruing from day to day: in practice it is appropriate for weekly and monthly losses as well.
3. The column headed "1" is for a series of payments at yearly intervals *at the end of each year* for *n* years. If you want an immediate payment as well, add 1.
4. The remaining columns similarly show the multiplier for a series of payments at intervals of two, three, four and so on years.
5. Thus at 2.5 per cent discount £100 paid after 10 years has a present value of £78.10;
   - £100 a year continuously over the next 10 years has a present value of £886;
   - £100 at the end of each of the next 10 years has a present value of £875;
   - £100 at the end of two, four, six, eight and 10 years has a present value of £432 (row 10, two-yearly column);
   - £100 at the end of three, six and nine years has a present value of £259 (row 9, three-yearly column); and
   - £100 now and after two, four, six and eight years (but not the 10th year) has a present value of £454 (row 8, two-yearly column, plus one).

# A6: Tables of deferred loss

## Introductory notes

Part 1

1. The first table that follows is intended for use when a claimant will suffer a loss over a specified number of years, but that loss will not start to run immediately. The figures in the table have been derived from first principles, but they are the same as combining Ogden Tables 27 and 28 at 2.5 per cent per annum.

2. For example:

    a. The claimant is now 30 years old. The Court has decided that he has a reduced expectation of life of 30 years, to the age of 60. For the last 10 years of his life he is expected to need nursing care at a cost of £7,500 a year. His nursing needs will therefore start in 20 years time.

    b. At 2.5 per cent per annum discount, the multiplier for a period of 10 years is 8.86 [Ogden Table 28].

    c. At 2.5 per cent per annum discount, a loss that will not occur for another 20 years should be discounted by multiplying it by 0.6103 [Ogden Table 27].

    d. The appropriate multiplier is therefore [8.86 × 0.6103] = 5.41 (to two decimal places).

    But see paras 20–33 of the Ogden notes.

3. The following points should also be remembered:

    a. Ogden Table 27 (Discounting Factors for Term Certain) gives the discount factor for a period of complete years. So, in the example above, where the date of trial is 23 August 2016, the need for nursing care is assumed to start on 23 August 2036.

    b. Ogden Table 28 (Multipliers for Pecuniary Loss for Term Certain) assumes that the loss will occur continuously throughout the year, e.g. weekly or monthly bills for nursing care.

## A6: Tables of deferred loss

**Combination grid for different terms certain and different deferment periods (Discount rate 2.5% per annum)**

| Years of loss | Years before loss starts to run | | | | | | | | | | | | | | | Years of loss |
|---|---|---|---|---|---|---|---|---|---|---|---|---|---|---|---|---|
| | 1 | 2 | 3 | 4 | 5 | 6 | 7 | 8 | 9 | 10 | 12.5 | 15 | 20 | 25 | 30 | 35 | 40 | |
| 1 | 0.96 | 0.94 | 0.92 | 0.89 | 0.87 | 0.85 | 0.83 | 0.81 | 0.79 | 0.77 | 0.73 | 0.68 | 0.60 | 0.53 | 0.47 | 0.42 | 0.37 | 1 |
| 2 | 1.90 | 1.86 | 1.81 | 1.77 | 1.72 | 1.68 | 1.64 | 1.60 | 1.56 | 1.52 | 1.43 | 1.35 | 1.19 | 1.05 | 0.93 | 0.82 | 0.73 | 2 |
| 3 | 2.82 | 2.75 | 2.69 | 2.62 | 2.56 | 2.49 | 2.43 | 2.37 | 2.32 | 2.26 | 2.12 | 2.00 | 1.76 | 1.56 | 1.38 | 1.22 | 1.08 | 3 |
| 4 | 3.72 | 3.63 | 3.54 | 3.45 | 3.37 | 3.28 | 3.20 | 3.13 | 3.05 | 2.98 | 2.80 | 2.63 | 2.32 | 2.05 | 1.82 | 1.60 | 1.42 | 4 |
| 5 | 4.59 | 4.48 | 4.37 | 4.26 | 4.16 | 4.06 | 3.96 | 3.86 | 3.77 | 3.67 | 3.45 | 3.25 | 2.87 | 2.54 | 2.24 | 1.98 | 1.75 | 5 |
| 6 | 5.44 | 5.31 | 5.18 | 5.05 | 4.93 | 4.81 | 4.69 | 4.58 | 4.47 | 4.36 | 4.10 | 3.85 | 3.40 | 3.01 | 2.66 | 2.35 | 2.08 | 6 |
| 7 | 6.27 | 6.12 | 5.97 | 5.82 | 5.68 | 5.54 | 5.41 | 5.28 | 5.15 | 5.02 | 4.72 | 4.44 | 3.92 | 3.47 | 3.06 | 2.71 | 2.39 | 7 |
| 8 | 7.08 | 6.91 | 6.74 | 6.58 | 6.42 | 6.26 | 6.11 | 5.96 | 5.81 | 5.67 | 5.33 | 5.01 | 4.43 | 3.92 | 3.46 | 3.06 | 2.70 | 8 |
| 9 | 7.87 | 7.68 | 7.49 | 7.31 | 7.13 | 6.96 | 6.79 | 6.62 | 6.46 | 6.30 | 5.93 | 5.57 | 4.92 | 4.35 | 3.85 | 3.40 | 3.01 | 9 |
| 10 | 8.64 | 8.43 | 8.23 | 8.03 | 7.83 | 7.64 | 7.45 | 7.27 | 7.10 | 6.92 | 6.51 | 6.12 | 5.41 | 4.78 | 4.22 | 3.73 | 3.30 | 10 |
| 11 | 9.40 | 9.17 | 8.94 | 8.73 | 8.51 | 8.31 | 8.10 | 7.91 | 7.71 | 7.53 | 7.07 | 6.65 | 5.88 | 5.20 | 4.59 | 4.06 | 3.59 | 11 |
| 12 | 10.13 | 9.89 | 9.64 | 9.41 | 9.18 | 8.96 | 8.74 | 8.52 | 8.32 | 8.11 | 7.63 | 7.17 | 6.34 | 5.60 | 4.95 | 4.38 | 3.87 | 12 |
| 13 | 10.85 | 10.58 | 10.33 | 10.07 | 9.83 | 9.59 | 9.35 | 9.13 | 8.90 | 8.69 | 8.17 | 7.68 | 6.79 | 6.00 | 5.30 | 4.69 | 4.14 | 13 |
| 14 | 11.55 | 11.27 | 10.99 | 10.72 | 10.46 | 10.21 | 9.96 | 9.71 | 9.48 | 9.25 | 8.69 | 8.17 | 7.22 | 6.38 | 5.64 | 4.99 | 4.41 | 14 |
| 15 | 12.23 | 11.93 | 11.64 | 11.36 | 11.08 | 10.81 | 10.55 | 10.29 | 10.04 | 9.79 | 9.21 | 8.66 | 7.65 | 6.76 | 5.98 | 5.28 | 4.67 | 15 |
| 16 | 12.90 | 12.58 | 12.27 | 11.97 | 11.68 | 11.40 | 11.12 | 10.85 | 10.58 | 10.33 | 9.71 | 9.13 | 8.07 | 7.13 | 6.30 | 5.57 | 4.92 | 16 |
| 17 | 13.54 | 13.21 | 12.89 | 12.58 | 12.27 | 11.97 | 11.68 | 11.39 | 11.12 | 10.85 | 10.20 | 9.59 | 8.47 | 7.49 | 6.62 | 5.85 | 5.17 | 17 |
| 18 | 14.18 | 13.83 | 13.49 | 13.17 | 12.84 | 12.53 | 12.23 | 11.93 | 11.64 | 11.35 | 10.67 | 10.03 | 8.87 | 7.84 | 6.93 | 6.12 | 5.41 | 18 |
| 19 | 14.80 | 14.43 | 14.08 | 13.74 | 13.40 | 13.08 | 12.76 | 12.45 | 12.14 | 11.85 | 11.14 | 10.47 | 9.25 | 8.18 | 7.23 | 6.39 | 5.65 | 19 |
| 20 | 15.40 | 15.02 | 14.66 | 14.30 | 13.95 | 13.61 | 13.28 | 12.95 | 12.64 | 12.33 | 11.59 | 10.90 | 9.63 | 8.51 | 7.52 | 6.65 | 5.88 | 20 |
| 21 | 15.99 | 15.60 | 15.22 | 14.84 | 14.48 | 14.13 | 13.78 | 13.45 | 13.12 | 12.80 | 12.03 | 11.31 | 10.00 | 8.84 | 7.81 | 6.90 | 6.10 | 21 |
| 22 | 16.56 | 16.16 | 15.76 | 15.38 | 15.00 | 14.64 | 14.28 | 13.93 | 13.59 | 13.26 | 12.47 | 11.72 | 10.36 | 9.16 | 8.09 | 7.15 | 6.32 | 22 |
| 23 | 17.12 | 16.70 | 16.29 | 15.90 | 15.51 | 15.13 | 14.76 | 14.40 | 14.05 | 13.71 | 12.89 | 12.12 | 10.71 | 9.47 | 8.37 | 7.39 | 6.54 | 23 |
| 24 | 17.67 | 17.24 | 16.81 | 16.40 | 16.00 | 15.61 | 15.23 | 14.86 | 14.50 | 14.15 | 13.30 | 12.50 | 11.05 | 9.77 | 8.63 | 7.63 | 6.74 | 24 |
| 25 | 18.20 | 17.75 | 17.32 | 16.90 | 16.49 | 16.09 | 15.69 | 15.31 | 14.94 | 14.57 | 13.70 | 12.88 | 11.38 | 10.06 | 8.89 | 7.86 | 6.95 | 25 |
| 26 | 18.72 | 18.26 | 17.82 | 17.38 | 16.96 | 16.54 | 16.14 | 15.75 | 15.36 | 14.99 | 14.09 | 13.25 | 11.71 | 10.35 | 9.15 | 8.08 | 7.15 | 26 |
| 27 | 19.23 | 18.76 | 18.30 | 17.85 | 17.42 | 16.99 | 16.58 | 16.17 | 15.78 | 15.39 | 14.47 | 13.61 | 12.03 | 10.63 | 9.39 | 8.30 | 7.34 | 27 |
| 28 | 19.72 | 19.24 | 18.77 | 18.31 | 17.87 | 17.43 | 17.00 | 16.59 | 16.19 | 15.79 | 14.85 | 13.96 | 12.34 | 10.90 | 9.64 | 8.52 | 7.53 | 28 |
| 29 | 20.20 | 19.71 | 19.23 | 18.76 | 18.30 | 17.86 | 17.42 | 17.00 | 16.58 | 16.18 | 15.21 | 14.30 | 12.64 | 11.17 | 9.87 | 8.73 | 7.71 | 29 |
| 30 | 20.67 | 20.17 | 19.68 | 19.20 | 18.73 | 18.27 | 17.83 | 17.39 | 16.97 | 16.55 | 15.56 | 14.63 | 12.93 | 11.43 | 10.10 | 8.93 | 7.89 | 30 |
| 31 | 21.13 | 20.62 | 20.12 | 19.62 | 19.15 | 18.68 | 18.22 | 17.78 | 17.35 | 16.92 | 15.91 | 14.96 | 13.22 | 11.68 | 10.33 | 9.13 | 8.07 | 31 |
| 32 | 21.58 | 21.06 | 20.54 | 20.04 | 19.55 | 19.08 | 18.61 | 18.16 | 17.71 | 17.28 | 16.25 | 15.27 | 13.50 | 11.93 | 10.55 | 9.32 | 8.24 | 32 |
| 33 | 22.02 | 21.48 | 20.96 | 20.45 | 19.95 | 19.46 | 18.99 | 18.52 | 18.07 | 17.63 | 16.58 | 15.58 | 13.77 | 12.17 | 10.76 | 9.51 | 8.41 | 33 |
| 34 | 22.45 | 21.90 | 21.36 | 20.84 | 20.33 | 19.84 | 19.35 | 18.88 | 18.42 | 17.97 | 16.90 | 15.89 | 14.04 | 12.41 | 10.97 | 9.69 | 8.57 | 34 |
| 35 | 22.86 | 22.30 | 21.76 | 21.23 | 20.71 | 20.21 | 19.71 | 19.23 | 18.76 | 18.31 | 17.21 | 16.18 | 14.30 | 12.64 | 11.17 | 9.87 | 8.73 | 35 |
| 36 | 23.27 | 22.70 | 22.15 | 21.61 | 21.08 | 20.57 | 20.06 | 19.57 | 19.10 | 18.63 | 17.52 | 16.47 | 14.55 | 12.86 | 11.37 | 10.05 | 8.88 | 36 |
| 37 | 23.66 | 23.09 | 22.52 | 21.97 | 21.44 | 20.92 | 20.41 | 19.91 | 19.42 | 18.95 | 17.81 | 16.75 | 14.80 | 13.08 | 11.56 | 10.22 | 9.03 | 37 |
| 38 | 24.05 | 23.46 | 22.89 | 22.33 | 21.79 | 21.26 | 20.74 | 20.23 | 19.74 | 19.26 | 18.11 | 17.02 | 15.04 | 13.30 | 11.75 | 10.39 | 9.18 | 38 |
| 39 | 24.43 | 23.83 | 23.25 | 22.68 | 22.13 | 21.59 | 21.06 | 20.55 | 20.05 | 19.56 | 18.39 | 17.29 | 15.28 | 13.51 | 11.94 | 10.55 | 9.32 | 39 |
| 40 | 24.80 | 24.19 | 23.60 | 23.02 | 22.46 | 21.92 | 21.38 | 20.86 | 20.35 | 19.85 | 18.67 | 17.55 | 15.51 | 13.71 | 12.12 | 10.71 | 9.47 | 40 |
| 41 | 25.15 | 24.54 | 23.94 | 23.36 | 22.79 | 22.23 | 21.69 | 21.16 | 20.65 | 20.14 | 18.94 | 17.80 | 15.73 | 13.91 | 12.29 | 10.86 | 9.60 | 41 |
| 42 | 25.50 | 24.88 | 24.28 | 23.68 | 23.11 | 22.54 | 21.99 | 21.46 | 20.93 | 20.42 | 19.20 | 18.05 | 15.95 | 14.10 | 12.46 | 11.02 | 9.74 | 42 |
| 43 | 25.85 | 25.22 | 24.60 | 24.00 | 23.42 | 22.84 | 22.29 | 21.74 | 21.21 | 20.70 | 19.46 | 18.29 | 16.17 | 14.29 | 12.63 | 11.16 | 9.87 | 43 |
| 44 | 26.18 | 25.54 | 24.92 | 24.31 | 23.72 | 23.14 | 22.57 | 22.02 | 21.49 | 20.96 | 19.71 | 18.53 | 16.38 | 14.47 | 12.79 | 11.31 | 9.99 | 44 |
| 45 | 26.50 | 25.86 | 25.23 | 24.61 | 24.01 | 23.43 | 22.85 | 22.30 | 21.75 | 21.22 | 19.95 | 18.76 | 16.58 | 14.65 | 12.95 | 11.45 | 10.12 | 45 |
| Years of loss | 1 | 2 | 3 | 4 | 5 | 6 | 7 | 8 | 9 | 10 | 12.5 | 15 | 20 | 25 | 30 | 35 | 40 | Years of loss |
| | Years before loss starts to run | | | | | | | | | | | | | | | | | |

A6: Tables of deferred loss

Part 2

4. The following tables are intended for use when a claimant will suffer a loss for the rest of life, but that loss will not start to run immediately. These tables allow for mortality and are therefore consistent with Ogden Tables 1 to 26. The period of deferment is represented by $m$. When $m$ is zero the factors correspond to Tables 1 and 2 of the Ogden Tables at the relevant ages. Some other combinations correspond to other tables in the Ogden Tables. For example, the multiplier for a male age 40 with a 20 year period of deferment is 11.08. This is the same as Table 19 of the Ogden Tables at age 40.

5. If a multiplier is required for a specific number of payments after a period of deferment, the combination table on the previous page can be used with mortality ignored.

6. If there is medical evidence of the particular claimant's life expectancy, it will usually be appropriate to follow the approach set out in paragraph 20 of the 7th edition of the Ogden Tables to find the effective age for which the expectation of life in accordance with the mortality tables underlying the Ogden Tables (from the 0.0% per annum column of Table 1 or 2 of the Ogden Tables as appropriate) would be equal to the deemed life expectancy. This effective age can then be used as the starting age in order to apply the following table to find a multiplier for a series of payments for life which is deferred for a given period.

7. For example, the claimant is a female aged 30 and a payment of £5,000 a year is expected to start after 15 years. The multiplier from the female tables at 2.5 per cent per annum for age 30 at the start and a period of deferment of 15 years is 18.19. The value of this loss is thus £5,000 × 18.19 = £90,950.

8. In another example the claimant is a male aged 45, who would have a normal expectation of life of 40.55 (from Table 1 of the Ogden Tables at 0.0% per annum). On the basis of medical evidence he is deemed to have an expectation of life of only 25 years. His deemed age is thus 61 (from Table 1 of Ogden at 0.0%). A multiplier is required for a continuous payment for the rest of life starting 10 years from now. The multipliers from the table below are 9.85 for a male aged 60 at the date of calculation and 5.52 for a male aged 70 at the date of calculation. For a male aged 61 at the date of calculation the multiplier required is $9.85 \times 9/10 + 5.52 \times 1/10 = 9.42$.

9. The following points should also be remembered:

   a. When applying the multipliers to claims for loss of earnings, this table (along with the Ogden Tables themselves) only take into account the discount rate and mortality. They do not take into accounts other factors such as employment status or disability and the impact that such factors may be expected to have on the likelihood of continuing to be employed up to normal retirement age. Where appropriate a discount should be applied for these contingencies other than mortality in accordance with Section B of the Explanatory Notes of the 7th edition of the Ogden Tables.

   b. The multipliers in the tables below assume that payments are made continually (or on a weekly or monthly basis) once they come into payment.

10. If a multiplier at 2.5 per cent per annum is required for future continuous payment for just $m$ years, this can be obtained by subtracting the relevant multiplier in the following tables for payments deferred for $m$ years from the corresponding whole life multiplier from Table 1 or 2 of the Ogden Tables.

**Multipliers at 2.5 per cent for future continuous annual payments deferred *m* years (Males)**

Starting age

| m | 0 | 10 | 20 | 30 | 40 | 50 | 60 | 70 | 80 |
|---|---|---|---|---|---|---|---|---|---|
| 0 | 35.41 | 34.08 | 32.10 | 29.60 | 26.52 | 22.69 | 18.30 | 13.44 | 8.09 |
| 1 | 34.43 | 33.09 | 31.11 | 28.62 | 25.54 | 21.70 | 17.31 | 12.47 | 7.14 |
| 2 | 33.47 | 32.13 | 30.15 | 27.66 | 24.57 | 20.75 | 16.36 | 11.53 | 6.26 |
| 3 | 32.54 | 31.19 | 29.21 | 26.72 | 23.64 | 19.81 | 15.44 | 10.64 | 5.45 |
| 4 | 31.63 | 30.27 | 28.29 | 25.80 | 22.73 | 18.91 | 14.55 | 9.79 | 4.72 |
| 5 | 30.74 | 29.38 | 27.40 | 24.91 | 21.84 | 18.03 | 13.69 | 8.97 | 4.06 |
| 6 | 29.87 | 28.51 | 26.53 | 24.04 | 20.97 | 17.18 | 12.87 | 8.21 | 3.46 |
| 7 | 29.02 | 27.66 | 25.68 | 23.20 | 20.13 | 16.35 | 12.07 | 7.47 | 2.93 |
| 8 | 28.20 | 26.83 | 24.85 | 22.37 | 19.31 | 15.55 | 11.30 | 6.78 | 2.45 |
| 9 | 27.39 | 26.02 | 24.04 | 21.57 | 18.52 | 14.77 | 10.56 | 6.13 | 2.04 |
| 10 | 26.60 | 25.23 | 23.26 | 20.79 | 17.74 | 14.01 | 9.85 | 5.52 | 1.67 |
| 11 | 25.84 | 24.46 | 22.49 | 20.02 | 16.99 | 13.28 | 9.17 | 4.94 | 1.36 |
| 12 | 25.09 | 23.71 | 21.74 | 19.28 | 16.25 | 12.57 | 8.51 | 4.40 | 1.08 |
| 13 | 24.36 | 22.98 | 21.01 | 18.56 | 15.54 | 11.88 | 7.88 | 3.90 | 0.86 |
| 14 | 23.65 | 22.26 | 20.30 | 17.85 | 14.84 | 11.22 | 7.28 | 3.44 | 0.66 |
| 15 | 22.95 | 21.57 | 19.61 | 17.17 | 14.17 | 10.58 | 6.70 | 3.01 | 0.51 |
| 20 | 19.73 | 18.33 | 16.40 | 13.99 | 11.08 | 7.69 | 4.22 | 1.38 | 0.10 |
| 25 | 16.89 | 15.49 | 13.58 | 11.23 | 8.43 | 5.31 | 2.38 | 0.48 | 0.01 |
| 30 | 14.38 | 12.98 | 11.11 | 8.83 | 6.19 | 3.41 | 1.14 | 0.11 | |
| 35 | 12.17 | 10.78 | 8.95 | 6.76 | 4.33 | 1.97 | 0.42 | 0.02 | |
| 40 | 10.22 | 8.84 | 7.08 | 5.01 | 2.83 | 0.98 | 0.11 | | |

**Multipliers at 2.5 per cent for future continuous annual payments deferred *m* years (Females)**

Starting age

| m | 0 | 10 | 20 | 30 | 40 | 50 | 60 | 70 | 80 |
|---|---|---|---|---|---|---|---|---|---|
| 0 | 35.94 | 34.75 | 32.97 | 30.68 | 27.76 | 24.14 | 19.83 | 14.87 | 9.07 |
| 1 | 34.96 | 33.76 | 31.98 | 29.69 | 26.78 | 23.15 | 18.85 | 13.90 | 8.10 |
| 2 | 34.00 | 32.80 | 31.02 | 28.73 | 25.81 | 22.19 | 17.89 | 12.95 | 7.20 |
| 3 | 33.06 | 31.86 | 30.08 | 27.79 | 24.88 | 21.26 | 16.96 | 12.04 | 6.36 |
| 4 | 32.15 | 30.94 | 29.16 | 26.87 | 23.96 | 20.35 | 16.06 | 11.17 | 5.58 |
| 5 | 31.26 | 30.04 | 28.27 | 25.98 | 23.07 | 19.46 | 15.19 | 10.33 | 4.87 |
| 6 | 30.39 | 29.17 | 27.40 | 25.11 | 22.20 | 18.60 | 14.35 | 9.53 | 4.21 |
| 7 | 29.54 | 28.32 | 26.54 | 24.26 | 21.36 | 17.77 | 13.53 | 8.76 | 3.62 |
| 8 | 28.71 | 27.49 | 25.72 | 23.43 | 20.53 | 16.95 | 12.74 | 8.03 | 3.07 |
| 9 | 27.91 | 26.68 | 24.91 | 22.62 | 19.73 | 16.16 | 11.98 | 7.33 | 2.59 |
| 10 | 27.12 | 25.89 | 24.12 | 21.84 | 18.95 | 15.39 | 11.24 | 6.66 | 2.16 |
| 11 | 26.35 | 25.12 | 23.35 | 21.07 | 18.19 | 14.65 | 10.53 | 6.03 | 1.78 |
| 12 | 25.61 | 24.37 | 22.60 | 20.32 | 17.45 | 13.92 | 9.84 | 5.44 | 1.44 |
| 13 | 24.88 | 23.63 | 21.86 | 19.59 | 16.72 | 13.22 | 9.18 | 4.88 | 1.16 |
| 14 | 24.16 | 22.92 | 21.15 | 18.88 | 16.02 | 12.54 | 8.54 | 4.35 | 0.91 |
| 15 | 23.47 | 22.22 | 20.45 | 18.19 | 15.34 | 11.88 | 7.92 | 3.86 | 0.71 |
| 20 | 20.24 | 18.98 | 17.22 | 14.98 | 12.19 | 8.86 | 5.21 | 1.89 | 0.16 |
| 25 | 17.39 | 16.12 | 14.38 | 12.17 | 9.46 | 6.32 | 3.10 | 0.72 | 0.02 |
| 30 | 14.87 | 13.60 | 11.87 | 9.71 | 7.12 | 4.22 | 1.58 | 0.19 | |
| 35 | 12.65 | 11.37 | 9.68 | 7.58 | 5.13 | 2.57 | 0.64 | 0.03 | |
| 40 | 10.68 | 9.42 | 7.76 | 5.74 | 3.48 | 1.36 | 0.18 | | |

# A7: Table of adjustments to multiplier for Fatal Accidents Acts dependency

These tables deal with factors to be applied in fatal accident cases to allow for the possibility that the deceased would not have survived until trial. These tables are derived from the Explanatory Notes of the Ogden Tables, para.64 onwards (approved as the correct approach by the Supreme Court in *Knauer v Ministry of Justice*[1]). They are set out here on one page for convenience.

**PRE-TRIAL damages** (factor to be applied to damages from date of accident to trial)

| Age of deceased at date of accident | Male | Period from accident to trial (or cessation of dependency if earlier) 3 | 6 | 9 | Female | 3 | 6 | 9 |
|---|---|---|---|---|---|---|---|---|
| 10 | | 1.00 | 1.00 | 1.00 | | 1.00 | 1.00 | 1.00 |
| 20 | | 1.00 | 1.00 | 1.00 | | 1.00 | 1.00 | 1.00 |
| 30 | | 1.00 | 1.00 | 0.99 | | 1.00 | 1.00 | 1.00 |
| 40 | | 1.00 | 0.99 | 0.99 | | 1.00 | 1.00 | 0.99 |
| 50 | | 0.99 | 0.99 | 0.98 | | 1.00 | 0.99 | 0.99 |
| 60 | | 0.99 | 0.97 | 0.94 | | 0.99 | 0.98 | 0.97 |
| 65 | | 0.98 | 0.95 | 0.91 | | 0.99 | 0.97 | 0.95 |
| 70 | | 0.97 | 0.92 | 0.86 | | 0.98 | 0.95 | 0.91 |
| 75 | | 0.94 | 0.87 | 0.78 | | 0.96 | 0.91 | 0.84 |
| 80 | | 0.90 | 0.79 | 0.67 | | 0.93 | 0.84 | 0.75 |

**POST-TRIAL damages** (factor to be applied to damages from date of trial to retirement age)

| Age of deceased at date of accident | Male | Period from accident to trial 3 | 6 | 9 | Female | 3 | 6 | 9 |
|---|---|---|---|---|---|---|---|---|
| 10 | | 1.00 | 1.00 | 1.00 | | 1.00 | 1.00 | 1.00 |
| 20 | | 1.00 | 1.00 | 0.99 | | 1.00 | 1.00 | 1.00 |
| 30 | | 1.00 | 0.99 | 0.99 | | 1.00 | 1.00 | 0.99 |
| 40 | | 0.99 | 0.99 | 0.98 | | 1.00 | 0.99 | 0.99 |
| 50 | | 0.99 | 0.97 | 0.95 | | 0.99 | 0.98 | 0.97 |
| 60 | | 0.97 | 0.93 | 0.88 | | 0.98 | 0.96 | 0.92 |
| 65 | | 0.96 | 0.90 | 0.82 | | 0.97 | 0.93 | 0.88 |
| 70 | | 0.93 | 0.84 | 0.71 | | 0.96 | 0.89 | 0.80 |
| 75 | | 0.88 | 0.73 | 0.55 | | 0.92 | 0.81 | 0.66 |
| 80 | | 0.83 | 0.59 | 0.37 | | 0.86 | 0.68 | 0.48 |

**POST-RETIREMENT damages** (for the period of dependency after retirement age)

1. First obtain the multiplier for the whole of life dependency by the following steps:

    (a) determine, from 0% tables, the expectation of life which the deceased would have had at the date of trial (or the shorter period for which the deceased would have provided the dependency);

    (b) determine the expected period for which the dependant would have been able to receive the dependency (for a widow, normally her life expectancy from 0% tables; for a child, normally the period until it reaches adulthood);

    (c) take the lesser of the two periods; and

    (d) treat the resulting period as a term certain and look up the multiplier for that period (Table A5, continuous loss column).

2. Obtain the multiplier for dependency from date of trial to retirement age. Do not adjust it for contingencies other than mortality. Do not apply the factors in the Post-Trial table above.

[1] [2016] UKSC 9.

## A7: Table of adjustments to multiplier for Fatal Accidents Acts dependency

3. Subtract the multiplier for dependency to retirement age (2) from the whole life multiplier (1). Multiply by the factor in the Post-Trial table above.

   Post-retirement multiplier = [Stage 1 figure *minus* Stage 2 figure] × Post-Trial factor.

# A8: The Ogden Tables

Actuarial tables with explanatory notes for use in personal injury and fatal accident cases.

Prepared by an Inter-Professional Working Party of Actuaries, Lawyers, Accountants and other interested parties.

7th edition prepared by the Government Actuary's Department.

| Table of Contents | Page |
|---|---|
| Introduction to 7th edition | 45 |
| Explanatory Notes | 49 |
| Section A: General | 49 |
| Section B: Contingencies other than mortality | 56 |
| Section C: Summary of personal injury applications | 63 |
| Section D: Application of tables to fatal accident cases | 68 |
| Section E: Concluding remarks | 79 |

**Tables 1–26**

| | |
|---|---|
| Table 1: Multipliers for pecuniary loss for life (males) | 80 |
| Table 2: Multipliers for pecuniary loss for life (females) | 82 |
| Table 3: Multipliers for loss of earnings to pension age 50 (males) | 84 |
| Table 4: Multipliers for loss of earnings to pension age 50 (females) | 85 |
| Table 5: Multipliers for loss of earnings to pension age 55 (males) | 86 |
| Table 6: Multipliers for loss of earnings to pension age 55 (females) | 87 |
| Table 7: Multipliers for loss of earnings to pension age 60 (males) | 88 |
| Table 8: Multipliers for loss of earnings to pension age 60 (females) | 89 |
| Table 9: Multipliers for loss of earnings to pension age 65 (males) | 90 |
| Table 10: Multipliers for loss of earnings to pension age 65 (females) | 91 |
| Table 11: Multipliers for loss of earnings to pension age 70 (males) | 92 |
| Table 12: Multipliers for loss of earnings to pension age 70 (females) | 93 |
| Table 13: Multipliers for loss of earnings to pension age 75 (males) | 94 |
| Table 14: Multipliers for loss of earnings to pension age 75 (females) | 95 |
| Table 15: Multipliers for loss of pension commencing age 50 (males) | 96 |
| Table 16: Multipliers for loss of pension commencing age 50 (females) | 97 |
| Table 17: Multipliers for loss of pension commencing age 55 (males) | 98 |
| Table 18: Multipliers for loss of pension commencing age 55 (females) | 99 |
| Table 19: Multipliers for loss of pension commencing age 60 (males) | 100 |

Table 20: Multipliers for loss of pension commencing age 60 (females)     102

Table 21: Multipliers for loss of pension commencing age 65 (males)     104

Table 22: Multipliers for loss of pension commencing age 65 (females)     106

Table 23: Multipliers for loss of pension commencing age 70 (males)     108

Table 24: Multipliers for loss of pension commencing age 70 (females)     110

Table 25: Multipliers for loss of pension commencing age 75 (males)     112

Table 26: Multipliers for loss of pension commencing age 75 (females)     114

**Tables 27 and 28 (Tables for term certain)**

Table 27: Discounting factors for term certain     116

Table 28: Multipliers for pecuniary loss for term certain     118

Actuarial formulae and basis     119

A8: The Ogden Tables

## Introduction to the 7th edition

*"When it comes to the explanatory notes we must make sure that they are readily comprehensible. We must assume the most stupid circuit judge in the country and before him are the two most stupid advocates. All three of them must be able to understand what we are saying"*

Sir Michael Ogden QC, on his explanatory notes to the 1st edition of the Ogden Tables.[1]

1. The Working Party has been eager to see a new set of these tables published, as there have been changes in the official projections of future mortality rates for the UK since the previous, 6th edition was published which produce significant changes in the values of some of the multipliers. The Working Party is grateful that the Ministry of Justice has agreed to fund the production of this edition of the Ogden Tables.

## Purpose of the tables

2. These tables are designed to assist those concerned with calculating lump sum damages for future losses in personal injury and fatal accident cases in the UK.

3. The methodology is long-established whereby multipliers are applied to the present day value of a future annual loss (net of tax in the case of a loss of earnings and pension) with the aim of producing a lump sum equivalent to the capitalised value of the future losses. In essence, the multiplier is the figure by which an annual loss is multiplied in order to calculate a capitalised sum, taking into account accelerated receipt, mortality risks and, in relation to claims for loss of earnings and pension, discounts for contingencies other than mortality.

4. This methodology was endorsed by the House of Lords in the famous case of **Wells v Wells**.[2] In that case the court determined that the discount rate should be based on the yields on Index Linked Government Stock. The discount rate is now fixed by the Lord Chancellor of the day pursuant to his powers under the Damages Act 1996. The above method was further endorsed by Lord Chancellor Irvine in his decision of July 2001, when he fixed the Discount Rate as being 2.5 per cent. He also gave his reasons for his decision, which reasons appear now to be less than happy in the light of the financial turmoil which has since occurred. I will deal with this below. In my view, this present rate is long out of date and does not reflect the substantial reduction in yields on Index Linked Government Stocks since 2001. The present Lord Chancellor Clarke has agreed to review it although his decision may not be available for several months.

## First decision of the Working Party

5. It was decided that, with funding now obtained, a new set of tables, based on the most recent mortality rates produced by the Office for National Statistics (ONS), with as few other revisions as possible, should be issued as quickly as was realistically achievable.

## Second decision of the Working Party

6. It was decided that, due to the passage of time and the changed circumstances since the tables were first produced, the text of the Explanatory Notes will require a substantial re-write in order to bolster

---

[1] Memoirs of Sir Michael Ogden QC, *Variety is the Spice of Legal Life*, p.182 (Lewes: The Book Guild, 2002).
[2] [1999] 1 A.C. 345.

its usefulness to practitioners. Not only is there a need to change the language, but the effect of other decided cases has made this a task of importance. The intention of the Working party is to accomplish this re-writing in the next (eighth) edition, which will rely on the further updated mortality projections due to be produced by the ONS later in 2011. It is hoped that the 8th edition will be available in autumn 2012.

**Third decision of the Working Party**

7. Developments in Guernsey and the review of the discount rate currently being carried out by the Lord Chancellor (see further, below, in respect of both matters) caused the Working Party to decide to include in this edition tables with discount rate columns which range between minus 2 per cent and plus 3 per cent.

8. It is not, we believe, the purpose of these tables or the role of the Working Party to advocate a discount rate, but merely to provide the tools so that, whatever the rate should be, personal injury and fatal accident claims may be quantified.

9. The revised spread of discount rates will assist comparison between lump sums and periodical payments, a process required by the Damages Act 1996, to be more accurately appreciated. The present value of periodical payments is substantially higher than lump sums calculated using the current discount rate of 2.5 per cent. Brooke L.J. remarked in para.34 of the *Flora v Wakom*[3] judgment: "The fact that these two quite different mechanisms now sit side by side in the same Act of Parliament does not in my judgment mean that the problems that infected the operation of the one should be allowed to infect the operation of the other." This imbalance is a factor which any Lord Chancellor ought to take into account.

**Fourth decision of the Working Party**

10. The Working Party decided not to increase further the number of tables to reflect different possible retirement ages. The multipliers for retirement ages which do not conform strictly with the five-yearly intervals between 50 and 75 can be calculated with reasonable accuracy by interpolation. We would be interested to learn of other views on this decision which might cause us to think again.

**Helmot v Simon**

11. The judgment in *Helmot v Simon*[4] in the Court of Appeal of the Island of Guernsey (September 14, 2010), presided over by Sumption J.A., could be truly described as a decision which has had after-effects. The results have rippled the waters within the English legal establishment, even though the decision creates no precedent in England.

12. The first point to make about the case is that the Damages Act 1996 (as amended) does not apply in Guernsey. Consequentially, neither the 2.5 per cent discount rate prescribed under the power provided by s.1 applies nor is there any power to make an award by way of a periodical payment.

13. The original lump sum award made at first instance on January 14, 2010 was for damages in the sum of £9.3 million plus interest. The court used a single discount rate of 1 per cent for all future losses. The claimant had argued for differential rates of 0.5 per cent for non-earnings-related losses and of

[3] [2006] EWCA Civ 1103; [2007] 1 W.L.R. 282.
[4] [2009–10] G.L.R. 465.

minus 1.5 per cent for earnings-related losses. Some eight months later these arguments succeeded on appeal and the final amount of the award was increased to more than £14 million. Permission has been granted to appeal the decision to the Privy Council.

14. The consequences in England and Wales have been profound. The Lord Chancellor has indicated his intention to reconsider the discount rate and at the time of writing is in the process of doing so. It has also emphasised the disparity between lump sum awards and the provision of periodical payments, to the detriment of lump sum awards, when the discount rate is inappropriate, it not having been revised for a period of 10 years.

**Mortality data**

15. Projections of future mortality rates are usually produced on a two-yearly basis by the ONS as part of the production of national population projections for the United Kingdom and its constituent countries. Multipliers published in the 6th edition of the Ogden Tables were calculated using mortality rates from the 2004-based projections; this new edition provides multipliers based on mortality rates from the most recent, 2008-based, projections. The 2006-based projections showed rather higher projected life expectancies at many ages than those in the 2004-based projections. The 2008-based projections suggest slightly higher projected life expectancies than those in the 2006-based projections, but which are of relatively little significance in terms of the values of the multipliers at most ages.

16. There is much debate among demographers about whether the factors that have led to the significant improvements in mortality in recent years can continue unabated, thus adding some uncertainty to any projections of future mortality. While the Working Party has continued to use the official projections made by the ONS of future mortality rates in the UK, we propose to monitor developments as new evidence becomes available.

**Contingencies other than mortality**

17. We have persuaded Dr Victoria Wass to join the Working Party. She has suggested changes to the definition of "disabled" and also clarified some of the language in the Explanatory Notes. We anticipate some further suggestions for amendment in the 8th edition.

18. The Working Party notes that there have been a number of cases in which judges have made significant adjustments to the suggested discount factors. In particular the approach of the trial judges to the calculation of future loss of earnings in ***Conner v Bradman***[5] and ***Clarke v Maltby***[6] has generated some debate. These issues will be discussed in detail when drafting the 8th edition and consideration will be given to whether or not the Explanatory Notes need amendment, especially as regards the circumstances in which it might be appropriate to depart from the suggested non-mortality reduction factors and the size of any adjustments that are made. In the meantime, practitioners performing such calculations are referred to the helpful article by Dr Wass, *"Discretion in the Application of the New Ogden Six Multipliers: The Case of Conner v Bradman and Company"*,[7] which highlights some of the relevant issues.

---

[5] [2007] EWHC 2789 (QB).
[6] [2010] EWHC 1201 (QB).
[7] [2008] J.P.I.L. 2, 154–163.

**Fatal Accidents Act calculations and the "Actuarially Recommended Approach"**

19. This is dealt with in detail in Section D of the Explanatory Notes. To those comments I would add one qualification which is that the Court of Appeal in **Fletcher v A Train & Sons Ltd**[8] was sufficiently concerned with the consequence of following the reasoning of the House of Lords in **Cookson v Knowles**[9] that it unanimously gave the unsuccessful appellant permission to appeal to the House of Lords on the point; the appeal was subsequently compromised.

20. The Scottish Parliament has since enacted the Damages (Scotland) Act 2011 dealing with the same point and in so doing has demonstrated that it agrees with the point that our predecessors had made on this topic.

21. Section 7(1)(d) of the Damages (Scotland) Act 2011 provides for the multiplier to be calculated at the date of the proof (trial) and the losses over the period between the fatal accident and the proof to be calculated separately, subject to a factor for possible early death, with interest added. Multipliers are determined from the tables based on the age of the deceased had he/she survived to the date of proof. This is the same as our actuarially recommended approach.

**Concluding remarks**

22. The changes to the Explanatory Notes in this edition are minor; it is the figures that have been updated.

23. As I have previously stated, the figures for the tables themselves are produced by the Government Actuary's Department according to long-established principles.

24. The other matters discussed are the subject of careful and detailed analysis by the members of the Working Party. Its discussions are never less than uninhibited and I am grateful to those members of the Working Party (listed inside the front cover) who give their time and energy to attend the meetings and ensure that all is done which ought to be done.

25. I begin to believe that the journey made by Jason and the Argonauts in search of the Golden Fleece is as nothing in comparison with the desire of those involved in these tables to make the assessment of future losses as simple and accurate as they possibly can be, whilst remaining as clear as we can be in explaining the actual process of calculating the figures. I am conscious that we may not always succeed in that ambition.

Robin de Wilde QC                                                                                                1 August 2012

---

[8] [2008] EWCA Civ 413; [2008] 4 All E.R. 699.
[9] [1979] A.C. 566.

A8: The Ogden Tables

**Explanatory Notes**

**Section A: General**

**Purpose of tables**

1. The tables have been prepared by the Government Actuary's Department. They provide an aid for those assessing the lump sum appropriate as compensation for a continuing future pecuniary loss or consequential expense or cost of care in personal injury and fatal accident cases.

**Application of tables**

2. The tables set out multipliers. These multipliers enable the user to assess the present capital value of future annual loss (net of tax) or annual expense calculated on the basis of various assumptions which are explained below. Accordingly, to find the present capital value of a given annual loss or expense, it is necessary to select the appropriate table, find the appropriate multiplier and then multiply the amount of the annual loss or expense by that figure.

3. Tables 1–26 deal with annual loss or annual expense extending over three different periods of time. In each case there are separate tables for men and women.

— In Tables 1 and 2 the loss or expense is assumed to begin immediately and to continue for the whole of the rest of the claimant's life.

— In Tables 3–14 the loss or expense is assumed to begin immediately but to continue only until the claimant's retirement or earlier death.

— In Tables 15–26 it is assumed that the annual loss or annual expense will not begin until the claimant reaches retirement but will then continue for the whole of the rest of his or her life. These tables all make due allowance for the chance that the claimant may not live to reach the age of retirement.

**Mortality assumptions**

4. The tables are based on a reasonable estimate of the future mortality likely to be experienced by average members of the population alive today and are based on projected mortality rates for the United Kingdom as a whole. The Office for National Statistics publishes population projections on a regular basis which include estimates of the extent of future improvements in mortality. Tables 1–26 in this edition show the multipliers which result from the application of these projected mortality rates which were derived from the principal 2008-based population projections for the United Kingdom, which were published in October 2009. (Further details of these projections can be found on the ONS website at: *http://www.ons.gov.uk/ons/rel/npp/national-population-projections/2008-based-projections/index/html.)*

5. The tables do not assume that the claimant dies after a period equating to the expectation of life, but take account of the possibilities that the claimant will live for different periods, e.g. die soon or live to be very old. The mortality assumptions relate to the general population of the United Kingdom. However, unless there is clear evidence in an individual case to support the view that the individual is atypical and will enjoy longer or shorter expectation of life, no further increase or reduction is required for mortality alone.

## Use of tables

6. To find the appropriate figure for the present value of a particular loss or expense, the user must first choose that table which relates to the period of loss or expense for which the individual claimant is to be compensated and to the gender of the claimant, or, where appropriate, the claimant's dependants.

7. If, for some reason, the facts in a particular case do not correspond with the assumptions on which one of the tables is based (e.g. it is known that the claimant will have a different retiring age from that assumed in the tables), then the tables can only be used if an appropriate allowance is made for this difference; for this purpose the assistance of an actuary should be sought, except for situations where specific guidance is given in these explanatory notes.

## Rate of return

8. The basis of the multipliers set out in the tables is that the lump sum will be invested and yield income (but that over the period in question the claimant will gradually reduce the capital sum, so that at the end of the period it is exhausted). Accordingly, an essential factor in arriving at the right figure is the choice of the appropriate rate of return.

9. The annual rate of return currently to be applied is 2.5 per cent (net of tax), as fixed by the Lord Chancellor on June 25, 2001, and reassessed on July 27, 2001, under the provisions of the Damages Act 1996 s.1. An annual rate of return of 2.5 per cent was also set for Scotland by the Scottish Ministers on February 8, 2002. The Lord Chancellor may make a fresh determination of this rate, after receiving advice from the Government Actuary and the Treasury (and, in Scotland, the Scottish Ministers after consultation with the Government Actuary). In order to allow the tables to continue to be used should a new discount rate be specified, the tables are accordingly shown for a range of possible annual rates of return ranging from −2 per cent to 3 per cent, in steps of 0.5 per cent, rather than the range 0.0 per cent to 5.0 per cent as in the 6th edition. This change has been made because multipliers at negative rates are useful for the financial evaluation of periodical payments in the exercise which is required by the Damages Act in all cases for comparison with lump sums. In addition, it is recognised that multipliers based on discount rates of more than 3 per cent are currently not generally required, and a recent case heard in the Channel Islands (**Helmot v Simon**[10]) has made an award based on negative discount rates.

10. The figures in the 0% column show the multiplier without any discount for interest and provide the expectations of life (Tables 1 and 2) or the expected period over which a person would have provided a dependency (up to retirement age Tables 3–14 or from pension age Tables 15–26). These are supplied to assist in the calculation of multipliers in Fatal Accidents Act cases (see Section D).

11. Section 1(2) of the Damages Act 1996 makes provision for the courts to make variations to the discount rate if any party to the proceedings shows that it is more appropriate in the case in question. Variations to the discount rate under this provision have, however, been rejected by the Court of Appeal in the cases of **Warriner v Warriner**[11] and **Cooke & Others v United Bristol Health Care & Others**.[12]

12. Previous editions of these tables explained how the current yields on index-linked government bonds could be used as an indicator of the appropriate real rate of return for valuing future income

---

[10] [2009–10] G.L.R. 465.
[11] [2002] EWCA Civ 81; [2002] 1 W.L.R. 1703.
[12] [2003] EWCA Civ 1370; [2004] 1 W.L.R. 251.

streams. Such considerations were endorsed by the House of Lords in **Wells v Wells** and the same argumentation was adopted by the Lord Chancellor when he set the rate on commencement of s.1 of the Damages Act 1996. In cases outwith the scope of these tables, the advice of an actuary should be sought.

**Different retirement ages**

13. In para.7 above, reference was made to the problem that will arise when the claimant's retiring age is different from that assumed in the tables. Such a problem may arise in valuing a loss or expense beginning immediately but ending at retirement; or in valuing a loss or expense which will not begin until the claimant reaches retirement but will then continue until death. Tables are provided for retirement ages of 50, 55, 60, 65, 70 and 75. Where the claimant's actual retiring age would have been between two of the retirement ages for which tables are provided, the correct multiplier can be obtained by consideration of the tables for retirement age immediately above and below the actual retirement age, keeping the period to retirement age the same. Thus a woman of 42 who would have retired at 58 can be considered as being in between the cases of a woman of 39 with a retirement age of 55 and a woman of 44 with a retirement age of 60. The steps to take are as follows:

(1) Determine between which retirement ages, for which tables are provided, the claimant's actual retirement age $R$ lies. Let the lower of these ages be $A$ and the higher be $B$.

(2) Determine how many years must be subtracted from the claimant's actual retirement age to get to $A$ and subtract that period from the claimant's age. If the claimant's age is $x$, the result of this calculation is $(x + A - R)$.

(3) Look up this new reduced age in the table corresponding to retirement age $A$ at the appropriate rate of return. Let the resulting multiplier be $M$.

(4) Determine how many years must be added to the claimant's actual retirement age to get to $B$ and add that period to the claimant's age. The result of this calculation is $(x + B - R)$.

(5) Look up this new increased age in the table corresponding to retirement age $B$ at the appropriate rate of return. Let the resulting multiplier be $N$.

(6) Interpolate between $M$ and $N$. In other words, calculate:

$(B - R) \times M + (R - A) \times N$

and divide the result by $[(B - R) + (R - A)]$, (or equivalently $[B - A]$).

14. In the example given in para.13, the steps would be as follows:

(1) $R$ is 58, $A$ is 55 and $B$ is 60.

(2) Subtracting three years from the claimant's age gives 39.

(3) Looking up age 39 in Table 6 (for retirement age 55) gives 13.10 at a rate of return of 2.5 per cent.

(4) Adding two years to the claimant's age gives 44.

(5) Looking up age 44 in Table 8 (for retirement age 60) gives 13.03 at a rate of return of 2.5 per cent.

(6) Calculating $2 \times 13.10 + 3 \times 13.03$ and dividing by $(60 - 58) + (58 - 55)$ [equals 5] gives 13.06 as the multiplier.

15. When the loss or expense to be valued is that from the date of retirement to death, and the claimant's date of retirement differs from that assumed in the tables, a different approach is necessary, involving the following three steps.

(1) Assume that there is a present loss which will continue for the rest of the claimant's life and from Table 1 or 2 establish the value of that loss or expense over the whole period from the date of assessment until the claimant's death.

(2) Establish the value of such loss or expense over the period from the date of assessment until the claimant's expected date of retirement following the procedure explained in paras 13 and 14, above.

(3) Subtract the second figure from the first. The balance remaining represents the present value of the claimant's loss or expense between retirement and death.

16. If the claimant's actual retirement age would have been earlier than 50, or later than 75, the advice of an actuary should be sought.

**Younger ages**

17. Tables 1 and 2, which concern pecuniary loss for life, and Tables 15–26, which concern loss of pension from retirement age, have been extended down to age 0. In some circumstances the multiplier at age 0 is slightly lower than that at age 1; this arises because of the relatively high incidence of deaths immediately after birth.

18. Tables for multipliers for loss of earnings (Tables 3–14) have not been extended below age 16. In order to determine the multiplier for loss of earnings for someone who has not yet started work, it is first necessary to determine an assumed age at which the claimant would have commenced work and to find the appropriate multiplier for that age from Tables 3–14, according to the assumed retirement age. This multiplier should then be multiplied by the deferment factor from Table 27 which corresponds to the appropriate rate of return and the period from the date of the trial to the date on which it is assumed that the claimant would have started work. A similar approach can be used for determining a multiplier for pecuniary loss for life where the loss is assumed to commence a fixed period of years from the date of the trial. For simplicity the factors in Table 27 relate purely to the impact of compound interest and ignore mortality. At ages below 30 this is a reasonable approximation but at higher ages it would normally be appropriate to allow explicitly for mortality and the advice of an actuary should be sought.

**Contingencies**

19. Tables 1–26 make reasonable provision for the levels of mortality which members of the population of the United Kingdom alive today may expect to experience in future. The tables do not take account of the other risks and vicissitudes of life, such as the possibility that the claimant would for periods have ceased to earn due to ill-health or loss of employment. Nor do they take account of the fact that many people cease work for substantial periods to care for children or other dependants. Section B suggests ways in which allowance may be made to the multipliers for loss of earnings, to allow for certain risks other than mortality.

**Impaired lives**

20. In some cases, medical evidence may be available which asserts that a claimant's health impairments are equivalent to adding a certain number of years to their current age, or to treating the

# A8: The Ogden Tables

individual as having a specific age different from their actual age. In such cases, Tables 1 and 2 can be used with respect to the deemed higher age. For the other tables the adjustment is not so straightforward, as adjusting the age will also affect the assumed retirement age, but the procedures described in paras 13–15 may be followed, or the advice of an actuary should be sought. In other cases, the medical evidence may state that the claimant is likely to live for a stated number of years. This is often then treated as requiring payment to be made for a fixed period equal to the stated life expectancy and using Table 28 to ascertain the value of the multiplier. In general, this is likely to give a multiplier which is too high since this approach does not allow for the distribution of deaths around the expected length of life. For a group of similarly impaired lives of the same age, some will die before the average life expectancy and some after; allowing for this spread of deaths results in a lower multiplier than assuming payment for a term certain equal to the life expectancy. In such cases, it is preferable to look up the age in the 0 per cent column in Tables 1 or 2 for which the value of the multiplier at 0 per cent is equal to the stated life expectancy. The relevant multipliers are then obtained from the relevant tables using this age. Take, for example, an impaired male life which is stated to have a life expectancy of 20 years. By interpolation, the age for which the multiplier in the 0 per cent column in Table 1 is 20 is:

$(20 - 19.74)/(20.57 - 19.74) \times 66 + (20.57 - 20)/(20.57 - 19.74) \times 67$

which equals 66.7 years.

The value of the whole of life multiplier is then obtained from the 2.5 per cent column of Table 1 for age 66.7 years:

$(67 - 66.7) \times 15.38 + (66.7 - 66) \times 14.90$

which equals 15.04 (compared to 15.78 for the value for a term certain of 20 years using the 2.5 per cent column of Table 28).

**Fixed period**

21. In cases where pecuniary loss is to be valued for a fixed period, the multipliers in Table 28 may be used. These make no allowance for mortality or any other contingency but assume that regular frequent payments (e.g. weekly or monthly) will continue throughout the period. These figures should in principle be adjusted if the periodicity of payment is less frequent, especially if the payments in question are annually in advance or in arrears.

**Variable future losses or expenses**

22. The tables do not provide an immediate answer when the annual future loss or expense is likely to change at given points in time in the future. The most common examples will be where:

(a) the claimant's lost earnings would have increased on a sliding scale or changed due to promotion; or

(b) the claimant's care needs are likely to change in the future, perhaps because it is anticipated that a family carer will not be able to continue to provide help.

In such situations it is usually necessary to split the overall multiplier, whether for working life or whole of life, into segments, and then to apply those smaller segmented multipliers to the multiplicand appropriate for each period.

There are a variety of methods which could be used for splitting a multiplier, especially where the age at which a payment is increased or decreased, or stops or begins, is one which is tabulated in Tables 1–26. The following examples serve to illustrate how multipliers might be split using the "apportionment method". This method can be extended for use in cases where none of the ages at which payments change are tabulated.

**Example 1—Variable future earnings**

23. The claimant is female, a graduate with a degree, aged 25 at date of settlement/trial. Her probable career progression, in the absence of injury, would have provided her with salary increases at ages 30, 35 and 40; thereafter she would have continued at the same level to age 60, when she would have stepped down from full-time work to work part-time until 70. Post-accident she is now incapable of working.

The multiplicands for lost future earnings are:

    Age 25–30:    £16,000 a year

    Age 30–35:    £25,000 a year

    Age 35–40:    £35,000 a year

    Age 40–60:    £40,000 a year

    Age 60–70:    £20,000 a year

The multipliers for each stage of her career are calculated as follows:

(1) The working-life will be 45 years and the Multiplier from Table 12 for that period taking into account mortality risks but without any discounts for any other contingencies will be 26.73.

(2) The multiplier for a term certain of 45 years (ignoring mortality risks) from Table 28 is 27.17.

(3) The multiplier from Table 28 should be split so that each individual segment of the whole working life period (45 years) is represented by a figure. So, the first five years is represented by a multiplier for a term certain of five years, namely 4.70; the next five years is represented by a multiplier of 4.16 (being the difference between the figure for a term certain of 10 years, namely 8.86 and the figure for a term certain of five years, namely 4.70); the next five years by 3.68 (i.e. the 15-year figure of 12.54 less the 10 year figure of 8.86); the next 20 years by 10.89 (i.e. the difference between the 35-year figure which is 23.43 and the 15-year figure of 12.54); then, the final 10 years by the balance of 3.74 (the residual figure being 27.17 less 23.43).

(4) Each of those smaller segmented multipliers can be shown as a percentage or fraction of the whole: so, for the first five years the segmented multiplier of 4.70 is 17.30 per cent of the whole figure of 27.17, and so on for each segment of the 45-year period.

(5) The working life multiplier from Table 12 can now be split up in identical proportions to the way in which the Table 28 multiplier has been treated above: thus the first five-year period is now represented by a multiplier of 4.62, which is calculated by taking 17.30 per cent of 26.73. Each segmented multiplier is calculated in the same way.

(6) Having now obtained multipliers for each segment of working life, taking into account mortality risks, it is then necessary to discount those figures for "contingencies other than mortality". The

## A8: The Ogden Tables

discount factor from Table C (using the column for a female, not disabled, with degree level education) is 0.89. So, the figure of 4.62 for the first five-year period now becomes 4.11 (i.e. 4.62 × 0.89). Again, treat each segmented multiplier in the same way.

(7) The multiplicand for each segment of working life is now multiplied by the appropriate segmented multiplier to calculate the loss for that period. The sum total of those losses represents the full sum for loss of future earnings (ignoring any mitigation).

(8) The figures are set out in tabular form below and give a total lump sum award of £716,260:

| Ages | Period (years) | Table 28 | % Split | Table 12 | Discounted Multipliers (Table C) (× 0.89) | Net Annual Earnings £ | £ Loss |
|---|---|---|---|---|---|---|---|
| 25–30 | 5 | 4.70 | 17.30 | 4.62 | 4.11 | 16,000 | 65,760 |
| 30–35 | 5 | 4.16 | 15.31 | 4.09 | 3.64 | 25,000 | 91,000 |
| 35–40 | 5 | 3.68 | 13.54 | 3.62 | 3.22 | 35,000 | 112,700 |
| 40–60 | 20 | 10.89 | 40.08 | 10.71 | 9.53 | 40,000 | 381,200 |
| 60–70 | 10 | 3.74 | 13.77 | 3.68 | 3.28 | 20,000 | 65,600 |
| Totals: | 45 years | 27.17 | 100.00 | 26.73 | 23.79 | | **716, 260** |

N.B. the figures in the above table have been rounded at each step of the calculation so the totals shown are not necessarily the sum of the individual multipliers in the columns

### Example 2—Variable future care costs

24. A male aged 20 years at the date of settlement/trial requires personal care support for life. He has a normal life expectation for his age. Significant changes in his care regime are anticipated at age 30 and again at age 50.

The multiplicands for care costs are:

Age 20–30: £30,000 a year

Age 30–50: £60,000 a year

Age 50 for rest of life: £80,000 a year

The multipliers for each stage of the care regime are calculated as follows:

(1) The life expectation will be 67.22 years (from the 0 per cent column of Table 1) and the multiplier for that period taking into account mortality risks (from Table 1) will be 32.10.

(2) The multiplier for a term certain of 67.22 years (ignoring mortality risks) from Table 28 lies between 32.75 (for 67 years) and 32.94 (for 68 years) and is calculated thus:

$(68 - 67.22) \times 32.75 + (67.22 - 67) \times 32.94 = 32.79.$

(3) The multiplier from Table 28 should be split so that each individual segment of the whole period of life expectation is represented by a figure. So, the first 10 years (20–30) are represented by a multiplier of 8.86; the next 20 years (30–50) are represented by a multiplier of 12.33 (being the difference between the 30-year figure of 21.19 and the 10-year figure of 8.86); then, the final

years (50 to death) are represented by the balance of 11.60 (being the difference between the term certain multiplier of 32.79 and the 30-year figure of 21.19).

(4) Each of those smaller segmented multipliers can be shown as a percentage or fraction of the whole: so, for the first 10 years the segmented multiplier of 8.86 is 27.02 per cent of the whole figure of 32.79, and so on for each segment of the life period.

(5) The life multiplier from Table 1 can now be split up in the way in which the Table 28 multiplier was treated above and in identical proportions: thus the first 10-year period is now represented by a multiplier of 8.67 which is calculated by taking 27.02 per cent of 32.10.

(6) The figures are set out in tabular form below and give a total lump sum award of £1,893,100:

| Age (years) | Table 28 (67.22 years) Split multipliers | % Split (of Table 28) figure | Table 1 (multiplier allowing for mortality) | Care costs £ a year | Total £ |
|---|---|---|---|---|---|
| 20–30 | 8.86 | 27.02% | 8.67 | 30,000 | 260,100 |
| 30–50 | 12.33 | 37.60% | 12.07 | 60,000 | 724,200 |
| 50 till death | 11.60 | 35.38% | 11.36 | 80,000 | 908,800 |
| Totals | 32.79 (no mortality discount) | 100.00% | 32.10 life multiplier | | **1,893,100** |

N.B. the figures in the above table have been rounded at each step of the calculation.

### Spouse's pensions

25. If doubt exists whether the tables are appropriate to a particular case which appears to present significant difficulties of substance, it would be prudent to take actuarial advice. This might be appropriate in relation to the level of spouse's benefits, if these are to be assessed, since these are not readily valued using Tables 1–26. As a rough rule of thumb, if spouse's benefits are to be included when valuing pension loss from normal pension age, the multipliers in Tables 15–26 should be increased by 5 per cent for a female claimant (i.e. benefits to the male spouse) and by 14 per cent for a male claimant if the spouse's pension would be half of the pension that the member was receiving at death. If the spouse's pension would be payable at a rate of two-thirds the member's pension at death the multipliers should be increased by 7 per cent for a female claimant and by 18 per cent for a male claimant.

### Section B: Contingencies other than mortality

26. As stated in para.19, the tables for loss of earnings (Tables 3–14) take no account of risks other than mortality. This section shows how the multipliers in these tables may be reduced to take account of these risks.

27. Tables of factors to be applied to the existing multipliers were first introduced in the 2nd edition of the Ogden Tables. These factors were based on work commissioned by the Institute of Actuaries and carried out by Professor S. Haberman and Mrs D. S. F. Bloomfield.[13] Although there was some debate within the actuarial profession about the details of the work, and in particular about the scope for developing it further, the findings were broadly accepted and were adopted by the Government

---

[13] "Work time lost to sickness, unemployment and stoppages: measurement and application" (1990) 117 *Journal of the Institute of Actuaries*, 533–595.

Actuary and the other actuaries who were members of the Working Party when the 2nd edition of the Tables was published and remained unchanged until the 6th edition.

28. Some related work was published in 2002 by Lewis, McNabb and Wass.[14] For the publication of the 6th edition of the Ogden Tables, the Ogden Working Party was involved in further research into the impact of contingencies other than mortality carried out by Professor Richard Verrall, Professor Steven Haberman and Mr Zoltan Butt of City University, London and, in a separate exercise, by Dr Victoria Wass of Cardiff University. Their findings were combined to produce the tables of factors given in section B of the 6th edition and repeated here.

29. The Haberman and Bloomfield paper relied on data from the Labour Force Surveys for 1973, 1977, 1981 and 1985 and English Life Tables No. 14 (1980–82). The Labour Force Survey (LFS) was originally designed to produce a periodic cross-sectional snapshot of the working age population and collects information on an extensive range of socio-economic and labour force characteristics. Since the winter of 1992/3, the LFS has been carried out on a quarterly basis, with respondents being included in the survey over five successive quarters. The research of Professor Verrall *et al.* and Dr Wass used data from the Labour Force Surveys conducted from 1998–2003 to estimate the probabilities of movement of males and females between different states of economic activity, dependent on age, sex, employment activity and level of disability. These probabilities permit the calculation of the expected periods in employment until retirement age, dependent on the initial starting state of economic activity, disability and educational attainment. These can then be discounted at the same discount rate that is used for obtaining the relevant multiplier from Tables 3–14, in order to give a multiplier which takes into account only those periods the claimant would be expected, on average, to be in work. These discounted working life expectancy multipliers can be compared to those obtained assuming the person remained in work throughout, to obtain reduction factors which give the expected proportion of time to retirement age which will be spent in employment.

30. The factors described in subsequent paragraphs are for use in calculating loss of earnings up to retirement age. The research work did not investigate the impact of contingencies other than mortality on the value of future pension rights. Some reduction to the multiplier for loss of pension would often be appropriate when a reduction is being applied for loss of earnings. This may be a smaller reduction than in the case of loss of earnings because the ill-health contingency (as opposed to the unemployment contingency) may give rise to significant ill-health retirement pension rights. A bigger reduction may be necessary in cases where there is significant doubt whether pension rights would have continued to accrue (to the extent not already allowed for in the post-retirement multiplier) or in cases where there may be doubt over the ability of the pension fund to pay promised benefits. In the case of a defined contribution pension scheme, loss of pension rights may be allowed for, simply by increasing the future earnings loss (adjusted for contingencies other than mortality) by the percentage of earnings which the employer contributes to the scheme represent.

31. The methodology proposed in paras 33–42 describes one method for dealing with contingencies other than mortality. If this methodology is followed, in many cases it will be appropriate to increase or reduce the discount in the tables to take account of the nature of a particular claimant's disabilities. It should be noted that the methodology does not take into account the pre-accident employment history. The methodology also provides for the possibility of valuing more appropriately the possible mitigation of loss of earnings in cases where the claimant is employed after the accident or is considered capable of being employed. This will in many cases enable a more accurate assessment to be made of the mitigation of loss. However, there may be some cases when the *Smith v Manchester Corporation* or *Blamire* approach remains applicable or otherwise where a precise mathematical approach is inapplicable.

---

[14] "Methods of calculating damages for loss of future earnings" (2002) 2 *Journal of Personal Injury Law*, 151–165.

32. The suggestions which follow are intended as a "ready reckoner" which provides an initial adjustment to the multipliers according to the employment status, disability status and educational attainment of the claimant when calculating awards for loss of earnings and for any mitigation of this loss in respect of potential future post-injury earnings. Such a ready reckoner cannot take into account all circumstances and it may be appropriate to argue for higher or lower adjustments in particular cases. In particular, it can be difficult to place a value on the possible mitigating income when considering the potential range of disabilities and their effect on post-work capability, even within the interpretation of disability set out in para.35. However, the methodology does offer a framework for consideration of a range of possible figures with the maximum being effectively provided by the post-injury multiplier assuming the claimant was not disabled and the minimum being the case where there is no realistic prospect of post-injury employment.

**The deduction for contingencies other than mortality**

33. Under this method, multipliers for loss of earnings obtained from Tables 3–14 are multiplied by factors to allow for the risk of periods of non-employment and absence from the workforce because of sickness.

34. The research by Professor Verrall et al. and Dr Wass referred to in paras 28 and 29 demonstrated that the key issues affecting a person's future working life are employment status, disability status and educational attainment.

35. The definitions of employed/not employed, disabled/not disabled and educational attainment used in this analysis and which should be used for determining which factors to apply to the multipliers to allow for contingencies other than mortality are as follows:

| | |
|---|---|
| Employed | Those who at the time of the accident are employed, self-employed or on a government training scheme. |
| Not employed | All others (including those temporarily out of work, full-time students and unpaid family workers). |
| Disabled | A person is classified as being disabled if all three of the following conditions in relation to the ill-health or disability are met: |

    (i)   the person has an illness or a disability which has lasted or is expected to last for over a year or is a progressive illness,

    (ii)  the person satisfies the Equality Act 2010 definition that the impact of the disability substantially limits the person's ability to carry out normal day to day activities, and

    (iii) their condition affects either the kind **or** the amount of paid work they can do.

| | |
|---|---|
| Not disabled | All others. |

Normal day to day activities are those which are carried out by most people on a daily basis, and we are interested in disabilities/health problems which have a substantial adverse effect on respondent's ability to carry out these activities.

There are several ways in which a disability or health problem may affect the respondent's day to day activities:

*Mobility*—for example, unable to travel short journeys as a passenger in a car, unable to walk other than at a slow pace or with jerky movements, difficulty in negotiating stairs, unable to use one or more forms of public transport, unable to go out of doors unaccompanied.

*Manual dexterity*—for example, loss of functioning in one or both hands, inability to use a knife and fork at the same time, or difficulty in pressing buttons on a keyboard.

*Physical co-ordination*—for example, the inability to feed or dress oneself; or to pour liquid from one vessel to another except with unusual slowness or concentration.

*Problems with bowel/bladder control*—for example, frequent or regular loss of control of the bladder or bowel. Occasional bedwetting is not considered a disability.

***Ability to lift, carry or otherwise move everyday objects (for example, books, kettles, light furniture)***—for example, inability to pick up a weight with one hand but not the other, or to carry a tray steadily.

*Speech*—for example, unable to communicate (clearly) orally with others, taking significantly longer to say things. A minor stutter, difficulty in speaking in front of an audience, or inability to speak a foreign language would not be considered impairments.

*Hearing*—for example, not being able to hear without the use of a hearing aid, the inability to understand speech under normal conditions or over the telephone.

*Eyesight*—for example, while wearing spectacles or contact lenses—being unable to pass the standard driving eyesight test, total inability to distinguish colours (excluding ordinary red/green colour blindness), or inability to read newsprint.

*Memory or ability to concentrate, learn or understand*—for example, intermittent loss of consciousness or confused behaviour, inability to remember names of family or friends, unable to write a cheque without assistance, or an inability to follow a recipe.

*Perception of risk of physical danger*—for example, reckless behaviour putting oneself or others at risk, mobility to cross the road safely. This excludes (significant) fear of heights or under-estimating risk of dangerous hobbies.

Three levels of educational attainment are defined for the purposes of the tables as follows:

D     Degree or equivalent or higher.

GE–A     GCSE grades A–C up to A levels or equivalents.

O     Below GCSE C or CSE 1 or equivalent or no qualifications.

The following table gives a more detailed breakdown of the allocation of various types of educational qualification to each of the three categories above and is based on the allocations used in the research by Professor Verrall, et al. and Dr Wass.

## Categories of highest educational attainment

| D<br>Degree or equivalent<br>or higher | GE–A<br>GCSE grades A–C<br>up to A levels<br>or equivalent | O<br>Below GCSE grade C<br>or CSE grade 1 or equivalent<br>or no qualifications |
|---|---|---|
| Any degree (first or higher)<br>Other higher education qualification below degree level<br>Diploma in higher education | A or AS level or equivalent<br>O level, GCSE grade A–C or equivalent | CSE below grade 1<br>GCSE below grade C |
| NVQ level 4 or 5 | NVQ level 2 or 3 | NVQ level 1 or equivalent |
| HNC/HND, BTEC higher, etc | BTEC/SCOTVEC first or general diploma<br>OND/ONC, BTEC/SCOTVEC national | BTEC first or general certificate<br>SCOTVEC modules or equivalent |
| RSA higher diploma | RSA diploma, advanced diploma or certificate | RSA other |
| Teaching, Nursing, etc | GNVQ intermediate or advanced | GNVQ/GVSQ foundation level |
|  | City and Guilds craft or advanced craft | City and Guilds other |
|  | SCE higher or equivalent Trade apprenticeship<br>Scottish 6th year certificate (CSYS) | YT/ YTP certificate<br><br>Other qualifications<br>No qualification<br>Don't know |

Note: "educational attainment" is used here as a proxy for skill level, so that those in professional occupations such as law, accountancy, nursing, etc. who do not have a degree ought to be treated as if they do have one.

36. The research also considered the extent to which a person's future working life expectancy is affected by individual circumstances such as occupation and industrial sector, geographical region and education. The researchers concluded that the most significant consideration was the highest level of education achieved by the claimant and that, if this was allowed for, the effect of the other factors was relatively small. As a result, the Working Party decided to propose adjustment factors which allow for employment status, disability status and educational attainment only. This is a change from earlier editions of the Ogden Tables where adjustments were made for types of occupation and for geographical region.

37. A separate assessment is made for: (a) the value of earnings the claimant would have received if the injury had not been suffered, and (b) the value of the claimant's earnings (if any) taking account of the injuries sustained. The risk of non-employment is significantly higher post-injury due to the impairment. The loss is arrived at by deducting (b) from (a).

38. In order to calculate the value of the earnings the claimant would have received, if the injury had not been suffered, the claimant's employment status and the disability status need to be determined as at the date of the accident (or the onset of the medical condition) giving rise to the claim, so that the correct table can be applied. For the calculation of future loss of earnings (based on actual pre-accident earnings and also future employment prospects), Tables A and C should be used for claimants who were not disabled at the time of the accident, and Tables B and D should be used for those with a pre-existing disability. In all of these tables the three left hand columns are for those who were employed at the time of the accident and the three right hand columns are for those who were not.

39. In order to calculate the value of the actual earnings that a claimant is likely to receive in the future (i.e. after settlement or trial), the employment status and the disability status need to be determined as at the date of settlement or trial. For claimants with a work-affecting disability at that point in time, Tables B and D should be used. The three left hand columns will apply in respect of claimants actually in employment at date of settlement or trial and the three right hand columns will apply in respect of those who remain non-employed at that point in time.

40. The factors in Tables A–D allow for the interruption of employment for bringing up children and caring for other dependants.

41. In the case of those who at the date of the accident have not yet reached the age at which it is likely they would have started work, the relevant factor will be chosen based on a number of assessments of the claimant's likely employment had the injury not occurred. The relevant factor from the tables would be chosen on the basis of the level of education the claimant would have been expected to have attained, the age at which it is likely the claimant would have started work, together with an assessment as to whether the claimant would have become employed or not. The work multiplier will also have to be discounted for early receipt using the appropriate factor from Table 27 for the number of years between the claimant's age at the date of trial and the age at which it is likely that he/she would have started work.

42. Tables A–D include factors up to age 54 only. For older ages the reduction factors increase towards 1 at retirement age for those who are employed and fall towards 0 for those who are not employed. However, where the claimant is older than 54, it is anticipated that the likely future course of employment status will be particularly dependent on individual circumstances, so that the use of factors based on averages would not be appropriate. Hence reduction factors are not provided for these older ages.

# A8: The Ogden Tables

### Table A
### Loss of earnings to pension age 65 (males—not disabled)

| Age at date of trial | Employed D | GE–A | O | Not employed D | GE–A | O |
|---|---|---|---|---|---|---|
| 16–19 |      | 0.90 | 0.85 |      | 0.85 | 0.82 |
| 20–24 | 0.92 | 0.92 | 0.87 | 0.89 | 0.88 | 0.83 |
| 25–29 | 0.93 | 0.92 | 0.89 | 0.89 | 0.88 | 0.82 |
| 30–34 | 0.92 | 0.91 | 0.89 | 0.87 | 0.86 | 0.81 |
| 35–39 | 0.90 | 0.90 | 0.89 | 0.85 | 0.84 | 0.80 |
| 40–44 | 0.88 | 0.88 | 0.88 | 0.82 | 0.81 | 0.78 |
| 45–49 | 0.86 | 0.86 | 0.86 | 0.77 | 0.77 | 0.74 |
| 50    | 0.83 | 0.83 | 0.83 | 0.72 | 0.72 | 0.70 |
| 51    | 0.82 | 0.82 | 0.82 | 0.70 | 0.70 | 0.68 |
| 52    | 0.81 | 0.81 | 0.81 | 0.67 | 0.67 | 0.66 |
| 53    | 0.80 | 0.80 | 0.80 | 0.63 | 0.63 | 0.63 |
| 54    | 0.79 | 0.79 | 0.79 | 0.59 | 0.59 | 0.59 |

### Table B
### Loss of earnings to pension age 65 (males—disabled)

| Age at date of trial | Employed D | GE–A | O | Not employed D | GE–A | O |
|---|---|---|---|---|---|---|
| 16–19 |      | 0.55 | 0.32 |      | 0.49 | 0.25 |
| 20–24 | 0.61 | 0.55 | 0.38 | 0.53 | 0.46 | 0.24 |
| 25–29 | 0.60 | 0.54 | 0.42 | 0.48 | 0.41 | 0.24 |
| 30–34 | 0.59 | 0.52 | 0.40 | 0.43 | 0.34 | 0.23 |
| 35–39 | 0.58 | 0.48 | 0.39 | 0.38 | 0.28 | 0.20 |
| 40–44 | 0.57 | 0.48 | 0.39 | 0.33 | 0.23 | 0.15 |
| 45–49 | 0.55 | 0.48 | 0.39 | 0.26 | 0.20 | 0.11 |
| 50    | 0.53 | 0.49 | 0.40 | 0.24 | 0.18 | 0.10 |
| 51    | 0.53 | 0.49 | 0.41 | 0.23 | 0.17 | 0.09 |
| 52    | 0.54 | 0.49 | 0.41 | 0.22 | 0.16 | 0.08 |
| 53    | 0.54 | 0.49 | 0.42 | 0.21 | 0.15 | 0.07 |
| 54    | 0.54 | 0.50 | 0.43 | 0.20 | 0.14 | 0.06 |

### Table C
### Loss of earnings to pension age 60 (females—not disabled)

| Age at date of trial | Employed D | GE–A | O | Not employed D | GE–A | O |
|---|---|---|---|---|---|---|
| 16–19 |      | 0.81 | 0.64 |      | 0.77 | 0.59 |
| 20–24 | 0.89 | 0.82 | 0.68 | 0.84 | 0.76 | 0.60 |
| 25–29 | 0.89 | 0.84 | 0.72 | 0.83 | 0.75 | 0.61 |
| 30–34 | 0.89 | 0.85 | 0.75 | 0.81 | 0.75 | 0.63 |
| 35–39 | 0.89 | 0.86 | 0.78 | 0.80 | 0.74 | 0.63 |
| 40–44 | 0.89 | 0.86 | 0.80 | 0.78 | 0.72 | 0.60 |
| 45–49 | 0.87 | 0.85 | 0.81 | 0.72 | 0.64 | 0.52 |
| 50    | 0.86 | 0.84 | 0.81 | 0.64 | 0.55 | 0.43 |
| 51    | 0.85 | 0.84 | 0.81 | 0.60 | 0.51 | 0.40 |
| 52    | 0.84 | 0.84 | 0.81 | 0.56 | 0.46 | 0.36 |
| 53    | 0.83 | 0.83 | 0.81 | 0.50 | 0.41 | 0.32 |
| 54    | 0.83 | 0.83 | 0.82 | 0.44 | 0.35 | 0.27 |

A8: The Ogden Tables

**Table D**
**Loss of earnings to pension age 60 (females—disabled)**

| Age at date of trial | Employed | | | Not employed | | |
|---|---|---|---|---|---|---|
| | D | GE–A | O | D | GE–A | O |
| 16–19 |      | 0.43 | 0.25 |      | 0.35 | 0.19 |
| 20–24 | 0.64 | 0.44 | 0.25 | 0.58 | 0.33 | 0.17 |
| 25–29 | 0.63 | 0.45 | 0.25 | 0.50 | 0.32 | 0.16 |
| 30–34 | 0.62 | 0.46 | 0.30 | 0.44 | 0.31 | 0.15 |
| 35–39 | 0.61 | 0.48 | 0.34 | 0.42 | 0.28 | 0.14 |
| 40–44 | 0.60 | 0.51 | 0.38 | 0.38 | 0.23 | 0.13 |
| 45–49 | 0.60 | 0.54 | 0.42 | 0.28 | 0.18 | 0.11 |
| 50    | 0.60 | 0.56 | 0.47 | 0.23 | 0.15 | 0.10 |
| 51    | 0.61 | 0.58 | 0.49 | 0.21 | 0.14 | 0.09 |
| 52    | 0.61 | 0.60 | 0.51 | 0.20 | 0.13 | 0.08 |
| 53    | 0.62 | 0.62 | 0.54 | 0.18 | 0.11 | 0.07 |
| 54    | 0.63 | 0.66 | 0.57 | 0.16 | 0.09 | 0.06 |

The factors in Tables A–D will need to be reviewed if the discount rate changes.

## Different pension ages

43. The factors in the preceding tables assume retirement at age 65 for males and age 60 for females. It is not possible to calculate expected working life times assuming alternative retirement ages from the LFS data, since the employment data in the LFS are collected only for the working population, assumed to be aged between 16 and 64 for males and between 16 and 59 for females. Where the retirement age is different from age 65 for males or age 60 for females, it is suggested that this should be ignored and the reduction factor and the adjustments thereto be taken from the above tables for the age of the claimant as at the date of trial with no adjustment, i.e. assume that the retirement age is age 65 for males and age 60 for females. However, if the retirement age is close to the age at the date of trial, then it may be more appropriate to take into account the circumstances of the individual case.

44. It should be noted that the reduction factors in Tables A, B, C and D are based on data for the period 1998–2003. Whilst the reduction factors and adjustments allow for the age-specific probabilities of moving into, or out of, employment over future working life time, based on data for the period 1998–2003, the methodology assumes that these probabilities remain constant over time; there is no allowance for changes in these age-specific probabilities beyond this period. It is also assumed that there will be no change in disability status or educational achievement after the date of the accident. Future changes in the probabilities of moving into, and out of, employment are especially difficult to predict with any certainty. It is the intention that the factors should be reassessed from time to time as new data becomes available.

## Section C: Summary of personal injury applications

45. To use the tables the guidance below should be followed:

(1) Choose the table relating to the appropriate sex of the claimant and period of loss or expense (e.g. loss for life, or loss of earnings to a set retirement age). Where loss of earnings is concerned, and none of the tables is relevant because the claimant's expected age of retirement differs from that assumed in the tables, the procedure in paras 13–16 of the explanatory notes should be followed.

(2) Choose the appropriate discount column (currently 2.5 per cent).

(3) In that column find the appropriate figure for the claimant's age at trial ("the basic multiplier").

**Loss of earnings**

(4) When calculating **loss of earnings**, the tables should be used when a multiplier/multiplicand approach is appropriate. If it is, the basic multiplier should be adjusted to take account of contingencies other than mortality. These contingencies include the claimant's employment and disability status and educational qualifications. The basic multiplier should be multiplied by the appropriate figure taken from Tables A–D. It may be necessary at this stage to modify the resulting figure further to allow for circumstances specific to the claimant.

This process gives "the adjusted table multiplier".

(5) Multiply the net annual loss (the multiplicand) by the adjusted table multiplier to arrive at a figure which represents the capitalised value of the future loss of earnings.

(6) If the claimant has a residual earning capacity, allowance should be made for any post-accident vulnerability on the labour market: the following paragraphs show one way of doing this, although there may still be cases where a conventional ***Smith v City of Manchester*** award is appropriate.

Where it is appropriate to do so, repeat steps 1–5 above, replacing the pre-accident employment and disability status with the post-accident employment and disability status in step 4 and replacing the net annual loss by the assumed new level of net earnings at step 5. It will only be necessary to reconsider the claimant's educational attainments if these have changed between the accident and the date of trial or settlement.

The result will represent the capitalised value of the claimant's likely post-accident earnings. It is important to note that, when carrying out this exercise, the *degree* of residual disability may have a different effect on residual earnings depending on its relevance to the claimant's likely field of work. For example, the loss of a leg may have less effect on a sedentary worker's earnings than on a manual worker's.

(7) Deduct the sum yielded by step 6 from that yielded by step 5 to obtain the net amount of loss of earnings allowing for residual earning capacity. Where the above methodology is used there will usually be no need for a separate ***Smith v City of Manchester*** award.

**Lifetime losses**

(8) Where a **loss** will continue **for life**, follow steps 1–3, above, to find the appropriate multiplier in the table.

Where the normal life expectancy given by the table is inapplicable the approach set out in para.20, using the lifetime tables rather than Table 28, is the correct approach.

(9) This figure may need adjustment to allow for the particular circumstances of the claimant.

(10) Multiply the annual loss or expense by the multiplier as adjusted.

**Variable annual losses**

(11) In cases where there will be different losses at different periods it may be necessary to split the multiplier. The approach set out at paras 22–24 should be followed.

## A8: The Ogden Tables

**Fixed period and deferred losses**

(12) Where a loss will continue over a fixed period, the appropriate multiplier can be found in Table 28.

(13) Where a loss will not commence until some future date, multiply the appropriate multiplier by a discount figure taken from Table 27 (the use of which is explained in para.18). This paragraph does not apply to loss of pensions, which have their own tables.

**Examples**

46. The following are examples of the use of the tables in illustrative personal injury cases with simplified assumptions.

**Example 3**

47. The claimant is female, aged 35 at the date of the trial. She has three A levels, but not a degree, and was in employment at the date of the accident at a salary of £25,000 a year net of tax. She was not disabled before the accident. As a result of her injuries, she is now disabled and has lost her job but has found part-time employment at a salary of £5,000 a year net of tax. Her loss of earnings to retirement age of 60 is assessed as follows:

(1) Look up Table 8 for loss of earnings to pension age 60 for females.

(2) The appropriate rate of return is determined to be 2.5 per cent (the rate currently set under s.1 of the Damages Act 1996).

(3) Table 8 shows that, on the basis of a 2.5 per cent rate of return, the multiplier for a female aged 35 is 18.43.

(4) Now take account of risks other than mortality. Allowing for the claimant being employed, not disabled and having achieved A levels at the date of trial, Table C would require 18.43 to be multiplied by 0.86, resulting in a revised multiplier of 15.85.

(5) The damages for loss of earnings are assessed as £396,250 (15.85 × £25,000).

(6) Allow for mitigation of loss of earnings in respect of post-injury earnings. As before, Table 8 shows that, on the basis of a 2.5 per cent rate of return, the multiplier for a female aged 35 is 18.43.

(7) Now take account of risks other than mortality. Allowing for the claimant being employed, disabled and having achieved A levels at the date of trial, Table D would require 18.43 to be multiplied by 0.48, resulting in a revised multiplier of 8.85.

(8) The amount of mitigation for post-injury earnings is assessed as £44,150 (8.85 × £5,000).

(9) Hence award for loss of earnings after allowing for mitigation is £396,250 − £44,250 = £352,00.

**Example 4**

48. The claimant is male, aged 48 at the date of the trial. He has no educational qualifications. His retirement age was 65, he was employed at the time of the accident and his pre-retirement multiplicand has been determined as £20,000 a year net of tax. He was not disabled before the accident.

As a result of his injuries, he is now disabled and has lost his job. The multiplicand for costs of care is deemed to be £50,000 a year. He is unemployed at the date of trial but has been assessed as capable of finding work with possible future earnings of £5,000 a year net of tax. His loss of earnings to retirement age of 65 is assessed as follows:

(1) Look up Table 9 for loss of earnings to pension age 65 for males.

(2) The appropriate rate of return is determined to be 2.5 per cent (the rate currently set under s.1 of the Damages Act 1996).

(3) Table 9 shows that, on the basis of a 2.5 per cent rate of return, the multiplier for a male aged 48 is 13.42.

(4) Now take account of risks other than mortality. Allowing for the claimant being employed, not disabled and having no educational qualifications at the date of trial, Table A would require 13.42 to be multiplied by 0.86, resulting in a revised multiplier of 11.54.

(5) The damages for loss of earnings are assessed as £230,800 (11.54 × £20,000).

(6) Allow for mitigation of loss of earnings in respect of post-injury earnings. As before, Table 9 shows that, on the basis of a 2.5 per cent rate of return, the multiplier for a male aged 48 is 13.42.

(7) Now take account of risks other than mortality. Allowing for the claimant being unemployed and disabled with no educational qualifications at the date of trial, Table B would require 13.42 to be multiplied by 0.11, resulting in a revised multiplier of 1.48.

(8) The amount of mitigation for post-injury earnings is assessed as £7,400 (1.48 × £5,000).

(9) Hence award for loss of earnings after allowing for mitigation is £230,800 − £7,400 = £223,400.

49. The damages for cost of care are assessed as follows:

(1) Look up Table 1 for the multiplier at age 48.

(2) The appropriate rate of return is 2.5 per cent.

(3) Table 1 shows that, on the basis of a 2.5 per cent rate of return, the multiplier at age 48 is 23.51.

(4) No adjustment is made for risks other than mortality.

(5) The damages for cost of care are assessed at £1,175,500 (23.51 × £50,000).

**Example 5**

50. The claimant is female, aged 14 at the date of the trial. She is expected to achieve a degree and to be in employment thereafter on a salary, in current terms, of £30,000 a year net of tax. She was not disabled before the accident. As a result of her injuries, she is now disabled—she is still expected to achieve a degree and to be in employment, but with an average salary in current terms of £20,000 net of tax. She will be aged 21 when she completes her degree. Her loss of earnings to retirement age of 60 is assessed as follows:

A8: The Ogden Tables

(1) Look up Table 8 for loss of earnings to pension age 60 for females.

(2) The appropriate rate of return is determined to be 2.5 per cent (the rate currently set under s.1 of the Damages Act 1996).

(3) Table 8 shows that, on the basis of a 2.5 per cent rate of return, the multiplier for a female graduate aged 21 is 24.83. This needs to be discounted back to age 14. The factor at 2.5 per cent for a period for deferment for seven years is 0.8413 from Table 27, giving a total multiplier of 24.83 × 0.8413 = 20.89.

(4) Now take account of risks other than mortality. Allowing for the claimant at age 21 assessed as achieving a degree, being employed and not disabled, Table C would require 20.89 to be multiplied by 0.89, resulting in a revised multiplier of 18.59.

(5) The damages for loss of earnings are assessed as £557,700 (18.59 × £30,000).

(6) Allow for mitigation of loss of earnings in respect of post-injury earnings. As before, Table 8 shows that, on the basis of a 2.5 per cent rate of return, the multiplier for a female graduate aged 21 is 24.83. As before, after discounting for seven years to age 14 the multiplier is reduced to 24.83 × 0.8413 = 20.89.

(7) Now take account of risks other than mortality. Allowing for the claimant at age 21 assessed as achieving a degree, being employed and disabled, Table D would require 20.89 to be multiplied by 0.64, resulting in a revised multiplier of 13.37.

(8) The amount of mitigation for post-injury earnings is assessed as £267,400 (13.37 × £20,000).

(9) Hence award for loss of earnings after allowing for mitigation is £557,700 − £267,400 = £290,300.

## Example 6

51. The claimant is male, aged 40 at the date of the trial. He has achieved O levels. He was unemployed at the time of the accident. His potential pre-retirement multiplicand has been determined as £15,000 a year net of tax. He was disabled before the accident. As a result of his injuries, he has been assessed as having no future prospect of employment. His loss of earnings to retirement age of 65 is assessed as follows:

(1) Look up Table 9 for loss of earnings to pension age 65 for males.

(2) The appropriate rate of return is determined to be 2.5 per cent (the rate currently set under s.1 of the Damages Act 1996).

(3) Table 9 shows that, on the basis of a 2.5 per cent rate of return, the multiplier for a male aged 40 is 18.09.

(4) Now take account of risks other than mortality. Allowing for the claimant being unemployed, disabled and having achieved O levels at the date of trial, Table A would require 18.09 to be multiplied by 0.23, resulting in a revised multiplier of 4.16.

(5) The damages for loss of earnings are assessed as £62,400 (4.16 × £15,000).

(6) As the claimant has been assessed as having no future prospect of employment following the accident, there is no mitigation of loss of earnings in respect of post-injury earnings.

(7) Hence award for loss of earnings after allowing for mitigation is £62,400.

## Section D: Application of tables to fatal accident cases

52. The current approach of the courts, except in Scotland, is to assess the multiplier as at the date of death (***Cookson v Knowles***[15]).

53. That approach was criticised by the Law Commission in their Report 263 (*Claims for Wrongful Death*). The Law Commission recommended that multipliers should be assessed as at the date of trial and that the multipliers derived from the Ogden Tables should only take effect from the date of trial. The Law Commission stressed that the current approach incorporates an actuarial flaw in that it incorporates a discount for early receipt in the period prior to trial or assessment.

54. The Working Party, then under the Chairmanship of the late Sir Michael Ogden QC, considered that the Law Commission's criticism was valid. In the Fourth Edition of the Tables published in August 2000, the Working Party set out guidance in Section D of the Explanatory Notes on how damages should be calculated in such cases. We refer to that guidance below as the actuarially recommended approach. We note that the actuarially recommended approach has been adopted in the Damages (Scotland) Act 2011. For further details see paras 20–21 in the Introduction.

55. However, the courts have considered themselves bound by ***Cookson v Knowles*** and hence have not followed the actuarially recommended approach (***White v Esab***,[16] ***H v S***[17] and ***Fletcher v A Train & Sons Ltd***[18]).

### The basic law in England and Wales

56. Under the Fatal Accidents Act the loss is that of the dependants, i.e. those who relied upon the deceased for support. They may claim that part of the deceased's income (whether earnings, pension, unearned income or state benefits) that the deceased would have spent on them. They may also claim the loss of the services such as DIY, domestic/household or childcare which the deceased would have undertaken and from which they would have benefited. The position of each dependant must be considered separately.

57. Each head of dependency must be considered separately. For each head of claim for each dependant the court calculates a multiplicand. This is calculated on the basis of what is known at the date of trial. For pre-trial losses, the actual loss to date of trial is calculated. Interest is added. For post-trial losses the multiplicand is calculated as at the date of trial.

58. A multiplier for the period of dependency is applied to the multiplicand to arrive at an overall lump sum for each head of dependency.

59. The remainder of section D deals with how to approach the calculations in fatal accident claims. Three approaches are put forward. Paragraphs 60–63 set out the current approach. The actuarially

---

[15] [1979] A.C. 556.
[16] [2002] P.I.Q.R. Q6.
[17] [2002] EWCA Civ. 792, [2003] Q.B. 965.
[18] [2008] EWCA Civ. 413, [2008] 4 All E.R. 699.

recommended approach is then set out at paras 64–81. Example 7 illustrates the application of both these approaches whilst Examples 8 and 9 show the actuarially recommended approach applied to more complex situations—these examples make up paras 82–87. The final paragraphs of section D, 88–90, offer an alternative approach using multipliers selected from the date of death.

**The current approach**

60. Under the approach currently followed by the courts, the multiplier is calculated as at the date of death. However, when making that calculation the court is entitled to take into account matters that have arisen between death and trial. For example, ***Williamson v Thorneycroft***[19] in which the deceased's widow died after her husband but before trial, her dependency terminated at her death. See also, ***Corbett v Barking, Havering & Brentwood HA***.[20]

61. There are two periods to be determined:

(i) the expected period from date of death in which the deceased would have been capable of providing the dependency; and

(ii) the expected period from the date of the death in which the dependant would have been able to receive the dependency.

The shorter of those two periods provides the basis for the multiplier.

62. In respect of each of those periods consideration must be given as to what discount should be made for contingencies other than mortality. The most obvious contingencies other than mortality fall into the following three categories:

(i) Factors relating to the deceased. For example, the deceased's health may have been such as to seriously affect his ability to provide services or work until retirement age. In relation to earnings the starting point for the adjustment factor should be the figures contained in Tables A–D.

(ii) Factors relating to the dependant. For example, at trial it may be proved that a dependant has a significantly reduced life expectancy.

(iii) Factors relating to the relationship of the deceased and the dependant. For example, an unmarried couple who were on the point of separation before the deceased died. See also s.3 (4) of the Act and ***Drew v Abassi***.[21]

63. The assessment of the multiplier involves the following steps:

(1) Determine the expected period from the date of death for which the deceased would have been capable of providing the dependency.

(2) Discount that period for early receipt using the appropriate table as at the date of death and a discount rate of 2.5 per cent.

(3) Apply any adjustment to the above figure to reflect contingencies other than mortality.

---

[19] [1940] 2 K.B. 658.
[20] [1991] 2 Q.B. 408.
[21] Court of Appeal, May 24, 1995.

(4) Determine the expected period from date of death for which the dependant would have been able to receive the dependency.

(5) Discount that period for early receipt using the appropriate table as at the date of death at a discount rate of 2.5 per cent.

(6) Apply any adjustment to the figure in (5) to reflect contingencies other than mortality.

(7) Take the lower of the figures in (3) and (6) above. That is the overall multiplier from date of death.

(8) Subtract the period elapsed from date of death to date of trial. Losses in this period will be treated as in effect special damages and will attract an award of interest.

(9) The balance of the multiplier will be the multiplier for the post-trial multiplicand.

**The actuarially recommended approach**

64. Whereas in personal injury cases the problem to be solved is that of setting a value on an income stream during the potential life of one person (the claimant), the situation is generally more complicated in fatal accident cases. Here the compensation is intended to reflect the value of an income stream during the lifetime of one or more dependants of the deceased (or the expected period for which the dependants would have expected to receive the dependency, if shorter) but limited according to the expectation of how long the deceased would have been able to provide the financial support, had he or she not been involved in the fatal accident.

65. In principle, therefore, the compensation for post-trial dependency should be based on the present value at the date of the trial of the dependency during the expected future joint lifetime of the deceased and the dependant or claimant (had the deceased survived naturally to the date of the trial), subject to any limitations on the period of dependency and any expected future changes in the level of dependency, for example, on attaining retirement age. In addition there should be compensation for the period between the date of accident and the date of trial.

66. A set of actuarial tables to make such calculations accurately would require tables similar to Tables 1–26 but for each combination of ages as at the date of the trial of the deceased and the dependant to whom compensation is to be paid. The Working Party concluded that this would not meet the criterion of simplicity of application which was a central objective of these tables and recommends that, in complex cases, or cases where the accuracy of the multiplier is thought by the parties to be of critical importance and material to the resulting amount of compensation (for example, in cases potentially involving very large claims where the level of the multiplicand is unambiguously established), the advice of a professionally qualified actuary should be sought. However, for the majority of cases, a certain amount of approximation will be appropriate, bearing in mind the need for a simple and streamlined process, and taking into consideration the other uncertainties in the determination of an appropriate level of compensation. The following paragraphs describe a methodology using Tables 1–26 which can be expected to yield satisfactory answers.

**(i) Damages for the period from the fatal accident to the date of trial**

67. The period of pre-trial dependency will normally be equal to the period between the date of the fatal accident and the date of the trial, substituting where appropriate the lower figure of the expected period for which the deceased would have provided the dependency, had he or she not been killed in

the accident, or if the period of dependency would have been limited in some way, for example, if the dependant is a child.

68. A deduction may be made for the risk that the deceased might have died anyway, in the period between the date of the fatal accident and the date at which the trial takes place. In many cases this deduction will be small and could usually be regarded as de minimis. The need for a deduction becomes more necessary the longer the period from the date of accident to the date of trial and the older the deceased at the date of death. As an illustration of the order of magnitude of the deduction, Table E shows some examples of factors by which the multiplier should be multiplied for different ages of the deceased and for different periods from the date of accident to the date of the trial.

**Table E**
**Factor by which pre-trial damages should be multiplied to allow for the likelihood that the deceased would not in any case have survived to provide the dependency for the full period to the date of trial**

| Age of deceased at date of accident | Period from date of accident to date of trial or date of cessation of dependency, if earlier (years) | | | | | |
|---|---|---|---|---|---|---|
| | Male deceased | | | Female deceased | | |
| | 3 | 6 | 9 | 3 | 6 | 9 |
| 10 | 1.00 | 1.00 | 1.00 | 1.00 | 1.00 | 1.00 |
| 20 | 1.00 | 1.00 | 1.00 | 1.00 | 1.00 | 1.00 |
| 30 | 1.00 | 1.00 | 0.99 | 1.00 | 1.00 | 1.00 |
| 40 | 1.00 | 0.99 | 0.99 | 1.00 | 1.00 | 0.99 |
| 50 | 0.99 | 0.99 | 0.98 | 1.00 | 0.99 | 0.99 |
| 60 | 0.99 | 0.97 | 0.94 | 0.99 | 0.98 | 0.97 |
| 65 | 0.98 | 0.95 | 0.91 | 0.99 | 0.97 | 0.95 |
| 70 | 0.97 | 0.92 | 0.86 | 0.98 | 0.95 | 0.91 |
| 75 | 0.94 | 0.87 | 0.78 | 0.96 | 0.91 | 0.84 |
| 80 | 0.90 | 0.79 | 0.67 | 0.93 | 0.84 | 0.75 |

N.B. The factor for a period of zero years is clearly 1.00. Factors for other ages and periods not shown in the table may be obtained approximately by interpolation.

69. The resultant multiplier, after application of any discount for the possibility of early death of the deceased before the date of trial, even had the accident not taken place, is to be applied to the multiplicand, which is determined in the usual way. Interest will then be added up to the date of trial on the basis of special damages.

### (ii) Damages from the date of trial to retirement age

70. The assessment of the multiplier involves the following steps:

(1) Determine the expected period from the date of the trial for which the deceased would have been able to provide the dependency (see para.71).

(2) Determine the expected period for which the dependant would have been able to receive the dependency (see paras 71 and 72).

(3) Take the lesser of the two periods.

(4) Treat the resulting period as a term certain for which the multiplier is to be determined and look up the figure in Table 28 for this period at the appropriate rate of interest.

(5) Apply any adjustment for contingencies other than mortality in accordance with section B.

(6) If necessary, make an allowance for the risk that the deceased might have died anyway before the date of the trial (see para.73).

71. The expected periods at (1) and (2) of para.70 may be obtained from the 0% column of the appropriate table at the back of this booklet. For (1), Tables 3–14 will be relevant, according to the sex of the deceased and the expected age of retirement. The age at which the table should be entered is the age which the deceased would have been at the date of the trial. For (2), Tables 1 and 2 can be used, according to the sex of the dependant and looking up the table at the age of the dependant at the date of the trial.

72. If the period for which the dependency would have continued is a short fixed period, as in the case of a child, the figure at (2) would be the outstanding period at the date of the trial.

73. A deduction may be made for the risk that the deceased might have died anyway before the date of trial. The need for such a deduction becomes more necessary the longer the period from the date of accident to the date of trial and the older the deceased at the date of death. As an illustration of the order of magnitude of the deduction, Table F shows some examples of the factor by which the multiplier, determined as above, should be multiplied for different ages of the deceased and for different periods from the date of accident to the date of the trial.

**Table F**
**Factor by which post-trial damages should be multiplied to allow for the likelihood that the deceased would not in any case have survived to the date of trial in order to provide any post-trial dependency**

| Age of deceased at date of accident | Period from date of accident to date of trial (years) | | | | | |
|---|---|---|---|---|---|---|
| | Male deceased | | | Female deceased | | |
| | 3 | 6 | 9 | 3 | 6 | 9 |
| 10 | 1.00 | 1.00 | 1.00 | 1.00 | 1.00 | 1.00 |
| 20 | 1.00 | 1.00 | 0.99 | 1.00 | 1.00 | 1.00 |
| 30 | 1.00 | 0.99 | 0.99 | 1.00 | 1.00 | 0.99 |
| 40 | 0.99 | 0.99 | 0.98 | 1.00 | 0.99 | 0.99 |
| 50 | 0.99 | 0.97 | 0.95 | 0.99 | 0.98 | 0.97 |
| 60 | 0.97 | 0.93 | 0.88 | 0.98 | 0.96 | 0.92 |
| 65 | 0.96 | 0.90 | 0.82 | 0.97 | 0.93 | 0.88 |
| 70 | 0.93 | 0.84 | 0.71 | 0.96 | 0.89 | 0.80 |
| 75 | 0.88 | 0.73 | 0.55 | 0.92 | 0.81 | 0.66 |
| 80 | 0.83 | 0.59 | 0.37 | 0.86 | 0.68 | 0.48 |

N.B. The factor for a period of zero years is clearly 1.00. Factors for other ages and periods not shown in the table may be obtained approximately by interpolation.

74. The resulting multiplier, after application of any discount for the possibility of early death of the deceased before the date of trial, even had the accident not taken place, is to be applied to the appropriate multiplicand, determined in relation to dependency as assessed for the period up to retirement age.

75. If there are several dependants, to whom damages are to be paid in respect of their own particular lifetime (or for a fixed period of dependency), separate multipliers should be determined for each and multiplied by the appropriate multiplicand using the procedure in paras 70–74. The total amount of damages is then obtained by adding the separate components. If a single multiplicand is determined, but the damages are to be shared among two or more dependants so long as they are each alive, or during a period of common dependency, then the multiplier will be calculated using the procedure in paras 70–74. However, at step (2) of para.70 the expected period will be the longest of the expected periods for which the dependency might last.

### (iii) Damages for the period of dependency after retirement age

76. The method described in paras 70–75 for pre-retirement age dependency cannot satisfactorily be applied directly to post-retirement age dependency with a sufficient degree of accuracy. We therefore propose a method which involves determining the multiplier by looking at dependency for the rest of life from the date of trial and then subtracting the multiplier for dependency up to retirement age.

77. The assessment of the multiplier for whole of life dependency involves the following steps:

(1) Determine the expectation of life which the deceased would have had as at the date of trial, or such lesser period for which the deceased would have been able to provide the dependency (see para.78).

(2) Determine the expected period for which the dependant would have been able to receive the dependency (see para.78).

(3) Take the lesser of the two periods.

(4) Treat the resulting period as a term certain for which the multiplier is to be determined and look up the figure in Table 28 for this period at the appropriate rate of interest.

78. The expected periods at (1) and (2) of para.77 may be obtained from the 0% column of the appropriate table at the back of this booklet. For (1), Tables 1 or 2 will be relevant, according to the sex of the deceased. The age at which the table should be entered is the age which the deceased would have attained at the date of the trial. For (2), Tables 1 and 2 can be used, according to the sex of the dependant and looking up the table at the age of the dependant at the date of the trial.

79. Deduct the corresponding multiplier for post-trial pre-retirement dependency, as determined in paras 70–75, but without any adjustment for contingencies other than mortality, or that the deceased may have died anyway before the date of trial. The result is the multiplier for post-retirement dependency, which must then be applied to the appropriate multiplicand, assessed in relation to dependency after retirement age. The adjustment for contingencies other than mortality in respect of the damages for the period of dependency after retirement age will often be less than that required for pre-retirement age damages (see para.30).

80. A deduction may finally be made for the risk that the deceased might have died anyway before the date of trial. The need for such a deduction becomes more necessary the longer the period from the date of accident to the date of trial and the older the deceased at the date of death. As an illustration of the order of magnitude of the deduction, Table F shows some examples of the factor by which the multiplier, determined as above, should be multiplied for different ages of the deceased and for different periods from the date of accident to the date of the trial. The factors for this purpose are exactly the same deductions as used in the calculation at paras 70–75.

81. The layout of paras 70–80 is based on the assumption that the dependency provided by the deceased would have changed at retirement age. This may not be appropriate in some cases, particularly in the important case of the deceased wife and mother whose contribution has been solely in the home or in the case of an adult child caring for an elderly parent or parents. In cases like this, where the deceased might have provided the dependency throughout their lifetime, paras 76–80 should be ignored and paras 70–75 used, with the difference that the expected period required at step (1) of para.70 should be a whole of life expectancy, taken from Tables 1 and 2. This is also the approach to use when the deceased was already a pensioner.

# A8: The Ogden Tables

**Examples**

82. Paragraphs 83 and 84 give calculations of damages awards for Example 7, calculated using first the current approach and then the actuarially recommended approach.

**Example 7**

83. The dependant is female, aged 38 at the date of the trial, which is taking place three years after the date of the fatal accident which killed her husband, at that time aged 37, on whom she was financially dependent. The deceased had A levels, was in employment and in good health with no disability at the time of the fatal accident. The dependant was, at the date of death, and is at the date of trial, in good health. Their relationship was stable. The court has determined a multiplicand of £30,000 up to the deceased's normal retirement age of 65 with no financial dependency post-age 65, nor any services dependency. The damages are to be calculated as follows:

**The current approach**

(1) The deceased would have been capable of providing the financial dependency to the dependant for the period of 28 years from the date of his death aged 37 to his 65th birthday.

(2) The appropriate Table is 9. Using the 2.5 per cent column the multiplier = 19.64.

(3) Adjustment factor for contingencies other than mortality (in accordance with section B) for an employed male aged 37 with A levels and who is not disabled = 0.9 to give a multiplier of 19.64 × 0.9 = 17.68.

(4) The expected period for which the dependant would have been able to receive the dependency was between the ages of 35 and 63.

(5) The appropriate Tables are 8 and 10, and using the 2.5 per cent column the multiplier = 19.91.

(6) The parties were married so section 3(4) does not apply. The relationship was stable. The dependant was and is in good health. The court is unlikely to make much of an adjustment to the figure in (5) above to reflect contingencies other than mortality.

(7) The lower of the two figures is that in (3) above, namely 17.68.

(8) The period that has elapsed between date of death and date of trial is three years. The pre-trial loss is therefore £30,000 × 3 = £90,000.

(9) Interest at half rate from date of death to date of trial: three years at 3 per cent a year = 9 per cent.
£90,000 × 9% = £8,100.

(10) The post-trial multiplier is 14.68 (17.68 − 3).

(11) The post trial loss is therefore 14.68 × £30,000 = £440,400.

(12) Total financial dependency is therefore £90,000 + £8,100 + £440,400 = £538,500.

## The actuarially recommended approach

84. Applying this approach to Example 7 set out above:

*Pre-trial damages*:

(1) Period between fatal accident and trial: three years.

(2) Factor for possible early death (Table E for male aged 37 and three years) = 1.00.

(3) Pre-trial damages = 3 × 1.00 × £30,000 = £90,000 (plus interest as special damages).

(4) Interest at half rate from date of death to date of trial: three years at 3 per cent a year = 9 per cent.
£90,000 × 9% = £8,100.

*Post-trial damages*:

(1) Expected period for which the deceased would have provided the dependency (Table 9 at 0 per cent for male aged 40, the age as at the date of trial): 24.13.

(2) Expected period for which the dependant would have been able to receive the dependency (Table 2 at 0 per cent for female aged 38): 51.38.

(3) Lesser of two periods at (1) and (2) = 24.13.

(4) Multiplier for term certain of 24.13 years at 2.5 per cent rate of return = 18.18.

(5) Adjustment factor for contingencies other than mortality (in accordance with section B) for an employed male aged 40 with A levels and who was not disabled = 0.88 to give a multiplier of 18.18 × 0.88 = 16.00.

(6) Adjustment factor for the risk that the deceased might have died anyway before the date of trial (Table F for male aged 37 and three years): 0.99 to give a multiplier of 16.00 × 0.99 = 15.84.

(7) Post-trial damages = 15.84 × £30,000 = £475,200.

(8) Total financial dependency is therefore £90,000 + £8,100 + £475,200 = £573,300.

85. Examples 8 and 9 in the following paragraphs set out two further examples to show the application of the actuarially recommended approach to more complex examples.

## Example 8

86. The dependant is female, aged 50 at the date of the trial, which is taking place four years after the date of the fatal accident which killed the man, at that time aged 47, on whom she was financially dependent. The deceased was in employment at the time of the fatal accident, was not disabled and had achieved A levels. The court has determined a multiplicand, up to the deceased's normal retirement age of 60, of £50,000 and has decided that post-retirement damages should be payable based on a multiplicand of £30,000. The damages are to be calculated as follows:

*Pre-trial damages*:

(1) Period between fatal accident and trial: four years.

(2) Factor for possible early death (Table E for male aged 47 and four years): 0.99.

(3) Pre-trial damages = 4 × 0.99 × £50,000 = £198,000 (plus interest as special damages).

*Post-trial pre-retirement damages*:

(1) Expected period for which the deceased would have provided the dependency (Table 7 at 0% for male aged 51, the age as at the date of trial): 8.81.

(2) Expected period for which the dependant would have been able to receive the dependency (Table 2 at 0 per cent for female aged 50): 38.73.

(3) Lesser of two periods at (1) and (2) = 8.81.

(4) Multiplier for term certain of 8.81 years at 2.5 per cent rate of return (interpolating between the values for 8 and 9 in Table 28) = (9 − 8.81) × 7.26 + (8.81 − 8) × 8.07 = 7.92.

(5) Adjustment factor for contingencies other than mortality (in accordance with section B) for an employed male aged 51 with A levels and who was not disabled = 0.82 to give a multiplier of 7.92 × 0.82 = 6.49.

(6) Adjustment factor for the risk that the deceased might have died anyway before the date of trial (Table F for male aged 47 and four years): 0.99 to give a multiplier of 6.49 × 0.99 = 6.43.

(7) Post-trial pre-retirement damages = 6.43 × £50,000 = £321,500.

*Post-retirement damages*:

(1) Expectation of life of deceased at date of trial (Table 1 at 0 per cent for male aged 51): 34.45.

(2) Expected period for which the dependant would have been able to receive the dependency (Table 2 at 0 per cent for female aged 50): 38.73.

(3) Lesser of two periods at (1) and (2) = 34.45.

(4) Multiplier for term certain of 34.45 years at 2.5 per cent rate of return (interpolating between the values for 34 and 35 in Table 28) = (35 − 34.45) × 23.01 + (34.45 − 34) × 23.43 = 23.20.

(5) Deduct multiplier for post-trial pre-retirement damages before application of adjustment factors for contingencies other than mortality and for the risk that the deceased might have died anyway before the date of trial: 23.20 − 7.92 = 15.28.

(6) Adjustment factor for the risk that the deceased might have died anyway before the date of trial (Table F for male aged 47 and four years): 0.99 to give a multiplier of 15.28 × 0.99 = 15.13.

(7) Post-retirement damages = 15.13 × £30,000 = £453,900.

**Example 9**

87. There are two dependants, respectively a child aged 10 and a male aged 41 at the date of the trial, which is taking place three years after the date of the fatal accident which killed the woman, at that

## A8: The Ogden Tables

time aged 35, on whom both were financially dependent. She had a degree and worked in London for a computer company. The court has determined a multiplicand, up to the deceased's normal retirement age of 62, of £50,000 for the male dependant and £10,000 for the child, up to the age of 21, and has decided that post-retirement damages should be payable based on a multiplicand of £20,000. The damages are to be calculated as follows:

*Pre-trial damages*:

(1) Period between fatal accident and trial: three years.

(2) Factor for possible early death (Table E for female aged 35 and three years): 1.00.

(3) Pre-trial damages = 3 × 1.00 × (£50,000 + £10,000) = £180,000 (plus interest as special damages).

*Post-trial pre-retirement damages*:

(1) Expected period for which the deceased would have provided the dependency should be based on female aged 38 at the date of trial with retirement age of 62. First calculate as though deceased were aged 36 and had retirement age of 60 (Table 8 at 0% for female aged 36): 23.66.

Then calculate as though deceased were aged 41 and had retirement age of 65 (Table 10 at 0 per cent for female aged 41): 23.47.

Interpolate for age 38 with retirement age of 62 = (3 × 23.66 + 2 × 23.47)/5 = 23.58.

(2) Expected period for which the male dependant would have been able to receive the dependency (Table 1 at 0 per cent for male aged 41): 44.71.

Expected period for which child would have been able to receive the dependency = 11.00.

(3) Lesser of two periods at (1) and (2) = 11.00 (in case of child)

= 23.58 (in case of man).

(4) Multiplier for term certain of 11 years at 2.5 per cent (Table 28): 9.63.

Multiplier for term certain of 23.58 years at 2.5 per cent rate of return (interpolating between the values for 23 and 24 in Table 28)

= (24 − 23.58) × 17.55 + (23.58 − 23) × 18.11 = 17.87.

(5) Adjustment factor for contingencies other than mortality (in accordance with section B) for an employed female aged 38 with a degree and who was not disabled = 0.89 (does not apply to child) to give a multiplier of 17.87 × 0.89 = 15.90.

(6) Adjustment factor for the risk that the deceased might have died anyway before the date of trial (Table F for female aged 35 and three years): 1.00, so multipliers are 9.63 and 15.90 respectively.

(7) Pre-retirement damages = 9.63 × £10,000 + 15.90 × £50,000

= £96,300 + £795,000 = £891,300.

*Post-retirement damages*:

(1) Expectation of life of deceased at date of trial (Table 2 at 0 per cent for female aged 38): 51.38.

(2) Expected period for which the dependant would have been able to receive the dependency (Table 1 at 0 per cent for male aged 41): 44.71 (no post retirement dependency for child).

(3) Lesser of two periods at (1) and (2) = 44.71.

(4) Multiplier for term certain of 44.71 years at 2.5 per cent rate of return (interpolating between the values for 42 and 43 in Table 28)

$= (45 - 44.71) \times 26.83 + (44.71 - 44) \times 27.17 = 27.07$.

(5) Deduct multiplier for post-trial pre-retirement damages before application of adjustment factors for contingencies other than mortality and for the risk that the deceased might have died anyway before the date of trial: $27.07 - 17.87 = 9.20$.

(6) Adjustment factor for the risk that the deceased might have died anyway before the date of trial (Table F for female aged 35 and three years) = 1.00, so multiplier is $9.20 \times 1.00 = 9.20$.

(7) Post-retirement damages = $9.20 \times £20,000 = £184,000$.

**An Alternative approach**

88. If the court wishes to select multipliers from the date of death, it is essential to ensure that the period before the trial does not include a discount for early receipt. This could be achieved by selecting multipliers from the 0% columns of the appropriate tables and then applying the discount for early receipt to the period after the trial (using the discount rate set under s.1 of the Damages Act 1996). The calculation of the multiplier involves the following steps:

(1) Determine the expected period for which the deceased would have provided the dependency at the date of death.

(2) Deduct the period between accidental death and date of trial to give post-trial period.

(3) Determine the expected post-trial period for which the dependant would have been able to receive the dependency.

(4) Take the lesser of two periods at (2) and (3).

(5) Take the multiplier for term certain for the period calculated at (4) at 2.5 per cent rate of return (from Table 28).

(6) Apply any adjustment factor to the figure in (5) to reflect contingencies other than mortality (in accordance with section B). This will give the multiplier for the post-trial multiplicand.

89. Applying this approach to Example 7 set out above:

(1) Expected period for which the deceased would have provided the dependency (Table 9 at 0 per cent for male aged 37, the age as at the date of death): 27.06.

(2) Deduct period between accidental death and date of trial of three years to give post-trial period: 24.06.

(3) Expected post-trial period for which the dependant would have been able to receive the dependency (Table 2 at 0 per cent for female aged 38): 51.38.

(4) Lesser of two periods at (2) and (3) = 24.06.

(5) Multiplier for term certain of 24.06 years at 2.5 per cent rate of return (Table 28) = 18.14.

(6) Adjustment factor for contingencies other than mortality (in accordance with section B) for an employed male aged 37 with A levels and who was not disabled = 0.90 to give a multiplier of 18.14 × 0.90 = 16.33.

(7) Pre-trial damages = 3 × £30,000 = £90,000 (plus interest as special damages of £8,100).

(8) Post-trial damages = 16.33 × £30,000 = £489,900.

(9) Total financial dependency therefore £90,000 + £8,100 + £489,900 = £588,000.

90. As can be seen, the three methodologies (the current approach, the actuarially recommended approach and this alternative approach) give three different amounts of damages in relation to Example 7, namely £538,500 for the current approach used by the courts, £573,300 using the actuarially recommended approach, and £588,000 using this alternative approach. The size of the disparities between the three methods depends on the length of the period between the date of death and the date of trial; if the example had assumed a period of six years then the differences would have been greater.

**Section E: Concluding remarks**

91. These tables are designed to assist the courts to arrive at suitable multipliers in a range of possible situations. However, they do not cover all possibilities and in more complex situations, such as where there are significant pension rights, advice should be sought from a Fellow of the Institute and Faculty of Actuaries.

GEORGE RUSSELL FIA
Deputy Government Actuary
London
August 2012

## Table 1: Multipliers for pecuniary loss for life (males)

| Age at date of trial | Multiplier calculated with allowance for projected mortality from the 2008–based population projections and rate of return of | | | | | | | | | | | Age at date of trial |
|---|---|---|---|---|---|---|---|---|---|---|---|---|
| | -2.0% | -1.5% | -1.0% | -0.5% | 0.0% | 0.5% | 1.0% | 1.5% | 2.0% | 2.5% | 3.0% | |
| 0 | 264.76 | 195.32 | 147.14 | 113.22 | 88.96 | 71.35 | 58.34 | 48.60 | 41.17 | 35.41 | 30.89 | 0 |
| 1 | 259.11 | 191.95 | 145.15 | 112.06 | 88.31 | 71.00 | 58.18 | 48.54 | 41.18 | 35.46 | 30.96 | 1 |
| 2 | 252.28 | 187.68 | 142.46 | 110.35 | 87.22 | 70.30 | 57.73 | 48.24 | 40.98 | 35.33 | 30.87 | 2 |
| 3 | 245.58 | 183.46 | 139.78 | 108.64 | 86.12 | 69.58 | 57.26 | 47.94 | 40.78 | 35.19 | 30.78 | 3 |
| 4 | 239.02 | 179.29 | 137.12 | 106.93 | 85.01 | 68.86 | 56.78 | 47.62 | 40.56 | 35.05 | 30.68 | 4 |
| 5 | 232.59 | 175.19 | 134.48 | 105.22 | 83.89 | 68.12 | 56.30 | 47.29 | 40.34 | 34.90 | 30.58 | 5 |
| 6 | 226.29 | 171.15 | 131.87 | 103.52 | 82.78 | 67.39 | 55.80 | 46.96 | 40.12 | 34.75 | 30.47 | 6 |
| 7 | 220.14 | 167.18 | 129.29 | 101.83 | 81.66 | 66.65 | 55.31 | 46.63 | 39.89 | 34.59 | 30.36 | 7 |
| 8 | 214.13 | 163.28 | 126.74 | 100.15 | 80.55 | 65.90 | 54.80 | 46.28 | 39.65 | 34.42 | 30.24 | 8 |
| 9 | 208.23 | 159.43 | 124.21 | 98.48 | 79.43 | 65.15 | 54.29 | 45.93 | 39.41 | 34.25 | 30.13 | 9 |
| 10 | 202.47 | 155.64 | 121.71 | 96.81 | 78.31 | 64.39 | 53.78 | 45.58 | 39.16 | 34.08 | 30.00 | 10 |
| 11 | 196.83 | 151.92 | 119.23 | 95.15 | 77.19 | 63.63 | 53.25 | 45.22 | 38.91 | 33.90 | 29.87 | 11 |
| 12 | 191.33 | 148.26 | 116.79 | 93.50 | 76.07 | 62.86 | 52.72 | 44.85 | 38.65 | 33.72 | 29.74 | 12 |
| 13 | 185.95 | 144.67 | 114.37 | 91.87 | 74.96 | 62.09 | 52.19 | 44.47 | 38.39 | 33.53 | 29.61 | 13 |
| 14 | 180.69 | 141.14 | 111.98 | 90.24 | 73.84 | 61.32 | 51.65 | 44.10 | 38.12 | 33.34 | 29.47 | 14 |
| 15 | 175.56 | 137.67 | 109.62 | 88.63 | 72.73 | 60.55 | 51.11 | 43.71 | 37.84 | 33.14 | 29.32 | 15 |
| 16 | 170.55 | 134.27 | 107.30 | 87.02 | 71.61 | 59.77 | 50.56 | 43.32 | 37.57 | 32.94 | 29.17 | 16 |
| 17 | 165.66 | 130.93 | 105.00 | 85.44 | 70.51 | 58.99 | 50.01 | 42.93 | 37.28 | 32.73 | 29.02 | 17 |
| 18 | 160.89 | 127.66 | 102.74 | 83.86 | 69.41 | 58.22 | 49.46 | 42.53 | 37.00 | 32.52 | 28.87 | 18 |
| 19 | 156.25 | 124.45 | 100.52 | 82.31 | 68.31 | 57.44 | 48.91 | 42.14 | 36.71 | 32.31 | 28.71 | 19 |
| 20 | 151.72 | 121.31 | 98.32 | 80.76 | 67.22 | 56.66 | 48.35 | 41.73 | 36.41 | 32.10 | 28.55 | 20 |
| 21 | 147.28 | 118.22 | 96.15 | 79.23 | 66.13 | 55.88 | 47.78 | 41.32 | 36.11 | 31.87 | 28.39 | 21 |
| 22 | 142.94 | 115.17 | 94.00 | 77.70 | 65.04 | 55.09 | 47.21 | 40.90 | 35.81 | 31.64 | 28.22 | 22 |
| 23 | 138.69 | 112.17 | 91.87 | 76.18 | 63.94 | 54.30 | 46.63 | 40.48 | 35.49 | 31.41 | 28.04 | 23 |
| 24 | 134.54 | 109.22 | 89.77 | 74.67 | 62.85 | 53.51 | 46.05 | 40.05 | 35.17 | 31.17 | 27.86 | 24 |
| 25 | 130.49 | 106.33 | 87.69 | 73.17 | 61.76 | 52.71 | 45.46 | 39.61 | 34.85 | 30.92 | 27.67 | 25 |
| 26 | 126.54 | 103.50 | 85.65 | 71.69 | 60.68 | 51.91 | 44.87 | 39.17 | 34.51 | 30.67 | 27.48 | 26 |
| 27 | 122.69 | 100.72 | 83.63 | 70.22 | 59.59 | 51.11 | 44.28 | 38.73 | 34.18 | 30.42 | 27.28 | 27 |
| 28 | 118.90 | 97.98 | 81.63 | 68.74 | 58.51 | 50.30 | 43.67 | 38.27 | 33.83 | 30.15 | 27.08 | 28 |
| 29 | 115.20 | 95.28 | 79.64 | 67.28 | 57.42 | 49.49 | 43.06 | 37.81 | 33.48 | 29.88 | 26.87 | 29 |
| 30 | 111.59 | 92.63 | 77.69 | 65.83 | 56.34 | 48.68 | 42.45 | 37.34 | 33.12 | 29.60 | 26.65 | 30 |
| 31 | 108.09 | 90.04 | 75.78 | 64.40 | 55.27 | 47.87 | 41.83 | 36.87 | 32.76 | 29.32 | 26.44 | 31 |
| 32 | 104.68 | 87.52 | 73.89 | 62.99 | 54.20 | 47.06 | 41.22 | 36.40 | 32.39 | 29.04 | 26.21 | 32 |
| 33 | 101.36 | 85.04 | 72.04 | 61.60 | 53.15 | 46.26 | 40.60 | 35.92 | 32.02 | 28.75 | 25.99 | 33 |
| 34 | 98.10 | 82.61 | 70.21 | 60.21 | 52.09 | 45.45 | 39.98 | 35.44 | 31.65 | 28.46 | 25.75 | 34 |
| 35 | 94.92 | 80.21 | 68.39 | 58.83 | 51.03 | 44.63 | 39.35 | 34.95 | 31.26 | 28.15 | 25.51 | 35 |
| 36 | 91.82 | 77.86 | 66.60 | 57.46 | 49.98 | 43.82 | 38.71 | 34.45 | 30.87 | 27.84 | 25.27 | 36 |
| 37 | 88.78 | 75.55 | 64.83 | 56.10 | 48.93 | 43.00 | 38.07 | 33.95 | 30.47 | 27.53 | 25.01 | 37 |
| 38 | 85.81 | 73.27 | 63.08 | 54.74 | 47.87 | 42.18 | 37.42 | 33.44 | 30.06 | 27.20 | 24.75 | 38 |
| 39 | 82.89 | 71.03 | 61.35 | 53.39 | 46.82 | 41.35 | 36.77 | 32.91 | 29.65 | 26.86 | 24.48 | 39 |
| 40 | 80.05 | 68.83 | 59.63 | 52.05 | 45.76 | 40.51 | 36.11 | 32.39 | 29.22 | 26.52 | 24.20 | 40 |
| 41 | 77.27 | 66.67 | 57.94 | 50.72 | 44.71 | 39.68 | 35.44 | 31.85 | 28.79 | 26.17 | 23.91 | 41 |
| 42 | 74.56 | 64.55 | 56.28 | 49.41 | 43.67 | 38.84 | 34.77 | 31.31 | 28.35 | 25.81 | 23.62 | 42 |
| 43 | 71.92 | 62.47 | 54.63 | 48.10 | 42.62 | 38.01 | 34.10 | 30.76 | 27.91 | 25.45 | 23.32 | 43 |
| 44 | 69.34 | 60.43 | 53.01 | 46.81 | 41.59 | 37.17 | 33.42 | 30.21 | 27.45 | 25.08 | 23.01 | 44 |
| 45 | 66.82 | 58.43 | 51.41 | 45.52 | 40.55 | 36.33 | 32.73 | 29.65 | 26.99 | 24.70 | 22.69 | 45 |
| 46 | 64.36 | 56.46 | 49.83 | 44.25 | 39.52 | 35.49 | 32.05 | 29.08 | 26.53 | 24.31 | 22.37 | 46 |
| 47 | 61.96 | 54.53 | 48.28 | 42.99 | 38.49 | 34.65 | 31.35 | 28.51 | 26.05 | 23.91 | 22.04 | 47 |
| 48 | 59.63 | 52.64 | 46.74 | 41.74 | 37.47 | 33.81 | 30.66 | 27.94 | 25.57 | 23.51 | 21.70 | 48 |
| 49 | 57.35 | 50.79 | 45.24 | 40.50 | 36.45 | 32.97 | 29.97 | 27.36 | 25.09 | 23.10 | 21.36 | 49 |
| 50 | 55.14 | 48.99 | 43.76 | 39.29 | 35.45 | 32.14 | 29.27 | 26.78 | 24.60 | 22.69 | 21.01 | 50 |
| 51 | 52.99 | 47.23 | 42.31 | 38.09 | 34.45 | 31.31 | 28.58 | 26.19 | 24.11 | 22.27 | 20.65 | 51 |
| 52 | 50.90 | 45.51 | 40.89 | 36.91 | 33.47 | 30.48 | 27.88 | 25.61 | 23.61 | 21.85 | 20.29 | 52 |
| 53 | 48.87 | 43.83 | 39.49 | 35.74 | 32.49 | 29.67 | 27.19 | 25.02 | 23.11 | 21.42 | 19.92 | 53 |
| 54 | 46.90 | 42.19 | 38.12 | 34.60 | 31.53 | 28.85 | 26.50 | 24.43 | 22.61 | 20.99 | 19.55 | 54 |

## Table 1: Multipliers for pecuniary loss for life (males) *continued*

| Age at date of trial | Multiplier calculated with allowance for projected mortality from the 2008–based population projections and rate of return of | | | | | | | | | | | Age at date of trial |
|---|---|---|---|---|---|---|---|---|---|---|---|---|
| | -2.0% | -1.5% | -1.0% | -0.5% | 0.0% | 0.5% | 1.0% | 1.5% | 2.0% | 2.5% | 3.0% | |
| 55 | 44.99 | 40.60 | 36.79 | 33.47 | 30.58 | 28.04 | 25.81 | 23.85 | 22.11 | 20.56 | 19.18 | 55 |
| 56 | 43.15 | 39.04 | 35.48 | 32.37 | 29.64 | 27.25 | 25.13 | 23.26 | 21.60 | 20.12 | 18.80 | 56 |
| 57 | 41.35 | 37.53 | 34.19 | 31.28 | 28.71 | 26.45 | 24.45 | 22.67 | 21.09 | 19.68 | 18.42 | 57 |
| 58 | 39.59 | 36.04 | 32.93 | 30.19 | 27.78 | 25.65 | 23.76 | 22.08 | 20.58 | 19.23 | 18.02 | 58 |
| 59 | 37.87 | 34.57 | 31.67 | 29.11 | 26.85 | 24.85 | 23.07 | 21.47 | 20.05 | 18.77 | 17.62 | 59 |
| 60 | 36.17 | 33.12 | 30.42 | 28.04 | 25.92 | 24.04 | 22.36 | 20.86 | 19.51 | 18.30 | 17.20 | 60 |
| 61 | 34.52 | 31.69 | 29.19 | 26.97 | 25.00 | 23.23 | 21.65 | 20.24 | 18.96 | 17.81 | 16.77 | 61 |
| 62 | 32.91 | 30.30 | 27.98 | 25.92 | 24.08 | 22.43 | 20.95 | 19.62 | 18.41 | 17.33 | 16.34 | 62 |
| 63 | 31.36 | 28.95 | 26.80 | 24.89 | 23.17 | 21.63 | 20.25 | 19.00 | 17.86 | 16.84 | 15.90 | 63 |
| 64 | 29.85 | 27.63 | 25.65 | 23.88 | 22.28 | 20.85 | 19.55 | 18.38 | 17.31 | 16.35 | 15.47 | 64 |
| 65 | 28.40 | 26.37 | 24.54 | 22.90 | 21.42 | 20.08 | 18.87 | 17.77 | 16.77 | 15.86 | 15.03 | 65 |
| 66 | 27.02 | 25.14 | 23.46 | 21.94 | 20.57 | 19.33 | 18.20 | 17.17 | 16.24 | 15.38 | 14.60 | 66 |
| 67 | 25.68 | 23.96 | 22.41 | 21.01 | 19.74 | 18.59 | 17.54 | 16.58 | 15.70 | 14.90 | 14.16 | 67 |
| 68 | 24.38 | 22.81 | 21.39 | 20.10 | 18.93 | 17.86 | 16.88 | 15.99 | 15.17 | 14.42 | 13.73 | 68 |
| 69 | 23.13 | 21.69 | 20.39 | 19.21 | 18.12 | 17.14 | 16.23 | 15.40 | 14.64 | 13.93 | 13.29 | 69 |
| 70 | 21.91 | 20.60 | 19.41 | 18.32 | 17.32 | 16.41 | 15.58 | 14.81 | 14.10 | 13.44 | 12.84 | 70 |
| 71 | 20.70 | 19.52 | 18.43 | 17.44 | 16.53 | 15.69 | 14.92 | 14.21 | 13.55 | 12.94 | 12.38 | 71 |
| 72 | 19.52 | 18.44 | 17.46 | 16.56 | 15.72 | 14.96 | 14.25 | 13.60 | 12.99 | 12.43 | 11.91 | 72 |
| 73 | 18.34 | 17.38 | 16.49 | 15.67 | 14.92 | 14.22 | 13.57 | 12.97 | 12.42 | 11.90 | 11.42 | 73 |
| 74 | 17.18 | 16.32 | 15.52 | 14.79 | 14.10 | 13.47 | 12.89 | 12.34 | 11.83 | 11.36 | 10.92 | 74 |
| 75 | 16.04 | 15.27 | 14.56 | 13.90 | 13.29 | 12.72 | 12.19 | 11.70 | 11.24 | 10.81 | 10.40 | 75 |
| 76 | 14.93 | 14.25 | 13.62 | 13.03 | 12.48 | 11.97 | 11.50 | 11.05 | 10.64 | 10.25 | 9.88 | 76 |
| 77 | 13.86 | 13.26 | 12.70 | 12.18 | 11.70 | 11.24 | 10.82 | 10.42 | 10.05 | 9.69 | 9.36 | 77 |
| 78 | 12.83 | 12.31 | 11.82 | 11.36 | 10.93 | 10.53 | 10.15 | 9.79 | 9.46 | 9.15 | 8.85 | 78 |
| 79 | 11.86 | 11.40 | 10.97 | 10.57 | 10.19 | 9.84 | 9.50 | 9.19 | 8.89 | 8.61 | 8.34 | 79 |
| 80 | 10.94 | 10.55 | 10.17 | 9.82 | 9.49 | 9.18 | 8.88 | 8.60 | 8.34 | 8.09 | 7.85 | 80 |
| 81 | 10.10 | 9.75 | 9.43 | 9.12 | 8.83 | 8.56 | 8.30 | 8.05 | 7.82 | 7.60 | 7.38 | 81 |
| 82 | 9.33 | 9.03 | 8.74 | 8.47 | 8.22 | 7.98 | 7.75 | 7.53 | 7.33 | 7.13 | 6.94 | 82 |
| 83 | 8.62 | 8.36 | 8.11 | 7.88 | 7.65 | 7.44 | 7.24 | 7.05 | 6.87 | 6.69 | 6.53 | 83 |
| 84 | 7.97 | 7.74 | 7.53 | 7.32 | 7.13 | 6.94 | 6.76 | 6.59 | 6.43 | 6.28 | 6.13 | 84 |
| 85 | 7.36 | 7.16 | 6.98 | 6.80 | 6.63 | 6.47 | 6.31 | 6.16 | 6.02 | 5.88 | 5.75 | 85 |
| 86 | 6.79 | 6.62 | 6.46 | 6.31 | 6.16 | 6.02 | 5.88 | 5.75 | 5.62 | 5.50 | 5.39 | 86 |
| 87 | 6.25 | 6.11 | 5.97 | 5.83 | 5.71 | 5.58 | 5.46 | 5.35 | 5.24 | 5.14 | 5.04 | 87 |
| 88 | 5.74 | 5.62 | 5.50 | 5.38 | 5.27 | 5.16 | 5.06 | 4.96 | 4.87 | 4.78 | 4.69 | 88 |
| 89 | 5.26 | 5.15 | 5.05 | 4.95 | 4.86 | 4.76 | 4.68 | 4.59 | 4.51 | 4.43 | 4.35 | 89 |
| 90 | 4.81 | 4.72 | 4.64 | 4.55 | 4.47 | 4.39 | 4.31 | 4.24 | 4.17 | 4.10 | 4.03 | 90 |
| 91 | 4.40 | 4.32 | 4.25 | 4.17 | 4.10 | 4.04 | 3.97 | 3.91 | 3.85 | 3.79 | 3.73 | 91 |
| 92 | 4.01 | 3.94 | 3.88 | 3.82 | 3.76 | 3.70 | 3.65 | 3.59 | 3.54 | 3.49 | 3.44 | 92 |
| 93 | 3.65 | 3.59 | 3.54 | 3.49 | 3.44 | 3.39 | 3.34 | 3.30 | 3.25 | 3.21 | 3.17 | 93 |
| 94 | 3.33 | 3.29 | 3.24 | 3.20 | 3.16 | 3.11 | 3.07 | 3.03 | 2.99 | 2.96 | 2.92 | 94 |
| 95 | 3.06 | 3.02 | 2.98 | 2.94 | 2.91 | 2.87 | 2.84 | 2.80 | 2.77 | 2.74 | 2.71 | 95 |
| 96 | 2.83 | 2.79 | 2.76 | 2.72 | 2.69 | 2.66 | 2.63 | 2.60 | 2.57 | 2.54 | 2.52 | 96 |
| 97 | 2.62 | 2.59 | 2.56 | 2.53 | 2.50 | 2.48 | 2.45 | 2.42 | 2.40 | 2.37 | 2.35 | 97 |
| 98 | 2.44 | 2.41 | 2.38 | 2.36 | 2.34 | 2.31 | 2.29 | 2.27 | 2.24 | 2.22 | 2.20 | 98 |
| 99 | 2.27 | 2.25 | 2.22 | 2.20 | 2.18 | 2.16 | 2.14 | 2.12 | 2.10 | 2.08 | 2.06 | 99 |
| 100 | 2.11 | 2.09 | 2.07 | 2.06 | 2.04 | 2.02 | 2.00 | 1.98 | 1.97 | 1.95 | 1.93 | 100 |

## Table 2: Multipliers for pecuniary loss for life (females)

| Age at date of trial | Multiplier calculated with allowance for projected mortality from the 2008–based population projections and rate of return of | | | | | | | | | | | Age at date of trial |
|---|---|---|---|---|---|---|---|---|---|---|---|---|
| | -2.0% | -1.5% | -1.0% | -0.5% | 0.0% | 0.5% | 1.0% | 1.5% | 2.0% | 2.5% | 3.0% | |
| 0 | 285.20 | 208.39 | 155.57 | 118.70 | 92.57 | 73.74 | 59.95 | 49.69 | 41.92 | 35.94 | 31.26 | 0 |
| 1 | 279.01 | 204.72 | 153.41 | 117.45 | 91.86 | 73.36 | 59.76 | 49.62 | 41.91 | 35.97 | 31.32 | 1 |
| 2 | 271.81 | 200.28 | 150.65 | 115.73 | 90.77 | 72.67 | 59.33 | 49.34 | 41.73 | 35.86 | 31.24 | 2 |
| 3 | 264.75 | 195.89 | 147.91 | 114.00 | 89.68 | 71.97 | 58.88 | 49.05 | 41.55 | 35.73 | 31.16 | 3 |
| 4 | 257.83 | 191.56 | 145.19 | 112.28 | 88.58 | 71.27 | 58.43 | 48.75 | 41.35 | 35.60 | 31.08 | 4 |
| 5 | 251.06 | 187.30 | 142.49 | 110.56 | 87.49 | 70.56 | 57.97 | 48.45 | 41.15 | 35.47 | 30.99 | 5 |
| 6 | 244.43 | 183.11 | 139.83 | 108.85 | 86.38 | 69.85 | 57.50 | 48.14 | 40.95 | 35.34 | 30.89 | 6 |
| 7 | 237.94 | 178.98 | 137.18 | 107.15 | 85.28 | 69.13 | 57.03 | 47.83 | 40.74 | 35.19 | 30.80 | 7 |
| 8 | 231.59 | 174.92 | 134.57 | 105.46 | 84.18 | 68.40 | 56.55 | 47.51 | 40.52 | 35.05 | 30.70 | 8 |
| 9 | 225.38 | 170.93 | 131.98 | 103.77 | 83.07 | 67.67 | 56.06 | 47.18 | 40.30 | 34.90 | 30.60 | 9 |
| 10 | 219.31 | 167.00 | 129.43 | 102.10 | 81.97 | 66.94 | 55.57 | 46.85 | 40.08 | 34.75 | 30.49 | 10 |
| 11 | 213.37 | 163.14 | 126.90 | 100.43 | 80.86 | 66.20 | 55.07 | 46.52 | 39.85 | 34.59 | 30.38 | 11 |
| 12 | 207.57 | 159.34 | 124.40 | 98.78 | 79.76 | 65.46 | 54.57 | 46.18 | 39.62 | 34.42 | 30.27 | 12 |
| 13 | 201.89 | 155.60 | 121.92 | 97.13 | 78.65 | 64.71 | 54.07 | 45.83 | 39.38 | 34.26 | 30.15 | 13 |
| 14 | 196.33 | 151.93 | 119.48 | 95.49 | 77.55 | 63.96 | 53.55 | 45.47 | 39.13 | 34.09 | 30.03 | 14 |
| 15 | 190.91 | 148.32 | 117.06 | 93.86 | 76.44 | 63.21 | 53.03 | 45.12 | 38.88 | 33.91 | 29.90 | 15 |
| 16 | 185.61 | 144.77 | 114.67 | 92.25 | 75.34 | 62.45 | 52.51 | 44.75 | 38.62 | 33.73 | 29.77 | 16 |
| 17 | 180.42 | 141.28 | 112.31 | 90.64 | 74.24 | 61.70 | 51.99 | 44.38 | 38.37 | 33.55 | 29.64 | 17 |
| 18 | 175.36 | 137.86 | 109.98 | 89.05 | 73.14 | 60.94 | 51.46 | 44.01 | 38.10 | 33.36 | 29.51 | 18 |
| 19 | 170.42 | 134.50 | 107.68 | 87.46 | 72.05 | 60.17 | 50.92 | 43.63 | 37.83 | 33.16 | 29.37 | 19 |
| 20 | 165.60 | 131.20 | 105.42 | 85.89 | 70.96 | 59.41 | 50.38 | 43.25 | 37.56 | 32.97 | 29.22 | 20 |
| 21 | 160.88 | 127.95 | 103.17 | 84.33 | 69.86 | 58.64 | 49.84 | 42.86 | 37.28 | 32.76 | 29.08 | 21 |
| 22 | 156.26 | 124.76 | 100.95 | 82.78 | 68.77 | 57.86 | 49.28 | 42.47 | 36.99 | 32.56 | 28.92 | 22 |
| 23 | 151.72 | 121.60 | 98.74 | 81.22 | 67.67 | 57.08 | 48.72 | 42.06 | 36.70 | 32.34 | 28.76 | 23 |
| 24 | 147.29 | 118.50 | 96.56 | 79.68 | 66.57 | 56.29 | 48.16 | 41.65 | 36.40 | 32.12 | 28.60 | 24 |
| 25 | 142.97 | 115.46 | 94.41 | 78.15 | 65.48 | 55.50 | 47.58 | 41.23 | 36.09 | 31.89 | 28.43 | 25 |
| 26 | 138.74 | 112.47 | 92.28 | 76.63 | 64.38 | 54.71 | 47.01 | 40.81 | 35.78 | 31.66 | 28.26 | 26 |
| 27 | 134.61 | 109.53 | 90.18 | 75.12 | 63.29 | 53.92 | 46.43 | 40.38 | 35.46 | 31.42 | 28.08 | 27 |
| 28 | 130.57 | 106.65 | 88.11 | 73.62 | 62.20 | 53.12 | 45.84 | 39.95 | 35.14 | 31.18 | 27.90 | 28 |
| 29 | 126.63 | 103.81 | 86.05 | 72.13 | 61.11 | 52.32 | 45.25 | 39.51 | 34.81 | 30.93 | 27.71 | 29 |
| 30 | 122.78 | 101.02 | 84.03 | 70.65 | 60.02 | 51.52 | 44.65 | 39.06 | 34.47 | 30.68 | 27.51 | 30 |
| 31 | 119.02 | 98.29 | 82.03 | 69.18 | 58.94 | 50.71 | 44.05 | 38.61 | 34.13 | 30.41 | 27.31 | 31 |
| 32 | 115.34 | 95.60 | 80.06 | 67.72 | 57.86 | 49.90 | 43.44 | 38.15 | 33.78 | 30.15 | 27.11 | 32 |
| 33 | 111.75 | 92.97 | 78.11 | 66.27 | 56.77 | 49.09 | 42.83 | 37.68 | 33.42 | 29.87 | 26.89 | 33 |
| 34 | 108.24 | 90.37 | 76.18 | 64.83 | 55.69 | 48.27 | 42.21 | 37.21 | 33.06 | 29.59 | 26.67 | 34 |
| 35 | 104.80 | 87.81 | 74.27 | 63.40 | 54.61 | 47.45 | 41.58 | 36.73 | 32.69 | 29.31 | 26.45 | 35 |
| 36 | 101.45 | 85.31 | 72.39 | 61.98 | 53.53 | 46.63 | 40.95 | 36.24 | 32.31 | 29.01 | 26.22 | 36 |
| 37 | 98.17 | 82.84 | 70.53 | 60.57 | 52.46 | 45.81 | 40.31 | 35.75 | 31.93 | 28.71 | 25.98 | 37 |
| 38 | 94.97 | 80.42 | 68.69 | 59.17 | 51.38 | 44.98 | 39.67 | 35.25 | 31.54 | 28.40 | 25.74 | 38 |
| 39 | 91.83 | 78.04 | 66.88 | 57.78 | 50.31 | 44.15 | 39.03 | 34.74 | 31.14 | 28.09 | 25.48 | 39 |
| 40 | 88.77 | 75.71 | 65.08 | 56.39 | 49.24 | 43.31 | 38.37 | 34.23 | 30.73 | 27.76 | 25.23 | 40 |
| 41 | 85.78 | 73.41 | 63.31 | 55.02 | 48.17 | 42.48 | 37.71 | 33.71 | 30.32 | 27.43 | 24.96 | 41 |
| 42 | 82.86 | 71.16 | 61.56 | 53.66 | 47.10 | 41.64 | 37.05 | 33.18 | 29.90 | 27.09 | 24.69 | 42 |
| 43 | 80.01 | 68.94 | 59.84 | 52.31 | 46.04 | 40.80 | 36.38 | 32.65 | 29.47 | 26.75 | 24.41 | 43 |
| 44 | 77.23 | 66.77 | 58.14 | 50.97 | 44.98 | 39.95 | 35.71 | 32.11 | 29.03 | 26.39 | 24.12 | 44 |
| 45 | 74.52 | 64.65 | 56.46 | 49.64 | 43.93 | 39.11 | 35.03 | 31.56 | 28.59 | 26.03 | 23.82 | 45 |
| 46 | 71.87 | 62.56 | 54.81 | 48.32 | 42.87 | 38.27 | 34.35 | 31.01 | 28.14 | 25.67 | 23.52 | 46 |
| 47 | 69.28 | 60.51 | 53.17 | 47.02 | 41.83 | 37.42 | 33.67 | 30.45 | 27.69 | 25.29 | 23.21 | 47 |
| 48 | 66.77 | 58.50 | 51.57 | 45.73 | 40.79 | 36.58 | 32.98 | 29.89 | 27.23 | 24.91 | 22.90 | 48 |
| 49 | 64.32 | 56.54 | 50.00 | 44.46 | 39.76 | 35.74 | 32.30 | 29.33 | 26.76 | 24.53 | 22.58 | 49 |
| 50 | 61.93 | 54.62 | 48.44 | 43.20 | 38.73 | 34.90 | 31.61 | 28.76 | 26.29 | 24.14 | 22.25 | 50 |
| 51 | 59.60 | 52.73 | 46.91 | 41.95 | 37.71 | 34.06 | 30.91 | 28.19 | 25.81 | 23.74 | 21.92 | 51 |
| 52 | 57.33 | 50.88 | 45.40 | 40.71 | 36.69 | 33.22 | 30.22 | 27.61 | 25.33 | 23.33 | 21.57 | 52 |
| 53 | 55.11 | 49.07 | 43.92 | 39.49 | 35.68 | 32.38 | 29.52 | 27.02 | 24.84 | 22.92 | 21.22 | 53 |
| 54 | 52.96 | 47.30 | 42.46 | 38.28 | 34.68 | 31.55 | 28.82 | 26.44 | 24.34 | 22.50 | 20.87 | 54 |

## Table 2: Multipliers for pecuniary loss for life (females) *continued*

| Age at date of trial | Multiplier calculated with allowance for projected mortality from the 2008–based population projections and rate of return of | | | | | | | | | | | Age at date of trial |
|---|---|---|---|---|---|---|---|---|---|---|---|---|
| | *-2.0%* | *-1.5%* | *-1.0%* | *-0.5%* | *0.0%* | *0.5%* | *1.0%* | *1.5%* | *2.0%* | *2.5%* | *3.0%* | |
| 55 | 50.86 | 45.57 | 41.02 | 37.09 | 33.68 | 30.71 | 28.12 | 25.84 | 23.84 | 22.07 | 20.51 | 55 |
| 56 | 48.83 | 43.88 | 39.61 | 35.91 | 32.69 | 29.88 | 27.42 | 25.25 | 23.34 | 21.64 | 20.14 | 56 |
| 57 | 46.84 | 42.22 | 38.23 | 34.75 | 31.71 | 29.05 | 26.72 | 24.65 | 22.83 | 21.21 | 19.76 | 57 |
| 58 | 44.89 | 40.60 | 36.86 | 33.59 | 30.74 | 28.22 | 26.01 | 24.05 | 22.31 | 20.76 | 19.37 | 58 |
| 59 | 42.99 | 38.99 | 35.50 | 32.44 | 29.76 | 27.39 | 25.29 | 23.43 | 21.78 | 20.30 | 18.98 | 59 |
| 60 | 41.12 | 37.41 | 34.16 | 31.30 | 28.78 | 26.55 | 24.57 | 22.81 | 21.24 | 19.83 | 18.57 | 60 |
| 61 | 39.30 | 35.86 | 32.83 | 30.16 | 27.80 | 25.70 | 23.84 | 22.18 | 20.69 | 19.35 | 18.15 | 61 |
| 62 | 37.52 | 34.33 | 31.52 | 29.03 | 26.83 | 24.86 | 23.11 | 21.54 | 20.13 | 18.86 | 17.72 | 62 |
| 63 | 35.79 | 32.84 | 30.24 | 27.92 | 25.86 | 24.02 | 22.38 | 20.90 | 19.57 | 18.37 | 17.28 | 63 |
| 64 | 34.11 | 31.39 | 28.98 | 26.83 | 24.91 | 23.19 | 21.65 | 20.26 | 19.01 | 17.87 | 16.84 | 64 |
| 65 | 32.50 | 29.99 | 27.76 | 25.77 | 23.98 | 22.38 | 20.93 | 19.63 | 18.45 | 17.38 | 16.40 | 65 |
| 66 | 30.94 | 28.64 | 26.58 | 24.73 | 23.07 | 21.58 | 20.23 | 19.00 | 17.89 | 16.88 | 15.96 | 66 |
| 67 | 29.44 | 27.32 | 25.43 | 23.72 | 22.18 | 20.78 | 19.52 | 18.38 | 17.34 | 16.39 | 15.52 | 67 |
| 68 | 27.99 | 26.05 | 24.30 | 22.72 | 21.29 | 20.00 | 18.83 | 17.76 | 16.78 | 15.89 | 15.07 | 68 |
| 69 | 26.57 | 24.80 | 23.19 | 21.74 | 20.42 | 19.22 | 18.13 | 17.13 | 16.22 | 15.39 | 14.62 | 69 |
| 70 | 25.19 | 23.57 | 22.10 | 20.76 | 19.55 | 18.44 | 17.43 | 16.50 | 15.65 | 14.87 | 14.15 | 70 |
| 71 | 23.83 | 22.35 | 21.01 | 19.79 | 18.67 | 17.65 | 16.72 | 15.86 | 15.07 | 14.35 | 13.68 | 71 |
| 72 | 22.47 | 21.14 | 19.92 | 18.81 | 17.79 | 16.85 | 16.00 | 15.20 | 14.48 | 13.80 | 13.18 | 72 |
| 73 | 21.13 | 19.93 | 18.83 | 17.82 | 16.89 | 16.04 | 15.25 | 14.53 | 13.86 | 13.24 | 12.66 | 73 |
| 74 | 19.80 | 18.72 | 17.73 | 16.82 | 15.99 | 15.21 | 14.50 | 13.84 | 13.23 | 12.66 | 12.13 | 74 |
| 75 | 18.48 | 17.53 | 16.64 | 15.83 | 15.08 | 14.38 | 13.74 | 13.14 | 12.58 | 12.06 | 11.58 | 75 |
| 76 | 17.20 | 16.35 | 15.57 | 14.84 | 14.17 | 13.55 | 12.97 | 12.43 | 11.92 | 11.45 | 11.01 | 76 |
| 77 | 15.95 | 15.21 | 14.51 | 13.87 | 13.28 | 12.72 | 12.20 | 11.72 | 11.27 | 10.84 | 10.45 | 77 |
| 78 | 14.75 | 14.10 | 13.50 | 12.93 | 12.40 | 11.91 | 11.45 | 11.02 | 10.62 | 10.24 | 9.88 | 78 |
| 79 | 13.62 | 13.05 | 12.52 | 12.03 | 11.56 | 11.13 | 10.72 | 10.34 | 9.98 | 9.64 | 9.32 | 79 |
| 80 | 12.56 | 12.07 | 11.61 | 11.17 | 10.77 | 10.38 | 10.02 | 9.69 | 9.37 | 9.07 | 8.78 | 80 |
| 81 | 11.58 | 11.15 | 10.75 | 10.37 | 10.02 | 9.68 | 9.36 | 9.06 | 8.78 | 8.51 | 8.26 | 81 |
| 82 | 10.67 | 10.30 | 9.95 | 9.62 | 9.31 | 9.02 | 8.74 | 8.48 | 8.23 | 7.99 | 7.76 | 82 |
| 83 | 9.83 | 9.51 | 9.21 | 8.92 | 8.65 | 8.39 | 8.15 | 7.92 | 7.70 | 7.49 | 7.29 | 83 |
| 84 | 9.06 | 8.78 | 8.52 | 8.27 | 8.03 | 7.81 | 7.59 | 7.39 | 7.19 | 7.01 | 6.83 | 84 |
| 85 | 8.34 | 8.10 | 7.87 | 7.65 | 7.45 | 7.25 | 7.06 | 6.88 | 6.71 | 6.55 | 6.40 | 85 |
| 86 | 7.66 | 7.45 | 7.25 | 7.07 | 6.89 | 6.72 | 6.56 | 6.40 | 6.25 | 6.11 | 5.97 | 86 |
| 87 | 7.01 | 6.84 | 6.67 | 6.51 | 6.36 | 6.21 | 6.07 | 5.93 | 5.80 | 5.68 | 5.56 | 87 |
| 88 | 6.41 | 6.26 | 6.11 | 5.98 | 5.85 | 5.72 | 5.60 | 5.48 | 5.37 | 5.26 | 5.16 | 88 |
| 89 | 5.84 | 5.71 | 5.59 | 5.47 | 5.36 | 5.25 | 5.15 | 5.05 | 4.95 | 4.86 | 4.77 | 89 |
| 90 | 5.31 | 5.20 | 5.10 | 5.00 | 4.90 | 4.81 | 4.72 | 4.64 | 4.55 | 4.47 | 4.40 | 90 |
| 91 | 4.82 | 4.73 | 4.64 | 4.55 | 4.47 | 4.40 | 4.32 | 4.25 | 4.18 | 4.11 | 4.04 | 91 |
| 92 | 4.37 | 4.29 | 4.22 | 4.15 | 4.08 | 4.01 | 3.95 | 3.89 | 3.83 | 3.77 | 3.71 | 92 |
| 93 | 3.97 | 3.90 | 3.84 | 3.78 | 3.72 | 3.67 | 3.61 | 3.56 | 3.51 | 3.46 | 3.41 | 93 |
| 94 | 3.62 | 3.56 | 3.51 | 3.46 | 3.41 | 3.36 | 3.31 | 3.27 | 3.22 | 3.18 | 3.14 | 94 |
| 95 | 3.32 | 3.27 | 3.23 | 3.18 | 3.14 | 3.10 | 3.06 | 3.02 | 2.98 | 2.94 | 2.91 | 95 |
| 96 | 3.06 | 3.02 | 2.98 | 2.94 | 2.91 | 2.87 | 2.84 | 2.80 | 2.77 | 2.74 | 2.71 | 96 |
| 97 | 2.84 | 2.80 | 2.77 | 2.74 | 2.70 | 2.67 | 2.64 | 2.61 | 2.58 | 2.56 | 2.53 | 97 |
| 98 | 2.64 | 2.61 | 2.58 | 2.55 | 2.52 | 2.49 | 2.47 | 2.44 | 2.42 | 2.39 | 2.37 | 98 |
| 99 | 2.45 | 2.42 | 2.40 | 2.37 | 2.35 | 2.32 | 2.30 | 2.28 | 2.26 | 2.23 | 2.21 | 99 |
| 100 | 2.27 | 2.25 | 2.22 | 2.20 | 2.18 | 2.16 | 2.14 | 2.12 | 2.10 | 2.08 | 2.06 | 100 |

## Table 3: Multipliers for loss of earnings to pension age 50 (males)

| Age at date of trial | Multiplier calculated with allowance for projected mortality from the 2008–based population projections and rate of return of | | | | | | | | | | | Age at date of trial |
|---|---|---|---|---|---|---|---|---|---|---|---|---|
| | *-2.0%* | *-1.5%* | *-1.0%* | *-0.5%* | *0.0%* | *0.5%* | *1.0%* | *1.5%* | *2.0%* | *2.5%* | *3.0%* | |
| 16 | 48.26 | 43.90 | 40.05 | 36.65 | 33.63 | 30.94 | 28.55 | 26.42 | 24.51 | 22.80 | 21.26 | 16 |
| 17 | 46.31 | 42.26 | 38.66 | 35.47 | 32.63 | 30.10 | 27.84 | 25.81 | 24.00 | 22.36 | 20.89 | 17 |
| 18 | 44.40 | 40.64 | 37.29 | 34.30 | 31.64 | 29.25 | 27.12 | 25.20 | 23.47 | 21.91 | 20.51 | 18 |
| 19 | 42.54 | 39.04 | 35.93 | 33.14 | 30.65 | 28.41 | 26.39 | 24.57 | 22.94 | 21.45 | 20.11 | 19 |
| 20 | 40.71 | 37.48 | 34.58 | 31.99 | 29.66 | 27.55 | 25.66 | 23.94 | 22.39 | 20.99 | 19.71 | 20 |
| 21 | 38.91 | 35.93 | 33.25 | 30.84 | 28.66 | 26.70 | 24.92 | 23.30 | 21.84 | 20.50 | 19.29 | 21 |
| 22 | 37.16 | 34.41 | 31.94 | 29.70 | 27.67 | 25.84 | 24.17 | 22.65 | 21.27 | 20.01 | 18.86 | 22 |
| 23 | 35.44 | 32.92 | 30.63 | 28.56 | 26.68 | 24.97 | 23.41 | 21.99 | 20.69 | 19.51 | 18.42 | 23 |
| 24 | 33.75 | 31.44 | 29.34 | 27.43 | 25.69 | 24.10 | 22.65 | 21.32 | 20.11 | 18.99 | 17.96 | 24 |
| 25 | 32.10 | 29.99 | 28.06 | 26.31 | 24.70 | 23.23 | 21.88 | 20.65 | 19.51 | 18.46 | 17.49 | 25 |
| 26 | 30.48 | 28.56 | 26.80 | 25.19 | 23.71 | 22.36 | 21.11 | 19.96 | 18.90 | 17.92 | 17.01 | 26 |
| 27 | 28.89 | 27.15 | 25.55 | 24.08 | 22.72 | 21.47 | 20.32 | 19.26 | 18.27 | 17.36 | 16.52 | 27 |
| 28 | 27.34 | 25.76 | 24.31 | 22.97 | 21.73 | 20.59 | 19.53 | 18.55 | 17.64 | 16.79 | 16.00 | 28 |
| 29 | 25.81 | 24.40 | 23.08 | 21.87 | 20.74 | 19.70 | 18.73 | 17.83 | 16.99 | 16.21 | 15.48 | 29 |
| 30 | 24.32 | 23.05 | 21.87 | 20.78 | 19.76 | 18.81 | 17.92 | 17.10 | 16.33 | 15.61 | 14.94 | 30 |
| 31 | 22.86 | 21.73 | 20.67 | 19.69 | 18.77 | 17.91 | 17.11 | 16.36 | 15.66 | 15.00 | 14.38 | 31 |
| 32 | 21.43 | 20.43 | 19.49 | 18.61 | 17.78 | 17.01 | 16.29 | 15.61 | 14.97 | 14.37 | 13.81 | 32 |
| 33 | 20.03 | 19.15 | 18.31 | 17.53 | 16.80 | 16.11 | 15.46 | 14.85 | 14.28 | 13.73 | 13.22 | 33 |
| 34 | 18.66 | 17.88 | 17.15 | 16.47 | 15.82 | 15.20 | 14.63 | 14.08 | 13.57 | 13.08 | 12.62 | 34 |
| 35 | 17.31 | 16.64 | 16.00 | 15.40 | 14.83 | 14.29 | 13.78 | 13.30 | 12.84 | 12.41 | 11.99 | 35 |
| 36 | 16.00 | 15.42 | 14.87 | 14.34 | 13.85 | 13.38 | 12.93 | 12.51 | 12.10 | 11.72 | 11.35 | 36 |
| 37 | 14.70 | 14.21 | 13.74 | 13.29 | 12.86 | 12.46 | 12.07 | 11.70 | 11.35 | 11.01 | 10.69 | 37 |
| 38 | 13.44 | 13.02 | 12.62 | 12.24 | 11.88 | 11.53 | 11.20 | 10.88 | 10.58 | 10.29 | 10.01 | 38 |
| 39 | 12.19 | 11.85 | 11.52 | 11.20 | 10.89 | 10.60 | 10.32 | 10.05 | 9.79 | 9.54 | 9.31 | 39 |
| 40 | 10.98 | 10.69 | 10.42 | 10.16 | 9.91 | 9.67 | 9.43 | 9.21 | 8.99 | 8.78 | 8.58 | 40 |
| 41 | 9.78 | 9.55 | 9.34 | 9.13 | 8.92 | 8.72 | 8.53 | 8.35 | 8.17 | 8.00 | 7.84 | 41 |
| 42 | 8.61 | 8.43 | 8.26 | 8.10 | 7.93 | 7.78 | 7.63 | 7.48 | 7.34 | 7.20 | 7.07 | 42 |
| 43 | 7.46 | 7.33 | 7.20 | 7.07 | 6.95 | 6.83 | 6.71 | 6.60 | 6.49 | 6.38 | 6.28 | 43 |
| 44 | 6.33 | 6.24 | 6.14 | 6.05 | 5.96 | 5.87 | 5.78 | 5.70 | 5.62 | 5.54 | 5.46 | 44 |
| 45 | 5.23 | 5.16 | 5.10 | 5.03 | 4.97 | 4.91 | 4.85 | 4.79 | 4.73 | 4.68 | 4.62 | 45 |
| 46 | 4.14 | 4.10 | 4.06 | 4.02 | 3.98 | 3.94 | 3.90 | 3.86 | 3.83 | 3.79 | 3.75 | 46 |
| 47 | 3.08 | 3.06 | 3.03 | 3.01 | 2.99 | 2.97 | 2.94 | 2.92 | 2.90 | 2.88 | 2.86 | 47 |
| 48 | 2.03 | 2.02 | 2.01 | 2.00 | 1.99 | 1.98 | 1.97 | 1.96 | 1.96 | 1.95 | 1.94 | 48 |
| 49 | 1.01 | 1.01 | 1.00 | 1.00 | 1.00 | 1.00 | 0.99 | 0.99 | 0.99 | 0.99 | 0.98 | 49 |

## Table 4: Multipliers for loss of earnings to pension age 50 (females)

| Age at date of trial | Multiplier calculated with allowance for projected mortality from the 2008–based population projections and rate of return of | | | | | | | | | | | Age at date of trial |
|---|---|---|---|---|---|---|---|---|---|---|---|---|
| | -2.0% | -1.5% | -1.0% | -0.5% | 0.0% | 0.5% | 1.0% | 1.5% | 2.0% | 2.5% | 3.0% | |
| 16 | 48.58 | 44.19 | 40.30 | 36.87 | 33.82 | 31.12 | 28.71 | 26.56 | 24.63 | 22.91 | 21.36 | 16 |
| 17 | 46.62 | 42.53 | 38.91 | 35.69 | 32.82 | 30.27 | 27.99 | 25.95 | 24.12 | 22.47 | 20.99 | 17 |
| 18 | 44.71 | 40.91 | 37.53 | 34.52 | 31.83 | 29.42 | 27.27 | 25.33 | 23.59 | 22.02 | 20.60 | 18 |
| 19 | 42.83 | 39.30 | 36.16 | 33.35 | 30.83 | 28.57 | 26.54 | 24.71 | 23.06 | 21.56 | 20.21 | 19 |
| 20 | 40.98 | 37.73 | 34.81 | 32.19 | 29.83 | 27.72 | 25.80 | 24.08 | 22.51 | 21.09 | 19.80 | 20 |
| 21 | 39.18 | 36.17 | 33.47 | 31.03 | 28.84 | 26.85 | 25.06 | 23.43 | 21.96 | 20.61 | 19.39 | 21 |
| 22 | 37.41 | 34.64 | 32.14 | 29.89 | 27.84 | 25.99 | 24.31 | 22.78 | 21.39 | 20.12 | 18.96 | 22 |
| 23 | 35.68 | 33.13 | 30.83 | 28.74 | 26.85 | 25.12 | 23.55 | 22.12 | 20.81 | 19.61 | 18.51 | 23 |
| 24 | 33.98 | 31.65 | 29.53 | 27.60 | 25.85 | 24.25 | 22.78 | 21.44 | 20.22 | 19.09 | 18.06 | 24 |
| 25 | 32.31 | 30.18 | 28.24 | 26.47 | 24.85 | 23.37 | 22.01 | 20.76 | 19.61 | 18.56 | 17.59 | 25 |
| 26 | 30.68 | 28.74 | 26.97 | 25.35 | 23.86 | 22.49 | 21.23 | 20.07 | 19.00 | 18.01 | 17.10 | 26 |
| 27 | 29.08 | 27.33 | 25.71 | 24.23 | 22.86 | 21.60 | 20.44 | 19.37 | 18.37 | 17.45 | 16.60 | 27 |
| 28 | 27.52 | 25.93 | 24.46 | 23.11 | 21.87 | 20.71 | 19.64 | 18.65 | 17.74 | 16.88 | 16.09 | 28 |
| 29 | 25.98 | 24.55 | 23.23 | 22.01 | 20.87 | 19.82 | 18.84 | 17.93 | 17.08 | 16.30 | 15.56 | 29 |
| 30 | 24.48 | 23.20 | 22.01 | 20.90 | 19.88 | 18.92 | 18.03 | 17.20 | 16.42 | 15.70 | 15.02 | 30 |
| 31 | 23.01 | 21.86 | 20.80 | 19.81 | 18.88 | 18.02 | 17.21 | 16.45 | 15.74 | 15.08 | 14.46 | 31 |
| 32 | 21.56 | 20.55 | 19.60 | 18.72 | 17.89 | 17.11 | 16.38 | 15.70 | 15.05 | 14.45 | 13.88 | 32 |
| 33 | 20.15 | 19.26 | 18.42 | 17.63 | 16.89 | 16.20 | 15.55 | 14.93 | 14.35 | 13.80 | 13.29 | 33 |
| 34 | 18.76 | 17.98 | 17.25 | 16.55 | 15.90 | 15.28 | 14.70 | 14.15 | 13.63 | 13.14 | 12.68 | 34 |
| 35 | 17.41 | 16.73 | 16.09 | 15.48 | 14.91 | 14.37 | 13.85 | 13.36 | 12.90 | 12.46 | 12.05 | 35 |
| 36 | 16.08 | 15.49 | 14.94 | 14.41 | 13.92 | 13.44 | 12.99 | 12.56 | 12.16 | 11.77 | 11.40 | 36 |
| 37 | 14.77 | 14.28 | 13.80 | 13.35 | 12.92 | 12.51 | 12.12 | 11.75 | 11.40 | 11.06 | 10.73 | 37 |
| 38 | 13.50 | 13.08 | 12.68 | 12.30 | 11.93 | 11.58 | 11.25 | 10.93 | 10.62 | 10.33 | 10.05 | 38 |
| 39 | 12.25 | 11.90 | 11.56 | 11.24 | 10.94 | 10.64 | 10.36 | 10.09 | 9.83 | 9.58 | 9.34 | 39 |
| 40 | 11.02 | 10.73 | 10.46 | 10.20 | 9.95 | 9.70 | 9.47 | 9.24 | 9.02 | 8.82 | 8.61 | 40 |
| 41 | 9.82 | 9.59 | 9.37 | 9.16 | 8.95 | 8.76 | 8.56 | 8.38 | 8.20 | 8.03 | 7.86 | 41 |
| 42 | 8.64 | 8.46 | 8.29 | 8.12 | 7.96 | 7.80 | 7.65 | 7.51 | 7.36 | 7.22 | 7.09 | 42 |
| 43 | 7.48 | 7.35 | 7.22 | 7.09 | 6.97 | 6.85 | 6.73 | 6.62 | 6.51 | 6.40 | 6.29 | 43 |
| 44 | 6.35 | 6.25 | 6.16 | 6.06 | 5.97 | 5.89 | 5.80 | 5.72 | 5.63 | 5.55 | 5.48 | 44 |
| 45 | 5.24 | 5.17 | 5.11 | 5.04 | 4.98 | 4.92 | 4.86 | 4.80 | 4.74 | 4.69 | 4.63 | 45 |
| 46 | 4.15 | 4.11 | 4.07 | 4.03 | 3.99 | 3.95 | 3.91 | 3.87 | 3.83 | 3.80 | 3.76 | 46 |
| 47 | 3.08 | 3.06 | 3.04 | 3.01 | 2.99 | 2.97 | 2.95 | 2.93 | 2.90 | 2.88 | 2.86 | 47 |
| 48 | 2.04 | 2.03 | 2.02 | 2.01 | 2.00 | 1.99 | 1.98 | 1.97 | 1.96 | 1.95 | 1.94 | 48 |
| 49 | 1.01 | 1.01 | 1.00 | 1.00 | 1.00 | 1.00 | 0.99 | 0.99 | 0.99 | 0.99 | 0.98 | 49 |

## Table 5: Multipliers for loss of earnings to pension age 55 (males)

| Age at date of trial | Multiplier calculated with allowance for projected mortality from the 2008–based population projections and rate of return of | | | | | | | | | | | Age at date of trial |
|---|---|---|---|---|---|---|---|---|---|---|---|---|
| | -2.0% | -1.5% | -1.0% | -0.5% | 0.0% | 0.5% | 1.0% | 1.5% | 2.0% | 2.5% | 3.0% | |
| 16 | 58.33 | 52.26 | 47.00 | 42.43 | 38.44 | 34.96 | 31.90 | 29.22 | 26.85 | 24.76 | 22.90 | 16 |
| 17 | 56.17 | 50.49 | 45.54 | 41.22 | 37.44 | 34.13 | 31.22 | 28.65 | 26.38 | 24.37 | 22.58 | 17 |
| 18 | 54.07 | 48.74 | 44.09 | 40.02 | 36.45 | 33.30 | 30.53 | 28.08 | 25.90 | 23.97 | 22.24 | 18 |
| 19 | 52.00 | 47.03 | 42.67 | 38.83 | 35.46 | 32.48 | 29.84 | 27.50 | 25.42 | 23.56 | 21.90 | 19 |
| 20 | 49.99 | 45.34 | 41.26 | 37.65 | 34.47 | 31.65 | 29.14 | 26.91 | 24.92 | 23.14 | 21.55 | 20 |
| 21 | 48.01 | 43.68 | 39.86 | 36.48 | 33.48 | 30.81 | 28.44 | 26.31 | 24.42 | 22.72 | 21.19 | 21 |
| 22 | 46.07 | 42.04 | 38.47 | 35.31 | 32.49 | 29.97 | 27.72 | 25.71 | 23.90 | 22.28 | 20.82 | 22 |
| 23 | 44.17 | 40.43 | 37.11 | 34.14 | 31.49 | 29.13 | 27.00 | 25.10 | 23.38 | 21.83 | 20.43 | 23 |
| 24 | 42.31 | 38.84 | 35.75 | 32.98 | 30.50 | 28.28 | 26.28 | 24.47 | 22.85 | 21.37 | 20.04 | 24 |
| 25 | 40.49 | 37.28 | 34.41 | 31.83 | 29.52 | 27.43 | 25.54 | 23.84 | 22.30 | 20.90 | 19.63 | 25 |
| 26 | 38.70 | 35.74 | 33.08 | 30.69 | 28.53 | 26.57 | 24.81 | 23.20 | 21.75 | 20.42 | 19.21 | 26 |
| 27 | 36.95 | 34.23 | 31.77 | 29.55 | 27.54 | 25.71 | 24.06 | 22.55 | 21.18 | 19.93 | 18.78 | 27 |
| 28 | 35.24 | 32.74 | 30.47 | 28.42 | 26.55 | 24.85 | 23.30 | 21.89 | 20.60 | 19.42 | 18.34 | 28 |
| 29 | 33.56 | 31.27 | 29.18 | 27.29 | 25.56 | 23.98 | 22.54 | 21.22 | 20.01 | 18.91 | 17.89 | 29 |
| 30 | 31.91 | 29.82 | 27.91 | 26.17 | 24.57 | 23.11 | 21.78 | 20.55 | 19.42 | 18.38 | 17.42 | 30 |
| 31 | 30.30 | 28.40 | 26.66 | 25.06 | 23.59 | 22.24 | 21.00 | 19.86 | 18.81 | 17.83 | 16.94 | 31 |
| 32 | 28.73 | 27.00 | 25.41 | 23.95 | 22.61 | 21.37 | 20.22 | 19.17 | 18.19 | 17.28 | 16.44 | 32 |
| 33 | 27.19 | 25.63 | 24.19 | 22.86 | 21.63 | 20.49 | 19.44 | 18.46 | 17.56 | 16.72 | 15.94 | 33 |
| 34 | 25.68 | 24.27 | 22.97 | 21.76 | 20.65 | 19.61 | 18.65 | 17.75 | 16.92 | 16.14 | 15.41 | 34 |
| 35 | 24.20 | 22.94 | 21.77 | 20.68 | 19.67 | 18.72 | 17.85 | 17.03 | 16.26 | 15.55 | 14.88 | 35 |
| 36 | 22.75 | 21.63 | 20.58 | 19.60 | 18.69 | 17.83 | 17.04 | 16.29 | 15.59 | 14.94 | 14.32 | 36 |
| 37 | 21.33 | 20.33 | 19.40 | 18.52 | 17.71 | 16.94 | 16.22 | 15.55 | 14.91 | 14.32 | 13.76 | 37 |
| 38 | 19.94 | 19.06 | 18.23 | 17.46 | 16.73 | 16.04 | 15.40 | 14.79 | 14.22 | 13.68 | 13.17 | 38 |
| 39 | 18.57 | 17.80 | 17.07 | 16.39 | 15.75 | 15.14 | 14.56 | 14.02 | 13.51 | 13.02 | 12.56 | 39 |
| 40 | 17.23 | 16.56 | 15.93 | 15.33 | 14.76 | 14.23 | 13.72 | 13.24 | 12.79 | 12.35 | 11.94 | 40 |
| 41 | 15.92 | 15.34 | 14.79 | 14.28 | 13.78 | 13.32 | 12.87 | 12.45 | 12.05 | 11.67 | 11.30 | 41 |
| 42 | 14.63 | 14.14 | 13.67 | 13.23 | 12.80 | 12.40 | 12.01 | 11.65 | 11.30 | 10.96 | 10.64 | 42 |
| 43 | 13.37 | 12.96 | 12.56 | 12.18 | 11.82 | 11.48 | 11.15 | 10.83 | 10.53 | 10.24 | 9.96 | 43 |
| 44 | 12.13 | 11.79 | 11.46 | 11.14 | 10.84 | 10.55 | 10.27 | 10.01 | 9.75 | 9.50 | 9.26 | 44 |
| 45 | 10.92 | 10.64 | 10.37 | 10.11 | 9.86 | 9.62 | 9.39 | 9.17 | 8.95 | 8.74 | 8.54 | 45 |
| 46 | 9.73 | 9.51 | 9.29 | 9.08 | 8.88 | 8.68 | 8.50 | 8.31 | 8.14 | 7.97 | 7.80 | 46 |
| 47 | 8.57 | 8.39 | 8.22 | 8.06 | 7.90 | 7.74 | 7.59 | 7.45 | 7.31 | 7.17 | 7.04 | 47 |
| 48 | 7.43 | 7.29 | 7.17 | 7.04 | 6.92 | 6.80 | 6.68 | 6.57 | 6.46 | 6.35 | 6.25 | 48 |
| 49 | 6.31 | 6.21 | 6.12 | 6.02 | 5.93 | 5.85 | 5.76 | 5.68 | 5.60 | 5.52 | 5.44 | 49 |
| 50 | 5.21 | 5.14 | 5.08 | 5.01 | 4.95 | 4.89 | 4.83 | 4.77 | 4.72 | 4.66 | 4.60 | 50 |
| 51 | 4.13 | 4.09 | 4.05 | 4.01 | 3.97 | 3.93 | 3.89 | 3.85 | 3.81 | 3.78 | 3.74 | 51 |
| 52 | 3.07 | 3.05 | 3.03 | 3.00 | 2.98 | 2.96 | 2.94 | 2.91 | 2.89 | 2.87 | 2.85 | 52 |
| 53 | 2.03 | 2.02 | 2.01 | 2.00 | 1.99 | 1.98 | 1.97 | 1.96 | 1.95 | 1.94 | 1.93 | 53 |
| 54 | 1.01 | 1.01 | 1.00 | 1.00 | 1.00 | 1.00 | 0.99 | 0.99 | 0.99 | 0.99 | 0.98 | 54 |

## Table 6: Multipliers for loss of earnings to pension age 55 (females)

| Age at date of trial | Multiplier calculated with allowance for projected mortality from the 2008–based population projections and rate of return of | | | | | | | | | | | Age at date of trial |
|---|---|---|---|---|---|---|---|---|---|---|---|---|
| | -2.0% | -1.5% | -1.0% | -0.5% | 0.0% | 0.5% | 1.0% | 1.5% | 2.0% | 2.5% | 3.0% | |
| 16 | 58.83 | 52.69 | 47.37 | 42.75 | 38.72 | 35.20 | 32.11 | 29.40 | 27.01 | 24.90 | 23.03 | 16 |
| 17 | 56.66 | 50.91 | 45.90 | 41.54 | 37.72 | 34.37 | 31.43 | 28.84 | 26.54 | 24.51 | 22.70 | 17 |
| 18 | 54.54 | 49.15 | 44.45 | 40.34 | 36.72 | 33.55 | 30.74 | 28.26 | 26.07 | 24.11 | 22.37 | 18 |
| 19 | 52.46 | 47.43 | 43.02 | 39.14 | 35.73 | 32.71 | 30.05 | 27.68 | 25.58 | 23.71 | 22.03 | 19 |
| 20 | 50.43 | 45.73 | 41.60 | 37.95 | 34.73 | 31.88 | 29.35 | 27.09 | 25.09 | 23.29 | 21.68 | 20 |
| 21 | 48.43 | 44.05 | 40.19 | 36.77 | 33.73 | 31.04 | 28.64 | 26.50 | 24.58 | 22.86 | 21.32 | 21 |
| 22 | 46.48 | 42.41 | 38.80 | 35.59 | 32.74 | 30.20 | 27.92 | 25.89 | 24.06 | 22.42 | 20.95 | 22 |
| 23 | 44.56 | 40.78 | 37.42 | 34.42 | 31.74 | 29.35 | 27.20 | 25.27 | 23.54 | 21.97 | 20.56 | 23 |
| 24 | 42.69 | 39.18 | 36.05 | 33.25 | 30.74 | 28.49 | 26.47 | 24.65 | 23.00 | 21.51 | 20.17 | 24 |
| 25 | 40.85 | 37.60 | 34.70 | 32.09 | 29.75 | 27.64 | 25.73 | 24.01 | 22.46 | 21.04 | 19.76 | 25 |
| 26 | 39.04 | 36.05 | 33.36 | 30.94 | 28.75 | 26.78 | 24.99 | 23.37 | 21.90 | 20.56 | 19.34 | 26 |
| 27 | 37.28 | 34.52 | 32.04 | 29.79 | 27.76 | 25.91 | 24.24 | 22.72 | 21.33 | 20.06 | 18.91 | 27 |
| 28 | 35.55 | 33.02 | 30.73 | 28.65 | 26.76 | 25.04 | 23.48 | 22.05 | 20.75 | 19.56 | 18.46 | 28 |
| 29 | 33.86 | 31.54 | 29.43 | 27.51 | 25.77 | 24.17 | 22.72 | 21.38 | 20.16 | 19.04 | 18.01 | 29 |
| 30 | 32.20 | 30.08 | 28.15 | 26.38 | 24.77 | 23.30 | 21.94 | 20.70 | 19.56 | 18.51 | 17.54 | 30 |
| 31 | 30.57 | 28.64 | 26.88 | 25.26 | 23.78 | 22.42 | 21.16 | 20.01 | 18.94 | 17.96 | 17.05 | 31 |
| 32 | 28.98 | 27.23 | 25.62 | 24.15 | 22.79 | 21.53 | 20.38 | 19.31 | 18.32 | 17.40 | 16.56 | 32 |
| 33 | 27.42 | 25.84 | 24.38 | 23.03 | 21.79 | 20.64 | 19.58 | 18.60 | 17.68 | 16.83 | 16.04 | 33 |
| 34 | 25.89 | 24.46 | 23.15 | 21.93 | 20.80 | 19.75 | 18.78 | 17.87 | 17.03 | 16.25 | 15.52 | 34 |
| 35 | 24.39 | 23.11 | 21.93 | 20.83 | 19.81 | 18.86 | 17.97 | 17.14 | 16.37 | 15.65 | 14.97 | 35 |
| 36 | 22.92 | 21.78 | 20.73 | 19.74 | 18.82 | 17.96 | 17.15 | 16.40 | 15.69 | 15.03 | 14.41 | 36 |
| 37 | 21.48 | 20.48 | 19.53 | 18.65 | 17.83 | 17.05 | 16.33 | 15.65 | 15.01 | 14.40 | 13.84 | 37 |
| 38 | 20.07 | 19.19 | 18.35 | 17.57 | 16.84 | 16.14 | 15.49 | 14.88 | 14.30 | 13.76 | 13.25 | 38 |
| 39 | 18.69 | 17.92 | 17.19 | 16.50 | 15.85 | 15.23 | 14.65 | 14.11 | 13.59 | 13.10 | 12.64 | 39 |
| 40 | 17.34 | 16.67 | 16.03 | 15.43 | 14.86 | 14.32 | 13.80 | 13.32 | 12.86 | 12.42 | 12.01 | 40 |
| 41 | 16.02 | 15.44 | 14.89 | 14.36 | 13.87 | 13.40 | 12.95 | 12.52 | 12.12 | 11.73 | 11.36 | 41 |
| 42 | 14.72 | 14.22 | 13.75 | 13.30 | 12.88 | 12.47 | 12.08 | 11.71 | 11.36 | 11.02 | 10.70 | 42 |
| 43 | 13.45 | 13.03 | 12.63 | 12.25 | 11.89 | 11.54 | 11.21 | 10.89 | 10.59 | 10.29 | 10.01 | 43 |
| 44 | 12.20 | 11.85 | 11.52 | 11.20 | 10.90 | 10.61 | 10.33 | 10.06 | 9.80 | 9.55 | 9.31 | 44 |
| 45 | 10.98 | 10.70 | 10.42 | 10.16 | 9.91 | 9.67 | 9.43 | 9.21 | 8.99 | 8.79 | 8.58 | 45 |
| 46 | 9.78 | 9.56 | 9.34 | 9.13 | 8.92 | 8.73 | 8.54 | 8.35 | 8.17 | 8.00 | 7.84 | 46 |
| 47 | 8.61 | 8.43 | 8.26 | 8.09 | 7.93 | 7.78 | 7.63 | 7.48 | 7.34 | 7.20 | 7.07 | 47 |
| 48 | 7.46 | 7.33 | 7.20 | 7.07 | 6.95 | 6.83 | 6.71 | 6.60 | 6.49 | 6.38 | 6.28 | 48 |
| 49 | 6.33 | 6.24 | 6.14 | 6.05 | 5.96 | 5.87 | 5.78 | 5.70 | 5.62 | 5.54 | 5.46 | 49 |
| 50 | 5.23 | 5.16 | 5.10 | 5.03 | 4.97 | 4.91 | 4.85 | 4.79 | 4.73 | 4.68 | 4.62 | 50 |
| 51 | 4.14 | 4.10 | 4.06 | 4.02 | 3.98 | 3.94 | 3.90 | 3.86 | 3.83 | 3.79 | 3.75 | 51 |
| 52 | 3.08 | 3.06 | 3.03 | 3.01 | 2.99 | 2.97 | 2.94 | 2.92 | 2.90 | 2.88 | 2.86 | 52 |
| 53 | 2.03 | 2.02 | 2.01 | 2.00 | 1.99 | 1.98 | 1.97 | 1.96 | 1.96 | 1.95 | 1.94 | 53 |
| 54 | 1.01 | 1.01 | 1.00 | 1.00 | 1.00 | 1.00 | 0.99 | 0.99 | 0.99 | 0.99 | 0.98 | 54 |

## Table 7: Multipliers for loss of earnings to pension age 60 (males)

| Age at date of trial | Multiplier calculated with allowance for projected mortality from the 2008–based population projections and rate of return of | | | | | | | | | | | Age at date of trial |
|---|---|---|---|---|---|---|---|---|---|---|---|---|
| | *-2.0%* | *-1.5%* | *-1.0%* | *-0.5%* | *0.0%* | *0.5%* | *1.0%* | *1.5%* | *2.0%* | *2.5%* | *3.0%* | |
| 16 | 69.28 | 61.13 | 54.18 | 48.26 | 43.18 | 38.81 | 35.03 | 31.77 | 28.93 | 26.46 | 24.29 | 16 |
| 17 | 66.90 | 59.22 | 52.65 | 47.02 | 42.18 | 38.00 | 34.38 | 31.24 | 28.50 | 26.11 | 24.01 | 17 |
| 18 | 64.58 | 57.34 | 51.13 | 45.79 | 41.18 | 37.19 | 33.73 | 30.71 | 28.07 | 25.75 | 23.72 | 18 |
| 19 | 62.30 | 55.49 | 49.63 | 44.57 | 40.19 | 36.38 | 33.06 | 30.17 | 27.62 | 25.39 | 23.42 | 19 |
| 20 | 60.08 | 53.68 | 48.15 | 43.36 | 39.20 | 35.57 | 32.40 | 29.62 | 27.17 | 25.02 | 23.11 | 20 |
| 21 | 57.90 | 51.89 | 46.68 | 42.15 | 38.21 | 34.75 | 31.72 | 29.06 | 26.71 | 24.64 | 22.80 | 21 |
| 22 | 55.76 | 50.13 | 45.23 | 40.95 | 37.21 | 33.93 | 31.04 | 28.50 | 26.25 | 24.25 | 22.47 | 22 |
| 23 | 53.66 | 48.40 | 43.79 | 39.76 | 36.22 | 33.11 | 30.36 | 27.93 | 25.77 | 23.85 | 22.14 | 23 |
| 24 | 51.61 | 46.69 | 42.37 | 38.57 | 35.23 | 32.28 | 29.66 | 27.35 | 25.28 | 23.44 | 21.80 | 24 |
| 25 | 49.60 | 45.01 | 40.96 | 37.40 | 34.24 | 31.45 | 28.97 | 26.76 | 24.79 | 23.02 | 21.44 | 25 |
| 26 | 47.64 | 43.35 | 39.57 | 36.22 | 33.25 | 30.61 | 28.26 | 26.16 | 24.28 | 22.59 | 21.08 | 26 |
| 27 | 45.71 | 41.72 | 38.19 | 35.06 | 32.27 | 29.77 | 27.55 | 25.56 | 23.77 | 22.16 | 20.71 | 27 |
| 28 | 43.82 | 40.12 | 36.83 | 33.90 | 31.28 | 28.93 | 26.83 | 24.94 | 23.24 | 21.71 | 20.32 | 28 |
| 29 | 41.97 | 38.54 | 35.48 | 32.74 | 30.29 | 28.09 | 26.10 | 24.32 | 22.70 | 21.25 | 19.92 | 29 |
| 30 | 40.15 | 36.99 | 34.14 | 31.59 | 29.30 | 27.24 | 25.37 | 23.69 | 22.16 | 20.78 | 19.52 | 30 |
| 31 | 38.38 | 35.46 | 32.83 | 30.46 | 28.32 | 26.39 | 24.64 | 23.05 | 21.61 | 20.29 | 19.10 | 31 |
| 32 | 36.65 | 33.96 | 31.53 | 29.33 | 27.34 | 25.53 | 23.89 | 22.40 | 21.04 | 19.80 | 18.67 | 32 |
| 33 | 34.96 | 32.48 | 30.24 | 28.21 | 26.36 | 24.68 | 23.15 | 21.75 | 20.47 | 19.30 | 18.23 | 33 |
| 34 | 33.30 | 31.03 | 28.97 | 27.09 | 25.38 | 23.82 | 22.39 | 21.09 | 19.89 | 18.79 | 17.78 | 34 |
| 35 | 31.67 | 29.60 | 27.71 | 25.98 | 24.40 | 22.96 | 21.63 | 20.42 | 19.30 | 18.27 | 17.32 | 35 |
| 36 | 30.07 | 28.19 | 26.46 | 24.88 | 23.43 | 22.09 | 20.87 | 19.74 | 18.69 | 17.73 | 16.84 | 36 |
| 37 | 28.51 | 26.80 | 25.23 | 23.78 | 22.45 | 21.22 | 20.09 | 19.04 | 18.08 | 17.18 | 16.35 | 37 |
| 38 | 26.98 | 25.43 | 24.01 | 22.69 | 21.48 | 20.35 | 19.31 | 18.34 | 17.45 | 16.61 | 15.84 | 38 |
| 39 | 25.48 | 24.08 | 22.80 | 21.60 | 20.50 | 19.47 | 18.52 | 17.63 | 16.81 | 16.04 | 15.32 | 39 |
| 40 | 24.00 | 22.76 | 21.60 | 20.52 | 19.52 | 18.59 | 17.72 | 16.91 | 16.15 | 15.44 | 14.78 | 40 |
| 41 | 22.56 | 21.45 | 20.41 | 19.45 | 18.54 | 17.70 | 16.91 | 16.17 | 15.48 | 14.84 | 14.23 | 41 |
| 42 | 21.15 | 20.16 | 19.24 | 18.38 | 17.57 | 16.81 | 16.10 | 15.43 | 14.80 | 14.21 | 13.66 | 42 |
| 43 | 19.76 | 18.90 | 18.08 | 17.31 | 16.59 | 15.92 | 15.28 | 14.68 | 14.11 | 13.58 | 13.07 | 43 |
| 44 | 18.41 | 17.65 | 16.93 | 16.26 | 15.62 | 15.02 | 14.45 | 13.91 | 13.41 | 12.93 | 12.47 | 44 |
| 45 | 17.08 | 16.42 | 15.79 | 15.20 | 14.64 | 14.12 | 13.61 | 13.14 | 12.69 | 12.26 | 11.85 | 45 |
| 46 | 15.78 | 15.21 | 14.67 | 14.16 | 13.67 | 13.21 | 12.77 | 12.35 | 11.95 | 11.58 | 11.22 | 46 |
| 47 | 14.50 | 14.02 | 13.56 | 13.12 | 12.70 | 12.30 | 11.92 | 11.55 | 11.21 | 10.88 | 10.56 | 47 |
| 48 | 13.26 | 12.85 | 12.46 | 12.08 | 11.73 | 11.38 | 11.06 | 10.75 | 10.45 | 10.16 | 9.89 | 48 |
| 49 | 12.03 | 11.69 | 11.37 | 11.05 | 10.75 | 10.47 | 10.19 | 9.93 | 9.67 | 9.43 | 9.19 | 49 |
| 50 | 10.83 | 10.56 | 10.29 | 10.03 | 9.78 | 9.55 | 9.32 | 9.10 | 8.88 | 8.68 | 8.48 | 50 |
| 51 | 9.66 | 9.44 | 9.22 | 9.01 | 8.81 | 8.62 | 8.43 | 8.25 | 8.08 | 7.91 | 7.75 | 51 |
| 52 | 8.51 | 8.34 | 8.17 | 8.00 | 7.84 | 7.69 | 7.54 | 7.40 | 7.26 | 7.12 | 6.99 | 52 |
| 53 | 7.38 | 7.25 | 7.12 | 7.00 | 6.87 | 6.76 | 6.64 | 6.53 | 6.42 | 6.32 | 6.21 | 53 |
| 54 | 6.27 | 6.18 | 6.08 | 5.99 | 5.90 | 5.82 | 5.73 | 5.65 | 5.57 | 5.49 | 5.41 | 54 |
| 55 | 5.18 | 5.12 | 5.05 | 4.99 | 4.93 | 4.87 | 4.81 | 4.75 | 4.69 | 4.64 | 4.58 | 55 |
| 56 | 4.12 | 4.07 | 4.03 | 3.99 | 3.95 | 3.91 | 3.87 | 3.84 | 3.80 | 3.76 | 3.73 | 56 |
| 57 | 3.06 | 3.04 | 3.02 | 2.99 | 2.97 | 2.95 | 2.93 | 2.91 | 2.89 | 2.86 | 2.84 | 57 |
| 58 | 2.03 | 2.02 | 2.01 | 2.00 | 1.99 | 1.98 | 1.97 | 1.96 | 1.95 | 1.94 | 1.93 | 58 |
| 59 | 1.01 | 1.00 | 1.00 | 1.00 | 1.00 | 0.99 | 0.99 | 0.99 | 0.99 | 0.98 | 0.98 | 59 |

## A8: The Ogden Tables

### Table 8: Multipliers for loss of earnings to pension age 60 (females)

| Age at date of trial | Multiplier calculated with allowance for projected mortality from the 2008–based population projections and rate of return of | | | | | | | | | | | Age at date of trial |
|---|---|---|---|---|---|---|---|---|---|---|---|---|
| | -2.0% | -1.5% | -1.0% | -0.5% | 0.0% | 0.5% | 1.0% | 1.5% | 2.0% | 2.5% | 3.0% | |
| 16 | 70.04 | 61.77 | 54.73 | 48.72 | 43.57 | 39.14 | 35.32 | 32.02 | 29.14 | 26.64 | 24.45 | 16 |
| 17 | 67.65 | 59.85 | 53.18 | 47.48 | 42.57 | 38.33 | 34.67 | 31.49 | 28.72 | 26.29 | 24.17 | 17 |
| 18 | 65.30 | 57.96 | 51.66 | 46.24 | 41.57 | 37.52 | 34.01 | 30.96 | 28.28 | 25.94 | 23.88 | 18 |
| 19 | 63.01 | 56.10 | 50.15 | 45.02 | 40.57 | 36.71 | 33.35 | 30.41 | 27.84 | 25.58 | 23.59 | 19 |
| 20 | 60.76 | 54.27 | 48.66 | 43.80 | 39.57 | 35.90 | 32.68 | 29.87 | 27.39 | 25.21 | 23.28 | 20 |
| 21 | 58.56 | 52.46 | 47.18 | 42.58 | 38.58 | 35.08 | 32.01 | 29.31 | 26.93 | 24.83 | 22.97 | 21 |
| 22 | 56.40 | 50.69 | 45.71 | 41.37 | 37.58 | 34.25 | 31.32 | 28.74 | 26.46 | 24.44 | 22.64 | 22 |
| 23 | 54.29 | 48.94 | 44.26 | 40.17 | 36.58 | 33.42 | 30.64 | 28.17 | 25.98 | 24.04 | 22.31 | 23 |
| 24 | 52.21 | 47.21 | 42.83 | 38.98 | 35.58 | 32.59 | 29.94 | 27.59 | 25.50 | 23.63 | 21.97 | 24 |
| 25 | 50.18 | 45.51 | 41.41 | 37.79 | 34.59 | 31.75 | 29.24 | 27.00 | 25.00 | 23.21 | 21.61 | 25 |
| 26 | 48.19 | 43.84 | 40.00 | 36.60 | 33.59 | 30.91 | 28.53 | 26.40 | 24.49 | 22.78 | 21.25 | 26 |
| 27 | 46.24 | 42.20 | 38.61 | 35.43 | 32.59 | 30.07 | 27.81 | 25.79 | 23.98 | 22.34 | 20.87 | 27 |
| 28 | 44.33 | 40.58 | 37.24 | 34.26 | 31.60 | 29.22 | 27.09 | 25.17 | 23.45 | 21.89 | 20.49 | 28 |
| 29 | 42.46 | 38.98 | 35.87 | 33.09 | 30.60 | 28.37 | 26.36 | 24.55 | 22.91 | 21.43 | 20.09 | 29 |
| 30 | 40.63 | 37.41 | 34.53 | 31.94 | 29.61 | 27.51 | 25.62 | 23.91 | 22.37 | 20.96 | 19.69 | 30 |
| 31 | 38.83 | 35.86 | 33.19 | 30.79 | 28.62 | 26.65 | 24.88 | 23.27 | 21.81 | 20.48 | 19.27 | 31 |
| 32 | 37.08 | 34.34 | 31.87 | 29.64 | 27.62 | 25.79 | 24.13 | 22.62 | 21.24 | 19.98 | 18.83 | 32 |
| 33 | 35.35 | 32.84 | 30.57 | 28.50 | 26.63 | 24.93 | 23.37 | 21.96 | 20.66 | 19.48 | 18.39 | 33 |
| 34 | 33.67 | 31.37 | 29.28 | 27.37 | 25.64 | 24.06 | 22.61 | 21.29 | 20.07 | 18.96 | 17.93 | 34 |
| 35 | 32.01 | 29.91 | 28.00 | 26.25 | 24.65 | 23.18 | 21.84 | 20.60 | 19.47 | 18.43 | 17.46 | 35 |
| 36 | 30.40 | 28.48 | 26.73 | 25.13 | 23.66 | 22.30 | 21.06 | 19.91 | 18.86 | 17.88 | 16.98 | 36 |
| 37 | 28.81 | 27.08 | 25.48 | 24.02 | 22.67 | 21.42 | 20.28 | 19.21 | 18.23 | 17.32 | 16.48 | 37 |
| 38 | 27.26 | 25.69 | 24.24 | 22.91 | 21.68 | 20.54 | 19.48 | 18.50 | 17.60 | 16.75 | 15.97 | 38 |
| 39 | 25.73 | 24.32 | 23.02 | 21.81 | 20.69 | 19.65 | 18.68 | 17.78 | 16.95 | 16.17 | 15.44 | 39 |
| 40 | 24.24 | 22.98 | 21.81 | 20.72 | 19.70 | 18.76 | 17.88 | 17.05 | 16.29 | 15.57 | 14.90 | 40 |
| 41 | 22.78 | 21.66 | 20.61 | 19.63 | 18.71 | 17.86 | 17.06 | 16.31 | 15.61 | 14.96 | 14.34 | 41 |
| 42 | 21.35 | 20.35 | 19.42 | 18.55 | 17.73 | 16.96 | 16.24 | 15.56 | 14.93 | 14.33 | 13.77 | 42 |
| 43 | 19.95 | 19.07 | 18.24 | 17.47 | 16.74 | 16.05 | 15.41 | 14.80 | 14.23 | 13.69 | 13.18 | 43 |
| 44 | 18.58 | 17.81 | 17.08 | 16.40 | 15.75 | 15.15 | 14.57 | 14.03 | 13.52 | 13.03 | 12.57 | 44 |
| 45 | 17.24 | 16.57 | 15.93 | 15.33 | 14.77 | 14.23 | 13.73 | 13.25 | 12.79 | 12.36 | 11.95 | 45 |
| 46 | 15.92 | 15.34 | 14.80 | 14.28 | 13.79 | 13.32 | 12.87 | 12.45 | 12.05 | 11.67 | 11.30 | 46 |
| 47 | 14.63 | 14.14 | 13.67 | 13.23 | 12.80 | 12.40 | 12.01 | 11.65 | 11.30 | 10.96 | 10.64 | 47 |
| 48 | 13.37 | 12.95 | 12.56 | 12.18 | 11.82 | 11.48 | 11.15 | 10.83 | 10.53 | 10.24 | 9.96 | 48 |
| 49 | 12.13 | 11.79 | 11.46 | 11.14 | 10.84 | 10.55 | 10.27 | 10.00 | 9.75 | 9.50 | 9.26 | 49 |
| 50 | 10.92 | 10.64 | 10.37 | 10.11 | 9.86 | 9.62 | 9.39 | 9.17 | 8.95 | 8.74 | 8.54 | 50 |
| 51 | 9.73 | 9.51 | 9.29 | 9.08 | 8.88 | 8.69 | 8.50 | 8.31 | 8.14 | 7.97 | 7.80 | 51 |
| 52 | 8.57 | 8.39 | 8.22 | 8.06 | 7.90 | 7.75 | 7.60 | 7.45 | 7.31 | 7.17 | 7.04 | 52 |
| 53 | 7.43 | 7.30 | 7.17 | 7.04 | 6.92 | 6.80 | 6.68 | 6.57 | 6.46 | 6.36 | 6.25 | 53 |
| 54 | 6.31 | 6.21 | 6.12 | 6.03 | 5.94 | 5.85 | 5.76 | 5.68 | 5.60 | 5.52 | 5.44 | 54 |
| 55 | 5.21 | 5.14 | 5.08 | 5.02 | 4.95 | 4.89 | 4.83 | 4.77 | 4.72 | 4.66 | 4.61 | 55 |
| 56 | 4.13 | 4.09 | 4.05 | 4.01 | 3.97 | 3.93 | 3.89 | 3.85 | 3.82 | 3.78 | 3.74 | 56 |
| 57 | 3.07 | 3.05 | 3.03 | 3.00 | 2.98 | 2.96 | 2.94 | 2.92 | 2.89 | 2.87 | 2.85 | 57 |
| 58 | 2.03 | 2.02 | 2.01 | 2.00 | 1.99 | 1.98 | 1.97 | 1.96 | 1.95 | 1.94 | 1.93 | 58 |
| 59 | 1.01 | 1.01 | 1.00 | 1.00 | 1.00 | 1.00 | 0.99 | 0.99 | 0.99 | 0.99 | 0.98 | 59 |

### Table 9: Multipliers for loss of earnings to pension age 65 (males)

| Age at date of trial | Multiplier calculated with allowance for projected mortality from the 2008–based population projections and rate of return of | | | | | | | | | | | Age at date of trial |
|---|---|---|---|---|---|---|---|---|---|---|---|---|
| | -2.0% | -1.5% | -1.0% | -0.5% | 0.0% | 0.5% | 1.0% | 1.5% | 2.0% | 2.5% | 3.0% | |
| 16 | 81.11 | 70.46 | 61.56 | 54.09 | 47.80 | 42.47 | 37.95 | 34.08 | 30.77 | 27.92 | 25.46 | 16 |
| 17 | 78.49 | 68.41 | 59.95 | 52.82 | 46.80 | 41.68 | 37.32 | 33.59 | 30.38 | 27.61 | 25.21 | 17 |
| 18 | 75.93 | 66.39 | 58.35 | 51.56 | 45.80 | 40.89 | 36.69 | 33.09 | 29.98 | 27.29 | 24.96 | 18 |
| 19 | 73.42 | 64.40 | 56.78 | 50.31 | 44.80 | 40.10 | 36.06 | 32.58 | 29.58 | 26.97 | 24.70 | 19 |
| 20 | 70.97 | 62.45 | 55.22 | 49.07 | 43.81 | 39.30 | 35.42 | 32.07 | 29.16 | 26.64 | 24.43 | 20 |
| 21 | 68.57 | 60.53 | 53.68 | 47.83 | 42.82 | 38.50 | 34.78 | 31.55 | 28.74 | 26.30 | 24.15 | 21 |
| 22 | 66.21 | 58.63 | 52.16 | 46.60 | 41.82 | 37.70 | 34.13 | 31.02 | 28.31 | 25.95 | 23.87 | 22 |
| 23 | 63.90 | 56.77 | 50.65 | 45.38 | 40.83 | 36.89 | 33.47 | 30.49 | 27.88 | 25.59 | 23.57 | 23 |
| 24 | 61.64 | 54.93 | 49.15 | 44.16 | 39.84 | 36.08 | 32.81 | 29.94 | 27.43 | 25.22 | 23.27 | 24 |
| 25 | 59.43 | 53.12 | 47.68 | 42.95 | 38.85 | 35.27 | 32.14 | 29.39 | 26.98 | 24.85 | 22.96 | 25 |
| 26 | 57.26 | 51.35 | 46.22 | 41.75 | 37.86 | 34.45 | 31.46 | 28.84 | 26.52 | 24.47 | 22.65 | 26 |
| 27 | 55.14 | 49.60 | 44.77 | 40.56 | 36.87 | 33.63 | 30.78 | 28.27 | 26.05 | 24.07 | 22.32 | 27 |
| 28 | 53.06 | 47.87 | 43.34 | 39.37 | 35.88 | 32.81 | 30.10 | 27.70 | 25.57 | 23.67 | 21.98 | 28 |
| 29 | 51.02 | 46.17 | 41.92 | 38.18 | 34.89 | 31.98 | 29.40 | 27.11 | 25.08 | 23.26 | 21.63 | 29 |
| 30 | 49.03 | 44.50 | 40.52 | 37.01 | 33.90 | 31.15 | 28.70 | 26.52 | 24.58 | 22.84 | 21.28 | 30 |
| 31 | 47.08 | 42.86 | 39.14 | 35.84 | 32.92 | 30.32 | 28.00 | 25.93 | 24.07 | 22.41 | 20.91 | 31 |
| 32 | 45.17 | 41.25 | 37.78 | 34.69 | 31.94 | 29.49 | 27.29 | 25.33 | 23.56 | 21.97 | 20.54 | 32 |
| 33 | 43.31 | 39.67 | 36.43 | 33.54 | 30.96 | 28.65 | 26.58 | 24.72 | 23.04 | 21.53 | 20.16 | 33 |
| 34 | 41.48 | 38.11 | 35.10 | 32.40 | 29.99 | 27.81 | 25.86 | 24.10 | 22.51 | 21.07 | 19.77 | 34 |
| 35 | 39.69 | 36.57 | 33.78 | 31.27 | 29.01 | 26.97 | 25.14 | 23.48 | 21.97 | 20.60 | 19.36 | 35 |
| 36 | 37.94 | 35.06 | 32.47 | 30.14 | 28.03 | 26.13 | 24.41 | 22.84 | 21.42 | 20.13 | 18.95 | 36 |
| 37 | 36.22 | 33.57 | 31.18 | 29.02 | 27.06 | 25.28 | 23.67 | 22.20 | 20.86 | 19.64 | 18.52 | 37 |
| 38 | 34.54 | 32.11 | 29.90 | 27.90 | 26.08 | 24.43 | 22.92 | 21.55 | 20.29 | 19.13 | 18.08 | 38 |
| 39 | 32.89 | 30.66 | 28.64 | 26.79 | 25.11 | 23.57 | 22.17 | 20.88 | 19.70 | 18.62 | 17.62 | 39 |
| 40 | 31.27 | 29.24 | 27.38 | 25.69 | 24.13 | 22.71 | 21.41 | 20.21 | 19.11 | 18.09 | 17.16 | 40 |
| 41 | 29.69 | 27.84 | 26.14 | 24.59 | 23.16 | 21.85 | 20.64 | 19.53 | 18.50 | 17.55 | 16.68 | 41 |
| 42 | 28.14 | 26.46 | 24.92 | 23.50 | 22.19 | 20.98 | 19.87 | 18.84 | 17.88 | 17.00 | 16.18 | 42 |
| 43 | 26.62 | 25.10 | 23.70 | 22.41 | 21.22 | 20.11 | 19.09 | 18.14 | 17.26 | 16.44 | 15.68 | 43 |
| 44 | 25.13 | 23.77 | 22.50 | 21.33 | 20.25 | 19.24 | 18.30 | 17.43 | 16.62 | 15.86 | 15.16 | 44 |
| 45 | 23.68 | 22.45 | 21.32 | 20.26 | 19.28 | 18.36 | 17.51 | 16.71 | 15.97 | 15.27 | 14.62 | 45 |
| 46 | 22.25 | 21.16 | 20.14 | 19.19 | 18.31 | 17.48 | 16.71 | 15.98 | 15.30 | 14.67 | 14.07 | 46 |
| 47 | 20.86 | 19.89 | 18.98 | 18.14 | 17.34 | 16.60 | 15.90 | 15.24 | 14.63 | 14.05 | 13.50 | 47 |
| 48 | 19.49 | 18.64 | 17.84 | 17.08 | 16.38 | 15.71 | 15.09 | 14.50 | 13.94 | 13.42 | 12.92 | 48 |
| 49 | 18.15 | 17.41 | 16.70 | 16.04 | 15.41 | 14.82 | 14.27 | 13.74 | 13.24 | 12.77 | 12.33 | 49 |
| 50 | 16.85 | 16.20 | 15.58 | 15.00 | 14.46 | 13.94 | 13.44 | 12.98 | 12.53 | 12.11 | 11.71 | 50 |
| 51 | 15.57 | 15.01 | 14.48 | 13.98 | 13.50 | 13.04 | 12.61 | 12.20 | 11.81 | 11.44 | 11.09 | 51 |
| 52 | 14.32 | 13.84 | 13.39 | 12.95 | 12.54 | 12.15 | 11.77 | 11.42 | 11.08 | 10.75 | 10.44 | 52 |
| 53 | 13.09 | 12.69 | 12.30 | 11.94 | 11.59 | 11.25 | 10.93 | 10.62 | 10.33 | 10.05 | 9.78 | 53 |
| 54 | 11.89 | 11.56 | 11.24 | 10.93 | 10.63 | 10.35 | 10.08 | 9.82 | 9.57 | 9.33 | 9.10 | 54 |
| 55 | 10.71 | 10.44 | 10.18 | 9.92 | 9.68 | 9.45 | 9.22 | 9.00 | 8.79 | 8.59 | 8.40 | 55 |
| 56 | 9.56 | 9.34 | 9.13 | 8.93 | 8.73 | 8.54 | 8.35 | 8.17 | 8.00 | 7.84 | 7.67 | 56 |
| 57 | 8.43 | 8.26 | 8.09 | 7.93 | 7.77 | 7.62 | 7.47 | 7.33 | 7.19 | 7.06 | 6.93 | 57 |
| 58 | 7.32 | 7.19 | 7.06 | 6.94 | 6.82 | 6.70 | 6.59 | 6.48 | 6.37 | 6.26 | 6.16 | 58 |
| 59 | 6.22 | 6.13 | 6.03 | 5.94 | 5.85 | 5.77 | 5.68 | 5.60 | 5.52 | 5.45 | 5.37 | 59 |
| 60 | 5.14 | 5.08 | 5.01 | 4.95 | 4.89 | 4.83 | 4.77 | 4.71 | 4.66 | 4.60 | 4.55 | 60 |
| 61 | 4.09 | 4.04 | 4.00 | 3.96 | 3.92 | 3.89 | 3.85 | 3.81 | 3.77 | 3.74 | 3.70 | 61 |
| 62 | 3.04 | 3.02 | 3.00 | 2.98 | 2.95 | 2.93 | 2.91 | 2.89 | 2.87 | 2.85 | 2.83 | 62 |
| 63 | 2.02 | 2.01 | 2.00 | 1.99 | 1.98 | 1.97 | 1.96 | 1.95 | 1.94 | 1.93 | 1.92 | 63 |
| 64 | 1.00 | 1.00 | 1.00 | 1.00 | 0.99 | 0.99 | 0.99 | 0.99 | 0.98 | 0.98 | 0.98 | 64 |

## A8: The Ogden Tables

**Table 10: Multipliers for loss of earnings to pension age 65 (females)**

| Age at date of trial | Multiplier calculated with allowance for projected mortality from the 2008–based population projections and rate of return of | | | | | | | | | | | Age at date of trial |
|---|---|---|---|---|---|---|---|---|---|---|---|---|
| | -2.0% | -1.5% | -1.0% | -0.5% | 0.0% | 0.5% | 1.0% | 1.5% | 2.0% | 2.5% | 3.0% | |
| 16 | 82.26 | 71.41 | 62.34 | 54.74 | 48.34 | 42.93 | 38.33 | 34.41 | 31.05 | 28.16 | 25.66 | 16 |
| 17 | 79.62 | 69.34 | 60.72 | 53.47 | 47.34 | 42.14 | 37.71 | 33.91 | 30.66 | 27.85 | 25.41 | 17 |
| 18 | 77.03 | 67.31 | 59.12 | 52.20 | 46.34 | 41.35 | 37.08 | 33.42 | 30.26 | 27.53 | 25.16 | 18 |
| 19 | 74.50 | 65.30 | 57.53 | 50.95 | 45.34 | 40.55 | 36.45 | 32.91 | 29.86 | 27.21 | 24.91 | 19 |
| 20 | 72.02 | 63.33 | 55.96 | 49.70 | 44.34 | 39.75 | 35.81 | 32.40 | 29.45 | 26.88 | 24.64 | 20 |
| 21 | 69.59 | 61.39 | 54.41 | 48.45 | 43.34 | 38.95 | 35.16 | 31.88 | 29.03 | 26.54 | 24.37 | 21 |
| 22 | 67.20 | 59.48 | 52.87 | 47.21 | 42.34 | 38.15 | 34.51 | 31.35 | 28.60 | 26.20 | 24.08 | 22 |
| 23 | 64.87 | 57.59 | 51.35 | 45.98 | 41.35 | 37.33 | 33.85 | 30.82 | 28.16 | 25.84 | 23.79 | 23 |
| 24 | 62.58 | 55.73 | 49.84 | 44.75 | 40.35 | 36.52 | 33.19 | 30.27 | 27.72 | 25.47 | 23.49 | 24 |
| 25 | 60.34 | 53.91 | 48.35 | 43.53 | 39.35 | 35.70 | 32.51 | 29.72 | 27.27 | 25.10 | 23.19 | 25 |
| 26 | 58.14 | 52.11 | 46.87 | 42.32 | 38.35 | 34.88 | 31.84 | 29.16 | 26.80 | 24.72 | 22.87 | 26 |
| 27 | 55.99 | 50.33 | 45.41 | 41.11 | 37.35 | 34.05 | 31.15 | 28.60 | 26.33 | 24.33 | 22.54 | 27 |
| 28 | 53.88 | 48.59 | 43.96 | 39.91 | 36.36 | 33.23 | 30.46 | 28.02 | 25.85 | 23.93 | 22.21 | 28 |
| 29 | 51.82 | 46.87 | 42.53 | 38.72 | 35.36 | 32.39 | 29.77 | 27.44 | 25.36 | 23.51 | 21.86 | 29 |
| 30 | 49.80 | 45.18 | 41.12 | 37.53 | 34.36 | 31.56 | 29.06 | 26.84 | 24.87 | 23.09 | 21.51 | 30 |
| 31 | 47.82 | 43.52 | 39.72 | 36.35 | 33.37 | 30.72 | 28.35 | 26.25 | 24.36 | 22.66 | 21.14 | 31 |
| 32 | 45.88 | 41.88 | 38.33 | 35.18 | 32.38 | 29.87 | 27.64 | 25.64 | 23.84 | 22.22 | 20.77 | 32 |
| 33 | 43.98 | 40.27 | 36.96 | 34.01 | 31.38 | 29.03 | 26.92 | 25.02 | 23.31 | 21.77 | 20.38 | 33 |
| 34 | 42.12 | 38.68 | 35.60 | 32.85 | 30.39 | 28.18 | 26.19 | 24.39 | 22.78 | 21.31 | 19.98 | 34 |
| 35 | 40.30 | 37.11 | 34.26 | 31.70 | 29.40 | 27.32 | 25.45 | 23.76 | 22.23 | 20.84 | 19.57 | 35 |
| 36 | 38.51 | 35.58 | 32.93 | 30.56 | 28.41 | 26.47 | 24.71 | 23.12 | 21.67 | 20.35 | 19.15 | 36 |
| 37 | 36.76 | 34.06 | 31.62 | 29.42 | 27.42 | 25.61 | 23.96 | 22.47 | 21.10 | 19.86 | 18.72 | 37 |
| 38 | 35.05 | 32.57 | 30.32 | 28.28 | 26.43 | 24.74 | 23.21 | 21.81 | 20.52 | 19.35 | 18.28 | 38 |
| 39 | 33.38 | 31.10 | 29.04 | 27.16 | 25.44 | 23.88 | 22.44 | 21.14 | 19.93 | 18.83 | 17.82 | 39 |
| 40 | 31.73 | 29.66 | 27.76 | 26.04 | 24.45 | 23.00 | 21.68 | 20.46 | 19.33 | 18.30 | 17.35 | 40 |
| 41 | 30.12 | 28.24 | 26.51 | 24.92 | 23.47 | 22.13 | 20.90 | 19.77 | 18.72 | 17.76 | 16.86 | 41 |
| 42 | 28.55 | 26.84 | 25.26 | 23.81 | 22.48 | 21.25 | 20.12 | 19.07 | 18.10 | 17.20 | 16.37 | 42 |
| 43 | 27.01 | 25.46 | 24.03 | 22.71 | 21.50 | 20.37 | 19.33 | 18.36 | 17.46 | 16.63 | 15.85 | 43 |
| 44 | 25.49 | 24.10 | 22.81 | 21.62 | 20.51 | 19.48 | 18.53 | 17.64 | 16.82 | 16.05 | 15.33 | 44 |
| 45 | 24.02 | 22.77 | 21.61 | 20.53 | 19.53 | 18.60 | 17.73 | 16.92 | 16.16 | 15.45 | 14.79 | 45 |
| 46 | 22.57 | 21.46 | 20.42 | 19.45 | 18.55 | 17.71 | 16.92 | 16.18 | 15.49 | 14.84 | 14.23 | 46 |
| 47 | 21.15 | 20.17 | 19.24 | 18.38 | 17.57 | 16.81 | 16.10 | 15.43 | 14.81 | 14.22 | 13.66 | 47 |
| 48 | 19.77 | 18.90 | 18.08 | 17.31 | 16.59 | 15.92 | 15.28 | 14.68 | 14.11 | 13.58 | 13.08 | 48 |
| 49 | 18.41 | 17.65 | 16.93 | 16.26 | 15.62 | 15.02 | 14.45 | 13.91 | 13.41 | 12.93 | 12.47 | 49 |
| 50 | 17.08 | 16.42 | 15.80 | 15.21 | 14.65 | 14.12 | 13.62 | 13.14 | 12.69 | 12.26 | 11.85 | 50 |
| 51 | 15.78 | 15.21 | 14.67 | 14.16 | 13.67 | 13.21 | 12.77 | 12.35 | 11.96 | 11.58 | 11.22 | 51 |
| 52 | 14.51 | 14.02 | 13.56 | 13.12 | 12.70 | 12.30 | 11.92 | 11.56 | 11.21 | 10.88 | 10.56 | 52 |
| 53 | 13.26 | 12.85 | 12.46 | 12.09 | 11.73 | 11.39 | 11.06 | 10.75 | 10.45 | 10.17 | 9.89 | 53 |
| 54 | 12.04 | 11.70 | 11.37 | 11.06 | 10.76 | 10.47 | 10.20 | 9.93 | 9.68 | 9.43 | 9.20 | 54 |
| 55 | 10.84 | 10.56 | 10.30 | 10.04 | 9.79 | 9.55 | 9.32 | 9.10 | 8.89 | 8.68 | 8.49 | 55 |
| 56 | 9.67 | 9.44 | 9.23 | 9.02 | 8.82 | 8.63 | 8.44 | 8.26 | 8.09 | 7.92 | 7.75 | 56 |
| 57 | 8.52 | 8.34 | 8.17 | 8.01 | 7.85 | 7.70 | 7.55 | 7.40 | 7.26 | 7.13 | 7.00 | 57 |
| 58 | 7.39 | 7.25 | 7.13 | 7.00 | 6.88 | 6.76 | 6.65 | 6.53 | 6.43 | 6.32 | 6.22 | 58 |
| 59 | 6.28 | 6.18 | 6.09 | 5.99 | 5.91 | 5.82 | 5.73 | 5.65 | 5.57 | 5.49 | 5.41 | 59 |
| 60 | 5.19 | 5.12 | 5.05 | 4.99 | 4.93 | 4.87 | 4.81 | 4.75 | 4.69 | 4.64 | 4.58 | 60 |
| 61 | 4.11 | 4.07 | 4.03 | 3.99 | 3.95 | 3.91 | 3.87 | 3.84 | 3.80 | 3.76 | 3.73 | 61 |
| 62 | 3.06 | 3.04 | 3.02 | 2.99 | 2.97 | 2.95 | 2.93 | 2.91 | 2.88 | 2.86 | 2.84 | 62 |
| 63 | 2.03 | 2.02 | 2.01 | 2.00 | 1.99 | 1.98 | 1.97 | 1.96 | 1.95 | 1.94 | 1.93 | 63 |
| 64 | 1.01 | 1.00 | 1.00 | 1.00 | 1.00 | 0.99 | 0.99 | 0.99 | 0.99 | 0.98 | 0.98 | 64 |

## Table 11: Multipliers for loss of earnings to pension age 70 (males)

| Age at date of trial | Multiplier calculated with allowance for projected mortality from the 2008–based population projections and rate of return of | | | | | | | | | | | Age at date of trial |
|---|---|---|---|---|---|---|---|---|---|---|---|---|
| | -2.0% | -1.5% | -1.0% | -0.5% | 0.0% | 0.5% | 1.0% | 1.5% | 2.0% | 2.5% | 3.0% | |
| 16 | 93.75 | 80.18 | 69.05 | 59.87 | 52.26 | 45.93 | 40.62 | 36.16 | 32.38 | 29.18 | 26.44 | 16 |
| 17 | 90.86 | 77.97 | 67.35 | 58.57 | 51.26 | 45.15 | 40.02 | 35.69 | 32.02 | 28.89 | 26.22 | 17 |
| 18 | 88.04 | 75.80 | 65.68 | 57.27 | 50.25 | 44.37 | 39.41 | 35.22 | 31.65 | 28.61 | 25.99 | 18 |
| 19 | 85.28 | 73.67 | 64.03 | 55.99 | 49.26 | 43.59 | 38.81 | 34.74 | 31.28 | 28.31 | 25.76 | 19 |
| 20 | 82.58 | 71.57 | 62.39 | 54.71 | 48.26 | 42.81 | 38.19 | 34.26 | 30.90 | 28.01 | 25.52 | 20 |
| 21 | 79.94 | 69.50 | 60.78 | 53.44 | 47.26 | 42.03 | 37.58 | 33.78 | 30.52 | 27.71 | 25.28 | 21 |
| 22 | 77.35 | 67.47 | 59.17 | 52.18 | 46.27 | 41.24 | 36.95 | 33.28 | 30.12 | 27.39 | 25.03 | 22 |
| 23 | 74.81 | 65.46 | 57.59 | 50.93 | 45.27 | 40.45 | 36.32 | 32.78 | 29.72 | 27.07 | 24.77 | 23 |
| 24 | 72.32 | 63.49 | 56.02 | 49.68 | 44.27 | 39.65 | 35.68 | 32.26 | 29.31 | 26.74 | 24.50 | 24 |
| 25 | 69.89 | 61.55 | 54.47 | 48.44 | 43.28 | 38.85 | 35.04 | 31.75 | 28.89 | 26.40 | 24.23 | 25 |
| 26 | 67.50 | 59.64 | 52.93 | 47.20 | 42.29 | 38.05 | 34.39 | 31.22 | 28.47 | 26.06 | 23.95 | 26 |
| 27 | 65.17 | 57.76 | 51.42 | 45.98 | 41.29 | 37.25 | 33.74 | 30.69 | 28.03 | 25.70 | 23.66 | 27 |
| 28 | 62.88 | 55.91 | 49.92 | 44.76 | 40.30 | 36.44 | 33.08 | 30.15 | 27.59 | 25.34 | 23.36 | 28 |
| 29 | 60.64 | 54.08 | 48.43 | 43.54 | 39.31 | 35.63 | 32.41 | 29.61 | 27.14 | 24.97 | 23.05 | 29 |
| 30 | 58.45 | 52.29 | 46.96 | 42.34 | 38.32 | 34.81 | 31.74 | 29.05 | 26.68 | 24.59 | 22.74 | 30 |
| 31 | 56.31 | 50.53 | 45.51 | 41.14 | 37.33 | 34.00 | 31.07 | 28.49 | 26.22 | 24.20 | 22.42 | 31 |
| 32 | 54.21 | 48.80 | 44.08 | 39.96 | 36.35 | 33.18 | 30.39 | 27.93 | 25.75 | 23.81 | 22.09 | 32 |
| 33 | 52.17 | 47.10 | 42.67 | 38.79 | 35.37 | 32.37 | 29.71 | 27.36 | 25.27 | 23.41 | 21.75 | 33 |
| 34 | 50.16 | 45.43 | 41.28 | 37.62 | 34.40 | 31.55 | 29.02 | 26.78 | 24.79 | 23.00 | 21.41 | 34 |
| 35 | 48.20 | 43.78 | 39.89 | 36.46 | 33.42 | 30.73 | 28.33 | 26.20 | 24.29 | 22.58 | 21.05 | 35 |
| 36 | 46.28 | 42.16 | 38.53 | 35.31 | 32.45 | 29.90 | 27.63 | 25.60 | 23.79 | 22.15 | 20.69 | 36 |
| 37 | 44.39 | 40.57 | 37.18 | 34.16 | 31.47 | 29.07 | 26.93 | 25.00 | 23.27 | 21.72 | 20.31 | 37 |
| 38 | 42.55 | 39.00 | 35.84 | 33.02 | 30.50 | 28.24 | 26.21 | 24.39 | 22.75 | 21.27 | 19.93 | 38 |
| 39 | 40.74 | 37.45 | 34.51 | 31.88 | 29.52 | 27.40 | 25.49 | 23.77 | 22.21 | 20.80 | 19.53 | 39 |
| 40 | 38.96 | 35.92 | 33.20 | 30.75 | 28.55 | 26.56 | 24.76 | 23.14 | 21.67 | 20.33 | 19.12 | 40 |
| 41 | 37.23 | 34.42 | 31.90 | 29.63 | 27.57 | 25.71 | 24.03 | 22.50 | 21.11 | 19.85 | 18.70 | 41 |
| 42 | 35.53 | 32.95 | 30.62 | 28.51 | 26.60 | 24.87 | 23.29 | 21.86 | 20.55 | 19.36 | 18.26 | 42 |
| 43 | 33.86 | 31.50 | 29.35 | 27.40 | 25.63 | 24.02 | 22.55 | 21.20 | 19.98 | 18.85 | 17.82 | 43 |
| 44 | 32.23 | 30.07 | 28.10 | 26.30 | 24.66 | 23.17 | 21.80 | 20.54 | 19.39 | 18.34 | 17.36 | 44 |
| 45 | 30.64 | 28.66 | 26.86 | 25.21 | 23.70 | 22.31 | 21.04 | 19.87 | 18.80 | 17.81 | 16.90 | 45 |
| 46 | 29.08 | 27.28 | 25.63 | 24.12 | 22.73 | 21.45 | 20.28 | 19.19 | 18.19 | 17.27 | 16.41 | 46 |
| 47 | 27.55 | 25.92 | 24.42 | 23.04 | 21.77 | 20.59 | 19.51 | 18.51 | 17.58 | 16.72 | 15.92 | 47 |
| 48 | 26.06 | 24.58 | 23.22 | 21.97 | 20.81 | 19.73 | 18.74 | 17.81 | 16.95 | 16.16 | 15.41 | 48 |
| 49 | 24.60 | 23.27 | 22.04 | 20.91 | 19.85 | 18.87 | 17.96 | 17.11 | 16.32 | 15.58 | 14.90 | 49 |
| 50 | 23.17 | 21.98 | 20.88 | 19.85 | 18.90 | 18.01 | 17.18 | 16.40 | 15.68 | 15.00 | 14.37 | 50 |
| 51 | 21.78 | 20.72 | 19.73 | 18.81 | 17.95 | 17.14 | 16.39 | 15.69 | 15.02 | 14.40 | 13.82 | 51 |
| 52 | 20.42 | 19.48 | 18.60 | 17.78 | 17.00 | 16.28 | 15.60 | 14.96 | 14.36 | 13.80 | 13.27 | 52 |
| 53 | 19.09 | 18.26 | 17.48 | 16.75 | 16.06 | 15.41 | 14.81 | 14.23 | 13.69 | 13.18 | 12.70 | 53 |
| 54 | 17.79 | 17.06 | 16.38 | 15.73 | 15.12 | 14.55 | 14.01 | 13.49 | 13.01 | 12.55 | 12.11 | 54 |
| 55 | 16.51 | 15.88 | 15.29 | 14.72 | 14.19 | 13.68 | 13.20 | 12.75 | 12.31 | 11.90 | 11.52 | 55 |
| 56 | 15.27 | 14.73 | 14.21 | 13.72 | 13.25 | 12.81 | 12.39 | 11.99 | 11.61 | 11.25 | 10.90 | 56 |
| 57 | 14.05 | 13.59 | 13.14 | 12.72 | 12.32 | 11.94 | 11.57 | 11.22 | 10.89 | 10.57 | 10.27 | 57 |
| 58 | 12.85 | 12.46 | 12.09 | 11.73 | 11.39 | 11.06 | 10.75 | 10.45 | 10.16 | 9.88 | 9.62 | 58 |
| 59 | 11.68 | 11.35 | 11.04 | 10.74 | 10.45 | 10.17 | 9.91 | 9.66 | 9.41 | 9.18 | 8.95 | 59 |
| 60 | 10.52 | 10.26 | 10.00 | 9.75 | 9.51 | 9.28 | 9.06 | 8.85 | 8.65 | 8.45 | 8.26 | 60 |
| 61 | 9.39 | 9.18 | 8.97 | 8.77 | 8.58 | 8.39 | 8.21 | 8.04 | 7.87 | 7.71 | 7.55 | 61 |
| 62 | 8.28 | 8.11 | 7.95 | 7.79 | 7.64 | 7.49 | 7.35 | 7.21 | 7.07 | 6.94 | 6.82 | 62 |
| 63 | 7.19 | 7.06 | 6.94 | 6.82 | 6.70 | 6.59 | 6.48 | 6.37 | 6.27 | 6.16 | 6.06 | 63 |
| 64 | 6.12 | 6.03 | 5.94 | 5.85 | 5.77 | 5.68 | 5.60 | 5.52 | 5.44 | 5.36 | 5.29 | 64 |
| 65 | 5.07 | 5.01 | 4.95 | 4.89 | 4.83 | 4.77 | 4.71 | 4.65 | 4.60 | 4.54 | 4.49 | 65 |
| 66 | 4.04 | 4.00 | 3.96 | 3.92 | 3.88 | 3.84 | 3.81 | 3.77 | 3.73 | 3.70 | 3.66 | 66 |
| 67 | 3.02 | 3.00 | 2.97 | 2.95 | 2.93 | 2.91 | 2.89 | 2.86 | 2.84 | 2.82 | 2.80 | 67 |
| 68 | 2.01 | 2.00 | 1.99 | 1.98 | 1.97 | 1.96 | 1.95 | 1.94 | 1.93 | 1.92 | 1.91 | 68 |
| 69 | 1.00 | 1.00 | 1.00 | 0.99 | 0.99 | 0.99 | 0.99 | 0.98 | 0.98 | 0.98 | 0.98 | 69 |

## A8: The Ogden Tables

**Table 12: Multipliers for loss of earnings to pension age 70 (females)**

| Age at date of trial | Multiplier calculated with allowance for projected mortality from the 2008–based population projections and rate of return of | | | | | | | | | | | Age at date of trial |
|---|---|---|---|---|---|---|---|---|---|---|---|---|
| | -2.0% | -1.5% | -1.0% | -0.5% | 0.0% | 0.5% | 1.0% | 1.5% | 2.0% | 2.5% | 3.0% | |
| 16 | 95.47 | 81.58 | 70.18 | 60.79 | 53.01 | 46.54 | 41.12 | 36.57 | 32.73 | 29.47 | 26.68 | 16 |
| 17 | 92.56 | 79.35 | 68.47 | 59.48 | 52.01 | 45.76 | 40.53 | 36.11 | 32.37 | 29.19 | 26.46 | 17 |
| 18 | 89.71 | 77.16 | 66.79 | 58.18 | 51.00 | 44.99 | 39.93 | 35.65 | 32.01 | 28.91 | 26.24 | 18 |
| 19 | 86.92 | 75.00 | 65.12 | 56.89 | 50.00 | 44.21 | 39.32 | 35.18 | 31.64 | 28.62 | 26.02 | 19 |
| 20 | 84.18 | 72.88 | 63.47 | 55.61 | 49.00 | 43.43 | 38.71 | 34.70 | 31.27 | 28.32 | 25.79 | 20 |
| 21 | 81.50 | 70.79 | 61.84 | 54.33 | 48.00 | 42.64 | 38.09 | 34.21 | 30.88 | 28.02 | 25.55 | 21 |
| 22 | 78.87 | 68.73 | 60.22 | 53.06 | 47.00 | 41.85 | 37.47 | 33.72 | 30.49 | 27.71 | 25.30 | 22 |
| 23 | 76.30 | 66.70 | 58.62 | 51.79 | 46.00 | 41.06 | 36.84 | 33.22 | 30.09 | 27.39 | 25.04 | 23 |
| 24 | 73.77 | 64.70 | 57.04 | 50.53 | 44.99 | 40.26 | 36.20 | 32.71 | 29.68 | 27.06 | 24.78 | 24 |
| 25 | 71.30 | 62.73 | 55.47 | 49.28 | 43.99 | 39.46 | 35.56 | 32.19 | 29.27 | 26.73 | 24.51 | 25 |
| 26 | 68.88 | 60.80 | 53.91 | 48.03 | 42.99 | 38.65 | 34.91 | 31.67 | 28.85 | 26.39 | 24.23 | 26 |
| 27 | 66.51 | 58.89 | 52.38 | 46.80 | 41.99 | 37.85 | 34.26 | 31.13 | 28.41 | 26.03 | 23.95 | 27 |
| 28 | 64.19 | 57.01 | 50.86 | 45.56 | 40.99 | 37.03 | 33.59 | 30.60 | 27.98 | 25.68 | 23.65 | 28 |
| 29 | 61.91 | 55.17 | 49.36 | 44.34 | 39.99 | 36.22 | 32.93 | 30.05 | 27.53 | 25.31 | 23.35 | 29 |
| 30 | 59.68 | 53.35 | 47.87 | 43.12 | 39.00 | 35.40 | 32.25 | 29.50 | 27.07 | 24.93 | 23.04 | 30 |
| 31 | 57.50 | 51.56 | 46.40 | 41.91 | 38.00 | 34.58 | 31.58 | 28.94 | 26.61 | 24.55 | 22.72 | 31 |
| 32 | 55.37 | 49.79 | 44.94 | 40.71 | 37.01 | 33.75 | 30.89 | 28.37 | 26.13 | 24.15 | 22.39 | 32 |
| 33 | 53.27 | 48.06 | 43.51 | 39.52 | 36.01 | 32.92 | 30.20 | 27.79 | 25.65 | 23.75 | 22.05 | 33 |
| 34 | 51.22 | 46.35 | 42.08 | 38.33 | 35.02 | 32.09 | 29.50 | 27.21 | 25.16 | 23.34 | 21.70 | 34 |
| 35 | 49.22 | 44.67 | 40.67 | 37.14 | 34.02 | 31.26 | 28.80 | 26.61 | 24.66 | 22.91 | 21.35 | 35 |
| 36 | 47.25 | 43.02 | 39.28 | 35.97 | 33.03 | 30.42 | 28.09 | 26.01 | 24.15 | 22.48 | 20.98 | 36 |
| 37 | 45.32 | 41.39 | 37.90 | 34.80 | 32.04 | 29.58 | 27.37 | 25.40 | 23.63 | 22.04 | 20.60 | 37 |
| 38 | 43.44 | 39.79 | 36.54 | 33.64 | 31.05 | 28.73 | 26.65 | 24.78 | 23.10 | 21.58 | 20.21 | 38 |
| 39 | 41.59 | 38.21 | 35.19 | 32.48 | 30.06 | 27.88 | 25.92 | 24.16 | 22.56 | 21.12 | 19.81 | 39 |
| 40 | 39.78 | 36.66 | 33.85 | 31.34 | 29.07 | 27.03 | 25.19 | 23.52 | 22.01 | 20.65 | 19.40 | 40 |
| 41 | 38.01 | 35.13 | 32.53 | 30.20 | 28.08 | 26.18 | 24.45 | 22.88 | 21.46 | 20.16 | 18.98 | 41 |
| 42 | 36.28 | 33.62 | 31.23 | 29.06 | 27.10 | 25.32 | 23.70 | 22.23 | 20.89 | 19.66 | 18.54 | 42 |
| 43 | 34.58 | 32.14 | 29.94 | 27.93 | 26.11 | 24.46 | 22.95 | 21.57 | 20.31 | 19.15 | 18.10 | 43 |
| 44 | 32.92 | 30.69 | 28.66 | 26.81 | 25.13 | 23.59 | 22.19 | 20.90 | 19.72 | 18.63 | 17.64 | 44 |
| 45 | 31.29 | 29.26 | 27.40 | 25.70 | 24.15 | 22.73 | 21.42 | 20.22 | 19.12 | 18.10 | 17.17 | 45 |
| 46 | 29.70 | 27.85 | 26.15 | 24.60 | 23.17 | 21.86 | 20.65 | 19.54 | 18.51 | 17.56 | 16.68 | 46 |
| 47 | 28.15 | 26.47 | 24.92 | 23.50 | 22.19 | 20.99 | 19.87 | 18.84 | 17.89 | 17.01 | 16.19 | 47 |
| 48 | 26.63 | 25.11 | 23.71 | 22.41 | 21.22 | 20.11 | 19.09 | 18.14 | 17.26 | 16.44 | 15.68 | 48 |
| 49 | 25.14 | 23.77 | 22.51 | 21.34 | 20.25 | 19.24 | 18.30 | 17.43 | 16.62 | 15.86 | 15.16 | 49 |
| 50 | 23.68 | 22.46 | 21.32 | 20.27 | 19.28 | 18.36 | 17.51 | 16.71 | 15.97 | 15.27 | 14.62 | 50 |
| 51 | 22.26 | 21.17 | 20.15 | 19.20 | 18.31 | 17.49 | 16.71 | 15.99 | 15.31 | 14.67 | 14.07 | 51 |
| 52 | 20.87 | 19.90 | 18.99 | 18.14 | 17.35 | 16.60 | 15.91 | 15.25 | 14.63 | 14.05 | 13.51 | 52 |
| 53 | 19.50 | 18.65 | 17.85 | 17.09 | 16.39 | 15.72 | 15.09 | 14.50 | 13.95 | 13.42 | 12.93 | 53 |
| 54 | 18.17 | 17.42 | 16.72 | 16.05 | 15.43 | 14.83 | 14.28 | 13.75 | 13.25 | 12.78 | 12.33 | 54 |
| 55 | 16.86 | 16.21 | 15.60 | 15.02 | 14.47 | 13.95 | 13.45 | 12.99 | 12.54 | 12.12 | 11.72 | 55 |
| 56 | 15.58 | 15.02 | 14.49 | 13.99 | 13.51 | 13.05 | 12.62 | 12.21 | 11.82 | 11.45 | 11.09 | 56 |
| 57 | 14.33 | 13.85 | 13.40 | 12.96 | 12.55 | 12.16 | 11.78 | 11.43 | 11.09 | 10.76 | 10.45 | 57 |
| 58 | 13.10 | 12.70 | 12.31 | 11.95 | 11.59 | 11.26 | 10.94 | 10.63 | 10.34 | 10.05 | 9.78 | 58 |
| 59 | 11.89 | 11.56 | 11.24 | 10.93 | 10.64 | 10.35 | 10.08 | 9.82 | 9.57 | 9.33 | 9.10 | 59 |
| 60 | 10.71 | 10.44 | 10.18 | 9.92 | 9.68 | 9.44 | 9.22 | 9.00 | 8.79 | 8.59 | 8.39 | 60 |
| 61 | 9.55 | 9.33 | 9.12 | 8.92 | 8.72 | 8.53 | 8.35 | 8.17 | 8.00 | 7.83 | 7.67 | 61 |
| 62 | 8.42 | 8.25 | 8.08 | 7.92 | 7.76 | 7.61 | 7.46 | 7.32 | 7.18 | 7.05 | 6.92 | 62 |
| 63 | 7.30 | 7.17 | 7.05 | 6.92 | 6.80 | 6.69 | 6.57 | 6.47 | 6.36 | 6.25 | 6.15 | 63 |
| 64 | 6.21 | 6.12 | 6.02 | 5.93 | 5.85 | 5.76 | 5.68 | 5.59 | 5.51 | 5.44 | 5.36 | 64 |
| 65 | 5.14 | 5.07 | 5.01 | 4.95 | 4.89 | 4.83 | 4.77 | 4.71 | 4.65 | 4.60 | 4.54 | 65 |
| 66 | 4.08 | 4.04 | 4.00 | 3.96 | 3.92 | 3.88 | 3.85 | 3.81 | 3.77 | 3.74 | 3.70 | 66 |
| 67 | 3.04 | 3.02 | 3.00 | 2.98 | 2.95 | 2.93 | 2.91 | 2.89 | 2.87 | 2.85 | 2.83 | 67 |
| 68 | 2.02 | 2.01 | 2.00 | 1.99 | 1.98 | 1.97 | 1.96 | 1.95 | 1.94 | 1.93 | 1.92 | 68 |
| 69 | 1.00 | 1.00 | 1.00 | 1.00 | 0.99 | 0.99 | 0.99 | 0.99 | 0.98 | 0.98 | 0.98 | 69 |

## Table 13: Multipliers for loss of earnings to pension age 75 (males)

| Age at date of trial | Multiplier calculated with allowance for projected mortality from the 2008–based population projections and rate of return of | | | | | | | | | | | Age at date of trial |
|---|---|---|---|---|---|---|---|---|---|---|---|---|
| | -2.0% | -1.5% | -1.0% | -0.5% | 0.0% | 0.5% | 1.0% | 1.5% | 2.0% | 2.5% | 3.0% | |
| 16 | 107.05 | 90.16 | 76.55 | 65.51 | 56.51 | 49.13 | 43.04 | 37.99 | 33.77 | 30.23 | 27.24 | 16 |
| 17 | 103.88 | 87.79 | 74.76 | 64.17 | 55.50 | 48.37 | 42.46 | 37.55 | 33.44 | 29.97 | 27.04 | 17 |
| 18 | 100.78 | 85.45 | 73.01 | 62.84 | 54.49 | 47.60 | 41.88 | 37.10 | 33.10 | 29.71 | 26.84 | 18 |
| 19 | 97.75 | 83.16 | 71.27 | 61.52 | 53.49 | 46.83 | 41.29 | 36.65 | 32.75 | 29.44 | 26.63 | 19 |
| 20 | 94.79 | 80.91 | 69.55 | 60.21 | 52.48 | 46.06 | 40.70 | 36.20 | 32.40 | 29.17 | 26.42 | 20 |
| 21 | 91.89 | 78.69 | 67.86 | 58.91 | 51.48 | 45.29 | 40.11 | 35.74 | 32.04 | 28.89 | 26.20 | 21 |
| 22 | 89.04 | 76.51 | 66.17 | 57.61 | 50.48 | 44.52 | 39.50 | 35.27 | 31.67 | 28.61 | 25.98 | 22 |
| 23 | 86.25 | 74.36 | 64.51 | 56.32 | 49.48 | 43.74 | 38.89 | 34.79 | 31.30 | 28.31 | 25.74 | 23 |
| 24 | 83.52 | 72.24 | 62.86 | 55.04 | 48.48 | 42.95 | 38.28 | 34.31 | 30.92 | 28.01 | 25.51 | 24 |
| 25 | 80.85 | 70.15 | 61.23 | 53.76 | 47.48 | 42.17 | 37.66 | 33.82 | 30.53 | 27.70 | 25.26 | 25 |
| 26 | 78.23 | 68.10 | 59.63 | 52.50 | 46.48 | 41.38 | 37.04 | 33.32 | 30.14 | 27.39 | 25.01 | 26 |
| 27 | 75.67 | 66.09 | 58.03 | 51.24 | 45.48 | 40.59 | 36.41 | 32.82 | 29.74 | 27.07 | 24.75 | 27 |
| 28 | 73.16 | 64.10 | 56.46 | 49.99 | 44.48 | 39.79 | 35.77 | 32.31 | 29.32 | 26.74 | 24.48 | 28 |
| 29 | 70.70 | 62.14 | 54.90 | 48.74 | 43.49 | 38.99 | 35.13 | 31.79 | 28.91 | 26.40 | 24.21 | 29 |
| 30 | 68.29 | 60.22 | 53.35 | 47.50 | 42.49 | 38.19 | 34.48 | 31.27 | 28.48 | 26.05 | 23.93 | 30 |
| 31 | 65.95 | 58.33 | 51.84 | 46.28 | 41.50 | 37.39 | 33.83 | 30.74 | 28.05 | 25.70 | 23.64 | 31 |
| 32 | 63.65 | 56.48 | 50.34 | 45.06 | 40.52 | 36.59 | 33.18 | 30.21 | 27.62 | 25.35 | 23.35 | 32 |
| 33 | 61.41 | 54.66 | 48.86 | 43.86 | 39.54 | 35.79 | 32.52 | 29.67 | 27.18 | 24.98 | 23.05 | 33 |
| 34 | 59.22 | 52.87 | 47.40 | 42.66 | 38.56 | 34.98 | 31.86 | 29.13 | 26.73 | 24.61 | 22.74 | 34 |
| 35 | 57.06 | 51.11 | 45.95 | 41.47 | 37.58 | 34.17 | 31.19 | 28.58 | 26.27 | 24.23 | 22.43 | 35 |
| 36 | 54.96 | 49.37 | 44.52 | 40.29 | 36.60 | 33.36 | 30.52 | 28.02 | 25.80 | 23.84 | 22.10 | 36 |
| 37 | 52.90 | 47.67 | 43.11 | 39.12 | 35.62 | 32.55 | 29.84 | 27.45 | 25.33 | 23.45 | 21.77 | 37 |
| 38 | 50.87 | 45.98 | 41.70 | 37.95 | 34.64 | 31.73 | 29.16 | 26.87 | 24.85 | 23.04 | 21.42 | 38 |
| 39 | 48.89 | 44.33 | 40.31 | 36.78 | 33.67 | 30.91 | 28.46 | 26.29 | 24.35 | 22.62 | 21.07 | 39 |
| 40 | 46.95 | 42.69 | 38.94 | 35.62 | 32.69 | 30.08 | 27.76 | 25.70 | 23.85 | 22.19 | 20.70 | 40 |
| 41 | 45.05 | 41.09 | 37.58 | 34.47 | 31.71 | 29.25 | 27.06 | 25.10 | 23.34 | 21.75 | 20.33 | 41 |
| 42 | 43.19 | 39.51 | 36.24 | 33.33 | 30.74 | 28.42 | 26.35 | 24.49 | 22.81 | 21.31 | 19.95 | 42 |
| 43 | 41.37 | 37.96 | 34.91 | 32.20 | 29.77 | 27.59 | 25.63 | 23.87 | 22.29 | 20.85 | 19.55 | 43 |
| 44 | 39.59 | 36.43 | 33.60 | 31.07 | 28.80 | 26.76 | 24.91 | 23.25 | 21.75 | 20.39 | 19.15 | 44 |
| 45 | 37.85 | 34.93 | 32.31 | 29.95 | 27.83 | 25.92 | 24.19 | 22.62 | 21.20 | 19.91 | 18.73 | 45 |
| 46 | 36.14 | 33.45 | 31.03 | 28.84 | 26.87 | 25.08 | 23.46 | 21.98 | 20.64 | 19.42 | 18.31 | 46 |
| 47 | 34.47 | 32.00 | 29.76 | 27.74 | 25.90 | 24.24 | 22.72 | 21.34 | 20.08 | 18.93 | 17.87 | 47 |
| 48 | 32.84 | 30.58 | 28.52 | 26.65 | 24.95 | 23.39 | 21.98 | 20.69 | 19.50 | 18.42 | 17.42 | 48 |
| 49 | 31.25 | 29.18 | 27.29 | 25.56 | 23.99 | 22.55 | 21.24 | 20.03 | 18.92 | 17.90 | 16.97 | 49 |
| 50 | 29.70 | 27.81 | 26.07 | 24.49 | 23.04 | 21.71 | 20.49 | 19.37 | 18.33 | 17.38 | 16.50 | 50 |
| 51 | 28.18 | 26.46 | 24.88 | 23.43 | 22.10 | 20.87 | 19.74 | 18.70 | 17.74 | 16.85 | 16.03 | 51 |
| 52 | 26.70 | 25.14 | 23.70 | 22.38 | 21.16 | 20.03 | 18.99 | 18.03 | 17.13 | 16.31 | 15.54 | 52 |
| 53 | 25.26 | 23.85 | 22.54 | 21.34 | 20.23 | 19.19 | 18.24 | 17.35 | 16.52 | 15.76 | 15.04 | 53 |
| 54 | 23.85 | 22.58 | 21.40 | 20.31 | 19.30 | 18.35 | 17.48 | 16.66 | 15.90 | 15.20 | 14.53 | 54 |
| 55 | 22.48 | 21.34 | 20.28 | 19.29 | 18.37 | 17.52 | 16.72 | 15.98 | 15.28 | 14.63 | 14.02 | 55 |
| 56 | 21.13 | 20.12 | 19.17 | 18.28 | 17.46 | 16.68 | 15.96 | 15.28 | 14.64 | 14.05 | 13.49 | 56 |
| 57 | 19.82 | 18.92 | 18.07 | 17.28 | 16.54 | 15.85 | 15.19 | 14.58 | 14.00 | 13.46 | 12.95 | 57 |
| 58 | 18.53 | 17.74 | 16.99 | 16.29 | 15.63 | 15.00 | 14.42 | 13.86 | 13.34 | 12.85 | 12.39 | 58 |
| 59 | 17.27 | 16.57 | 15.91 | 15.29 | 14.71 | 14.16 | 13.63 | 13.14 | 12.67 | 12.23 | 11.81 | 59 |
| 60 | 16.03 | 15.42 | 14.85 | 14.30 | 13.79 | 13.30 | 12.84 | 12.40 | 11.99 | 11.60 | 11.22 | 60 |
| 61 | 14.81 | 14.29 | 13.79 | 13.32 | 12.87 | 12.45 | 12.04 | 11.66 | 11.29 | 10.95 | 10.61 | 61 |
| 62 | 13.62 | 13.18 | 12.75 | 12.35 | 11.96 | 11.59 | 11.24 | 10.91 | 10.59 | 10.28 | 9.99 | 62 |
| 63 | 12.46 | 12.09 | 11.73 | 11.38 | 11.05 | 10.74 | 10.44 | 10.15 | 9.88 | 9.61 | 9.36 | 63 |
| 64 | 11.33 | 11.02 | 10.72 | 10.43 | 10.15 | 9.89 | 9.63 | 9.39 | 9.15 | 8.93 | 8.71 | 64 |
| 65 | 10.22 | 9.97 | 9.72 | 9.48 | 9.25 | 9.03 | 8.82 | 8.61 | 8.42 | 8.23 | 8.04 | 65 |
| 66 | 9.14 | 8.93 | 8.73 | 8.54 | 8.36 | 8.18 | 8.00 | 7.83 | 7.67 | 7.52 | 7.36 | 66 |
| 67 | 8.08 | 7.92 | 7.76 | 7.61 | 7.46 | 7.32 | 7.18 | 7.04 | 6.91 | 6.79 | 6.66 | 67 |
| 68 | 7.04 | 6.91 | 6.79 | 6.67 | 6.56 | 6.45 | 6.34 | 6.24 | 6.14 | 6.04 | 5.94 | 68 |
| 69 | 6.01 | 5.92 | 5.83 | 5.74 | 5.66 | 5.58 | 5.50 | 5.42 | 5.34 | 5.27 | 5.19 | 69 |
| 70 | 4.99 | 4.93 | 4.87 | 4.81 | 4.75 | 4.69 | 4.63 | 4.58 | 4.52 | 4.47 | 4.42 | 70 |
| 71 | 3.98 | 3.94 | 3.90 | 3.86 | 3.83 | 3.79 | 3.75 | 3.72 | 3.68 | 3.65 | 3.61 | 71 |
| 72 | 2.98 | 2.96 | 2.94 | 2.92 | 2.89 | 2.87 | 2.85 | 2.83 | 2.81 | 2.79 | 2.77 | 72 |
| 73 | 1.99 | 1.98 | 1.97 | 1.96 | 1.95 | 1.94 | 1.93 | 1.92 | 1.91 | 1.90 | 1.89 | 73 |
| 74 | 1.00 | 0.99 | 0.99 | 0.99 | 0.99 | 0.98 | 0.98 | 0.98 | 0.98 | 0.97 | 0.97 | 74 |

## Table 14: Multipliers for loss of earnings to pension age 75 (females)

| Age at date of trial | \-2.0% | \-1.5% | \-1.0% | \-0.5% | 0.0% | 0.5% | 1.0% | 1.5% | 2.0% | 2.5% | 3.0% | Age at date of trial |
|---|---|---|---|---|---|---|---|---|---|---|---|---|
| | Multiplier calculated with allowance for projected mortality from the 2008–based population projections and rate of return of | | | | | | | | | | | |
| 16 | 109.63 | 92.19 | 78.15 | 66.79 | 57.53 | 49.95 | 43.70 | 38.52 | 34.21 | 30.59 | 27.53 | 16 |
| 17 | 106.42 | 89.80 | 76.36 | 65.44 | 56.52 | 49.19 | 43.13 | 38.09 | 33.88 | 30.34 | 27.34 | 17 |
| 18 | 103.28 | 87.44 | 74.59 | 64.11 | 55.51 | 48.43 | 42.55 | 37.65 | 33.55 | 30.08 | 27.15 | 18 |
| 19 | 100.20 | 85.12 | 72.84 | 62.78 | 54.51 | 47.66 | 41.97 | 37.21 | 33.21 | 29.82 | 26.95 | 19 |
| 20 | 97.19 | 82.84 | 71.11 | 61.47 | 53.50 | 46.90 | 41.38 | 36.76 | 32.86 | 29.56 | 26.74 | 20 |
| 21 | 94.24 | 80.59 | 69.39 | 60.15 | 52.50 | 46.13 | 40.79 | 36.30 | 32.51 | 29.28 | 26.53 | 21 |
| 22 | 91.35 | 78.38 | 67.69 | 58.85 | 51.49 | 45.35 | 40.19 | 35.84 | 32.15 | 29.00 | 26.31 | 22 |
| 23 | 88.51 | 76.19 | 66.01 | 57.55 | 50.49 | 44.57 | 39.58 | 35.37 | 31.78 | 28.71 | 26.08 | 23 |
| 24 | 85.73 | 74.04 | 64.34 | 56.25 | 49.48 | 43.79 | 38.97 | 34.89 | 31.40 | 28.42 | 25.85 | 24 |
| 25 | 83.01 | 71.93 | 62.69 | 54.97 | 48.48 | 43.00 | 38.35 | 34.40 | 31.02 | 28.12 | 25.61 | 25 |
| 26 | 80.34 | 69.84 | 61.06 | 53.69 | 47.47 | 42.21 | 37.73 | 33.91 | 30.63 | 27.81 | 25.37 | 26 |
| 27 | 77.73 | 67.79 | 59.45 | 52.42 | 46.47 | 41.41 | 37.10 | 33.41 | 30.23 | 27.49 | 25.11 | 27 |
| 28 | 75.17 | 65.77 | 57.85 | 51.15 | 45.46 | 40.62 | 36.47 | 32.90 | 29.83 | 27.17 | 24.85 | 28 |
| 29 | 72.67 | 63.79 | 56.27 | 49.90 | 44.46 | 39.82 | 35.83 | 32.39 | 29.42 | 26.84 | 24.59 | 29 |
| 30 | 70.22 | 61.83 | 54.71 | 48.65 | 43.46 | 39.01 | 35.18 | 31.87 | 29.00 | 26.50 | 24.31 | 30 |
| 31 | 67.82 | 59.91 | 53.17 | 47.40 | 42.46 | 38.20 | 34.53 | 31.34 | 28.57 | 26.15 | 24.03 | 31 |
| 32 | 65.47 | 58.01 | 51.64 | 46.17 | 41.46 | 37.40 | 33.87 | 30.81 | 28.13 | 25.79 | 23.74 | 32 |
| 33 | 63.16 | 56.15 | 50.13 | 44.94 | 40.46 | 36.58 | 33.21 | 30.26 | 27.69 | 25.43 | 23.44 | 33 |
| 34 | 60.91 | 54.31 | 48.63 | 43.72 | 39.47 | 35.77 | 32.54 | 29.72 | 27.24 | 25.06 | 23.13 | 34 |
| 35 | 58.70 | 52.51 | 47.15 | 42.51 | 38.47 | 34.95 | 31.86 | 29.16 | 26.78 | 24.68 | 22.82 | 35 |
| 36 | 56.54 | 50.73 | 45.69 | 41.30 | 37.47 | 34.12 | 31.18 | 28.59 | 26.31 | 24.29 | 22.49 | 36 |
| 37 | 54.42 | 48.98 | 44.24 | 40.10 | 36.48 | 33.30 | 30.49 | 28.02 | 25.83 | 23.89 | 22.16 | 37 |
| 38 | 52.35 | 47.26 | 42.81 | 38.91 | 35.49 | 32.47 | 29.80 | 27.44 | 25.34 | 23.48 | 21.81 | 38 |
| 39 | 50.32 | 45.57 | 41.40 | 37.73 | 34.49 | 31.64 | 29.10 | 26.85 | 24.85 | 23.06 | 21.46 | 39 |
| 40 | 48.33 | 43.90 | 40.00 | 36.55 | 33.50 | 30.80 | 28.40 | 26.26 | 24.35 | 22.63 | 21.10 | 40 |
| 41 | 46.38 | 42.26 | 38.61 | 35.38 | 32.51 | 29.96 | 27.69 | 25.65 | 23.83 | 22.20 | 20.73 | 41 |
| 42 | 44.48 | 40.64 | 37.24 | 34.22 | 31.53 | 29.12 | 26.97 | 25.04 | 23.31 | 21.75 | 20.34 | 42 |
| 43 | 42.61 | 39.06 | 35.89 | 33.06 | 30.54 | 28.28 | 26.25 | 24.42 | 22.78 | 21.29 | 19.95 | 43 |
| 44 | 40.79 | 37.49 | 34.55 | 31.92 | 29.55 | 27.43 | 25.52 | 23.79 | 22.24 | 20.82 | 19.55 | 44 |
| 45 | 39.00 | 35.96 | 33.23 | 30.78 | 28.57 | 26.58 | 24.79 | 23.16 | 21.69 | 20.35 | 19.13 | 45 |
| 46 | 37.26 | 34.45 | 31.93 | 29.65 | 27.59 | 25.73 | 24.05 | 22.52 | 21.13 | 19.86 | 18.71 | 46 |
| 47 | 35.55 | 32.97 | 30.64 | 28.53 | 26.62 | 24.88 | 23.30 | 21.87 | 20.56 | 19.36 | 18.27 | 47 |
| 48 | 33.88 | 31.51 | 29.37 | 27.42 | 25.64 | 24.03 | 22.56 | 21.21 | 19.98 | 18.86 | 17.83 | 48 |
| 49 | 32.25 | 30.08 | 28.11 | 26.31 | 24.67 | 23.18 | 21.81 | 20.55 | 19.40 | 18.34 | 17.37 | 49 |
| 50 | 30.66 | 28.68 | 26.87 | 25.22 | 23.71 | 22.32 | 21.05 | 19.88 | 18.81 | 17.82 | 16.90 | 50 |
| 51 | 29.10 | 27.30 | 25.65 | 24.14 | 22.75 | 21.47 | 20.29 | 19.20 | 18.20 | 17.28 | 16.42 | 51 |
| 52 | 27.58 | 25.94 | 24.44 | 23.06 | 21.78 | 20.61 | 19.52 | 18.52 | 17.59 | 16.73 | 15.93 | 52 |
| 53 | 26.08 | 24.61 | 23.25 | 21.99 | 20.83 | 19.75 | 18.75 | 17.83 | 16.97 | 16.17 | 15.43 | 53 |
| 54 | 24.63 | 23.30 | 22.07 | 20.93 | 19.87 | 18.89 | 17.98 | 17.13 | 16.34 | 15.60 | 14.91 | 54 |
| 55 | 23.20 | 22.01 | 20.91 | 19.88 | 18.92 | 18.03 | 17.20 | 16.42 | 15.69 | 15.02 | 14.38 | 55 |
| 56 | 21.81 | 20.75 | 19.76 | 18.83 | 17.97 | 17.16 | 16.41 | 15.70 | 15.04 | 14.42 | 13.84 | 56 |
| 57 | 20.45 | 19.50 | 18.62 | 17.80 | 17.02 | 16.30 | 15.62 | 14.98 | 14.38 | 13.81 | 13.28 | 57 |
| 58 | 19.11 | 18.28 | 17.50 | 16.77 | 16.08 | 15.43 | 14.82 | 14.25 | 13.70 | 13.19 | 12.71 | 58 |
| 59 | 17.80 | 17.07 | 16.39 | 15.74 | 15.13 | 14.56 | 14.02 | 13.50 | 13.02 | 12.56 | 12.12 | 59 |
| 60 | 16.52 | 15.88 | 15.29 | 14.72 | 14.19 | 13.68 | 13.20 | 12.75 | 12.32 | 11.91 | 11.52 | 60 |
| 61 | 15.26 | 14.71 | 14.20 | 13.71 | 13.24 | 12.80 | 12.38 | 11.98 | 11.60 | 11.24 | 10.89 | 61 |
| 62 | 14.03 | 13.56 | 13.12 | 12.70 | 12.30 | 11.92 | 11.56 | 11.21 | 10.88 | 10.56 | 10.26 | 62 |
| 63 | 12.83 | 12.43 | 12.06 | 11.70 | 11.36 | 11.04 | 10.72 | 10.42 | 10.14 | 9.86 | 9.60 | 63 |
| 64 | 11.65 | 11.33 | 11.01 | 10.71 | 10.43 | 10.15 | 9.89 | 9.63 | 9.39 | 9.16 | 8.93 | 64 |
| 65 | 10.50 | 10.24 | 9.98 | 9.73 | 9.50 | 9.27 | 9.05 | 8.84 | 8.63 | 8.43 | 8.24 | 65 |
| 66 | 9.38 | 9.16 | 8.96 | 8.76 | 8.57 | 8.38 | 8.20 | 8.03 | 7.86 | 7.70 | 7.54 | 66 |
| 67 | 8.28 | 8.11 | 7.95 | 7.79 | 7.64 | 7.49 | 7.35 | 7.21 | 7.07 | 6.94 | 6.81 | 67 |
| 68 | 7.19 | 7.07 | 6.94 | 6.82 | 6.70 | 6.59 | 6.48 | 6.37 | 6.27 | 6.17 | 6.07 | 68 |
| 69 | 6.13 | 6.04 | 5.95 | 5.86 | 5.77 | 5.69 | 5.60 | 5.52 | 5.44 | 5.37 | 5.29 | 69 |
| 70 | 5.08 | 5.01 | 4.95 | 4.89 | 4.83 | 4.77 | 4.71 | 4.66 | 4.60 | 4.55 | 4.49 | 70 |
| 71 | 4.04 | 4.00 | 3.96 | 3.92 | 3.88 | 3.85 | 3.81 | 3.77 | 3.73 | 3.70 | 3.66 | 71 |
| 72 | 3.02 | 3.00 | 2.97 | 2.95 | 2.93 | 2.91 | 2.89 | 2.86 | 2.84 | 2.82 | 2.80 | 72 |
| 73 | 2.01 | 2.00 | 1.99 | 1.98 | 1.97 | 1.96 | 1.95 | 1.94 | 1.93 | 1.92 | 1.91 | 73 |
| 74 | 1.00 | 1.00 | 1.00 | 0.99 | 0.99 | 0.99 | 0.99 | 0.98 | 0.98 | 0.98 | 0.98 | 74 |

## Table 15: Multipliers for loss of pension commencing age 50 (males)

| Age at date of trial | Multiplier calculated with allowance for projected mortality from the 2008–based population projections and rate of return of | | | | | | | | | | | Age at date of trial |
|---|---|---|---|---|---|---|---|---|---|---|---|---|
| | -2.0% | -1.5% | -1.0% | -0.5% | 0.0% | 0.5% | 1.0% | 1.5% | 2.0% | 2.5% | 3.0% | |
| 0 | 179.64 | 121.70 | 83.09 | 57.16 | 39.61 | 27.64 | 19.42 | 13.74 | 9.78 | 7.00 | 5.04 | 0 |
| 1 | 176.24 | 120.05 | 82.40 | 56.99 | 39.70 | 27.85 | 19.67 | 13.99 | 10.01 | 7.20 | 5.21 | 1 |
| 2 | 172.05 | 117.83 | 81.32 | 56.54 | 39.59 | 27.92 | 19.83 | 14.17 | 10.19 | 7.37 | 5.36 | 2 |
| 3 | 167.93 | 115.64 | 80.24 | 56.09 | 39.49 | 27.99 | 19.98 | 14.35 | 10.37 | 7.54 | 5.51 | 3 |
| 4 | 163.90 | 113.48 | 79.16 | 55.63 | 39.37 | 28.06 | 20.13 | 14.53 | 10.56 | 7.72 | 5.67 | 4 |
| 5 | 159.97 | 111.36 | 78.10 | 55.18 | 39.26 | 28.12 | 20.28 | 14.72 | 10.75 | 7.89 | 5.83 | 5 |
| 6 | 156.12 | 109.27 | 77.05 | 54.73 | 39.14 | 28.19 | 20.43 | 14.91 | 10.94 | 8.08 | 5.99 | 6 |
| 7 | 152.36 | 107.22 | 76.01 | 54.28 | 39.03 | 28.25 | 20.59 | 15.10 | 11.14 | 8.26 | 6.16 | 7 |
| 8 | 148.69 | 105.21 | 74.99 | 53.83 | 38.91 | 28.32 | 20.74 | 15.29 | 11.33 | 8.45 | 6.34 | 8 |
| 9 | 145.10 | 103.23 | 73.98 | 53.39 | 38.80 | 28.38 | 20.90 | 15.48 | 11.54 | 8.65 | 6.52 | 9 |
| 10 | 141.59 | 101.28 | 72.97 | 52.95 | 38.68 | 28.44 | 21.05 | 15.68 | 11.74 | 8.84 | 6.70 | 10 |
| 11 | 138.17 | 99.37 | 71.98 | 52.51 | 38.56 | 28.51 | 21.21 | 15.87 | 11.95 | 9.05 | 6.89 | 11 |
| 12 | 134.83 | 97.50 | 71.01 | 52.07 | 38.44 | 28.57 | 21.36 | 16.07 | 12.16 | 9.26 | 7.08 | 12 |
| 13 | 131.57 | 95.66 | 70.04 | 51.64 | 38.33 | 28.63 | 21.52 | 16.28 | 12.38 | 9.47 | 7.28 | 13 |
| 14 | 128.40 | 93.86 | 69.10 | 51.21 | 38.21 | 28.70 | 21.68 | 16.48 | 12.60 | 9.69 | 7.48 | 14 |
| 15 | 125.31 | 92.10 | 68.16 | 50.79 | 38.10 | 28.76 | 21.85 | 16.69 | 12.82 | 9.91 | 7.69 | 15 |
| 16 | 122.29 | 90.37 | 67.24 | 50.38 | 37.99 | 28.83 | 22.01 | 16.90 | 13.05 | 10.14 | 7.91 | 16 |
| 17 | 119.35 | 88.68 | 66.34 | 49.96 | 37.88 | 28.89 | 22.17 | 17.12 | 13.29 | 10.37 | 8.13 | 17 |
| 18 | 116.49 | 87.02 | 65.46 | 49.56 | 37.77 | 28.96 | 22.34 | 17.34 | 13.53 | 10.61 | 8.36 | 18 |
| 19 | 113.71 | 85.41 | 64.59 | 49.16 | 37.67 | 29.03 | 22.52 | 17.56 | 13.77 | 10.86 | 8.60 | 19 |
| 20 | 111.01 | 83.83 | 63.74 | 48.78 | 37.57 | 29.11 | 22.69 | 17.79 | 14.02 | 11.11 | 8.85 | 20 |
| 21 | 108.37 | 82.28 | 62.90 | 48.39 | 37.46 | 29.18 | 22.87 | 18.02 | 14.28 | 11.37 | 9.10 | 21 |
| 22 | 105.78 | 80.76 | 62.06 | 48.00 | 37.36 | 29.26 | 23.04 | 18.25 | 14.53 | 11.63 | 9.36 | 22 |
| 23 | 103.25 | 79.25 | 61.24 | 47.62 | 37.26 | 29.33 | 23.22 | 18.49 | 14.80 | 11.90 | 9.62 | 23 |
| 24 | 100.79 | 77.78 | 60.42 | 47.24 | 37.16 | 29.40 | 23.40 | 18.73 | 15.06 | 12.18 | 9.90 | 24 |
| 25 | 98.39 | 76.35 | 59.63 | 46.86 | 37.06 | 29.48 | 23.58 | 18.97 | 15.34 | 12.46 | 10.18 | 25 |
| 26 | 96.06 | 74.95 | 58.85 | 46.50 | 36.96 | 29.56 | 23.77 | 19.22 | 15.62 | 12.76 | 10.47 | 26 |
| 27 | 93.80 | 73.57 | 58.08 | 46.14 | 36.87 | 29.64 | 23.96 | 19.47 | 15.90 | 13.06 | 10.77 | 27 |
| 28 | 91.57 | 72.22 | 57.32 | 45.77 | 36.77 | 29.71 | 24.14 | 19.72 | 16.19 | 13.36 | 11.08 | 28 |
| 29 | 89.39 | 70.88 | 56.56 | 45.41 | 36.68 | 29.79 | 24.33 | 19.98 | 16.49 | 13.67 | 11.39 | 29 |
| 30 | 87.27 | 69.58 | 55.82 | 45.06 | 36.58 | 29.87 | 24.52 | 20.24 | 16.79 | 13.99 | 11.72 | 30 |
| 31 | 85.23 | 68.32 | 55.10 | 44.71 | 36.50 | 29.96 | 24.72 | 20.51 | 17.10 | 14.33 | 12.05 | 31 |
| 32 | 83.24 | 67.09 | 54.41 | 44.38 | 36.42 | 30.05 | 24.93 | 20.79 | 17.42 | 14.67 | 12.40 | 32 |
| 33 | 81.32 | 65.90 | 53.73 | 44.06 | 36.35 | 30.15 | 25.14 | 21.07 | 17.75 | 15.02 | 12.77 | 33 |
| 34 | 79.44 | 64.72 | 53.05 | 43.74 | 36.27 | 30.24 | 25.35 | 21.36 | 18.08 | 15.38 | 13.14 | 34 |
| 35 | 77.60 | 63.57 | 52.39 | 43.42 | 36.20 | 30.34 | 25.56 | 21.65 | 18.42 | 15.75 | 13.52 | 35 |
| 36 | 75.82 | 62.44 | 51.74 | 43.11 | 36.13 | 30.44 | 25.78 | 21.95 | 18.77 | 16.13 | 13.92 | 36 |
| 37 | 74.08 | 61.34 | 51.09 | 42.81 | 36.06 | 30.54 | 26.00 | 22.25 | 19.12 | 16.51 | 14.32 | 37 |
| 38 | 72.37 | 60.25 | 50.46 | 42.50 | 35.99 | 30.64 | 26.22 | 22.55 | 19.49 | 16.91 | 14.74 | 38 |
| 39 | 70.70 | 59.18 | 49.83 | 42.19 | 35.92 | 30.74 | 26.45 | 22.86 | 19.85 | 17.32 | 15.17 | 39 |
| 40 | 69.07 | 58.13 | 49.21 | 41.89 | 35.85 | 30.85 | 26.67 | 23.18 | 20.23 | 17.74 | 15.62 | 40 |
| 41 | 67.49 | 57.11 | 48.61 | 41.60 | 35.79 | 30.96 | 26.91 | 23.50 | 20.62 | 18.17 | 16.08 | 41 |
| 42 | 65.95 | 56.11 | 48.01 | 41.31 | 35.73 | 31.07 | 27.14 | 23.83 | 21.01 | 18.61 | 16.55 | 42 |
| 43 | 64.46 | 55.14 | 47.44 | 41.03 | 35.68 | 31.18 | 27.39 | 24.16 | 21.42 | 19.07 | 17.04 | 43 |
| 44 | 63.01 | 54.19 | 46.87 | 40.76 | 35.63 | 31.30 | 27.63 | 24.51 | 21.84 | 19.54 | 17.55 | 44 |
| 45 | 61.60 | 53.26 | 46.32 | 40.49 | 35.58 | 31.42 | 27.89 | 24.86 | 22.26 | 20.02 | 18.07 | 45 |
| 46 | 60.22 | 52.36 | 45.77 | 40.23 | 35.54 | 31.55 | 28.14 | 25.22 | 22.70 | 20.52 | 18.62 | 46 |
| 47 | 58.88 | 51.47 | 45.24 | 39.98 | 35.50 | 31.68 | 28.41 | 25.59 | 23.15 | 21.03 | 19.18 | 47 |
| 48 | 57.59 | 50.62 | 44.73 | 39.73 | 35.47 | 31.83 | 28.69 | 25.97 | 23.62 | 21.56 | 19.76 | 48 |
| 49 | 56.34 | 49.79 | 44.23 | 39.50 | 35.46 | 31.98 | 28.97 | 26.37 | 24.10 | 22.11 | 20.37 | 49 |
| 50 | 55.14 | 48.99 | 43.76 | 39.29 | 35.45 | 32.14 | 29.27 | 26.78 | 24.60 | 22.69 | 21.01 | 50 |

## Table 16: Multipliers for loss of pension commencing age 50 (females)

| Age at date of trial | Multiplier calculated with allowance for projected mortality from the 2008–based population projections and rate of return of | | | | | | | | | | | Age at date of trial |
|---|---|---|---|---|---|---|---|---|---|---|---|---|
| | -2.0% | -1.5% | -1.0% | -0.5% | 0.0% | 0.5% | 1.0% | 1.5% | 2.0% | 2.5% | 3.0% | |
| 0 | 199.59 | 134.37 | 91.19 | 62.37 | 42.98 | 29.85 | 20.87 | 14.70 | 10.42 | 7.43 | 5.33 | 0 |
| 1 | 195.74 | 132.49 | 90.40 | 62.16 | 43.07 | 30.06 | 21.13 | 14.95 | 10.65 | 7.64 | 5.51 | 1 |
| 2 | 191.18 | 130.11 | 89.25 | 61.69 | 42.97 | 30.15 | 21.30 | 15.16 | 10.85 | 7.82 | 5.67 | 2 |
| 3 | 186.71 | 127.75 | 88.10 | 61.23 | 42.87 | 30.24 | 21.48 | 15.36 | 11.05 | 8.00 | 5.83 | 3 |
| 4 | 182.34 | 125.44 | 86.97 | 60.76 | 42.77 | 30.32 | 21.65 | 15.56 | 11.26 | 8.19 | 6.00 | 4 |
| 5 | 178.06 | 123.16 | 85.85 | 60.30 | 42.67 | 30.41 | 21.82 | 15.77 | 11.46 | 8.39 | 6.17 | 5 |
| 6 | 173.88 | 120.92 | 84.74 | 59.84 | 42.56 | 30.49 | 22.00 | 15.97 | 11.67 | 8.58 | 6.35 | 6 |
| 7 | 169.79 | 118.72 | 83.65 | 59.38 | 42.46 | 30.58 | 22.17 | 16.18 | 11.89 | 8.78 | 6.53 | 7 |
| 8 | 165.80 | 116.55 | 82.56 | 58.92 | 42.36 | 30.66 | 22.35 | 16.40 | 12.10 | 8.99 | 6.72 | 8 |
| 9 | 161.89 | 114.43 | 81.49 | 58.47 | 42.25 | 30.75 | 22.53 | 16.61 | 12.33 | 9.20 | 6.91 | 9 |
| 10 | 158.08 | 112.34 | 80.43 | 58.02 | 42.15 | 30.83 | 22.70 | 16.83 | 12.55 | 9.42 | 7.11 | 10 |
| 11 | 154.36 | 110.29 | 79.39 | 57.57 | 42.04 | 30.92 | 22.89 | 17.05 | 12.78 | 9.64 | 7.31 | 11 |
| 12 | 150.73 | 108.28 | 78.36 | 57.12 | 41.94 | 31.00 | 23.07 | 17.27 | 13.01 | 9.86 | 7.52 | 12 |
| 13 | 147.17 | 106.30 | 77.34 | 56.68 | 41.83 | 31.08 | 23.25 | 17.50 | 13.25 | 10.09 | 7.73 | 13 |
| 14 | 143.71 | 104.36 | 76.34 | 56.24 | 41.73 | 31.17 | 23.43 | 17.73 | 13.49 | 10.33 | 7.95 | 14 |
| 15 | 140.33 | 102.45 | 75.35 | 55.81 | 41.62 | 31.25 | 23.62 | 17.96 | 13.74 | 10.57 | 8.18 | 15 |
| 16 | 137.02 | 100.58 | 74.37 | 55.38 | 41.52 | 31.34 | 23.81 | 18.20 | 13.99 | 10.82 | 8.41 | 16 |
| 17 | 133.80 | 98.75 | 73.41 | 54.95 | 41.42 | 31.42 | 24.00 | 18.44 | 14.25 | 11.07 | 8.65 | 17 |
| 18 | 130.66 | 96.95 | 72.46 | 54.53 | 41.32 | 31.51 | 24.19 | 18.68 | 14.51 | 11.33 | 8.90 | 18 |
| 19 | 127.60 | 95.19 | 71.52 | 54.11 | 41.22 | 31.60 | 24.38 | 18.92 | 14.78 | 11.60 | 9.16 | 19 |
| 20 | 124.61 | 93.47 | 70.61 | 53.70 | 41.12 | 31.69 | 24.58 | 19.18 | 15.05 | 11.87 | 9.42 | 20 |
| 21 | 121.70 | 91.78 | 69.70 | 53.30 | 41.03 | 31.78 | 24.78 | 19.43 | 15.32 | 12.15 | 9.69 | 21 |
| 22 | 118.85 | 90.11 | 68.80 | 52.89 | 40.93 | 31.87 | 24.97 | 19.69 | 15.61 | 12.44 | 9.97 | 22 |
| 23 | 116.05 | 88.47 | 67.91 | 52.48 | 40.82 | 31.96 | 25.17 | 19.94 | 15.89 | 12.73 | 10.25 | 23 |
| 24 | 113.32 | 86.85 | 67.03 | 52.08 | 40.72 | 32.05 | 25.37 | 20.21 | 16.18 | 13.03 | 10.54 | 24 |
| 25 | 110.66 | 85.27 | 66.16 | 51.68 | 40.62 | 32.14 | 25.57 | 20.47 | 16.48 | 13.33 | 10.85 | 25 |
| 26 | 108.06 | 83.73 | 65.31 | 51.28 | 40.53 | 32.23 | 25.78 | 20.74 | 16.78 | 13.65 | 11.16 | 26 |
| 27 | 105.53 | 82.21 | 64.47 | 50.89 | 40.43 | 32.32 | 25.99 | 21.02 | 17.09 | 13.97 | 11.48 | 27 |
| 28 | 103.06 | 80.72 | 63.64 | 50.50 | 40.33 | 32.41 | 26.19 | 21.29 | 17.40 | 14.30 | 11.81 | 28 |
| 29 | 100.65 | 79.26 | 62.82 | 50.12 | 40.24 | 32.50 | 26.41 | 21.58 | 17.72 | 14.64 | 12.14 | 29 |
| 30 | 98.30 | 77.82 | 62.02 | 49.74 | 40.15 | 32.60 | 26.62 | 21.86 | 18.05 | 14.98 | 12.49 | 30 |
| 31 | 96.01 | 76.42 | 61.23 | 49.37 | 40.06 | 32.69 | 26.84 | 22.15 | 18.38 | 15.33 | 12.85 | 31 |
| 32 | 93.78 | 75.05 | 60.46 | 49.00 | 39.97 | 32.79 | 27.06 | 22.45 | 18.73 | 15.70 | 13.22 | 32 |
| 33 | 91.61 | 73.71 | 59.69 | 48.64 | 39.88 | 32.89 | 27.28 | 22.75 | 19.07 | 16.07 | 13.61 | 33 |
| 34 | 89.48 | 72.38 | 58.93 | 48.28 | 39.79 | 32.99 | 27.50 | 23.05 | 19.43 | 16.45 | 14.00 | 34 |
| 35 | 87.39 | 71.08 | 58.18 | 47.92 | 39.70 | 33.09 | 27.73 | 23.36 | 19.79 | 16.84 | 14.40 | 35 |
| 36 | 85.37 | 69.81 | 57.45 | 47.57 | 39.62 | 33.19 | 27.96 | 23.68 | 20.16 | 17.24 | 14.82 | 36 |
| 37 | 83.40 | 68.57 | 56.73 | 47.22 | 39.54 | 33.29 | 28.19 | 24.00 | 20.53 | 17.65 | 15.25 | 37 |
| 38 | 81.47 | 67.35 | 56.02 | 46.87 | 39.45 | 33.40 | 28.43 | 24.32 | 20.92 | 18.07 | 15.69 | 38 |
| 39 | 79.59 | 66.15 | 55.31 | 46.53 | 39.37 | 33.50 | 28.66 | 24.65 | 21.31 | 18.50 | 16.14 | 39 |
| 40 | 77.75 | 64.97 | 54.62 | 46.19 | 39.29 | 33.61 | 28.90 | 24.99 | 21.71 | 18.95 | 16.61 | 40 |
| 41 | 75.96 | 63.82 | 53.94 | 45.86 | 39.22 | 33.72 | 29.15 | 25.33 | 22.11 | 19.40 | 17.10 | 41 |
| 42 | 74.22 | 62.69 | 53.27 | 45.54 | 39.14 | 33.83 | 29.40 | 25.67 | 22.53 | 19.87 | 17.60 | 42 |
| 43 | 72.53 | 61.59 | 52.62 | 45.22 | 39.07 | 33.95 | 29.65 | 26.03 | 22.96 | 20.35 | 18.11 | 43 |
| 44 | 70.88 | 60.52 | 51.98 | 44.90 | 39.01 | 34.07 | 29.91 | 26.39 | 23.40 | 20.84 | 18.64 | 44 |
| 45 | 69.28 | 59.47 | 51.35 | 44.60 | 38.94 | 34.19 | 30.17 | 26.76 | 23.85 | 21.35 | 19.19 | 45 |
| 46 | 67.72 | 58.45 | 50.74 | 44.30 | 38.89 | 34.32 | 30.44 | 27.14 | 24.31 | 21.87 | 19.76 | 46 |
| 47 | 66.20 | 57.45 | 50.14 | 44.01 | 38.83 | 34.45 | 30.72 | 27.53 | 24.78 | 22.41 | 20.35 | 47 |
| 48 | 64.73 | 56.48 | 49.56 | 43.73 | 38.79 | 34.59 | 31.01 | 27.93 | 25.27 | 22.97 | 20.96 | 48 |
| 49 | 63.31 | 55.54 | 48.99 | 43.46 | 38.76 | 34.74 | 31.30 | 28.34 | 25.77 | 23.54 | 21.59 | 49 |
| 50 | 61.93 | 54.62 | 48.44 | 43.20 | 38.73 | 34.90 | 31.61 | 28.76 | 26.29 | 24.14 | 22.25 | 50 |

A8: The Ogden Tables

## Table 17: Multipliers for loss of pension commencing age 55 (males)

| Age at date of trial | Multiplier calculated with allowance for projected mortality from the 2008–based population projections and rate of return of | | | | | | | | | | | Age at date of trial |
|---|---|---|---|---|---|---|---|---|---|---|---|---|
| | -2.0% | -1.5% | -1.0% | -0.5% | 0.0% | 0.5% | 1.0% | 1.5% | 2.0% | 2.5% | 3.0% | |
| 0 | 165.74 | 111.07 | 74.94 | 50.90 | 34.80 | 23.94 | 16.57 | 11.54 | 8.08 | 5.69 | 4.02 | 0 |
| 1 | 162.56 | 109.52 | 74.30 | 50.73 | 34.87 | 24.11 | 16.78 | 11.74 | 8.26 | 5.85 | 4.16 | 1 |
| 2 | 158.64 | 107.46 | 73.29 | 50.31 | 34.76 | 24.17 | 16.90 | 11.89 | 8.41 | 5.98 | 4.27 | 2 |
| 3 | 154.79 | 105.43 | 72.29 | 49.89 | 34.65 | 24.22 | 17.02 | 12.04 | 8.56 | 6.12 | 4.39 | 3 |
| 4 | 151.03 | 103.43 | 71.30 | 49.47 | 34.54 | 24.27 | 17.15 | 12.19 | 8.71 | 6.26 | 4.52 | 4 |
| 5 | 147.35 | 101.46 | 70.32 | 49.05 | 34.43 | 24.31 | 17.27 | 12.34 | 8.86 | 6.40 | 4.64 | 5 |
| 6 | 143.76 | 99.52 | 69.35 | 48.63 | 34.32 | 24.36 | 17.39 | 12.49 | 9.02 | 6.54 | 4.77 | 6 |
| 7 | 140.25 | 97.62 | 68.39 | 48.22 | 34.20 | 24.41 | 17.52 | 12.64 | 9.17 | 6.69 | 4.90 | 7 |
| 8 | 136.83 | 95.76 | 67.44 | 47.80 | 34.09 | 24.45 | 17.64 | 12.80 | 9.33 | 6.84 | 5.04 | 8 |
| 9 | 133.48 | 93.92 | 66.51 | 47.39 | 33.97 | 24.50 | 17.77 | 12.96 | 9.50 | 7.00 | 5.18 | 9 |
| 10 | 130.21 | 92.11 | 65.58 | 46.98 | 33.86 | 24.54 | 17.89 | 13.11 | 9.66 | 7.15 | 5.32 | 10 |
| 11 | 127.02 | 90.34 | 64.67 | 46.57 | 33.74 | 24.59 | 18.02 | 13.27 | 9.83 | 7.32 | 5.47 | 11 |
| 12 | 123.91 | 88.61 | 63.77 | 46.17 | 33.63 | 24.63 | 18.14 | 13.44 | 10.00 | 7.48 | 5.62 | 12 |
| 13 | 120.87 | 86.91 | 62.88 | 45.77 | 33.51 | 24.68 | 18.27 | 13.60 | 10.18 | 7.65 | 5.78 | 13 |
| 14 | 117.91 | 85.24 | 62.00 | 45.37 | 33.40 | 24.72 | 18.40 | 13.77 | 10.35 | 7.82 | 5.94 | 14 |
| 15 | 115.03 | 83.61 | 61.14 | 44.98 | 33.29 | 24.77 | 18.53 | 13.94 | 10.53 | 8.00 | 6.10 | 15 |
| 16 | 112.22 | 82.01 | 60.30 | 44.60 | 33.17 | 24.81 | 18.66 | 14.11 | 10.72 | 8.18 | 6.27 | 16 |
| 17 | 109.49 | 80.45 | 59.47 | 44.22 | 33.06 | 24.86 | 18.79 | 14.28 | 10.90 | 8.37 | 6.45 | 17 |
| 18 | 106.83 | 78.92 | 58.65 | 43.84 | 32.96 | 24.91 | 18.93 | 14.46 | 11.10 | 8.56 | 6.63 | 18 |
| 19 | 104.24 | 77.42 | 57.85 | 43.47 | 32.85 | 24.96 | 19.07 | 14.64 | 11.29 | 8.75 | 6.81 | 19 |
| 20 | 101.73 | 75.97 | 57.07 | 43.11 | 32.75 | 25.02 | 19.21 | 14.82 | 11.49 | 8.95 | 7.00 | 20 |
| 21 | 99.28 | 74.54 | 56.29 | 42.76 | 32.65 | 25.07 | 19.35 | 15.01 | 11.70 | 9.16 | 7.20 | 21 |
| 22 | 96.87 | 73.13 | 55.52 | 42.40 | 32.55 | 25.12 | 19.49 | 15.19 | 11.90 | 9.37 | 7.40 | 22 |
| 23 | 94.52 | 71.74 | 54.76 | 42.04 | 32.45 | 25.17 | 19.63 | 15.38 | 12.11 | 9.58 | 7.61 | 23 |
| 24 | 92.23 | 70.38 | 54.02 | 41.69 | 32.34 | 25.23 | 19.77 | 15.58 | 12.33 | 9.80 | 7.82 | 24 |
| 25 | 90.00 | 69.05 | 53.28 | 41.34 | 32.24 | 25.28 | 19.92 | 15.77 | 12.54 | 10.02 | 8.04 | 25 |
| 26 | 87.84 | 67.76 | 52.56 | 41.00 | 32.15 | 25.34 | 20.07 | 15.97 | 12.77 | 10.25 | 8.27 | 26 |
| 27 | 85.73 | 66.49 | 51.86 | 40.67 | 32.06 | 25.40 | 20.22 | 16.17 | 13.00 | 10.49 | 8.50 | 27 |
| 28 | 83.67 | 65.24 | 51.16 | 40.33 | 31.96 | 25.45 | 20.37 | 16.38 | 13.23 | 10.73 | 8.74 | 28 |
| 29 | 81.64 | 64.01 | 50.46 | 39.99 | 31.86 | 25.51 | 20.52 | 16.58 | 13.46 | 10.97 | 8.98 | 29 |
| 30 | 79.68 | 62.81 | 49.78 | 39.66 | 31.76 | 25.56 | 20.67 | 16.79 | 13.70 | 11.23 | 9.24 | 30 |
| 31 | 77.78 | 61.65 | 49.12 | 39.35 | 31.68 | 25.63 | 20.83 | 17.01 | 13.95 | 11.49 | 9.50 | 31 |
| 32 | 75.95 | 60.52 | 48.48 | 39.04 | 31.60 | 25.69 | 20.99 | 17.23 | 14.20 | 11.76 | 9.77 | 32 |
| 33 | 74.17 | 59.42 | 47.86 | 38.74 | 31.52 | 25.77 | 21.16 | 17.46 | 14.46 | 12.03 | 10.05 | 33 |
| 34 | 72.42 | 58.34 | 47.24 | 38.44 | 31.44 | 25.84 | 21.33 | 17.69 | 14.73 | 12.32 | 10.34 | 34 |
| 35 | 70.72 | 57.27 | 46.62 | 38.15 | 31.36 | 25.91 | 21.50 | 17.92 | 15.00 | 12.61 | 10.64 | 35 |
| 36 | 69.07 | 56.24 | 46.03 | 37.86 | 31.29 | 25.98 | 21.68 | 18.16 | 15.28 | 12.90 | 10.94 | 36 |
| 37 | 67.45 | 55.22 | 45.44 | 37.57 | 31.22 | 26.06 | 21.85 | 18.40 | 15.56 | 13.21 | 11.26 | 37 |
| 38 | 65.87 | 54.22 | 44.85 | 37.29 | 31.14 | 26.13 | 22.03 | 18.65 | 15.85 | 13.52 | 11.58 | 38 |
| 39 | 64.33 | 53.23 | 44.27 | 37.00 | 31.07 | 26.21 | 22.21 | 18.89 | 16.14 | 13.84 | 11.91 | 39 |
| 40 | 62.82 | 52.27 | 43.70 | 36.72 | 31.00 | 26.28 | 22.38 | 19.14 | 16.44 | 14.17 | 12.26 | 40 |
| 41 | 61.36 | 51.33 | 43.15 | 36.45 | 30.93 | 26.36 | 22.57 | 19.40 | 16.74 | 14.50 | 12.61 | 41 |
| 42 | 59.93 | 50.41 | 42.60 | 36.18 | 30.86 | 26.45 | 22.76 | 19.66 | 17.06 | 14.85 | 12.98 | 42 |
| 43 | 58.55 | 49.51 | 42.07 | 35.92 | 30.80 | 26.53 | 22.95 | 19.93 | 17.38 | 15.21 | 13.36 | 43 |
| 44 | 57.21 | 48.64 | 41.55 | 35.66 | 30.74 | 26.62 | 23.15 | 20.21 | 17.71 | 15.57 | 13.75 | 44 |
| 45 | 55.90 | 47.78 | 41.04 | 35.41 | 30.69 | 26.71 | 23.35 | 20.49 | 18.04 | 15.95 | 14.15 | 45 |
| 46 | 54.63 | 46.95 | 40.54 | 35.16 | 30.64 | 26.81 | 23.55 | 20.77 | 18.39 | 16.34 | 14.57 | 46 |
| 47 | 53.39 | 46.14 | 40.05 | 34.93 | 30.59 | 26.91 | 23.76 | 21.06 | 18.74 | 16.74 | 15.00 | 47 |
| 48 | 52.20 | 45.35 | 39.58 | 34.70 | 30.55 | 27.01 | 23.98 | 21.37 | 19.11 | 17.15 | 15.45 | 48 |
| 49 | 51.04 | 44.58 | 39.12 | 34.48 | 30.52 | 27.12 | 24.20 | 21.68 | 19.49 | 17.58 | 15.92 | 49 |
| 50 | 49.93 | 43.85 | 38.68 | 34.27 | 30.50 | 27.25 | 24.44 | 22.00 | 19.88 | 18.03 | 16.40 | 50 |
| 51 | 48.86 | 43.14 | 38.26 | 34.08 | 30.49 | 27.38 | 24.69 | 22.34 | 20.29 | 18.49 | 16.91 | 51 |
| 52 | 47.83 | 42.46 | 37.86 | 33.91 | 30.49 | 27.53 | 24.95 | 22.69 | 20.72 | 18.98 | 17.44 | 52 |
| 53 | 46.84 | 41.81 | 37.48 | 33.74 | 30.50 | 27.68 | 25.22 | 23.06 | 21.16 | 19.48 | 17.99 | 53 |
| 54 | 45.90 | 41.19 | 37.12 | 33.60 | 30.53 | 27.86 | 25.51 | 23.44 | 21.62 | 20.01 | 18.57 | 54 |
| 55 | 44.99 | 40.60 | 36.79 | 33.47 | 30.58 | 28.04 | 25.81 | 23.85 | 22.11 | 20.56 | 19.18 | 55 |

## Table 18: Multipliers for loss of pension commencing age 55 (females)

| Age at date of trial | Multiplier calculated with allowance for projected mortality from the 2008–based population projections and rate of return of | | | | | | | | | | | Age at date of trial |
|---|---|---|---|---|---|---|---|---|---|---|---|---|
| | -2.0% | -1.5% | -1.0% | -0.5% | 0.0% | 0.5% | 1.0% | 1.5% | 2.0% | 2.5% | 3.0% | |
| 0 | 185.47 | 123.56 | 82.90 | 56.01 | 38.10 | 26.08 | 17.97 | 12.46 | 8.69 | 6.09 | 4.30 | 0 |
| 1 | 181.85 | 121.80 | 82.16 | 55.81 | 38.16 | 26.26 | 18.19 | 12.68 | 8.88 | 6.26 | 4.44 | 1 |
| 2 | 177.57 | 119.58 | 81.09 | 55.37 | 38.06 | 26.33 | 18.33 | 12.84 | 9.05 | 6.41 | 4.57 | 2 |
| 3 | 173.37 | 117.38 | 80.03 | 54.94 | 37.96 | 26.40 | 18.48 | 13.01 | 9.21 | 6.56 | 4.69 | 3 |
| 4 | 169.26 | 115.23 | 78.98 | 54.51 | 37.86 | 26.47 | 18.62 | 13.18 | 9.38 | 6.71 | 4.83 | 4 |
| 5 | 165.25 | 113.10 | 77.94 | 54.08 | 37.76 | 26.54 | 18.76 | 13.35 | 9.55 | 6.87 | 4.97 | 5 |
| 6 | 161.33 | 111.01 | 76.92 | 53.65 | 37.66 | 26.60 | 18.91 | 13.52 | 9.72 | 7.03 | 5.11 | 6 |
| 7 | 157.49 | 108.96 | 75.90 | 53.22 | 37.56 | 26.67 | 19.05 | 13.69 | 9.89 | 7.19 | 5.25 | 7 |
| 8 | 153.74 | 106.95 | 74.89 | 52.79 | 37.45 | 26.73 | 19.20 | 13.87 | 10.07 | 7.36 | 5.40 | 8 |
| 9 | 150.08 | 104.96 | 73.90 | 52.37 | 37.35 | 26.80 | 19.35 | 14.04 | 10.25 | 7.53 | 5.55 | 9 |
| 10 | 146.51 | 103.02 | 72.92 | 51.95 | 37.24 | 26.86 | 19.49 | 14.22 | 10.44 | 7.70 | 5.71 | 10 |
| 11 | 143.02 | 101.11 | 71.95 | 51.53 | 37.14 | 26.93 | 19.64 | 14.41 | 10.63 | 7.88 | 5.87 | 11 |
| 12 | 139.61 | 99.24 | 71.00 | 51.12 | 37.04 | 26.99 | 19.79 | 14.59 | 10.82 | 8.06 | 6.04 | 12 |
| 13 | 136.29 | 97.39 | 70.05 | 50.71 | 36.93 | 27.06 | 19.94 | 14.78 | 11.01 | 8.25 | 6.21 | 13 |
| 14 | 133.04 | 95.59 | 69.12 | 50.30 | 36.83 | 27.12 | 20.09 | 14.97 | 11.21 | 8.44 | 6.38 | 14 |
| 15 | 129.87 | 93.82 | 68.21 | 49.90 | 36.72 | 27.19 | 20.25 | 15.16 | 11.41 | 8.63 | 6.56 | 15 |
| 16 | 126.78 | 92.08 | 67.30 | 49.50 | 36.62 | 27.26 | 20.40 | 15.35 | 11.61 | 8.83 | 6.75 | 16 |
| 17 | 123.76 | 90.37 | 66.41 | 49.10 | 36.52 | 27.32 | 20.55 | 15.55 | 11.82 | 9.03 | 6.94 | 17 |
| 18 | 120.82 | 88.70 | 65.53 | 48.71 | 36.42 | 27.39 | 20.71 | 15.75 | 12.03 | 9.24 | 7.13 | 18 |
| 19 | 117.96 | 87.07 | 64.67 | 48.32 | 36.32 | 27.46 | 20.87 | 15.95 | 12.25 | 9.46 | 7.34 | 19 |
| 20 | 115.17 | 85.47 | 63.82 | 47.94 | 36.23 | 27.53 | 21.03 | 16.16 | 12.47 | 9.68 | 7.54 | 20 |
| 21 | 112.45 | 83.90 | 62.98 | 47.56 | 36.13 | 27.60 | 21.20 | 16.37 | 12.70 | 9.90 | 7.76 | 21 |
| 22 | 109.78 | 82.35 | 62.15 | 47.19 | 36.03 | 27.67 | 21.36 | 16.58 | 12.93 | 10.13 | 7.98 | 22 |
| 23 | 107.16 | 80.82 | 61.33 | 46.81 | 35.93 | 27.73 | 21.52 | 16.79 | 13.16 | 10.37 | 8.20 | 23 |
| 24 | 104.61 | 79.32 | 60.51 | 46.43 | 35.83 | 27.80 | 21.68 | 17.00 | 13.40 | 10.61 | 8.43 | 24 |
| 25 | 102.12 | 77.86 | 59.71 | 46.06 | 35.73 | 27.87 | 21.85 | 17.22 | 13.64 | 10.85 | 8.67 | 25 |
| 26 | 99.70 | 76.42 | 58.92 | 45.69 | 35.63 | 27.94 | 22.02 | 17.44 | 13.88 | 11.10 | 8.92 | 26 |
| 27 | 97.34 | 75.01 | 58.15 | 45.33 | 35.54 | 28.01 | 22.19 | 17.67 | 14.13 | 11.36 | 9.17 | 27 |
| 28 | 95.02 | 73.63 | 57.38 | 44.97 | 35.44 | 28.08 | 22.36 | 17.89 | 14.39 | 11.62 | 9.43 | 28 |
| 29 | 92.77 | 72.27 | 56.62 | 44.61 | 35.34 | 28.15 | 22.53 | 18.12 | 14.65 | 11.89 | 9.70 | 29 |
| 30 | 90.58 | 70.94 | 55.88 | 44.26 | 35.25 | 28.22 | 22.71 | 18.36 | 14.91 | 12.17 | 9.97 | 30 |
| 31 | 88.45 | 69.65 | 55.15 | 43.92 | 35.16 | 28.29 | 22.88 | 18.60 | 15.18 | 12.45 | 10.26 | 31 |
| 32 | 86.37 | 68.38 | 54.44 | 43.58 | 35.07 | 28.37 | 23.06 | 18.84 | 15.46 | 12.74 | 10.55 | 32 |
| 33 | 84.34 | 67.13 | 53.73 | 43.24 | 34.98 | 28.45 | 23.24 | 19.09 | 15.74 | 13.04 | 10.85 | 33 |
| 34 | 82.35 | 65.90 | 53.03 | 42.90 | 34.89 | 28.52 | 23.43 | 19.33 | 16.03 | 13.35 | 11.16 | 34 |
| 35 | 80.41 | 64.70 | 52.34 | 42.57 | 34.80 | 28.60 | 23.61 | 19.59 | 16.32 | 13.66 | 11.48 | 35 |
| 36 | 78.53 | 63.52 | 51.66 | 42.24 | 34.72 | 28.67 | 23.80 | 19.84 | 16.62 | 13.98 | 11.80 | 36 |
| 37 | 76.69 | 62.37 | 51.00 | 41.92 | 34.63 | 28.75 | 23.99 | 20.10 | 16.92 | 14.30 | 12.14 | 37 |
| 38 | 74.89 | 61.24 | 50.34 | 41.60 | 34.55 | 28.83 | 24.18 | 20.37 | 17.23 | 14.64 | 12.49 | 38 |
| 39 | 73.14 | 60.13 | 49.69 | 41.28 | 34.46 | 28.91 | 24.37 | 20.64 | 17.55 | 14.98 | 12.85 | 39 |
| 40 | 71.43 | 59.04 | 49.05 | 40.97 | 34.38 | 29.00 | 24.57 | 20.91 | 17.87 | 15.34 | 13.22 | 40 |
| 41 | 69.76 | 57.97 | 48.43 | 40.66 | 34.30 | 29.08 | 24.77 | 21.19 | 18.20 | 15.70 | 13.60 | 41 |
| 42 | 68.14 | 56.93 | 47.81 | 40.35 | 34.23 | 29.17 | 24.97 | 21.47 | 18.54 | 16.07 | 13.99 | 42 |
| 43 | 66.56 | 55.91 | 47.21 | 40.05 | 34.15 | 29.25 | 25.17 | 21.76 | 18.88 | 16.45 | 14.39 | 43 |
| 44 | 65.03 | 54.92 | 46.62 | 39.76 | 34.08 | 29.35 | 25.38 | 22.05 | 19.23 | 16.84 | 14.81 | 44 |
| 45 | 63.54 | 53.95 | 46.04 | 39.48 | 34.02 | 29.44 | 25.60 | 22.35 | 19.60 | 17.25 | 15.24 | 45 |
| 46 | 62.09 | 53.00 | 45.47 | 39.20 | 33.95 | 29.54 | 25.82 | 22.66 | 19.97 | 17.66 | 15.68 | 46 |
| 47 | 60.68 | 52.07 | 44.91 | 38.93 | 33.89 | 29.64 | 26.04 | 22.97 | 20.35 | 18.09 | 16.14 | 47 |
| 48 | 59.31 | 51.18 | 44.38 | 38.66 | 33.84 | 29.75 | 26.27 | 23.30 | 20.74 | 18.53 | 16.62 | 48 |
| 49 | 57.99 | 50.31 | 43.85 | 38.41 | 33.80 | 29.87 | 26.51 | 23.63 | 21.14 | 18.99 | 17.12 | 49 |
| 50 | 56.70 | 49.46 | 43.35 | 38.17 | 33.76 | 29.99 | 26.76 | 23.97 | 21.56 | 19.46 | 17.63 | 50 |
| 51 | 55.46 | 48.63 | 42.85 | 37.93 | 33.73 | 30.12 | 27.01 | 24.32 | 21.99 | 19.95 | 18.16 | 51 |
| 52 | 54.25 | 47.83 | 42.37 | 37.70 | 33.70 | 30.25 | 27.27 | 24.68 | 22.43 | 20.45 | 18.71 | 52 |
| 53 | 53.08 | 47.05 | 41.90 | 37.49 | 33.68 | 30.40 | 27.54 | 25.06 | 22.88 | 20.97 | 19.29 | 53 |
| 54 | 51.95 | 46.30 | 41.45 | 37.28 | 33.68 | 30.55 | 27.83 | 25.44 | 23.35 | 21.51 | 19.88 | 54 |
| 55 | 50.86 | 45.57 | 41.02 | 37.09 | 33.68 | 30.71 | 28.12 | 25.84 | 23.84 | 22.07 | 20.51 | 55 |

## Table 19: Multipliers for loss of pension commencing age 60 (males)

| Age at date of trial | Multiplier calculated with allowance for projected mortality from the 2008–based population projections and rate of return of ||||||||||| Age at date of trial |
|---|---|---|---|---|---|---|---|---|---|---|---|---|
| | -2.0% | -1.5% | -1.0% | -0.5% | 0.0% | 0.5% | 1.0% | 1.5% | 2.0% | 2.5% | 3.0% | |
| 0 | 150.59 | 99.76 | 66.49 | 44.58 | 30.06 | 20.38 | 13.89 | 9.52 | 6.56 | 4.54 | 3.16 | 0 |
| 1 | 147.63 | 98.33 | 65.89 | 44.41 | 30.10 | 20.52 | 14.06 | 9.69 | 6.70 | 4.66 | 3.26 | 1 |
| 2 | 144.02 | 96.44 | 64.97 | 44.02 | 30.00 | 20.55 | 14.16 | 9.80 | 6.82 | 4.77 | 3.35 | 2 |
| 3 | 140.47 | 94.58 | 64.06 | 43.63 | 29.89 | 20.59 | 14.26 | 9.92 | 6.94 | 4.88 | 3.44 | 3 |
| 4 | 137.00 | 92.74 | 63.15 | 43.25 | 29.78 | 20.62 | 14.35 | 10.04 | 7.06 | 4.98 | 3.54 | 4 |
| 5 | 133.61 | 90.93 | 62.25 | 42.86 | 29.67 | 20.65 | 14.45 | 10.16 | 7.18 | 5.10 | 3.63 | 5 |
| 6 | 130.29 | 89.16 | 61.36 | 42.47 | 29.56 | 20.68 | 14.54 | 10.28 | 7.30 | 5.21 | 3.73 | 6 |
| 7 | 127.06 | 87.42 | 60.49 | 42.09 | 29.45 | 20.71 | 14.64 | 10.40 | 7.42 | 5.32 | 3.83 | 7 |
| 8 | 123.91 | 85.71 | 59.63 | 41.71 | 29.34 | 20.74 | 14.74 | 10.52 | 7.55 | 5.44 | 3.94 | 8 |
| 9 | 120.82 | 84.03 | 58.77 | 41.33 | 29.22 | 20.77 | 14.84 | 10.65 | 7.68 | 5.56 | 4.05 | 9 |
| 10 | 117.81 | 82.38 | 57.93 | 40.95 | 29.11 | 20.80 | 14.93 | 10.77 | 7.81 | 5.68 | 4.16 | 10 |
| 11 | 114.87 | 80.76 | 57.09 | 40.58 | 29.00 | 20.82 | 15.03 | 10.90 | 7.94 | 5.81 | 4.27 | 11 |
| 12 | 112.01 | 79.17 | 56.27 | 40.21 | 28.88 | 20.85 | 15.13 | 11.03 | 8.07 | 5.94 | 4.39 | 12 |
| 13 | 109.22 | 77.62 | 55.46 | 39.84 | 28.77 | 20.88 | 15.23 | 11.16 | 8.21 | 6.07 | 4.50 | 13 |
| 14 | 106.50 | 76.10 | 54.67 | 39.48 | 28.66 | 20.91 | 15.33 | 11.29 | 8.35 | 6.20 | 4.63 | 14 |
| 15 | 103.85 | 74.61 | 53.88 | 39.12 | 28.55 | 20.94 | 15.43 | 11.42 | 8.49 | 6.34 | 4.75 | 15 |
| 16 | 101.27 | 73.15 | 53.11 | 38.77 | 28.44 | 20.96 | 15.53 | 11.55 | 8.63 | 6.48 | 4.88 | 16 |
| 17 | 98.76 | 71.72 | 52.36 | 38.42 | 28.33 | 20.99 | 15.63 | 11.69 | 8.78 | 6.62 | 5.02 | 17 |
| 18 | 96.32 | 70.32 | 51.61 | 38.07 | 28.23 | 21.03 | 15.74 | 11.83 | 8.93 | 6.77 | 5.15 | 18 |
| 19 | 93.94 | 68.96 | 50.88 | 37.74 | 28.12 | 21.06 | 15.84 | 11.97 | 9.08 | 6.92 | 5.30 | 19 |
| 20 | 91.64 | 67.63 | 50.17 | 37.41 | 28.02 | 21.09 | 15.95 | 12.11 | 9.24 | 7.08 | 5.44 | 20 |
| 21 | 89.39 | 66.33 | 49.47 | 37.08 | 27.92 | 21.13 | 16.06 | 12.26 | 9.40 | 7.23 | 5.59 | 21 |
| 22 | 87.18 | 65.04 | 48.77 | 36.75 | 27.82 | 21.16 | 16.17 | 12.41 | 9.56 | 7.40 | 5.74 | 22 |
| 23 | 85.02 | 63.77 | 48.08 | 36.42 | 27.72 | 21.19 | 16.28 | 12.55 | 9.72 | 7.56 | 5.90 | 23 |
| 24 | 82.92 | 62.54 | 47.40 | 36.09 | 27.62 | 21.23 | 16.39 | 12.70 | 9.89 | 7.73 | 6.06 | 24 |
| 25 | 80.88 | 61.33 | 46.73 | 35.78 | 27.52 | 21.26 | 16.50 | 12.86 | 10.06 | 7.90 | 6.23 | 25 |
| 26 | 78.91 | 60.15 | 46.08 | 35.46 | 27.42 | 21.30 | 16.61 | 13.01 | 10.23 | 8.08 | 6.40 | 26 |
| 27 | 76.98 | 59.00 | 45.44 | 35.16 | 27.33 | 21.34 | 16.73 | 13.17 | 10.41 | 8.26 | 6.58 | 27 |
| 28 | 75.09 | 57.86 | 44.80 | 34.85 | 27.23 | 21.37 | 16.84 | 13.33 | 10.59 | 8.45 | 6.76 | 28 |
| 29 | 73.23 | 56.74 | 44.17 | 34.54 | 27.13 | 21.41 | 16.96 | 13.49 | 10.77 | 8.63 | 6.95 | 29 |
| 30 | 71.44 | 55.65 | 43.55 | 34.24 | 27.04 | 21.44 | 17.08 | 13.65 | 10.96 | 8.83 | 7.14 | 30 |
| 31 | 69.70 | 54.59 | 42.95 | 33.95 | 26.95 | 21.48 | 17.20 | 13.82 | 11.15 | 9.03 | 7.34 | 31 |
| 32 | 68.02 | 53.56 | 42.37 | 33.66 | 26.86 | 21.53 | 17.32 | 13.99 | 11.35 | 9.23 | 7.54 | 32 |
| 33 | 66.40 | 52.56 | 41.80 | 33.39 | 26.79 | 21.58 | 17.45 | 14.17 | 11.55 | 9.45 | 7.75 | 33 |
| 34 | 64.81 | 51.58 | 41.24 | 33.12 | 26.71 | 21.63 | 17.58 | 14.35 | 11.76 | 9.66 | 7.97 | 34 |
| 35 | 63.25 | 50.61 | 40.68 | 32.84 | 26.63 | 21.67 | 17.71 | 14.53 | 11.96 | 9.89 | 8.20 | 35 |
| 36 | 61.74 | 49.67 | 40.14 | 32.58 | 26.55 | 21.72 | 17.85 | 14.72 | 12.18 | 10.11 | 8.43 | 36 |
| 37 | 60.27 | 48.75 | 39.60 | 32.31 | 26.47 | 21.78 | 17.98 | 14.90 | 12.40 | 10.35 | 8.66 | 37 |
| 38 | 58.83 | 47.84 | 39.07 | 32.05 | 26.40 | 21.83 | 18.12 | 15.09 | 12.62 | 10.58 | 8.91 | 38 |
| 39 | 57.42 | 46.95 | 38.55 | 31.79 | 26.32 | 21.88 | 18.25 | 15.28 | 12.84 | 10.83 | 9.16 | 39 |
| 40 | 56.04 | 46.07 | 38.03 | 31.53 | 26.24 | 21.93 | 18.39 | 15.48 | 13.07 | 11.08 | 9.42 | 40 |
| 41 | 54.71 | 45.22 | 37.53 | 31.28 | 26.17 | 21.98 | 18.53 | 15.68 | 13.31 | 11.33 | 9.68 | 41 |
| 42 | 53.42 | 44.38 | 37.04 | 31.03 | 26.10 | 22.03 | 18.67 | 15.88 | 13.55 | 11.60 | 9.96 | 42 |
| 43 | 52.16 | 43.57 | 36.55 | 30.79 | 26.03 | 22.09 | 18.82 | 16.09 | 13.80 | 11.87 | 10.24 | 43 |
| 44 | 50.93 | 42.78 | 36.08 | 30.55 | 25.97 | 22.15 | 18.97 | 16.30 | 14.05 | 12.15 | 10.54 | 44 |
| 45 | 49.74 | 42.01 | 35.62 | 30.32 | 25.91 | 22.22 | 19.12 | 16.51 | 14.31 | 12.44 | 10.84 | 45 |
| 46 | 48.58 | 41.25 | 35.16 | 30.09 | 25.85 | 22.28 | 19.28 | 16.73 | 14.57 | 12.73 | 11.15 | 46 |
| 47 | 47.46 | 40.51 | 34.72 | 29.87 | 25.79 | 22.35 | 19.44 | 16.96 | 14.84 | 13.03 | 11.48 | 47 |
| 48 | 46.37 | 39.80 | 34.29 | 29.65 | 25.74 | 22.42 | 19.60 | 17.19 | 15.12 | 13.35 | 11.81 | 48 |
| 49 | 45.32 | 39.10 | 33.87 | 29.45 | 25.70 | 22.50 | 19.77 | 17.43 | 15.41 | 13.67 | 12.16 | 49 |
| 50 | 44.30 | 38.43 | 33.47 | 29.26 | 25.66 | 22.59 | 19.95 | 17.68 | 15.71 | 14.01 | 12.52 | 50 |
| 51 | 43.33 | 37.79 | 33.09 | 29.07 | 25.64 | 22.69 | 20.14 | 17.94 | 16.03 | 14.36 | 12.90 | 51 |
| 52 | 42.39 | 37.17 | 32.72 | 28.91 | 25.62 | 22.79 | 20.34 | 18.21 | 16.35 | 14.72 | 13.30 | 52 |
| 53 | 41.49 | 36.58 | 32.37 | 28.75 | 25.62 | 22.91 | 20.55 | 18.49 | 16.69 | 15.11 | 13.71 | 53 |
| 54 | 40.63 | 36.01 | 32.04 | 28.61 | 25.63 | 23.04 | 20.77 | 18.79 | 17.04 | 15.50 | 14.14 | 54 |

**Table 19: Multipliers for loss of pension commencing age 60 (males)** *continued*

| Age at date of trial | Multiplier calculated with allowance for projected mortality from the 2008–based population projections and rate of return of | | | | | | | | | | | Age at date of trial |
|---|---|---|---|---|---|---|---|---|---|---|---|---|
| | -2.0% | -1.5% | -1.0% | -0.5% | 0.0% | 0.5% | 1.0% | 1.5% | 2.0% | 2.5% | 3.0% | |
| 55 | 39.81 | 35.48 | 31.73 | 28.48 | 25.65 | 23.18 | 21.01 | 19.10 | 17.41 | 15.92 | 14.60 | 55 |
| 56 | 39.03 | 34.97 | 31.45 | 28.37 | 25.69 | 23.33 | 21.26 | 19.43 | 17.80 | 16.36 | 15.07 | 56 |
| 57 | 38.29 | 34.49 | 31.18 | 28.28 | 25.74 | 23.50 | 21.52 | 19.77 | 18.21 | 16.82 | 15.57 | 57 |
| 58 | 37.56 | 34.02 | 30.92 | 28.20 | 25.80 | 23.68 | 21.79 | 20.12 | 18.63 | 17.29 | 16.09 | 58 |
| 59 | 36.86 | 33.56 | 30.67 | 28.12 | 25.86 | 23.86 | 22.07 | 20.49 | 19.06 | 17.79 | 16.64 | 59 |
| 60 | 36.17 | 33.12 | 30.42 | 28.04 | 25.92 | 24.04 | 22.36 | 20.86 | 19.51 | 18.30 | 17.20 | 60 |

### Table 20: Multipliers for loss of pension commencing age 60 (females)

| Age at date of trial | Multiplier calculated with allowance for projected mortality from the 2008–based population projections and rate of return of | | | | | | | | | | | Age at date of trial |
|---|---|---|---|---|---|---|---|---|---|---|---|---|
| | -2.0% | -1.5% | -1.0% | -0.5% | 0.0% | 0.5% | 1.0% | 1.5% | 2.0% | 2.5% | 3.0% | |
| 0 | 169.99 | 112.01 | 74.27 | 49.55 | 33.26 | 22.45 | 15.24 | 10.40 | 7.14 | 4.92 | 3.41 | 0 |
| 1 | 166.62 | 110.38 | 73.58 | 49.35 | 33.30 | 22.59 | 15.42 | 10.58 | 7.30 | 5.06 | 3.52 | 1 |
| 2 | 162.64 | 108.33 | 72.60 | 48.95 | 33.20 | 22.65 | 15.53 | 10.71 | 7.43 | 5.17 | 3.62 | 2 |
| 3 | 158.74 | 106.30 | 71.62 | 48.55 | 33.10 | 22.70 | 15.65 | 10.85 | 7.56 | 5.29 | 3.72 | 3 |
| 4 | 154.93 | 104.31 | 70.66 | 48.15 | 33.00 | 22.75 | 15.77 | 10.98 | 7.69 | 5.41 | 3.83 | 4 |
| 5 | 151.21 | 102.36 | 69.71 | 47.75 | 32.90 | 22.80 | 15.88 | 11.12 | 7.83 | 5.54 | 3.93 | 5 |
| 6 | 147.57 | 100.43 | 68.76 | 47.36 | 32.80 | 22.85 | 16.00 | 11.26 | 7.97 | 5.66 | 4.04 | 6 |
| 7 | 144.01 | 98.54 | 67.83 | 46.96 | 32.70 | 22.89 | 16.11 | 11.40 | 8.11 | 5.79 | 4.16 | 7 |
| 8 | 140.54 | 96.68 | 66.91 | 46.57 | 32.60 | 22.94 | 16.23 | 11.54 | 8.25 | 5.92 | 4.27 | 8 |
| 9 | 137.14 | 94.85 | 65.99 | 46.18 | 32.49 | 22.99 | 16.35 | 11.69 | 8.39 | 6.06 | 4.39 | 9 |
| 10 | 133.83 | 93.06 | 65.09 | 45.79 | 32.39 | 23.03 | 16.47 | 11.83 | 8.54 | 6.20 | 4.51 | 10 |
| 11 | 130.60 | 91.31 | 64.21 | 45.41 | 32.29 | 23.08 | 16.59 | 11.98 | 8.69 | 6.34 | 4.64 | 11 |
| 12 | 127.45 | 89.58 | 63.33 | 45.02 | 32.18 | 23.13 | 16.71 | 12.13 | 8.84 | 6.48 | 4.77 | 12 |
| 13 | 124.36 | 87.89 | 62.47 | 44.65 | 32.08 | 23.17 | 16.83 | 12.28 | 9.00 | 6.63 | 4.90 | 13 |
| 14 | 121.36 | 86.23 | 61.62 | 44.27 | 31.98 | 23.22 | 16.95 | 12.43 | 9.16 | 6.78 | 5.04 | 14 |
| 15 | 118.43 | 84.60 | 60.77 | 43.90 | 31.88 | 23.27 | 17.07 | 12.58 | 9.32 | 6.93 | 5.18 | 15 |
| 16 | 115.57 | 83.00 | 59.95 | 43.53 | 31.78 | 23.31 | 17.19 | 12.74 | 9.48 | 7.09 | 5.32 | 16 |
| 17 | 112.78 | 81.44 | 59.13 | 43.16 | 31.67 | 23.36 | 17.32 | 12.90 | 9.65 | 7.25 | 5.47 | 17 |
| 18 | 110.06 | 79.90 | 58.33 | 42.80 | 31.58 | 23.41 | 17.44 | 13.06 | 9.82 | 7.42 | 5.62 | 18 |
| 19 | 107.41 | 78.40 | 57.53 | 42.45 | 31.48 | 23.46 | 17.57 | 13.22 | 9.99 | 7.58 | 5.78 | 19 |
| 20 | 104.83 | 76.93 | 56.76 | 42.10 | 31.38 | 23.51 | 17.70 | 13.38 | 10.17 | 7.76 | 5.94 | 20 |
| 21 | 102.32 | 75.49 | 55.99 | 41.75 | 31.29 | 23.56 | 17.83 | 13.55 | 10.35 | 7.93 | 6.11 | 21 |
| 22 | 99.85 | 74.07 | 55.23 | 41.40 | 31.19 | 23.61 | 17.96 | 13.72 | 10.53 | 8.12 | 6.28 | 22 |
| 23 | 97.44 | 72.67 | 54.48 | 41.05 | 31.09 | 23.66 | 18.09 | 13.89 | 10.71 | 8.30 | 6.45 | 23 |
| 24 | 95.08 | 71.29 | 53.73 | 40.70 | 30.99 | 23.70 | 18.22 | 14.06 | 10.90 | 8.49 | 6.63 | 24 |
| 25 | 92.79 | 69.95 | 53.00 | 40.36 | 30.89 | 23.75 | 18.35 | 14.24 | 11.09 | 8.68 | 6.82 | 25 |
| 26 | 90.55 | 68.63 | 52.28 | 40.03 | 30.79 | 23.80 | 18.48 | 14.41 | 11.29 | 8.88 | 7.01 | 26 |
| 27 | 88.37 | 67.34 | 51.57 | 39.69 | 30.70 | 23.85 | 18.62 | 14.59 | 11.49 | 9.08 | 7.20 | 27 |
| 28 | 86.24 | 66.07 | 50.87 | 39.36 | 30.60 | 23.90 | 18.75 | 14.77 | 11.69 | 9.29 | 7.41 | 28 |
| 29 | 84.17 | 64.83 | 50.18 | 39.03 | 30.51 | 23.95 | 18.89 | 14.96 | 11.90 | 9.50 | 7.61 | 29 |
| 30 | 82.15 | 63.61 | 49.50 | 38.71 | 30.41 | 24.00 | 19.03 | 15.15 | 12.11 | 9.71 | 7.83 | 30 |
| 31 | 80.18 | 62.43 | 48.84 | 38.39 | 30.32 | 24.05 | 19.17 | 15.34 | 12.32 | 9.94 | 8.04 | 31 |
| 32 | 78.27 | 61.26 | 48.19 | 38.08 | 30.23 | 24.11 | 19.31 | 15.53 | 12.54 | 10.16 | 8.27 | 32 |
| 33 | 76.40 | 60.12 | 47.54 | 37.77 | 30.14 | 24.16 | 19.45 | 15.72 | 12.76 | 10.40 | 8.50 | 33 |
| 34 | 74.57 | 59.00 | 46.90 | 37.46 | 30.05 | 24.22 | 19.60 | 15.92 | 12.99 | 10.64 | 8.74 | 34 |
| 35 | 72.79 | 57.90 | 46.27 | 37.15 | 29.96 | 24.27 | 19.74 | 16.12 | 13.22 | 10.88 | 8.99 | 35 |
| 36 | 71.05 | 56.82 | 45.66 | 36.85 | 29.88 | 24.33 | 19.89 | 16.33 | 13.45 | 11.13 | 9.24 | 36 |
| 37 | 69.36 | 55.77 | 45.05 | 36.55 | 29.79 | 24.38 | 20.04 | 16.53 | 13.69 | 11.38 | 9.50 | 37 |
| 38 | 67.71 | 54.73 | 44.45 | 36.26 | 29.71 | 24.44 | 20.19 | 16.74 | 13.94 | 11.65 | 9.77 | 38 |
| 39 | 66.10 | 53.72 | 43.86 | 35.97 | 29.62 | 24.50 | 20.34 | 16.96 | 14.19 | 11.92 | 10.04 | 39 |
| 40 | 64.53 | 52.73 | 43.28 | 35.68 | 29.54 | 24.56 | 20.50 | 17.17 | 14.44 | 12.19 | 10.32 | 40 |
| 41 | 63.00 | 51.75 | 42.70 | 35.39 | 29.46 | 24.62 | 20.65 | 17.39 | 14.70 | 12.47 | 10.62 | 41 |
| 42 | 61.51 | 50.80 | 42.14 | 35.11 | 29.38 | 24.68 | 20.81 | 17.62 | 14.97 | 12.76 | 10.92 | 42 |
| 43 | 60.06 | 49.87 | 41.59 | 34.84 | 29.30 | 24.74 | 20.97 | 17.85 | 15.24 | 13.06 | 11.23 | 43 |
| 44 | 58.65 | 48.97 | 41.06 | 34.57 | 29.23 | 24.81 | 21.14 | 18.08 | 15.52 | 13.36 | 11.55 | 44 |
| 45 | 57.28 | 48.08 | 40.53 | 34.31 | 29.16 | 24.88 | 21.31 | 18.32 | 15.80 | 13.68 | 11.88 | 45 |
| 46 | 55.95 | 47.21 | 40.01 | 34.05 | 29.09 | 24.95 | 21.48 | 18.56 | 16.09 | 14.00 | 12.22 | 46 |
| 47 | 54.65 | 46.37 | 39.50 | 33.79 | 29.02 | 25.02 | 21.65 | 18.81 | 16.39 | 14.33 | 12.57 | 47 |
| 48 | 53.40 | 45.55 | 39.01 | 33.55 | 28.97 | 25.10 | 21.84 | 19.06 | 16.70 | 14.67 | 12.94 | 48 |
| 49 | 52.19 | 44.75 | 38.54 | 33.32 | 28.92 | 25.19 | 22.03 | 19.33 | 17.01 | 15.03 | 13.32 | 49 |
| 50 | 51.01 | 43.98 | 38.07 | 33.09 | 28.87 | 25.28 | 22.22 | 19.60 | 17.34 | 15.39 | 13.71 | 50 |
| 51 | 49.86 | 43.22 | 37.62 | 32.87 | 28.83 | 25.38 | 22.42 | 19.87 | 17.67 | 15.77 | 14.11 | 51 |
| 52 | 48.76 | 42.49 | 37.17 | 32.65 | 28.79 | 25.47 | 22.62 | 20.16 | 18.02 | 16.16 | 14.53 | 52 |
| 53 | 47.68 | 41.78 | 36.75 | 32.45 | 28.76 | 25.58 | 22.83 | 20.45 | 18.38 | 16.56 | 14.97 | 53 |
| 54 | 46.65 | 41.09 | 36.34 | 32.26 | 28.74 | 25.70 | 23.06 | 20.76 | 18.74 | 16.98 | 15.43 | 54 |

## A8: The Ogden Tables

**Table 20: Multipliers for loss of pension commencing age 60 (females)** *continued*

| Age at date of trial | Multiplier calculated with allowance for projected mortality from the 2008-based population projections and rate of return of | | | | | | | | | | | Age at date of trial |
|---|---|---|---|---|---|---|---|---|---|---|---|---|
| | *-2.0%* | *-1.5%* | *-1.0%* | *-0.5%* | *0.0%* | *0.5%* | *1.0%* | *1.5%* | *2.0%* | *2.5%* | *3.0%* | |
| 55 | 45.65 | 40.43 | 35.94 | 32.08 | 28.73 | 25.82 | 23.29 | 21.07 | 19.13 | 17.41 | 15.90 | 55 |
| 56 | 44.69 | 39.79 | 35.57 | 31.91 | 28.73 | 25.95 | 23.53 | 21.40 | 19.52 | 17.86 | 16.39 | 56 |
| 57 | 43.76 | 39.18 | 35.20 | 31.75 | 28.73 | 26.09 | 23.78 | 21.74 | 19.93 | 18.33 | 16.91 | 57 |
| 58 | 42.86 | 38.57 | 34.85 | 31.59 | 28.74 | 26.24 | 24.04 | 22.09 | 20.35 | 18.81 | 17.44 | 58 |
| 59 | 41.98 | 37.99 | 34.50 | 31.44 | 28.76 | 26.39 | 24.30 | 22.44 | 20.79 | 19.31 | 17.99 | 59 |
| 60 | 41.12 | 37.41 | 34.16 | 31.30 | 28.78 | 26.55 | 24.57 | 22.81 | 21.24 | 19.83 | 18.57 | 60 |

## Table 21: Multipliers for loss of pension commencing age 65 (males)

| Age at date of trial | Multiplier calculated with allowance for projected mortality from the 2008-based population projections and rate of return of | | | | | | | | | | | Age at date of trial |
|---|---|---|---|---|---|---|---|---|---|---|---|---|
| | *-2.0%* | *-1.5%* | *-1.0%* | *-0.5%* | *0.0%* | *0.5%* | *1.0%* | *1.5%* | *2.0%* | *2.5%* | *3.0%* | |
| 0 | 134.16 | 87.81 | 57.78 | 38.22 | 25.41 | 16.98 | 11.40 | 7.69 | 5.21 | 3.54 | 2.42 | 0 |
| 1 | 131.46 | 86.50 | 57.23 | 38.06 | 25.44 | 17.08 | 11.53 | 7.82 | 5.32 | 3.64 | 2.50 | 1 |
| 2 | 128.17 | 84.80 | 56.40 | 37.70 | 25.33 | 17.10 | 11.60 | 7.91 | 5.41 | 3.72 | 2.57 | 2 |
| 3 | 124.95 | 83.11 | 55.57 | 37.35 | 25.23 | 17.12 | 11.67 | 8.00 | 5.50 | 3.80 | 2.64 | 3 |
| 4 | 121.80 | 81.45 | 54.76 | 37.00 | 25.12 | 17.14 | 11.75 | 8.09 | 5.59 | 3.88 | 2.71 | 4 |
| 5 | 118.72 | 79.82 | 53.95 | 36.64 | 25.01 | 17.15 | 11.82 | 8.18 | 5.68 | 3.97 | 2.78 | 5 |
| 6 | 115.71 | 78.22 | 53.15 | 36.29 | 24.90 | 17.17 | 11.89 | 8.27 | 5.78 | 4.05 | 2.85 | 6 |
| 7 | 112.78 | 76.65 | 52.36 | 35.95 | 24.80 | 17.18 | 11.96 | 8.36 | 5.87 | 4.14 | 2.93 | 7 |
| 8 | 109.92 | 75.11 | 51.59 | 35.60 | 24.69 | 17.20 | 12.03 | 8.46 | 5.97 | 4.23 | 3.01 | 8 |
| 9 | 107.13 | 73.60 | 50.82 | 35.26 | 24.58 | 17.21 | 12.11 | 8.55 | 6.07 | 4.32 | 3.09 | 9 |
| 10 | 104.40 | 72.11 | 50.06 | 34.91 | 24.47 | 17.22 | 12.18 | 8.65 | 6.17 | 4.41 | 3.17 | 10 |
| 11 | 101.74 | 70.65 | 49.31 | 34.57 | 24.36 | 17.23 | 12.25 | 8.74 | 6.27 | 4.51 | 3.26 | 11 |
| 12 | 99.15 | 69.23 | 48.57 | 34.24 | 24.25 | 17.25 | 12.32 | 8.84 | 6.37 | 4.60 | 3.34 | 12 |
| 13 | 96.62 | 67.83 | 47.84 | 33.91 | 24.14 | 17.26 | 12.39 | 8.94 | 6.47 | 4.70 | 3.43 | 13 |
| 14 | 94.16 | 66.46 | 47.13 | 33.58 | 24.03 | 17.27 | 12.47 | 9.04 | 6.58 | 4.80 | 3.52 | 14 |
| 15 | 91.77 | 65.12 | 46.43 | 33.25 | 23.92 | 17.28 | 12.54 | 9.14 | 6.68 | 4.91 | 3.62 | 15 |
| 16 | 89.44 | 63.81 | 45.74 | 32.93 | 23.82 | 17.30 | 12.62 | 9.24 | 6.79 | 5.01 | 3.71 | 16 |
| 17 | 87.17 | 62.53 | 45.06 | 32.61 | 23.71 | 17.31 | 12.69 | 9.34 | 6.90 | 5.12 | 3.81 | 17 |
| 18 | 84.97 | 61.27 | 44.39 | 32.30 | 23.61 | 17.33 | 12.77 | 9.45 | 7.02 | 5.23 | 3.91 | 18 |
| 19 | 82.83 | 60.05 | 43.74 | 32.00 | 23.51 | 17.34 | 12.85 | 9.55 | 7.13 | 5.34 | 4.02 | 19 |
| 20 | 80.75 | 58.86 | 43.10 | 31.70 | 23.41 | 17.36 | 12.93 | 9.66 | 7.25 | 5.46 | 4.13 | 20 |
| 21 | 78.72 | 57.69 | 42.47 | 31.40 | 23.31 | 17.38 | 13.01 | 9.77 | 7.37 | 5.58 | 4.24 | 21 |
| 22 | 76.73 | 56.54 | 41.84 | 31.10 | 23.21 | 17.39 | 13.09 | 9.88 | 7.49 | 5.70 | 4.35 | 22 |
| 23 | 74.79 | 55.40 | 41.22 | 30.80 | 23.11 | 17.41 | 13.17 | 9.99 | 7.61 | 5.82 | 4.47 | 23 |
| 24 | 72.90 | 54.29 | 40.61 | 30.51 | 23.01 | 17.42 | 13.25 | 10.11 | 7.74 | 5.95 | 4.59 | 24 |
| 25 | 71.06 | 53.21 | 40.01 | 30.22 | 22.91 | 17.44 | 13.33 | 10.22 | 7.87 | 6.08 | 4.71 | 25 |
| 26 | 69.28 | 52.16 | 39.43 | 29.94 | 22.82 | 17.46 | 13.41 | 10.34 | 8.00 | 6.21 | 4.83 | 26 |
| 27 | 67.55 | 51.13 | 38.86 | 29.66 | 22.73 | 17.48 | 13.50 | 10.46 | 8.13 | 6.34 | 4.97 | 27 |
| 28 | 65.85 | 50.11 | 38.29 | 29.38 | 22.63 | 17.50 | 13.58 | 10.58 | 8.26 | 6.48 | 5.10 | 28 |
| 29 | 64.18 | 49.10 | 37.72 | 29.10 | 22.53 | 17.51 | 13.66 | 10.69 | 8.40 | 6.62 | 5.23 | 29 |
| 30 | 62.57 | 48.13 | 37.17 | 28.82 | 22.44 | 17.53 | 13.75 | 10.82 | 8.54 | 6.76 | 5.38 | 30 |
| 31 | 61.01 | 47.18 | 36.64 | 28.56 | 22.35 | 17.55 | 13.83 | 10.94 | 8.68 | 6.91 | 5.52 | 31 |
| 32 | 59.50 | 46.27 | 36.12 | 28.30 | 22.26 | 17.58 | 13.93 | 11.07 | 8.83 | 7.07 | 5.67 | 32 |
| 33 | 58.05 | 45.38 | 35.61 | 28.06 | 22.18 | 17.61 | 14.02 | 11.20 | 8.98 | 7.22 | 5.83 | 33 |
| 34 | 56.62 | 44.50 | 35.11 | 27.81 | 22.10 | 17.63 | 14.12 | 11.34 | 9.14 | 7.38 | 5.99 | 34 |
| 35 | 55.23 | 43.64 | 34.61 | 27.56 | 22.02 | 17.66 | 14.21 | 11.47 | 9.29 | 7.55 | 6.15 | 35 |
| 36 | 53.87 | 42.80 | 34.13 | 27.32 | 21.94 | 17.69 | 14.31 | 11.61 | 9.45 | 7.72 | 6.32 | 36 |
| 37 | 52.56 | 41.97 | 33.65 | 27.08 | 21.87 | 17.72 | 14.41 | 11.75 | 9.61 | 7.89 | 6.49 | 37 |
| 38 | 51.26 | 41.16 | 33.18 | 26.84 | 21.79 | 17.75 | 14.50 | 11.89 | 9.78 | 8.07 | 6.67 | 38 |
| 39 | 50.00 | 40.37 | 32.71 | 26.60 | 21.71 | 17.77 | 14.60 | 12.03 | 9.95 | 8.24 | 6.85 | 39 |
| 40 | 48.77 | 39.59 | 32.25 | 26.36 | 21.63 | 17.80 | 14.70 | 12.18 | 10.12 | 8.43 | 7.04 | 40 |
| 41 | 47.58 | 38.83 | 31.80 | 26.13 | 21.55 | 17.83 | 14.80 | 12.32 | 10.29 | 8.62 | 7.24 | 41 |
| 42 | 46.42 | 38.09 | 31.36 | 25.91 | 21.48 | 17.86 | 14.90 | 12.47 | 10.47 | 8.81 | 7.44 | 42 |
| 43 | 45.30 | 37.36 | 30.93 | 25.69 | 21.41 | 17.90 | 15.01 | 12.63 | 10.65 | 9.01 | 7.64 | 43 |
| 44 | 44.21 | 36.66 | 30.51 | 25.47 | 21.34 | 17.93 | 15.12 | 12.78 | 10.84 | 9.21 | 7.86 | 44 |
| 45 | 43.15 | 35.97 | 30.09 | 25.26 | 21.27 | 17.97 | 15.23 | 12.94 | 11.03 | 9.43 | 8.08 | 45 |
| 46 | 42.11 | 35.30 | 29.69 | 25.05 | 21.21 | 18.01 | 15.34 | 13.10 | 11.22 | 9.64 | 8.30 | 46 |
| 47 | 41.11 | 34.64 | 29.29 | 24.85 | 21.15 | 18.05 | 15.46 | 13.27 | 11.42 | 9.86 | 8.54 | 47 |
| 48 | 40.14 | 34.01 | 28.91 | 24.65 | 21.09 | 18.10 | 15.57 | 13.44 | 11.63 | 10.09 | 8.78 | 48 |
| 49 | 39.20 | 33.39 | 28.53 | 24.46 | 21.04 | 18.15 | 15.70 | 13.62 | 11.84 | 10.33 | 9.03 | 49 |
| 50 | 38.29 | 32.79 | 28.18 | 24.28 | 20.99 | 18.20 | 15.83 | 13.80 | 12.07 | 10.58 | 9.29 | 50 |
| 51 | 37.42 | 32.22 | 27.83 | 24.11 | 20.96 | 18.27 | 15.97 | 13.99 | 12.29 | 10.83 | 9.56 | 51 |
| 52 | 36.58 | 31.67 | 27.50 | 23.96 | 20.93 | 18.34 | 16.11 | 14.19 | 12.53 | 11.10 | 9.85 | 52 |
| 53 | 35.78 | 31.14 | 27.19 | 23.81 | 20.91 | 18.41 | 16.26 | 14.40 | 12.78 | 11.37 | 10.15 | 53 |
| 54 | 35.01 | 30.64 | 26.89 | 23.67 | 20.90 | 18.50 | 16.42 | 14.62 | 13.04 | 11.66 | 10.46 | 54 |

**Table 21: Multipliers for loss of pension commencing age 65 (males)** *continued*

| Age at date of trial | Multiplier calculated with allowance for projected mortality from the 2008–based population projections and rate of return of | | | | | | | | | | | Age at date of trial |
|---|---|---|---|---|---|---|---|---|---|---|---|---|
| | −2.0% | −1.5% | −1.0% | −0.5% | 0.0% | 0.5% | 1.0% | 1.5% | 2.0% | 2.5% | 3.0% | |
| 55 | 34.28 | 30.15 | 26.61 | 23.55 | 20.90 | 18.60 | 16.59 | 14.85 | 13.31 | 11.97 | 10.78 | 55 |
| 56 | 33.59 | 29.70 | 26.35 | 23.44 | 20.91 | 18.71 | 16.78 | 15.09 | 13.60 | 12.29 | 11.13 | 56 |
| 57 | 32.92 | 29.27 | 26.10 | 23.35 | 20.94 | 18.83 | 16.97 | 15.34 | 13.90 | 12.62 | 11.49 | 57 |
| 58 | 32.28 | 28.85 | 25.87 | 23.26 | 20.97 | 18.95 | 17.18 | 15.60 | 14.21 | 12.97 | 11.86 | 58 |
| 59 | 31.65 | 28.44 | 25.64 | 23.17 | 21.00 | 19.08 | 17.38 | 15.87 | 14.53 | 13.32 | 12.25 | 59 |
| 60 | 31.03 | 28.04 | 25.41 | 23.09 | 21.03 | 19.21 | 17.59 | 16.14 | 14.85 | 13.69 | 12.65 | 60 |
| 61 | 30.43 | 27.65 | 25.19 | 23.01 | 21.07 | 19.35 | 17.81 | 16.43 | 15.19 | 14.08 | 13.07 | 61 |
| 62 | 29.87 | 27.28 | 24.99 | 22.94 | 21.12 | 19.50 | 18.04 | 16.73 | 15.55 | 14.48 | 13.51 | 62 |
| 63 | 29.34 | 26.94 | 24.81 | 22.90 | 21.20 | 19.67 | 18.29 | 17.05 | 15.93 | 14.91 | 13.98 | 63 |
| 64 | 28.85 | 26.63 | 24.65 | 22.88 | 21.29 | 19.86 | 18.56 | 17.39 | 16.33 | 15.37 | 14.49 | 64 |
| 65 | 28.40 | 26.37 | 24.54 | 22.90 | 21.42 | 20.08 | 18.87 | 17.77 | 16.77 | 15.86 | 15.03 | 65 |

### Table 22: Multipliers for loss of pension commencing age 65 (females)

| Age at date of trial | Multiplier calculated with allowance for projected mortality from the 2008–based population projections and rate of return of | | | | | | | | | | | Age at date of trial |
|---|---|---|---|---|---|---|---|---|---|---|---|---|
| | -2.0% | -1.5% | -1.0% | -0.5% | 0.0% | 0.5% | 1.0% | 1.5% | 2.0% | 2.5% | 3.0% | |
| 0 | 153.09 | 99.71 | 65.31 | 43.01 | 28.47 | 18.95 | 12.67 | 8.52 | 5.75 | 3.90 | 2.66 | 0 |
| 1 | 149.98 | 98.22 | 64.68 | 42.82 | 28.50 | 19.06 | 12.81 | 8.66 | 5.87 | 4.00 | 2.74 | 1 |
| 2 | 146.34 | 96.35 | 63.78 | 42.45 | 28.40 | 19.10 | 12.90 | 8.76 | 5.98 | 4.09 | 2.82 | 2 |
| 3 | 142.77 | 94.51 | 62.90 | 42.08 | 28.30 | 19.13 | 12.99 | 8.87 | 6.08 | 4.19 | 2.90 | 3 |
| 4 | 139.29 | 92.70 | 62.02 | 41.72 | 28.21 | 19.16 | 13.08 | 8.98 | 6.18 | 4.28 | 2.98 | 4 |
| 5 | 135.88 | 90.92 | 61.16 | 41.36 | 28.11 | 19.20 | 13.17 | 9.08 | 6.29 | 4.38 | 3.06 | 5 |
| 6 | 132.55 | 89.17 | 60.30 | 40.99 | 28.01 | 19.23 | 13.26 | 9.19 | 6.40 | 4.47 | 3.14 | 6 |
| 7 | 129.30 | 87.45 | 59.46 | 40.63 | 27.91 | 19.26 | 13.35 | 9.30 | 6.51 | 4.57 | 3.23 | 7 |
| 8 | 126.13 | 85.76 | 58.62 | 40.27 | 27.81 | 19.29 | 13.45 | 9.41 | 6.62 | 4.68 | 3.32 | 8 |
| 9 | 123.03 | 84.10 | 57.80 | 39.92 | 27.70 | 19.32 | 13.54 | 9.53 | 6.73 | 4.78 | 3.41 | 9 |
| 10 | 120.00 | 82.48 | 56.98 | 39.56 | 27.60 | 19.35 | 13.63 | 9.64 | 6.85 | 4.89 | 3.50 | 10 |
| 11 | 117.06 | 80.89 | 56.18 | 39.21 | 27.50 | 19.38 | 13.72 | 9.75 | 6.97 | 4.99 | 3.60 | 11 |
| 12 | 114.18 | 79.32 | 55.39 | 38.87 | 27.40 | 19.41 | 13.81 | 9.87 | 7.08 | 5.11 | 3.69 | 12 |
| 13 | 111.37 | 77.79 | 54.61 | 38.52 | 27.30 | 19.44 | 13.90 | 9.99 | 7.20 | 5.22 | 3.79 | 13 |
| 14 | 108.63 | 76.28 | 53.84 | 38.18 | 27.20 | 19.47 | 14.00 | 10.11 | 7.33 | 5.33 | 3.90 | 14 |
| 15 | 105.96 | 74.81 | 53.08 | 37.84 | 27.10 | 19.50 | 14.09 | 10.23 | 7.45 | 5.45 | 4.00 | 15 |
| 16 | 103.35 | 73.36 | 52.33 | 37.50 | 27.00 | 19.53 | 14.19 | 10.35 | 7.58 | 5.57 | 4.11 | 16 |
| 17 | 100.81 | 71.94 | 51.59 | 37.17 | 26.90 | 19.56 | 14.28 | 10.47 | 7.71 | 5.70 | 4.23 | 17 |
| 18 | 98.33 | 70.55 | 50.86 | 36.84 | 26.80 | 19.59 | 14.38 | 10.60 | 7.84 | 5.82 | 4.34 | 18 |
| 19 | 95.92 | 69.19 | 50.15 | 36.52 | 26.71 | 19.62 | 14.47 | 10.72 | 7.97 | 5.95 | 4.46 | 19 |
| 20 | 93.58 | 67.87 | 49.45 | 36.20 | 26.61 | 19.65 | 14.57 | 10.85 | 8.11 | 6.09 | 4.58 | 20 |
| 21 | 91.29 | 66.56 | 48.76 | 35.88 | 26.52 | 19.69 | 14.67 | 10.98 | 8.25 | 6.22 | 4.71 | 21 |
| 22 | 89.05 | 65.28 | 48.07 | 35.56 | 26.42 | 19.72 | 14.77 | 11.11 | 8.39 | 6.36 | 4.84 | 22 |
| 23 | 86.86 | 64.01 | 47.39 | 35.24 | 26.32 | 19.74 | 14.87 | 11.24 | 8.53 | 6.50 | 4.97 | 23 |
| 24 | 84.71 | 62.77 | 46.72 | 34.93 | 26.23 | 19.77 | 14.97 | 11.38 | 8.68 | 6.65 | 5.11 | 24 |
| 25 | 82.63 | 61.55 | 46.06 | 34.62 | 26.13 | 19.80 | 15.07 | 11.51 | 8.83 | 6.79 | 5.25 | 25 |
| 26 | 80.60 | 60.37 | 45.41 | 34.31 | 26.03 | 19.83 | 15.17 | 11.65 | 8.98 | 6.94 | 5.39 | 26 |
| 27 | 78.62 | 59.20 | 44.77 | 34.01 | 25.94 | 19.86 | 15.27 | 11.79 | 9.13 | 7.10 | 5.54 | 27 |
| 28 | 76.69 | 58.06 | 44.14 | 33.71 | 25.84 | 19.89 | 15.38 | 11.93 | 9.29 | 7.26 | 5.69 | 28 |
| 29 | 74.81 | 56.94 | 43.52 | 33.41 | 25.75 | 19.93 | 15.48 | 12.07 | 9.44 | 7.42 | 5.84 | 29 |
| 30 | 72.98 | 55.84 | 42.91 | 33.12 | 25.66 | 19.96 | 15.58 | 12.21 | 9.61 | 7.58 | 6.00 | 30 |
| 31 | 71.20 | 54.77 | 42.32 | 32.83 | 25.57 | 19.99 | 15.69 | 12.36 | 9.77 | 7.75 | 6.17 | 31 |
| 32 | 69.46 | 53.73 | 41.73 | 32.54 | 25.48 | 20.03 | 15.80 | 12.51 | 9.94 | 7.92 | 6.34 | 32 |
| 33 | 67.77 | 52.70 | 41.15 | 32.26 | 25.39 | 20.06 | 15.91 | 12.66 | 10.11 | 8.10 | 6.51 | 33 |
| 34 | 66.12 | 51.69 | 40.58 | 31.98 | 25.30 | 20.09 | 16.02 | 12.81 | 10.28 | 8.28 | 6.69 | 34 |
| 35 | 64.50 | 50.70 | 40.01 | 31.70 | 25.21 | 20.13 | 16.13 | 12.97 | 10.46 | 8.47 | 6.88 | 35 |
| 36 | 62.93 | 49.73 | 39.45 | 31.43 | 25.13 | 20.16 | 16.24 | 13.12 | 10.64 | 8.66 | 7.06 | 36 |
| 37 | 61.41 | 48.78 | 38.91 | 31.15 | 25.04 | 20.20 | 16.35 | 13.28 | 10.83 | 8.85 | 7.26 | 37 |
| 38 | 59.91 | 47.85 | 38.37 | 30.89 | 24.95 | 20.23 | 16.47 | 13.44 | 11.01 | 9.05 | 7.46 | 38 |
| 39 | 58.46 | 46.94 | 37.84 | 30.62 | 24.87 | 20.27 | 16.58 | 13.61 | 11.20 | 9.25 | 7.67 | 39 |
| 40 | 57.04 | 46.05 | 37.32 | 30.36 | 24.79 | 20.31 | 16.70 | 13.77 | 11.40 | 9.46 | 7.88 | 40 |
| 41 | 55.66 | 45.17 | 36.80 | 30.10 | 24.70 | 20.35 | 16.81 | 13.94 | 11.60 | 9.67 | 8.10 | 41 |
| 42 | 54.31 | 44.32 | 36.30 | 29.84 | 24.62 | 20.38 | 16.93 | 14.11 | 11.80 | 9.89 | 8.32 | 42 |
| 43 | 53.01 | 43.48 | 35.81 | 29.59 | 24.54 | 20.43 | 17.05 | 14.29 | 12.00 | 10.12 | 8.55 | 43 |
| 44 | 51.74 | 42.67 | 35.33 | 29.35 | 24.47 | 20.47 | 17.18 | 14.46 | 12.22 | 10.35 | 8.79 | 44 |
| 45 | 50.50 | 41.88 | 34.85 | 29.11 | 24.40 | 20.51 | 17.31 | 14.65 | 12.43 | 10.58 | 9.04 | 45 |
| 46 | 49.30 | 41.10 | 34.39 | 28.87 | 24.32 | 20.56 | 17.44 | 14.83 | 12.65 | 10.83 | 9.29 | 46 |
| 47 | 48.13 | 40.34 | 33.93 | 28.64 | 24.26 | 20.61 | 17.57 | 15.02 | 12.88 | 11.08 | 9.55 | 47 |
| 48 | 47.00 | 39.61 | 33.49 | 28.42 | 24.19 | 20.66 | 17.70 | 15.22 | 13.11 | 11.33 | 9.82 | 48 |
| 49 | 45.91 | 38.89 | 33.06 | 28.20 | 24.14 | 20.72 | 17.85 | 15.42 | 13.35 | 11.60 | 10.10 | 49 |
| 50 | 44.85 | 38.20 | 32.64 | 27.99 | 24.08 | 20.78 | 17.99 | 15.62 | 13.60 | 11.88 | 10.40 | 50 |
| 51 | 43.82 | 37.52 | 32.23 | 27.79 | 24.03 | 20.85 | 18.14 | 15.83 | 13.85 | 12.16 | 10.70 | 51 |
| 52 | 42.82 | 36.86 | 31.84 | 27.59 | 23.99 | 20.92 | 18.29 | 16.05 | 14.12 | 12.45 | 11.01 | 52 |
| 53 | 41.85 | 36.22 | 31.45 | 27.40 | 23.95 | 20.99 | 18.45 | 16.27 | 14.38 | 12.75 | 11.33 | 53 |
| 54 | 40.92 | 35.60 | 31.08 | 27.22 | 23.91 | 21.07 | 18.62 | 16.50 | 14.66 | 13.06 | 11.67 | 54 |

**Table 22: Multipliers for loss of pension commencing age 65 (females)** *continued*

| Age at date of trial | Multiplier calculated with allowance for projected mortality from the 2008–based population projections and rate of return of | | | | | | | | | | | Age at date of trial |
|---|---|---|---|---|---|---|---|---|---|---|---|---|
| | *–2.0%* | *–1.5%* | *–1.0%* | *–0.5%* | *0.0%* | *0.5%* | *1.0%* | *1.5%* | *2.0%* | *2.5%* | *3.0%* | |
| 55 | 40.02 | 35.01 | 30.73 | 27.05 | 23.89 | 21.16 | 18.80 | 16.74 | 14.95 | 13.39 | 12.02 | 55 |
| 56 | 39.16 | 34.44 | 30.38 | 26.89 | 23.87 | 21.26 | 18.98 | 16.99 | 15.25 | 13.73 | 12.38 | 56 |
| 57 | 38.32 | 33.88 | 30.05 | 26.74 | 23.86 | 21.36 | 19.17 | 17.25 | 15.56 | 14.08 | 12.76 | 57 |
| 58 | 37.51 | 33.34 | 29.73 | 26.59 | 23.86 | 21.46 | 19.36 | 17.51 | 15.88 | 14.44 | 13.16 | 58 |
| 59 | 36.72 | 32.81 | 29.42 | 26.45 | 23.85 | 21.57 | 19.56 | 17.78 | 16.21 | 14.81 | 13.56 | 59 |
| 60 | 35.94 | 32.29 | 29.10 | 26.31 | 23.85 | 21.68 | 19.76 | 18.06 | 16.54 | 15.19 | 13.98 | 60 |
| 61 | 35.18 | 31.78 | 28.80 | 26.17 | 23.85 | 21.79 | 19.97 | 18.34 | 16.89 | 15.59 | 14.42 | 61 |
| 62 | 34.46 | 31.29 | 28.51 | 26.04 | 23.86 | 21.91 | 20.18 | 18.63 | 17.25 | 16.00 | 14.87 | 62 |
| 63 | 33.76 | 30.83 | 28.23 | 25.93 | 23.88 | 22.05 | 20.41 | 18.94 | 17.62 | 16.43 | 15.35 | 63 |
| 64 | 33.10 | 30.39 | 27.98 | 25.83 | 23.92 | 22.20 | 20.66 | 19.27 | 18.02 | 16.89 | 15.86 | 64 |
| 65 | 32.50 | 29.99 | 27.76 | 25.77 | 23.98 | 22.38 | 20.93 | 19.63 | 18.45 | 17.38 | 16.40 | 65 |

## Table 23: Multipliers for loss of pension commencing age 70 (males)

| Age at date of trial | Multiplier calculated with allowance for projected mortality from the 2008–based population projections and rate of return of | | | | | | | | | | | Age at date of trial |
|---|---|---|---|---|---|---|---|---|---|---|---|---|
| | *-2.0%* | *-1.5%* | *-1.0%* | *-0.5%* | *0.0%* | *0.5%* | *1.0%* | *1.5%* | *2.0%* | *2.5%* | *3.0%* | |
| 0 | 116.52 | 75.30 | 48.89 | 31.89 | 20.90 | 13.76 | 9.09 | 6.04 | 4.02 | 2.69 | 1.81 | 0 |
| 1 | 114.10 | 74.13 | 48.39 | 31.74 | 20.91 | 13.83 | 9.19 | 6.13 | 4.11 | 2.76 | 1.87 | 1 |
| 2 | 111.17 | 72.62 | 47.66 | 31.42 | 20.81 | 13.84 | 9.24 | 6.20 | 4.17 | 2.82 | 1.91 | 2 |
| 3 | 108.30 | 71.12 | 46.93 | 31.10 | 20.70 | 13.84 | 9.29 | 6.27 | 4.24 | 2.88 | 1.96 | 3 |
| 4 | 105.50 | 69.65 | 46.20 | 30.78 | 20.60 | 13.85 | 9.34 | 6.33 | 4.31 | 2.94 | 2.02 | 4 |
| 5 | 102.76 | 68.21 | 45.49 | 30.47 | 20.50 | 13.85 | 9.39 | 6.40 | 4.37 | 3.00 | 2.07 | 5 |
| 6 | 100.08 | 66.80 | 44.78 | 30.16 | 20.39 | 13.85 | 9.44 | 6.46 | 4.44 | 3.06 | 2.12 | 6 |
| 7 | 97.48 | 65.41 | 44.09 | 29.84 | 20.29 | 13.85 | 9.49 | 6.53 | 4.51 | 3.13 | 2.18 | 7 |
| 8 | 94.95 | 64.05 | 43.40 | 29.54 | 20.19 | 13.85 | 9.54 | 6.60 | 4.58 | 3.19 | 2.23 | 8 |
| 9 | 92.47 | 62.71 | 42.72 | 29.23 | 20.08 | 13.85 | 9.59 | 6.67 | 4.65 | 3.26 | 2.29 | 9 |
| 10 | 90.04 | 61.40 | 42.05 | 28.92 | 19.97 | 13.85 | 9.64 | 6.74 | 4.73 | 3.33 | 2.35 | 10 |
| 11 | 87.69 | 60.11 | 41.39 | 28.62 | 19.87 | 13.85 | 9.69 | 6.81 | 4.80 | 3.39 | 2.41 | 11 |
| 12 | 85.39 | 58.86 | 40.74 | 28.32 | 19.76 | 13.85 | 9.74 | 6.88 | 4.87 | 3.46 | 2.47 | 12 |
| 13 | 83.16 | 57.63 | 40.10 | 28.02 | 19.66 | 13.85 | 9.79 | 6.95 | 4.95 | 3.54 | 2.54 | 13 |
| 14 | 80.98 | 56.42 | 39.47 | 27.73 | 19.56 | 13.85 | 9.84 | 7.02 | 5.02 | 3.61 | 2.60 | 14 |
| 15 | 78.87 | 55.24 | 38.85 | 27.44 | 19.45 | 13.85 | 9.89 | 7.09 | 5.10 | 3.68 | 2.67 | 15 |
| 16 | 76.81 | 54.09 | 38.25 | 27.15 | 19.35 | 13.85 | 9.94 | 7.16 | 5.18 | 3.76 | 2.74 | 16 |
| 17 | 74.80 | 52.96 | 37.65 | 26.87 | 19.25 | 13.85 | 9.99 | 7.24 | 5.26 | 3.84 | 2.81 | 17 |
| 18 | 72.86 | 51.86 | 37.06 | 26.59 | 19.15 | 13.85 | 10.05 | 7.31 | 5.34 | 3.92 | 2.88 | 18 |
| 19 | 70.97 | 50.79 | 36.49 | 26.32 | 19.06 | 13.85 | 10.10 | 7.39 | 5.43 | 4.00 | 2.95 | 19 |
| 20 | 69.13 | 49.74 | 35.93 | 26.05 | 18.96 | 13.85 | 10.15 | 7.47 | 5.51 | 4.08 | 3.03 | 20 |
| 21 | 67.34 | 48.71 | 35.38 | 25.79 | 18.87 | 13.85 | 10.21 | 7.55 | 5.60 | 4.17 | 3.11 | 21 |
| 22 | 65.59 | 47.70 | 34.82 | 25.52 | 18.77 | 13.85 | 10.26 | 7.63 | 5.69 | 4.25 | 3.19 | 22 |
| 23 | 63.88 | 46.71 | 34.28 | 25.25 | 18.67 | 13.85 | 10.31 | 7.70 | 5.77 | 4.34 | 3.27 | 23 |
| 24 | 62.22 | 45.74 | 33.75 | 24.99 | 18.58 | 13.85 | 10.37 | 7.78 | 5.86 | 4.43 | 3.36 | 24 |
| 25 | 60.60 | 44.79 | 33.22 | 24.74 | 18.48 | 13.86 | 10.42 | 7.87 | 5.96 | 4.52 | 3.44 | 25 |
| 26 | 59.04 | 43.87 | 32.71 | 24.48 | 18.39 | 13.86 | 10.48 | 7.95 | 6.05 | 4.62 | 3.53 | 26 |
| 27 | 57.52 | 42.97 | 32.21 | 24.24 | 18.30 | 13.86 | 10.54 | 8.03 | 6.14 | 4.71 | 3.63 | 27 |
| 28 | 56.02 | 42.07 | 31.71 | 23.99 | 18.21 | 13.86 | 10.59 | 8.12 | 6.24 | 4.81 | 3.72 | 28 |
| 29 | 54.56 | 41.20 | 31.22 | 23.74 | 18.11 | 13.86 | 10.65 | 8.20 | 6.34 | 4.91 | 3.82 | 29 |
| 30 | 53.15 | 40.34 | 30.73 | 23.49 | 18.02 | 13.87 | 10.70 | 8.29 | 6.44 | 5.01 | 3.92 | 30 |
| 31 | 51.78 | 39.52 | 30.27 | 23.26 | 17.93 | 13.87 | 10.76 | 8.38 | 6.54 | 5.12 | 4.02 | 31 |
| 32 | 50.46 | 38.72 | 29.81 | 23.03 | 17.85 | 13.88 | 10.82 | 8.47 | 6.64 | 5.23 | 4.12 | 32 |
| 33 | 49.19 | 37.94 | 29.37 | 22.81 | 17.77 | 13.89 | 10.89 | 8.56 | 6.75 | 5.34 | 4.23 | 33 |
| 34 | 47.94 | 37.18 | 28.93 | 22.59 | 17.69 | 13.90 | 10.95 | 8.66 | 6.86 | 5.45 | 4.35 | 34 |
| 35 | 46.72 | 36.43 | 28.50 | 22.37 | 17.61 | 13.91 | 11.02 | 8.75 | 6.97 | 5.57 | 4.46 | 35 |
| 36 | 45.54 | 35.70 | 28.08 | 22.15 | 17.53 | 13.92 | 11.08 | 8.85 | 7.08 | 5.69 | 4.58 | 36 |
| 37 | 44.39 | 34.98 | 27.66 | 21.94 | 17.45 | 13.93 | 11.15 | 8.95 | 7.20 | 5.81 | 4.70 | 37 |
| 38 | 43.26 | 34.27 | 27.24 | 21.72 | 17.37 | 13.94 | 11.21 | 9.04 | 7.32 | 5.93 | 4.82 | 38 |
| 39 | 42.16 | 33.58 | 26.84 | 21.51 | 17.30 | 13.95 | 11.28 | 9.14 | 7.43 | 6.06 | 4.95 | 39 |
| 40 | 41.09 | 32.90 | 26.43 | 21.30 | 17.22 | 13.95 | 11.34 | 9.24 | 7.55 | 6.19 | 5.08 | 40 |
| 41 | 40.05 | 32.24 | 26.04 | 21.10 | 17.14 | 13.97 | 11.41 | 9.35 | 7.68 | 6.32 | 5.22 | 41 |
| 42 | 39.04 | 31.60 | 25.66 | 20.90 | 17.07 | 13.98 | 11.48 | 9.45 | 7.80 | 6.46 | 5.36 | 42 |
| 43 | 38.06 | 30.97 | 25.28 | 20.70 | 16.99 | 13.99 | 11.55 | 9.56 | 7.93 | 6.60 | 5.50 | 43 |
| 44 | 37.11 | 30.36 | 24.92 | 20.51 | 16.92 | 14.01 | 11.62 | 9.67 | 8.06 | 6.74 | 5.65 | 44 |
| 45 | 36.18 | 29.76 | 24.56 | 20.32 | 16.85 | 14.02 | 11.69 | 9.78 | 8.20 | 6.89 | 5.80 | 45 |
| 46 | 35.28 | 29.18 | 24.20 | 20.13 | 16.79 | 14.04 | 11.77 | 9.89 | 8.33 | 7.04 | 5.96 | 46 |
| 47 | 34.41 | 28.61 | 23.86 | 19.95 | 16.72 | 14.06 | 11.85 | 10.01 | 8.47 | 7.19 | 6.12 | 47 |
| 48 | 33.57 | 28.06 | 23.52 | 19.77 | 16.66 | 14.08 | 11.92 | 10.13 | 8.62 | 7.35 | 6.29 | 48 |
| 49 | 32.75 | 27.52 | 23.19 | 19.60 | 16.60 | 14.10 | 12.01 | 10.25 | 8.77 | 7.52 | 6.46 | 49 |
| 50 | 31.96 | 27.01 | 22.88 | 19.43 | 16.55 | 14.13 | 12.09 | 10.38 | 8.92 | 7.69 | 6.64 | 50 |
| 51 | 31.21 | 26.51 | 22.58 | 19.28 | 16.51 | 14.17 | 12.19 | 10.51 | 9.08 | 7.87 | 6.83 | 51 |
| 52 | 30.48 | 26.03 | 22.29 | 19.13 | 16.47 | 14.21 | 12.28 | 10.65 | 9.25 | 8.05 | 7.02 | 52 |
| 53 | 29.79 | 25.57 | 22.01 | 19.00 | 16.43 | 14.25 | 12.39 | 10.79 | 9.42 | 8.24 | 7.23 | 53 |
| 54 | 29.12 | 25.13 | 21.75 | 18.87 | 16.41 | 14.30 | 12.50 | 10.94 | 9.60 | 8.44 | 7.44 | 54 |

## Table 23: Multipliers for loss of pension commencing age 70 (males) *continued*

| Age at date of trial | \-2.0% | \-1.5% | \-1.0% | \-0.5% | 0.0% | 0.5% | 1.0% | 1.5% | 2.0% | 2.5% | 3.0% | Age at date of trial |
|---|---|---|---|---|---|---|---|---|---|---|---|---|
| 55 | 28.48 | 24.71 | 21.50 | 18.75 | 16.39 | 14.36 | 12.61 | 11.10 | 9.79 | 8.65 | 7.66 | 55 |
| 56 | 27.88 | 24.32 | 21.27 | 18.65 | 16.39 | 14.43 | 12.74 | 11.27 | 9.99 | 8.88 | 7.90 | 56 |
| 57 | 27.30 | 23.94 | 21.05 | 18.55 | 16.39 | 14.51 | 12.88 | 11.45 | 10.20 | 9.11 | 8.15 | 57 |
| 58 | 26.74 | 23.58 | 20.84 | 18.46 | 16.40 | 14.59 | 13.02 | 11.63 | 10.42 | 9.35 | 8.40 | 58 |
| 59 | 26.19 | 23.22 | 20.63 | 18.38 | 16.40 | 14.68 | 13.16 | 11.82 | 10.64 | 9.59 | 8.67 | 59 |
| 60 | 25.65 | 22.86 | 20.42 | 18.29 | 16.41 | 14.76 | 13.30 | 12.01 | 10.86 | 9.85 | 8.94 | 60 |
| 61 | 25.13 | 22.52 | 20.22 | 18.20 | 16.42 | 14.84 | 13.44 | 12.20 | 11.10 | 10.11 | 9.23 | 61 |
| 62 | 24.63 | 22.19 | 20.03 | 18.13 | 16.44 | 14.94 | 13.60 | 12.41 | 11.34 | 10.38 | 9.52 | 62 |
| 63 | 24.16 | 21.88 | 19.86 | 18.07 | 16.47 | 15.04 | 13.77 | 12.63 | 11.60 | 10.67 | 9.84 | 63 |
| 64 | 23.72 | 21.60 | 19.71 | 18.03 | 16.52 | 15.17 | 13.95 | 12.86 | 11.87 | 10.98 | 10.18 | 64 |
| 65 | 23.33 | 21.35 | 19.59 | 18.01 | 16.59 | 15.31 | 14.16 | 13.12 | 12.17 | 11.32 | 10.54 | 65 |
| 66 | 22.97 | 21.14 | 19.50 | 18.02 | 16.69 | 15.48 | 14.39 | 13.40 | 12.50 | 11.68 | 10.93 | 66 |
| 67 | 22.66 | 20.96 | 19.44 | 18.06 | 16.81 | 15.68 | 14.65 | 13.71 | 12.86 | 12.07 | 11.36 | 67 |
| 68 | 22.38 | 20.82 | 19.40 | 18.12 | 16.96 | 15.90 | 14.93 | 14.05 | 13.24 | 12.50 | 11.82 | 68 |
| 69 | 22.13 | 20.70 | 19.40 | 18.21 | 17.13 | 16.15 | 15.24 | 14.42 | 13.66 | 12.96 | 12.31 | 69 |
| 70 | 21.91 | 20.60 | 19.41 | 18.32 | 17.32 | 16.41 | 15.58 | 14.81 | 14.10 | 13.44 | 12.84 | 70 |

Multiplier calculated with allowance for projected mortality from the 2008–based population projections and rate of return of

## Table 24: Multipliers for loss of pension commencing age 70 (females)

| Age at date of trial | Multiplier calculated with allowance for projected mortality from the 2008–based population projections and rate of return of | | | | | | | | | | | Age at date of trial |
|---|---|---|---|---|---|---|---|---|---|---|---|---|
| | -2.0% | -1.5% | -1.0% | -0.5% | 0.0% | 0.5% | 1.0% | 1.5% | 2.0% | 2.5% | 3.0% | |
| 0 | 134.74 | 86.70 | 56.06 | 36.43 | 23.78 | 15.60 | 10.28 | 6.80 | 4.52 | 3.01 | 2.02 | 0 |
| 1 | 131.93 | 85.35 | 55.49 | 36.25 | 23.79 | 15.68 | 10.38 | 6.91 | 4.61 | 3.09 | 2.08 | 1 |
| 2 | 128.66 | 83.68 | 54.69 | 35.92 | 23.69 | 15.70 | 10.45 | 6.99 | 4.69 | 3.16 | 2.14 | 2 |
| 3 | 125.45 | 82.03 | 53.90 | 35.58 | 23.60 | 15.72 | 10.52 | 7.07 | 4.77 | 3.23 | 2.20 | 3 |
| 4 | 122.32 | 80.42 | 53.12 | 35.25 | 23.50 | 15.74 | 10.58 | 7.15 | 4.85 | 3.30 | 2.25 | 4 |
| 5 | 119.26 | 78.83 | 52.35 | 34.93 | 23.41 | 15.76 | 10.65 | 7.23 | 4.93 | 3.37 | 2.32 | 5 |
| 6 | 116.28 | 77.27 | 51.59 | 34.60 | 23.31 | 15.77 | 10.72 | 7.31 | 5.01 | 3.44 | 2.38 | 6 |
| 7 | 113.36 | 75.74 | 50.83 | 34.27 | 23.21 | 15.79 | 10.78 | 7.39 | 5.09 | 3.52 | 2.44 | 7 |
| 8 | 110.51 | 74.23 | 50.09 | 33.95 | 23.11 | 15.80 | 10.85 | 7.48 | 5.18 | 3.59 | 2.51 | 8 |
| 9 | 107.73 | 72.75 | 49.35 | 33.63 | 23.01 | 15.82 | 10.92 | 7.56 | 5.26 | 3.67 | 2.57 | 9 |
| 10 | 105.03 | 71.30 | 48.63 | 33.31 | 22.92 | 15.83 | 10.98 | 7.65 | 5.35 | 3.75 | 2.64 | 10 |
| 11 | 102.39 | 69.89 | 47.92 | 33.00 | 22.82 | 15.85 | 11.05 | 7.73 | 5.43 | 3.83 | 2.71 | 11 |
| 12 | 99.81 | 68.49 | 47.21 | 32.68 | 22.72 | 15.86 | 11.12 | 7.82 | 5.52 | 3.92 | 2.79 | 12 |
| 13 | 97.30 | 67.13 | 46.52 | 32.37 | 22.62 | 15.87 | 11.18 | 7.91 | 5.61 | 4.00 | 2.86 | 13 |
| 14 | 94.85 | 65.79 | 45.83 | 32.07 | 22.53 | 15.89 | 11.25 | 8.00 | 5.71 | 4.09 | 2.94 | 14 |
| 15 | 92.46 | 64.48 | 45.16 | 31.76 | 22.43 | 15.90 | 11.32 | 8.09 | 5.80 | 4.17 | 3.01 | 15 |
| 16 | 90.13 | 63.19 | 44.49 | 31.46 | 22.33 | 15.92 | 11.39 | 8.18 | 5.89 | 4.26 | 3.09 | 16 |
| 17 | 87.86 | 61.93 | 43.84 | 31.16 | 22.24 | 15.93 | 11.46 | 8.27 | 5.99 | 4.36 | 3.18 | 17 |
| 18 | 85.65 | 60.70 | 43.19 | 30.86 | 22.14 | 15.95 | 11.53 | 8.36 | 6.09 | 4.45 | 3.26 | 18 |
| 19 | 83.51 | 59.49 | 42.56 | 30.57 | 22.05 | 15.96 | 11.60 | 8.46 | 6.19 | 4.55 | 3.35 | 19 |
| 20 | 81.42 | 58.32 | 41.94 | 30.29 | 21.96 | 15.98 | 11.67 | 8.55 | 6.29 | 4.64 | 3.44 | 20 |
| 21 | 79.38 | 57.16 | 41.33 | 30.00 | 21.86 | 15.99 | 11.74 | 8.65 | 6.40 | 4.74 | 3.53 | 21 |
| 22 | 77.38 | 56.02 | 40.72 | 29.72 | 21.77 | 16.01 | 11.81 | 8.75 | 6.50 | 4.85 | 3.62 | 22 |
| 23 | 75.43 | 54.90 | 40.12 | 29.43 | 21.67 | 16.02 | 11.88 | 8.85 | 6.61 | 4.95 | 3.72 | 23 |
| 24 | 73.52 | 53.80 | 39.52 | 29.15 | 21.58 | 16.03 | 11.95 | 8.94 | 6.71 | 5.06 | 3.82 | 24 |
| 25 | 71.67 | 52.72 | 38.94 | 28.87 | 21.48 | 16.05 | 12.03 | 9.04 | 6.82 | 5.16 | 3.92 | 25 |
| 26 | 69.86 | 51.67 | 38.37 | 28.60 | 21.39 | 16.06 | 12.10 | 9.14 | 6.93 | 5.28 | 4.03 | 26 |
| 27 | 68.11 | 50.64 | 37.80 | 28.32 | 21.30 | 16.07 | 12.17 | 9.25 | 7.05 | 5.39 | 4.13 | 27 |
| 28 | 66.39 | 49.63 | 37.25 | 28.05 | 21.21 | 16.09 | 12.24 | 9.35 | 7.16 | 5.50 | 4.24 | 28 |
| 29 | 64.72 | 48.64 | 36.70 | 27.79 | 21.11 | 16.10 | 12.32 | 9.46 | 7.28 | 5.62 | 4.36 | 29 |
| 30 | 63.09 | 47.68 | 36.16 | 27.52 | 21.03 | 16.12 | 12.39 | 9.56 | 7.40 | 5.74 | 4.47 | 30 |
| 31 | 61.51 | 46.73 | 35.63 | 27.27 | 20.94 | 16.13 | 12.47 | 9.67 | 7.52 | 5.87 | 4.59 | 31 |
| 32 | 59.98 | 45.81 | 35.11 | 27.01 | 20.85 | 16.15 | 12.55 | 9.78 | 7.65 | 6.00 | 4.72 | 32 |
| 33 | 58.48 | 44.91 | 34.60 | 26.76 | 20.76 | 16.16 | 12.62 | 9.89 | 7.77 | 6.13 | 4.84 | 33 |
| 34 | 57.02 | 44.02 | 34.10 | 26.51 | 20.68 | 16.18 | 12.70 | 10.00 | 7.90 | 6.26 | 4.97 | 34 |
| 35 | 55.59 | 43.14 | 33.60 | 26.26 | 20.59 | 16.20 | 12.78 | 10.12 | 8.03 | 6.39 | 5.10 | 35 |
| 36 | 54.20 | 42.29 | 33.11 | 26.01 | 20.50 | 16.21 | 12.86 | 10.23 | 8.16 | 6.53 | 5.24 | 36 |
| 37 | 52.85 | 41.45 | 32.63 | 25.77 | 20.42 | 16.23 | 12.94 | 10.35 | 8.30 | 6.67 | 5.38 | 37 |
| 38 | 51.53 | 40.64 | 32.16 | 25.53 | 20.33 | 16.25 | 13.02 | 10.46 | 8.44 | 6.82 | 5.53 | 38 |
| 39 | 50.24 | 39.83 | 31.69 | 25.29 | 20.25 | 16.26 | 13.10 | 10.58 | 8.57 | 6.97 | 5.67 | 39 |
| 40 | 48.99 | 39.05 | 31.23 | 25.06 | 20.17 | 16.28 | 13.18 | 10.70 | 8.72 | 7.12 | 5.83 | 40 |
| 41 | 47.77 | 38.28 | 30.78 | 24.82 | 20.08 | 16.30 | 13.27 | 10.83 | 8.86 | 7.27 | 5.98 | 41 |
| 42 | 46.58 | 37.53 | 30.34 | 24.60 | 20.00 | 16.32 | 13.35 | 10.95 | 9.01 | 7.43 | 6.14 | 42 |
| 43 | 45.43 | 36.80 | 29.90 | 24.37 | 19.93 | 16.34 | 13.44 | 11.08 | 9.16 | 7.59 | 6.31 | 43 |
| 44 | 44.31 | 36.08 | 29.48 | 24.15 | 19.85 | 16.36 | 13.52 | 11.21 | 9.31 | 7.76 | 6.48 | 44 |
| 45 | 43.23 | 35.39 | 29.06 | 23.94 | 19.78 | 16.39 | 13.61 | 11.34 | 9.47 | 7.93 | 6.66 | 45 |
| 46 | 42.17 | 34.70 | 28.65 | 23.73 | 19.70 | 16.41 | 13.70 | 11.47 | 9.63 | 8.11 | 6.84 | 46 |
| 47 | 41.14 | 34.04 | 28.25 | 23.52 | 19.63 | 16.44 | 13.80 | 11.61 | 9.80 | 8.29 | 7.03 | 47 |
| 48 | 40.14 | 33.39 | 27.86 | 23.32 | 19.57 | 16.47 | 13.89 | 11.75 | 9.97 | 8.47 | 7.22 | 48 |
| 49 | 39.18 | 32.77 | 27.49 | 23.12 | 19.51 | 16.50 | 13.99 | 11.90 | 10.14 | 8.67 | 7.42 | 49 |
| 50 | 38.25 | 32.16 | 27.12 | 22.93 | 19.45 | 16.54 | 14.10 | 12.05 | 10.32 | 8.86 | 7.63 | 50 |
| 51 | 37.34 | 31.56 | 26.76 | 22.75 | 19.39 | 16.57 | 14.20 | 12.20 | 10.51 | 9.07 | 7.84 | 51 |
| 52 | 36.46 | 30.99 | 26.41 | 22.57 | 19.34 | 16.62 | 14.31 | 12.36 | 10.69 | 9.28 | 8.06 | 52 |
| 53 | 35.61 | 30.43 | 26.07 | 22.40 | 19.29 | 16.66 | 14.42 | 12.52 | 10.89 | 9.49 | 8.30 | 53 |
| 54 | 34.79 | 29.89 | 25.74 | 22.23 | 19.25 | 16.71 | 14.54 | 12.69 | 11.09 | 9.72 | 8.53 | 54 |

## Table 24: Multipliers for loss of pension commencing age 70 (females) *continued*

| Age at date of trial | Multiplier calculated with allowance for projected mortality from the 2008–based population projections and rate of return of | | | | | | | | | | | Age at date of trial |
|---|---|---|---|---|---|---|---|---|---|---|---|---|
| | *–2.0%* | *–1.5%* | *–1.0%* | *–0.5%* | *0.0%* | *0.5%* | *1.0%* | *1.5%* | *2.0%* | *2.5%* | *3.0%* | |
| 55 | 34.00 | 29.36 | 25.43 | 22.08 | 19.21 | 16.77 | 14.67 | 12.86 | 11.30 | 9.95 | 8.78 | 55 |
| 56 | 33.24 | 28.86 | 25.12 | 21.93 | 19.19 | 16.83 | 14.80 | 13.04 | 11.52 | 10.19 | 9.04 | 56 |
| 57 | 32.51 | 28.37 | 24.83 | 21.79 | 19.16 | 16.89 | 14.93 | 13.23 | 11.74 | 10.44 | 9.31 | 57 |
| 58 | 31.79 | 27.90 | 24.54 | 21.65 | 19.14 | 16.96 | 15.07 | 13.42 | 11.97 | 10.70 | 9.59 | 58 |
| 59 | 31.10 | 27.43 | 24.26 | 21.51 | 19.12 | 17.03 | 15.21 | 13.61 | 12.21 | 10.97 | 9.88 | 59 |
| 60 | 30.41 | 26.97 | 23.98 | 21.37 | 19.10 | 17.10 | 15.35 | 13.81 | 12.44 | 11.24 | 10.17 | 60 |
| 61 | 29.74 | 26.52 | 23.71 | 21.24 | 19.08 | 17.17 | 15.49 | 14.01 | 12.69 | 11.52 | 10.48 | 61 |
| 62 | 29.10 | 26.09 | 23.44 | 21.11 | 19.06 | 17.25 | 15.64 | 14.22 | 12.94 | 11.81 | 10.80 | 62 |
| 63 | 28.48 | 25.67 | 23.19 | 21.00 | 19.06 | 17.33 | 15.80 | 14.43 | 13.21 | 12.11 | 11.13 | 63 |
| 64 | 27.90 | 25.28 | 22.96 | 20.90 | 19.07 | 17.43 | 15.97 | 14.67 | 13.49 | 12.43 | 11.48 | 64 |
| 65 | 27.36 | 24.92 | 22.75 | 20.82 | 19.10 | 17.55 | 16.17 | 14.92 | 13.79 | 12.78 | 11.86 | 65 |
| 66 | 26.86 | 24.60 | 22.58 | 20.77 | 19.15 | 17.69 | 16.38 | 15.19 | 14.12 | 13.15 | 12.26 | 66 |
| 67 | 26.40 | 24.30 | 22.43 | 20.74 | 19.22 | 17.85 | 16.61 | 15.49 | 14.47 | 13.54 | 12.69 | 67 |
| 68 | 25.97 | 24.04 | 22.30 | 20.73 | 19.32 | 18.03 | 16.87 | 15.81 | 14.84 | 13.96 | 13.15 | 68 |
| 69 | 25.57 | 23.79 | 22.19 | 20.74 | 19.43 | 18.23 | 17.14 | 16.15 | 15.24 | 14.40 | 13.64 | 69 |
| 70 | 25.19 | 23.57 | 22.10 | 20.76 | 19.55 | 18.44 | 17.43 | 16.50 | 15.65 | 14.87 | 14.15 | 70 |

## Table 25: Multipliers for loss of pension commencing age 75 (males)

| Age at date of trial | Multiplier calculated with allowance for projected mortality from the 2008–based population projections and rate of return of | | | | | | | | | | | Age at date of trial |
|---|---|---|---|---|---|---|---|---|---|---|---|---|
| | -2.0% | -1.5% | -1.0% | -0.5% | 0.0% | 0.5% | 1.0% | 1.5% | 2.0% | 2.5% | 3.0% | |
| 0 | 97.81 | 62.36 | 39.93 | 25.68 | 16.58 | 10.74 | 6.99 | 4.57 | 2.99 | 1.97 | 1.30 | 0 |
| 1 | 95.69 | 61.34 | 39.49 | 25.52 | 16.56 | 10.79 | 7.06 | 4.63 | 3.05 | 2.02 | 1.34 | 1 |
| 2 | 93.15 | 60.03 | 38.85 | 25.24 | 16.47 | 10.79 | 7.09 | 4.68 | 3.10 | 2.06 | 1.37 | 2 |
| 3 | 90.66 | 58.74 | 38.22 | 24.97 | 16.37 | 10.78 | 7.12 | 4.73 | 3.15 | 2.10 | 1.41 | 3 |
| 4 | 88.23 | 57.47 | 37.59 | 24.69 | 16.28 | 10.77 | 7.16 | 4.77 | 3.19 | 2.14 | 1.44 | 4 |
| 5 | 85.86 | 56.23 | 36.98 | 24.41 | 16.18 | 10.76 | 7.19 | 4.82 | 3.24 | 2.19 | 1.48 | 5 |
| 6 | 83.55 | 55.01 | 36.37 | 24.14 | 16.08 | 10.75 | 7.22 | 4.86 | 3.29 | 2.23 | 1.52 | 6 |
| 7 | 81.31 | 53.82 | 35.77 | 23.86 | 15.98 | 10.74 | 7.25 | 4.91 | 3.33 | 2.27 | 1.55 | 7 |
| 8 | 79.12 | 52.65 | 35.18 | 23.59 | 15.88 | 10.73 | 7.28 | 4.95 | 3.38 | 2.32 | 1.59 | 8 |
| 9 | 76.97 | 51.50 | 34.59 | 23.32 | 15.79 | 10.72 | 7.31 | 5.00 | 3.43 | 2.36 | 1.63 | 9 |
| 10 | 74.89 | 50.37 | 34.02 | 23.06 | 15.69 | 10.71 | 7.34 | 5.05 | 3.48 | 2.41 | 1.67 | 10 |
| 11 | 72.85 | 49.27 | 33.45 | 22.79 | 15.59 | 10.70 | 7.37 | 5.09 | 3.53 | 2.46 | 1.71 | 11 |
| 12 | 70.88 | 48.19 | 32.89 | 22.53 | 15.49 | 10.69 | 7.40 | 5.14 | 3.58 | 2.50 | 1.76 | 12 |
| 13 | 68.96 | 47.14 | 32.34 | 22.27 | 15.39 | 10.67 | 7.43 | 5.19 | 3.63 | 2.55 | 1.80 | 13 |
| 14 | 67.09 | 46.10 | 31.80 | 22.02 | 15.29 | 10.66 | 7.46 | 5.23 | 3.68 | 2.60 | 1.84 | 14 |
| 15 | 65.27 | 45.10 | 31.27 | 21.76 | 15.20 | 10.65 | 7.49 | 5.28 | 3.74 | 2.65 | 1.89 | 15 |
| 16 | 63.50 | 44.11 | 30.75 | 21.51 | 15.10 | 10.64 | 7.52 | 5.33 | 3.79 | 2.71 | 1.94 | 16 |
| 17 | 61.78 | 43.15 | 30.24 | 21.27 | 15.01 | 10.63 | 7.55 | 5.38 | 3.85 | 2.76 | 1.98 | 17 |
| 18 | 60.12 | 42.21 | 29.74 | 21.03 | 14.92 | 10.62 | 7.58 | 5.43 | 3.90 | 2.81 | 2.03 | 18 |
| 19 | 58.50 | 41.29 | 29.25 | 20.79 | 14.82 | 10.61 | 7.61 | 5.48 | 3.96 | 2.87 | 2.08 | 19 |
| 20 | 56.93 | 40.40 | 28.77 | 20.55 | 14.74 | 10.60 | 7.65 | 5.53 | 4.02 | 2.92 | 2.13 | 20 |
| 21 | 55.40 | 39.52 | 28.29 | 20.32 | 14.65 | 10.59 | 7.68 | 5.59 | 4.08 | 2.98 | 2.19 | 21 |
| 22 | 53.90 | 38.66 | 27.82 | 20.09 | 14.55 | 10.58 | 7.71 | 5.64 | 4.13 | 3.04 | 2.24 | 22 |
| 23 | 52.44 | 37.81 | 27.36 | 19.86 | 14.46 | 10.57 | 7.74 | 5.69 | 4.19 | 3.10 | 2.30 | 23 |
| 24 | 51.02 | 36.99 | 26.90 | 19.63 | 14.37 | 10.55 | 7.77 | 5.74 | 4.25 | 3.16 | 2.35 | 24 |
| 25 | 49.64 | 36.18 | 26.46 | 19.41 | 14.28 | 10.54 | 7.81 | 5.80 | 4.31 | 3.22 | 2.41 | 25 |
| 26 | 48.31 | 35.40 | 26.02 | 19.19 | 14.20 | 10.53 | 7.84 | 5.85 | 4.38 | 3.29 | 2.47 | 26 |
| 27 | 47.02 | 34.64 | 25.60 | 18.98 | 14.11 | 10.52 | 7.87 | 5.91 | 4.44 | 3.35 | 2.53 | 27 |
| 28 | 45.74 | 33.88 | 25.17 | 18.76 | 14.02 | 10.51 | 7.90 | 5.96 | 4.51 | 3.42 | 2.60 | 28 |
| 29 | 44.50 | 33.14 | 24.75 | 18.54 | 13.93 | 10.50 | 7.94 | 6.01 | 4.57 | 3.48 | 2.66 | 29 |
| 30 | 43.30 | 32.41 | 24.34 | 18.33 | 13.85 | 10.49 | 7.97 | 6.07 | 4.64 | 3.55 | 2.73 | 30 |
| 31 | 42.14 | 31.71 | 23.94 | 18.13 | 13.76 | 10.48 | 8.00 | 6.13 | 4.70 | 3.62 | 2.79 | 31 |
| 32 | 41.02 | 31.04 | 23.56 | 17.93 | 13.69 | 10.48 | 8.04 | 6.19 | 4.77 | 3.69 | 2.86 | 32 |
| 33 | 39.94 | 30.38 | 23.18 | 17.74 | 13.61 | 10.47 | 8.08 | 6.25 | 4.85 | 3.77 | 2.94 | 33 |
| 34 | 38.89 | 29.74 | 22.81 | 17.54 | 13.53 | 10.47 | 8.12 | 6.31 | 4.92 | 3.84 | 3.01 | 34 |
| 35 | 37.86 | 29.10 | 22.44 | 17.35 | 13.45 | 10.46 | 8.15 | 6.37 | 4.99 | 3.92 | 3.09 | 35 |
| 36 | 36.86 | 28.49 | 22.08 | 17.16 | 13.38 | 10.46 | 8.19 | 6.43 | 5.07 | 4.00 | 3.16 | 36 |
| 37 | 35.88 | 27.88 | 21.73 | 16.98 | 13.30 | 10.45 | 8.23 | 6.50 | 5.14 | 4.08 | 3.24 | 37 |
| 38 | 34.93 | 27.29 | 21.38 | 16.79 | 13.23 | 10.44 | 8.27 | 6.56 | 5.22 | 4.16 | 3.33 | 38 |
| 39 | 34.00 | 26.71 | 21.03 | 16.61 | 13.15 | 10.44 | 8.31 | 6.62 | 5.30 | 4.24 | 3.41 | 39 |
| 40 | 33.10 | 26.14 | 20.69 | 16.43 | 13.07 | 10.43 | 8.34 | 6.69 | 5.38 | 4.33 | 3.49 | 40 |
| 41 | 32.22 | 25.58 | 20.36 | 16.25 | 13.00 | 10.43 | 8.38 | 6.75 | 5.46 | 4.42 | 3.58 | 41 |
| 42 | 31.38 | 25.04 | 20.04 | 16.07 | 12.93 | 10.42 | 8.42 | 6.82 | 5.54 | 4.51 | 3.67 | 42 |
| 43 | 30.55 | 24.51 | 19.72 | 15.90 | 12.86 | 10.42 | 8.46 | 6.89 | 5.62 | 4.60 | 3.77 | 43 |
| 44 | 29.75 | 24.00 | 19.41 | 15.73 | 12.79 | 10.42 | 8.50 | 6.96 | 5.71 | 4.69 | 3.86 | 44 |
| 45 | 28.98 | 23.50 | 19.10 | 15.57 | 12.72 | 10.41 | 8.55 | 7.03 | 5.79 | 4.79 | 3.96 | 45 |
| 46 | 28.22 | 23.01 | 18.80 | 15.41 | 12.65 | 10.41 | 8.59 | 7.10 | 5.88 | 4.88 | 4.06 | 46 |
| 47 | 27.49 | 22.53 | 18.51 | 15.25 | 12.59 | 10.41 | 8.63 | 7.17 | 5.97 | 4.99 | 4.17 | 47 |
| 48 | 26.78 | 22.07 | 18.23 | 15.09 | 12.52 | 10.41 | 8.68 | 7.25 | 6.07 | 5.09 | 4.28 | 48 |
| 49 | 26.10 | 21.62 | 17.95 | 14.94 | 12.46 | 10.42 | 8.73 | 7.33 | 6.16 | 5.20 | 4.39 | 49 |
| 50 | 25.44 | 21.18 | 17.68 | 14.80 | 12.41 | 10.43 | 8.78 | 7.41 | 6.26 | 5.31 | 4.50 | 50 |
| 51 | 24.80 | 20.77 | 17.43 | 14.66 | 12.36 | 10.44 | 8.83 | 7.49 | 6.37 | 5.42 | 4.62 | 51 |
| 52 | 24.20 | 20.37 | 17.18 | 14.53 | 12.31 | 10.45 | 8.89 | 7.58 | 6.48 | 5.54 | 4.75 | 52 |
| 53 | 23.61 | 19.98 | 16.95 | 14.41 | 12.27 | 10.47 | 8.96 | 7.67 | 6.59 | 5.67 | 4.88 | 53 |
| 54 | 23.05 | 19.61 | 16.72 | 14.29 | 12.23 | 10.50 | 9.02 | 7.77 | 6.70 | 5.80 | 5.02 | 54 |

## Table 25: Multipliers for loss of pension commencing age 75 (males) *continued*

| Age at date of trial | Multiplier calculated with allowance for projected mortality from the 2008–based population projections and rate of return of | | | | | | | | | | | Age at date of trial |
|---|---|---|---|---|---|---|---|---|---|---|---|---|
| | *-2.0%* | *-1.5%* | *-1.0%* | *-0.5%* | *0.0%* | *0.5%* | *1.0%* | *1.5%* | *2.0%* | *2.5%* | *3.0%* | |
| 55 | 22.52 | 19.26 | 16.51 | 14.18 | 12.20 | 10.53 | 9.09 | 7.87 | 6.83 | 5.93 | 5.16 | 55 |
| 56 | 22.01 | 18.93 | 16.31 | 14.08 | 12.18 | 10.56 | 9.17 | 7.98 | 6.96 | 6.08 | 5.31 | 56 |
| 57 | 21.53 | 18.61 | 16.12 | 13.99 | 12.17 | 10.60 | 9.26 | 8.10 | 7.09 | 6.23 | 5.47 | 57 |
| 58 | 21.06 | 18.30 | 15.94 | 13.91 | 12.16 | 10.65 | 9.34 | 8.21 | 7.23 | 6.38 | 5.64 | 58 |
| 59 | 20.60 | 18.00 | 15.76 | 13.82 | 12.15 | 10.69 | 9.43 | 8.33 | 7.38 | 6.54 | 5.81 | 59 |
| 60 | 20.15 | 17.70 | 15.58 | 13.73 | 12.13 | 10.74 | 9.52 | 8.45 | 7.52 | 6.70 | 5.98 | 60 |
| 61 | 19.71 | 17.41 | 15.40 | 13.65 | 12.12 | 10.78 | 9.61 | 8.58 | 7.67 | 6.87 | 6.16 | 61 |
| 62 | 19.29 | 17.13 | 15.23 | 13.57 | 12.12 | 10.84 | 9.71 | 8.71 | 7.83 | 7.04 | 6.35 | 62 |
| 63 | 18.89 | 16.86 | 15.08 | 13.51 | 12.12 | 10.89 | 9.81 | 8.85 | 7.99 | 7.23 | 6.55 | 63 |
| 64 | 18.52 | 16.62 | 14.94 | 13.45 | 12.13 | 10.96 | 9.92 | 8.99 | 8.16 | 7.42 | 6.76 | 64 |
| 65 | 18.18 | 16.40 | 14.82 | 13.41 | 12.16 | 11.05 | 10.05 | 9.16 | 8.35 | 7.63 | 6.99 | 65 |
| 66 | 17.87 | 16.21 | 14.73 | 13.40 | 12.21 | 11.15 | 10.20 | 9.34 | 8.56 | 7.86 | 7.23 | 66 |
| 67 | 17.60 | 16.04 | 14.65 | 13.40 | 12.28 | 11.27 | 10.36 | 9.53 | 8.79 | 8.11 | 7.50 | 67 |
| 68 | 17.35 | 15.90 | 14.60 | 13.42 | 12.37 | 11.41 | 10.54 | 9.75 | 9.03 | 8.38 | 7.78 | 68 |
| 69 | 17.12 | 15.78 | 14.56 | 13.46 | 12.47 | 11.56 | 10.73 | 9.98 | 9.30 | 8.67 | 8.09 | 69 |
| 70 | 16.92 | 15.67 | 14.54 | 13.51 | 12.58 | 11.72 | 10.94 | 10.23 | 9.58 | 8.97 | 8.42 | 70 |
| 71 | 16.72 | 15.57 | 14.53 | 13.57 | 12.70 | 11.90 | 11.17 | 10.49 | 9.87 | 9.30 | 8.77 | 71 |
| 72 | 16.53 | 15.48 | 14.52 | 13.64 | 12.83 | 12.08 | 11.40 | 10.77 | 10.18 | 9.64 | 9.14 | 72 |
| 73 | 16.36 | 15.40 | 14.52 | 13.71 | 12.97 | 12.28 | 11.64 | 11.05 | 10.51 | 10.00 | 9.53 | 73 |
| 74 | 16.19 | 15.33 | 14.53 | 13.80 | 13.12 | 12.49 | 11.90 | 11.36 | 10.86 | 10.39 | 9.95 | 74 |
| 75 | 16.04 | 15.27 | 14.56 | 13.90 | 13.29 | 12.72 | 12.19 | 11.70 | 11.24 | 10.81 | 10.40 | 75 |

## Table 26: Multipliers for loss of pension commencing age 75 (females)

| Age at date of trial | Multiplier calculated with allowance for projected mortality from the 2008–based population projections and rate of return of | | | | | | | | | | | Age at date of trial |
|---|---|---|---|---|---|---|---|---|---|---|---|---|
| | -2.0% | -1.5% | -1.0% | -0.5% | 0.0% | 0.5% | 1.0% | 1.5% | 2.0% | 2.5% | 3.0% | |
| 0 | 114.99 | 73.05 | 46.61 | 29.87 | 19.22 | 12.42 | 8.06 | 5.25 | 3.43 | 2.25 | 1.48 | 0 |
| 1 | 112.51 | 71.86 | 46.09 | 29.69 | 19.21 | 12.48 | 8.13 | 5.33 | 3.50 | 2.31 | 1.53 | 1 |
| 2 | 109.64 | 70.40 | 45.40 | 29.40 | 19.12 | 12.48 | 8.18 | 5.38 | 3.56 | 2.36 | 1.57 | 2 |
| 3 | 106.83 | 68.96 | 44.71 | 29.10 | 19.02 | 12.49 | 8.23 | 5.44 | 3.61 | 2.41 | 1.61 | 3 |
| 4 | 104.08 | 67.55 | 44.02 | 28.81 | 18.93 | 12.49 | 8.27 | 5.50 | 3.67 | 2.46 | 1.65 | 4 |
| 5 | 101.41 | 66.16 | 43.35 | 28.52 | 18.84 | 12.49 | 8.32 | 5.56 | 3.73 | 2.51 | 1.69 | 5 |
| 6 | 98.79 | 64.80 | 42.69 | 28.23 | 18.75 | 12.50 | 8.36 | 5.62 | 3.79 | 2.56 | 1.74 | 6 |
| 7 | 96.24 | 63.47 | 42.03 | 27.94 | 18.65 | 12.50 | 8.41 | 5.67 | 3.84 | 2.61 | 1.78 | 7 |
| 8 | 93.75 | 62.16 | 41.38 | 27.66 | 18.56 | 12.50 | 8.45 | 5.73 | 3.90 | 2.67 | 1.83 | 8 |
| 9 | 91.32 | 60.87 | 40.74 | 27.37 | 18.46 | 12.50 | 8.50 | 5.79 | 3.97 | 2.72 | 1.88 | 9 |
| 10 | 88.95 | 59.61 | 40.11 | 27.09 | 18.37 | 12.50 | 8.54 | 5.85 | 4.03 | 2.78 | 1.92 | 10 |
| 11 | 86.65 | 58.38 | 39.49 | 26.82 | 18.28 | 12.50 | 8.59 | 5.92 | 4.09 | 2.84 | 1.97 | 11 |
| 12 | 84.41 | 57.17 | 38.88 | 26.54 | 18.18 | 12.51 | 8.63 | 5.98 | 4.15 | 2.90 | 2.03 | 12 |
| 13 | 82.21 | 55.99 | 38.27 | 26.26 | 18.09 | 12.51 | 8.68 | 6.04 | 4.22 | 2.96 | 2.08 | 13 |
| 14 | 80.08 | 54.83 | 37.68 | 25.99 | 18.00 | 12.51 | 8.72 | 6.10 | 4.28 | 3.02 | 2.13 | 14 |
| 15 | 78.00 | 53.69 | 37.09 | 25.73 | 17.91 | 12.51 | 8.77 | 6.16 | 4.35 | 3.08 | 2.19 | 15 |
| 16 | 75.98 | 52.58 | 36.52 | 25.46 | 17.81 | 12.51 | 8.81 | 6.23 | 4.42 | 3.14 | 2.24 | 16 |
| 17 | 74.00 | 51.48 | 35.95 | 25.20 | 17.72 | 12.51 | 8.86 | 6.29 | 4.49 | 3.21 | 2.30 | 17 |
| 18 | 72.08 | 50.42 | 35.39 | 24.94 | 17.63 | 12.51 | 8.90 | 6.36 | 4.55 | 3.27 | 2.36 | 18 |
| 19 | 70.22 | 49.37 | 34.84 | 24.68 | 17.54 | 12.51 | 8.95 | 6.42 | 4.63 | 3.34 | 2.42 | 19 |
| 20 | 68.41 | 48.36 | 34.31 | 24.43 | 17.45 | 12.51 | 9.00 | 6.49 | 4.70 | 3.41 | 2.48 | 20 |
| 21 | 66.64 | 47.36 | 33.78 | 24.18 | 17.36 | 12.51 | 9.05 | 6.56 | 4.77 | 3.48 | 2.55 | 21 |
| 22 | 64.91 | 46.38 | 33.26 | 23.93 | 17.27 | 12.51 | 9.09 | 6.63 | 4.85 | 3.55 | 2.61 | 22 |
| 23 | 63.22 | 45.41 | 32.73 | 23.68 | 17.18 | 12.51 | 9.14 | 6.69 | 4.92 | 3.63 | 2.68 | 23 |
| 24 | 61.56 | 44.46 | 32.22 | 23.43 | 17.09 | 12.51 | 9.18 | 6.76 | 4.99 | 3.70 | 2.75 | 24 |
| 25 | 59.96 | 43.53 | 31.71 | 23.18 | 17.00 | 12.51 | 9.23 | 6.83 | 5.07 | 3.78 | 2.82 | 25 |
| 26 | 58.40 | 42.63 | 31.22 | 22.94 | 16.91 | 12.51 | 9.28 | 6.90 | 5.15 | 3.85 | 2.89 | 26 |
| 27 | 56.88 | 41.74 | 30.73 | 22.70 | 16.82 | 12.51 | 9.32 | 6.97 | 5.23 | 3.93 | 2.97 | 27 |
| 28 | 55.40 | 40.87 | 30.25 | 22.47 | 16.74 | 12.50 | 9.37 | 7.04 | 5.31 | 4.01 | 3.04 | 28 |
| 29 | 53.96 | 40.02 | 29.78 | 22.23 | 16.65 | 12.50 | 9.42 | 7.12 | 5.39 | 4.10 | 3.12 | 29 |
| 30 | 52.56 | 39.19 | 29.32 | 22.00 | 16.56 | 12.50 | 9.47 | 7.19 | 5.47 | 4.18 | 3.20 | 30 |
| 31 | 51.20 | 38.38 | 28.86 | 21.78 | 16.48 | 12.50 | 9.52 | 7.26 | 5.56 | 4.27 | 3.28 | 31 |
| 32 | 49.88 | 37.59 | 28.42 | 21.55 | 16.39 | 12.51 | 9.57 | 7.34 | 5.65 | 4.35 | 3.37 | 32 |
| 33 | 48.59 | 36.82 | 27.98 | 21.33 | 16.31 | 12.51 | 9.62 | 7.42 | 5.73 | 4.44 | 3.45 | 33 |
| 34 | 47.33 | 36.05 | 27.55 | 21.11 | 16.23 | 12.51 | 9.67 | 7.49 | 5.82 | 4.54 | 3.54 | 34 |
| 35 | 46.10 | 35.30 | 27.12 | 20.89 | 16.14 | 12.51 | 9.72 | 7.57 | 5.91 | 4.63 | 3.63 | 35 |
| 36 | 44.91 | 34.57 | 26.70 | 20.68 | 16.06 | 12.51 | 9.77 | 7.65 | 6.00 | 4.73 | 3.73 | 36 |
| 37 | 43.75 | 33.86 | 26.29 | 20.47 | 15.98 | 12.51 | 9.82 | 7.73 | 6.10 | 4.82 | 3.82 | 37 |
| 38 | 42.62 | 33.16 | 25.88 | 20.26 | 15.90 | 12.51 | 9.87 | 7.81 | 6.19 | 4.92 | 3.92 | 38 |
| 39 | 41.52 | 32.48 | 25.48 | 20.05 | 15.82 | 12.51 | 9.92 | 7.89 | 6.29 | 5.02 | 4.02 | 39 |
| 40 | 40.44 | 31.81 | 25.09 | 19.84 | 15.73 | 12.51 | 9.97 | 7.97 | 6.39 | 5.13 | 4.13 | 40 |
| 41 | 39.40 | 31.15 | 24.70 | 19.64 | 15.66 | 12.51 | 10.03 | 8.05 | 6.49 | 5.23 | 4.23 | 41 |
| 42 | 38.38 | 30.51 | 24.32 | 19.44 | 15.58 | 12.52 | 10.08 | 8.14 | 6.59 | 5.34 | 4.34 | 42 |
| 43 | 37.40 | 29.89 | 23.95 | 19.24 | 15.50 | 12.52 | 10.13 | 8.22 | 6.69 | 5.45 | 4.46 | 43 |
| 44 | 36.44 | 29.28 | 23.59 | 19.05 | 15.43 | 12.52 | 10.19 | 8.31 | 6.80 | 5.57 | 4.57 | 44 |
| 45 | 35.52 | 28.69 | 23.23 | 18.86 | 15.35 | 12.53 | 10.25 | 8.40 | 6.90 | 5.69 | 4.69 | 45 |
| 46 | 34.61 | 28.10 | 22.88 | 18.68 | 15.28 | 12.53 | 10.31 | 8.49 | 7.01 | 5.81 | 4.82 | 46 |
| 47 | 33.73 | 27.54 | 22.54 | 18.49 | 15.21 | 12.54 | 10.36 | 8.58 | 7.13 | 5.93 | 4.94 | 47 |
| 48 | 32.89 | 26.99 | 22.21 | 18.32 | 15.14 | 12.55 | 10.43 | 8.68 | 7.24 | 6.06 | 5.07 | 48 |
| 49 | 32.07 | 26.46 | 21.88 | 18.15 | 15.08 | 12.56 | 10.49 | 8.78 | 7.36 | 6.19 | 5.21 | 49 |
| 50 | 31.27 | 25.94 | 21.57 | 17.98 | 15.02 | 12.58 | 10.56 | 8.88 | 7.48 | 6.32 | 5.35 | 50 |
| 51 | 30.50 | 25.43 | 21.26 | 17.81 | 14.96 | 12.59 | 10.62 | 8.98 | 7.61 | 6.46 | 5.49 | 51 |
| 52 | 29.75 | 24.94 | 20.96 | 17.65 | 14.90 | 12.61 | 10.69 | 9.09 | 7.74 | 6.60 | 5.64 | 52 |
| 53 | 29.03 | 24.47 | 20.67 | 17.50 | 14.85 | 12.63 | 10.77 | 9.20 | 7.87 | 6.75 | 5.80 | 53 |
| 54 | 28.33 | 24.01 | 20.39 | 17.35 | 14.80 | 12.66 | 10.84 | 9.31 | 8.01 | 6.90 | 5.96 | 54 |

**Table 26: Multipliers for loss of pension commencing age 75 (females)** *continued*

| Age at date of trial | Multiplier calculated with allowance for projected mortality from the 2008–based population projections and rate of return of | | | | | | | | | | | Age at date of trial |
|---|---|---|---|---|---|---|---|---|---|---|---|---|
| | −2.0% | −1.5% | −1.0% | −0.5% | 0.0% | 0.5% | 1.0% | 1.5% | 2.0% | 2.5% | 3.0% | |
| 55 | 27.66 | 23.56 | 20.12 | 17.21 | 14.76 | 12.69 | 10.92 | 9.43 | 8.15 | 7.06 | 6.12 | 55 |
| 56 | 27.02 | 23.14 | 19.86 | 17.08 | 14.72 | 12.72 | 11.01 | 9.55 | 8.30 | 7.22 | 6.30 | 56 |
| 57 | 26.39 | 22.72 | 19.60 | 16.95 | 14.69 | 12.75 | 11.10 | 9.67 | 8.45 | 7.39 | 6.48 | 57 |
| 58 | 25.78 | 22.32 | 19.36 | 16.83 | 14.66 | 12.79 | 11.19 | 9.80 | 8.60 | 7.56 | 6.66 | 58 |
| 59 | 25.19 | 21.92 | 19.11 | 16.70 | 14.62 | 12.83 | 11.28 | 9.93 | 8.76 | 7.74 | 6.85 | 59 |
| 60 | 24.61 | 21.53 | 18.87 | 16.57 | 14.59 | 12.86 | 11.37 | 10.06 | 8.92 | 7.92 | 7.05 | 60 |
| 61 | 24.04 | 21.14 | 18.63 | 16.45 | 14.55 | 12.90 | 11.46 | 10.19 | 9.08 | 8.11 | 7.25 | 61 |
| 62 | 23.49 | 20.77 | 18.40 | 16.33 | 14.52 | 12.94 | 11.55 | 10.33 | 9.25 | 8.30 | 7.46 | 62 |
| 63 | 22.96 | 20.41 | 18.17 | 16.22 | 14.50 | 12.99 | 11.65 | 10.47 | 9.43 | 8.50 | 7.68 | 63 |
| 64 | 22.46 | 20.07 | 17.97 | 16.12 | 14.48 | 13.04 | 11.76 | 10.63 | 9.62 | 8.71 | 7.91 | 64 |
| 65 | 22.00 | 19.76 | 17.78 | 16.04 | 14.49 | 13.11 | 11.89 | 10.79 | 9.82 | 8.94 | 8.16 | 65 |
| 66 | 21.56 | 19.48 | 17.62 | 15.97 | 14.51 | 13.20 | 12.03 | 10.98 | 10.03 | 9.19 | 8.42 | 66 |
| 67 | 21.16 | 19.22 | 17.48 | 15.93 | 14.54 | 13.30 | 12.18 | 11.17 | 10.27 | 9.45 | 8.71 | 67 |
| 68 | 20.79 | 18.98 | 17.36 | 15.90 | 14.59 | 13.41 | 12.35 | 11.39 | 10.51 | 9.72 | 9.01 | 68 |
| 69 | 20.44 | 18.76 | 17.25 | 15.88 | 14.65 | 13.54 | 12.53 | 11.61 | 10.78 | 10.02 | 9.33 | 69 |
| 70 | 20.11 | 18.55 | 17.15 | 15.87 | 14.72 | 13.67 | 12.72 | 11.85 | 11.05 | 10.33 | 9.66 | 70 |
| 71 | 19.78 | 18.35 | 17.05 | 15.87 | 14.79 | 13.81 | 12.91 | 12.09 | 11.34 | 10.65 | 10.01 | 71 |
| 72 | 19.46 | 18.14 | 16.95 | 15.86 | 14.86 | 13.95 | 13.11 | 12.34 | 11.63 | 10.98 | 10.38 | 72 |
| 73 | 19.13 | 17.93 | 16.84 | 15.84 | 14.93 | 14.08 | 13.31 | 12.59 | 11.93 | 11.32 | 10.75 | 73 |
| 74 | 18.80 | 17.72 | 16.74 | 15.83 | 15.00 | 14.23 | 13.51 | 12.86 | 12.24 | 11.68 | 11.15 | 74 |
| 75 | 18.48 | 17.53 | 16.64 | 15.83 | 15.08 | 14.38 | 13.74 | 13.14 | 12.58 | 12.06 | 11.58 | 75 |

## Table 27: Discounting factors for term certain

| Term | Factor to discount value of multiplier for a period of deferment | | | | | | | | | | | Term |
|---|---|---|---|---|---|---|---|---|---|---|---|---|
| | *-2.0%* | *-1.5%* | *-1.0%* | *-0.5%* | *0.0%* | *0.5%* | *1.0%* | *1.5%* | *2.0%* | *2.5%* | *3.0%* | |
| 1 | 1.0204 | 1.0152 | 1.0101 | 1.0050 | 1.0000 | 0.9950 | 0.9901 | 0.9852 | 0.9804 | 0.9756 | 0.9709 | 1 |
| 2 | 1.0412 | 1.0307 | 1.0203 | 1.0101 | 1.0000 | 0.9901 | 0.9803 | 0.9707 | 0.9612 | 0.9518 | 0.9426 | 2 |
| 3 | 1.0625 | 1.0464 | 1.0306 | 1.0152 | 1.0000 | 0.9851 | 0.9706 | 0.9563 | 0.9423 | 0.9286 | 0.9151 | 3 |
| 4 | 1.0842 | 1.0623 | 1.0410 | 1.0203 | 1.0000 | 0.9802 | 0.9610 | 0.9422 | 0.9238 | 0.9060 | 0.8885 | 4 |
| 5 | 1.1063 | 1.0785 | 1.0515 | 1.0254 | 1.0000 | 0.9754 | 0.9515 | 0.9283 | 0.9057 | 0.8839 | 0.8626 | 5 |
| 6 | 1.1289 | 1.0949 | 1.0622 | 1.0305 | 1.0000 | 0.9705 | 0.9420 | 0.9145 | 0.8880 | 0.8623 | 0.8375 | 6 |
| 7 | 1.1519 | 1.1116 | 1.0729 | 1.0357 | 1.0000 | 0.9657 | 0.9327 | 0.9010 | 0.8706 | 0.8413 | 0.8131 | 7 |
| 8 | 1.1754 | 1.1285 | 1.0837 | 1.0409 | 1.0000 | 0.9609 | 0.9235 | 0.8877 | 0.8535 | 0.8207 | 0.7894 | 8 |
| 9 | 1.1994 | 1.1457 | 1.0947 | 1.0461 | 1.0000 | 0.9561 | 0.9143 | 0.8746 | 0.8368 | 0.8007 | 0.7664 | 9 |
| 10 | 1.2239 | 1.1632 | 1.1057 | 1.0514 | 1.0000 | 0.9513 | 0.9053 | 0.8617 | 0.8203 | 0.7812 | 0.7441 | 10 |
| 11 | 1.2489 | 1.1809 | 1.1169 | 1.0567 | 1.0000 | 0.9466 | 0.8963 | 0.8489 | 0.8043 | 0.7621 | 0.7224 | 11 |
| 12 | 1.2743 | 1.1989 | 1.1282 | 1.0620 | 1.0000 | 0.9419 | 0.8874 | 0.8364 | 0.7885 | 0.7436 | 0.7014 | 12 |
| 13 | 1.3004 | 1.2171 | 1.1396 | 1.0673 | 1.0000 | 0.9372 | 0.8787 | 0.8240 | 0.7730 | 0.7254 | 0.6810 | 13 |
| 14 | 1.3269 | 1.2356 | 1.1511 | 1.0727 | 1.0000 | 0.9326 | 0.8700 | 0.8118 | 0.7579 | 0.7077 | 0.6611 | 14 |
| 15 | 1.3540 | 1.2545 | 1.1627 | 1.0781 | 1.0000 | 0.9279 | 0.8613 | 0.7999 | 0.7430 | 0.6905 | 0.6419 | 15 |
| 16 | 1.3816 | 1.2736 | 1.1745 | 1.0835 | 1.0000 | 0.9233 | 0.8528 | 0.7880 | 0.7284 | 0.6736 | 0.6232 | 16 |
| 17 | 1.4098 | 1.2930 | 1.1863 | 1.0889 | 1.0000 | 0.9187 | 0.8444 | 0.7764 | 0.7142 | 0.6572 | 0.6050 | 17 |
| 18 | 1.4386 | 1.3126 | 1.1983 | 1.0944 | 1.0000 | 0.9141 | 0.8360 | 0.7649 | 0.7002 | 0.6412 | 0.5874 | 18 |
| 19 | 1.4679 | 1.3326 | 1.2104 | 1.0999 | 1.0000 | 0.9096 | 0.8277 | 0.7536 | 0.6864 | 0.6255 | 0.5703 | 19 |
| 20 | 1.4979 | 1.3529 | 1.2226 | 1.1054 | 1.0000 | 0.9051 | 0.8195 | 0.7425 | 0.6730 | 0.6103 | 0.5537 | 20 |
| 21 | 1.5285 | 1.3735 | 1.2350 | 1.1110 | 1.0000 | 0.9006 | 0.8114 | 0.7315 | 0.6598 | 0.5954 | 0.5375 | 21 |
| 22 | 1.5596 | 1.3944 | 1.2475 | 1.1166 | 1.0000 | 0.8961 | 0.8034 | 0.7207 | 0.6468 | 0.5809 | 0.5219 | 22 |
| 23 | 1.5915 | 1.4157 | 1.2601 | 1.1222 | 1.0000 | 0.8916 | 0.7954 | 0.7100 | 0.6342 | 0.5667 | 0.5067 | 23 |
| 24 | 1.6240 | 1.4372 | 1.2728 | 1.1278 | 1.0000 | 0.8872 | 0.7876 | 0.6995 | 0.6217 | 0.5529 | 0.4919 | 24 |
| 25 | 1.6571 | 1.4591 | 1.2856 | 1.1335 | 1.0000 | 0.8828 | 0.7798 | 0.6892 | 0.6095 | 0.5394 | 0.4776 | 25 |
| 26 | 1.6909 | 1.4814 | 1.2986 | 1.1392 | 1.0000 | 0.8784 | 0.7720 | 0.6790 | 0.5976 | 0.5262 | 0.4637 | 26 |
| 27 | 1.7254 | 1.5039 | 1.3117 | 1.1449 | 1.0000 | 0.8740 | 0.7644 | 0.6690 | 0.5859 | 0.5134 | 0.4502 | 27 |
| 28 | 1.7606 | 1.5268 | 1.3250 | 1.1507 | 1.0000 | 0.8697 | 0.7568 | 0.6591 | 0.5744 | 0.5009 | 0.4371 | 28 |
| 29 | 1.7966 | 1.5501 | 1.3384 | 1.1565 | 1.0000 | 0.8653 | 0.7493 | 0.6494 | 0.5631 | 0.4887 | 0.4243 | 29 |
| 30 | 1.8332 | 1.5737 | 1.3519 | 1.1623 | 1.0000 | 0.8610 | 0.7419 | 0.6398 | 0.5521 | 0.4767 | 0.4120 | 30 |
| 31 | 1.8706 | 1.5976 | 1.3656 | 1.1681 | 1.0000 | 0.8567 | 0.7346 | 0.6303 | 0.5412 | 0.4651 | 0.4000 | 31 |
| 32 | 1.9088 | 1.6220 | 1.3793 | 1.1740 | 1.0000 | 0.8525 | 0.7273 | 0.6210 | 0.5306 | 0.4538 | 0.3883 | 32 |
| 33 | 1.9478 | 1.6467 | 1.3933 | 1.1799 | 1.0000 | 0.8482 | 0.7201 | 0.6118 | 0.5202 | 0.4427 | 0.3770 | 33 |
| 34 | 1.9875 | 1.6717 | 1.4074 | 1.1858 | 1.0000 | 0.8440 | 0.7130 | 0.6028 | 0.5100 | 0.4319 | 0.3660 | 34 |
| 35 | 2.0281 | 1.6972 | 1.4216 | 1.1918 | 1.0000 | 0.8398 | 0.7059 | 0.5939 | 0.5000 | 0.4214 | 0.3554 | 35 |
| 36 | 2.0695 | 1.7230 | 1.4359 | 1.1978 | 1.0000 | 0.8356 | 0.6989 | 0.5851 | 0.4902 | 0.4111 | 0.3450 | 36 |
| 37 | 2.1117 | 1.7493 | 1.4504 | 1.2038 | 1.0000 | 0.8315 | 0.6920 | 0.5764 | 0.4806 | 0.4011 | 0.3350 | 37 |
| 38 | 2.1548 | 1.7759 | 1.4651 | 1.2098 | 1.0000 | 0.8274 | 0.6852 | 0.5679 | 0.4712 | 0.3913 | 0.3252 | 38 |
| 39 | 2.1988 | 1.8030 | 1.4799 | 1.2159 | 1.0000 | 0.8232 | 0.6784 | 0.5595 | 0.4619 | 0.3817 | 0.3158 | 39 |
| 40 | 2.2437 | 1.8304 | 1.4948 | 1.2220 | 1.0000 | 0.8191 | 0.6717 | 0.5513 | 0.4529 | 0.3724 | 0.3066 | 40 |
| 41 | 2.2894 | 1.8583 | 1.5099 | 1.2282 | 1.0000 | 0.8151 | 0.6650 | 0.5431 | 0.4440 | 0.3633 | 0.2976 | 41 |
| 42 | 2.3362 | 1.8866 | 1.5252 | 1.2343 | 1.0000 | 0.8110 | 0.6584 | 0.5351 | 0.4353 | 0.3545 | 0.2890 | 42 |
| 43 | 2.3838 | 1.9153 | 1.5406 | 1.2405 | 1.0000 | 0.8070 | 0.6519 | 0.5272 | 0.4268 | 0.3458 | 0.2805 | 43 |
| 44 | 2.4325 | 1.9445 | 1.5561 | 1.2468 | 1.0000 | 0.8030 | 0.6454 | 0.5194 | 0.4184 | 0.3374 | 0.2724 | 44 |
| 45 | 2.4821 | 1.9741 | 1.5719 | 1.2530 | 1.0000 | 0.7990 | 0.6391 | 0.5117 | 0.4102 | 0.3292 | 0.2644 | 45 |
| 46 | 2.5328 | 2.0042 | 1.5877 | 1.2593 | 1.0000 | 0.7950 | 0.6327 | 0.5042 | 0.4022 | 0.3211 | 0.2567 | 46 |
| 47 | 2.5845 | 2.0347 | 1.6038 | 1.2657 | 1.0000 | 0.7910 | 0.6265 | 0.4967 | 0.3943 | 0.3133 | 0.2493 | 47 |
| 48 | 2.6372 | 2.0657 | 1.6200 | 1.2720 | 1.0000 | 0.7871 | 0.6203 | 0.4894 | 0.3865 | 0.3057 | 0.2420 | 48 |
| 49 | 2.6911 | 2.0971 | 1.6363 | 1.2784 | 1.0000 | 0.7832 | 0.6141 | 0.4821 | 0.3790 | 0.2982 | 0.2350 | 49 |
| 50 | 2.7460 | 2.1291 | 1.6529 | 1.2848 | 1.0000 | 0.7793 | 0.6080 | 0.4750 | 0.3715 | 0.2909 | 0.2281 | 50 |
| 51 | 2.8020 | 2.1615 | 1.6696 | 1.2913 | 1.0000 | 0.7754 | 0.6020 | 0.4680 | 0.3642 | 0.2838 | 0.2215 | 51 |
| 52 | 2.8592 | 2.1944 | 1.6864 | 1.2978 | 1.0000 | 0.7716 | 0.5961 | 0.4611 | 0.3571 | 0.2769 | 0.2150 | 52 |
| 53 | 2.9175 | 2.2278 | 1.7035 | 1.3043 | 1.0000 | 0.7677 | 0.5902 | 0.4543 | 0.3501 | 0.2702 | 0.2088 | 53 |
| 54 | 2.9771 | 2.2617 | 1.7207 | 1.3109 | 1.0000 | 0.7639 | 0.5843 | 0.4475 | 0.3432 | 0.2636 | 0.2027 | 54 |
| 55 | 3.0378 | 2.2962 | 1.7381 | 1.3174 | 1.0000 | 0.7601 | 0.5785 | 0.4409 | 0.3365 | 0.2572 | 0.1968 | 55 |

## Table 27: Discounting factors for term certain *continued*

| Term | \-2.0% | \-1.5% | \-1.0% | \-0.5% | 0.0% | 0.5% | 1.0% | 1.5% | 2.0% | 2.5% | 3.0% | Term |
|---|---|---|---|---|---|---|---|---|---|---|---|---|
| 56 | 3.0998 | 2.3312 | 1.7556 | 1.3241 | 1.0000 | 0.7563 | 0.5728 | 0.4344 | 0.3299 | 0.2509 | 0.1910 | 56 |
| 57 | 3.1631 | 2.3667 | 1.7733 | 1.3307 | 1.0000 | 0.7525 | 0.5671 | 0.4280 | 0.3234 | 0.2448 | 0.1855 | 57 |
| 58 | 3.2277 | 2.4027 | 1.7913 | 1.3374 | 1.0000 | 0.7488 | 0.5615 | 0.4217 | 0.3171 | 0.2388 | 0.1801 | 58 |
| 59 | 3.2935 | 2.4393 | 1.8094 | 1.3441 | 1.0000 | 0.7451 | 0.5560 | 0.4154 | 0.3109 | 0.2330 | 0.1748 | 59 |
| 60 | 3.3607 | 2.4764 | 1.8276 | 1.3509 | 1.0000 | 0.7414 | 0.5504 | 0.4093 | 0.3048 | 0.2273 | 0.1697 | 60 |
| 61 | 3.4293 | 2.5141 | 1.8461 | 1.3577 | 1.0000 | 0.7377 | 0.5450 | 0.4032 | 0.2988 | 0.2217 | 0.1648 | 61 |
| 62 | 3.4993 | 2.5524 | 1.8647 | 1.3645 | 1.0000 | 0.7340 | 0.5396 | 0.3973 | 0.2929 | 0.2163 | 0.1600 | 62 |
| 63 | 3.5707 | 2.5913 | 1.8836 | 1.3713 | 1.0000 | 0.7304 | 0.5343 | 0.3914 | 0.2872 | 0.2111 | 0.1553 | 63 |
| 64 | 3.6436 | 2.6308 | 1.9026 | 1.3782 | 1.0000 | 0.7267 | 0.5290 | 0.3856 | 0.2816 | 0.2059 | 0.1508 | 64 |
| 65 | 3.7180 | 2.6708 | 1.9218 | 1.3852 | 1.0000 | 0.7231 | 0.5237 | 0.3799 | 0.2761 | 0.2009 | 0.1464 | 65 |
| 66 | 3.7938 | 2.7115 | 1.9412 | 1.3921 | 1.0000 | 0.7195 | 0.5185 | 0.3743 | 0.2706 | 0.1960 | 0.1421 | 66 |
| 67 | 3.8713 | 2.7528 | 1.9608 | 1.3991 | 1.0000 | 0.7159 | 0.5134 | 0.3688 | 0.2653 | 0.1912 | 0.1380 | 67 |
| 68 | 3.9503 | 2.7947 | 1.9806 | 1.4061 | 1.0000 | 0.7124 | 0.5083 | 0.3633 | 0.2601 | 0.1865 | 0.1340 | 68 |
| 69 | 4.0309 | 2.8373 | 2.0007 | 1.4132 | 1.0000 | 0.7088 | 0.5033 | 0.3580 | 0.2550 | 0.1820 | 0.1301 | 69 |
| 70 | 4.1132 | 2.8805 | 2.0209 | 1.4203 | 1.0000 | 0.7053 | 0.4983 | 0.3527 | 0.2500 | 0.1776 | 0.1263 | 70 |
| 71 | 4.1971 | 2.9243 | 2.0413 | 1.4275 | 1.0000 | 0.7018 | 0.4934 | 0.3475 | 0.2451 | 0.1732 | 0.1226 | 71 |
| 72 | 4.2827 | 2.9689 | 2.0619 | 1.4346 | 1.0000 | 0.6983 | 0.4885 | 0.3423 | 0.2403 | 0.1690 | 0.1190 | 72 |
| 73 | 4.3702 | 3.0141 | 2.0827 | 1.4418 | 1.0000 | 0.6948 | 0.4837 | 0.3373 | 0.2356 | 0.1649 | 0.1156 | 73 |
| 74 | 4.4593 | 3.0600 | 2.1038 | 1.4491 | 1.0000 | 0.6914 | 0.4789 | 0.3323 | 0.2310 | 0.1609 | 0.1122 | 74 |
| 75 | 4.5503 | 3.1066 | 2.1250 | 1.4564 | 1.0000 | 0.6879 | 0.4741 | 0.3274 | 0.2265 | 0.1569 | 0.1089 | 75 |
| 76 | 4.6432 | 3.1539 | 2.1465 | 1.4637 | 1.0000 | 0.6845 | 0.4694 | 0.3225 | 0.2220 | 0.1531 | 0.1058 | 76 |
| 77 | 4.7380 | 3.2019 | 2.1682 | 1.4710 | 1.0000 | 0.6811 | 0.4648 | 0.3178 | 0.2177 | 0.1494 | 0.1027 | 77 |
| 78 | 4.8347 | 3.2507 | 2.1901 | 1.4784 | 1.0000 | 0.6777 | 0.4602 | 0.3131 | 0.2134 | 0.1457 | 0.0997 | 78 |
| 79 | 4.9333 | 3.3002 | 2.2122 | 1.4859 | 1.0000 | 0.6743 | 0.4556 | 0.3084 | 0.2092 | 0.1422 | 0.0968 | 79 |
| 80 | 5.0340 | 3.3504 | 2.2345 | 1.4933 | 1.0000 | 0.6710 | 0.4511 | 0.3039 | 0.2051 | 0.1387 | 0.0940 | 80 |

## Table 28: Multipliers for pecuniary loss for term certain

| Term | Multiplier for regular frequent payments for a term certain at rate of return of | | | | | | | | | | | Term |
|---|---|---|---|---|---|---|---|---|---|---|---|---|
| | *-2.0%* | *-1.5%* | *-1.0%* | *-0.5%* | *0.0%* | *0.5%* | *1.0%* | *1.5%* | *2.0%* | *2.5%* | *3.0%* | |
| 1 | 1.01 | 1.01 | 1.01 | 1.00 | 1.00 | 1.00 | 1.00 | 0.99 | 0.99 | 0.99 | 0.99 | 1 |
| 2 | 2.04 | 2.03 | 2.02 | 2.01 | 2.00 | 1.99 | 1.98 | 1.97 | 1.96 | 1.95 | 1.94 | 2 |
| 3 | 3.09 | 3.07 | 3.05 | 3.02 | 3.00 | 2.98 | 2.96 | 2.93 | 2.91 | 2.89 | 2.87 | 3 |
| 4 | 4.17 | 4.12 | 4.08 | 4.04 | 4.00 | 3.96 | 3.92 | 3.88 | 3.85 | 3.81 | 3.77 | 4 |
| 5 | 5.26 | 5.19 | 5.13 | 5.06 | 5.00 | 4.94 | 4.88 | 4.82 | 4.76 | 4.70 | 4.65 | 5 |
| 6 | 6.38 | 6.28 | 6.18 | 6.09 | 6.00 | 5.91 | 5.82 | 5.74 | 5.66 | 5.58 | 5.50 | 6 |
| 7 | 7.52 | 7.38 | 7.25 | 7.12 | 7.00 | 6.88 | 6.76 | 6.65 | 6.54 | 6.43 | 6.32 | 7 |
| 8 | 8.68 | 8.50 | 8.33 | 8.16 | 8.00 | 7.84 | 7.69 | 7.54 | 7.40 | 7.26 | 7.12 | 8 |
| 9 | 9.87 | 9.64 | 9.42 | 9.21 | 9.00 | 8.80 | 8.61 | 8.42 | 8.24 | 8.07 | 7.90 | 9 |
| 10 | 11.08 | 10.80 | 10.52 | 10.25 | 10.00 | 9.75 | 9.52 | 9.29 | 9.07 | 8.86 | 8.66 | 10 |
| 11 | 12.32 | 11.97 | 11.63 | 11.31 | 11.00 | 10.70 | 10.42 | 10.15 | 9.88 | 9.63 | 9.39 | 11 |
| 12 | 13.58 | 13.16 | 12.75 | 12.37 | 12.00 | 11.65 | 11.31 | 10.99 | 10.68 | 10.39 | 10.10 | 12 |
| 13 | 14.87 | 14.37 | 13.89 | 13.43 | 13.00 | 12.59 | 12.19 | 11.82 | 11.46 | 11.12 | 10.79 | 13 |
| 14 | 16.18 | 15.59 | 15.03 | 14.50 | 14.00 | 13.52 | 13.07 | 12.64 | 12.23 | 11.84 | 11.46 | 14 |
| 15 | 17.52 | 16.84 | 16.19 | 15.58 | 15.00 | 14.45 | 13.93 | 13.44 | 12.98 | 12.54 | 12.12 | 15 |
| 16 | 18.89 | 18.10 | 17.36 | 16.66 | 16.00 | 15.38 | 14.79 | 14.24 | 13.71 | 13.22 | 12.75 | 16 |
| 17 | 20.28 | 19.38 | 18.54 | 17.75 | 17.00 | 16.30 | 15.64 | 15.02 | 14.43 | 13.88 | 13.36 | 17 |
| 18 | 21.71 | 20.69 | 19.73 | 18.84 | 18.00 | 17.22 | 16.48 | 15.79 | 15.14 | 14.53 | 13.96 | 18 |
| 19 | 23.16 | 22.01 | 20.94 | 19.93 | 19.00 | 18.13 | 17.31 | 16.55 | 15.83 | 15.17 | 14.54 | 19 |
| 20 | 24.64 | 23.35 | 22.15 | 21.04 | 20.00 | 19.03 | 18.14 | 17.30 | 16.51 | 15.78 | 15.10 | 20 |
| 21 | 26.16 | 24.71 | 23.38 | 22.15 | 21.00 | 19.94 | 18.95 | 18.03 | 17.18 | 16.39 | 15.65 | 21 |
| 22 | 27.70 | 26.10 | 24.62 | 23.26 | 22.00 | 20.84 | 19.76 | 18.76 | 17.83 | 16.97 | 16.17 | 22 |
| 23 | 29.28 | 27.50 | 25.88 | 24.38 | 23.00 | 21.73 | 20.56 | 19.48 | 18.47 | 17.55 | 16.69 | 23 |
| 24 | 30.88 | 28.93 | 27.14 | 25.50 | 24.00 | 22.62 | 21.35 | 20.18 | 19.10 | 18.11 | 17.19 | 24 |
| 25 | 32.53 | 30.38 | 28.42 | 26.63 | 25.00 | 23.50 | 22.13 | 20.87 | 19.72 | 18.65 | 17.67 | 25 |
| 26 | 34.20 | 31.85 | 29.71 | 27.77 | 26.00 | 24.38 | 22.91 | 21.56 | 20.32 | 19.19 | 18.14 | 26 |
| 27 | 35.91 | 33.34 | 31.02 | 28.91 | 27.00 | 25.26 | 23.68 | 22.23 | 20.91 | 19.71 | 18.60 | 27 |
| 28 | 37.65 | 34.86 | 32.34 | 30.06 | 28.00 | 26.13 | 24.44 | 22.90 | 21.49 | 20.21 | 19.04 | 28 |
| 29 | 39.43 | 36.40 | 33.67 | 31.21 | 29.00 | 27.00 | 25.19 | 23.55 | 22.06 | 20.71 | 19.47 | 29 |
| 30 | 41.24 | 37.96 | 35.01 | 32.37 | 30.00 | 27.86 | 25.94 | 24.20 | 22.62 | 21.19 | 19.89 | 30 |
| 31 | 43.10 | 39.54 | 36.37 | 33.54 | 31.00 | 28.72 | 26.67 | 24.83 | 23.17 | 21.66 | 20.30 | 31 |
| 32 | 44.99 | 41.15 | 37.74 | 34.71 | 32.00 | 29.58 | 27.41 | 25.46 | 23.70 | 22.12 | 20.69 | 32 |
| 33 | 46.91 | 42.79 | 39.13 | 35.89 | 33.00 | 30.43 | 28.13 | 26.07 | 24.23 | 22.57 | 21.08 | 33 |
| 34 | 48.88 | 44.45 | 40.53 | 37.07 | 34.00 | 31.27 | 28.85 | 26.68 | 24.74 | 23.01 | 21.45 | 34 |
| 35 | 50.89 | 46.13 | 41.95 | 38.26 | 35.00 | 32.12 | 29.56 | 27.28 | 25.25 | 23.43 | 21.81 | 35 |
| 36 | 52.94 | 47.84 | 43.37 | 39.45 | 36.00 | 32.95 | 30.26 | 27.87 | 25.74 | 23.85 | 22.16 | 36 |
| 37 | 55.03 | 49.58 | 44.82 | 40.65 | 37.00 | 33.79 | 30.95 | 28.45 | 26.23 | 24.26 | 22.50 | 37 |
| 38 | 57.16 | 51.34 | 46.28 | 41.86 | 38.00 | 34.62 | 31.64 | 29.02 | 26.70 | 24.65 | 22.83 | 38 |
| 39 | 59.34 | 53.13 | 47.75 | 43.07 | 39.00 | 35.44 | 32.32 | 29.58 | 27.17 | 25.04 | 23.15 | 39 |
| 40 | 61.56 | 54.95 | 49.24 | 44.29 | 40.00 | 36.26 | 33.00 | 30.14 | 27.63 | 25.42 | 23.46 | 40 |
| 41 | 63.83 | 56.79 | 50.74 | 45.52 | 41.00 | 37.08 | 33.67 | 30.69 | 28.08 | 25.78 | 23.76 | 41 |
| 42 | 66.14 | 58.66 | 52.26 | 46.75 | 42.00 | 37.89 | 34.33 | 31.23 | 28.52 | 26.14 | 24.06 | 42 |
| 43 | 68.50 | 60.56 | 53.79 | 47.99 | 43.00 | 38.70 | 34.98 | 31.76 | 28.95 | 26.49 | 24.34 | 43 |
| 44 | 70.91 | 62.49 | 55.34 | 49.23 | 44.00 | 39.51 | 35.63 | 32.28 | 29.37 | 26.83 | 24.62 | 44 |
| 45 | 73.36 | 64.45 | 56.90 | 50.48 | 45.00 | 40.31 | 36.27 | 32.80 | 29.78 | 27.17 | 24.88 | 45 |
| 46 | 75.87 | 66.44 | 58.48 | 51.74 | 46.00 | 41.10 | 36.91 | 33.30 | 30.19 | 27.49 | 25.15 | 46 |
| 47 | 78.43 | 68.46 | 60.08 | 53.00 | 47.00 | 41.90 | 37.54 | 33.80 | 30.59 | 27.81 | 25.40 | 47 |
| 48 | 81.04 | 70.51 | 61.69 | 54.27 | 48.00 | 42.69 | 38.16 | 34.30 | 30.98 | 28.12 | 25.64 | 48 |
| 49 | 83.70 | 72.59 | 63.32 | 55.54 | 49.00 | 43.47 | 38.78 | 34.78 | 31.36 | 28.42 | 25.88 | 49 |
| 50 | 86.42 | 74.70 | 64.96 | 56.82 | 50.00 | 44.25 | 39.39 | 35.26 | 31.74 | 28.72 | 26.11 | 50 |
| 51 | 89.20 | 76.85 | 66.62 | 58.11 | 51.00 | 45.03 | 40.00 | 35.73 | 32.10 | 29.00 | 26.34 | 51 |
| 52 | 92.03 | 79.03 | 68.30 | 59.41 | 52.00 | 45.80 | 40.60 | 36.20 | 32.47 | 29.28 | 26.56 | 52 |
| 53 | 94.92 | 81.24 | 69.99 | 60.71 | 53.00 | 46.57 | 41.19 | 36.66 | 32.82 | 29.56 | 26.77 | 53 |
| 54 | 97.86 | 83.48 | 71.71 | 62.01 | 54.00 | 47.34 | 41.78 | 37.11 | 33.17 | 29.82 | 26.97 | 54 |
| 55 | 100.87 | 85.76 | 73.44 | 63.33 | 55.00 | 48.10 | 42.36 | 37.55 | 33.51 | 30.08 | 27.17 | 55 |

### Table 28: Multipliers for pecuniary loss for term certain *continued*

| Term | \-2.0% | \-1.5% | \-1.0% | \-0.5% | 0.0% | 0.5% | 1.0% | 1.5% | 2.0% | 2.5% | 3.0% | Term |
|---|---|---|---|---|---|---|---|---|---|---|---|---|
| 56 | 103.94 | 88.08 | 75.18 | 64.65 | 56.00 | 48.86 | 42.93 | 37.99 | 33.84 | 30.34 | 27.37 | 56 |
| 57 | 107.07 | 90.43 | 76.95 | 65.98 | 57.00 | 49.61 | 43.50 | 38.42 | 34.17 | 30.59 | 27.56 | 57 |
| 58 | 110.27 | 92.81 | 78.73 | 67.31 | 58.00 | 50.36 | 44.07 | 38.84 | 34.49 | 30.83 | 27.74 | 58 |
| 59 | 113.53 | 95.23 | 80.53 | 68.65 | 59.00 | 51.11 | 44.63 | 39.26 | 34.80 | 31.06 | 27.92 | 59 |
| 60 | 116.85 | 97.69 | 82.35 | 70.00 | 60.00 | 51.85 | 45.18 | 39.67 | 35.11 | 31.29 | 28.09 | 60 |
| 61 | 120.25 | 100.18 | 84.19 | 71.35 | 61.00 | 52.59 | 45.73 | 40.08 | 35.41 | 31.52 | 28.26 | 61 |
| 62 | 123.71 | 102.72 | 86.04 | 72.71 | 62.00 | 53.33 | 46.27 | 40.48 | 35.70 | 31.74 | 28.42 | 62 |
| 63 | 127.25 | 105.29 | 87.91 | 74.08 | 63.00 | 54.06 | 46.81 | 40.88 | 36.00 | 31.95 | 28.58 | 63 |
| 64 | 130.85 | 107.90 | 89.81 | 75.46 | 64.00 | 54.79 | 47.34 | 41.26 | 36.28 | 32.16 | 28.73 | 64 |
| 65 | 134.53 | 110.55 | 91.72 | 76.84 | 65.00 | 55.52 | 47.86 | 41.65 | 36.56 | 32.36 | 28.88 | 65 |
| 66 | 138.29 | 113.24 | 93.65 | 78.23 | 66.00 | 56.24 | 48.39 | 42.02 | 36.83 | 32.56 | 29.02 | 66 |
| 67 | 142.12 | 115.97 | 95.60 | 79.62 | 67.00 | 56.95 | 48.90 | 42.40 | 37.10 | 32.75 | 29.16 | 67 |
| 68 | 146.03 | 118.75 | 97.57 | 81.03 | 68.00 | 57.67 | 49.41 | 42.76 | 37.36 | 32.94 | 29.30 | 68 |
| 69 | 150.02 | 121.56 | 99.56 | 82.44 | 69.00 | 58.38 | 49.92 | 43.12 | 37.62 | 33.13 | 29.43 | 69 |
| 70 | 154.10 | 124.42 | 101.57 | 83.85 | 70.00 | 59.09 | 50.42 | 43.48 | 37.87 | 33.31 | 29.56 | 70 |
| 71 | 158.25 | 127.32 | 103.61 | 85.28 | 71.00 | 59.79 | 50.91 | 43.83 | 38.12 | 33.48 | 29.68 | 71 |
| 72 | 162.49 | 130.27 | 105.66 | 86.71 | 72.00 | 60.49 | 51.41 | 44.17 | 38.36 | 33.65 | 29.80 | 72 |
| 73 | 166.82 | 133.26 | 107.73 | 88.15 | 73.00 | 61.19 | 51.89 | 44.51 | 38.60 | 33.82 | 29.92 | 73 |
| 74 | 171.23 | 136.30 | 109.82 | 89.59 | 74.00 | 61.88 | 52.37 | 44.85 | 38.83 | 33.98 | 30.03 | 74 |
| 75 | 175.74 | 139.38 | 111.94 | 91.04 | 75.00 | 62.57 | 52.85 | 45.18 | 39.06 | 34.14 | 30.15 | 75 |
| 76 | 180.33 | 142.51 | 114.07 | 92.50 | 76.00 | 63.26 | 53.32 | 45.50 | 39.29 | 34.30 | 30.25 | 76 |
| 77 | 185.02 | 145.69 | 116.23 | 93.97 | 77.00 | 63.94 | 53.79 | 45.82 | 39.51 | 34.45 | 30.36 | 77 |
| 78 | 189.81 | 148.92 | 118.41 | 95.45 | 78.00 | 64.62 | 54.25 | 46.14 | 39.72 | 34.60 | 30.46 | 78 |
| 79 | 194.69 | 152.19 | 120.61 | 96.93 | 79.00 | 65.29 | 54.71 | 46.45 | 39.93 | 34.74 | 30.56 | 79 |
| 80 | 199.68 | 155.52 | 122.83 | 98.42 | 80.00 | 65.97 | 55.16 | 46.75 | 40.14 | 34.88 | 30.65 | 80 |

## ACTUARIAL FORMULAE AND BASIS

**The functions tabulated are:**

| | | | |
|---|---|---|---|
| Tables 1 and 2 | $\bar{a}_x$ | Tables 17 and 18 | $_{(55-x)|}\bar{a}_x$ |
| Tables 3 and 4 | $\bar{a}_{x:\overline{50-x|}}$ | Tables 19 and 20 | $_{(60-x)|}\bar{a}_x$ |
| Tables 5 and 6 | $\bar{a}_{x:\overline{55-x|}}$ | Tables 21 and 22 | $_{(65-x)|}\bar{a}_x$ |
| Tables 7 and 8 | $\bar{a}_{x:\overline{60-x|}}$ | Tables 23 and 24 | $_{(70-x)|}\bar{a}_x$ |
| Tables 9 and 10 | $\bar{a}_{x:\overline{65-x|}}$ | Tables 25 and 26 | $_{(75-x)|}\bar{a}_x$ |
| Tables 11 and 12 | $\bar{a}_{x:\overline{70-x|}}$ | Table 27 | $1/(1+i)^n$ |
| Tables 13 and 14 | $\bar{a}_{x:\overline{75-x|}}$ | Table 28 | $a_{\overline{n|}}$ |
| Tables 15 and 16 | $_{(50-x)|}\bar{a}_x$ | | |

- Mortality assumptions for 2008-based official population projections for the United Kingdom.
- Loadings: None.
- Rate of return: As stated in the tables.

## Table 28: Multipliers for pecuniary loss for term certain

| Term | \-2.0% | \-1.5% | \-1.0% | \-0.5% | 0.0% | 0.5% | 1.0% | 1.5% | 2.0% | 2.5% | 3.0% | Term |
|---|---|---|---|---|---|---|---|---|---|---|---|---|
| 1 | 1.01 | 1.01 | 1.01 | 1.00 | 1.00 | 1.00 | 1.00 | 0.99 | 0.99 | 0.99 | 0.99 | 1 |
| 2 | 2.04 | 2.03 | 2.02 | 2.01 | 2.00 | 1.99 | 1.98 | 1.97 | 1.96 | 1.95 | 1.94 | 2 |
| 3 | 3.09 | 3.07 | 3.05 | 3.02 | 3.00 | 2.98 | 2.96 | 2.93 | 2.91 | 2.89 | 2.87 | 3 |
| 4 | 4.17 | 4.12 | 4.08 | 4.04 | 4.00 | 3.96 | 3.92 | 3.88 | 3.85 | 3.81 | 3.77 | 4 |
| 5 | 5.26 | 5.19 | 5.13 | 5.06 | 5.00 | 4.94 | 4.88 | 4.82 | 4.76 | 4.70 | 4.65 | 5 |
| 6 | 6.38 | 6.28 | 6.18 | 6.09 | 6.00 | 5.91 | 5.82 | 5.74 | 5.66 | 5.58 | 5.50 | 6 |
| 7 | 7.52 | 7.38 | 7.25 | 7.12 | 7.00 | 6.88 | 6.76 | 6.65 | 6.54 | 6.43 | 6.32 | 7 |
| 8 | 8.68 | 8.50 | 8.33 | 8.16 | 8.00 | 7.84 | 7.69 | 7.54 | 7.40 | 7.26 | 7.12 | 8 |
| 9 | 9.87 | 9.64 | 9.42 | 9.21 | 9.00 | 8.80 | 8.61 | 8.42 | 8.24 | 8.07 | 7.90 | 9 |
| 10 | 11.08 | 10.80 | 10.52 | 10.25 | 10.00 | 9.75 | 9.52 | 9.29 | 9.07 | 8.86 | 8.66 | 10 |
| 11 | 12.32 | 11.97 | 11.63 | 11.31 | 11.00 | 10.70 | 10.42 | 10.15 | 9.88 | 9.63 | 9.39 | 11 |
| 12 | 13.58 | 13.16 | 12.75 | 12.37 | 12.00 | 11.65 | 11.31 | 10.99 | 10.68 | 10.39 | 10.10 | 12 |
| 13 | 14.87 | 14.37 | 13.89 | 13.43 | 13.00 | 12.59 | 12.19 | 11.82 | 11.46 | 11.12 | 10.79 | 13 |
| 14 | 16.18 | 15.59 | 15.03 | 14.50 | 14.00 | 13.52 | 13.07 | 12.64 | 12.23 | 11.84 | 11.46 | 14 |
| 15 | 17.52 | 16.84 | 16.19 | 15.58 | 15.00 | 14.45 | 13.93 | 13.44 | 12.98 | 12.54 | 12.12 | 15 |
| 16 | 18.89 | 18.10 | 17.36 | 16.66 | 16.00 | 15.38 | 14.79 | 14.24 | 13.71 | 13.22 | 12.75 | 16 |
| 17 | 20.28 | 19.38 | 18.54 | 17.75 | 17.00 | 16.30 | 15.64 | 15.02 | 14.43 | 13.88 | 13.36 | 17 |
| 18 | 21.71 | 20.69 | 19.73 | 18.84 | 18.00 | 17.22 | 16.48 | 15.79 | 15.14 | 14.53 | 13.96 | 18 |
| 19 | 23.16 | 22.01 | 20.94 | 19.93 | 19.00 | 18.13 | 17.31 | 16.55 | 15.83 | 15.17 | 14.54 | 19 |
| 20 | 24.64 | 23.35 | 22.15 | 21.04 | 20.00 | 19.03 | 18.14 | 17.30 | 16.51 | 15.78 | 15.10 | 20 |
| 21 | 26.16 | 24.71 | 23.38 | 22.15 | 21.00 | 19.94 | 18.95 | 18.03 | 17.18 | 16.39 | 15.65 | 21 |
| 22 | 27.70 | 26.10 | 24.62 | 23.26 | 22.00 | 20.84 | 19.76 | 18.76 | 17.83 | 16.97 | 16.17 | 22 |
| 23 | 29.28 | 27.50 | 25.88 | 24.38 | 23.00 | 21.73 | 20.56 | 19.48 | 18.47 | 17.55 | 16.69 | 23 |
| 24 | 30.88 | 28.93 | 27.14 | 25.50 | 24.00 | 22.62 | 21.35 | 20.18 | 19.10 | 18.11 | 17.19 | 24 |
| 25 | 32.53 | 30.38 | 28.42 | 26.63 | 25.00 | 23.50 | 22.13 | 20.87 | 19.72 | 18.65 | 17.67 | 25 |
| 26 | 34.20 | 31.85 | 29.71 | 27.77 | 26.00 | 24.38 | 22.91 | 21.56 | 20.32 | 19.19 | 18.14 | 26 |
| 27 | 35.91 | 33.34 | 31.02 | 28.91 | 27.00 | 25.26 | 23.68 | 22.23 | 20.91 | 19.71 | 18.60 | 27 |
| 28 | 37.65 | 34.86 | 32.34 | 30.06 | 28.00 | 26.13 | 24.44 | 22.90 | 21.49 | 20.21 | 19.04 | 28 |
| 29 | 39.43 | 36.40 | 33.67 | 31.21 | 29.00 | 27.00 | 25.19 | 23.55 | 22.06 | 20.71 | 19.47 | 29 |
| 30 | 41.24 | 37.96 | 35.01 | 32.37 | 30.00 | 27.86 | 25.94 | 24.20 | 22.62 | 21.19 | 19.89 | 30 |
| 31 | 43.10 | 39.54 | 36.37 | 33.54 | 31.00 | 28.72 | 26.67 | 24.83 | 23.17 | 21.66 | 20.30 | 31 |
| 32 | 44.99 | 41.15 | 37.74 | 34.71 | 32.00 | 29.58 | 27.41 | 25.46 | 23.70 | 22.12 | 20.69 | 32 |
| 33 | 46.91 | 42.79 | 39.13 | 35.89 | 33.00 | 30.43 | 28.13 | 26.07 | 24.23 | 22.57 | 21.08 | 33 |
| 34 | 48.88 | 44.45 | 40.53 | 37.07 | 34.00 | 31.27 | 28.85 | 26.68 | 24.74 | 23.01 | 21.45 | 34 |
| 35 | 50.89 | 46.13 | 41.95 | 38.26 | 35.00 | 32.12 | 29.56 | 27.28 | 25.25 | 23.43 | 21.81 | 35 |
| 36 | 52.94 | 47.84 | 43.37 | 39.45 | 36.00 | 32.95 | 30.26 | 27.87 | 25.74 | 23.85 | 22.16 | 36 |
| 37 | 55.03 | 49.58 | 44.82 | 40.65 | 37.00 | 33.79 | 30.95 | 28.45 | 26.23 | 24.26 | 22.50 | 37 |
| 38 | 57.16 | 51.34 | 46.28 | 41.86 | 38.00 | 34.62 | 31.64 | 29.02 | 26.70 | 24.65 | 22.83 | 38 |
| 39 | 59.34 | 53.13 | 47.75 | 43.07 | 39.00 | 35.44 | 32.32 | 29.58 | 27.17 | 25.04 | 23.15 | 39 |
| 40 | 61.56 | 54.95 | 49.24 | 44.29 | 40.00 | 36.26 | 33.00 | 30.14 | 27.63 | 25.42 | 23.46 | 40 |
| 41 | 63.83 | 56.79 | 50.74 | 45.52 | 41.00 | 37.08 | 33.67 | 30.69 | 28.08 | 25.78 | 23.76 | 41 |
| 42 | 66.14 | 58.66 | 52.26 | 46.75 | 42.00 | 37.89 | 34.33 | 31.23 | 28.52 | 26.14 | 24.06 | 42 |
| 43 | 68.50 | 60.56 | 53.79 | 47.99 | 43.00 | 38.70 | 34.98 | 31.76 | 28.95 | 26.49 | 24.34 | 43 |
| 44 | 70.91 | 62.49 | 55.34 | 49.23 | 44.00 | 39.51 | 35.63 | 32.28 | 29.37 | 26.83 | 24.62 | 44 |
| 45 | 73.36 | 64.45 | 56.90 | 50.48 | 45.00 | 40.31 | 36.27 | 32.80 | 29.78 | 27.17 | 24.88 | 45 |
| 46 | 75.87 | 66.44 | 58.48 | 51.74 | 46.00 | 41.10 | 36.91 | 33.30 | 30.19 | 27.49 | 25.15 | 46 |
| 47 | 78.43 | 68.46 | 60.08 | 53.00 | 47.00 | 41.90 | 37.54 | 33.80 | 30.59 | 27.81 | 25.40 | 47 |
| 48 | 81.04 | 70.51 | 61.69 | 54.27 | 48.00 | 42.69 | 38.16 | 34.30 | 30.98 | 28.12 | 25.64 | 48 |
| 49 | 83.70 | 72.59 | 63.32 | 55.54 | 49.00 | 43.47 | 38.78 | 34.78 | 31.36 | 28.42 | 25.88 | 49 |
| 50 | 86.42 | 74.70 | 64.96 | 56.82 | 50.00 | 44.25 | 39.39 | 35.26 | 31.74 | 28.72 | 26.11 | 50 |
| 51 | 89.20 | 76.85 | 66.62 | 58.11 | 51.00 | 45.03 | 40.00 | 35.73 | 32.10 | 29.00 | 26.34 | 51 |
| 52 | 92.03 | 79.03 | 68.30 | 59.41 | 52.00 | 45.80 | 40.60 | 36.20 | 32.47 | 29.28 | 26.56 | 52 |
| 53 | 94.92 | 81.24 | 69.99 | 60.71 | 53.00 | 46.57 | 41.19 | 36.66 | 32.82 | 29.56 | 26.77 | 53 |
| 54 | 97.86 | 83.48 | 71.71 | 62.01 | 54.00 | 47.34 | 41.78 | 37.11 | 33.17 | 29.82 | 26.97 | 54 |
| 55 | 100.87 | 85.76 | 73.44 | 63.33 | 55.00 | 48.10 | 42.36 | 37.55 | 33.51 | 30.08 | 27.17 | 55 |

## Table 28: Multipliers for pecuniary loss for term certain *continued*

| Term | \-2.0% | \-1.5% | \-1.0% | \-0.5% | 0.0% | 0.5% | 1.0% | 1.5% | 2.0% | 2.5% | 3.0% | Term |
|---|---|---|---|---|---|---|---|---|---|---|---|---|
| | Multiplier for regular frequent payments for a term certain at rate of return of | | | | | | | | | | | |
| 56 | 103.94 | 88.08 | 75.18 | 64.65 | 56.00 | 48.86 | 42.93 | 37.99 | 33.84 | 30.34 | 27.37 | 56 |
| 57 | 107.07 | 90.43 | 76.95 | 65.98 | 57.00 | 49.61 | 43.50 | 38.42 | 34.17 | 30.59 | 27.56 | 57 |
| 58 | 110.27 | 92.81 | 78.73 | 67.31 | 58.00 | 50.36 | 44.07 | 38.84 | 34.49 | 30.83 | 27.74 | 58 |
| 59 | 113.53 | 95.23 | 80.53 | 68.65 | 59.00 | 51.11 | 44.63 | 39.26 | 34.80 | 31.06 | 27.92 | 59 |
| 60 | 116.85 | 97.69 | 82.35 | 70.00 | 60.00 | 51.85 | 45.18 | 39.67 | 35.11 | 31.29 | 28.09 | 60 |
| 61 | 120.25 | 100.18 | 84.19 | 71.35 | 61.00 | 52.59 | 45.73 | 40.08 | 35.41 | 31.52 | 28.26 | 61 |
| 62 | 123.71 | 102.72 | 86.04 | 72.71 | 62.00 | 53.33 | 46.27 | 40.48 | 35.70 | 31.74 | 28.42 | 62 |
| 63 | 127.25 | 105.29 | 87.91 | 74.08 | 63.00 | 54.06 | 46.81 | 40.88 | 36.00 | 31.95 | 28.58 | 63 |
| 64 | 130.85 | 107.90 | 89.81 | 75.46 | 64.00 | 54.79 | 47.34 | 41.26 | 36.28 | 32.16 | 28.73 | 64 |
| 65 | 134.53 | 110.55 | 91.72 | 76.84 | 65.00 | 55.52 | 47.86 | 41.65 | 36.56 | 32.36 | 28.88 | 65 |
| 66 | 138.29 | 113.24 | 93.65 | 78.23 | 66.00 | 56.24 | 48.39 | 42.02 | 36.83 | 32.56 | 29.02 | 66 |
| 67 | 142.12 | 115.97 | 95.60 | 79.62 | 67.00 | 56.95 | 48.90 | 42.40 | 37.10 | 32.75 | 29.16 | 67 |
| 68 | 146.03 | 118.75 | 97.57 | 81.03 | 68.00 | 57.67 | 49.41 | 42.76 | 37.36 | 32.94 | 29.30 | 68 |
| 69 | 150.02 | 121.56 | 99.56 | 82.44 | 69.00 | 58.38 | 49.92 | 43.12 | 37.62 | 33.13 | 29.43 | 69 |
| 70 | 154.10 | 124.42 | 101.57 | 83.85 | 70.00 | 59.09 | 50.42 | 43.48 | 37.87 | 33.31 | 29.56 | 70 |
| 71 | 158.25 | 127.32 | 103.61 | 85.28 | 71.00 | 59.79 | 50.91 | 43.83 | 38.12 | 33.48 | 29.68 | 71 |
| 72 | 162.49 | 130.27 | 105.66 | 86.71 | 72.00 | 60.49 | 51.41 | 44.17 | 38.36 | 33.65 | 29.80 | 72 |
| 73 | 166.82 | 133.26 | 107.73 | 88.15 | 73.00 | 61.19 | 51.89 | 44.51 | 38.60 | 33.82 | 29.92 | 73 |
| 74 | 171.23 | 136.30 | 109.82 | 89.59 | 74.00 | 61.88 | 52.37 | 44.85 | 38.83 | 33.98 | 30.03 | 74 |
| 75 | 175.74 | 139.38 | 111.94 | 91.04 | 75.00 | 62.57 | 52.85 | 45.18 | 39.06 | 34.14 | 30.15 | 75 |
| 76 | 180.33 | 142.51 | 114.07 | 92.50 | 76.00 | 63.26 | 53.32 | 45.50 | 39.29 | 34.30 | 30.25 | 76 |
| 77 | 185.02 | 145.69 | 116.23 | 93.97 | 77.00 | 63.94 | 53.79 | 45.82 | 39.51 | 34.45 | 30.36 | 77 |
| 78 | 189.81 | 148.92 | 118.41 | 95.45 | 78.00 | 64.62 | 54.25 | 46.14 | 39.72 | 34.60 | 30.46 | 78 |
| 79 | 194.69 | 152.19 | 120.61 | 96.93 | 79.00 | 65.29 | 54.71 | 46.45 | 39.93 | 34.74 | 30.56 | 79 |
| 80 | 199.68 | 155.52 | 122.83 | 98.42 | 80.00 | 65.97 | 55.16 | 46.75 | 40.14 | 34.88 | 30.65 | 80 |

## ACTUARIAL FORMULAE AND BASIS

**The functions tabulated are:**

| | | | |
|---|---|---|---|
| Tables 1 and 2 | $\bar{a}_x$ | Tables 17 and 18 | $_{(55-x)|}\bar{a}_x$ |
| Tables 3 and 4 | $\bar{a}_{x:\overline{50-x|}}$ | Tables 19 and 20 | $_{(60-x)|}\bar{a}_x$ |
| Tables 5 and 6 | $\bar{a}_{x:\overline{55-x|}}$ | Tables 21 and 22 | $_{(65-x)|}\bar{a}_x$ |
| Tables 7 and 8 | $\bar{a}_{x:\overline{60-x|}}$ | Tables 23 and 24 | $_{(70-x)|}\bar{a}_x$ |
| Tables 9 and 10 | $\bar{a}_{x:\overline{65-x|}}$ | Tables 25 and 26 | $_{(75-x)|}\bar{a}_x$ |
| Tables 11 and 12 | $\bar{a}_{x:\overline{70-x|}}$ | Table 27 | $1/(1+i)^n$ |
| Tables 13 and 14 | $\bar{a}_{x:\overline{75-x|}}$ | Table 28 | $a_{\overline{n|}}$ |
| Tables 15 and 16 | $_{(50-x)|}\bar{a}_x$ | | |

- Mortality assumptions for 2008-based official population projections for the United Kingdom.
- Loadings: None.
- Rate of return: As stated in the tables.

# A9: The Lord Chancellor's statement, 27 July 2001

THE LORD CHANCELLOR'S DEPARTMENT
Discount Rate
Setting the Discount Rate
Lord Chancellor's Reasons
July 27, 2001

## Introduction

On June 25, 2001 I made the Damages (Personal Injury) Order 2001 ("the 2001 Order") pursuant to s.1 of the Damages Act 1996. In setting a rate of 2.5% in the 2001 Order I had regard to what I believed to be the accurate figure for the average gross redemption yield on Index-Linked Government Stock for the three years leading up to June 8, 2001. Following my announcement of the discount rate, questions were raised as to the correctness of the three-year average yield figure upon which I had relied.

These questions led me to have the information about the three-year average yield figure checked thoroughly. Those checks revealed certain limited inaccuracies in the information underlying the average yield figure on which I had based my reasoning in making the 2001 Order. In the light of the correction of that average yield figure, I think it right that I should consider completely afresh, on the basis of the accurate average yield figure, what rate I should have set when I made the 2001 Order on June 25, 2001, in order to determine whether the 2001 Order should be withdrawn.

## Decision

Having considered all the material available to me, including the accurate, corrected average yield figure, I have come to the conclusion that a discount rate of 2.5% was the appropriate rate to set. Therefore, I do not consider that the 2001 Order should be withdrawn. This statement sets out my reasons for coming to that conclusion.

## Reasons

In determining the discount rate, I have applied the appropriate legal principle laid down authoritatively by the courts, and in particular by the House of Lords in *Wells v Wells*.[1]

I also consider that it is highly desirable to exercise my powers under the Act so as to produce a situation in which claimants and defendants may have a reasonably clear idea about the impact of the discount rate upon their cases, so as to facilitate negotiation of settlements and the presentation of cases in court. In order to promote this objective, I have concluded that I should:

a  set a single rate to cover all cases. This accords with the solution adopted by the House of Lords in *Wells v Wells*. It will eliminate scope for uncertainty and argument about the applicable rate. Similarly, I consider it is preferable to have a fixed rate, which promotes certainty and which avoids the complexity and extra costs that a formula would entail;

b  set a rate which is easy for all parties and their lawyers to apply in practice and which reflects the fact that the rate is bound to be applied in a range of different circumstances over a period of time.

---

[1] [1999] 1 A.C. 345.

## A9: The Lord Chancellor's statement, 27 July 2001

For this reason, I consider it appropriate to set the discount rate to the nearest half per cent, so as to ensure that the figure will be suitable for use in conjunction with the Ogden Tables, which are a ready means for parties to take into account actuarial factors in computing the quantum of damages;

c set a rate which should obtain for the foreseeable future. I consider it would be very detrimental to the reasonable certainty which is necessary to promote the just and efficient resolution of disputes (by settlement as well as by hearing in court) to make frequent changes to the discount rate. Therefore, whilst I will remain ready to review the discount rate whenever I find there is a significant and established change in the relevant real rates of return to be expected, I do not propose to tinker with the rate frequently to take account of every transient shift in market conditions.

(I consider that the reasoning and conclusions in the above paragraph, which appeared in my original reasons for setting the discount rate in the 2001 Order, continue to apply.)

The principle which I must strive to apply is clear: " . . . the object of the award of damages for future expenditure is to place the injured party as nearly as possible in the same financial position he or she would have been in but for the accident. The aim is to award such a sum of money as will amount to no more, and at the same time no less, than the net loss." (*Wells v Wells* at 390A–B per Lord Hope of Craighead). I acknowledge that claimants who have suffered severe injuries are not in the position of ordinary investors. Such claimants have a pressing need for a dependable source of income to meet the costs of their future care. It is accordingly unrealistic to require severely injured claimants to take even moderate risks when they invest their damages awards.

Setting a single rate to cover all cases, whilst highly desirable for the reasons given above, has the effect that the discount rate has to cover a wide variety of different cases, and claimants with widely differing personal and financial characteristics. Moreover, as has become clear from the consultation exercise (including responses by expert financial analysts to questions which I posed them), the real rate of return on investments of any character (including investments in Index-Linked Government Securities) involves making assumptions for the future about a wide variety of factors affecting the economy as a whole, including for example the likely rate of inflation. In these circumstances, it is inevitable that any approach to setting the discount rate must be fairly broad-brush. Put shortly, there can be no single "right" answer as to what rate should be set. Since it is in the context of larger awards, intended to cover longer periods, that there is the greatest risk of serious discrepancies between the level of compensation and the actual losses incurred if the discount rate set is not appropriate, I have had this type of award particularly in mind when considering the level at which the discount rate should be set. (The above paragraphs also formed a part of my original reasons for setting the discount rate, and I consider that they continue to apply.)

The House of Lords in *Wells v Wells* determined the real rate of return obtainable by claimants through low-risk investment by reference to the gross redemption yields on Index-Linked Government Stock. Their Lordships assumed that a claimant would use his damages award to purchase the right portfolio of Index-Linked Government Stock to ensure that in future years the sums which he received from his portfolio by way of coupon payments and payments on redemption would be sufficient to meet his financial needs. The risk that an early sale of Index-Linked Government Stock might cause capital losses was removed by assuming that such a claimant would hold all his Index-Linked Government Stock until redemption.

The House of Lords thought it appropriate to set the discount rate by reference to the average yields on Index-Linked Government Stock. There is no single correct method by which this average yield may be calculated. Among other factors, the calculation will depend upon the length of the period under consideration, the stocks which are to be included within the average, the inflation assumption made and the form of average taken.

## A9: The Lord Chancellor's statement, 27 July 2001

The majority of their Lordships considered it appropriate to set a discount rate by taking a three-year average of Index-Linked Government Stock yields. I agree that, having regard to the benefits to be obtained in setting the discount rate for the foreseeable future, three years is an appropriate period over which to take an average. I note that Lord Lloyd of Berwick preferred a one-year period; this confirms the need for judgements to be made in determining the appropriate average yield.

It appears from the speech of Lord Hope at 393E–F that his Lordship had regard to an average of gross redemption yields on Index-Linked Government Stock with lives of over five years. He did not give reasons for adopting that particular approach. I am aware that this approach has also been favoured by the Ogden Working Party. However, having regard to the basic reasoning of the House of Lords in *Wells v Wells*, I do not consider that I am obliged to follow it. As noted above, the House of Lords in *Wells v Wells* assumed that a claimant would generally hold all his Index-Linked Government Stock until redemption. Further, as was stated by Lord Clyde at 395H–396A, it was to be assumed that in each year of loss a proportion of the capital would have to be used. If these two assumptions are to be rendered consistent then it will be necessary for the claimant to purchase Index-Linked Government Stock which will mature in the short term, for otherwise the claimant would have to sell a proportion of his Index-Linked Government Stock prior to redemption in order to realise, in the short term, some of the capital value of his investments. Some claimants, whose losses extend over periods of about five years or so or less, would have to purchase all or most of their Index-Linked Government Stock (if that is what they chose to do with the damages paid to them) in this category of stock. I have therefore decided that it is proper to take an average over all Index-Linked Government Stock rather than to exclude Index-Linked Government Stock with less than five years to maturity.

Nevertheless, I consider that it would be inappropriate to include the gross redemption yields of such stock which is very near maturity ("near maturity ILGS"—which is stock for which the nominal value of the final coupon and redemption payments have become known with certainty). The gross redemption yield on such near maturity ILGS is a nominal yield rather than a real yield. Accordingly, I asked for a calculation of the size of the real yield element in the gross redemption yields of the near maturity ILGS and have included those real yields within my calculation of the average yield.

The average yield figure upon which Lord Hope relied at 393E–F in *Wells v Wells* was based on an inflation assumption of 5%. I consider that, given both the current rate of inflation and the Government's policy aim of maintaining that rate within an upper limit of 2.5%, an assumption of 3% is to be preferred for present purposes.

The House of Lords in *Wells v Wells* did not discuss what form of average should be taken of Index-Linked Government Stock yields. One method is to take an average which is weighted in accordance with the market value of each stock. To my mind, such a weighted average is not relevant to the present circumstances, as the choice of Index-Linked Government Stock portfolio which is necessary to ensure that the future financial needs of a claimant are adequately and promptly met does not depend upon the prevailing market values of Index-Linked Government Stock. I have therefore decided that it is appropriate to take a simple average of Index-Linked Government Stock yields.

A calculation of the simple average of the gross redemption yields of an Index-Linked Government Stock (with an appropriate adjustment for the yields of near maturity ILGS) at an assumed rate of inflation of 3% produces an average yield figure of 2.46%. Accordingly, I conclude that the net average yield on Index-Linked Government Stock, as adjusted to take account of tax, lies in the range between 2% and 2.5%. In my opinion, following *Wells v Wells*, the discount rate should be set within this range. Further, given that the rate is to be set to the nearest 0.5%, it is clear that the discount rate should either be 2% or 2.5%. I do not consider that the choice whether a rate of 2% or one of 2.5% is appropriate is a simple arithmetical matter, nor that *Wells v Wells* requires me to set one rate or the other. I must have regard to the basic principle to which I have referred above, and I have taken account of matters which I consider are relevant to the setting of a discount rate which is just as between claimants as a group and defendants as a group.

In the light of all the information now available to me, and considering the matter completely afresh, I have decided that on June 25, 2001 I should have set the discount rate at 2.5%.

In doing so, I have noted that the real rate of return to be expected from Index-Linked Government Securities tends to be higher the lower the rate of inflation is assumed to be (figures at assumed rates of inflation of 3% and 5% are readily available for comparison). The average gross redemption yield figure of 2.46% assumes an inflation figure of 3% extending into the future. But over recent years inflation has been kept close to or below the 2.5% target set by the Government, and Government policy and the function of the Bank of England remains firmly to maintain inflation according to that target. Although economists differ as to what inflation rates may be expected for the future, I note that the market's general expectation as to the rate of inflation for the future (as implied by market valuations of gilts) is well below 3%. I consider that it is reasonable to assume an inflation rate for the foreseeable future somewhere below 3%, and this in turn provides comfort that a discount rate set at 2.5% is reasonable. (The above paragraph and the larger part of the following four paragraphs were contained in my original reasons for setting the discount rate. They set out considerations which I consider continue to apply).

I am further supported in my conclusion that a discount rate of 2.5% is reasonable by indications that the rate of return in respect of Index-Linked Government Securities does not represent a pure and undistorted measure of the real rate of return which markets would afford in relation to investments with minimal risk which have emerged from the information which was provided in the responses to the consultation paper and the responses from expert financial analysts which I obtained, and by consideration of rates of return on other investments which are available at low risk to claimants. I have treated the following points as significant.

First, some responses to the consultation maintained that the market in Index-Linked Government Securities is at present distorted so that the prevailing yields are artificially low, and do not necessarily give a reliable indication of the real rate of return which markets would afford in relation to investments with minimal risk. The expert financial analysts whom I consulted concurred that the market is distorted at present. This appears to be a result of the minimum funding requirement introduced by the Pensions Act 1995 (which has, in effect, created additional demand for such securities on the part of pension funds) combined with a reduced supply of government securities generally, as the Government has reduced the national debt. The market in Index-Linked Government Securities has changed significantly since *Wells v Wells* was argued and decided. It is widely held that the continuing high demand for Index-Linked Government Stock and the scarcity of supply has led to yields being artificially low as compared with both past record and the yields presently available on similar investment instruments issued by other, comparable, national governments. I consider that the fact that yields in Index-Linked Government Stock appear to be artificially low at present militates against the suggestion that these yields over recent years should be taken as the sole indication of the rates of return that can be achieved through low risk investment in the market. Also, I consider that there is some reasonable prospect of a return to higher rates of return in respect of Index-Linked Government Stock when the Government's already announced plans to abolish the minimum funding requirement are carried into effect. Any distorting effect of the minimum funding requirement would be expected to be particularly pronounced in relation to the longer maturity stocks, whose yields have recently been lower than shorter maturity stocks.

Second, I have noted that the Court of Protection, even in the wake of *Wells v Wells*, has continued to invest, on the behalf of claimants, in multi-asset portfolios, including an equity element. Investment in this manner could be expected to produce real rates of return well in excess of 2.5%. The Court of Protection has specific responsibility to ensure that the financial needs of those for whose benefit it acts will be met, ie its investment objectives are closely similar to those of the prudent claimant which the House of Lords identified in *Wells v Wells*. The Court of Protection takes competent financial advice as to the investment strategy which will best secure those objectives. Despite the decision of the House of Lords in *Wells v Wells* to set the discount rate by reference to yields on Index-Linked Government Securities, the Court of Protection has continued its former policy, with the agreement of the families concerned, of investing in portfolios comprising of a mixture of equities, gilts and cash. Master Lush of the Court of Protection has stated that none of the families of the Court's patients have chosen to invest in Index-Linked Government Stock since *Wells v Wells*, despite having been offered that option. Thus it appears that there are sensible, low risk investment strategies available to claimants which would enable them comfortably to achieve a real rate of return at 2.5% or above, without their being unduly exposed to risk in the equity markets. Although the House of Lords in *Wells v Wells* chose not to be guided by the practice of the Court of Protection, this was principally on the grounds that what the Court of Protection might do in the future was uncertain, and not on the grounds that its practice was irrelevant. I consider it is appropriate to take account of what has happened in the period since that decision.

Third, I consider that it is likely that real claimants with a large award of compensation, who sought investment advice and instructed their advisers as to the particular investment objectives which they needed to fulfil (as they could reasonably be expected to do) would not be advised to invest solely or even primarily in Index-Linked Government Securities, but rather in a mixed portfolio, in which any investment risk would be managed so as to be very low. This view is supported by the experience of the Court of Protection as to the independent financial advice they receive. It is also supported by the responses of the expert financial analysts whom I have consulted. No one responding to the consultation identified a single case in which the claimant had invested solely in Index-Linked Government Securities and doubts were expressed as to whether there was any such case. This suggests that setting the discount rate at 2.5% would not place an intolerable burden on claimants to take on excessive, i.e. moderate or above, risk in the equity markets, and would be a rate more likely to accord with real expectations of returns, particularly at the higher end of awards.

Finally, in deciding that a single rate of 2.5% should have been set by me on June 25, 2001, I have borne in mind that it will, of course, remain open for the Courts under s.1(2) of the Damages Act 1996 to adopt a different rate in any particular case if there are exceptional circumstances which justify it in doing so.

Irvine of Lairg
Lord Chancellor
July 27, 2001

# Group B
*Damages*

B1: General damages table following *Heil v Rankin* and *Simmons v Castle*

B2: Bereavement damages

B3: *Auty v National Coal Board* (pension claims)

B4: *Roberts v Johnstone* (accommodation claims)

B5: Periodical payments

B6: Step-by-step guide to finding the annual estimates for hourly pay in ASHE SOC 2000 6115

# Group B
*Damages*

**B1:** General damages table following *Heil v Rankin* and *Simmons v Castle*

**B2:** Bereavement damages

**B3:** *Auty v National Coal Board* (pension claims)

**B4:** *Roberts v Johnstone* (accommodation claims)

**B5:** Periodical payments

**B6:** Step-by-step guide to finding the annual estimates for hourly pay in ASHE SOC 2000 6115

# B1: General damages table following *Heil v Rankin* and *Simmons v Castle*

**General introduction**

On the following pages are tables for use in updating awards of general damages in the light of the Court of Appeal's judgments in *Heil v Rankin*[1] and in *Simmons v Castle*.[2] At Table E1 will be found a Retail Prices Index table and at Table E2 an inflation table.

1. Annexed to the Court of Appeal's judgment in *Heil* was a rather smudged graph provided to show "very approximately" the scale of the increase. The line is a shallow curve. In discussion after judgment was given, their Lordships said that they had not intended to lay down a mathematical formula. We must therefore assume that the top line was intended to fit around what had actually been done in *Heil* (i.e. nothing) and the other seven cases.

2. Despite this, and with a little diffidence (though some confidence), we suggest the following formula. It is calculated on the following assumptions—

    a. the highest award of general damages at 23 March 2000 was around £150,000: awards of this amount or higher were increased by $33\frac{1}{3}$ per cent;

    b. there is no increase in awards that were worth up to £10,000 before that date; and

    c. the uplift is 0% at £10,000 and rises *in a straight line* to $33\frac{1}{3}$ per cent.

3. To find the value of an *old* award in *new* terms, that award must first be updated to 23 March 2000 using the Retail Prices Index (reproduced below), in the usual way. Let us call this updated figure A. The formula is:

$$£A + [£A-10,000/420,000 \times £A]$$

    The part in square brackets is the *Heil* uplift.

4. In *Simmons v Castle* the Court of Appeal decided that general damages for personal injury (and certain other losses) will increase by 10 per cent (as proposed in the Final Report on Civil Litigation Costs by Sir Rupert Jackson), unless the claimant falls within s.44(6) of the Legal Aid, Sentencing and Punishment of Offenders Act 2012[3]. The effect of this is that in a case where the claimant entered into a Conditional Fee Agreement before 1 April 2013, he recovers the success fee as part of his costs (as before) but does not get the 10 per cent increase in general damages: in any other case the claimant gets the 10 per cent increase in damages but does not get the success fee.

5. For example:

    a. On January 26, 1988, McNeill J awarded the claimant in *Chan v Chan* general damages of £75,000.

    b. Updating £75,000 to 23 March 2000 in line with the Retail Prices Index gives £122,250.

    c. Subtract £10,000 from £122,250, and divide it by £420,000. This gives $112,250/420,000$ = 0.27. This is the percentage uplift.

    d. Applying this uplift to the original award gives [0.27 × £122,250] = £33,008.

---

[1] [2000] 2 W.L.R. 1173.
[2] [2012] EWCA Civ 1039 and [2012] EWCA Civ 1288.
[3] In *Summers v Bundy* [2016] EWCA Civ 126, the Court held that cases within s.44(6) are the only exception and the judge has no discretion to dispense with the uplift in other cases.

B1: General damages table following *Heil v Rankin* and *Simmons v Castle*

e. The award in *Chan v Chan* was therefore worth [£122,250 + £33,008] = **£155,258** on 23 March 2000.

f. The £155,258 should then be updated from 23 March 2000 to the present and, unless s.44(6) applies, it should also be increased by 10 per cent. Multiply by [present RPI] × 1.10 / [RPI March 2000].

6. Because the degree of uplift varies with the size of the old award, it is inaccurate to apply the *Heil v Rankin* uplift to a figure already adjusted for inflation to a date later than 23 March 2000. The *Simmons v Castle* uplift of 10 per cent does not depend on the size of the award. In June 2016 the RPI was 263.1.

## TO UPDATE A PRE-*HEIL v RANKIN* AWARD

The table on this page shows the factor to allow for inflation from an earlier judgment date to 23 March 2000. The table overleaf shows the appropriate new figure, following *Heil v Rankin* in relation to the conventional level of damages at £1,000 intervals up to £150,000.

Note that the uplift should be applied to the damages adjusted for inflation to 23 March 2000, thus:

(1) Damages awarded, say, January 1990 × Inflation increase 1 January 1990–23 March 2000 (from first table) = old award as at 23 March 2000.

(2) Award uplifted under *Heil v Rankin* (from second table).

(3) Then multiply by an inflation uplift from 23 March 2000 onwards to the date of trial; plus the additional 10 per cent (unless s.44(6) applies).

### TABLE TO UPDATE FOR INFLATION TO MARCH 2000

| | J | F | M | A | M | J | J | A | S | O | N | D | |
|---|---|---|---|---|---|---|---|---|---|---|---|---|---|
| 1980 | 2.708 | 2.670 | 2.634 | 2.547 | 2.524 | 2.500 | 2.480 | 2.474 | 2.459 | 2.443 | 2.424 | 2.411 | 1980 |
| 1981 | 2.396 | 2.374 | 2.339 | 2.274 | 2.259 | 2.246 | 2.236 | 2.220 | 2.207 | 2.187 | 2.165 | 2.151 | 1981 |
| 1982 | 2.139 | 2.138 | 2.120 | 2.078 | 2.063 | 2.057 | 2.057 | 2.056 | 2.057 | 2.047 | 2.037 | 2.041 | 1982 |
| 1983 | 2.038 | 2.030 | 2.026 | 1.998 | 1.990 | 1.985 | 1.974 | 1.965 | 1.957 | 1.950 | 1.943 | 1.938 | 1983 |
| 1984 | 1.939 | 1.931 | 1.925 | 1.900 | 1.893 | 1.888 | 1.890 | 1.872 | 1.869 | 1.857 | 1.852 | 1.853 | 1984 |
| 1985 | 1.846 | 1.832 | 1.815 | 1.777 | 1.769 | 1.765 | 1.768 | 1.764 | 1.765 | 1.762 | 1.756 | 1.753 | 1985 |
| 1986 | 1.750 | 1.743 | 1.741 | 1.724 | 1.721 | 1.722 | 1.727 | 1.722 | 1.713 | 1.710 | 1.696 | 1.690 | 1986 |
| 1987 | 1.684 | 1.677 | 1.674 | 1.654 | 1.653 | 1.653 | 1.654 | 1.649 | 1.645 | 1.637 | 1.629 | 1.630 | 1987 |
| 1988 | 1.630 | 1.624 | 1.618 | 1.592 | 1.586 | 1.580 | 1.578 | 1.561 | 1.554 | 1.538 | 1.531 | 1.527 | 1988 |
| 1989 | 1.517 | 1.506 | 1.500 | 1.473 | 1.464 | 1.459 | 1.458 | 1.454 | 1.444 | 1.433 | 1.421 | 1.418 | 1989 |
| 1990 | 1.409 | 1.401 | 1.387 | 1.346 | 1.334 | 1.329 | 1.328 | 1.315 | 1.302 | 1.292 | 1.295 | 1.296 | 1990 |
| 1991 | 1.293 | 1.286 | 1.282 | 1.265 | 1.261 | 1.256 | 1.259 | 1.256 | 1.251 | 1.246 | 1.242 | 1.241 | 1991 |
| 1992 | 1.242 | 1.236 | 1.232 | 1.213 | 1.209 | 1.209 | 1.213 | 1.212 | 1.208 | 1.204 | 1.205 | 1.210 | 1992 |
| 1993 | 1.221 | 1.213 | 1.209 | 1.198 | 1.193 | 1.194 | 1.197 | 1.192 | 1.187 | 1.188 | 1.189 | 1.187 | 1993 |
| 1994 | 1.192 | 1.185 | 1.182 | 1.168 | 1.164 | 1.164 | 1.169 | 1.164 | 1.161 | 1.160 | 1.159 | 1.153 | 1994 |
| 1995 | 1.153 | 1.146 | 1.142 | 1.130 | 1.126 | 1.124 | 1.129 | 1.123 | 1.118 | 1.124 | 1.124 | 1.117 | 1995 |
| 1996 | 1.121 | 1.116 | 1.112 | 1.104 | 1.101 | 1.101 | 1.105 | 1.100 | 1.095 | 1.095 | 1.094 | 1.091 | 1996 |
| 1997 | 1.091 | 1.086 | 1.084 | 1.077 | 1.073 | 1.069 | 1.069 | 1.062 | 1.057 | 1.056 | 1.055 | 1.053 | 1997 |
| 1998 | 1.056 | 1.051 | 1.047 | 1.036 | 1.030 | 1.031 | 1.033 | 1.029 | 1.024 | 1.024 | 1.024 | 1.024 | 1998 |
| 1999 | 1.031 | 1.029 | 1.026 | 1.019 | 1.017 | 1.017 | 1.020 | 1.018 | 1.013 | 1.011 | 1.010 | 1.007 | 1999 |
| 2000 | 1.011 | 1.005 | | | | | | | | | | | 2000 |
| | J | F | M | A | M | J | J | A | S | O | N | D | |

B1: General damages table following *Heil v Rankin* and *Simmons v Castle*

## UPLIFT FOR INFLATION, AND *SIMMONS v CASTLE*, FROM MARCH 2000 TO THE DATE OF TRIAL

The Retail Prices Index on 23 March 2000 was 168.4. 168.4 ÷ 110% = 153.1. In June 2016 the RPI was 263.1.

The uplift for inflation from March 2000 is calculated as follows:

£award × (RPI at date of trial) / 153.1. (Note that using the figure of 153.1 already takes account of the *Simmons v Castle* 10 per cent uplift.)

For an award that was worth £5,000 in March 2000, this would give at June 2016:

£5,000 × 263.1 / 153.1 = £8,592.

| Month | 2016 | | | | | | 2017 | | | | | |
|---|---|---|---|---|---|---|---|---|---|---|---|---|
| | Jul | Aug | Sep | Oct | Nov | Dec | Jan | Feb | Mar | Apr | May | Jun | Jul |
| Current RPI | | | | | | | | | | | | | |
| Uplift (current RPI ÷ 153.1) | | | | | | | | | | | | | |

## TABLE OF UPLIFTS FOLLOWING *HEIL v RANKIN*

| Old | New | Old | New | Old | New |
|---|---|---|---|---|---|
| 0–10,000 | No change | 57,000 | 63,378 | 104,000 | 127,276 |
| 11,000 | 11,026 | 58,000 | 64,628 | 105,000 | 128,745 |
| 12,000 | 12,057 | 59,000 | 65,883 | 106,000 | 130,229 |
| 13,000 | 13,092 | 60,000 | 67,142 | 107,000 | 131,712 |
| 14,000 | 14,133 | 61,000 | 68,407 | 108,000 | 133,200 |
| 15,000 | 15,178 | 62,000 | 69,676 | 109,000 | 134,693 |
| 16,000 | 16,228 | 63,000 | 70,949 | 110,000 | 136,190 |
| 17,000 | 17,283 | 64,000 | 72,228 | 111,000 | 137,693 |
| 18,000 | 18,342 | 65,000 | 73,511 | 112,000 | 139,200 |
| 19,000 | 19,407 | 66,000 | 74,799 | 113,000 | 140,712 |
| 20,000 | 20,476 | 67,000 | 76,092 | 114,000 | 142,229 |
| 21,000 | 21,549 | 68,000 | 77,390 | 115,000 | 143,750 |
| 22,000 | 22,628 | 69,000 | 78,692 | 116,000 | 142,276 |
| 23,000 | 23,711 | 70,000 | 79,999 | 117,000 | 146,807 |
| 24,000 | 24,799 | 71,000 | 81,311 | 118,000 | 148,343 |
| 25,000 | 25,892 | 72,000 | 82,628 | 119,000 | 149,883 |
| 26,000 | 26,990 | 73,000 | 83,950 | 120,000 | 151,428 |
| 27,000 | 28,092 | 74,000 | 85,276 | 121,000 | 152,979 |
| 28,000 | 29,199 | 75,000 | 86,607 | 122,000 | 154,533 |
| 29,000 | 30,311 | 76,000 | 87,942 | 123,000 | 156,093 |
| 30,000 | 31,428 | 77,000 | 89,283 | 124,000 | 157,657 |
| 31,000 | 32,550 | 78,000 | 90,629 | 125,000 | 159,226 |
| 32,000 | 33,676 | 79,000 | 91,979 | 126,000 | 160,800 |
| 33,000 | 34,807 | 80,000 | 93,333 | 127,000 | 162,379 |
| 34,000 | 35,942 | 81,000 | 94,693 | 128,000 | 163,962 |
| 35,000 | 37,083 | 82,000 | 96,057 | 129,000 | 165,549 |
| 36,000 | 38,228 | 83,000 | 97,426 | 130,000 | 167,143 |
| 37,000 | 39,378 | 84,000 | 98,800 | 131,000 | 168,740 |
| 38,000 | 40,533 | 85,000 | 100,179 | 132,000 | 170,343 |
| 39,000 | 41,692 | 86,000 | 101,562 | 133,000 | 171,950 |
| 40,000 | 42,857 | 87,000 | 102,945 | 134,000 | 173,562 |

B1: General damages table following *Heil v Rankin* and *Simmons v Castle*

## TABLE OF UPLIFTS FOLLOWING *HEIL v RANKIN continued*

| Old | New | Old | New | Old | New |
|---|---|---|---|---|---|
| 41,000 | 44,026 | 88,000 | 104,343 | 135,000 | 175,179 |
| 42,000 | 45,199 | 89,000 | 105,740 | 136,000 | 176,800 |
| 43,000 | 46,378 | 90,000 | 107,142 | 137,000 | 178,426 |
| 44,000 | 47,561 | 91,000 | 108,549 | 138,000 | 180,057 |
| 45,000 | 48,750 | 92,000 | 109,961 | 139,000 | 181,692 |
| 46,000 | 49,942 | 93,000 | 111,378 | 140,000 | 183,333 |
| 47,000 | 51,140 | 94,000 | 112,800 | 141,000 | 184,978 |
| 48,000 | 52,342 | 95,000 | 114,226 | 142,000 | 186,628 |
| 49,000 | 53,549 | 96,000 | 115,657 | 143,000 | 188,283 |
| 50,000 | 54,761 | 97,000 | 117,092 | 144,000 | 189,942 |
| 51,000 | 55,978 | 98,000 | 118,533 | 145,000 | 191,607 |
| 52,000 | 57,200 | 99,000 | 119,978 | 146,000 | 193,276 |
| 53,000 | 58,426 | 100,000 | 121,428 | 147,000 | 194,949 |
| 54,000 | 59,657 | 101,000 | 122,883 | 148,000 | 196,628 |
| 55,000 | 60,892 | 102,000 | 124,342 | 149,000 | 198,311 |
| 56,000 | 62,133 | 103,000 | 125,807 | 150,000 | 200,000 |

### TO UPDATE A POST-*HEIL v RANKIN*, BUT PRE-*SIMMONS v CASTLE*, AWARD

Awards since *Heil v Rankin* but before the *Simmons v Castle* uplift (generally awards between 23 March 2000 and 1 April 2013), should be updated in this way:

£award × 1.1 × (RPI at date of trial)/(RPI at date of award)

For an award that was worth £5,000 in June 2008, this would give at June 2016 (unless s.44(6) applies):

£5,000 × 1.1 × 263.1 / 216.8 = £6,675

### TO UPDATE A POST-*SIMMONS v CASTLE* AWARD

Awards which already include the *Simmons v Castle* uplift (generally awards since 1 April 2013 unless s.44(6) applied to them), should be updated in this way:

£award × (RPI at date of trial)/(RPI at date of award)

For an award that was worth £5,000 in June 2013, this would give at June 2016:

£5,000 × 263.1 / 249.7 = £5,268

# B2: Bereavement damages

1. Damages for bereavement are awarded under s.1A of the Fatal Accidents Act 1976. This is a fixed sum, set by statute as amended (see below).

2. The claim for bereavement damages can only be brought by:

    (i) a bereaved spouse, or

    (ii) where the deceased was a minor who never married, by:
    (a) either of his parents if the deceased was legitimate; or
    (b) the mother if the deceased was illegitimate.

3. Where there is a claim for damages for bereavement for the benefit of the parents of the deceased, s.1A(4) of the Fatal Accidents Act 1976 provides that:

    "The sum awarded shall be divided equally between them (subject to any deduction falling to be made in respect of costs not recovered from the defendant)."

    Where the parents are divorced or separated and only one parent makes the claim, that parent will hold half of the bereavement damages on trust for the other parent.

4. The Administration of Justice Act 1982 contains a provision (at s.1A(5)) for the Lord Chancellor to vary the statutory sum. The original statute fixed the sum at £3,500, and that was raised by four subsequent statutory instruments (SI 1990/2575, SI 2002/644, SI 2007/3488 and SI 2013/510). Hence the relevant dates and statutory sums are as follows:

    | | |
    |---|---:|
    | – if the death was before 1 January 1983, the award is | **nil** |
    | – if the death was between 1 January 1983 and 31 March 1991, the award is | **£3,500** |
    | – if the death was between 1 April 1991 and 31 March 2002, the award is | **£7,500** |
    | – if the death was between 1 April 2002 and 31 December 2007, the award is | **£10,000** |
    | – if the death was between 1 January 2008 and 31 March 2013, the award is | **£11,800** |
    | – if the death was on or after 1 April 2013, the award is | **£12,980** |

5. The claimant is entitled to interest on bereavement damages from the date of death to the date of trial or settlement of the action—see *Prior v Hastie*.[1]

---

[1] [1987] C.L.Y. 1219.

# B3: *Auty v National Coal Board* (pension claims)

In *Wells v Wells*, the House of Lords made only passing reference to the calculation of future pension losses. The implication is that the multipliers for such losses are to be taken from the Ogden Tables, as are those for pecuniary losses for life and for loss of earnings. There is no justification for adopting a different approach. Since the mid-1980s, pension claims have often been based on the principles set out in *Auty v National Coal Board*.[1] This analysis is a guide to those principles, but is included with the caution that the method of selecting multipliers and discount factors has been superseded by *Wells v Wells*.

It is important to remember that the trial judge in *Auty* was not working from the Ogden Tables, but from a table of life expectation. Here is the calculation carried out in *Auty*:

1. The net annual pension loss after tax: £443.
2. The claimant and his wife were both aged 34 at the date of trial.
3. The life tables showed that the claimant's life expectation beyond the age of 65 was 6.68 years, and his wife's life expectation beyond the age of 65 was 12.26 years. She was therefore expected to survive him by 5.58 years. She was entitled to a two-thirds widow's pension, so the judge added two-thirds of 5.58 years (i.e. 3.72 years) to the claimant's life expectancy beyond 65 of 6.68 to give a total period of loss of 10.4 years.
4. **First step**: the judge considered an appropriate multiplier (at a 5 per cent discount rate) for 10.4 years to be seven. This is the equivalent of the discounting calculation that would now be performed (at 2.5 per cent) by using the Ogden Tables.
5. The basic pension loss at 65 was therefore [7 × £443] = £3,101.
6. Loss of lump sum gratuity: £1,899.
7. Total capital value of loss at retirement age [£3,101 + £1,899] = £5,000.
8. **Second step**: Mr Auty was 34 years old. He was therefore being compensated for his pension loss 31 years prematurely. The judge discounted the sum of £5,000 at 5 per cent over 31 years, leaving £1,100. This discount would now be performed by Ogden Table 27 at 2.5 per cent.
9. **Third step**: The judge discounted the pension claim by a further 27 per cent for contingencies. This brought the sum of £1,100 down to £800. Of this step the Court of Appeal said[2]:

    "The discount for imponderables which the judge made in Auty's case was 27 per cent. The judge said that the imponderables included voluntary wastage, redundancy, dismissal, supervening ill-health, disablement or death before 65, and said that death was the major discount."

10. Add value of loss of death in service benefit (£200).
11. Total value of award: **£1,000**.

Note: The three steps bring the annual pension element alone (ignoring the lump sum and the death in service benefit) down to below £500. If one simply applied the Ogden Tables and a 2.5 per cent discount rate to the above annual pension loss the claimant would receive [7.98 × £443] = £3,535, before contingencies. It should also be noted that, when using the Ogden Tables, no further discount should be made in the contingencies deduction for mortality, as this is incorporated into the Ogden Tables, so applying a further contingency discount would amount to a "double discount".

Employment tribunals have developed a different approach to the calculation of pension loss. Those interested are referred to the guidelines in Sneath, Sara, Daykin and Gallop, *Industrial Tribunals: Compensation for loss of pension rights* (2003, 3rd edn) HMSO, approved by the Employment Appeal Tribunal in *Benson v Dairy Crest*.[3]

---

[1] [1985] 1 All E.R. 930.
[2] Waller LJ in *Auty*, at 937.
[3] (EAT/192/89).

# B4: *Roberts v Johnstone* (accommodation claims)

1. Seriously injured claimants will often require special accommodation which may have to be adapted for their particular needs. This will often mean that they have to move to a more expensive house. The applicable principles of law were set out by the Court of Appeal in *Roberts v Johnstone*.[1]

2. **Example**: A paraplegic claimant lives in an unsuitable house with a market value of £150,000. She wishes to buy a more suitable house for £230,000 and alter it (because of her disabilities) at a cost of £20,000. The alterations will not (in themselves) make any difference to the value of the adapted house. The claimant will continue to live in the adapted house for the rest of her life and the agreed life multiplier is 10. Following *Roberts v Johnstone*, the claim for accommodation costs is calculated as follows:

    (i) Costs of adaption: **£20,000**
    Recovered in full because wholly attributable to injuries and will not add value to the house.

    (ii) Costs of moving house: **£10,000**
    Recovered in full if the claimant would not have moved house but for the accident.

    (iii) Loss of Use of Capital:
    As a result of the move, the claimant is obliged to invest in the house, thereby foregoing the use of a part of her capital. The discount rate of 2.5 per cent is taken as the annual loss caused by this. Hence the claim is:

    £80,000 (extra cost of the house) × 2.5% (discount rate) × 10 (agreed life multiplier) = **£20,000**

    Note that the claimant does not recover the full additional capital cost of the house; if she did, the estate would derive a windfall benefit.

    (iv) Extra Annual Costs of Accommodation:
    If the costs of living in the more expensive house are higher, the claimant can claim them. Items might include council tax, decorating costs and water charges. If these costs were £500 p.a., the claim would be:

    £500 (extra annual costs) × 10 (agreed life multiplier) = **£5,000**

3. The total claim for accommodation in the example is therefore **£55,000**.

4. If the discount rate is varied from the present figure of 2.5 per cent, *Roberts v Johnstone* claims will also change. For instance, if the rate were to be reduced to 1 per cent, the calculation of loss of capital in para.2 (iii), above, would be £80,000 × 1% × 10 = £8,000.

---

[1] [1989] Q.B. 878.

# B5: Periodical payments

**The circumstances in which a periodical payment should be made**

The Damages Act 1996 as amended now empowers the Court to order Periodical Payments for future losses. Provisions dealing with the making of a periodical payments order are contained in CPR rr.41.4 to 41.10 and the attendant Practice Directions. Rule 41.7 provides that:

"When considering–

(a) its indication as to whether periodical payments or a lump sum is likely to be the more appropriate form for all or part of an award of damages under rule 41.6; or

(b) whether to make an order under section 2(1)(a) of the 1996 Act,

the court shall have regard to all the circumstances of the case and in particular the form of award which best meets the claimant's needs, having regard to the factors set out in Practice Direction 41B."

The factors involved are derived from the Practice Direction supplementing Part 41 which provides that:

"The factors which the court shall have regard to under rule 41.7 include–

(1) the scale of the annual payments taking into account any deduction for contributory negligence;

(2) the form of award preferred by the claimant including–

(a) the reasons for the claimant's preference; and

(b) the nature of any financial advice received by the claimant when considering the form of award; and

(3) the form of award preferred by the defendant including the reasons for the defendant's preference."

Practitioners representing claimants may wish to obtain financial advice in order to decide whether or not to ask the Court to make an award for Periodical Payments. Such advice will be particularly useful in difficult cases such as those involving incomplete recovery (contributory negligence or agreed reduction of damages for litigation risk in a clinical negligence claim).

**Circumstances in which periodical payments are not available**

Section 2(3) of the 1996 Act provides that:

"(3) A court may not make an order for periodical payments unless satisfied that the continuity of payment under the order is reasonably secure."

Continuity of payment will only be secure in three situations, each dignified by its own sub-clause in subsection 2(4):

"(4) For the purposes of subsection (3) the continuity of payment under an order is reasonably secure if–

(a) it is protected by a guarantee given under section 6 of or the Schedule to this Act,

(b) it is protected by a scheme under section 213 of the Financial Services and Markets Act 2000 (compensation) (whether or not as modified by section 4 of this Act), or

(c) the source of payment is a government or health service body."

The effect of this is that Periodical Payments will not be available unless the defendant is either a government body (such as the NHSLA) or a UK insurer within one of the two statutory schemes. Hence practitioners must ascertain whether or not the defendant is within those schemes well before the matter comes to trial or settlement meeting.

## The indexation of periodical payments

Section 2(8) of the Damages Act 1996 (as amended) provides that orders for periodical payments are to be treated as providing for the amount of the payment ordered to vary with the Retail Prices Index ("RPI"). However, section 2(9) of the Damages Act 1996 then stipulates that an order for periodical payments may include provision disapplying section 2(8) or modifying its effect.

In *Thompstone v Tameside and Glossop NHS Trust* [2008] AER 72, the Court of Appeal held that the appropriate means of indexation of future costs of care and case management would be by reference to ASHE 6115 (see next section of *Facts & Figures*) which was the most reliable way of "tracking" changes to these costs.

Consequently, the ASHE 6115 indexation will apply to periodical payments in respect of future care and case management. The Retail Prices Index will be used for future losses which are goods-based (such as future equipment and assistive technology). In *Sarwar v Ali and Motor Insurers Bureau* [2007] LS Law Med 375, Lloyd Jones J awarded a periodical payment for future losses of earnings and index-linked the loss by reference to the ASHE aggregated earnings data for male full-time employees. Theoretically, it would be possible for a party to contend for another means of indexation, although to our knowledge this has not been successfully attempted in a reported case.

## "Model Order" for periodical payments

The leading case is now *RH v University Hospitals Bristol NHS Foundation Trust* [2013] EWHC 229. Swift J held that since there had been a change in statistical methodology used to generate the ASHE 6115 indexation, there was a need to adapt the previous model order made by Sir Christopher Holland on 2 December 2008, which is reported at [2009] P.I.Q.R. P153. The model order approved in *RH* may be used for periodical payments and it deals with the complex issues of indexation and changes to payments caused by that indexation. The NHSLA continues to uprate indexed payments on December 15 each year although other defendants and insurers may have different preferences. Clearly, the starting date must be set at sufficient distance to allow its satisfactory introduction; this is likely to be more protracted if the claimant has a deputy.

## Is the claimant still alive?

In *Long v Norwich Union* [2009] EWHC 715 QB, Mackay J held that a claimant was not entitled to recover the costs of proving that he was still alive at the date of periodical payment. The court held that this cost would be covered by the award for the costs of deputyship; alternatively, it might be said that the modest costs of this type borne by the claimant would be covered by the interest generated on the advance payments to be made under the order.

# B6: Step-by-step guide to finding the annual estimates for hourly pay in ASHE SOC 2000 6115

The data collection point for the Annual Survey of Hours and Earnings (ASHE) is April each year. The data are collected over the summer and the first release of estimates takes place in November/December of that year. These are provisional estimates which are revised and published as final estimates the following November/December. The following estimates were published for ASHE SOC2000 on 22 November 2012, 12 December 2013, 19 November 2014 and 18 November 2015. Estimates for 2015 are provisional and will be replaced by final estimates in November/December 2016.

**ASHE SOC 2000 6115 Centile estimates for hourly earnings £ for UK employees 2011–2015**

| Centile | 10 | 20 | 25 | 30 | 40 | 50 | 60 | 70 | 75 | 80 | 90 |
|---|---|---|---|---|---|---|---|---|---|---|---|
| ASHE 6115 2011 Final release | 6.05 | 6.44 | 6.65 | 6.87 | 7.28 | 7.83 | 8.45 | 9.17 | 9.67 | 10.22 | 11.92 |
| ASHE 6115 2012 Final release | 6.21 | 6.57 | 6.80 | 7.00 | 7.44 | 7.92 | 8.51 | 9.21 | 9.69 | 10.25 | 11.97 |
| ASHE 6115 2013 Final release | 6.30 | 6.61 | 6.80 | 7.00 | 7.40 | 7.91 | 8.50 | 9.22 | 9.73 | 10.29 | 12.02 |
| ASHE 6115 2014 Final release | 6.41 | 6.74 | 6.94 | 7.12 | 7.53 | 8.00 | 8.55 | 9.23 | 9.72 | 10.21 | 11.95 |
| ASHE 6115 2015 First release | 6.64 | 6.98 | 7.11 | 7.30 | 7.72 | 8.18 | 8.73 | 9.45 | 9.88 | 10.38 | 12.21 |

*Source:* ONS, ASHE

ASHE estimates are only available online. They can be found on the website of the Office for National Statistics (ONS). This website was redesigned and launched on 25 February 2016. Step-by-step instructions to locate estimates for ASHE SOC 2000 6115 are provided. You need not follow all these instructions each time you consult the tables as you can either download the tables as an Excel file or you can save the web link to the tables in Bookmarks.

Reclassification of occupational categories occurs every 10 years. Estimates from 2011 final are based on the Standard Occupational Classification (SOC) 2010 weights. When calculating a growth rate, care must be taken that estimates in different years are made on the basis of the same occupational weights. When comparing earnings in any year from 2011 onwards with 2011, use the 2011 final release. When comparing earnings in any year before 2011, use the 2011 first release.

The classification for carers changed in SOC 2010 to include two separate categories, ASHE 6145 care workers and home carers and ASHE 6146 senior care workers. For the purposes of the indexation of future care, the new classification for carers should be ignored and the older classification based on SOC 2000 6115 used instead. The occupational earnings tables for SOC 2000 6115 can be found at Table 26. The title for this table is Care Workers (SOC) ASHE: Table 26.

1. Find the home page of the Office for National Statistics (ONS) at *www.ons.gov.uk*

2. Type in ASHE Care Workers in the search box at the top of this page and click Search.

3. Refine the search using the menu on the left hand side by checking the box for Datasets.

4. The title for this Table is Care Workers (SOC) ASHE: Table 26.

5. Clicking on the table title opens a new menu containing tables for care workers from 2011 to 2015. Clicking on the table title for each year will open a .zip file.

## B6: Step-by-step guide to finding the annual estimates for hourly pay in ASHE SOC 2000 6115

6. Opening the .zip file will produce a contents list of Excel files each of which contain a different set of earnings estimates for carers.

7. Hourly pay for carers is in Care Workers (SOC 6145 and 6146—equivalent to SOC 2000 6115) Table 26.5a Hourly Pay—Gross. You may need to expand the "name" column to see the full narrative. A double-click on the table title will take you to a worksheet in an Excel file. If you are sure that you have located the file that you want, save it using File–> Save in Excel. The description within the table is "Care workers, home carers and senior care workers".

8. Once in the Excel file, check the bottom tab. "All" refers to all employees (male and female, part- and full-time).

9. Read across the centile estimates. Shading indicates the reliability of the estimate. Where the estimate of the error is less than five per cent (reliable), there is no shading. ASHE 6115 estimates are normally reliable due to a large sample size. The key to the shading can be found at the bottom and at the right hand side of the table.

10. If you have not already saved this file at step 7 above, this table can be saved now, either in part or in full. If the file is saved before the final release in November/December 2016, make a note that the 2015 estimates are provisional. They will be replaced in the final release under the same title.

11. Details of any changes to the estimates and/or to the step-by-step guide which occur after publication of *Facts & Figures 2016/17* and links to sources of further information on reclassification can be found on *www.victoriawass-laboureconomics.co.uk under Indexation*.

This guide has been prepared by Dr Victoria Wass, Cardiff Business School, April 2016.

### B6: Step-by-step guide to finding the annual estimates for hourly pay in ASHE SOC 2000 6115

6. Opening the .zip file will produce a contents list of Excel files each of which contain a different set of earnings estimates for carers.

7. Hourly pay for carers is in Care Workers (SOC 6145 and 6146—equivalent to SOC 2000 6115) Table 26.5a Hourly Pay—Gross. You may need to expand the "name" column to see the full narrative. A double-click on the table title will take you to a worksheet in an Excel file. If you are sure that you have located the file that you want, save it using File–> Save in Excel. The description within the table is "Care workers, home carers and senior care workers".

8. Once in the Excel file, check the bottom tab. "All" refers to all employees (male and female, part- and full-time).

9. Read across the centile estimates. Shading indicates the reliability of the estimate. Where the estimate of the error is less than five per cent (reliable), there is no shading. ASHE 6115 estimates are normally reliable due to a large sample size. The key to the shading can be found at the bottom and at the right hand side of the table.

10. If you have not already saved this file at step 7 above, this table can be saved now, either in part or in full. If the file is saved before the final release in November/December 2016, make a note that the 2015 estimates are provisional. They will be replaced in the final release under the same title.

11. Details of any changes to the estimates and/or to the step-by-step guide which occur after publication of *Facts & Figures 2016/17* and links to sources of further information on reclassification can be found on *www.victoriawass-laboureconomics.co.uk under Indexation*.

This guide has been prepared by Dr Victoria Wass, Cardiff Business School, April 2016.

# Group C
*Interest Rates*

C1: **Interest base rates**

C2: **Real and nominal interest rates and price inflation**

C3: **Special investment account rates**

C4: **Special and general damages interest**

C5: **Base rate + 10 per cent**

C6: **Number of days between two dates**

C7: **Decimal years**

C8: **Judgment debt interest rates (England and Wales)**

C9: **Judicial rates of interest (Scotland)**

# Group C
## Interest Rates

| | |
|---|---|
| C1 | Inter-bank base rates |
| C2 | Real and nominal interest rates and price inflation |
| C3 | Special investment account rates |
| C4 | Special and general damages interest |
| C5 | Base rate + 1.0 per cent |
| C6 | Number of days between two dates |
| C7 | Decimal years |
| C8 | Judgment debt interest rates (England and Wales) |
| C9 | Judicial rates of interest (Scotland) |

# C1: Interest base rates

**Introductory notes**

1. The data for this table are obtained from retail banks Barclays, Lloyds TSB, HSBC and National Westminster.

2. Where these banks' base rates did not change on the same day, an average rate is shown (and asterisked in the table).

3. Since 3 August 2006, these retail banks' base rates have been identical to the Bank of England's Official Bank Rate.

| Date | New rate (%) | Date | New rate (%) | Date | New rate (%) |
|---|---|---|---|---|---|
| **1982** | | **1986** | | 25 March | 12.50 |
| 2 August | 11.50 | 9 January | 12.50 | 12 April | 12.00 |
| 18 August | 11.00 | 19 March | 11.50 | 24 May | 11.50 |
| 31 August | 10.50 | 8 April | 11.25* | 12 July | 11.00 |
| 7 October | 10.00 | 9 April | 11.00 | 4 September | 10.50 |
| 14 October | 9.50 | 24 April | 10.50 | | |
| 4 November | 9.00 | 27 May | 10.00 | **1992** | |
| 26 November | 10.125* | 14 October | 11.00 | 5 May | 10.00 |
| | | | | 16 September | 12.00 |
| **1983** | | **1987** | | 17 September | 10.00 |
| 12 January | 11.00 | 10 March | 10.50 | 22 September | 9.00 |
| 15 March | 10.50 | 19 March | 10.00 | 16 October | 8.00 |
| 15 April | 10.00 | 29 April | 9.50 | 13 November | 7.00 |
| 15 June | 9.50 | 11 May | 9.00 | | |
| 4 October | 9.00 | 7 August | 10.00 | **1993** | |
| | | 26 October | 9.50 | 26 January | 6.00 |
| **1984** | | 5 November | 9.00 | 23 November | 5.50 |
| 7 March | 8.875* | 4 December | 8.50 | | |
| 15 March | 8.625* | | | **1994** | |
| 10 May | 9.125* | **1988** | | 8 February | 5.25 |
| 27 June | 9.25 | 2 February | 9.00 | 12 September | 5.75 |
| 9 July | 10.00 | 17 March | 8.50 | 7 December | 6.25 |
| 11 July | 11.00* | 11 April | 8.00 | | |
| 12 July | 12.00 | 18 May | 7.50 | **1995** | |
| 9 August | 11.50 | 3 June | 8.00 | 2 February | 6.75 |
| 10 August | 11.00 | 6 June | 8.25* | 13 December | 6.50 |
| 20 August | 10.50 | 7 June | 8.50 | | |
| 7 November | 10.00 | 22 June | 9.00 | **1996** | |
| 20 November | 9.875* | 29 June | 9.50 | 18 January | 6.25 |
| 23 November | 9.625* | 5 July | 10.00 | 8 March | 6.00 |
| | | 19 July | 10.50 | 6 June | 5.75 |
| **1985** | | 8 August | 10.75* | 30 October | 6.00 |
| 11 January | 10.50 | 9 August | 11.00 | | |
| 14 January | 12.00 | 25 August | 11.50 | **1997** | |
| 28 January | 14.00 | 26 August | 12.00 | 7 May | 6.25 |
| 20 March | 13.75* | 25 November | 13.00 | 9 June | 6.50 |
| 21 March | 13.50 | | | 11 July | 6.75 |
| 29 March | 13.25* | **1989** | | 8 August | 7.00 |
| 2 April | 13.125* | 24 May | 14.00 | 7 November | 7.25 |
| 12 April | 12.875* | 5 October | 15.00 | | |
| 19 April | 12.675* | | | **1998** | |
| 12 June | 12.50 | **1990** | | 5 June | 7.50 |
| 7 July | 12.25* | 8 October | 14.00 | 9 October | 7.25 |
| 16 July | 12.00 | | | 6 November | 6.75 |
| 29 July | 11.75* | **1991** | | 11 December | 6.25 |
| 30 July | 11.50 | 13 February | 13.50 | | |
| | | 27 February | 13.00 | | |

## C1: Interest base rates

| Date | New rate (%) | Date | New rate (%) | Date | New rate (%) |
|---|---|---|---|---|---|
| **1999** | | 8 November | 4.00 | **2007** | |
| 8 January | 6.00 | **2003** | | 11 January | 5.25 |
| 5 February | 5.50 | 7 February | 3.75 | 10 May | 5.50 |
| 8 April | 5.25 | 10 July | 3.50 | 5 July | 5.75 |
| 10 June | 5.00 | 6 November | 3.75 | 6 December | 5.50 |
| 8 September | 5.25 | **2004** | | **2008** | |
| 4 November | 5.50 | 5 February | 4.00 | 7 February | 5.25 |
| **2000** | | 6 May | 4.25 | 10 April | 5.00 |
| 13 January | 5.75 | 10 June | 4.50 | 8 October | 4.50 |
| 10 February | 6.00 | 5 August | 4.75 | 6 November | 3.00 |
| **2001** | | **2005** | | 4 December | 2.00 |
| 8 February | 5.75 | 4 August | 4.50 | **2009** | |
| 5 April | 5.50 | **2006** | | 8 January | 1.50 |
| 10 May | 5.25 | 3 August | 4.75 | 5 February | 1.00 |
| 2 August | 5.00 | 9 November | 5.00 | 5 March | 0.50 |
| 18 September | 4.75 | | | | |
| 4 October | 4.50 | | | | |

# C2: Real and nominal interest rates and price inflation

## Introductory notes

1. Price inflation is calculated as the rate of change of the Retail Prices Index.
2. The nominal interest rate is based on the rate on 20-year British Government Securities.
3. No account has been taken of tax in these figures.

|  | Price Inflation % | Nominal Interest Rate % | Real Interest Rate % |
|---|---|---|---|
| 1980 | 18.03 | 13.78 | (4.25) |
| 1981 | 11.88 | 14.74 | 2.86 |
| 1982 | 8.70 | 12.88 | 4.18 |
| 1983 | 4.44 | 10.80 | 6.36 |
| 1984 | 5.01 | 10.69 | 5.68 |
| 1985 | 6.04 | 10.62 | 4.58 |
| 1986 | 3.40 | 9.87 | 6.47 |
| 1987 | 4.16 | 9.47 | 5.31 |
| 1988 | 4.92 | 9.36 | 4.44 |
| 1989 | 7.79 | 9.58 | 1.79 |
| 1990 | 9.44 | 11.08 | 1.64 |
| 1991 | 5.91 | 9.92 | 4.01 |
| 1992 | 3.73 | 9.12 | 5.39 |
| 1993 | 1.57 | 7.87 | 6.30 |
| 1994 | 2.48 | 8.05 | 5.57 |
| 1995 | 3.41 | 8.26 | 4.85 |
| 1996 | 2.44 | 8.10 | 5.66 |
| 1997 | 3.12 | 7.09 | 3.97 |
| 1998 | 3.42 | 5.45 | 2.03 |
| 1999 | 1.56 | 4.70 | 3.14 |
| 2000 | 2.93 | 4.70 | 1.77 |
| 2001 | 1.84 | 4.78 | 2.94 |
| 2002 | 1.62 | 4.83 | 3.21 |
| 2003 | 2.91 | 4.64 | 1.73 |
| 2004 | 2.96 | 4.78 | 1.82 |
| 2005 | 2.84 | 4.39 | 1.55 |
| 2006 | 3.20 | 4.29 | 1.09 |
| 2007 | 4.26 | 4.73 | 0.47 |
| 2008 | 4.00 | 4.68 | 0.68 |
| 2009 | (0.53) | 4.25 | 4.78 |
| 2010 | 4.61 | 4.24 | (0.37) |
| 2011 | 5.21 | 3.83 | (1.38) |
| 2012 | 3.22 | 2.86 | (0.36) |
| 2013 | 3.05 | 3.19 | 0.14 |
| 2014 | 2.38 | 3.10 | 0.72 |
| 2015 | 0.98 | 2.41 | 1.43 |
| Averages: | | | |
| 1980–89 | 7.44 | 11.18 | 3.74 |
| 1990–99 | 3.71 | 7.96 | 4.25 |
| 2000–09 | 2.60 | 4.61 | 2.01 |
| 2010–15 | 3.24 | 3.27 | 0.03 |

C2: Real and nominal interest rates and price inflation

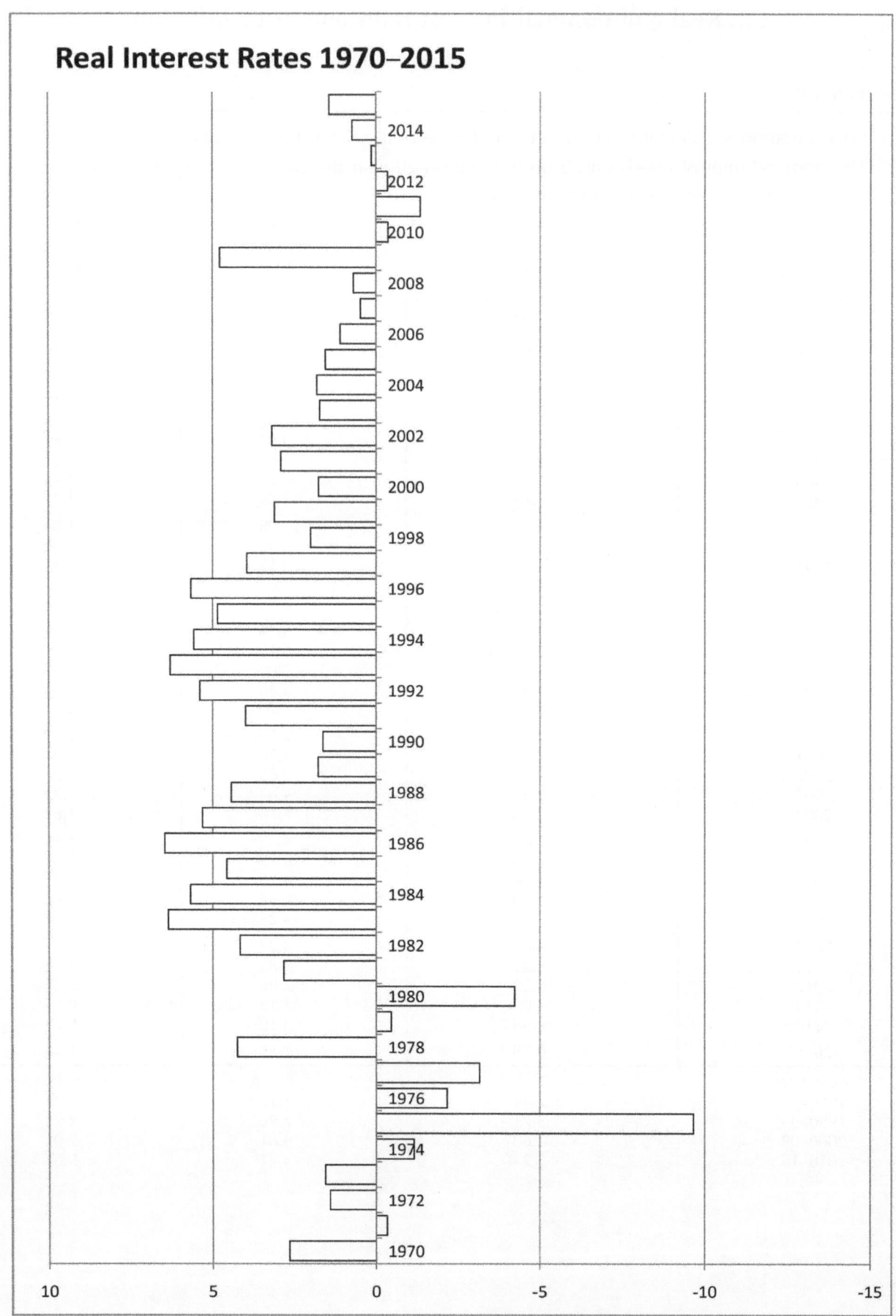

# C3: Special investment account rates

## Introductory notes

This is a composite table including both the Short-term Investment Account rate and the succeeding High Court Special Investment Account rate.

The manner of crediting interest is set out in Court Fund Rules 1987 r.27. Interest accruing to a special investment account is credited without the deduction of income tax.

| From: | | % |
|---|---|---|
| 1 October | 1965 | 5.0 |
| 1 September | 1966 | 5.5 |
| 1 March | 1968 | 6.0 |
| 1 March | 1969 | 6.5 |
| 1 March | 1970 | 7.0 |
| 1 March | 1971 | 7.5 |
| 1 March | 1973 | 8.0 |
| 1 March | 1974 | 9.0 |
| 1 February | 1977 | 10.0 |
| 1 March | 1979 | 12.5 |
| 1 January | 1980 | 15.0 |
| 1 January | 1981 | 12.5 |
| 1 December | 1981 | 15.0 |
| 1 March | 1982 | 14.0 |
| 1 July | 1982 | 13.0 |
| 1 April | 1983 | 12.5 |
| 1 April | 1984 | 12.0 |
| 1 August | 1986 | 11.5 |
| 1 January | 1987 | 12.25 |
| 1 April | 1987 | 11.75 |
| 1 November | 1987 | 11.25 |
| 1 December | 1987 | 11.0 |
| 1 May | 1988 | 9.5 |
| 1 August | 1988 | 11.0 |
| 1 November | 1988 | 12.25 |
| 1 January | 1989 | 13.0 |
| 1 November | 1989 | 14.25 |
| 1 April | 1991 | 12.0 |
| 1 October | 1991 | 10.25 |
| 1 February | 1993 | 8.0 |
| 1 August | 1999 | 7.0 |
| 1 February | 2002 | 6.0 |
| 1 February | 2009 | 3.0 |
| 1 June | 2009 | 1.5 |
| 1 July | 2009 | 0.5 |

# C4: Special and general damages interest

## Introductory notes

### Special damages

The appropriate rate of interest for special damages is the rate, over the period for which the interest is awarded, which is payable on the court special account. This rate was reduced to 0.5 per cent on 1 July 2009. Interest since June 1987 has been paid daily on a 1/365th basis, even in a leap year such as 2016.

In cases of continuing special damages, half the appropriate rate from the date of injury to the date of trial is awarded. In cases where the special damages have ceased and are thus limited to a finite period, there are conflicting Court of Appeal decisions as to whether the award should be half the appropriate rate from injury to trial (*Dexter v Courtaulds*[1]) or the full special account rate from a date within the period to which the special damages are limited (*Prokop v DHSS*[2]).

The relevant rates since 1965 are set out in Table C3.

The table on the next page records the total of these rates from January 1981. In the left-hand column is shown the month from the first day of which interest is assumed to run. The right-hand column shows the percentage interest accumulated from the first day of each month to 30 June 2016.

Continued use may be made of this table by adding to the figures in it 1/365th of the special account rate for each day from 1 July 2016 onwards, using Table C6, which records the number of days between two dates in a two-year period.

Suppose that interest runs from 1 January 2001 to 13 October 2016. The total to 30 June 2016 is 54.24 per cent (see Table C4). From Table C6, July 1 to October 13 is 286–182 days = 104 days, but add 1 day as both days are to be included = 105 days. If the rate remains at 0.5 per cent p.a., the appropriate addition will be 0.5 per cent × 105/365 = 0.14 per cent. Thus the grand total from 1 January 2001 to 13 October 2016 will be 54.24 + 0.14 = 54.38 per cent.

### General damages

In personal injury cases, the normal rate of interest on general damages for pain, suffering and loss of amenity was by convention two per cent per annum. In *Lawrence v Chief Constable of Staffordshire*[3] the Court of Appeal held that in spite of *Wells v Wells*,[4] the rate should remain at two per cent. Interest runs from the date of service of proceedings.

---

[1] [1984] 1 All E.R. 70.
[2] [1985] C.L.Y. 1037.
[3] CA, transcript 29 June 2000.
[4] [1999] A.C. 345.

## C4: Special and general damages interest

**Table of cumulative interest at the special account rate from the first day of each month to 30 June 2016.**

|  | 1981 | 1982 | 1983 | 1984 | 1985 | 1986 | 1987 | 1988 | 1989 | 1990 |
|---|---|---|---|---|---|---|---|---|---|---|
| January | 264.47 | 251.76 | 238.10 | 225.48 | 213.32 | 201.32 | 189.53 | 177.76 | 166.90 | 153.69 |
| February | 263.41 | 250.49 | 237.00 | 224.42 | 212.30 | 200.30 | 188.49 | 176.83 | 165.80 | 152.48 |
| March | 262.45 | 249.34 | 236.00 | 223.43 | 211.38 | 199.38 | 187.55 | 175.96 | 164.80 | 151.39 |
| April | 261.39 | 248.15 | 234.90 | 222.36 | 210.36 | 198.36 | 186.51 | 175.02 | 163.70 | 150.18 |
| May | 260.36 | 247.00 | 233.87 | 221.38 | 209.38 | 197.38 | 185.55 | 174.12 | 162.63 | 149.01 |
| June | 259.30 | 245.81 | 232.81 | 220.36 | 208.36 | 196.36 | 184.55 | 173.31 | 161.53 | 147.80 |
| July | 258.28 | 244.66 | 231.78 | 219.37 | 207.37 | 195.37 | 183.58 | 172.53 | 160.46 | 146.63 |
| August | 257.21 | 243.55 | 230.72 | 218.35 | 206.35 | 194.35 | 182.58 | 171.72 | 159.35 | 145.42 |
| September | 256.15 | 242.45 | 229.66 | 217.33 | 205.33 | 193.38 | 181.59 | 170.79 | 158.25 | 144.21 |
| October | 255.12 | 241.38 | 228.63 | 216.35 | 204.35 | 192.43 | 180.62 | 169.88 | 157.18 | 143.04 |
| November | 254.06 | 240.28 | 227.57 | 215.33 | 203.33 | 191.45 | 179.62 | 168.95 | 156.08 | 141.83 |
| December | 253.04 | 239.21 | 226.54 | 214.34 | 202.34 | 190.51 | 178.70 | 167.94 | 154.90 | 140.65 |
|  | **1991** | **1992** | **1993** | **1994** | **1995** | **1996** | **1997** | **1998** | **1999** | **2000** |
| January | 139.44 | 127.33 | 117.05 | 108.86 | 100.86 | 92.86 | 84.84 | 76.84 | 68.84 | 61.26 |
| February | 138.23 | 126.46 | 116.18 | 108.18 | 100.18 | 92.18 | 84.16 | 76.16 | 68.16 | 60.66 |
| March | 137.14 | 125.65 | 115.57 | 107.57 | 99.57 | 91.55 | 83.55 | 75.55 | 67.55 | 60.11 |
| April | 135.93 | 124.78 | 114.89 | 106.89 | 98.89 | 90.87 | 82.87 | 74.87 | 66.87 | 59.51 |
| May | 134.94 | 123.93 | 114.23 | 106.23 | 98.23 | 90.21 | 82.21 | 74.21 | 66.21 | 58.94 |
| June | 133.93 | 123.06 | 113.55 | 105.55 | 97.55 | 89.53 | 81.53 | 73.53 | 65.53 | 58.34 |
| July | 132.94 | 122.22 | 112.89 | 104.89 | 96.89 | 88.87 | 80.87 | 72.87 | 64.87 | 57.77 |
| August | 131.92 | 121.35 | 112.22 | 104.22 | 96.22 | 88.19 | 80.19 | 72.19 | 64.19 | 57.17 |
| September | 130.90 | 120.48 | 111.54 | 103.54 | 95.54 | 87.51 | 79.51 | 71.51 | 63.60 | 56.58 |
| October | 129.91 | 119.64 | 110.88 | 102.88 | 94.88 | 86.86 | 78.86 | 70.86 | 63.02 | 56.00 |
| November | 129.04 | 118.77 | 110.20 | 102.20 | 94.20 | 86.18 | 78.18 | 70.18 | 62.43 | 55.41 |
| December | 128.20 | 117.92 | 109.54 | 101.54 | 93.54 | 85.52 | 77.52 | 69.52 | 61.85 | 54.83 |
|  | **2001** | **2002** | **2003** | **2004** | **2005** | **2006** | **2007** | **2008** | **2009** | **2010** |
| January | 54.24 | 47.24 | 41.15 | 35.15 | 29.14 | 23.14 | 17.14 | 11.14 | 5.12 | 3.25 |
| February | 53.65 | 46.65 | 40.65 | 34.65 | 28.63 | 22.63 | 16.63 | 10.63 | 4.61 | 3.21 |
| March | 53.11 | 46.18 | 40.18 | 34.17 | 28.17 | 22.17 | 16.17 | 10.15 | 4.38 | 3.17 |
| April | 52.51 | 45.68 | 39.68 | 33.66 | 27.66 | 21.66 | 15.66 | 9.64 | 4.13 | 3.13 |
| May | 51.94 | 45.18 | 39.18 | 33.17 | 27.17 | 21.17 | 15.17 | 9.15 | 3.88 | 3.09 |
| June | 51.34 | 44.67 | 38.67 | 32.66 | 26.66 | 20.66 | 14.66 | 8.64 | 3.63 | 3.04 |
| July | 50.77 | 44.18 | 38.18 | 32.16 | 26.16 | 20.16 | 14.16 | 8.15 | 3.50 | 3.00 |
| August | 50.17 | 43.67 | 37.67 | 31.65 | 25.65 | 19.65 | 13.65 | 7.64 | 3.46 | 2.96 |
| September | 49.58 | 43.16 | 37.16 | 31.14 | 25.14 | 19.14 | 13.14 | 7.13 | 3.42 | 2.92 |
| October | 49.00 | 42.67 | 36.67 | 30.65 | 24.65 | 18.65 | 12.65 | 6.63 | 3.38 | 2.88 |
| November | 48.41 | 42.16 | 36.16 | 30.14 | 24.14 | 18.14 | 12.14 | 6.12 | 3.33 | 2.83 |
| December | 47.83 | 41.66 | 35.66 | 29.65 | 23.65 | 17.65 | 11.65 | 5.63 | 3.29 | 2.79 |
|  | **2011** | **2012** | **2013** | **2014** | **2015** | **2016** | | | | |
| January | 2.75 | 2.25 | 1.75 | 1.25 | 0.75 | 0.25 | | | | |
| February | 2.71 | 2.21 | 1.71 | 1.21 | 0.71 | 0.21 | | | | |
| March | 2.67 | 2.17 | 1.67 | 1.17 | 0.67 | 0.17 | | | | |
| April | 2.63 | 2.13 | 1.63 | 1.13 | 0.63 | 0.12 | | | | |
| May | 2.59 | 2.08 | 1.58 | 1.08 | 0.58 | 0.08 | | | | |
| June | 2.54 | 2.04 | 1.54 | 1.04 | 0.54 | 0.04 | | | | |
| July | 2.50 | 2.00 | 1.50 | 1.00 | 0.50 | | | | | |
| August | 2.46 | 1.96 | 1.46 | 0.96 | 0.46 | | | | | |
| September | 2.42 | 1.92 | 1.42 | 0.92 | 0.42 | | | | | |
| October | 2.38 | 1.88 | 1.38 | 0.88 | 0.38 | | | | | |
| November | 2.33 | 1.83 | 1.33 | 0.83 | 0.33 | | | | | |
| December | 2.29 | 1.79 | 1.29 | 0.79 | 0.29 | | | | | |

If the rate remains at 0.5 per cent, interest to the last day of successive later months can be found to a date after 30 June 2016 by adding the figure from the following table:

|  | 2016 | 2017 |
|---|---|---|
| January |  | 0.29 |
| February |  | 0.33 |
| March |  | 0.38 |
| April |  | 0.42 |
| May |  | 0.46 |
| June |  | 0.50 |
| July | 0.04 |  |
| August | 0.08 |  |
| September | 0.13 |  |
| October | 0.17 |  |
| November | 0.21 |  |
| December | 0.25 |  |

# C5: Base rate + 10 per cent

## Introductory notes

1. Under the Civil Procedure Rules 1998 r.36.21, where the judgment against a defendant is more advantageous to the claimant than the proposals in a claimant's Part 36 offer, the court may order interest on the sum awarded and on the costs, for some or all of the period starting with the latest date on which the defendant could have accepted the Part 36 offer without needing the permission of the court, at a rate not exceeding 10 per cent above base rate. In *All-in-One Design & Build Ltd v Motcomb Estates Ltd*,[1] it was held that r.36.21 is not ultra vires.

2. Rule 36.21(4) provides that where the rule applies, the court will make those orders unless it considers it unjust to do so; sub-rule (5) sets out the factors to be considered in deciding whether it would be unjust.

3. Since November 1997 base rates plus 10 per cent have been as follows:

|      |              | Rate + 10% |      |              | Rate + 10% |      |             | Rate + 10% |
|------|--------------|------------|------|--------------|------------|------|-------------|------------|
| 1997 | 7 November   | 17.25%     | 2001 | 5 April      | 15.50%     | 2006 | 3 August    | 14.75%     |
| 1998 | 5 June       | 17.50%     |      | 10 May       | 15.25%     |      | 9 November  | 15.00%     |
|      | 9 October    | 17.25%     |      | 2 August     | 15.00%     | 2007 | 11 January  | 15.25%     |
|      | 6 November   | 16.75%     |      | 18 September | 14.75%     |      | 10 May      | 15.50%     |
|      | 11 December  | 16.25%     |      | 4 October    | 14.50%     |      | 5 July      | 15.75%     |
| 1999 | 8 January    | 16.00%     |      | 8 November   | 14.00%     |      | 6 December  | 15.50%     |
|      | 5 February   | 15.50%     | 2003 | 7 February   | 13.75%     | 2008 | 7 February  | 15.25%     |
|      | 8 April      | 15.25%     |      | 10 July      | 13.50%     |      | 10 April    | 15.00%     |
|      | 10 June      | 15.00%     |      | 6 November   | 13.75%     |      | 8 October   | 14.50%     |
|      | 8 September  | 15.25%     | 2004 | 5 February   | 14.00%     |      | 6 November  | 13.00%     |
|      | 4 November   | 15.50%     |      | 6 May        | 14.25%     |      | 4 December  | 12.00%     |
| 2000 | 13 January   | 15.75%     |      | 10 June      | 14.50%     | 2009 | 8 January   | 11.50%     |
|      | 10 February  | 16.00%     |      | 5 August     | 14.75%     |      | 5 February  | 11.00%     |
| 2001 | 8 February   | 15.75%     | 2005 | 4 August     | 14.50%     |      | 5 March     | 10.50%     |

The following table shows cumulative interest at 10 per cent above base rate from the first day of each month until 30 June 2016. Interest for parts of a month can be found by following the method in the notes to Table C4.

|           | 2005   | 2006   | 2007   | 2008  | 2009  | 2010  | 2011  | 2012  | 2013  | 2014  | 2015  | 2016 |
|-----------|--------|--------|--------|-------|-------|-------|-------|-------|-------|-------|-------|------|
| January   | 138.38 | 123.73 | 109.09 | 93.58 | 78.91 | 68.26 | 57.76 | 47.26 | 36.74 | 26.24 | 15.74 | 5.24 |
| February  | 137.12 | 122.50 | 107.80 | 92.27 | 77.92 | 67.37 | 56.87 | 46.37 | 35.84 | 25.34 | 14.84 | 4.34 |
| March     | 135.99 | 121.39 | 106.63 | 91.05 | 77.07 | 66.57 | 56.07 | 45.54 | 35.04 | 24.54 | 14.04 | 3.51 |
| April     | 134.74 | 120.15 | 105.34 | 89.76 | 76.18 | 65.68 | 55.18 | 44.65 | 34.15 | 23.65 | 13.15 | 2.62 |
| May       | 133.53 | 118.96 | 104.08 | 88.53 | 75.31 | 64.81 | 54.31 | 43.78 | 33.28 | 22.78 | 12.28 | 1.75 |
| June      | 132.27 | 117.73 | 102.77 | 87.26 | 74.42 | 63.92 | 53.42 | 42.89 | 32.39 | 21.89 | 11.39 | 0.86 |
| July      | 131.06 | 116.54 | 101.50 | 86.03 | 73.56 | 63.06 | 52.56 | 42.03 | 31.53 | 21.03 | 10.53 |      |
| August    | 129.81 | 115.31 | 100.16 | 84.76 | 72.67 | 62.17 | 51.67 | 41.14 | 30.64 | 20.14 | 9.64  |      |
| September | 128.58 | 114.06 | 98.83  | 83.49 | 71.77 | 61.27 | 50.77 | 40.25 | 29.75 | 19.25 | 8.75  |      |
| October   | 127.38 | 112.84 | 97.53  | 82.26 | 70.91 | 60.41 | 49.91 | 39.38 | 28.88 | 18.38 | 7.88  |      |
| November  | 126.15 | 111.59 | 96.19  | 81.02 | 70.02 | 59.52 | 49.02 | 38.49 | 27.99 | 17.49 | 6.99  |      |
| December  | 124.96 | 110.36 | 94.90  | 79.93 | 69.16 | 58.66 | 48.16 | 37.63 | 27.13 | 16.63 | 6.13  |      |

---

[1] *The Times*, 4 April 2000.

If there are no further changes of rate after that on 5 March 2009, interest to the last day of successive later months can be found to a date after 30 June 2016 by adding the figure from the following table:

|  | 2016 | 2017 |
|---|---|---|
| January |  | 6.18 |
| February |  | 6.99 |
| March |  | 7.88 |
| April |  | 8.75 |
| May |  | 9.64 |
| June |  | 10.50 |
| July | 0.89 |  |
| August | 1.78 |  |
| September | 2.65 |  |
| October | 3.54 |  |
| November | 4.40 |  |
| December | 5.29 |  |

# C6: Number of days between two dates

## Introductory notes

Deduct the number of the opening date from the number of the closing date (where necessary adding a day for 29 February).
Example: 14 October–19 March (where the February is not a leap year) is 443 – 287 = 156 days.
Note that the calculation produces the *interval* between the two dates; so that it includes the first date and excludes the last date. For example, 1 January to 31 January is calculated as 31 – 1 = 30 days, not 31. If the last date is to be included then "add 1" to the number of days.

### Day numbers

| Day of month | Jan | Feb | Mar | Apr | May | Jun | Jul | Aug | Sep | Oct | Nov | Dec | Jan | Feb | Mar | Apr | May | Jun | Jul | Aug | Sep | Oct | Nov | Dec | Day of month |
|---|---|---|---|---|---|---|---|---|---|---|---|---|---|---|---|---|---|---|---|---|---|---|---|---|---|
| 1 | 1 | 32 | 60 | 91 | 121 | 152 | 182 | 213 | 244 | 274 | 305 | 335 | 366 | 397 | 425 | 456 | 486 | 517 | 547 | 578 | 609 | 639 | 670 | 700 | 1 |
| 2 | 2 | 33 | 61 | 92 | 122 | 153 | 183 | 214 | 245 | 275 | 306 | 336 | 367 | 398 | 426 | 457 | 487 | 518 | 548 | 579 | 610 | 640 | 671 | 701 | 2 |
| 3 | 3 | 34 | 62 | 93 | 123 | 154 | 184 | 215 | 246 | 276 | 307 | 337 | 368 | 399 | 427 | 458 | 488 | 519 | 549 | 580 | 611 | 641 | 672 | 702 | 3 |
| 4 | 4 | 35 | 63 | 94 | 124 | 155 | 185 | 216 | 247 | 277 | 308 | 338 | 369 | 400 | 428 | 459 | 489 | 520 | 550 | 581 | 612 | 642 | 673 | 703 | 4 |
| 5 | 5 | 36 | 64 | 95 | 125 | 156 | 186 | 217 | 248 | 278 | 309 | 339 | 370 | 401 | 429 | 460 | 490 | 521 | 551 | 582 | 613 | 643 | 674 | 704 | 5 |
| 6 | 6 | 37 | 65 | 96 | 126 | 157 | 187 | 218 | 249 | 279 | 310 | 340 | 371 | 402 | 430 | 461 | 491 | 522 | 552 | 583 | 614 | 644 | 675 | 705 | 6 |
| 7 | 7 | 38 | 66 | 97 | 127 | 158 | 188 | 219 | 250 | 280 | 311 | 341 | 372 | 403 | 431 | 462 | 492 | 523 | 553 | 584 | 615 | 645 | 676 | 706 | 7 |
| 8 | 8 | 39 | 67 | 98 | 128 | 159 | 189 | 220 | 251 | 281 | 312 | 342 | 373 | 404 | 432 | 463 | 493 | 524 | 554 | 585 | 616 | 646 | 677 | 707 | 8 |
| 9 | 9 | 40 | 68 | 99 | 129 | 160 | 190 | 221 | 252 | 282 | 313 | 343 | 374 | 405 | 433 | 464 | 494 | 525 | 555 | 586 | 617 | 647 | 678 | 708 | 9 |
| 10 | 10 | 41 | 69 | 100 | 130 | 161 | 191 | 222 | 253 | 283 | 314 | 344 | 375 | 406 | 434 | 465 | 495 | 526 | 556 | 587 | 618 | 648 | 679 | 709 | 10 |
| 11 | 11 | 42 | 70 | 101 | 131 | 162 | 192 | 223 | 254 | 284 | 315 | 345 | 376 | 407 | 435 | 466 | 496 | 527 | 557 | 588 | 619 | 649 | 680 | 710 | 11 |
| 12 | 12 | 43 | 71 | 102 | 132 | 163 | 193 | 224 | 255 | 285 | 316 | 346 | 377 | 408 | 436 | 467 | 497 | 528 | 558 | 589 | 620 | 650 | 681 | 711 | 12 |
| 13 | 13 | 44 | 72 | 103 | 133 | 164 | 194 | 225 | 256 | 286 | 317 | 347 | 378 | 409 | 437 | 468 | 498 | 529 | 559 | 590 | 621 | 651 | 682 | 712 | 13 |
| 14 | 14 | 45 | 73 | 104 | 134 | 165 | 195 | 226 | 257 | 287 | 318 | 348 | 379 | 410 | 438 | 469 | 499 | 530 | 560 | 591 | 622 | 652 | 683 | 713 | 14 |
| 15 | 15 | 46 | 74 | 105 | 135 | 166 | 196 | 227 | 258 | 288 | 319 | 349 | 380 | 411 | 439 | 470 | 500 | 531 | 561 | 592 | 623 | 653 | 684 | 714 | 15 |
| 16 | 16 | 47 | 75 | 106 | 136 | 167 | 197 | 228 | 259 | 289 | 320 | 350 | 381 | 412 | 440 | 471 | 501 | 532 | 562 | 593 | 624 | 654 | 685 | 715 | 16 |
| 17 | 17 | 48 | 76 | 107 | 137 | 168 | 198 | 229 | 260 | 290 | 321 | 351 | 382 | 413 | 441 | 472 | 502 | 533 | 563 | 594 | 625 | 655 | 686 | 716 | 17 |
| 18 | 18 | 49 | 77 | 108 | 138 | 169 | 199 | 230 | 261 | 291 | 322 | 352 | 383 | 414 | 442 | 473 | 503 | 534 | 564 | 595 | 626 | 656 | 687 | 717 | 18 |
| 19 | 19 | 50 | 78 | 109 | 139 | 170 | 200 | 231 | 262 | 292 | 323 | 353 | 384 | 415 | 443 | 474 | 504 | 535 | 565 | 596 | 627 | 657 | 688 | 718 | 19 |
| 20 | 20 | 51 | 79 | 110 | 140 | 171 | 201 | 232 | 263 | 293 | 324 | 354 | 385 | 416 | 444 | 475 | 505 | 536 | 566 | 597 | 628 | 658 | 689 | 719 | 20 |
| 21 | 21 | 52 | 80 | 111 | 141 | 172 | 202 | 233 | 264 | 294 | 325 | 355 | 386 | 417 | 445 | 476 | 506 | 537 | 567 | 598 | 629 | 659 | 690 | 720 | 21 |
| 22 | 22 | 53 | 81 | 112 | 142 | 173 | 203 | 234 | 265 | 295 | 326 | 356 | 387 | 418 | 446 | 477 | 507 | 538 | 568 | 599 | 630 | 660 | 691 | 721 | 22 |
| 23 | 23 | 54 | 82 | 113 | 143 | 174 | 204 | 235 | 266 | 296 | 327 | 357 | 388 | 419 | 447 | 478 | 508 | 539 | 569 | 600 | 631 | 661 | 692 | 722 | 23 |
| 24 | 24 | 55 | 83 | 114 | 144 | 175 | 205 | 236 | 267 | 297 | 328 | 358 | 389 | 420 | 448 | 479 | 509 | 540 | 570 | 601 | 632 | 662 | 693 | 723 | 24 |
| 25 | 25 | 56 | 84 | 115 | 145 | 176 | 206 | 237 | 268 | 298 | 329 | 359 | 390 | 421 | 449 | 480 | 510 | 541 | 571 | 602 | 633 | 663 | 694 | 724 | 25 |
| 26 | 26 | 57 | 85 | 116 | 146 | 177 | 207 | 238 | 269 | 299 | 330 | 360 | 391 | 422 | 450 | 481 | 511 | 542 | 572 | 603 | 634 | 664 | 695 | 725 | 26 |
| 27 | 27 | 58 | 86 | 117 | 147 | 178 | 208 | 239 | 270 | 300 | 331 | 361 | 392 | 423 | 451 | 482 | 512 | 543 | 573 | 604 | 635 | 665 | 696 | 726 | 27 |
| 28 | 28 | 59 | 87 | 118 | 148 | 179 | 209 | 240 | 271 | 301 | 332 | 362 | 393 | 424 | 452 | 483 | 513 | 544 | 574 | 605 | 636 | 666 | 697 | 727 | 28 |
| 29 | 29 |  | 88 | 119 | 149 | 180 | 210 | 241 | 272 | 302 | 333 | 363 | 394 |  | 453 | 484 | 514 | 545 | 575 | 606 | 637 | 667 | 698 | 728 | 29 |
| 30 | 30 |  | 89 | 120 | 150 | 181 | 211 | 242 | 273 | 303 | 334 | 364 | 395 |  | 454 | 485 | 515 | 546 | 576 | 607 | 638 | 668 | 699 | 729 | 30 |
| 31 | 31 |  | 90 |  | 151 |  | 212 | 243 |  | 304 |  | 365 | 396 |  | 455 |  | 516 |  | 577 | 608 |  | 669 |  | 730 | 31 |

# C7: Decimal years

An alternative way of calculating interest is with a table expressing intervals as decimals of a year. It is in some respects simpler than using Table C6 (Number of Days) as it avoids the need to divide by 365.

The first table below gives days, weeks and months as decimals of a year.

The second table gives the period between corresponding days of two months, with the earlier month down the left-hand side and the later month across the top. Thus from the two figures in bold one sees that from 1 April–1 June is 0.167 years; from 1 June to the next 1 April is 0.833 years. The calculation again produces the *interval* between the dates: 1 January to 1 February is 31 days (not 32).

## Days, weeks and months expressed as decimals of a year

**Days**

| | | | | | | | | | | | | | | | | | | | |
|---|---|---|---|---|---|---|---|---|---|---|---|---|---|---|---|---|---|---|---|
| 1 | 0.003 | 2 | 0.005 | 3 | 0.008 | 4 | 0.011 | 5 | 0.014 | 6 | 0.016 | 7 | 0.019 | 8 | 0.022 | 9 | 0.025 | 10 | 0.027 |
| 11 | 0.030 | 12 | 0.033 | 13 | 0.036 | 14 | 0.038 | 15 | 0.041 | 16 | 0.044 | 17 | 0.047 | 18 | 0.049 | 19 | 0.052 | 20 | 0.055 |
| 21 | 0.058 | 22 | 0.060 | 23 | 0.063 | 24 | 0.066 | 25 | 0.068 | 26 | 0.071 | 27 | 0.074 | 28 | 0.077 | 29 | 0.079 | 30 | 0.082 |

**Weeks**

| | | | | | | | | | | | | | | | | | | | |
|---|---|---|---|---|---|---|---|---|---|---|---|---|---|---|---|---|---|---|---|
| 1 | 0.019 | 2 | 0.038 | 3 | 0.058 | 4 | 0.077 | 5 | 0.096 | 6 | 0.115 | 7 | 0.134 | 8 | 0.153 | 9 | 0.173 | 10 | 0.192 |

**Months**

| | | | | | | | |
|---|---|---|---|---|---|---|---|
| 28 days | 0.077 | 29 days | 0.079 | 30 days | 0.082 | 31 days | 0.085 |

## Intervals between corresponding days of months as decimals of a year

| Earlier month | Later month | | | | | |
|---|---|---|---|---|---|---|
| | Jan | Feb | Mar | Apr | May | Jun |
| Jan | 1.000 | 0.085 | 0.162 | 0.247 | 0.329 | 0.414 |
| Feb | 0.915 | 1.000 | 0.077 | 0.162 | 0.244 | 0.329 |
| Mar | 0.838 | 0.923 | 1.000 | 0.085 | 0.167 | 0.252 |
| Apr | 0.753 | 0.838 | 0.915 | 1.000 | 0.082 | **0.167** |
| May | 0.671 | 0.756 | 0.833 | 0.918 | 1.000 | 0.085 |
| Jun | 0.586 | 0.671 | 0.748 | **0.833** | 0.915 | 1.000 |
| Jul | 0.504 | 0.589 | 0.666 | 0.751 | 0.833 | 0.918 |
| Aug | 0.419 | 0.504 | 0.581 | 0.666 | 0.748 | 0.833 |
| Sept | 0.334 | 0.419 | 0.496 | 0.581 | 0.663 | 0.748 |
| Oct | 0.252 | 0.337 | 0.414 | 0.499 | 0.581 | 0.666 |
| Nov | 0.167 | 0.252 | 0.329 | 0.414 | 0.496 | 0.581 |
| Dec | 0.085 | 0.170 | 0.247 | 0.332 | 0.414 | 0.499 |

| Earlier month | Jul | Aug | Sept | Oct | Nov | Dec |
|---|---|---|---|---|---|---|
| Jan | 0.496 | 0.581 | 0.666 | 0.748 | 0.833 | 0.915 |
| Feb | 0.411 | 0.496 | 0.581 | 0.663 | 0.748 | 0.830 |
| Mar | 0.334 | 0.419 | 0.504 | 0.586 | 0.671 | 0.753 |
| Apr | 0.249 | 0.334 | 0.419 | 0.501 | 0.586 | 0.668 |
| May | 0.167 | 0.252 | 0.337 | 0.419 | 0.504 | 0.586 |
| Jun | 0.082 | 0.167 | 0.252 | 0.334 | 0.419 | 0.501 |
| Jul | 1.000 | 0.085 | 0.170 | 0.252 | 0.337 | 0.419 |
| Aug | 0.915 | 1.000 | 0.085 | 0.167 | 0.252 | 0.334 |
| Sept | 0.830 | 0.915 | 1.000 | 0.082 | 0.167 | 0.249 |
| Oct | 0.748 | 0.833 | 0.918 | 1.000 | 0.085 | 0.167 |
| Nov | 0.663 | 0.748 | 0.833 | 0.915 | 1.000 | 0.082 |
| Dec | 0.581 | 0.666 | 0.751 | 0.833 | 0.918 | 1.000 |

Example: to calculate interest at eight per cent from 3 June 2016 to 15 April 2017

| | | | |
|---|---|---|---|
| 3 June to 15 June | = 12 days | = 0.033 years | |
| 15 June to 15 April the following year | | = 0.833 | |
| Total     3.6.14 to 15.4.15 | | = 0.866 years | |
| Interest at 8% from 3.6.14 to 15.4.15 | | = 0.866 × 8 | = 6.928% |

## C8: Judgment debt interest rates (England and Wales)

**Introductory notes**

Interest rates under the Judgments Act 1838 s.17.

This table sets out the interest rates as determined by the Judgment Debts (Rate of Interest) Orders. Such orders are made under the Administration of Justice Act 1970 s.44.

By virtue of The County Courts (Interest on Judgment Debts) Order 1991, the general rule is that every judgment debt of not less than £5,000 carries interest from the date on which it was given, at the same rate as that payable on High Court judgments.

| From | At % | Order |
| --- | --- | --- |
| 20 April 1971 | 7.5 | SI 1971/491 |
| 1 March 1977 | 10 | SI 1977/141 |
| 3 December 1979 | 12.5 | SI 1979/1382 |
| 9 June 1980 | 15 | SI 1980/672 |
| 8 June 1982 | 14 | SI 1982/696 |
| 10 November 1982 | 12 | SI 1982/1427 |
| 16 April 1985 | 15 | SI 1985/437 |
| 1 April 1993 to date | 8 | SI 1993/564 |

## C9: Judicial rates of interest (Scotland)

| From | At % | Act of Sederunt |
| --- | --- | --- |
| 4 May 1965 | 5 | SI 1965/321 |
| 6 January 1970 | 7 | SI 1969/1819 |
| 7 January 1975 | 11 | SI 1974/2090 |
| 5 April 1983 | 12 | SI 1983/398 |
| 16 August 1985 | 15 | SI 1985/1178 |
| 1 April 1993 to date | 8 | SI 1993/770 and SI 1994/1443 |

# Group D
*Investment*

D1: Share price index (FTSE 100)

D2: Graph of share price index

D3: Index-linked stock

# D1: Share price index (FTSE 100)

FTSE® 100 (on last day of month)

|  | 1987 | 1988 | 1989 | 1990 | 1991 | 1992 | 1993 | 1994 |
|---|---|---|---|---|---|---|---|---|
| January | 1808.3 | 1790.8 | 2051.8 | 2337.3 | 2170.3 | 2571.2 | 2807.2 | 3491.8 |
| February | 1979.2 | 1768.8 | 2002.4 | 2255.4 | 2380.9 | 2562.1 | 2868.0 | 3328.1 |
| March | 1997.6 | 1742.5 | 2075.0 | 2247.9 | 2456.5 | 2440.1 | 2878.7 | 3086.4 |
| April | 2050.5 | 1802.2 | 2118.0 | 2103.4 | 2486.2 | 2654.1 | 2813.1 | 3125.3 |
| May | 2203.0 | 1784.5 | 2114.4 | 2345.1 | 2499.5 | 2707.6 | 2840.7 | 2970.5 |
| June | 2284.1 | 1857.6 | 2151.0 | 2374.6 | 2414.8 | 2521.2 | 2900.0 | 2919.2 |
| July | 2360.9 | 1853.6 | 2297.0 | 2326.2 | 2588.8 | 2399.6 | 2926.5 | 3082.6 |
| August | 2249.7 | 1753.6 | 2387.9 | 2162.8 | 2645.7 | 2312.6 | 3100.0 | 3251.3 |
| September | 2366.0 | 1826.5 | 2299.4 | 1990.2 | 2621.7 | 2553.0 | 3037.5 | 3026.3 |
| October | 1749.8 | 1852.4 | 2142.6 | 2050.3 | 2566.0 | 2658.3 | 3171.0 | 3097.4 |
| November | 1579.9 | 1792.4 | 2276.8 | 2149.4 | 2420.2 | 2778.8 | 3166.9 | 3081.4 |
| December | 1713.9 | 1793.1 | 2422.7 | 2143.5 | 2493.1 | 2846.5 | 3418.4 | 3065.5 |

|  | 1995 | 1996 | 1997 | 1998 | 1999 | 200 | 2001 | 2002 |
|---|---|---|---|---|---|---|---|---|
| January | 2991.6 | 3759.3 | 4275.8 | 5458.5 | 5896.0 | 6268.5 | 6297.5 | 5164.8 |
| February | 3009.3 | 3727.6 | 4308.3 | 5767.3 | 6175.1 | 6232.6 | 5917.9 | 5101.0 |
| March | 3137.9 | 3699.7 | 4312.9 | 5932.2 | 6295.3 | 6540.2 | 5633.7 | 5271.8 |
| April | 3216.7 | 3817.9 | 4436.0 | 5928.4 | 6552.2 | 6327.4 | 5967.0 | 5165.6 |
| May | 3319.4 | 3747.8 | 4621.3 | 5870.7 | 6226.2 | 6359.4 | 5796.2 | 5085.1 |
| June | 3314.6 | 3711.0 | 4604.6 | 5832.6 | 6318.5 | 6312.7 | 5642.5 | 4656.4 |
| July | 3463.3 | 3703.2 | 4907.5 | 5837.1 | 6231.9 | 6365.3 | 5529.1 | 4246.2 |
| August | 3477.8 | 3867.6 | 4817.5 | 5249.4 | 6246.4 | 6672.7 | 5345.0 | 4227.3 |
| September | 3508.2 | 3953.7 | 5244.2 | 5064.4 | 6029.8 | 6294.2 | 4903.4 | 3721.8 |
| October | 3529.1 | 3979.1 | 4842.3 | 5438.4 | 6255.7 | 6438.4 | 5039.7 | 4039.7 |
| November | 3664.3 | 4058.0 | 4831.8 | 5743.9 | 6597.2 | 6142.2 | 5203.6 | 4169.4 |
| December | 3689.3 | 4118.5 | 5135.5 | 5882.6 | 6930.2 | 6222.5 | 5217.4 | 3940.4 |

|  | 2003 | 2004 | 2005 | 2006 | 2007 | 2008 | 2009 | 2010 |
|---|---|---|---|---|---|---|---|---|
| January | 3567.4 | 4390.7 | 4852.3 | 5760.3 | 6203.1 | 5879.8 | 4149.6 | 5188.5 |
| February | 3655.6 | 4492.2 | 4968.5 | 5791.5 | 6171.5 | 5884.3 | 3830.1 | 5354.5 |
| March | 3613.3 | 4385.7 | 4894.4 | 5964.6 | 6308.0 | 5702.1 | 3926.1 | 5679.6 |
| April | 3926.0 | 4489.7 | 4801.7 | 6023.1 | 6449.2 | 6087.3 | 4243.7 | 5553.5 |
| May | 4048.1 | 4430.7 | 4964.0 | 5723.8 | 6621.5 | 6053.5 | 4417.9 | 5188.4 |
| June | 4031.2 | 4464.1 | 5113.2 | 5833.4 | 6607.9 | 5625.9 | 4249.2 | 4916.9 |
| July | 4157.0 | 4413.1 | 5282.3 | 5928.3 | 6360.1 | 5411.9 | 4608.4 | 5258.0 |
| August | 4161.1 | 4459.3 | 5296.9 | 5906.1 | 6303.3 | 5636.6 | 4908.9 | 5225.2 |
| September | 4091.3 | 4570.8 | 5477.7 | 5960.8 | 6466.8 | 4902.5 | 5133.9 | 5548.6 |
| October | 4287.6 | 4624.2 | 5317.3 | 6129.2 | 6721.6 | 4377.3 | 5044.6 | 5675.2 |
| November | 4342.6 | 4703.2 | 5423.2 | 6048.8 | 6432.5 | 4288.0 | 5190.7 | 5528.3 |
| December | 4476.9 | 4814.3 | 5618.8 | 6220.8 | 6456.9 | 4434.2 | 5412.9 | 5899.9 |

|  | 2011 | 2012 | 2013 | 2014 | 2015 | 2016 |
|---|---|---|---|---|---|---|
| January | 5862.9 | 5681.6 | 6276.9 | 6510.4 | 6749.4 | 6083.8 |
| February | 5994.0 | 5871.5 | 6360.8 | 6809.7 | 6946.7 | 6097.1 |
| March | 5908.8 | 5768.5 | 6411.7 | 6598.4 | 6773.0 | 6091.2 |
| April | 6069.9 | 5737.8 | 6430.1 | 6780.0 | 6960.6 | 6241.9 |
| May | 5990.0 | 5320.9 | 6583.1 | 6844.5 | 6984.4 | 6230.8 |
| June | 5945.7 | 5571.2 | 6215.5 | 6743.9 | 6521.0 | |
| July | 5815.2 | 5635.3 | 6621.1 | 6730.1 | 6696.3 | |
| August | 5394.5 | 5711.5 | 6412.9 | 6819.8 | 6247.9 | |
| September | 5128.5 | 5742.1 | 6462.2 | 6622.7 | 6061.6 | |
| October | 5544.2 | 5782.7 | 6731.4 | 6546.5 | 6361.1 | |
| November | 5505.4 | 5866.8 | 6650.6 | 6722.6 | 6356.1 | |
| December | 5572.3 | 5897.8 | 6749.1 | 6566.1 | 6242.3 | |

## D2: Graph of share price index

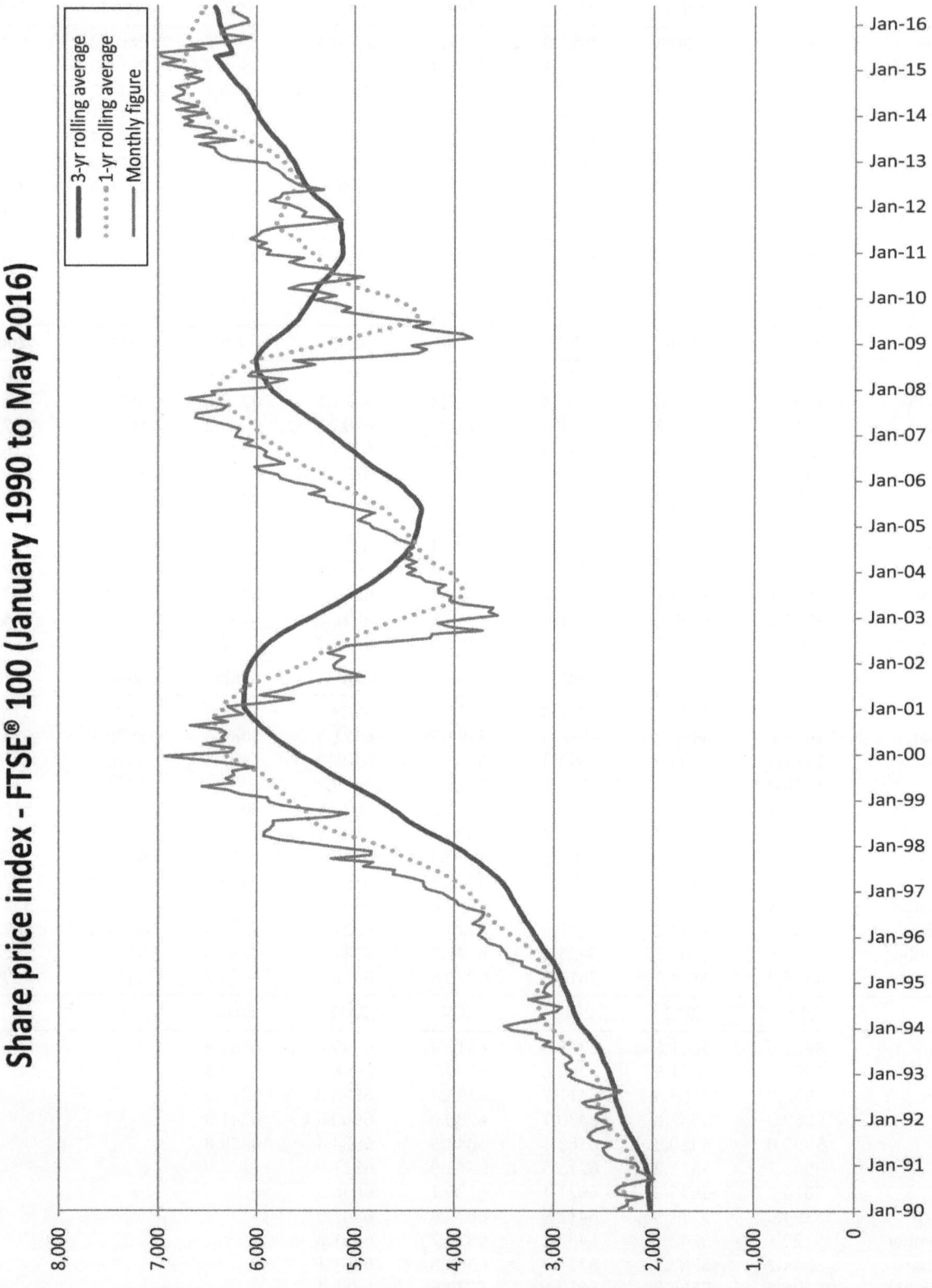

# D3: Index-linked stock

**Return on index-linked government securities**

|  | 2002 | | 2003 | | 2004 | | 2005 | | 2006 | |
|---|---|---|---|---|---|---|---|---|---|---|
|  | Gross % | Net % | Gross % | Net % | Gross % | Net % | Gross % | Net % | Gross % | Net % |
| January | 2.36% | 2.01% | 1.99% | 1.69% | 1.97% | 1.68% | 1.69% | 1.44% | 1.04% | 0.79% |
| February | 2.35% | 2.00% | 1.87% | 1.59% | 1.84% | 1.56% | 1.68% | 1.43% | 1.05% | 0.80% |
| March | 2.36% | 2.01% | 1.94% | 1.65% | 1.75% | 1.49% | 1.69% | 1.44% | 1.25% | 1.00% |
| April | 2.38% | 2.03% | 2.00% | 1.70% | 1.91% | 1.62% | 1.64% | 1.39% | 1.44% | 1.19% |
| May | 2.34% | 1.99% | 1.82% | 1.55% | 1.99% | 1.69% | 1.62% | 1.37% | 1.42% | 1.17% |
| June | 2.23% | 1.89% | 1.85% | 1.57% | 1.96% | 1.67% | 1.46% | 1.21% | 1.50% | 1.25% |
| July | 2.41% | 2.05% | 2.06% | 1.75% | 2.00% | 1.70% | 1.57% | 1.32% | 1.31% | 1.06% |
| August | 2.12% | 1.80% | 2.02% | 1.72% | 1.84% | 1.56% | 1.38% | 1.13% | 1.18% | 0.93% |
| September | 2.10% | 1.78% | 1.93% | 1.64% | 1.79% | 1.53% | 1.40% | 1.15% | 1.22% | 0.97% |
| October | 2.22% | 1.89% | 2.19% | 1.86% | 1.77% | 1.51% | 1.37% | 1.12% | 1.10% | 0.85% |
| November | 2.35% | 2.00% | 2.19% | 1.86% | 1.70% | 1.44% | 1.30% | 1.05% | 1.11% | 0.86% |
| December | 2.11% | 1.79% | 1.92% | 1.63% | 1.62% | 1.37% | 1.14% | 0.89% | 1.29% | 1.04% |

|  | 2007 | | 2008 | | 2009 | | 2010 | | 2011 | |
|---|---|---|---|---|---|---|---|---|---|---|
|  | Gross % | Net % | Gross % | Net % | Gross % | Net % | Gross % | Net % | Gross % | Net % |
| January | 1.50% | 1.25% | 0.98% | 0.73% | 1.03% | 0.88% | 0.76% | 0.61% | 0.72% | 0.57% |
| February | 1.27% | 1.02% | 0.95% | 0.70% | 1.26% | 1.11% | 0.81% | 0.66% | 0.64% | 0.49% |
| March | 1.45% | 1.20% | 0.87% | 0.62% | 1.05% | 0.90% | 0.68% | 0.53% | 0.66% | 0.51% |
| April | 1.70% | 1.45% | 0.99% | 0.74% | 1.09% | 0.94% | 0.72% | 0.57% | 0.57% | 0.42% |
| May | 1.75% | 1.50% | 1.06% | 0.81% | 0.99% | 0.84% | 0.76% | 0.61% | 0.53% | 0.38% |
| June | 1.74% | 1.49% | 0.92% | 0.67% | 0.88% | 0.73% | 0.71% | 0.56% | 0.51% | 0.36% |
| July | 1.54% | 1.29% | 1.01% | 0.76% | 0.96% | 0.81% | 0.84% | 0.69% | 0.35% | 0.20% |
| August | 1.37% | 1.12% | 0.64% | 0.39% | 0.74% | 0.59% | 0.51% | 0.36% | 0.38% | 0.23% |
| September | 1.39% | 1.14% | 1.01% | 0.76% | 0.73% | 0.58% | 0.51% | 0.36% | 0.18% | 0.03% |
| October | 1.36% | 1.11% | 1.61% | 1.36% | 0.60% | 0.45% | 0.63% | 0.48% | 0.24% | 0.09% |
| November | 1.17% | 0.92% | 1.73% | 1.48% | 0.52% | 0.37% | 0.65% | 0.50% | −0.11% | −0.26% |
| December | 1.06% | 0.81% | 1.02% | 0.77% | 0.72% | 0.57% | 0.52% | 0.37% | −0.23% | −0.38% |

|  | 2012 | | 2013 | | 2014 | | 2015 | | 2016 | |
|---|---|---|---|---|---|---|---|---|---|---|
|  | Gross % | Net % | Gross % | Net % | Gross % | Net % | Gross % | Net % | Gross % | Net % |
| January | −0.23% | −0.38% | −0.24% | −0.39% | −0.01% | −0.16% | −0.95% | −1.10% | −0.89% | −1.04% |
| February | −0.15% | −0.30% | −0.23% | −0.38% | −0.02% | −0.17% | −0.73% | −0.88% | −0.90% | −1.05% |
| March | −0.09% | −0.24% | −0.41% | −0.56% | −0.08% | −0.23% | −0.92% | −1.07% | −0.97% | −1.12% |
| April | −0.06% | −0.21% | −0.45% | −0.60% | −0.11% | −0.26% | −0.87% | −1.02% | −0.84% | −0.99% |
| May | −0.18% | −0.33% | −0.27% | −0.42% | −0.15% | −0.30% | −0.86% | −1.01% | −0.92% | −1.07% |
| June | −0.08% | −0.23% | −0.01% | −0.16% | −0.10% | −0.25% | −0.73% | −0.88% | −1.40% | −1.55% |
| July | −0.09% | −0.24% | −0.03% | −0.18% | −0.14% | −0.29% | −0.83% | −0.98% | | |
| August | −0.10% | −0.25% | −0.02% | −0.17% | −0.41% | −0.56% | −0.79% | −0.94% | | |
| September | 0.11% | −0.04% | −0.02% | −0.17% | −0.35% | −0.50% | −0.81% | −0.96% | | |
| October | 0.11% | −0.04% | −0.08% | −0.23% | −0.42% | −0.57% | −0.74% | −0.89% | | |
| November | −0.01% | −0.16% | −0.05% | −0.20% | −0.66% | −0.81% | −0.81% | −0.96% | | |
| December | −0.05% | −0.20% | 0.05% | −0.10% | −0.73% | −0.88% | −0.64% | −0.79% | | |

**Notes:**

1. The above table shows the average month end gross redemption yields of British Government index-linked stocks with over five years to maturity.

2. Up to and including December 2014 the figures in the above table assume 3 per cent inflation (the standard assumption in recent years), by interpolation of the 0 per cent and 5 per cent published figures for inflation (Source: *Financial Times* or FT website).

3. From January 2015 the figures in the above table allow for 3 per cent inflation in eight-month lagged Gilts (those issued prior to 1 April 2005) and no adjustment for inflation in three-month lagged Gilts (those issued from 1 April 2005), in accordance with the UK Debt Management Office's calculations.

D3: Index-linked stock

4. The net percentage yield shown above up to and including 2004 is stated after deducting tax at 15 per cent (this was the assumption used in *Wells v Wells* and by the Lord Chancellor when he set the discount rate in 2001).

5. From 2005 to 2008 (inclusive) a fixed deduction of 0.25 per cent has been allowed for tax instead of a percentage. This is because, in spite of reducing yields in this period, taxable interest remained high in this period so that applying a percentage to the combined gross yield would understate the deduction for tax. The actual average tax rate will vary depending on the size of the award.

6. From 2009 a fixed deduction of 0.15 per cent has been allowed for tax. The average income tax deduction on taxable interest has been calculated by expert accountants as ranging from 0 per cent to 0.30 per cent depending on the size of the award, so 0.15 per cent is adopted as the midpoint of the range.

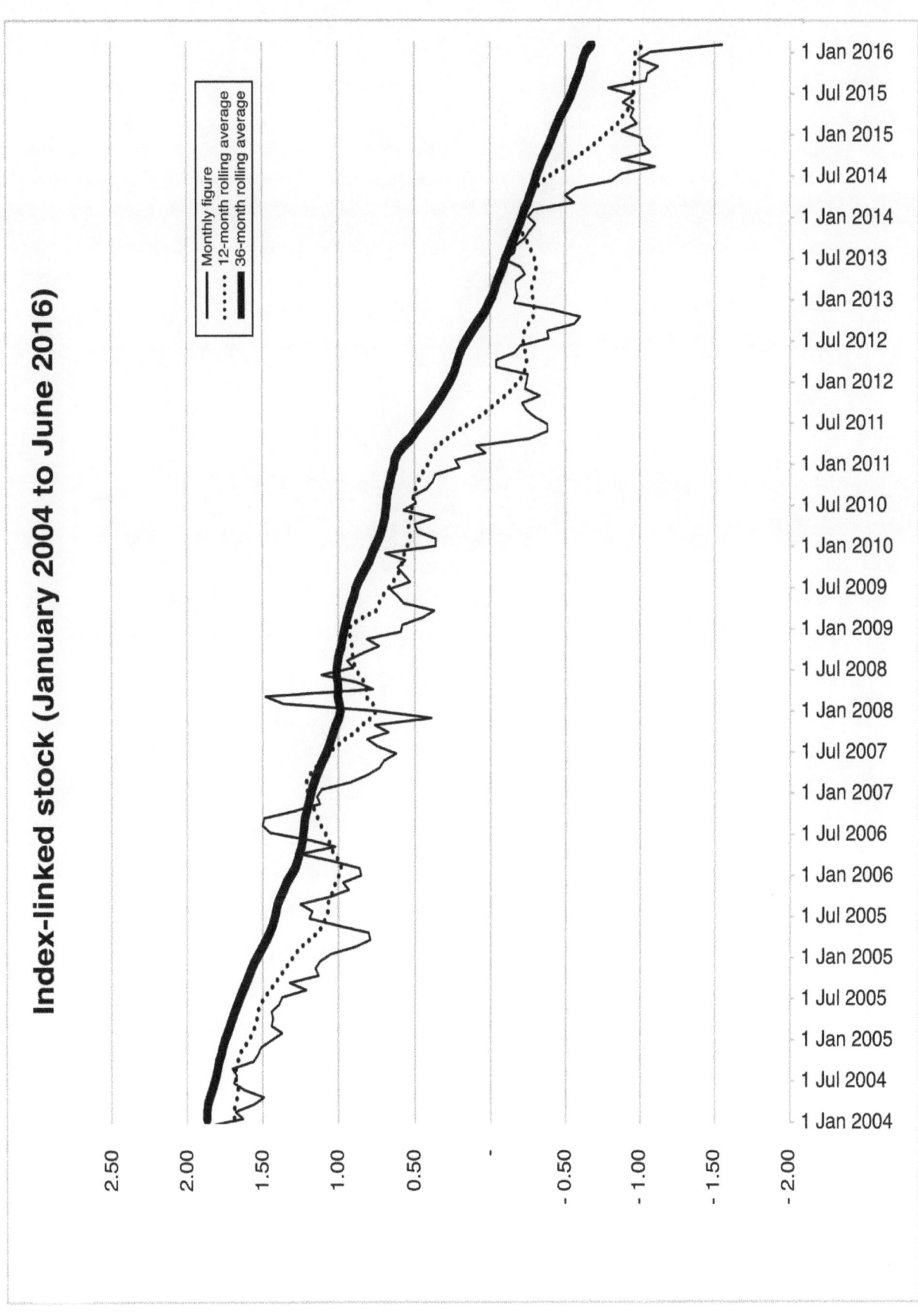

# Group E
*Prices*

- **E1:** Retail Prices Index
- **E2:** Inflation table
- **E3:** House price indices
- **E4:** Average semi-detached house prices by region
- **E5:** How prices have changed over 12 years

## E1: Retail Prices Index

| | Jan | Feb | Mar | Apr | May | June | July | Aug | Sept | Oct | Nov | Dec | |
|---|---|---|---|---|---|---|---|---|---|---|---|---|---|
| 2016 | 258.8 | 260.0 | 261.1 | 261.4 | 262.1 | 263.1 | 258.6 | 259.8 | 259.6 | 259.5 | 259.8 | 260.6 | 2016 |
| 2015 | 255.4 | 256.7 | 257.1 | 258.0 | 258.5 | 258.9 | 258.0 | 257.0 | 257.6 | 257.7 | 257.1 | 257.5 | 2015 |
| 2014 | 252.6 | 254.2 | 254.8 | 255.7 | 255.9 | 256.3 | 256.0 | 257.0 | 257.6 | 257.9 | 252.1 | 253.4 | 2014 |
| 2013 | 245.8 | 247.6 | 248.7 | 249.5 | 250.0 | 249.7 | 249.7 | 251.0 | 251.9 | 251.9 | 252.1 | 253.4 | 2013 |
| 2012 | 238.0 | 239.9 | 240.8 | 242.5 | 242.4 | 241.8 | 242.1 | 243.0 | 244.2 | 245.6 | 245.6 | 246.8 | 2012 |
| 2011 | 229.0 | 231.3 | 232.5 | 234.4 | 235.2 | 235.2 | 234.7 | 236.1 | 237.9 | 238.0 | 238.5 | 239.4 | 2011 |
| 2010 | 217.9 | 219.2 | 220.7 | 222.8 | 223.6 | 224.1 | 223.6 | 224.5 | 225.3 | 225.8 | 226.8 | 228.4 | 2010 |
| 2009 | 210.1 | 211.4 | 211.3 | 211.5 | 212.8 | 213.4 | 213.4 | 214.4 | 215.3 | 216.0 | 216.6 | 218.0 | 2009 |
| 2008 | 209.8 | 211.4 | 212.1 | 214.0 | 215.1 | 216.8 | 216.5 | 217.2 | 218.4 | 217.7 | 216.0 | 212.9 | 2008 |
| 2007 | 201.6 | 203.1 | 204.4 | 205.4 | 206.2 | 207.3 | 206.1 | 207.3 | 208.0 | 208.9 | 209.7 | 210.9 | 2007 |
| 2006 | 193.4 | 194.2 | 195.0 | 196.5 | 197.7 | 198.5 | 198.5 | 199.2 | 200.1 | 200.4 | 201.1 | 202.7 | 2006 |
| 2005 | 188.9 | 189.6 | 190.5 | 191.6 | 192.0 | 192.2 | 192.2 | 192.6 | 193.1 | 193.3 | 193.6 | 194.1 | 2005 |
| 2004 | 183.1 | 183.8 | 184.6 | 185.7 | 186.5 | 186.8 | 186.8 | 187.4 | 188.1 | 188.6 | 189.0 | 189.9 | 2004 |
| 2003 | 178.4 | 179.3 | 179.9 | 181.2 | 181.5 | 181.3 | 181.3 | 181.6 | 182.5 | 182.6 | 182.7 | 183.5 | 2003 |
| 2002 | 173.3 | 173.8 | 174.5 | 175.7 | 176.2 | 176.2 | 175.9 | 176.4 | 177.6 | 177.9 | 178.2 | 178.5 | 2002 |
| 2001 | 171.1 | 172.0 | 172.2 | 173.1 | 174.2 | 174.4 | 173.3 | 174.0 | 174.6 | 174.3 | 173.6 | 173.4 | 2001 |
| 2000 | 166.6 | 167.5 | 168.4 | 170.1 | 170.7 | 171.1 | 170.5 | 170.5 | 171.7 | 171.6 | 172.1 | 172.2 | 2000 |
| 1999 | 163.4 | 163.7 | 164.1 | 165.2 | 165.6 | 165.6 | 165.1 | 165.5 | 166.2 | 166.5 | 166.7 | 167.3 | 1999 |
| 1998 | 159.5 | 160.3 | 160.8 | 162.6 | 163.5 | 163.4 | 163.0 | 163.7 | 164.4 | 164.5 | 164.4 | 164.4 | 1998 |
| 1997 | 154.4 | 155.0 | 155.4 | 156.3 | 156.9 | 157.5 | 157.5 | 158.5 | 159.3 | 159.5 | 159.6 | 160.0 | 1997 |
| 1996 | 150.2 | 150.9 | 151.5 | 152.6 | 152.9 | 153.0 | 152.4 | 153.1 | 153.8 | 153.8 | 153.9 | 154.4 | 1996 |
| 1995 | 146.0 | 146.9 | 147.5 | 149.0 | 149.6 | 149.8 | 149.1 | 149.9 | 150.6 | 149.8 | 149.8 | 150.7 | 1995 |
| 1994 | 141.3 | 142.1 | 142.5 | 144.2 | 144.7 | 144.7 | 144.0 | 144.7 | 145.0 | 145.2 | 145.3 | 146.0 | 1994 |
| 1993 | 137.9 | 138.8 | 139.3 | 140.6 | 141.1 | 141.0 | 140.7 | 141.3 | 141.9 | 141.8 | 141.6 | 141.9 | 1993 |
| 1992 | 135.6 | 136.3 | 136.7 | 138.8 | 139.3 | 139.3 | 138.8 | 138.9 | 139.4 | 139.9 | 139.7 | 139.2 | 1992 |
| 1991 | 130.2 | 130.9 | 131.4 | 133.1 | 133.5 | 134.1 | 133.8 | 134.1 | 134.6 | 135.1 | 135.6 | 135.7 | 1991 |
| 1990 | 119.5 | 120.2 | 121.4 | 125.1 | 126.2 | 126.7 | 126.8 | 128.1 | 129.3 | 130.3 | 130.0 | 129.9 | 1990 |
| 1989 | 111.0 | 111.8 | 112.3 | 114.3 | 115.0 | 115.4 | 115.5 | 115.8 | 116.6 | 117.5 | 118.5 | 118.8 | 1989 |
| 1988 | 103.3 | 103.7 | 104.1 | 105.8 | 106.2 | 106.6 | 106.7 | 107.9 | 108.4 | 109.5 | 110.0 | 110.3 | 1988 |
| 1987 | 100.0 | 100.4 | 100.6 | 101.8 | 101.9 | 101.9 | 101.8 | 102.1 | 102.4 | 102.9 | 103.4 | 103.3 | 1987 |
| 1986 | 96.25 | 96.60 | 96.73 | 97.67 | 97.85 | 97.79 | 97.52 | 97.82 | 98.30 | 98.45 | 99.29 | 99.62 | 1986 |
| 1985 | 91.20 | 91.94 | 92.80 | 94.78 | 95.21 | 95.41 | 95.23 | 95.49 | 95.44 | 95.59 | 95.92 | 96.05 | 1985 |
| 1984 | 86.84 | 87.20 | 87.48 | 88.64 | 88.97 | 89.20 | 89.10 | 89.94 | 90.11 | 90.67 | 90.95 | 90.87 | 1984 |
| 1983 | 82.61 | 82.97 | 83.12 | 84.28 | 84.64 | 84.84 | 85.30 | 85.68 | 86.06 | 86.36 | 86.67 | 86.89 | 1983 |
| 1982 | 78.73 | 78.76 | 79.44 | 81.04 | 81.62 | 81.85 | 81.88 | 81.90 | 81.85 | 82.26 | 82.66 | 82.51 | 1982 |
| 1981 | 70.29 | 70.93 | 71.99 | 74.07 | 74.55 | 74.98 | 75.31 | 75.87 | 76.30 | 76.98 | 77.79 | 78.28 | 1981 |
| 1980 | 62.18 | 63.07 | 63.93 | 66.11 | 66.72 | 67.35 | 67.91 | 68.06 | 68.49 | 68.92 | 69.48 | 69.86 | 1980 |
| 1979 | 52.52 | 52.95 | 53.38 | 54.30 | 54.73 | 55.67 | 58.07 | 58.53 | 59.11 | 59.72 | 60.25 | 60.68 | 1979 |
| 1978 | 48.04 | 48.31 | 48.62 | 49.33 | 49.61 | 49.99 | 50.22 | 50.54 | 50.75 | 50.98 | 51.33 | 51.76 | 1978 |
| 1977 | 43.70 | 44.13 | 44.56 | 45.70 | 46.06 | 46.54 | 46.59 | 46.82 | 47.07 | 47.28 | 47.50 | 47.76 | 1977 |
| | Jan | Feb | Mar | Apr | May | June | July | Aug | Sept | Oct | Nov | Dec | |

## E1: Retail Prices Index

| | Jan | Feb | Mar | Apr | May | June | July | Aug | Sept | Oct | Nov | Dec | |
|---|---|---|---|---|---|---|---|---|---|---|---|---|---|
| 1976 | 37.49 | 37.97 | 38.17 | 38.91 | 39.34 | 39.54 | 39.62 | 40.18 | 40.71 | 41.44 | 42.03 | 42.59 | 1976 |
| 1975 | 30.39 | 30.90 | 31.51 | 32.72 | 34.09 | 34.75 | 35.11 | 35.31 | 35.61 | 36.12 | 36.55 | 37.01 | 1975 |
| 1974 | 25.35 | 25.78 | 26.01 | 26.89 | 27.28 | 27.55 | 27.81 | 27.83 | 28.14 | 28.69 | 29.20 | 29.63 | 1974 |
| 1973 | 22.64 | 22.78 | 22.92 | 23.35 | 23.52 | 23.64 | 23.75 | 23.82 | 24.03 | 24.50 | 24.69 | 24.87 | 1973 |
| 1972 | 21.01 | 21.12 | 21.19 | 21.38 | 21.49 | 21.63 | 21.70 | 21.87 | 21.99 | 22.30 | 22.37 | 22.49 | 1972 |
| 1971 | 19.43 | 19.53 | 19.69 | 20.11 | 20.25 | 20.39 | 20.51 | 20.52 | 20.55 | 20.67 | 20.79 | 20.89 | 1971 |
| 1970 | 17.91 | 18.00 | 18.11 | 18.38 | 18.44 | 18.49 | 18.62 | 18.61 | 18.70 | 18.90 | 19.03 | 19.16 | 1970 |
| 1969 | 17.06 | 17.15 | 17.22 | 17.41 | 17.38 | 17.46 | 17.46 | 17.42 | 17.47 | 17.60 | 17.64 | 17.76 | 1969 |
| 1968 | 16.07 | 16.15 | 16.20 | 16.49 | 16.51 | 16.57 | 16.59 | 16.61 | 16.63 | 16.71 | 16.74 | 16.97 | 1968 |
| 1967 | 15.66 | 15.67 | 15.67 | 15.79 | 15.78 | 15.85 | 15.75 | 15.71 | 15.70 | 15.82 | 15.91 | 16.02 | 1967 |
| 1966 | 15.11 | 15.12 | 15.15 | 15.33 | 15.44 | 15.48 | 15.41 | 15.50 | 15.48 | 15.52 | 15.61 | 15.63 | 1966 |
| 1965 | 14.47 | 14.47 | 14.52 | 14.80 | 14.85 | 14.89 | 14.89 | 14.92 | 14.93 | 14.95 | 15.01 | 15.08 | 1965 |
| 1964 | 13.84 | 13.85 | 13.90 | 14.02 | 14.14 | 14.19 | 14.19 | 14.25 | 14.25 | 14.26 | 14.38 | 14.43 | 1964 |
| 1963 | 13.57 | 13.69 | 13.71 | 13.74 | 13.73 | 13.73 | 13.65 | 13.61 | 13.65 | 13.71 | 13.74 | 13.77 | 1963 |
| 1962 | 13.22 | 13.23 | 13.28 | 13.47 | 13.51 | 13.60 | 13.55 | 13.43 | 13.41 | 13.40 | 13.45 | 13.52 | 1962 |
| 1961 | 12.63 | 12.63 | 12.68 | 12.74 | 12.78 | 12.89 | 12.89 | 13.01 | 12.99 | 13.01 | 13.15 | 13.17 | 1961 |
| 1960 | 12.36 | 12.36 | 12.34 | 12.41 | 12.41 | 12.47 | 12.50 | 12.42 | 12.43 | 12.53 | 12.59 | 12.62 | 1960 |
| 1959 | 12.42 | 12.41 | 12.41 | 12.32 | 12.27 | 12.29 | 12.26 | 12.29 | 12.23 | 12.28 | 12.37 | 12.40 | 1959 |
| 1958 | 12.16 | 12.10 | 12.19 | 12.33 | 12.28 | 12.40 | 12.20 | 12.18 | 12.19 | 12.31 | 12.35 | 12.40 | 1958 |
| 1957 | 11.74 | 11.73 | 11.71 | 11.75 | 11.77 | 11.89 | 11.99 | 11.97 | 11.93 | 12.05 | 12.11 | 12.17 | 1957 |
| 1956 | 11.25 | 11.25 | 11.39 | 11.55 | 11.53 | 11.52 | 11.47 | 11.51 | 11.48 | 11.55 | 11.60 | 11.63 | 1956 |
| 1955 | 10.70 | 10.70 | 10.70 | 10.76 | 10.74 | 10.97 | 11.00 | 10.93 | 11.00 | 11.11 | 11.29 | 11.29 | 1955 |
| 1954 | 10.28 | 10.26 | 10.35 | 10.39 | 10.36 | 10.42 | 10.60 | 10.53 | 10.51 | 10.56 | 10.61 | 10.66 | 1954 |
| 1953 | 10.14 | 10.17 | 10.24 | 10.33 | 10.30 | 10.35 | 10.35 | 10.29 | 10.27 | 10.27 | 10.30 | 10.26 | 1953 |
| 1952 | 9.71 | 9.72 | 9.77 | 9.93 | 9.93 | 10.09 | 10.08 | 10.02 | 10.00 | 10.09 | 10.08 | 10.15 | 1952 |
| 1951 | 8.60 | 8.68 | 8.74 | 8.88 | 9.10 | 9.13 | 9.27 | 9.31 | 9.38 | 9.44 | 9.48 | 9.54 | 1951 |
| 1950 | 8.28 | 8.30 | 8.32 | 8.35 | 8.37 | 8.33 | 8.33 | 8.30 | 8.35 | 8.44 | 8.47 | 8.52 | 1950 |
| 1949 | 7.99 | 8.01 | 7.98 | 7.96 | 8.11 | 8.14 | 8.15 | 8.16 | 8.19 | 8.23 | 8.23 | 8.25 | 1949 |
| 1948 | 7.64 | 7.78 | 7.80 | 7.91 | 7.90 | 8.04 | 7.92 | 7.92 | 7.93 | 7.95 | 7.97 | 7.98 | 1948 |
| 1947 | – | – | – | – | – | 7.33 | 7.38 | 7.34 | 7.37 | 7.43 | 7.58 | 7.60 | 1947 |
| | Jan | Feb | Mar | Apr | May | June | July | Aug | Sept | Oct | Nov | Dec | |

**Source:** Office for National Statistics licensed under the Open Government Licence V.I.O.

**Note:**

To calculate the equivalent value of a lump sum, divide by the RPI at the time and multiply the result by the current RPI. Thus £460 in June 1981 would be calculated as:

$$\left(\frac{460}{74.98}\right) \times \text{current RPI}$$

to show the relative value of that amount in "today's money".

# E2: Inflation table

**Introductory notes**

The table shows the value each January in earlier years equivalent to £1 in January 2016, after taking account of inflation over time.

Price inflation is measured by reference to the Retail Prices Index.

| Year | Multiplier | Year | Multiplier |
|---|---|---|---|
| 1948 | 33.88 | 1983 | 3.13 |
| 1949 | 32.39 | 1984 | 2.98 |
| 1950 | 31.27 | 1985 | 2.84 |
| 1951 | 30.10 | 1986 | 2.69 |
| 1952 | 26.64 | 1987 | 2.59 |
| 1953 | 25.52 | 1988 | 2.51 |
| 1954 | 25.18 | 1989 | 2.33 |
| 1955 | 24.18 | 1990 | 2.17 |
| 1956 | 23.01 | 1991 | 1.99 |
| 1957 | 22.04 | 1992 | 1.91 |
| 1958 | 21.28 | 1993 | 1.88 |
| 1959 | 20.84 | 1994 | 1.83 |
| 1960 | 20.94 | 1995 | 1.77 |
| 1961 | 20.49 | 1996 | 1.72 |
| 1962 | 19.58 | 1997 | 1.68 |
| 1963 | 19.07 | 1998 | 1.62 |
| 1964 | 18.70 | 1999 | 1.58 |
| 1965 | 17.88 | 2000 | 1.55 |
| 1966 | 17.13 | 2001 | 1.51 |
| 1967 | 16.53 | 2002 | 1.49 |
| 1968 | 16.10 | 2003 | 1.45 |
| 1969 | 15.17 | 2004 | 1.41 |
| 1970 | 14.45 | 2005 | 1.37 |
| 1971 | 13.32 | 2006 | 1.34 |
| 1972 | 12.32 | 2007 | 1.28 |
| 1973 | 11.43 | 2008 | 1.23 |
| 1974 | 10.21 | 2009 | 1.23 |
| 1975 | 8.52 | 2010 | 1.19 |
| 1976 | 6.90 | 2011 | 1.13 |
| 1977 | 5.92 | 2012 | 1.09 |
| 1978 | 5.39 | 2013 | 1.05 |
| 1979 | 4.93 | 2014 | 1.02 |
| 1980 | 4.16 | 2015 | 1.01 |
| 1981 | 3.68 | 2016 | 1.00 |
| 1982 | 3.29 | | |

# E3: House price indices

## Introductory notes

1. There are several price indices available in April 2016. These include the Halifax, Nationwide, the Financial Times, the Royal Institute of Chartered Surveyors, Hometrack, Rightmove, the Government Index and the Land Registry index.

2. The editors of *Facts & Figures* have used the Halifax table in previous editions and continue to do so. The Index Year for the Halifax table is 1983. In certain circumstances, the data offered by other indices may be useful. For example the Land Registry figures are broken down regionally and contain information about the numbers of first-time buyers. However, they exclude cash purchases which account for about a quarter of all transactions. Each table has strengths and weaknesses of this sort.

3. None of the indices should be treated as definitive. They can only be used as guides to the movement of prices over longer periods of time. Readers should be cautious about over-interpreting the analysis of short-term price changes.

**All Houses**

| Year | U.K. | | |
|---|---|---|---|
| | Index | % | Average Price £ |
| 92 | 208.1 | −5.6 | 64,309 |
| 93 | 202.1 | −2.9 | 62,455 |
| 94 | 203.1 | 0.5 | 62,750 |
| 95 | 199.6 | −1.7 | 61,666 |
| 96 | 208.6 | 4.5 | 64,441 |
| 97 | 221.7 | 6.3 | 68,504 |
| 98 | 233.7 | 5.4 | 72,196 |
| 99 | 250.5 | 7.2 | 77,405 |
| 00 | 275.1 | 9.8 | 85,005 |
| 01 | 298.6 | 8.5 | 92,256 |
| 02 | 350.6 | 17.4 | 108,342 |
| 03 | 429.1 | 22.4 | 132,589 |
| 04 | 507.6 | 18.3 | 156,831 |
| 05 | 536.6 | 5.7 | 165,807 |
| 06 | 581.3 | 8.3 | 179,601 |
| 07 | 635.9 | 9.4 | 196,478 |
| 08 | 585.9 | −7.9 | 181,032 |
| 09 | 524.6 | −10.5 | 162,085 |
| 10 | 539.6 | 2.9 | 166,739 |
| 11 | 525.4 | −2.6 | 162,322 |
| 12 | 522.1 | −0.6 | 161,308 |
| 13 | 547.0 | 4.77 | 169,003 |
| 14 | 593.5 | 8.51 | 183,391 |
| 15 | 648.4 | 9.2 | 200,329 |

## E3: House price indices

| Year | North Index | % | Yorks/Humb Index | % | N. West Index | % | E. Midlands Index | % |
|---|---|---|---|---|---|---|---|---|
| 92 | 210.1 | −1.6 | 231.9 | −3.6 | 226.1 | −4.3 | 214.4 | −5.9 |
| 93 | 206.3 | −1.8 | 228.3 | −1.6 | 219.3 | −3.0 | 208.3 | −2.8 |
| 94 | 203.6 | −1.3 | 226.3 | −0.9 | 215.8 | −1.6 | 209.1 | 0.4 |
| 95 | 195.9 | −3.8 | 219.2 | −3.1 | 207.8 | −3.7 | 203.9 | −2.5 |
| 96 | 201.9 | 3.1 | 224.5 | 2.4 | 210.7 | 1.4 | 209.4 | 2.7 |
| 97 | 206.5 | 2.3 | 228.5 | 1.8 | 216.7 | 2.9 | 221.5 | 5.8 |
| 98 | 211.2 | 2.3 | 229.8 | 0.5 | 220.4 | 1.7 | 229.9 | 3.8 |
| 99 | 220.1 | 4.2 | 236.5 | 2.9 | 231.0 | 4.8 | 244.8 | 6.5 |
| 00 | 221.9 | 0.8 | 243.9 | 3.2 | 242.6 | 5.0 | 265.0 | 8.2 |
| 01 | 234.0 | 5.5 | 257.5 | 5.6 | 255.7 | 5.4 | 287.3 | 8.4 |
| 02 | 271.4 | 16.0 | 297.7 | 15.6 | 292.8 | 14.5 | 361.7 | 25.9 |
| 03 | 370.6 | 36.5 | 395.6 | 32.9 | 366.3 | 25.1 | 457.5 | 26.5 |
| 04 | 490.3 | 32.3 | 495.0 | 25.1 | 472.8 | 29.1 | 541.4 | 18.3 |
| 05 | 533.3 | 8.8 | 549.3 | 11.0 | 523.7 | 10.8 | 564.9 | 4.3 |
| 06 | 567.3 | 6.4 | 602.4 | 9.7 | 565.1 | 7.9 | 599.4 | 6.1 |
| 07 | 601.8 | 6.1 | 640.5 | 6.3 | 596.8 | 5.6 | 632.4 | 5.5 |
| 08 | 547.2 | −9.1 | 580.0 | −9.5 | 558.3 | −6.5 | 582.0 | −8.0 |
| 09 | 500.2 | −8.6 | 526.3 | −9.3 | 492.8 | −11.7 | 518.2 | −11.0 |
| 10 | 511.5 | 2.3 | 538.2 | 2.3 | 486.7 | −1.3 | 541.7 | 4.5 |
| 11 | 483.1 | −5.6 | 513.2 | −4.6 | 485.0 | −0.4 | 517.9 | −4.4 |
| 12 | 478.1 | −1.0 | 509.1 | −0.8 | 468.6 | −3.4 | 523.1 | 1.0 |
| 13 | 496.8 | 3.9 | 527.3 | 3.6 | 501.9 | 7.1 | 539.2 | 3.1 |
| 14 | 507.7 | 2.2 | 562.1 | 6.6 | 540.4 | 7.7 | 584.3 | 8.4 |
| 15 | 548.0 | 7.9 | 615.6 | 9.5 | 573.4 | 6.1 | 633.3 | 8.4 |

| Year | W. Midlands Index | % | E. Anglia Index | % | S. West Index | % | S. East Index | % |
|---|---|---|---|---|---|---|---|---|
| 92 | 229.4 | −4.6 | 198.5 | −7.4 | 193.9 | −7.8 | 192.8 | −8.5 |
| 93 | 219.1 | −4.5 | 193.2 | −2.7 | 185.9 | −4.1 | 186.4 | −3.3 |
| 94 | 218.3 | −0.4 | 195.8 | 1.3 | 186.6 | 1.5 | 189.8 | 1.8 |
| 95 | 215.6 | −1.2 | 193.5 | −1.1 | 186.1 | −1.3 | 190.3 | 0.3 |
| 96 | 224.6 | 4.2 | 197.7 | 2.1 | 195.1 | 4.8 | 199.9 | 5.0 |
| 97 | 237.3 | 5.6 | 211.0 | 6.7 | 209.7 | 7.5 | 221.2 | 10.7 |
| 98 | 250.0 | 5.4 | 224.4 | 6.4 | 226.4 | 8.0 | 244.2 | 10.4 |
| 99 | 254.7 | 1.9 | 241.1 | 7.5 | 248.8 | 9.9 | 271.2 | 11.0 |
| 00 | 282.2 | 10.8 | 279.7 | 16.0 | 291.0 | 17.0 | 318.3 | 17.4 |
| 01 | 301.5 | 6.8 | 322.6 | 15.4 | 327.8 | 12.6 | 354.7 | 11.4 |
| 02 | 363.7 | 20.7 | 386.0 | 19.6 | 403.4 | 23.0 | 413.7 | 16.6 |
| 03 | 460.7 | 26.7 | 465.0 | 20.5 | 477.7 | 18.4 | 483.8 | 17.0 |
| 04 | 540.5 | 17.3 | 522.3 | 12.3 | 545.4 | 14.2 | 528.8 | 9.3 |
| 05 | 565.4 | 4.6 | 536.0 | 2.6 | 552.6 | 1.3 | 537.0 | 1.5 |
| 06 | 602.8 | 6.6 | 581.1 | 8.4 | 587.5 | 6.3 | 571.2 | 6.4 |
| 07 | 640.4 | 6.2 | 637.3 | 9.7 | 641.9 | 9.3 | 636.9 | 11.5 |
| 08 | 591.9 | −7.6 | 600.8 | −5.7 | 583.2 | −9.1 | 588.6 | −7.6 |
| 09 | 534.1 | −9.8 | 520.2 | −13.4 | 540.0 | −7.4 | 532.1 | −9.6 |
| 10 | 549.5 | 2.9 | 540.9 | 4.0 | 568.5 | 5.3 | 561.4 | 5.5 |
| 11 | 530.9 | −3.4 | 544.1 | 0.6 | 547.3 | −3.7 | 553.1 | −1.5 |
| 12 | 528.8 | −0.4 | 540.7 | −0.6 | 553.1 | 1.1 | 558.8 | 1.0 |
| 13 | 540.7 | 2.3 | 551.1 | 1.9 | 565.8 | 2.3 | 591 | 5.8 |
| 14 | 574.3 | 6.2 | 601.2 | 9.1 | 610.5 | 7.9 | 654.6 | 10.8 |
| 15 | 624.9 | 8.8 | 682.4 | 13.5 | 646.5 | 5.9 | 725.2 | 10.8 |

| Year | Gr. London Index | % | Wales Index | % | Scotland Index | % | N. Ireland Index | % |
|---|---|---|---|---|---|---|---|---|
| 92 | 202.0 | −9.4 | 207.7 | −4.3 | 193.2 | 0.2 | 145.5 | −1.0 |
| 93 | 192.0 | −4.9 | 204.5 | −1.6 | 196.4 | 1.6 | 151.7 | 4.3 |
| 94 | 195.5 | 1.8 | 201.9 | −1.2 | 199.4 | 1.6 | 162.1 | 6.9 |
| 95 | 194.9 | −0.4 | 194.2 | −3.8 | 199.4 | 0.0 | 172.8 | 6.6 |
| 96 | 212.4 | 9.0 | 205.5 | 5.9 | 204.9 | 2.8 | 204.5 | 18.3 |
| 97 | 246.3 | 16.0 | 212.0 | 3.1 | 204.7 | 0.1 | 210.6 | 3.0 |
| 98 | 272.3 | 10.5 | 220.2 | 3.8 | 209.8 | 2.5 | 235.6 | 11.9 |
| 99 | 317.9 | 16.8 | 232.3 | 5.5 | 212.8 | 1.4 | 248.8 | 5.6 |
| 00 | 373.6 | 17.5 | 245.0 | 5.5 | 214.2 | 0.7 | 264.4 | 6.3 |
| 01 | 428.3 | 14.7 | 263.8 | 7.7 | 220.0 | 2.7 | 296.8 | 12.2 |
| 02 | 499.4 | 16.6 | 299.8 | 13.6 | 238.5 | 8.4 | 307.4 | 3.6 |
| 03 | 563.3 | 12.8 | 397.2 | 32.5 | 274.5 | 15.1 | 340.3 | 10.7 |
| 04 | 608.5 | 8.0 | 516.3 | 30.0 | 330.6 | 20.4 | 397.9 | 16.9 |
| 05 | 621.4 | 2.1 | 553.7 | 7.3 | 375.7 | 13.6 | 486.0 | 22.1 |
| 06 | 680.9 | 9.6 | 589.7 | 6.5 | 421.7 | 12.2 | 581.3 | 32.6 |
| 07 | 777.6 | 14.2 | 640.7 | 8.7 | 488.2 | 15.8 | 844.5 | 31.1 |
| 08 | 705.3 | −9.3 | 579.4 | −9.6 | 478.2 | −2.1 | 679.2 | −19.6 |
| 09 | 622.0 | −11.8 | 512.0 | −11.6 | 426.6 | −10.8 | 563.7 | −17.0 |
| 10 | 659.9 | 6.1 | 530.3 | 3.6 | 421.4 | −1.2 | 506.2 | −10.2 |
| 11 | 659.6 | 0.0 | 521.5 | −1.7 | 406.8 | −3.5 | 444.1 | −12.3 |
| 12 | 674.4 | 2.2 | 505.6 | −3.0 | 384.2 | −5.5 | 405.4 | −8.7 |
| 13 | 737.2 | 9.3 | 557.3 | 10.2 | 400.5 | 4.2 | 368.9 | −9.0 |
| 14 | 855.2 | 16.0 | 572.8 | 2.8 | 430.2 | 7.4 | 430.8 | 16.8 |
| 15 | 995.1 | 16.4 | 585.9 | 2.3 | 463.3 | 7.7 | 452.0 | 4.9 |

## E4: Average semi-detached house prices by region

Prices are as of first quarter of 2016.

| Region | £ |
|---|---|
| North | 146,862 |
| North West | 171,145 |
| West Midlands | 180,253 |
| South East | 339,378 |
| South West | 238,765 |
| Greater London | 546,511 |
| Yorkshire & Humberside | 154,155 |
| East Midlands | 155,763 |
| East Anglia | 214,976 |

## E5: How prices have changed over 12 years

PRICE COMPARISON 2004–2016

| Item | Price in 2004 | Price in 2016 | % change | Source |
|---|---|---|---|---|
| Milk (pint) | 35p | 45p | 28.6% | ONS |
| Loaf of white sliced bread (800g) | 65p | £1.00 | 53.8% | ONS |
| Eggs (a dozen) | £1.55 | £2.00 | 29% | ONS |
| Sugar (kg) | 74p | £1.40 | 89.2% | ONS |
| Draught lager (pint) | £2.33 | £3.67 | 57.5% | ONS |
| Cigarettes (20) | £4.39 | £9.16 | 108.7% | ONS |
| Unleaded petrol per litre | 81.49p | 110.24p | 35.3% | ONS |
| House prices (All UK) | £161,742 | £200,329 | 23.9% | ONS |
| Weekly State Pension | £79.60 | £115.95 | 45.7% | Royal London |
| Price of gold (per ounce) | £223.56 | £880.31 | 293.8% | Goldprice.org |
| Price of oil (per barrel) | $37.66 | $47.10 | 25.1% | Inflationdata.com |
| McDonald's Big Mac | £2.23 | £2.89 | 29.6% | Big-mac-index.com |

Read more: http://www.thisismoney.co.uk/historic-inflation-calculator#ixzz1Bm4ygOL6

# Group F
*Earnings*

**F1:** Earnings losses in personal injury and fatal accident cases

**F2:** Payroll documents

**F3:** National minimum wage

**F4:** Regional unemployment statistics

**F5:** Average weekly earnings index

**F6:** Average weekly earnings

**F7:** Average earnings statistics

**F8:** Public sector comparable earnings

**F9:** Public sector earnings websites

# F1: Earnings losses in personal injury and fatal accident cases

1. **Purpose of note**

   The purpose of this note is to provide some basic guidance on what information to request from a claimant in order to make an initial assessment as to whether an earnings loss is likely to arise.

2. **Nature of occupation**

   Identify at an early stage into which category of occupation the claimant falls:

   **Employment**
   — Employee without ownership rights.
   — Director/shareholder (of private company).

   **Self-employment**
   — Sole trader.
   — Partner.

3. **Relevant dates**

   For the purposes of proposing the periods for which information should be requested, relevant dates will be identified as follows:

   **For an individual in employment**
   (References here are to tax years ending on 5 April although the tax for many salaried employees will often effectively run from 1 April to 31 March.)

   D1   6 April three years before D2
   D2   5 April immediately preceding D3
   D3   Incident date
   D4   5 April immediately preceding D5
   D5   Present time

   **For business accounts**
   D6   Date of beginning of accounting period three years before D7
   D7   Date of end of accounting period immediately preceding D3
   D8   Date of end of accounting period immediately preceding D5

   A full three years' pre-accident financial information should often be sufficient (having regard to the need for proportionality), although documentation for a longer period may be appropriate if it emerges that business results have been volatile.

   **For an individual in employment**

| D1 | | D2 | [ D3 Incident ] | | D4 | D5 |
|---|---|---|---|---|---|---|
| 6 April   5 April | 6 April   5 April | 6 April   5 April | 6 April   5 April | 6 April   5 April | 6 April   5 April | 6 April   Present time |
| Tax year −3 | Tax year −2 | Tax year −1 | Tax year 0 | Tax year +1 | Current tax year −1 | Current tax year |

Sweet & Maxwell

F1: Earnings losses in personal injury and fatal accident cases

**For business accounts**

| D6 | | D7 | [ D3 Incident ] | | D8 | D5 |
|---|---|---|---|---|---|---|
| Beginning   End | Beginning   End | Beginning   End | Beginning   End | Beginning   End | Beginning            End | Beginning        Present time |
| Accounts year −3 | Accounts year −2 | Accounts year −1 | Accounts year 0 | Accounts year +1 | Current accounts year −1 | Current accounts year |

4. **Employment: Employee without ownership rights**

   This is the likely category for most employees—but excluding in particular those who are directors and/or shareholders with a degree of control over private companies.

   In the absence of detailed representations from the employer, or from an employment expert, the earnings history may be the only useful guide to potential earnings but for the incident giving rise to the claim.

   The most useful documentation will usually be a comprehensive set of pay advices (monthly, sometimes four-weekly, or weekly) because these may be expected to show:

   - basic pay level (and dates/amounts of periodic increases),
   - overtime (if paid) and any other regular or periodic enhancements,
   - bonuses (and dates/amounts paid),
   - sick pay (and dates), and
   - employee pension contributions.

   Request:

   - **Pay advices (whether from employment or subsequent pension) from D1 to D5.**
   - **Details of benefits other than pay for each tax year between D1 and D2 and for each tax year since D2.**

5. **Employment: Director/shareholders**

   This category relates mainly to those individuals who have a degree of ownership or control, probably in a private company, and whose remuneration as such may not be a fair reflection of the personal reward available from the business.

   For instance:

   - profits may have been drawn by way of dividend for reasons of tax efficiency; or
   - profits (which the claimant could have drawn) have been re-invested in the business.

   It may well be appropriate to assess loss along the lines that would be adopted in relation to a sole trader or partner, that is:

   - first to identify whether a business loss has occurred that is attributable to the claim incident, and
   - if so, go on to identify the share of the business loss suffered personally by the claimant.

   In such a case, it will often be appropriate to review not only the remuneration history of the individual but also the dividend history. Benefits history may also be important.

Request:

*Regarding the business*

- **full accounts (including detailed profit and loss accounts) from D6 to D8,**

  and consider requesting

- **figures for monthly (preferably) or quarterly sales from D6 to D5.**
  (Important if the claimant's role is likely to have influenced sales levels; the figures should show trends and seasonality, etc.)

*Regarding the claimant*

- **pay advices (whether from employment or pension) from D1 to D5, and**
- **tax returns from D1 to D4.**
  (Mainly to check remuneration and dividends received in each tax year, but also benefits and any personal pension contributions, etc.)

6. **Self-employment: Sole trader**

   Request:

   - **full accounts from D6 to D8,**
   - **figures for monthly or quarterly sales from D6 to D5, and**
   - **tax returns from D1 to D4.**
     (Mainly to check private usage deductions from business expenses, capital allowances, personal pension contributions, etc.)

7. **Self-employment: Partner**

   Approach will be:

   - first to identify whether a business loss has occurred that is attributable to the claim incident, and
   - if so, go on to identify the share of the business loss suffered personally by the claimant.

   Request:

   *Regarding the business*

   - **full partnership accounts from D6 to D8, and**
   - **figures for monthly (preferably) or quarterly sales from D6 to D5.**

   *Regarding the claimant*

   - **personal tax returns from D1 to D4.**
     (Mainly to check personal pension contributions, etc.)

8. **Benefits other than pay (employees)**

   In the first instance, it is probably sufficient simply to ask, in relation to any employee (including a company director), for:

   - **details of any non-pecuniary benefits in employment, and any pension benefits.**

## 9. Other points

- **Company searches**

Searches of small UK limited companies seldom yield helpful results as regards accounts because the contents of the accounts to be filed are invariably in abbreviated form, sometimes only a balance sheet.

In cases where there are doubts about full disclosure, a search may be useful in identifying whether a claimant has more directorships than advised, or possibly a history of connections with insolvent companies.

- **Permanent Health Insurance income**

Where a claimant receives insurance money through his employer, this will usually be evident from review of the pay advices.

As to whether credit needs to be given by the claimant for such insurance money for claim purposes will probably depend on the nature of the underlying policy. See *Gaca v Pirelli General plc*.[1]

- **Ill-health pension**

Where a claimant receives an ill-health pension following an incident, this should again be evident from review of the pay advices.

Generally, no credit is to be given for actual pension in a loss of earnings claim: *Parry v Cleaver*.[2]

- **Partnerships**

There may be cases where the profit-sharing arrangements do not reflect the realistic commercial input of the respective partners. This issue may arise particularly where spouses are business partners. The court may be prepared to put aside the historic arrangements in assessing loss: *Ward v Newalls Insulation Co Ltd*.[3]

---

[1] [2004] 1 W.L.R. 2683.
[2] [1970] A.C. 1.
[3] [1998] 1 W.L.R. 1722.

# F2: Payroll documents

## SPECIMEN PAY ADVICE

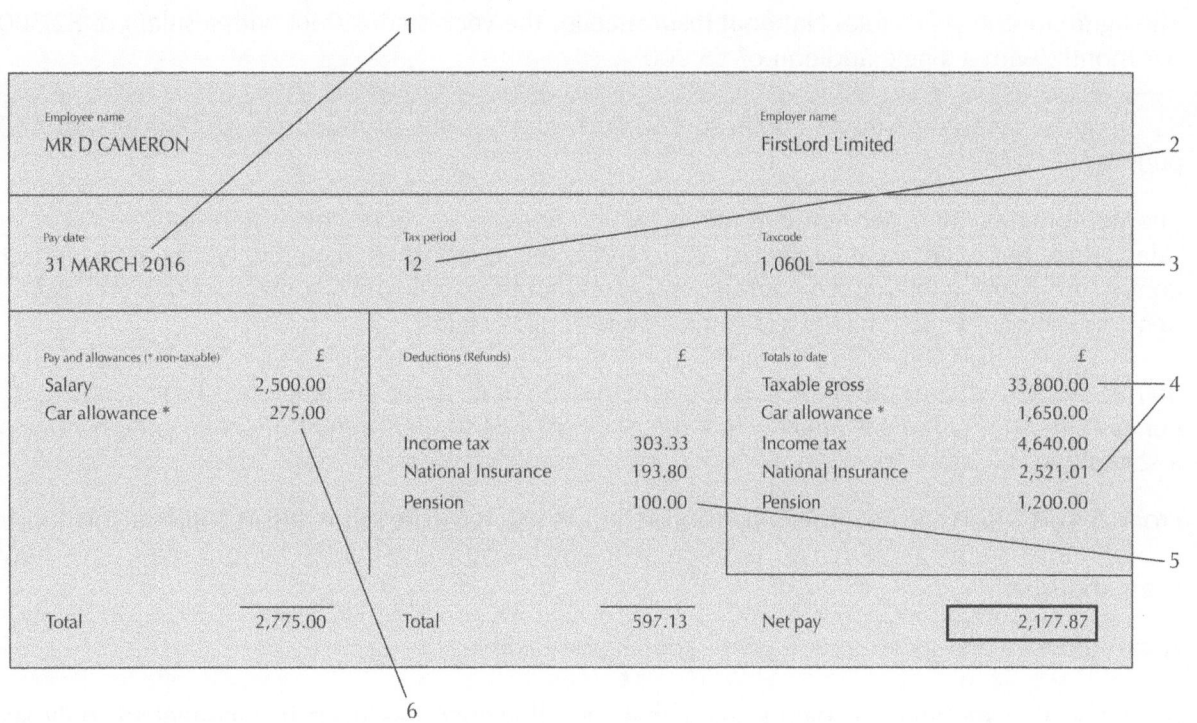

### Points to note

1. As good a starting point as any is usually a pay advice at the end of the **last full tax year**, but try also to obtain all subsequent pay advices whether to date of trial in a personal injury case or to date of death if a fatal accident.

2. It is worth bearing in mind that some employers pay every four weeks, and on rare occasions every two weeks, rather than necessarily monthly or weekly. The tax period should help to identify payment frequency.

3. The tax code, **1060L**, represents the basic tax allowance of £10,600. This indicates that the tax inspector has no reason to make any adjustment to the standard code to collect additional tax due in the year.

   This in turn implies that the employee has no taxable benefits from the employer.

   The most common taxable benefits are probably health insurance cover and those related to private use of motor vehicles.

   By way of example, were the employee enjoying taxable benefits to a value of £1,000 p.a., the code could be expected to be 960L. Application of this code would result in the tax due on the benefit being collected under PAYE over the course of the tax year.

4. In the illustration shown above, the **gross taxable income** figure requires some reconciliation to other figures.

## F2: Payroll documents

The year-end figures suggest that salary has probably been running consistently at £2,500 per month (i.e. £30,000 per annum), with a £100 per month pension contribution. That would produce a taxable total of £28,800 in the year, suggesting that there has been additional pay of £5,000 in arriving at the taxable gross figure of £33,800.

The figure for the year's total **National Insurance** for the year is consistent with a salary of £2,500 per month, with a single addition of £5,000.

So the gross taxable seems to comprise £30,000 salary, a one-off bonus of £5,000 less £1,200 pension contributions.

5   The combination of a **pension deduction,** which appears to represent exactly four per cent of salary, together with the fact that it can readily be established that the National Insurance contributions are at contracted out rates, suggests that the employee is a member of a final salary pension scheme, which may give rise to a pension loss claim.

(In the case of a money purchase pension scheme, the deductions are made less basic rate tax, 20 per cent in 2015/16, so it is unlikely that the amount of £100.00 is a monthly contribution to such a scheme.)

From 2016/17 tax year, final salary pension schemes will have the same rate of National Insurance contributions as money purchase pension schemes because the contracted-out rates have now been abolished.

6   A **car allowance** is shown, but it is marked as non-taxable.

Note also that the totals to date suggest that the allowance has been in payment for only six months in the year.

Generally, if an allowance is non-taxable, it is unlikely to represent a valuable benefit. Perhaps the car allowance in this case is a fixed level reimbursement of business costs on a prescribed formula, which will be adjusted after the year-end in accordance with actual business mileage or the like.

Nevertheless it would be worth establishing why the car allowance was not in payment throughout the year.

# F3: National Minimum Wage and National Living Wage

**Introductory notes**

1. The National Minimum Wage became law on 1 April 1999 and the National Living Wage became law on 1 April 2016.

2. The National Minimum Wage is the minimum amount of pay to which workers over a specified age are entitled. Up to 30 September 2004, the minimum age was 18. Since 1 October 2004 a new rate has been available to workers under 18 who are no longer of compulsory school age. The National Living Wage was introduced on 1 April 2016 for workers aged 25 and older. The National Minimum Wage still applies for workers aged under 25.

3. Most adult workers who are resident in the UK, who have a written, oral or implied contract and who are not genuinely self-employed, are entitled to the National Minimum Wage or National Living Wage.

4. The National Minimum Wage and National Living Wage are enforced by HM Revenue and Customs.

5. There are currently four levels of National Minimum Wage: a development rate for those aged between 18 and 20; a main rate for workers aged between 21 and 24; from 1 October 2004, a rate for workers under 18 who are no longer of compulsory school age; and, from 1 October 2010, an apprentice minimum wage (see note 8, below).

6. The main rate was extended to workers aged 21 or over from October 2010. Prior to that the qualifying age for the main rate was 22. Correspondingly the development rate has been available to those aged between 18 and 20 from October 2010. Prior to that it was available to those aged between 18 and 21.

7. A development rate available, subject to various conditions, to workers aged 22 or over who started a new job with a new employer and did accredited training, being a course approved by the UK government to obtain a vocational qualification, was abolished for pay reference periods starting on or after 1 October 2006. When applicable, the accredited training rate could only be paid for the first six months of the new job, after which the National Minimum Wage main rate applied.

8. A new apprentice minimum wage was introduced with effect from 1 October 2010, available to apprentices aged under 19, or apprentices aged 19 or over but in the first year of their apprenticeship.

9. The government has announced that they will align the National Minimum Wage and National Living Wages cycles so that both rates are amended in April each year. This will take effect from April 2017.

F3: National Minimum Wage and National Living Wage

**National Minimum Wage**

|  | Pay reference periods starting on or after 1 October | | | | | | |
|---|---|---|---|---|---|---|---|
|  | 2010 £/hr | 2011 £/hr | 2012 £/hr | 2013 £/hr | 2014 £/hr | 2015 £/hr | 2016 £/hr |
| Workers under 18 who are no longer of compulsory school age (notes 2 and 5) | 3.64 | 3.68 | 3.68 | 3.72 | 3.79 | 3.87 | 4.00 |
| Development rate for workers aged 18 to 20 years (from October 2010) (notes 5 and 6) | 4.92 | 4.98 | 4.98 | 5.03 | 5.13 | 5.30 | 5.55 |
| Rate for apprentices aged under 19, or 19 or over but in the first year of their apprenticeship (note 8) | 2.50 | 2.60 | 2.65 | 2.68 | 2.73 | 3.30 | 3.40 |
| **Main rate** for workers aged 21 or over from October 2010 and for workers aged 21 to 24 years from April 2016 (notes 2, 5, and 9) | 5.93 | 6.08 | 6.19 | 6.31 | 6.50 | 6.70 | 6.95 |

**National Living Wage**

|  | Pay reference periods starting on or after 1 April | | | | | | |
|---|---|---|---|---|---|---|---|
|  | 2010 £/hr | 2011 £/hr | 2012 £/hr | 2013 £/hr | 2014 £/hr | 2015 £/hr | 2016 £/hr |
| For workers aged 25 or over from April 2016 (see note 2) | n/a | n/a | n/a | n/a | n/a | n/a | 7.20 |

# F4: Regional unemployment statistics

In previous years, tables showing the average duration of claims for Jobseeker's Allowance have been drawn from the Office of National Statistics Economic and Labour Market Review. This is no longer being produced.

The tables below have been based on data available on the Nomis website for March 2016.

**North East**
Median duration
(weeks)

| Age | Female | Male | All |
|---|---|---|---|
| Under 17 | 4.0 | 0.0 | 1.0 |
| 17 | 6.0 | 7.0 | 7.0 |
| 18 | 12.8 | 11.1 | 11.8 |
| 19 | 14.4 | 15.9 | 15.4 |
| 20–24 | 17.5 | 17.0 | 17.2 |
| 25–29 | 19.1 | 19.0 | 19.0 |
| 30–34 | 20.0 | 19.1 | 19.4 |
| 35–39 | 19.5 | 20.4 | 20.1 |
| 40–44 | 19.5 | 21.6 | 20.8 |
| 45–49 | 18.7 | 22.5 | 21.4 |
| 50–54 | 19.2 | 21.9 | 21.0 |
| 55–59 | 19.8 | 22.0 | 21.3 |
| 60+ | 20.0 | 19.3 | 19.5 |

**North West**
Median duration
(weeks)

| Age | Female | Male | All |
|---|---|---|---|
| Under 17 | 4.0 | 1.0 | 6.0 |
| 17 | 4.8 | 4.3 | 4.5 |
| 18 | 8.5 | 8.3 | 8.4 |
| 19 | 12.2 | 12.8 | 12.7 |
| 20–24 | 15.4 | 15.1 | 15.2 |
| 25–29 | 18.7 | 18.2 | 18.4 |
| 30–34 | 20.2 | 19.9 | 20.0 |
| 35–39 | 22.7 | 21.7 | 22.1 |
| 40–44 | 24.0 | 23.0 | 23.4 |
| 45–49 | 23.2 | 26.4 | 25.0 |
| 50–54 | 22.2 | 26.2 | 24.6 |
| 55–59 | 21.7 | 32.0 | 25.8 |
| 60+ | 21.3 | 24.8 | 23.6 |

**Yorkshire and the Humber**
Median duration
(weeks)

| Age | Female | Male | All |
|---|---|---|---|
| Under 17 | 1.0 | 2.0 | 2.0 |
| 17 | 5.0 | 3.2 | 3.7 |
| 18 | 8.8 | 8.9 | 8.8 |
| 19 | 14.7 | 13.3 | 13.9 |
| 20–24 | 15.1 | 15.2 | 15.2 |
| 25–29 | 18.7 | 17.1 | 17.7 |
| 30–34 | 20.9 | 18.5 | 19.4 |
| 35–39 | 22.4 | 21.0 | 21.5 |
| 40–44 | 23.4 | 24.1 | 23.8 |
| 45–49 | 24.8 | 25.9 | 25.5 |
| 50–54 | 22.7 | 25.9 | 24.7 |
| 55–59 | 22.5 | 27.9 | 25.3 |
| 60+ | 23.9 | 25.0 | 24.7 |

**East Midlands**
Median duration
(weeks)

| Age | Female | Male | All |
|---|---|---|---|
| Under 17 | 3.0 | 1.0 | 3.0 |
| 17 | 5.3 | 4.5 | 5.0 |
| 18 | 11.1 | 12.2 | 11.7 |
| 19 | 15.5 | 13.4 | 14.3 |
| 20–24 | 16.3 | 14.7 | 15.3 |
| 25–29 | 17.9 | 15.8 | 16.6 |
| 30–34 | 16.9 | 17.1 | 17.0 |
| 35–39 | 19.7 | 17.9 | 18.6 |
| 40–44 | 19.8 | 20.9 | 20.5 |
| 45–49 | 22.4 | 21.9 | 22.1 |
| 50–54 | 20.5 | 22.8 | 21.9 |
| 55–59 | 21.6 | 24.6 | 23.6 |
| 60+ | 23.7 | 22.2 | 22.7 |

F4: Regional unemployment statistics

### West Midlands
Median duration (weeks)

| Age | Female | Male | All |
|---|---|---|---|
| Under 17 | 4.0 | 2.7 | 3.0 |
| 17 | 6.0 | 6.0 | 6.0 |
| 18 | 10.8 | 10.1 | 10.4 |
| 19 | 16.7 | 15.2 | 15.8 |
| 20–24 | 18.4 | 18.6 | 18.6 |
| 25–29 | 23.5 | 22.7 | 23.0 |
| 30–34 | 22.2 | 24.8 | 23.7 |
| 35–39 | 24.6 | 25.4 | 25.1 |
| 40–44 | 27.5 | 31.4 | 29.8 |
| 45–49 | 27.0 | 35.6 | 32.3 |
| 50–54 | 24.5 | 43.6 | 34.5 |
| 55–59 | 26.3 | 43.0 | 35.7 |
| 60+ | 27.2 | 31.8 | 30.1 |

### East
Median duration (weeks)

| Age | Female | Male | All |
|---|---|---|---|
| Under 17 | 6.0 | 0.7 | 4.0 |
| 17 | 5.4 | 6.0 | 5.8 |
| 18 | 8.2 | 8.5 | 8.4 |
| 19 | 12.0 | 11.7 | 11.8 |
| 20–24 | 12.4 | 12.5 | 12.5 |
| 25–29 | 14.5 | 13.6 | 13.9 |
| 30–34 | 13.6 | 13.9 | 13.8 |
| 35–39 | 16.3 | 15.5 | 15.8 |
| 40–44 | 17.6 | 17.9 | 17.8 |
| 45–49 | 17.7 | 19.5 | 18.7 |
| 50–54 | 18.0 | 22.2 | 20.6 |
| 55–59 | 17.9 | 22.3 | 20.6 |
| 60+ | 17.6 | 20.2 | 19.3 |

### London
Median duration (weeks)

| Age | Female | Male | All |
|---|---|---|---|
| Under 17 | 2.0 | 1.0 | 4.0 |
| 17 | 6.0 | 5.5 | 5.6 |
| 18 | 6.9 | 8.8 | 8.2 |
| 19 | 11.6 | 11.2 | 11.4 |
| 20–24 | 12.2 | 12.8 | 12.6 |
| 25–29 | 14.9 | 14.9 | 14.9 |
| 30–34 | 16.5 | 16.8 | 16.6 |
| 35–39 | 18.8 | 18.6 | 18.7 |
| 40–44 | 20.9 | 20.5 | 20.7 |
| 45–49 | 22.7 | 23.8 | 23.3 |
| 50–54 | 22.7 | 27.4 | 24.9 |
| 55–59 | 24.1 | 29.6 | 26.6 |
| 60+ | 25.9 | 31.7 | 29.5 |

### South East
Median duration (weeks)

| Age | Female | Male | All |
|---|---|---|---|
| Under 17 | 3.3 | 4.0 | 3.5 |
| 17 | 3.8 | 4.0 | 4.0 |
| 18 | 7.9 | 9.3 | 8.7 |
| 19 | 12.1 | 12.8 | 12.6 |
| 20–24 | 12.5 | 14.1 | 13.5 |
| 25–29 | 14.3 | 13.8 | 14.0 |
| 30–34 | 14.0 | 13.8 | 13.9 |
| 35–39 | 16.3 | 15.6 | 15.9 |
| 40–44 | 16.3 | 17.5 | 17.0 |
| 45–49 | 17.5 | 20.2 | 19.1 |
| 50–54 | 17.7 | 21.4 | 19.9 |
| 55–59 | 17.7 | 22.0 | 20.3 |
| 60+ | 17.7 | 19.8 | 19.1 |

### South West
Median duration (weeks)

| Age | Female | Male | All |
|---|---|---|---|
| Under 17 | 4.0 | 6.0 | 6.0 |
| 17 | 5.0 | 6.0 | 5.7 |
| 18 | 9.1 | 11.5 | 10.6 |
| 19 | 13.4 | 14.0 | 13.8 |
| 20–24 | 12.0 | 15.0 | 13.8 |
| 25–29 | 12.7 | 13.9 | 13.4 |
| 30–34 | 13.0 | 12.7 | 12.8 |
| 35–39 | 13.8 | 15.1 | 14.6 |
| 40–44 | 14.6 | 16.7 | 15.9 |
| 45–49 | 15.2 | 18.1 | 17.0 |
| 50–54 | 13.9 | 20.3 | 17.7 |
| 55–59 | 16.5 | 20.5 | 18.9 |
| 60+ | 14.8 | 17.9 | 16.8 |

### England
Median duration (weeks)

| Age | Female | Male | All |
|---|---|---|---|
| Under 17 | 3.7 | 3.6 | 3.7 |
| 17 | 5.2 | 5.2 | 5.2 |
| 18 | 9.2 | 9.7 | 9.5 |
| 19 | 13.7 | 13.3 | 13.4 |
| 20–24 | 14.5 | 15.0 | 14.8 |
| 25–29 | 17.1 | 16.8 | 16.9 |
| 30–34 | 17.7 | 17.8 | 17.8 |
| 35–39 | 19.6 | 19.5 | 19.5 |
| 40–44 | 20.7 | 21.4 | 21.1 |
| 45–49 | 21.5 | 23.6 | 22.7 |
| 50–54 | 20.7 | 24.9 | 23.2 |
| 55–59 | 21.4 | 25.8 | 24.1 |
| 60+ | 21.7 | 23.6 | 23.0 |

## F4: Regional unemployment statistics

### Wales
#### Median duration (weeks)

| Age | Female | Male | All |
|---|---|---|---|
| Under 17 | 1.0 | 0.0 | 1.0 |
| 17 | 2.5 | 4.0 | 3.4 |
| 18 | 10.8 | 10.1 | 10.4 |
| 19 | 16.9 | 14.9 | 15.8 |
| 20–24 | 21.2 | 20.9 | 21.0 |
| 25–29 | 20.6 | 20.1 | 20.3 |
| 30–34 | 21.7 | 22.4 | 22.1 |
| 35–39 | 22.3 | 23.4 | 22.9 |
| 40–44 | 23.0 | 25.5 | 24.4 |
| 45–49 | 25.4 | 26.4 | 25.9 |
| 50–54 | 24.1 | 28.3 | 25.9 |
| 55–59 | 24.9 | 32.4 | 29.3 |
| 60+ | 24.1 | 25.7 | 25.1 |

### Scotland
#### Median duration (weeks)

| Age | Female | Male | All |
|---|---|---|---|
| Under 17 | 3.8 | 4.7 | 4.0 |
| 17 | 5.8 | 8.9 | 8.2 |
| 18 | 11.2 | 10.1 | 10.6 |
| 19 | 14.0 | 14.5 | 14.3 |
| 20–24 | 14.7 | 15.6 | 15.4 |
| 25–29 | 16.3 | 18.3 | 17.7 |
| 30–34 | 17.5 | 18.5 | 18.1 |
| 35–39 | 18.8 | 21.3 | 20.5 |
| 40–44 | 21.8 | 23.3 | 22.7 |
| 45–49 | 22.9 | 25.9 | 24.8 |
| 50–54 | 20.4 | 26.8 | 24.4 |
| 55–59 | 20.0 | 26.0 | 24.1 |
| 60+ | 24.5 | 22.7 | 23.2 |

### Northern Ireland
#### Median duration (weeks)

| Age | Female | Male | All |
|---|---|---|---|
| Under 17 | 0.0 | 0.0 | 0.0 |
| 17 | 5.0 | 4.7 | 4.8 |
| 18 | 15.4 | 12.6 | 13.7 |
| 19 | 16.8 | 18.6 | 17.9 |
| 20–24 | 23.2 | 23.8 | 23.6 |
| 25–29 | 22.3 | 28.2 | 26.2 |
| 30–34 | 24.5 | 29.1 | 27.6 |
| 35–39 | 28.8 | 34.2 | 32.5 |
| 40–44 | 37.6 | 45.8 | 42.7 |
| 45–49 | 38.8 | 56.7 | 49.2 |
| 50–54 | 43.0 | 51.7 | 48.4 |
| 55–59 | 35.7 | 55.5 | 47.3 |
| 60+ | 38.7 | 55.5 | 48.9 |

### United Kingdom
#### Median duration (weeks)

| Age | Female | Male | All |
|---|---|---|---|
| Under 17 | 3.7 | 4.0 | 3.8 |
| 17 | 5.3 | 5.6 | 5.4 |
| 18 | 9.9 | 10.0 | 10.0 |
| 19 | 14.3 | 14.2 | 14.2 |
| 20–24 | 15.5 | 16.2 | 16.0 |
| 25–29 | 17.5 | 17.9 | 17.7 |
| 30–34 | 18.2 | 18.8 | 18.6 |
| 35–39 | 20.0 | 20.5 | 20.3 |
| 40–44 | 21.3 | 22.5 | 22.0 |
| 45–49 | 22.3 | 24.7 | 23.7 |
| 50–54 | 21.5 | 25.7 | 24.0 |
| 55–59 | 22.0 | 27.3 | 24.9 |
| 60+ | 22.6 | 24.3 | 23.8 |

## F4: Regional unemployment statistics

Labour Force Survey (November–January 2016)

Thousands, seasonally adjusted

| | Total aged 16-64 | Economically active | | | | | | | Employment | | | | | | | | Unemployment | | | | | |
|---|---|---|---|---|---|---|---|---|---|---|---|---|---|---|---|---|---|---|---|---|---|---|
| | | Total | | Men | | Women | | Total | | Men | | | Women | | | Total | | Men | | Women | | |
| | Level | Level | Rate (%)* | Level | Rate(%)* | Level | Rate (%)* | Level | Rate (%)* | Level | Rate (%)* | Level | Rate (%)* | Level | Rate (%)** | Level | Rate (%)** | Level | Rate (%)** | |
| | 1 | 2 | 3 | 4 | 5 | 6 | 7 | 8 | 9 | 10 | 11 | 12 | 13 | 14 | 15 | 16 | 17 | 18 | 19 |
| North East | 1661 | 1272 | 76.6 | 666 | 81.1 | 606 | 72.2 | 1,172 | 70.6 | 610 | 74.3 | 562 | 66.9 | 100 | 7.9 | 56 | 8.4 | 44 | 7.2 |
| North West | 4,515 | 3,478 | 77 | 1,841 | 82 | 1,637 | 72.1 | 3,303 | 73.2 | 1,746 | 77.7 | 1,557 | 68.7 | 175 | 5 | 96 | 5.2 | 79 | 4.8 |
| Yorkshire & the Humber | 3,387 | 2,598 | 76.7 | 1,388 | 82.1 | 1,210 | 74.1 | 2,436 | 71.9 | 1,289 | 76.2 | 1,147 | 67.6 | 162 | 6.2 | 99 | 7.1 | 63 | 5.2 |
| East Midlands | 2,902 | 2,264 | 78 | 1,204 | 83.4 | 1,060 | 72.7 | 2,162 | 74.5 | 1,151 | 77 | 1,011 | 65.1 | 103 | 5.6 | 53 | 5.9 | 50 | 5.3 |
| West Midlands | 3,547 | 2,672 | 75.3 | 1,451 | 81.9 | 1,221 | 68.8 | 2,521 | 71.1 | 1,365 | 77 | 1,156 | 65.1 | 151 | 5.6 | 86 | 5.9 | 65 | 5.3 |
| East | 3,707 | 3,002 | 81 | 1,596 | 86.7 | 1,406 | 75.4 | 2,891 | 78 | 1,541 | 83.7 | 1,350 | 72.3 | 112 | 3.7 | 55 | 3.4 | 57 | 4 |
| London | 5,788 | 4,493 | 77.6 | 2,449 | 84.8 | 2,044 | 70.4 | 4,208 | 72.7 | 2,303 | 79.8 | 1,906 | 65.7 | 285 | 6.3 | 146 | 6 | 139 | 6.8 |
| South East | 5,488 | 4,449 | 81.1 | 2,349 | 86.2 | 2,100 | 76 | 4,275 | 77.9 | 2,260 | 82.9 | 2,014 | 72.9 | 174 | 3.9 | 88 | 3.8 | 86 | 4.1 |
| South West | 3,290 | 2,641 | 80.3 | 1,383 | 84.7 | 1,259 | 76 | 2,538 | 77.1 | 1,327 | 81.3 | 1,211 | 73.1 | 103 | 3.9 | 55 | 4 | 48 | 3.8 |
| England | 34,285 | 26,870 | 78.4 | 14,327 | 84 | 12,543 | 72.8 | 25,506 | 74.1 | 13,592 | 79.7 | 11,913 | 69.2 | 1,364 | 5.1 | 734 | 5.1 | 630 | 5 |
| Wales | 1,911 | 1,445 | 75.6 | 764 | 80.2 | 681 | 71.1 | 1,366 | 71.5 | 716 | 75.2 | 650 | 67.8 | 80 | 5.5 | 48 | 6.3 | 32 | 4.6 |
| Scotland | 3,413 | 2,712 | 79.5 | 1,393 | 83.5 | 1,318 | 75.6 | 2,542 | 74.5 | 1,293 | 77.5 | 1,249 | 71.6 | 170 | 6.3 | 100 | 7.2 | 70 | 5.3 |
| N Ireland | 1,167 | 858 | 73.6 | 464 | 80.4 | 394 | 66.9 | 805 | 69 | 434 | 75.1 | 372 | 63.1 | 53 | 6.2 | 30 | 6.5 | 22 | 5.7 |
| United Kingdom[1] | | | | | | | | | | | | | | | | | | | |

Relationship between columns: 2 = 4+6 = 8+14; 8 = 10+12; 14 = 16+18

[1] Due to slight methodological differences between the way the national and regional LFS estimates have been interim adjusted for the 2001 Census, there may be small differences between the UK totals and the sum of the regional components.

* Denominator = all persons of working age
** Denominator = Total economically active

Data source: Labour Force Survey
Labour market statistics enquiries: labour.market@ons.gov.uk

## Labour Force Survey

The table reports headline labour market indicators for the UK and its constituent regions and nations. These are reported for the working age population (16–64 years) and include the number economically active in the working age population, the number in employment or self-employment (or government employment scheme) and the number unemployed. The statistics are derived from the Labour Force Survey (LFS) for November to January 2016. Updated statistics are available on NOMIS (*www.nomisweb.co.uk*). The UK statistics are reported in Table A02 and the regional statistics are reported in Tables HI01 to HI11.

Unemployment is defined using the ILO definition and includes those who were without work during the reference week but who are currently available for work and who were either actively seeking work in the past four weeks or who had already found a job to start within the next three months. This definition of unemployment is independent of whether or not the individual is eligible to claim benefit.

Those who are either employed or unemployed (and looking for work) are defined as economically active. The economically inactive are calculated by the difference between the estimate in column 1, the working age population and the estimate in column 2, the economically active working age population. Many people who are disabled will be inactive rather than unemployed.

Non-employment includes unemployment and inactivity. It is the difference between column 1 and column 8.

## Claimant Count v ILO Unemployment

Along with a large number of other countries, the United Kingdom publishes two defined measures of unemployment that complement each other.

One comes from a monthly count of those claiming unemployment-related benefits. This administrative measure is known as the "Claimant Count".

The other comes from a quarterly survey of households, the Labour Force Survey (LFS). This survey measure is accepted as an international standard because it is based on methods recommended by the International Labour Organisation (ILO). It is known as the $p$ and is used by the European Union (EU) and the Organisation for Economic Co-operation and Development (OECD).

Both measures have their advantages and disadvantages.

The advantage of the Claimant Count is that it is available quickly and monthly and because it is a 100 per cent count, it also provides precise information on very small areas.

The ILO measure on the other hand, as well as being internationally standard, springs from a data source (the Labour Force Survey) which allows unemployment to be analysed in the context of other labour market information and a variety of demographic characteristics.

A disadvantage of the Claimant Count is that it can be affected if there are changes to the benefit system from which it is derived.

Although changes in the benefit system may also affect the labour market behaviour of respondents to the LFS, the ILO definition itself is entirely independent of the benefit system. Comparatively the LFS results, based on the ILO measure, are not reliable for areas smaller than counties or the larger local authority districts, because of sample size restrictions. Estimates of less than 10,000 persons unemployed (after grossing up) are not shown in published tables because they are subject to unacceptably high sampling error and are, therefore, unreliable.

This said, government statistics apply recognised statistical procedures in order to minimise these disadvantages and maintain the relevance of both measures as accurate labour market indicators.

F4: Regional unemployment statistics

## Claimant Count Rates

| Area | 2006 | 2007 | 2008 | 2009 | 2010 | 2011 | 2012 | 2013 | 2014 | 2015 |
|---|---|---|---|---|---|---|---|---|---|---|
| North East | 4.1 | 4.1 | 4.5 | 6.9 | 6.7 | 4.7 | 5.4 | 5.4 | 4.2 | 4.0 |
| North West | 3.4 | 3.2 | 3.4 | 5.4 | 5.2 | 4.0 | 4.4 | 4.2 | 3.2 | 2.2 |
| Yorkshire and the Humber | 3.4 | 3.1 | 3.4 | 5.7 | 5.6 | 4.2 | 4.7 | 4.7 | 3.8 | 3.2 |
| East Midlands | 2.9 | 2.6 | 2.8 | 4.9 | 4.6 | 3.4 | 3.7 | 3.6 | 2.7 | 2.2 |
| West Midlands | 3.9 | 3.8 | 3.9 | 6.3 | 5.9 | 4.6 | 4.7 | 4.5 | 3.6 | 3.0 |
| East | 2.3 | 2.1 | 2.2 | 4.0 | 3.8 | 2.9 | 3.0 | 3.0 | 2.2 | 1.6 |
| London | 3.5 | 3.0 | 2.8 | 4.3 | 4.5 | 4.0 | 4.1 | 3.9 | 2.9 | 2.1 |
| South East | 1.9 | 1.6 | 1.7 | 3.3 | 3.1 | 2.5 | 2.5 | 2.4 | 1.8 | 1.3 |
| South West | 1.8 | 1.6 | 1.7 | 3.4 | 3.1 | 2.5 | 2.6 | 2.5 | 1.9 | 1.3 |
| England | 2.9 | 2.7 | 2.8 | 4.7 | 4.5 | 3.7 | 3.9 | 3.7 | 2.9 | 2.1 |
| Wales | 3.1 | 2.9 | 3.3 | 5.5 | 5.2 | 3.8 | 4.0 | 4.0 | 3.4 | 3.2 |
| Scotland | 3.2 | 2.8 | 2.9 | 4.6 | 4.9 | 4.0 | 4.2 | 4.0 | 3.2 | 2.9 |
| Northern Ireland | 3.2 | 2.8 | 3.1 | 5.5 | 6.4 | 6.1 | 5.3 | 5.5 | 4.9 | 5.1 |
| **United Kingdom** | **3.0** | **2.7** | **2.8** | **4.7** | **4.6** | **3.7** | **3.9** | **3.7** | **2.9** | **2.3** |

Percentages, seasonally adjusted annual averages

## ILO Unemployment Rates

| Area | 2006 | 2007 | 2008 | 2009 | 2010 | 2011 | 2012 | 2013 | 2014 | 2015 |
|---|---|---|---|---|---|---|---|---|---|---|
| North East | 6.6 | 5.8 | 8.6 | 9.5 | 10.2 | 9.8 | 10.8 | 10.0 | 9.7 | 7.7 |
| North West | 5.2 | 5.9 | 7.7 | 8.5 | 7.7 | 8.5 | 9.5 | 8.2 | 8.3 | 6.2 |
| Yorkshire and the Humber | 5.7 | 5.5 | 7.1 | 9.6 | 9.3 | 8.7 | 9.7 | 9.3 | 8.8 | 6.0 |
| East Midlands | 5.2 | 5.7 | 6.4 | 7.8 | 8.0 | 7.9 | 8.3 | 8.0 | 7.2 | 5.0 |
| West Midlands | 5.8 | 6.3 | 7.9 | 9.5 | 9.9 | 8.7 | 8.5 | 9.5 | 8.4 | 6.5 |
| East | 4.8 | 5.0 | 5.5 | 6.6 | 6.2 | 6.7 | 6.6 | 6.9 | 5.9 | 5.1 |
| London | 7.8 | 6.4 | 7.5 | 8.9 | 9.4 | 9.4 | 8.9 | 8.7 | 8.2 | 6.2 |
| South East | 4.5 | 4.6 | 4.8 | 6.4 | 6.3 | 5.7 | 6.3 | 6.8 | 5.3 | 4.5 |
| South West | 3.7 | 3.9 | 5.1 | 6.4 | 6.3 | 5.7 | 5.9 | 6.4 | 6.0 | 4.5 |
| England | 5.5 | 5.4 | 6.6 | 8.0 | 7.9 | 7.8 | 8.1 | 8.0 | 7.3 | 5.6 |
| Wales | 3.7 | 5.1 | 7.6 | 6.4 | 8.7 | 7.9 | 9.0 | 8.3 | 6.9 | 6.2 |
| Scotland | 5.2 | 4.6 | 5.1 | 7.8 | 8.1 | 7.7 | 7.9 | 7.5 | 7.1 | 5.9 |
| Northern Ireland | 4.4 | 4.0 | 5.7 | 6.4 | 8.0 | 7.1 | 6.9 | 8.3 | 7.7 | 6.0 |
| **United Kingdom** | **5.6** | **5.3** | **6.5** | **8.0** | **8.0** | **7.8** | **8.1** | **8.0** | **7.3** | **5.6** |

Percentages, Spring each year, seasonally adjusted

# F5: Average weekly earnings index

## Average weekly earnings index

Whole economy, excluding bonuses and arrears of pay, and seasonally adjusted.

|  | 2000 | 2001 | 2002 | 2003 | 2004 | 2005 |
|---|---|---|---|---|---|---|
| January | 99.0 | 102.5 | 107.1 | 110.8 | 114.6 | 119.3 |
| February | 98.9 | 102.5 | 107.9 | 111.1 | 114.7 | 119.5 |
| March | 98.7 | 103.2 | 108.1 | 111.3 | 115.1 | 120.2 |
| April | 98.7 | 104.0 | 108.4 | 111.7 | 115.6 | 120.6 |
| May | 99.3 | 104.1 | 108.4 | 112.0 | 116.0 | 120.8 |
| June | 99.4 | 104.3 | 109.1 | 112.2 | 116.3 | 121.2 |
| July | 99.7 | 105.0 | 109.3 | 112.5 | 116.7 | 121.9 |
| August | 100.1 | 105.7 | 109.0 | 112.9 | 117.2 | 122.4 |
| September | 100.9 | 105.8 | 109.3 | 113.3 | 117.4 | 122.8 |
| October | 101.3 | 106.2 | 109.5 | 113.6 | 118.0 | 123.0 |
| November | 101.7 | 106.6 | 109.8 | 114.0 | 118.3 | 123.3 |
| December | 102.2 | 106.7 | 109.8 | 114.5 | 119.1 | 123.6 |
| Yearly Average | 100.0 | 104.7 | 108.8 | 112.5 | 116.6 | 121.6 |

|  | 2006 | 2007 | 2008 | 2009 | 2010 | 2011 |
|---|---|---|---|---|---|---|
| January | 124.2 | 128.9 | 134.2 | 138.0 | 140.5 | 143.6 |
| February | 124.6 | 129.4 | 134.8 | 138.3 | 140.4 | 143.3 |
| March | 124.8 | 130.0 | 135.3 | 138.2 | 141.1 | 143.4 |
| April | 125.0 | 130.1 | 136.3 | 138.7 | 140.7 | 143.6 |
| May | 125.7 | 131.0 | 135.9 | 138.9 | 140.6 | 143.8 |
| June | 126.3 | 131.6 | 136.3 | 139.0 | 141.0 | 143.8 |
| July | 126.3 | 132.1 | 136.7 | 138.6 | 141.6 | 144.0 |
| August | 126.5 | 132.7 | 137.0 | 138.8 | 141.9 | 144.1 |
| September | 127.1 | 132.9 | 137.3 | 139.1 | 142.2 | 144.6 |
| October | 127.9 | 132.9 | 137.8 | 139.2 | 142.3 | 144.9 |
| November | 128.2 | 133.6 | 137.9 | 139.3 | 142.6 | 145.2 |
| December | 128.7 | 133.8 | 138.0 | 139.8 | 142.5 | 145.2 |
| Yearly Average | 126.3 | 131.6 | 136.5 | 138.8 | 141.5 | 144.1 |

|  | 2012 | 2013 | 2014 | 2015 | 2016 |
|---|---|---|---|---|---|
| January | 145.0 | 146.6 | 149.2 | 151.5 | 155.0 |
| February | 145.8 | 146.8 | 148.6 | 152.1 | 155.6 |
| March | 146.2 | 147.0 | 148.5 | 152.7 | 155.4 |
| April | 146.0 | 148.0 | 148.7 | 152.9 | |
| May | 146.3 | 147.9 | 148.9 | 153.1 | |
| June | 146.6 | 147.9 | 149.2 | 153.4 | |
| July | 146.6 | 148.1 | 149.3 | 153.6 | |
| August | 147.2 | 148.1 | 149.7 | 153.6 | |
| September | 146.8 | 148.0 | 150.7 | 153.5 | |
| October | 146.8 | 148.3 | 151.2 | 153.7 | |
| November | 147.3 | 148.3 | 150.9 | 154.2 | |
| December | 147.0 | 148.9 | 151.3 | 154.5 | |
| Yearly Average | 146.5 | 147.8 | 149.7 | 153.2 | |

ONS index reference: K54L

# F6: Average weekly earnings

These figures are the average (mean) gross weekly earnings of full-time employees on adult rates whose pay was not affected by absence.

|        | Men   | Women |
|--------|-------|-------|
|        | £     | £     |
| 1985   | 192.4 | 126.4 |
| 1986   | 207.5 | 137.2 |
| 1987   | 224.0 | 148.1 |
| 1988   | 245.8 | 164.2 |
| 1989   | 269.5 | 182.3 |
| 1990   | 295.6 | 201.5 |
| 1991   | 318.9 | 222.4 |
| 1992   | 340.1 | 241.1 |
| 1993   | 353.5 | 252.6 |
| 1994   | 362.1 | 261.5 |
| 1995   | 374.6 | 269.8 |
| 1996   | 391.6 | 283.0 |
| 1997   | 408.7 | 297.2 |
| 1998   | 427.1 | 309.6 |
| 1999   | 442.4 | 326.5 |
| 2000   | 453.3 | 337.6 |
| 2001   | 490.3 | 366.9 |
| 2002   | 513.8 | 383.2 |
| 2003   | 525.0 | 396.0 |
| 2004   | 556.8 | 420.2 |
| 2005   | 569.0 | 435.2 |
| 2006   | 589.8 | 450.0 |
| 2007   | 605.0 | 463.8 |
| 2008   | 634.0 | 484.4 |
| 2009   | 643.0 | 501.2 |
| 2010   | 653.3 | 513.1 |
| 2011   | 658.4 | 515.5 |
| 2012   | 660.7 | 525.1 |
| 2013   | 677.0 | 533.0 |
| 2014   | 674.0 | 539.3 |
| 2015(p)| 680.0 | 547.1 |

Until 2004 these figures were taken from the New Earnings Survey.
In 2004 the Annual Survey of Hours and Earnings (ASHE) was developed to replace the New Earnings Survey.
The above ASHE figures are taken from 14.1a revised tables other than the latest year which is provisional (p).
Both the New Earnings Survey and ASHE are published by HMSO.

# F7: Average Earnings Statistics

**Introductory notes**

1. It will usually be possible to obtain agreement, or a direction, that the earnings shown in the Annual Survey of Hours and Earnings (ASHE) may be adduced in evidence without formal proof but occasionally it may be necessary to adduce formal proof. This is done by calling a witness from the Office for National Statistics (ONS).

2. ASHE provides information about the levels, distribution and make-up of earnings and hours of paid work for employees. The data are collected and published by the ONS. ASHE replaced the New Earnings Survey (NES) in 2004.

3. ASHE is based upon a one per cent sample of employees taken from HM Revenue and Customs PAYE records. ASHE does not cover the self-employed nor employees not paid in the reference period.

4. ASHE is collected in April of each year and is published as a first release the following November/December. A second and final release is published in November/December a year later and includes any revisions to the estimates which may be required. The revisions are usually small.

5. The tables reproduced here relate to a sample restricted to full-time employees on adult rates of pay whose pay was not affected by absence. The estimates are disaggregated by sex and by a four-digit occupational classification. They are first release estimates for 2015. They were published by the ONS on 18 November 2015.

6. The earnings information relates to weekly and annual gross pay before tax, national insurance or other deductions and excludes payments in kind. Earnings are reported for full-time employees who are defined as those who work more than 30 paid hours per week.

7. Two measures of typical earnings are reported, the mean and median. The median is ONS's preferred measure of average earnings as it is less affected by the relatively small number of very high earners which skews the distribution of earnings. The median provides a better indication of typical earnings than does the mean.

8. It is helpful to understand the Standard Occupational Classification (SOC) as an ordered taxonomy of jobs in which narrowly defined jobs at the four-digit level (unit groups) are included within a wider definition at the three-digit level which in turn are included within a wider category at the two-digit level and a still wider category at the one-digit level. The hierarchy is based upon the concepts of the type of job and on the level of skill. There are 369 four digit occupational unit groups in SOC 2010 which cluster to form 90 minor groups, 25 sub-major groups and nine major groups. As an example, Rail Travel Assistants, 6215, are included within the three-digit group Leisure and Travel Services (621) and at the two-digit level, within Leisure, Travel and Related Personal Service Occupations (62), and, at the one-digit level, within Caring, Leisure and other Personal Service Occupations (6). The abbreviation "n.e.c." stands for "not elsewhere classified".

9. Reclassification of occupational categories occurs every 10 years and occurred in ASHE 2011 released in March 2012. For 2011 there is a dual set of tables, one using the SOC 2000 and the second using the SOC 2010.

10. Statistics derived from samples are called "estimates" because they estimate the population parameters that we are interested in. All sample estimates are subject to a degree of unreliability

## F7: Average Earnings Statistics

due to sampling variation. This is measured by ONS in the form of the coefficient of variation (CV) and is published in the series of Tables b which accompany the sample estimates in the series of Tables a. The CV is the ratio of the standard error of the estimate to the estimate itself. The smaller is the CV, the higher the precision (or quality) of the estimate. The ONS define four standards of reliability in relation to the size of the CV: less than five per cent, 5–10 per cent, 10–20 per cent, and greater than 20 per cent. An estimate with a CV of less than five per cent is the most reliable. Estimates with CVs of greater than 20 per cent are considered insufficiently reliable and are not published. Those in between are shaded in the ONS publication, though not in the reproduction here.

11. Tables of ASHE estimates are published online where alternative breakdowns can be found, for example by region, age group, industrial sector etc. and at 10 points across the earnings distribution. In November/December 2016, the estimates published online for 2015 will be the revised final release ones. A further advantage of the online source is the shading according to the levels of reliability referred to in 10 above. The tables can be found on the website of the ONS. ONS launched a new website on 25 February 2016. Step-by-step instructions to find the estimates produced here are provided below. You need not follow these step-by-step instructions each time you consult the tables as you can either download the tables as an Excel file or you can save the web link to bookmarks/favourites.

12. Find the home page of the ONS at *www.ons.gov.uk*

13. Type ASHE in the search box at the top of this page and click Search.

14. Refine the search using the menu on the left-hand side by checking the box for Datasets.

15. Scroll down the list of tables to the table title "Occupation (4 digit SOC) -ASHE:Table14". Clicking on the table title will open a .zip file.

16. Opening the .zip file will produce a contents list of Excel files, each of which contains different tables of earnings estimates.

17. Weekly pay by occupational group is in Table 14.1a Weekly Pay—Gross. A double-click on the table title will take you to a worksheet in an Excel file. If you are sure that you have located the file that you want, save it using File → Save in Excel. Weekly pay is measured for the reference week in April.

18. Annual pay by occupational group is in Table 14.7a Annual Pay—Gross. A double-click on the table title will take you to a worksheet in an Excel file. Annual estimates are provided for the tax year that ended in April in the reference year.

19. Note that all files marked with a file extension "b" report the coefficient of variation on the estimate (see 10 above).

20. Once in the Excel file, check the bottom tabs. Choose "Male Full-time" or "Female Full-time" to view the tables reproduced here. The median is reported in column 3 and the mean in column 5.

20. The shading indicates the reliability of the estimate. Where the estimate of the error is less than five per cent, there is no shading. The key to the shading can be found at the bottom and at the right-hand side of the table. The shading is not reproduced here.

21. If you have not already saved this file at step 17 above, this table can be saved now either in part or in full. If the file is saved prior to the final release, make a note that the 2015 estimates are provisional. They will be replaced in the final release in November/December 2016 under the same title.

This guide has been prepared by Dr Victoria Wass, Cardiff Business School, April 2016.

## Full-time males employees on adult rates (where pay was not affected by absence) in UK

n.e.c. = not elsewhere classified
X = unreliable

| Occupation SOC 2010 | SOC Code | Gross Weekly Pay (in April) 2015 | | Gross Annual Pay in tax year 2015/16 | |
|---|---|---|---|---|---|
| | | Median £ | Mean £ | Median £ | Mean £ |
| All employees | | 567.2 | 680.0 | 29,934 | 37,123 |
| **Managers, directors and senior officials** | 1 | 857.8 | 1,050.5 | 44,829 | 61,373 |
| Corporate managers and directors | 11 | 905.3 | 1,101.4 | 47,714 | 64,673 |
| Chief executives and senior officials | 111 | 1,724.9 | 1,979.7 | 95,074 | 135,427 |
| Chief executives and senior officials | 1115 | 1,775.9 | 2,032.7 | 98,838 | 139,533 |
| Elected officers and representatives | 1116 | X | 878.8 | X | 40,757 |
| Production managers and directors | 112 | 862.5 | 1,000.2 | 45,107 | 55,741 |
| Production managers and directors in manufacturing | 1121 | 881.6 | 1,018.5 | 46,257 | 56,751 |
| Production managers and directors in construction | 1122 | 826.4 | 911.2 | 43,143 | 51,080 |
| Production managers and directors in mining and energy | 1123 | 825.1 | 997.0 | 42,929 | 53,810 |
| Functional managers and directors | 113 | 1,245.7 | 1,392.3 | 66,745 | 84,564 |
| Financial managers and directors | 1131 | 1,331.9 | 1,529.7 | 74,129 | 94,966 |
| Marketing and sales directors | 1132 | 1,386.3 | 1,489.4 | 77,177 | 93,858 |
| Purchasing managers and directors | 1133 | 956.6 | 1,017.7 | 48,607 | 56,042 |
| Advertising and public relations directors | 1134 | X | 1,404.5 | X | 74,412 |
| Human resource managers and directors | 1135 | 958.5 | 1,103.6 | 52,235 | 63,419 |
| Information technology and telecommunications directors | 1136 | 1,252.7 | 1,295.7 | 65,881 | 72,063 |
| Functional managers and directors n.e.c. | 1139 | 1,149.9 | 1,286.2 | 58,428 | 75,947 |
| Financial institution managers and directors | 115 | 1,201.4 | 1,544.9 | 66,120 | 95,135 |
| Financial institution managers and directors | 1150 | 1,201.4 | 1,544.9 | 66,120 | 95,135 |
| Managers and directors in transport and logistics | 116 | 613.3 | 695.0 | 32,674 | 37,130 |
| Managers and directors in transport and distribution | 1161 | 705.6 | 823.1 | 38,602 | 44,154 |
| Managers and directors in storage and warehousing | 1162 | 564.2 | 611.3 | 30,125 | 32,622 |
| Senior officers in protective services | 117 | 1,078.2 | 1,165.7 | 58,305 | 60,862 |
| Officers in armed forces | 1171 | | | | |
| Senior police officers | 1172 | 1,149.7 | 1,211.7 | 61,935 | 62,128 |
| Senior officers in fire, ambulance, prison and related services | 1173 | 952.4 | 1,075.1 | 47,471 | 58,306 |
| Health and social services managers and directors | 118 | 902.5 | 1,003.3 | 46,253 | 52,833 |
| Health services and public health managers and directors | 1181 | 950.2 | 1,006.9 | 49,468 | 53,678 |
| Social services managers and directors | 1184 | 748.5 | 990.4 | 41,572 | 49,676 |
| Managers and directors in retail and wholesale | 119 | 566.8 | 659.5 | 30,183 | 37,070 |
| Managers and directors in retail and wholesale | 1190 | 566.8 | 659.5 | 30,183 | 37,070 |
| Other managers and proprietors | 12 | 589.8 | 703.7 | 31,880 | 38,772 |
| Managers and proprietors in agriculture related services | 121 | 560.2 | 644.1 | 29,897 | 35,008 |
| Managers and proprietors in agriculture and horticulture | 1211 | 579.0 | 665.3 | 30,214 | 35,884 |
| Managers and proprietors in forestry, fishing and related services | 1213 | X | 565.5 | X | 31,952 |
| Managers and proprietors in hospitality and leisure services | 122 | 503.8 | 590.1 | 27,299 | 32,369 |
| Hotel and accommodation managers and proprietors | 1221 | 536.7 | 655.1 | 28,944 | 36,825 |
| Restaurant and catering establishment managers and proprietors | 1223 | 457.0 | 489.1 | 25,173 | 27,605 |
| Publicans and managers of licensed premises | 1224 | 437.4 | 483.2 | X | 26,779 |
| Leisure and sports managers | 1225 | 558.6 | 660.9 | 28,968 | 35,952 |
| Travel agency managers and proprietors | 1226 | X | X | X | X |
| Managers and proprietors in health and care services | 124 | 671.9 | 703.3 | 35,493 | 36,821 |
| Health care practice managers | 1241 | 696.6 | 713.5 | 39,732 | 41,744 |
| Residential, day and domiciliary care managers and proprietors | 1242 | 645.4 | 701.4 | 34,602 | 36,121 |
| Managers and proprietors in other services | 125 | 645.9 | 771.6 | 34,219 | 42,547 |
| Property, housing and estate managers | 1251 | 710.4 | 791.9 | 37,096 | 44,991 |

## Full-time males employees on adult rates (where pay was not affected by absence) in UK

n.e.c. = not elsewhere classified
X = unreliable

| Occupation SOC 2010 | SOC Code | Gross Weekly Pay (in April) 2015 | | Gross Annual Pay in tax year 2015/16 | |
|---|---|---|---|---|---|
| | | Median £ | Mean £ | Median £ | Mean £ |
| Garage managers and proprietors | 1252 | 605.5 | 772.3 | 33,120 | 40,924 |
| Hairdressing and beauty salon managers and proprietors | 1253 | X | 470.5 | X | 27,488 |
| Shopkeepers and proprietors – wholesale and retail | 1254 | 530.8 | 694.7 | X | X |
| Waste disposal and environmental services managers | 1255 | 640.2 | 814.3 | 35,158 | 43,419 |
| Managers and proprietors in other services n.e.c. | 1259 | 612.4 | 753.6 | 31,876 | 40,446 |
| **Professional occupations** | 2 | 768.2 | 861.3 | 40,128 | 46,160 |
| Science, research, engineering and technology professionals | 21 | 771.1 | 828.8 | 40,773 | 44,289 |
| Natural and social science professionals | 211 | 716.7 | 793.0 | 37,857 | 43,530 |
| Chemical scientists | 2111 | 657.0 | 732.7 | 36,676 | 41,113 |
| Biological scientists and biochemists | 2112 | 767.1 | 825.1 | 40,753 | 45,048 |
| Physical scientists | 2113 | 759.8 | 975.9 | 39,147 | 55,979 |
| Social and humanities scientists | 2114 | 604.6 | 636.5 | 30,882 | 33,279 |
| Natural and social science professionals n.e.c. | 2119 | 686.2 | 729.7 | 36,752 | 38,877 |
| Engineering professionals | 212 | 771.2 | 812.4 | 40,313 | 42,972 |
| Civil engineers | 2121 | 753.3 | 814.2 | 41,014 | 43,397 |
| Mechanical engineers | 2122 | 807.2 | 871.0 | 42,610 | 45,722 |
| Electrical engineers | 2123 | 830.3 | 871.0 | 42,656 | 45,293 |
| Electronics engineers | 2124 | 816.7 | 886.5 | 41,569 | 47,246 |
| Design and development engineers | 2126 | 743.3 | 779.7 | 38,477 | 41,487 |
| Production and process engineers | 2127 | 729.4 | 777.6 | 38,546 | 40,313 |
| Engineering professionals n.e.c. | 2129 | 782.6 | 811.4 | 41,033 | 43,133 |
| Information technology and telecommunications professionals | 213 | 789.3 | 843.9 | 41,598 | 45,150 |
| IT specialist managers | 2133 | 880.6 | 956.9 | 46,063 | 50,419 |
| IT project and programme managers | 2134 | 974.2 | 987.5 | 53,079 | 52,803 |
| IT business analysts, architects and systems designers | 2135 | 845.1 | 899.4 | 43,981 | 47,917 |
| Programmers and software development professionals | 2136 | 757.6 | 786.0 | 39,988 | 42,042 |
| Web design and development professionals | 2137 | 539.3 | 566.6 | 29,930 | 31,815 |
| Information technology and telecommunications professionals n.e.c. | 2139 | 752.8 | 813.6 | 40,670 | 42,868 |
| Conservation and environmental professionals | 214 | 644.8 | 676.3 | 33,154 | 34,554 |
| Conservation professionals | 2141 | 665.5 | 664.9 | 34,991 | 33,993 |
| Environment professionals | 2142 | 630.7 | 679.4 | 32,225 | 34,705 |
| Research and development managers | 215 | 891.3 | 1,007.1 | 45,459 | 56,680 |
| Research and development managers | 2150 | 891.3 | 1,007.1 | 45,459 | 56,680 |
| Health professionals | 22 | 789.9 | 1,023.1 | 40,964 | 55,588 |
| Health professionals | 221 | 1,079.4 | 1,289.9 | 66,892 | 75,318 |
| Medical practitioners | 2211 | 1,356.0 | 1,491.8 | 88,866 | 90,580 |
| Psychologists | 2212 | 733.0 | 834.0 | X | 46,113 |
| Pharmacists | 2213 | 854.2 | 883.3 | 45,390 | 47,807 |
| Ophthalmic opticians | 2214 | 734.5 | 859.3 | X | 42,173 |
| Dental practitioners | 2215 | X | 1,196.6 | X | 79,518 |
| Veterinarians | 2216 | 764.5 | 765.6 | X | 41,784 |
| Medical radiographers | 2217 | 677.2 | 740.9 | 35,683 | 39,321 |
| Podiatrists | 2218 | 665.5 | 658.6 | 32,876 | 33,046 |
| Health professionals n.e.c. | 2219 | 668.4 | 686.0 | 35,222 | 37,937 |
| Therapy professionals | 222 | 584.3 | 670.4 | 30,337 | 35,988 |
| Physiotherapists | 2221 | 581.6 | 693.0 | 30,345 | 37,628 |
| Occupational therapists | 2222 | 574.5 | 592.6 | 28,451 | 29,747 |
| Speech and language therapists | 2223 | | | | |
| Therapy professionals n.e.c. | 2229 | 584.1 | 617.8 | X | 34,355 |
| Nursing and midwifery professionals | 223 | 624.7 | 658.2 | 32,701 | 32,810 |
| Nurses | 2231 | 623.8 | 657.5 | 32,690 | 32,782 |
| Midwives | 2232 | 693.3 | 777.6 | X | 36,996 |

## Full-time males employees on adult rates (where pay was not affected by absence) in UK

n.e.c. = not elsewhere classified
X = unreliable

| Occupation SOC 2010 | SOC Code | Gross Weekly Pay (in April) 2015 | | Gross Annual Pay in tax year 2015/16 | |
|---|---|---|---|---|---|
| | | Median £ | Mean £ | Median £ | Mean £ |
| Teaching and educational professionals | 23 | 761.4 | 813.5 | 39,917 | 42,732 |
| Teaching and educational professionals | 231 | 762.3 | 813.7 | 39,928 | 42,749 |
| Higher education teaching professionals | 2311 | 934.2 | 1,010.5 | 48,990 | 52,648 |
| Further education teaching professionals | 2312 | 696.0 | 724.6 | 35,751 | 37,421 |
| Secondary education teaching professionals | 2314 | 742.5 | 757.1 | 38,687 | 39,290 |
| Primary and nursery education teaching professionals | 2315 | 683.5 | 686.7 | 36,233 | 36,619 |
| Special needs education teaching professionals | 2316 | 712.6 | 687.0 | 36,831 | 34,709 |
| Senior professionals of educational establishments | 2317 | 1,132.0 | 1,188.6 | 57,417 | 60,317 |
| Education advisers and school inspectors | 2318 | 637.7 | 651.4 | X | 32,513 |
| Teaching and other educational professionals n.e.c. | 2319 | 555.5 | 602.4 | 29,370 | 31,152 |
| Business, media and public service professionals | 24 | 762.8 | 865.3 | 39,210 | 47,143 |
| Legal professionals | 241 | 899.6 | 1,149.4 | 46,649 | 65,635 |
| Barristers and judges | 2412 | X | 1,033.4 | X | 55,197 |
| Solicitors | 2413 | 776.7 | 954.5 | 41,193 | 51,164 |
| Legal professionals n.e.c. | 2419 | 1,392.4 | 1,567.0 | 73,281 | 92,102 |
| Business, research and administrative professionals | 242 | 816.6 | 909.5 | 42,387 | 50,588 |
| Chartered and certified accountants | 2421 | 802.8 | 851.5 | 41,734 | 47,424 |
| Management consultants and business analysts | 2423 | 844.8 | 928.9 | 43,622 | 51,587 |
| Business and financial project management professionals | 2424 | 911.3 | 1,001.7 | 47,427 | 55,937 |
| Actuaries, economists and statisticians | 2425 | 950.2 | 1,158.8 | X | 73,727 |
| Business and related research professionals | 2426 | 640.8 | 675.4 | 33,322 | 35,165 |
| Business, research and administrative professionals n.e.c. | 2429 | 707.6 | 774.7 | 36,870 | 41,039 |
| Architects, town planners and surveyors | 243 | 719.0 | 794.6 | 36,460 | 41,796 |
| Architects | 2431 | 793.6 | 877.7 | X | 48,154 |
| Town planning officers | 2432 | 682.8 | 666.8 | X | X |
| Quantity surveyors | 2433 | 805.2 | 829.2 | 40,718 | 42,350 |
| Chartered surveyors | 2434 | 682.3 | 756.0 | 35,199 | 39,749 |
| Chartered architectural technologists | 2435 | 572.0 | 690.2 | X | 35,191 |
| Construction project managers and related professionals | 2436 | 714.6 | 799.5 | 35,689 | 42,034 |
| Welfare professionals | 244 | 573.7 | 578.3 | 29,310 | 29,508 |
| Social workers | 2442 | 654.1 | 654.1 | 32,933 | 33,166 |
| Probation officers | 2443 | 609.8 | 636.6 | 30,648 | 31,767 |
| Clergy | 2444 | 462.2 | 505.9 | 24,710 | 26,333 |
| Welfare professionals n.e.c. | 2449 | 596.2 | 615.7 | 29,778 | 31,012 |
| Librarians and related professionals | 245 | 494.0 | 566.0 | 26,105 | 30,115 |
| Librarians | 2451 | X | 587.1 | 27,503 | 31,547 |
| Archivists and curators | 2452 | 492.4 | 535.5 | 25,397 | 28,196 |
| Quality and regulatory professionals | 246 | 750.2 | 837.6 | 38,336 | 45,065 |
| Quality control and planning engineers | 2461 | 690.0 | 736.9 | 35,984 | 37,856 |
| Quality assurance and regulatory professionals | 2462 | 798.0 | 922.0 | 41,201 | 51,411 |
| Environmental health professionals | 2463 | 669.4 | 699.3 | 34,805 | 35,828 |
| Media professionals | 247 | 651.6 | 739.6 | 33,518 | 38,770 |
| Journalists, newspaper and periodical editors | 2471 | 644.9 | 725.3 | 32,765 | 37,610 |
| Public relations professionals | 2472 | 600.3 | 678.6 | 31,915 | 36,684 |
| Advertising accounts managers and creative directors | 2473 | 783.5 | 851.8 | X | X |
| **Associate professional and technical occupations** | 3 | 635.0 | 724.1 | 33,955 | 39,981 |
| Science, engineering and technology associate professionals | 31 | 564.4 | 601.9 | 29,573 | 31,799 |
| Science, engineering and production technicians | 311 | 571.7 | 599.6 | 29,720 | 31,612 |
| Laboratory technicians | 3111 | 452.9 | 511.1 | 24,427 | 27,260 |
| Electrical and electronics technicians | 3112 | 603.5 | 615.0 | 29,712 | 30,740 |
| Engineering technicians | 3113 | 681.9 | 701.7 | 34,820 | 36,389 |
| Building and civil engineering technicians | 3114 | 560.1 | 565.4 | 28,715 | 30,678 |

F7: Average Earnings Statistics

**Full-time males employees on adult rates (where pay was not affected by absence) in UK**

n.e.c. = not elsewhere classified
X = unreliable

| Occupation SOC 2010 | SOC Code | Gross Weekly Pay (in April) 2015 | | Gross Annual Pay in tax year 2015/16 | |
|---|---|---|---|---|---|
| | | Median £ | Mean £ | Median £ | Mean £ |
| Quality assurance technicians | 3115 | 529.7 | 569.0 | 27,736 | 29,470 |
| Planning, process and production technicians | 3116 | 616.9 | 671.2 | 32,543 | 35,871 |
| Science, engineering and production technicians n.e.c. | 3119 | 518.0 | 543.1 | 26,940 | 28,826 |
| Draughtspersons and related architectural technicians | 312 | 544.0 | 586.5 | 28,203 | 31,093 |
| Architectural and town planning technicians | 3124 | 548.4 | 572.2 | 28,951 | 30,578 |
| Draughtspersons | 3122 | 536.5 | 592.4 | 27,913 | 31,259 |
| Information technology technicians | 313 | 555.8 | 608.9 | 29,289 | 32,249 |
| IT operations technicians | 3131 | 549.5 | 624.3 | 29,781 | 33,211 |
| IT user support technicians | 3132 | 562.2 | 598.3 | 29,222 | 31,572 |
| Health and social care associate professionals | 32 | 535.2 | 566.4 | 28,138 | 29,485 |
| Health associate professionals | 321 | 668.4 | 670.2 | 34,744 | 34,785 |
| Paramedics | 3213 | 731.9 | 770.1 | 37,702 | 39,425 |
| Dispensing opticians | 3216 | X | 668.9 | X | 33,760 |
| Pharmaceutical technicians | 3217 | 514.4 | 546.6 | 28,478 | 29,073 |
| Medical and dental technicians | 3218 | 578.8 | 607.5 | 29,941 | 31,852 |
| Health associate professionals n.e.c. | 3219 | 483.0 | 524.8 | 23,604 | 27,443 |
| Welfare and housing associate professionals | 323 | 479.1 | 505.9 | 25,092 | 26,165 |
| Youth and community workers | 3231 | 494.6 | 519.5 | 25,810 | 26,953 |
| Child and early years officers | 3233 | 472.0 | 469.3 | 24,677 | 25,129 |
| Housing officers | 3234 | 530.3 | 527.5 | 26,884 | 27,004 |
| Counsellors | 3235 | 505.1 | 537.6 | X | 26,472 |
| Welfare and housing associate professionals n.e.c. | 3239 | 447.7 | 489.5 | X | 25,177 |
| Protective service occupations | 33 | 719.7 | 737.2 | 37,270 | 38,083 |
| Protective service occupations | 331 | 719.7 | 737.2 | 37,270 | 38,083 |
| NCOs and other ranks | 3311 | | | | |
| Police officers (sergeant and below) | 3312 | 770.6 | 798.4 | 40,907 | 41,469 |
| Fire service officers (watch manager and below) | 3313 | 646.6 | 663.2 | 32,254 | 33,451 |
| Prison service officers (below principal officer) | 3314 | 551.1 | 564.3 | 29,372 | 29,378 |
| Police community support officers | 3315 | 520.9 | 525.9 | 26,524 | 27,312 |
| Protective service associate professionals n.e.c. | 3319 | 664.7 | 700.9 | 35,411 | 37,604 |
| Culture, media and sports occupations | 34 | 521.4 | 676.1 | 27,577 | 38,187 |
| Artistic, literary and media occupations | 341 | 594.2 | 642.1 | 31,381 | 34,374 |
| Artists | 3411 | 431.3 | 484.8 | 22,893 | 25,763 |
| Authors, writers and translators | 3412 | 569.5 | 631.2 | 31,652 | 34,349 |
| Actors, entertainers and presenters | 3413 | 695.3 | 721.2 | 37,632 | 39,699 |
| Dancers and choreographers | 3414 | | | | |
| Musicians | 3415 | 649.8 | 661.9 | 35,821 | 36,061 |
| Arts officers, producers and directors | 3416 | 735.4 | 771.0 | 41,313 | 42,775 |
| Photographers, audio-visual and broadcasting equipment operators | 3417 | 496.2 | 558.3 | 26,298 | 29,193 |
| Design occupations | 342 | 507.8 | 550.0 | 27,451 | 28,950 |
| Graphic designers | 3421 | 479.1 | 525.6 | 25,097 | 27,585 |
| Product, clothing and related designers | 3422 | 598.8 | 604.0 | 31,988 | 31,997 |
| Sports and fitness occupations | 344 | 429.8 | X | 22,059 | X |
| Sports players | 3441 | X | X | X | X |
| Sports coaches, instructors and officials | 3442 | 434.6 | 502.6 | 22,229 | 25,021 |
| Fitness instructors | 3443 | 346.4 | 364.7 | 17,064 | 18,479 |
| Business and public service associate professionals | 35 | 670.8 | 792.9 | 36,738 | 45,570 |
| Transport associate professionals | 351 | 1,646.1 | 1,631.2 | 81,646 | 80,213 |
| Air traffic controllers | 3511 | 1,701.0 | 1,673.2 | 86,694 | 84,360 |
| Aircraft pilots and flight engineers | 3512 | 1,808.8 | 1,877.7 | 85,476 | 88,069 |
| Ship and hovercraft officers | 3513 | 565.3 | 673.9 | X | 38,409 |
| Legal associate professionals | 352 | 574.9 | 688.4 | 30,537 | 38,682 |
| Legal associate professionals | 3520 | 574.9 | 688.4 | 30,537 | 38,682 |
| Business, finance and related associate professionals | 353 | 684.2 | 821.6 | 37,023 | 49,766 |

## F7: Average Earnings Statistics

**Full-time males employees on adult rates (where pay was not affected by absence) in UK**

n.e.c. = not elsewhere classified
X = unreliable

| Occupation SOC 2010 | SOC Code | Gross Weekly Pay (in April) 2015 Median £ | Mean £ | Gross Annual Pay in tax year 2015/16 Median £ | Mean £ |
| --- | --- | --- | --- | --- | --- |
| Estimators, valuers and assessors | 3531 | 586.4 | 700.6 | 32,146 | 38,981 |
| Brokers | 3532 | 1,267.3 | 1,679.7 | X | 135,697 |
| Insurance underwriters | 3533 | 694.9 | 905.2 | 36,687 | 53,057 |
| Finance and investment analysts and advisers | 3534 | 663.1 | 807.9 | 37,237 | 48,659 |
| Taxation experts | 3535 | 864.8 | 933.4 | 45,302 | 50,681 |
| Importers and exporters | 3536 | 560.5 | 675.9 | 29,520 | 33,910 |
| Financial and accounting technicians | 3537 | 840.8 | 948.3 | 44,508 | 53,030 |
| Financial accounts managers | 3538 | 763.4 | 894.5 | 40,964 | 54,022 |
| Business and related associate professionals n.e.c. | 3539 | 574.9 | 643.5 | 30,922 | 35,497 |
| Sales, marketing and related associate professionals | 354 | 715.1 | 812.9 | 39,210 | 46,545 |
| Buyers and procurement officers | 3541 | 608.5 | 656.2 | 32,081 | 34,464 |
| Business sales executives | 3542 | 569.2 | 650.5 | 31,818 | 37,372 |
| Marketing associate professionals | 3543 | 562.4 | 637.9 | 30,740 | 36,621 |
| Estate agents and auctioneers | 3544 | 487.9 | 546.7 | 25,475 | 30,456 |
| Sales accounts and business development managers | 3545 | 845.2 | 939.5 | 45,955 | 53,866 |
| Conference and exhibition managers and organisers | 3546 | 510.6 | 542.5 | 26,743 | 28,042 |
| Conservation and environmental associate professionals | 355 | 461.5 | 507.8 | 23,711 | 25,891 |
| Conservation and environmental associate professionals | 3550 | 461.5 | 507.8 | 23,711 | 25,891 |
| Public services and other associate professionals | 356 | 575.0 | 630.4 | 30,882 | 34,627 |
| Public service associate professionals | 3561 | 618.4 | 661.4 | 33,135 | 36,574 |
| Human resources and industrial relations officers | 3562 | 517.9 | 599.0 | 29,286 | 35,018 |
| Vocational and industrial trainers and instructors | 3563 | 554.1 | 601.2 | 29,642 | 32,186 |
| Careers advisers and vocational guidance specialists | 3564 | 497.3 | 552.5 | 27,270 | 29,152 |
| Inspectors of standards and regulations | 3565 | 603.9 | 638.9 | 30,567 | 32,805 |
| Health and safety officers | 3567 | 699.5 | 722.0 | 35,325 | 37,464 |
| **Administrative and secretarial occupations** | 4 | 448.2 | 498.5 | 23,855 | 26,601 |
| Administrative occupations | 41 | 451.2 | 501.6 | 23,978 | 26,752 |
| Administrative occupations: Government and related organisations | 411 | 469.0 | 498.8 | 24,852 | 26,337 |
| National government administrative occupations | 4112 | 445.4 | 482.2 | 24,056 | 25,731 |
| Local government administrative occupations | 4113 | 505.4 | 525.0 | 26,110 | 27,047 |
| Officers of non-governmental organisations | 4114 | 633.3 | 670.1 | 35,404 | 35,006 |
| Administrative occupations: Finance | 412 | 460.0 | 514.9 | 24,332 | 28,319 |
| Credit controllers | 4121 | 408.4 | 489.5 | 23,090 | 26,326 |
| Book-keepers, payroll managers and wages clerks | 4122 | 497.8 | 549.0 | 26,995 | 30,949 |
| Bank and post office clerks | 4123 | 441.6 | 486.3 | 23,436 | 26,568 |
| Finance officers | 4124 | 485.5 | 541.2 | 24,695 | 29,186 |
| Financial administrative occupations n.e.c. | 4129 | 422.6 | 470.6 | 21,548 | 24,631 |
| Administrative occupations: Records | 413 | 450.1 | 479.9 | 23,537 | 25,113 |
| Records clerks and assistants | 4131 | 460.0 | 499.3 | 24,379 | 26,347 |
| Pensions and insurance clerks and assistants | 4132 | 429.3 | 450.1 | 22,248 | 23,577 |
| Stock control clerks and assistants | 4133 | 426.1 | 452.5 | 21,855 | 23,586 |
| Transport and distribution clerks and assistants | 4134 | 493.5 | 523.2 | 25,615 | 27,193 |
| Library clerks and assistants | 4135 | 362.1 | 390.9 | 19,186 | 21,471 |
| Human resources administrative occupations | 4138 | 419.0 | 461.3 | 21,625 | 24,080 |
| Other administrative occupations | 415 | 399.7 | 464.0 | 21,171 | 23,723 |
| Sales administrators | 4151 | 402.5 | 423.2 | 22,648 | 23,044 |
| Other administrative occupations n.e.c. | 4159 | 399.4 | 467.9 | 21,105 | 23,796 |
| Administrative occupations: Office managers and supervisors | 416 | 611.9 | 662.4 | 32,852 | 36,442 |
| Office managers | 4161 | 638.4 | 683.5 | 34,987 | 38,157 |
| Office supervisors | 4162 | 544.7 | 563.4 | 27,463 | 28704 |
| Secretarial and related occupations | 42 | 373.0 | 438.3 | X | 23,587 |
| Secretarial and related occupations | 421 | 373.0 | 438.3 | X | 23,587 |
| Medical secretaries | 4211 | X | X | X | X |

## F7: Average Earnings Statistics

**Full-time males employees on adult rates (where pay was not affected by absence) in UK**

n.e.c. = not elsewhere classified
X = unreliable

| Occupation SOC 2010 | SOC Code | Gross Weekly Pay (in April) 2015 | | Gross Annual Pay in tax year 2015/16 | |
|---|---|---|---|---|---|
| | | Median £ | Mean £ | Median £ | Mean £ |
| Legal secretaries | 4212 | 351.7 | 363.5 | | |
| School secretaries | 4213 | 430.3 | 411.3 | 21,284 | 21,754 |
| Company secretaries | 4124 | X | 774.3 | X | 44,492 |
| Personal assistants and other secretaries | 4215 | 530.2 | 533.5 | 26,439 | 27,498 |
| Receptionists | 4216 | 327.3 | 344.7 | 16,359 | 17,458 |
| Typists and related keyboard occupations | 4217 | 368.0 | 418.3 | X | X |
| **Skilled trades occupations** | 5 | 500.0 | 538.3 | 26,224 | 27,926 |
| Skilled agricultural and related trades | 51 | 366.5 | 392.8 | 19,023 | 20,182 |
| Agricultural and related trades | 511 | 366.5 | 392.8 | 19,023 | 20,182 |
| Farmers | 5111 | 489.8 | 532.0 | 24,932 | 26,807 |
| Horticultural trades | 5112 | X | 428.0 | 17,624 | 19,966 |
| Gardeners and landscape gardeners | 5113 | 365.0 | 381.3 | 18,868 | 19,749 |
| Groundsmen and greenkeepers | 5114 | 357.0 | 375.3 | 18,725 | 19,523 |
| Agricultural and fishing trades n.e.c. | 5119 | 424.9 | 435.3 | 20,955 | 21,904 |
| Skilled metal, electrical and electronic trades | 52 | 552.5 | 589.8 | 28,862 | 30,455 |
| Metal forming, welding and related trades | 521 | 514.0 | 571.3 | 26,024 | 28,851 |
| Smiths and forge workers | 5211 | X | X | X | X |
| Moulders, core makers and die casters | 5212 | X | 500.5 | X | 24,089 |
| Sheet metal workers | 5213 | 504.7 | 555.6 | 23,623 | 27,096 |
| Metal plate workers, and riveters | 5214 | 569.4 | 622.4 | 29,637 | 31,191 |
| Welding trades | 5215 | 487.3 | 551.0 | 25,492 | 28,144 |
| Pipe fitters | 5216 | X | 788.9 | 39,211 | 38,408 |
| Metal machining, fitting and instrument making trades | 522 | 556.5 | 595.8 | 28,819 | 30,516 |
| Metal machining setters and setter-operators | 5221 | 516.1 | 554.3 | 26,467 | 28,150 |
| Tool makers, tool fitters and markers-out | 5222 | 513.0 | 545.6 | 26,586 | 27,785 |
| Metal working production and maintenance fitters | 5223 | 565.1 | 604.2 | 29,408 | 31,052 |
| Precision instrument makers and repairers | 5224 | 529.1 | 574.9 | 29,490 | 29,799 |
| Air conditioning and refrigeration engineers | 5225 | 609.6 | 643.1 | 31,312 | 32,064 |
| Vehicle trades | 523 | 499.9 | 525.2 | 25,733 | 27,320 |
| Vehicle technicians, mechanics and electricians | 5231 | 484.3 | 501.4 | 25,037 | 25,860 |
| Vehicle body builders and repairers | 5232 | 495.7 | 505.6 | 25,044 | 26,509 |
| Vehicle paint technicians | 5234 | 468.7 | 505.1 | 23,754 | 25,321 |
| Aircraft maintenance and related trades | 3235 | 644.5 | 667.3 | 33,564 | 34,881 |
| Boat and ship builders and repairers | 3236 | 500.7 | 517.6 | X | 29,897 |
| Rail and rolling stock builders and repairers | 5237 | 836.1 | 847.8 | 43,906 | 46,411 |
| Electrical and electronic trades | 524 | 574.9 | 607.8 | 30,169 | 31,666 |
| Electricians and electrical fitters | 5241 | 585.6 | 615.7 | 30,433 | 31,476 |
| Telecommunications engineers | 5242 | 601.8 | 642.7 | 32,010 | 33,971 |
| TV, video and audio engineers | 5244 | 498.8 | 541.7 | 27,354 | 28,562 |
| IT engineers | 5245 | 478.7 | 545.1 | 26,521 | 28,891 |
| Electrical and electronic trades n.e.c. | 5249 | 571.4 | 600.3 | 29,413 | 31,678 |
| Skilled metal, electrical and electronic trades supervisors | 525 | 638.4 | 689.3 | 33,036 | 36,331 |
| Skilled metal, electrical and electronic trades supervisors | 5250 | 638.4 | 689.3 | 33,036 | 36,331 |
| Skilled construction and building trades | 53 | 499.4 | 532.9 | 26,094 | 27,231 |
| Construction and building trades | 531 | 489.3 | 516.2 | 25,727 | 26,255 |
| Steel erectors | 5311 | 479.7 | 543.8 | 27,202 | 28,324 |
| Bricklayers and masons | 5312 | 469.5 | 498.3 | 25,254 | 25,763 |
| Roofers, roof tilers and slaters | 5313 | 450.0 | 479.3 | 23,087 | 24,037 |
| Plumbers and heating ventilating engineers | 5314 | 549.7 | 554.3 | 29,162 | 28,870 |
| Carpenters and joiners | 5315 | 490.0 | 507.3 | 25,757 | 25,876 |
| Glaziers, window fabricators and fitters | 5316 | 416.2 | 428.0 | 21,225 | 21,323 |
| Construction and building trades n.e.c. | 5319 | 498.1 | 561.8 | 25,399 | 27,285 |
| Building finishing trades | 532 | 450.4 | 479.1 | 23,598 | 24,399 |
| Plasterers | 5321 | 440.9 | 447.4 | 23,409 | 22,976 |

## Full-time males employees on adult rates (where pay was not affected by absence) in UK

n.e.c. = not elsewhere classified
X = unreliable

| Occupation SOC 2010 | SOC Code | Gross Weekly Pay (in April) 2015 | | Gross Annual Pay in tax year 2015/16 | |
|---|---|---|---|---|---|
| | | Median £ | Mean £ | Median £ | Mean £ |
| Floorers and wall tilers | 5322 | 490.3 | 554.5 | 26,458 | 27,410 |
| Painters and decorators | 5323 | 446.5 | 465.7 | 22,735 | 23,852 |
| Construction and building trades supervisors | 533 | 632.6 | 675.3 | 32,923 | 35,047 |
| Construction and building trades supervisors | 5330 | 632.6 | 675.3 | 32,923 | 35,047 |
| Textiles, printing and other skilled trades | 54 | 384.5 | 413.2 | 20,385 | 21,646 |
| Textiles and garments trades | 541 | 421.3 | 458.3 | 22,962 | 23,377 |
| Weavers and knitters | 5411 | 401.8 | 481.6 | 21,499 | 23,295 |
| Upholsterers | 5412 | 398.6 | 420.9 | 22,104 | 22,059 |
| Footwear and leather working trades | 5413 | 434.1 | 462.5 | 22,950 | 23,365 |
| Tailors and dressmakers | 5414 | 460.3 | 477.2 | 24,720 | 23,833 |
| Textiles, garments and related trades n.e.c. | 5419 | X | 560.1 | X | 27,938 |
| Printing trades | 542 | 475.3 | 506.6 | 25,127 | 26,370 |
| Pre-press technicians | 5421 | 474.7 | 535.3 | 24,970 | 27,588 |
| Printers | 5422 | 521.6 | 535.1 | 26,330 | 27,396 |
| Print finishing and binding workers | 5423 | 413.8 | 429.1 | 22,118 | 22,895 |
| Food preparation and hospitality trades | 543 | 366.8 | 388.0 | 19,000 | 20,175 |
| Butchers | 5431 | 354.3 | 369.8 | 18,581 | 19,458 |
| Bakers and flour confectioners | 5432 | 356.1 | 379.2 | 18,779 | 19,559 |
| Fishmongers and poultry dressers | 5433 | 319.2 | 365.2 | 15,998 | 17,928 |
| Chefs | 5434 | 368.6 | 386.9 | 19,057 | 20,059 |
| Cooks | 5435 | 338.0 | 364.5 | 17,354 | 18,667 |
| Catering and bar managers | 5436 | 401.2 | 430.5 | 20,668 | 22,801 |
| Other skilled trades | 544 | 425.0 | 474.2 | 21,530 | 23,876 |
| Glass and ceramics makers, decorators and finishers | 5441 | 370.5 | 461.1 | 20,421 | 23,836 |
| Furniture makers and other craft woodworkers | 5442 | 415.0 | 446.4 | 21,470 | 22,548 |
| Florists | 5443 | | | | |
| Other skilled trades n.e.c. | 5449 | 457.3 | 502.9 | 21,608 | 25,158 |
| **Caring, leisure and other service occupations** | 6 | 373.3 | 406.8 | 19,513 | 20,826 |
| Caring personal service occupations | 61 | 364.7 | 384.7 | 18,725 | 19,382 |
| Childcare and related personal services | 612 | 318.7 | 346.4 | 16,306 | 17,817 |
| Nursery nurses and assistants | 6121 | 325.7 | 345.9 | X | 17,297 |
| Childminders and related occupations | 6122 | | | | |
| Playworkers | 6123 | X | 387.8 | X | 19,636 |
| Teaching assistants | 6125 | 308.1 | 333.6 | 15,435 | 17,611 |
| Educational support assistants | 6126 | 351.9 | 369.1 | 17,341 | 18,396 |
| Animal care and control services | 613 | 370.4 | 374.5 | 18,486 | 19,050 |
| Veterinary nurses | 6131 | | | | |
| Pest control officers | 6132 | 388.7 | 389.9 | 20,028 | 19,858 |
| Animal care services occupations n.e.c. | 6139 | 349.6 | 368.7 | 17,280 | 18,894 |
| Caring personal services | 614 | 370.6 | 391.7 | 19,084 | 19,648 |
| Nursing auxiliaries and assistants | 6141 | 381.1 | 404.0 | 19,413 | 20,020 |
| Ambulance staff (excluding paramedics) | 6142 | 438.3 | 457.7 | 23,574 | 24,707 |
| Dental nurses | 6143 | 350.0 | 375.9 | 18,044 | 19,498 |
| Houseparents and residential wardens | 6144 | 474.3 | 494.6 | 25,334 | 25,748 |
| Care workers and home carers | 6145 | 343.7 | 367.8 | 17,582 | 18,130 |
| Senior care workers | 6146 | 372.2 | 402.1 | 20,232 | 21,326 |
| Care escorts | 6147 | 387.9 | 426.6 | 19,280 | 19,669 |
| Undertakers, mortuary and crematorium assistants | 6148 | 431.4 | 441.5 | 21,903 | 21,961 |
| Leisure, travel and related personal service occupations | 62 | 399.0 | 446.4 | 20,882 | 23,224 |
| Leisure and travel services | 621 | 452.5 | 510.7 | 24,842 | 26,509 |
| Sports and leisure assistants | 6211 | 341.8 | 354.4 | 17,238 | 17,567 |
| Travel agents | 385.4 | 6212 | 497.5 | 24,467 | X |
| Air travel assistants | 6214 | 466.7 | 531.1 | 25,061 | 25,916 |
| Rail travel assistants | 6215 | 632.0 | 665.8 | 33,575 | 34,183 |
| Leisure and travel service occupations n.e.c. | 6219 | 403.3 | 498.8 | X | 23,072 |
| Hairdressers and related services | 622 | 274.8 | 303.1 | 14,634 | 16,474 |

F7: Average Earnings Statistics

**Full-time males employees on adult rates (where pay was not affected by absence) in UK**

n.e.c. = not elsewhere classified
X = unreliable

| Occupation SOC 2010 | SOC Code | Gross Weekly Pay (in April) 2015 | | Gross Annual Pay in tax year 2015/16 | |
|---|---|---|---|---|---|
| | | Median £ | Mean £ | Median £ | Mean £ |
| Hairdressers and barbers | 6221 | 271.2 | 292.7 | 13,804 | 15,083 |
| Beauticians and related occupations | 6222 | 301.5 | 333.4 | 21,865 | 22,452 |
| Housekeeping and related services | 623 | 378.4 | 392.6 | 19,742 | 20,407 |
| Housekeepers and related occupations | 6231 | 288.9 | 357.3 | X | 20,008 |
| Caretakers | 6232 | 378.8 | 395.5 | 19,750 | 20,433 |
| Cleaning and housekeeping managers and supervisors | 624 | 373.2 | 414.2 | 20,634 | 21,071 |
| Cleaning and housekeeping managers and supervisors | 6240 | 373.2 | 414.2 | 20,634 | 21,071 |
| **Sales and customer service occupations** | 7 | 357.4 | 400.9 | 18,585 | 20,764 |
| Sales occupations | 71 | 343.9 | 378.4 | 17,793 | 19,349 |
| Sales assistants and retail cashiers | 711 | 331.8 | 366.6 | 16,860 | 18,486 |
| Sales and retail assistants | 7111 | 332.3 | 369.3 | 16,835 | 18,506 |
| Retail cashiers and check-out operators | 7112 | 296.2 | 308.1 | 15,290 | 15,528 |
| Telephone salespersons | 7113 | 376.4 | 382.8 | 20,281 | 20,503 |
| Pharmacy and other dispensing assistants | 7114 | 310.8 | 331.8 | 15,910 | 16,674 |
| Vehicle and parts salespersons and advisers | 7115 | 383.3 | 416.7 | 21,179 | 22,621 |
| Sales related occupations | 712 | 373.3 | 414.2 | 19,831 | 22,375 |
| Collector salespersons and credit agents | 7121 | X | 438.4 | X | X |
| Debt, rent and other cash collectors | 7122 | 339.6 | 373.9 | 18,384 | 19,268 |
| Roundspersons and van salespersons | 7123 | 410.7 | 421.4 | 22,336 | 22,764 |
| Market and street traders and assistants | 7124 | X | X | X | X |
| Merchandisers and window dressers | 7125 | 420.8 | 449.2 | 20,544 | 22,656 |
| Sales related occupations n.e.c. | 7129 | 383.3 | 433.0 | 20,136 | 25,650 |
| Sales supervisors | 713 | 390.3 | 418.5 | 20,663 | 21,621 |
| Sales supervisors | 7130 | 390.3 | 418.5 | 20,663 | 21,621 |
| Customer service occupations | 72 | 392.6 | 446.5 | 21,166 | 23,683 |
| Customer service occupations | 721 | 371.5 | 406.9 | 19,748 | 21,277 |
| Call and contact centre occupations | 7211 | 327.2 | 359.1 | X | 18,517 |
| Telephonists | 7213 | 367.2 | 394.3 | 18,890 | 19,789 |
| Communication operators | 7214 | 552.5 | 550.4 | 30,013 | 29,515 |
| Market research interviewers | 7215 | 412.2 | 436.1 | X | 16,934 |
| Customer service occupations n.e.c. | 7219 | 377.2 | 408.6 | 20,138 | 21,447 |
| Customer service managers and supervisors | 722 | 583.1 | 630.5 | 30,411 | 33,453 |
| Customer service managers and supervisors | 7220 | 583.1 | 630.5 | 30,411 | 33,453 |
| **Process, plant and machine operatives** | 8 | 473.5 | 509.5 | 24,429 | 25,934 |
| Process, plant and machine operatives | 81 | 448.8 | 489.0 | 23,625 | 25,428 |
| Process operatives | 811 | 409.4 | 451.2 | 21,577 | 23,566 |
| Food, drink and tobacco process operatives | 8111 | 373.5 | 403.3 | 19,131 | 20,525 |
| Glass and ceramics process operatives | 8112 | 407.2 | 489.5 | 23,560 | 25,734 |
| Textile process operatives | 8113 | 431.6 | 459.1 | 22,464 | 23,198 |
| Chemical and related process operatives | 8114 | 507.1 | 557.4 | 27,834 | 30,577 |
| Rubber process operatives | 8115 | 493.6 | 490.1 | 30,008 | 28,947 |
| Plastics process operatives | 8116 | 432.5 | 489.6 | 22,480 | 25,476 |
| Metal making and treating process operatives | 8117 | 484.1 | 523.3 | 24,625 | 26,772 |
| Electroplaters | 8118 | 444.8 | 477.1 | 22,444 | 24,340 |
| Process operatives n.e.c. | 8119 | 488.5 | 505.6 | 28,072 | 27,246 |
| Plant and machine operatives | 812 | 454.5 | 493.8 | 23,677 | 25,296 |
| Paper and wood machine operatives | 8121 | 397.5 | 433.5 | 20,122 | 21,704 |
| Coal mine operatives | 8122 | 608.3 | 722.9 | 29,937 | 34,754 |
| Quarry workers and related operatives | 8123 | 679.2 | 695.8 | 29,999 | 33,905 |
| Energy plant operatives | 8124 | 557.2 | 600.7 | X | 30,897 |
| Metal working machine operatives | 8125 | 416.4 | 451.4 | 21,843 | 23,408 |
| Water and sewerage plant operatives | 8126 | 520.0 | 552.8 | 30,504 | 31,968 |
| Printing machine assistants | 8127 | 421.4 | 445.3 | 22,003 | 22,932 |
| Plant and machine operatives n.e.c. | 8129 | 441.1 | 510.0 | 24,065 | 25,875 |

## Full-time males employees on adult rates (where pay was not affected by absence) in UK

n.e.c. = not elsewhere classified
X = unreliable

| Occupation SOC 2010 | SOC Code | Gross Weekly Pay (in April) 2015 | | Gross Annual Pay in tax year 2015/16 | |
|---|---|---|---|---|---|
| | | Median £ | Mean £ | Median £ | Mean £ |
| Assemblers and routine operatives | 813 | 454.0 | 503.1 | 24,185 | 26,250 |
| Assemblers (electrical and electronic products) | 8131 | 437.7 | 471.1 | 22,885 | 23,332 |
| Assemblers (vehicles and metal goods) | 8132 | 598.4 | 622.8 | 33,033 | 32,684 |
| Routine inspectors and testers | 8133 | 473.7 | 508.1 | 25,307 | 26,734 |
| Weighers, graders and sorters | 8134 | 382.6 | 410.9 | 19,429 | 21,367 |
| Tyre, exhaust and windscreen fitters | 8135 | 381.1 | 414.2 | 18,684 | 20,340 |
| Sewing machinists | 3137 | 330.9 | 342.8 | 19,084 | 18,658 |
| Assemblers and routine operatives n.e.c. | 3139 | 408.5 | 441.4 | 21,614 | 22,940 |
| Construction operatives | 814 | 493.1 | 515.5 | 25,916 | 26,821 |
| Scaffolders, stagers and riggers | 8141 | 606.4 | 608.6 | 30,071 | 30,820 |
| Road construction operatives | 8142 | 516.7 | 532.6 | 25,589 | 26,634 |
| Rail construction and maintenance operatives | 8143 | 636.9 | 649.8 | 34,213 | 35,426 |
| Construction operatives n.e.c. | 8149 | 465.0 | 473.0 | 24,310 | 24,705 |
| Transport and mobile machine drivers and operatives | 82 | 490.6 | 526.4 | 25,002 | 26,365 |
| Road transport drivers | 821 | 478.8 | 496.2 | 24,085 | 24,682 |
| Large goods vehicle drivers | 8211 | 546.0 | 556.8 | 27,363 | 27,310 |
| Van drivers | 8212 | 400.0 | 436.7 | 20,520 | 21,775 |
| Bus and coach drivers | 8213 | 476.8 | 506.2 | 24,247 | 25,558 |
| Taxi and cab drivers and chauffeurs | 8214 | 389.3 | 445.6 | 22,632 | 23,488 |
| Driving instructors | 8215 | X | 676.4 | X | 35,562 |
| Mobile machine drivers and operatives | 822 | 489.6 | 553.3 | 25,930 | 26,718 |
| Crane drivers | 8221 | 636.7 | 661.1 | 34,230 | 34,955 |
| Fork-lift truck drivers | 8222 | 412.5 | 518.3 | 20,503 | 22,458 |
| Agricultural machinery drivers | 8223 | 567.3 | 563.2 | 30,893 | 28,963 |
| Mobile machine drivers and operatives n.e.c. | 8229 | 521.1 | 550.2 | 26,538 | 27,093 |
| Other drivers and transport operatives | 823 | 853.5 | 809.8 | 44,503 | 41,179 |
| Train and tram drivers | 8231 | 952.2 | 977.2 | 49,945 | 49,355 |
| Marine and waterways transport operatives | 8232 | 650.0 | 682.6 | 38,169 | 37,252 |
| Air transport operatives | 8233 | 516.9 | 565.5 | 24,985 | 27,224 |
| Rail transport operatives | 8234 | 774.1 | 789.8 | 41,312 | 41,332 |
| Other drivers and transport operatives n.e.c. | 8239 | 524.0 | 520.4 | 27,333 | 27,215 |
| **Elementary occupations** | 9 | 367.4 | 397.9 | 19,510 | 20,451 |
| Elementary trades and related occupations | 91 | 372.6 | 402.3 | 19,610 | 20,830 |
| Elementary agricultural occupations | 911 | 372.2 | 404.1 | 19,521 | 20,590 |
| Farm workers | 9111 | 383.3 | 410.0 | 20,527 | 21,402 |
| Forestry workers | 9112 | 396.2 | 427.3 | 20,675 | 22,639 |
| Fishing and other elementary agriculture occupations n.e.c. | 9119 | 346.1 | 385.3 | X | 18,480 |
| Elementary construction occupations | 912 | 400.0 | 435.5 | 21,156 | 22,084 |
| Elementary construction occupations | 9120 | 400.0 | 435.5 | 21,156 | 22,084 |
| Elementary process plant occupations | 913 | 363.2 | 390.7 | 19,276 | 20,484 |
| Industrial cleaning process occupations | 9132 | 339.1 | 365.1 | 18,293 | 18,909 |
| Packers, bottlers, canners and fillers | 9134 | 345.2 | 369.6 | 18,626 | 19,839 |
| Elementary process plant occupations n.e.c. | 9139 | 378.9 | 408.3 | 19,893 | 21,091 |
| Elementary administration and service occupations | 92 | 365.9 | 396.7 | 19,460 | 20,351 |
| Elementary administration occupations | 921 | 465.6 | 491.3 | 24,488 | 25,117 |
| Postal workers, mail sorters, messengers and couriers | 9211 | 481.7 | 508.5 | 24,875 | 25,731 |
| Elementary administration occupations n.e.c. | 9219 | 318.0 | 344.2 | 16,978 | 18,524 |
| Elementary cleaning occupations | 923 | 328.4 | 344.3 | 17,022 | 17,421 |
| Window cleaners | 9231 | 320.5 | 339.3 | 17,635 | 18,409 |
| Street cleaners | 9232 | 337.6 | 350.2 | 18,129 | 17,790 |
| Cleaners and domestics | 9233 | 313.9 | 329.0 | 15,893 | 16,317 |
| Launderers, dry cleaners and pressers | 9234 | 310.6 | 324.1 | 15,483 | 16,032 |
| Refuse and salvage occupations | 9235 | 378.1 | 398.5 | 19,671 | 20,570 |
| Vehicle valeters and cleaners | 9236 | 309.3 | 322.0 | X | 16,119 |
| Elementary cleaning occupations n.e.c. | 9239 | 283.8 | 333.5 | 15,503 | 19,230 |
| Elementary security occupations | 924 | 420.9 | 438.7 | 21,304 | 22,163 |

## F7: Average Earnings Statistics

**Full-time males employees on adult rates (where pay was not affected by absence) in UK**

n.e.c. = not elsewhere classified
X = unreliable

| Occupation SOC 2010 | SOC Code | Gross Weekly Pay (in April) 2015 | | Gross Annual Pay in tax year 2015/16 | |
|---|---|---|---|---|---|
| | | Median £ | Mean £ | Median £ | Mean £ |
| Security guards and related occupations | 9241 | 431.5 | 443.6 | 21,565 | 22,446 |
| Parking and civil enforcement occupations | 9242 | 373.9 | 393.7 | 19,098 | 19,927 |
| School midday and crossing patrol occupations | 9244 | 331.5 | 385.6 | X | 20,399 |
| Elementary security occupations n.e.c. | 9249 | 412.3 | 442.1 | 20,928 | 22,016 |
| Elementary sales occupations | 925 | 301.0 | 326.0 | 15,441 | 16,592 |
| Shelf fillers | 9251 | 302.3 | 329.3 | 15,475 | 16,676 |
| Elementary sales occupations n.e.c. | 9259 | 276.0 | 285.1 | 14,460 | 14,719 |
| Elementary storage occupations | 926 | 374.2 | 409.3 | 19,809 | 20,802 |
| Elementary storage occupations | 9260 | 374.2 | 409.3 | 19,809 | 20,802 |
| Other elementary services occupations | 927 | 284.7 | 298.3 | 14,393 | 14,671 |
| Hospital porters | 9271 | 388.3 | 382.2 | 20,052 | 19,915 |
| Kitchen and catering assistants | 9272 | 285.0 | 297.4 | 14,254 | 14,426 |
| Waiters and waitresses | 9273 | 268.0 | 288.5 | X | 13,960 |
| Bar staff | 9274 | 279.1 | 288.7 | X | X |
| Leisure and theme park attendants | 9275 | 273.4 | 295.5 | 14,982 | 15,967 |
| Other elementary services occupations n.e.c. | 9279 | 296.2 | 315.8 | 15,900 | 16,588 |
| Not Classified | | | | | |

Source: *Annual Survey of Hours and Earnings, Office for National Statistics*, Tables 14.1a and 14.7a.

**Full-time Females employees on adult rates (where pay was not affected by absence) in UK**

n.e.c. = not elsewhere classified
X = unreliable

| Occupation SOC 2010 | SOC Code | Gross Weekly Pay (in April) 2015 | | Gross Annual Pay in tax year 2015/16 | |
|---|---|---|---|---|---|
| | | Median £ | Mean £ | Median £ | Mean £ |
| All employees | | 471.2 | 547.1 | 24,202 | 28,388 |
| **Managers, directors and senior officials** | 1 | 667.8 | 796.3 | 34,266 | 42,961 |
| Corporate managers and directors | 11 | 719.3 | 856.4 | 37,269 | 46,403 |
| Chief executives and senior officials | 111 | 1,174.4 | 1,268.5 | 63,218 | 72,563 |
| Chief executives and senior officials | 1115 | 1,179.4 | 1,313.9 | 63,235 | 75,770 |
| Elected officers and representatives | 1116 | X | X | X | X |
| Production managers and directors | 112 | 709.8 | 849.0 | 37,210 | 45,887 |
| Production managers and directors in manufacturing | 1121 | 713.3 | 847.2 | 37,267 | 45,391 |
| Production managers and directors in construction | 1122 | 647.9 | 853.2 | X | X |
| Production managers and directors in mining and energy | 1123 | X | 1,148.4 | X | X |
| Functional managers and directors | 113 | 920.1 | 1,046.1 | 47,581 | 57,785 |
| Financial managers and directors | 1131 | 931.0 | 1,033.0 | 47,483 | 58,524 |
| Marketing and sales directors | 1132 | 1,219.3 | 1,353.9 | X | 75,555 |
| Purchasing managers and directors | 1133 | 824.0 | 877.9 | 40,785 | 46,076 |
| Advertising and public relations directors | 1134 | 1,163.1 | 1,131.7 | 50,843 | 55,134 |
| Human resource managers and directors | 1135 | 838.5 | 931.7 | 42,594 | 50,540 |
| Information technology and telecommunications directors | 1136 | 1,245.2 | 1,256.8 | X | 65,114 |
| Functional managers and directors n.e.c. | 1139 | 925.9 | 989.7 | 48,077 | 54,859 |
| Financial institution managers and directors | 115 | 767.6 | 1,018.3 | 40,959 | 56,700 |
| Financial institution managers and directors | 1150 | 767.6 | 1,018.3 | 40,959 | 56,700 |
| Managers and directors in transport and logistics | 116 | 532.7 | 599.8 | 27,218 | 31,194 |
| Managers and directors in transport and distribution | 1161 | 621.1 | 714.4 | 31,617 | 38,751 |
| Managers and directors in storage and warehousing | 1162 | 480.6 | 556.2 | 25,094 | 28,428 |
| Senior officers in protective services | 117 | 1,044.3 | 1,061.2 | 57,066 | 52,950 |
| Officers in armed forces | 1171 | | | | |
| Senior police officers | 1172 | 1,153.0 | 1,185.9 | 60,203 | 59,637 |
| Senior officers in fire, ambulance, prison and related services | 1173 | X | 923.5 | X | 45,382 |
| Health and social services managers and directors | 118 | 785.1 | 874.5 | 40,501 | 46,127 |
| Health services and public health managers and directors | 1181 | 848.2 | 953.1 | 41,687 | 49,824 |
| Social services managers and directors | 1184 | 705.4 | 743.5 | 36,906 | 39,578 |
| Managers and directors in retail and wholesale | 119 | 405.7 | 472.4 | 20,676 | 24,593 |
| Managers and directors in retail and wholesale | 1190 | 405.7 | 472.4 | 20,676 | 24,593 |
| Other managers and proprietors | 12 | 526.7 | 583.3 | 26,971 | 30,698 |
| Managers and proprietors in agriculture related services | 121 | 544.7 | 544.1 | 28,175 | 28,735 |
| Managers and proprietors in agriculture and horticulture | 1211 | 581.5 | 585.7 | 29,264 | 30,683 |
| Managers and proprietors in forestry, fishing and related services | 1213 | | | | |
| Managers and proprietors in hospitality and leisure services | 122 | 451.2 | 486.4 | 23,092 | 25,476 |
| Hotel and accommodation managers and proprietors | 1221 | 412.2 | 475.1 | 22,988 | 26,402 |
| Restaurant and catering establishment managers and proprietors | 1223 | 438.5 | 445.1 | 21,479 | 22,124 |
| Publicans and managers of licensed premises | 1224 | 384.2 | 469.1 | X | 25,535 |
| Leisure and sports managers | 1225 | 516.7 | 569.3 | 26,953 | 29,162 |
| Travel agency managers and proprietors | 1226 | 441.0 | 531.2 | 32,210 | 33,830 |
| Managers and proprietors in health and care services | 124 | 589.4 | 637.2 | 30,924 | 33,691 |
| Health care practice managers | 1241 | 583.4 | 625.7 | 29,858 | 32,323 |
| Residential, day and domiciliary care managers and proprietors | 1242 | 588.1 | 639.9 | 30,925 | 34,042 |
| Managers and proprietors in other services | 125 | 535.7 | 614.8 | 27,672 | 32,043 |

F7: Average Earnings Statistics

**Full-time Females employees on adult rates (where pay was not affected by absence) in UK**

n.e.c. = not elsewhere classified
X = unreliable

| Occupation SOC 2010 | SOC Code | Gross Weekly Pay (in April) 2015 | | Gross Annual Pay in tax year 2015/16 | |
|---|---|---|---|---|---|
| | | Median £ | Mean £ | Median £ | Mean £ |
| Property, housing and estate managers | 1251 | 568.1 | 618.0 | 28,397 | 31,763 |
| Garage managers and proprietors | 1252 | X | 473.0 | X | X |
| Hairdressing and beauty salon managers and proprietors | 1253 | 386.4 | 432.7 | 20,404 | 21,646 |
| Shopkeepers and proprietors – wholesale and retail | 1254 | X | X | X | X |
| Waste disposal and environmental services managers | 1255 | 697.6 | 756.9 | X | 38,577 |
| Managers and proprietors in other services n.e.c. | 1259 | 509.7 | 623.7 | 26,633 | 33,064 |
| **Professional occupations** | 2 | 668.3 | 712.6 | 34,229 | 36,526 |
| Science, research, engineering and technology professionals | 21 | 689.2 | 732.6 | 35,647 | 38,835 |
| Natural and social science professionals | 211 | 661.3 | 709.4 | 34,780 | 37,855 |
| Chemical scientists | 2111 | 545.4 | 579.1 | 27,326 | 28,939 |
| Biological scientists and biochemists | 2112 | 670.8 | 718.9 | 34,152 | 37,581 |
| Physical scientists | 2113 | 710.1 | 681.5 | 37,739 | 37,700 |
| Social and humanities scientists | 2114 | X | X | X | X |
| Natural and social science professionals n.e.c. | 2119 | 692.3 | 730.8 | 36,438 | 40,671 |
| Engineering professionals | 212 | 691.1 | 744.4 | 35,200 | 37,562 |
| Civil engineers | 2121 | 673.8 | 719.6 | 33,844 | 35,518 |
| Mechanical engineers | 2122 | 800.8 | 848.5 | 37,608 | 41,033 |
| Electrical engineers | 2123 | 906.7 | 925.2 | 45,589 | 50,696 |
| Electronics engineers | 2124 | | | | |
| Design and development engineers | 2126 | 580.4 | 670.8 | 33,250 | 35,177 |
| Production and process engineers | 2127 | 689.9 | 744.1 | 33,129 | 35,154 |
| Engineering professionals n.e.c. | 2129 | 673.9 | 742.1 | 35,780 | 37,798 |
| Information technology and telecommunications professionals | 213 | 699.6 | 745.6 | 36,683 | 40,457 |
| IT specialist managers | 2133 | 755.7 | 816.8 | 38,280 | 44,426 |
| IT project and programme managers | 2134 | 840.0 | 895.0 | X | 51,334 |
| IT business analysts, architects and systems designers | 2135 | 665.8 | 744.7 | 37,839 | 41,521 |
| Programmers and software development professionals | 2136 | 706.8 | 732.5 | 36,654 | 39,533 |
| Web design and development professionals | 2137 | 569.2 | 582.0 | 28,544 | 29,116 |
| Information technology and telecommunications professionals n.e.c. | 2139 | 642.6 | 688.7 | 33,197 | 35,675 |
| Conservation and environment professionals | 214 | 572.9 | 593.7 | 29,003 | 30,985 |
| Conservation professionals | 2141 | 533.1 | 556.3 | 29,217 | 29,941 |
| Environment professionals | 2142 | 573.8 | 607.2 | 28,368 | 31,354 |
| Research and development managers | 215 | 752.6 | 813.0 | 40,169 | 42,779 |
| Research and development managers | 2150 | 752.6 | 813.0 | 40,169 | 42,779 |
| Health professionals | 22 | 641.7 | 706.3 | 32,552 | 35,301 |
| Health professionals | 221 | 807.1 | 951.6 | 40,412 | 50,119 |
| Medical practitioners | 2211 | 989.7 | 1,181.8 | 58,795 | 65,650 |
| Psychologists | 2212 | 727.0 | 753.3 | 38,757 | 39,181 |
| Pharmacists | 2213 | 732.5 | 718.3 | 38,475 | 41,994 |
| Ophthalmic opticians | 2214 | 748.7 | 742.6 | 36,329 | 37,778 |
| Dental practitioners | 2215 | 876.7 | 901.6 | 53,769 | 50,792 |
| Veterinarians | 2216 | 734.7 | 801.3 | 36,822 | 41,899 |
| Medical radiographers | 2217 | 663.5 | 676.9 | 34,247 | 34,931 |
| Podiatrists | 2218 | 548.3 | 599.9 | 28,996 | 30,532 |
| Health professionals n.e.c. | 2219 | 640.8 | 640.7 | 32,154 | 32,557 |
| Therapy professionals | 222 | 602.4 | 629.9 | 31,378 | 32,472 |
| Physiotherapists | 2221 | 608.9 | 634.7 | 31,541 | 32,829 |
| Occupational therapists | 2222 | 599.7 | 599.1 | 31,102 | 31,150 |
| Speech and language therapists | 2223 | 548.6 | 613.8 | 29,079 | 33,189 |
| Therapy professionals n.e.c. | 2229 | 687.9 | 717.9 | 35,158 | 34,453 |
| Nursing and midwifery professionals | 223 | 615.0 | 634.6 | 31,517 | 31,537 |
| Nurses | 2231 | 612.2 | 631.3 | 31,236 | 31,305 |

## Full-time Females employees on adult rates (where pay was not affected by absence) in UK

n.e.c. = not elsewhere classified
X = unreliable

| Occupation SOC 2010 | SOC Code | Gross Weekly Pay (in April) 2015 | | Gross Annual Pay in tax year 2015/16 | |
|---|---|---|---|---|---|
| | | Median £ | Mean £ | Median £ | Mean £ |
| Midwives | 2232 | 668.4 | 691.4 | 34,876 | 35,320 |
| Teaching and educational professionals | 23 | 683.4 | 698.2 | 35,477 | 35,807 |
| Teaching and educational professionals | 231 | 683.4 | 698.2 | 35,477 | 35,807 |
| Higher education teaching professionals | 2311 | 880.7 | 886.1 | 45,444 | 45,961 |
| Further education teaching professionals | 2312 | 655.9 | 672.5 | 33,573 | 34,464 |
| Secondary education teaching professionals | 2314 | 705.7 | 693.6 | 37,142 | 35,845 |
| Primary and nursery education teaching professionals | 2315 | 668.3 | 647.4 | 34,010 | 32,719 |
| Special needs education teaching professionals | 2316 | 694.5 | 676.1 | 37,754 | 35,839 |
| Senior professionals of educational establishments | 2317 | 939.1 | 922.5 | 46,338 | 46,219 |
| Education advisers and school inspectors | 2318 | 631.4 | 701.7 | 34,634 | 36,358 |
| Teaching and other educational professionals n.e.c. | 2319 | 479.1 | 519.1 | 24,724 | 26,872 |
| Business, media and public service professionals | 24 | 670.8 | 734.5 | 34,285 | 38,590 |
| Legal professionals | 241 | 833.1 | 938.5 | 42,405 | 50,592 |
| Barristers and judges | 2412 | 677.8 | 777.6 | 36,110 | 40,010 |
| Solicitors | 2413 | 735.2 | 788.9 | 37,958 | 41,809 |
| Legal professionals n.e.c. | 2419 | 1,218.0 | 1,256.4 | X | 69,231 |
| Business, research and administrative professionals | 242 | 692.3 | 750.3 | 35,872 | 39,971 |
| Chartered and certified accountants | 2421 | 669.6 | 710.9 | 34,939 | 37,138 |
| Management consultants and business analysts | 2423 | 733.2 | 792.2 | 38,528 | 43,437 |
| Business and financial project management professionals | 2424 | 750.1 | 810.2 | 37,748 | 43,370 |
| Actuaries, economists and statisticians | 2425 | 828.5 | 885.1 | 41,262 | 45,418 |
| Business and related research professionals | 2426 | 600.7 | 606.6 | 30,300 | 30,791 |
| Business, research and administrative professionals n.e.c. | 2429 | 667.6 | 725.0 | 34,771 | 37,638 |
| Architects, town planners and surveyors | 243 | 632.4 | 662.0 | 32,500 | 34,497 |
| Architects | 2431 | 632.4 | 674.9 | 33,000 | 35,058 |
| Town planning officers | 2432 | 661.7 | 684.3 | 34,788 | 35,784 |
| Quantity surveyors | 2433 | X | 707.6 | 36,912 | 39,668 |
| Chartered surveyors | 2434 | 634.5 | 649.7 | 29,925 | 33,671 |
| Chartered architectural technologists | 2435 | | | | |
| Construction project managers and related professionals | 2436 | 566.9 | 611.8 | 27,613 | 29,527 |
| Welfare professionals | 244 | 632.7 | 625.2 | 31,720 | 31,385 |
| Social workers | 2442 | 644.9 | 639.6 | 32,122 | 32,039 |
| Probation officers | 2443 | 488.8 | 560.8 | 30,611 | 32,316 |
| Clergy | 2444 | 433.7 | 474.1 | 22,492 | 23,749 |
| Welfare professionals n.e.c. | 2449 | 593.4 | 584.2 | 31,726 | 29,567 |
| Librarians and related professionals n.e.c. | 245 | 515.6 | 559.1 | 26,077 | 28,635 |
| Librarians | 2451 | 507.8 | 550.0 | 25,396 | 28,001 |
| Archivists and curators | 2452 | 519.7 | 580.1 | 26,777 | 30,094 |
| Quality and regulatory professionals | 246 | 708.4 | 764.3 | 36,927 | 40,336 |
| Quality control and planning engineers | 2461 | 670.8 | 674.2 | 35,923 | 36,309 |
| Quality assurance and regulatory professionals | 2462 | 732.4 | 797.3 | 38,274 | 41,752 |
| Environmental health professionals | 2463 | 667.8 | 681.4 | 34,712 | 35,382 |
| Media professionals | 247 | 570.8 | 626.0 | 30,099 | 32,169 |
| Journalists, newspaper and periodical editors | 2471 | 566.5 | 638.3 | 28,906 | 31,817 |
| Public relations professionals | 2472 | 561.5 | 599.2 | 30,375 | 31,606 |
| Advertising accounts managers and creative directors | 2473 | 592.0 | 643.4 | 30,616 | 33,659 |
| **Associate professional and technical occupations** | 3 | 536.6 | 596.1 | 28,002 | 31,689 |
| Science, engineering and technology associate professionals | 31 | 472.2 | 505.7 | 24,528 | 26,373 |
| Science, engineering and production technicians | 311 | 445.7 | 474.6 | 23,077 | 24,676 |
| Laboratory technicians | 3111 | 369.6 | 403.5 | 19,084 | 21,167 |
| Electrical and electronics technicians | 3112 | X | 421.0 | X | 18,684 |
| Engineering technicians | 3113 | 587.3 | 634.4 | 29,593 | 33,144 |

## F7: Average Earnings Statistics

**Full-time Females employees on adult rates (where pay was not affected by absence) in UK**

n.e.c. = not elsewhere classified
X = unreliable

| Occupation SOC 2010 | SOC Code | Gross Weekly Pay (in April) 2015 | | Gross Annual Pay in tax year 2015/16 | |
|---|---|---|---|---|---|
| | | Median £ | Mean £ | Median £ | Mean £ |
| Building and civil engineering technicians | 3114 | 563.5 | 558.5 | 28,861 | 29,271 |
| Quality assurance technicians | 3115 | 490.8 | 518.5 | 25,899 | 27,228 |
| Planning, process and production technicians | 3116 | 498.5 | 541.5 | 24,430 | 26,087 |
| Science, engineering and production technicians n.e.c. | 3119 | 397.9 | 432.6 | 21,682 | 22,816 |
| Draughtspersons and related architectural technicians | 312 | 514.2 | 520.4 | X | X |
| Architectural and town planning technicians | 3121 | 514.6 | 519.7 | X | X |
| Draughtspersons | 3122 | 477.5 | 521.4 | 27,188 | 28,545 |
| Information technology technicians | 313 | 503.1 | 540.8 | 26,716 | 28,275 |
| IT operations technicians | 3131 | 516.3 | 563.7 | 28,010 | 29,858 |
| IT user support technicians | 3132 | 491.5 | 522.0 | 25,323 | 26,913 |
| Health and social care associate professionals | 32 | 469.3 | 493.6 | 23,975 | 25,077 |
| Health associate professionals | 321 | 465.0 | 528.3 | 23,405 | 26,751 |
| Paramedics | 3213 | 685.1 | 736.6 | 35,167 | 36,213 |
| Dispensing opticians | 3216 | 449.5 | 482.1 | 22,940 | 25,281 |
| Pharmaceutical technicians | 3217 | 402.6 | 428.0 | 20,498 | 22,379 |
| Medical and dental technicians | 3218 | 496.4 | 531.7 | 22,887 | 26,498 |
| Health associate professionals n.e.c. | 3219 | 503.1 | 539.2 | X | 26,619 |
| Welfare and housing associate professionals | 323 | 470.2 | 484.0 | 24,017 | 24,605 |
| Youth and community workers | 3231 | 493.9 | 500.9 | 25,058 | 25,302 |
| Child and early years officers | 3233 | 450.8 | 466.7 | 23,695 | 24,369 |
| Housing officers | 3234 | 498.4 | 503.7 | 25,087 | 25,147 |
| Counsellors | 3235 | 472.2 | 498.7 | 24,155 | 25,926 |
| Welfare and housing associate professionals n.e.c. | 3239 | 446.5 | 464.1 | 22,912 | 23,580 |
| Protective service occupations | 33 | 660.0 | 664.7 | 34,324 | 34,279 |
| Protective service occupations | 331 | 660.0 | 664.7 | 34,324 | 34,279 |
| NCOs and other ranks | 3311 | | | | |
| Police officers (sergeant and below) | 3312 | 719.7 | 718.1 | 37,383 | 36,745 |
| Fire service officers (watch manager and below) | 3313 | 604.4 | 629.4 | 31,255 | 32,652 |
| Prison service officers (below principal officer) | 3314 | 458.7 | 501.0 | 25,276 | 26,532 |
| Police community support officers | 3315 | 505.9 | 506.4 | 26,182 | 26,159 |
| Protective service associate professionals n.e.c. | 3319 | 655.8 | 663.7 | 32,204 | 34,743 |
| Culture, media and sports occupations | 34 | 489.5 | 533.7 | 26,188 | 28,156 |
| Artistic, literary and media occupations | 341 | 536.6 | 609.1 | 28,143 | 31,558 |
| Artists | 3411 | X | 630.4 | X | X |
| Authors, writers and translators | 3412 | 487.6 | 601.7 | 26,784 | 32,417 |
| Actors, entertainers and presenters | 3413 | | | | |
| Dancers and choreographers | 3414 | X | X | X | X |
| Musicians | 3415 | 555.0 | 580.0 | 26,843 | 28,957 |
| Arts officers, producers and directors | 3416 | 676.5 | 715.9 | 35,397 | 37,175 |
| Photographers, audio-visual and broadcasting equipment operators | 3417 | 448.1 | 440.1 | 20,954 | 21,877 |
| Design occupations | 342 | 483.8 | 503.3 | 26,267 | 27,363 |
| Graphic designers | 3421 | 460.0 | 479.9 | X | X |
| Product, clothing and related designers | 3422 | 501.0 | 527.8 | 27,556 | 29,143 |
| Sports and fitness occupations | 344 | 421.7 | 447.3 | 21,562 | 22,467 |
| Sports players | 3441 | 414.9 | 463.0 | | |
| Sports coaches, instructors and officials | 3442 | 439.7 | 468.2 | 22,771 | 23,154 |
| Fitness instructors | 3443 | 330.7 | 403.2 | X | 21,612 |
| Business and public service associate professionals | 35 | 555.8 | 627.1 | 29,247 | 33,867 |
| Transport associate professionals | 351 | X | 1,272.4 | X | 61,823 |
| Air traffic controllers | 3511 | X | 1,266.4 | X | 62,868 |
| Aircraft pilots and flight engineers | 3512 | | | | |
| Ship and hovercraft officers | 3513 | | | | |
| Legal associate professionals | 352 | 488.7 | 537.3 | 24,691 | 28,077 |
| Legal associate professionals | 3520 | 488.7 | 537.3 | 24,691 | 28,077 |

**Full-time Females employees on adult rates (where pay was not affected by absence) in UK**

n.e.c. = not elsewhere classified
X = unreliable

| Occupation SOC 2010 | SOC Code | Gross Weekly Pay (in April) 2015 | | Gross Annual Pay in tax year 2015/16 | |
|---|---|---|---|---|---|
| | | Median £ | Mean £ | Median £ | Mean £ |
| Business, finance and related associate professionals | 353 | 566.7 | 643.9 | 29,733 | 35,423 |
| Estimators, valuers and assessors | 3531 | 500.1 | 534.6 | 26,442 | 29,278 |
| Brokers | 3532 | X | X | X | X |
| Insurance underwriters | 3533 | 577.4 | 646.9 | 29,103 | 35,766 |
| Finance and investment analysts and advisers | 3534 | 633.3 | 721.5 | 33,452 | 40,821 |
| Taxation experts | 3535 | 856.6 | 975.7 | X | 52,385 |
| Importers and exporters | 3536 | 507.6 | 554.7 | X | 29,659 |
| Financial and accounting technicians | 3537 | 646.2 | 775.7 | 32,377 | 44,293 |
| Financial accounts managers | 3538 | 632.2 | 668.5 | 32,560 | 35,849 |
| Business and related associate professionals n.e.c. | 3539 | 491.3 | 522.3 | 25,502 | 26,546 |
| Sales, marketing and related associate professionals | 354 | 581.1 | 666.5 | 30,776 | 36,359 |
| Buyers and procurement officers | 3541 | 582.1 | 618.8 | 29,875 | 32,099 |
| Business sales executives | 3542 | 478.9 | 539.2 | 26,580 | 30,361 |
| Marketing associate professionals | 3543 | 493.8 | 515.0 | 25,965 | 27,270 |
| Estate agents and auctioneers | 3544 | 417.3 | 487.5 | 21,025 | 26,664 |
| Sales accounts and business development managers | 3545 | 718.7 | 803.4 | 38,247 | 43,846 |
| Conference and exhibition managers and organisers | 3546 | 483.5 | 534.6 | 26,094 | 28,370 |
| Conservation and environmental associate professionals | 355 | 390.5 | 444.9 | 19,339 | 22,229 |
| Conservation and environmental associate professionals | 3550 | 390.5 | 444.9 | 19,339 | 22,229 |
| Public services and other associate professionals | 356 | 525.4 | 552.6 | 27,457 | 29,028 |
| Public service associate professionals | 3561 | 535.3 | 564.7 | 27,917 | 29,500 |
| Human resources and industrial relations officers | 3562 | 519.2 | 545.8 | 27,498 | 28,721 |
| Vocational and industrial trainers and instructors | 3563 | 499.0 | 528.7 | 25,921 | 27,243 |
| Careers advisers and vocational guidance specialists | 3564 | 522.4 | 530.8 | 24,757 | 26,442 |
| Inspectors of standards and regulations | 3565 | 530.8 | 578.4 | 26,697 | 29,496 |
| Health and safety officers | 3567 | 591.1 | 704.2 | 29,687 | 40,735 |
| **Administrative and secretarial occupations** | 4 | 404.1 | 441.3 | 20,995 | 22,824 |
| Administrative occupations | 41 | 405.3 | 442.2 | 21,065 | 22,821 |
| Administrative occupations: Government and related organisations | 411 | 423.9 | 448.8 | 22,310 | 23,313 |
| National government administrative occupations | 4112 | 419.1 | 443.1 | 21,909 | 23,207 |
| Local government administrative occupations | 4113 | 439.7 | 455.5 | 22,910 | 23,263 |
| Officers of non-governmental organisations | 4114 | 448.4 | 485.5 | 23,420 | 25,765 |
| Administrative occupations: Finance | 412 | 420.3 | 452.5 | 21,757 | 23,516 |
| Credit controllers | 4121 | 412.0 | 435.8 | 21,401 | 23,216 |
| Book-keepers, payroll managers and wages clerks | 4122 | 425.7 | 471.2 | 22,183 | 24,366 |
| Bank and post office clerks | 4123 | 404.8 | 432.1 | 21,564 | 22,866 |
| Finance officers | 4124 | 460.8 | 465.0 | 23,869 | 23,951 |
| Financial administrative occupations n.e.c. | 4129 | 402.5 | 425.5 | 20,523 | 21,975 |
| Administrative occupations: Records | 413 | 387.0 | 419.7 | 20,090 | 21,527 |
| Records clerks and assistants | 4131 | 382.0 | 415.4 | 19,691 | 21,235 |
| Pensions and insurance clerks and assistants | 4132 | 405.1 | 436.8 | 20,446 | 22,618 |
| Stock control clerks and assistants | 4133 | 382.4 | 414.5 | 20,224 | 21,628 |
| Transport and distribution clerks and assistants | 4134 | 423.1 | 456.0 | 22,314 | 23,209 |
| Library clerks and assistants | 4135 | 366.1 | 400.5 | 19,133 | 20,425 |
| Human resources administrative occupations | 4138 | 386.9 | 403.1 | 19,537 | 20,489 |
| Other administrative occupations | 415 | 377.8 | 411.5 | 19,399 | 20,796 |
| Sales administrators | 4151 | 383.3 | 397.9 | 20,019 | 20,902 |
| Other administrative occupations n.e.c. | 4159 | 376.2 | 412.9 | 19,330 | 20,785 |
| Administrative occupations: Office managers and supervisors | 416 | 519.7 | 562.0 | 27,659 | 29,333 |
| Office managers | 4161 | 536.3 | 572.8 | 28,183 | 29,873 |
| Office supervisors | 4162 | 463.1 | 485.7 | 24,069 | 25,546 |
| Secretarial and related occupations | 42 | 398.9 | 437.9 | 20,483 | 22,837 |
| Secretarial and related occupations | 421 | 398.9 | 437.9 | 20,483 | 22,837 |

F7: Average Earnings Statistics

**Full-time Females employees on adult rates (where pay was not affected by absence) in UK**

n.e.c. = not elsewhere classified
X = unreliable

| Occupation SOC 2010 | SOC Code | Gross Weekly Pay (in April) 2015 | | Gross Annual Pay in tax year 2015/16 | |
|---|---|---|---|---|---|
| | | Median £ | Mean £ | Median £ | Mean £ |
| Medical secretaries | 4211 | 416.7 | 413.1 | 21,769 | 21,294 |
| Legal secretaries | 4212 | 392.9 | 426.7 | 20,155 | 22,405 |
| School secretaries | 4213 | 387.2 | 412.7 | 19,445 | 21,128 |
| Company secretaries | 4214 | 469.5 | 568.9 | 24,482 | 32,103 |
| Personal assistants and other secretaries | 4215 | 488.3 | 519.9 | 25,023 | 26,963 |
| Receptionists | 4216 | 325.2 | 338.6 | 16,673 | 17,349 |
| Typists and related keyboard occupations | 4217 | 365.7 | 390.8 | X | 20,125 |
| **Skilled trades occupations** | 5 | 360.1 | 398.2 | 17,959 | 20,218 |
| Skilled agricultural and related trades | 51 | 399.4 | 416.3 | 19,169 | 19,836 |
| Agricultural and related trades | 511 | 399.4 | 416.3 | 19,169 | 19,836 |
| Farmers | 5111 | | | | |
| Horticultural trades | 5112 | 363.4 | 411.0 | X | 17,837 |
| Gardeners and landscape gardeners | 5113 | 393.6 | 422.7 | 18,739 | 19,973 |
| Groundsmen and gamekeepers | 5114 | 356.1 | 386.8 | 18,093 | 18,955 |
| Agricultural and fishing trades n.e.c. | 5119 | | | | |
| Skilled metal, electrical and electronic trades | 52 | 467.2 | 509.7 | 25,089 | 26,152 |
| Metal forming, welding and related trades | 521 | 278.6 | 303.8 | 13,151 | 14,872 |
| Smiths and forge workers | 5211 | | | | |
| Moulders, core makers and die casters | 5212 | | | | |
| Sheet metal workers | 5213 | | | | |
| Metal plate workers, and riveters | 5214 | | | | |
| Welding trades | 5215 | | | | |
| Pipe fitters | 5216 | | | | |
| Metal machining, fitting and instrument making trades | 522 | 447.1 | 474.4 | 19,704 | 23,422 |
| Metal machining setters and setter-operators | 5221 | 347.9 | 406.0 | X | 20,250 |
| Tool makers, tool fitters and markers-out | 5222 | | | | |
| Metal working production and maintenance fitters | 5223 | 460.6 | 492.8 | X | 23,611 |
| Precision instrument makers and repairers | 5224 | 442.2 | 475.8 | X | X |
| Air conditioning and refrigeration engineers | 5225 | | | | |
| Vehicle trades | 523 | 389.5 | 442.0 | X | 21,775 |
| Vehicle technicians, mechanics and electricians | 5231 | 334.4 | 380.1 | X | 18,242 |
| Vehicle body builders and repairers | 5232 | | | | |
| Vehicle paint technicians | 5234 | | | | |
| Aircraft maintenance and related trades | 5235 | X | 461.0 | X | X |
| Boat and ship builders and repairers | 5236 | | | | |
| Rail and rolling stock builders and repairers | 5237 | | | | |
| Electrical and electronic trades | 524 | 543.0 | 580.4 | 29,382 | 31,815 |
| Electricians and electrical fitters | 5241 | X | 554.3 | X | 29,353 |
| Telecommunications engineers | 5242 | 524.5 | 492.7 | 26,518 | 25,243 |
| TV, video and audio engineers | 5244 | | | | |
| IT engineers | 5245 | X | X | X | X |
| Electrical and electronic trades n.e.c. | 5249 | 589.3 | 614.1 | 31,747 | 33,998 |
| Skilled metal, electrical and electronic trades supervisors | 525 | 532.3 | 620.7 | 28,299 | 32,904 |
| Skilled metal, electrical and electronic trades supervisors | 5250 | 532.3 | 620.7 | 28,299 | 32,904 |
| Skilled construction and building trades | 53 | 415.1 | 467.4 | X | 23,644 |
| Construction and building trades | 531 | X | 486.3 | X | 23,554 |
| Steel erectors | 5311 | | | | |
| Bricklayers and masons | 5312 | | | | |
| Roofers, roof tilers and slaters | 5313 | | | | |
| Plumbers and heating and ventilating engineers | 5314 | X | 481.9 | X | 23,480 |
| Carpenters and joiners | 5315 | | | | |
| Glaziers, window fabricators and fitters | 5316 | | | | |
| Construction and building trades n.e.c. | 5319 | X | X | X | X |
| Building finishing trades | 532 | X | 427.4 | X | 22,724 |

*210*     PNBA

## Full-time Females employees on adult rates (where pay was not affected by absence) in UK

n.e.c. = not elsewhere classified
X = unreliable

| Occupation SOC 2010 | SOC Code | Gross Weekly Pay (in April) 2015 | | Gross Annual Pay in tax year 2015/16 | |
|---|---|---|---|---|---|
| | | Median £ | Mean £ | Median £ | Mean £ |
| Plasterers | 5321 | | | | |
| Floorers and wall tilers | 5322 | | | | |
| Painters and decorators | 5323 | 319.5 | 369.3 | | |
| Construction and building trades supervisors | 533 | 436.2 | 462.3 | X | 24,900 |
| Construction and building trades supervisors | 5330 | 436.2 | 462.3 | X | 24,900 |
| Textiles, printing and other skilled trades | 54 | 346.0 | 364.4 | 17,400 | 18,436 |
| Textiles and garments trades | 541 | 341.5 | 348.7 | X | X |
| Weavers and knitters | 5411 | | | | |
| Upholsterers | 5412 | 261.5 | 307.7 | 13,399 | 15,091 |
| Footwear and leather working trades | 5413 | 345.6 | 379.6 | 15,304 | 17,261 |
| Tailors and dressmakers | 5414 | | | | |
| Textiles, garments and related trades n.e.c. | 5419 | | | | |
| Printing trades | 542 | 346.7 | 374.1 | 17,954 | 19,296 |
| Pre-press technicians | 5421 | 377.7 | 378.9 | 19,255 | 19,630 |
| Printers | 5422 | X | 431.8 | X | 22,349 |
| Print finishing and binding workers | 5423 | 318.3 | 356.2 | 17,327 | 18,238 |
| Food preparation and hospitality trades | 543 | 345.0 | 361.6 | 17,503 | 18,431 |
| Butchers | 5431 | 363.4 | 413.5 | 19,308 | 19,234 |
| Bakers and flour confectioners | 5432 | 318.2 | 349.5 | 15,985 | 17,030 |
| Fishmongers and poultry dressers | 5433 | 292.7 | 322.7 | 15,742 | 16,149 |
| Chefs | 5434 | 355.4 | 370.9 | 18,008 | 19,153 |
| Cooks | 5435 | 293.3 | 300.8 | 15,117 | 15,429 |
| Catering and bar managers | 5436 | 377.7 | 394.7 | 18,694 | 20,161 |
| Other skilled trades | 544 | 355.0 | 402.0 | 17,300 | 20,086 |
| Glass and ceramics makers, decorators and finishers | 5441 | 307.6 | 330.9 | 16,079 | 17,429 |
| Furniture makers and other craft woodworkers | 5442 | 365.1 | 390.9 | X | X |
| Florists | 5443 | 285.9 | 339.7 | 15,783 | 16,990 |
| Other skilled trades n.e.c. | 5449 | 345.9 | 461.6 | X | 24,028 |
| **Caring, leisure and other service occupations** | 6 | 331.1 | 354.4 | 16,517 | 17,249 |
| Caring personal service occupations | 61 | 331.6 | 351.3 | 16,481 | 17,053 |
| Childcare and related personal services | 612 | 304.7 | 321.4 | 15,234 | 16,010 |
| Nursery nurses and assistants | 6121 | 293.7 | 312.9 | 14,512 | 15,458 |
| Childminders and related occupations | 6122 | 359.3 | 374.7 | 18,472 | 19,529 |
| Playworkers | 6123 | 307.1 | 332.3 | 15,402 | 16,661 |
| Teaching assistants | 6125 | 311.3 | 323.7 | 15,635 | 16,194 |
| Educational support assistants | 6126 | 305.5 | 319.0 | 15,213 | 15,943 |
| Animal care and control services | 613 | 352.0 | 357.2 | 18,017 | 18,904 |
| Veterinary nurses | 6131 | 378.6 | 387.9 | 18,069 | 19,168 |
| Pest control officers | 6132 | | | | |
| Animal care services occupations n.e.c. | 6139 | 308.1 | 328.8 | 17,434 | 18,524 |
| Caring personal services | 614 | 344.5 | 365.0 | 17,119 | 17,512 |
| Nursing auxiliaries and assistants | 6141 | 372.5 | 385.9 | 18,654 | 18,685 |
| Ambulance staff (excluding paramedics) | 6142 | 448.5 | 473.2 | 21,685 | 23,882 |
| Dental nurses | 6143 | 340.4 | 364.3 | 17,462 | 18,283 |
| Houseparents and residential wardens | 6144 | 392.8 | 433.9 | 20,163 | 21,101 |
| Care workers and home carers | 6145 | 323.9 | 348.0 | 15,736 | 16,332 |
| Senior care workers | 6146 | 354.1 | 370.5 | 17,040 | 18,289 |
| Care escorts | 6147 | 241.6 | 264.3 | 12,272 | 13,541 |
| Undertakers, mortuary and crematorium assistants | 6148 | 487.8 | 497.5 | 25,636 | 25,222 |
| Leisure, travel and related personal service occupations | 62 | 325.8 | 377.1 | 16,847 | 18,651 |
| Leisure and travel services | 621 | 374.8 | 416.4 | 19,214 | 21,055 |
| Sports and leisure assistants | 6211 | 302.2 | 333.5 | 15,398 | 16,896 |
| Travel agents | 6212 | 346.7 | 370.8 | X | 19,053 |
| Air travel assistants | 6214 | 423.5 | 459.9 | X | 22,178 |
| Rail travel assistants | 6215 | 618.2 | 651.6 | 32,692 | 32,932 |
| Leisure and travel service occupations n.e.c. | 6219 | 304.2 | 430.9 | 15,247 | 20,360 |

F7: Average Earnings Statistics

**Full-time Females employees on adult rates (where pay was not affected by absence) in UK**

n.e.c. = not elsewhere classified
X = unreliable

| Occupation SOC 2010 | SOC Code | Gross Weekly Pay (in April) 2015 | | Gross Annual Pay in tax year 2015/16 | |
|---|---|---|---|---|---|
| | | Median £ | Mean £ | Median £ | Mean £ |
| Hairdressers and related services | 622 | 291.4 | 333.8 | 14,522 | 15,632 |
| Hairdressers and barbers | 6221 | 275.8 | 336.1 | 13,797 | 14,780 |
| Beauticians and related occupations | 6222 | 312.9 | 329.9 | 15,709 | 17,287 |
| Housekeeping and related services | 623 | 328.7 | 367.3 | 16,863 | 18,424 |
| Housekeepers and related occupations | 6231 | 311.2 | 347.8 | 16,457 | 17,649 |
| Caretakers | 6232 | 374.4 | 407.3 | 18,450 | 20,138 |
| Cleaning and housekeeping managers and supervisors | 624 | 330.0 | 362.8 | 15,723 | 18,009 |
| Cleaning and housekeeping managers and supervisors | 6240 | 330.0 | 362.8 | 15,723 | 18,009 |
| **Sales and customer service occupations** | 7 | 333.3 | 365.1 | 16,829 | 18,357 |
| Sales occupations | 71 | 306.6 | 334.1 | 15,325 | 16,632 |
| Sales assistants and retail cashiers | 711 | 293.5 | 319.8 | 14,546 | 15,788 |
| Sales and retail assistants | 7111 | 294.5 | 322.9 | 14,436 | 15,787 |
| Retail cashiers and check-out operators | 7112 | 270.7 | 287.1 | 13,799 | 14,289 |
| Telephone salespersons | 7113 | 361.3 | 376.6 | 18,822 | 19,908 |
| Pharmacy and other dispensing assistants | 7114 | 293.4 | 303.0 | 15,309 | 15,694 |
| Vehicle and parts salespersons and advisers | 7115 | | | | |
| Sales related occupations | 712 | 392.5 | 434.9 | 21,302 | 22,850 |
| Collector salespersons and credit agents | 7121 | 297.8 | 334.0 | X | 20,474 |
| Debt, rent and other cash collectors | 7122 | 354.3 | 375.9 | 18,186 | 19,593 |
| Roundspersons and van salespersons | 7123 | | | | |
| Market and street traders and assistants | 7124 | | | | |
| Merchandisers and window dressers | 7125 | 440.8 | 492.0 | 22,221 | 24,041 |
| Sales related occupations n.e.c. | 7129 | 391.5 | 418.2 | 22,198 | X |
| Sales supervisors | 713 | 348.8 | 374.5 | 17,552 | 18,740 |
| Sales supervisors | 7130 | 348.8 | 374.5 | 17,552 | 18,740 |
| Customer service occupations | 72 | 382.0 | 416.1 | 19,696 | 21,280 |
| Customer service occupations | 721 | 364.2 | 388.0 | 18,934 | 19,801 |
| Call and contact centre occupations | 7211 | 324.4 | 341.2 | 17,032 | 17,492 |
| Telephonists | 7213 | 361.5 | 382.4 | 19,365 | 19,715 |
| Communication operators | 7214 | 532.9 | 532.6 | 28,680 | 28,572 |
| Market research interviewers | 7215 | X | 323.5 | X | X |
| Customer service occupations n.e.c. | 7219 | 366.1 | 389.9 | 19,042 | 19,818 |
| Customer service managers and supervisors | 722 | 505.9 | 538.4 | 25,432 | 27,516 |
| Customer service managers and supervisors | 7220 | 505.9 | 538.4 | 25,432 | 27,516 |
| **Process, plant and machine operatives** | 8 | 332.9 | 375.4 | 16,996 | 18,991 |
| Process, plant and machine operatives | 81 | 327.9 | 357.6 | 16,760 | 18,071 |
| Process operatives | 811 | 311.6 | 333.0 | 16,272 | 17,121 |
| Food, drink and tobacco process operatives | 8111 | 305.2 | 327.6 | 15,849 | 16,779 |
| Glass and ceramics process operatives | 8112 | X | 351.2 | 16,477 | 16,932 |
| Textile process operatives | 8113 | 345.2 | 336.4 | 17,083 | 17,051 |
| Chemical and related process operatives | 8114 | 356.5 | 386.3 | 18,686 | 20,083 |
| Rubber process operatives | 8115 | | | | |
| Plastics process operatives | 8116 | 323.1 | 386.5 | 17,027 | 20,004 |
| Metal making and treating process operatives | 8117 | | | | |
| Electroplaters | 8118 | | | | |
| Process operatives n.e.c. | 8119 | 298.9 | 293.9 | 16,096 | 16,104 |
| Plant and machine operatives | 812 | 334.0 | 366.4 | 17,264 | 18,793 |
| Paper and wood machine operatives | 8121 | 312.9 | 323.4 | 15,992 | 16,788 |
| Coal mine operatives | 8122 | | | | |
| Quarry workers and related operatives | 8123 | | | | |
| Energy plant operatives | 8124 | X | X | | |
| Metal working machine operatives | 8125 | 361.4 | 378.5 | 18,216 | 19,297 |
| Water and sewerage plant operatives | 8126 | X | X | X | X |
| Printing machine assistants | 8127 | 330.9 | 334.3 | 17,305 | 18,358 |

## Full-time Females employees on adult rates (where pay was not affected by absence) in UK

n.e.c. = not elsewhere classified
X = unreliable

| Occupation SOC 2010 | SOC Code | Gross Weekly Pay (in April) 2015 | | Gross Annual Pay in tax year 2015/16 | |
|---|---|---|---|---|---|
| | | Median £ | Mean £ | Median £ | Mean £ |
| Plant and machine operatives n.e.c. | 8129 | X | 453.8 | X | 21,603 |
| Assemblers and routine operatives | 813 | 339.8 | 372.8 | 16,912 | 18,423 |
| Assemblers (electrical and electronic products) | 8131 | 349.9 | 375.0 | 18,943 | 19,239 |
| Assemblers (vehicles and metal goods) | 8132 | X | 547.0 | 22,298 | 24,798 |
| Routine inspectors and testers | 8133 | 372.2 | 398.9 | 18,488 | 19,682 |
| Weighers, graders and sorters | 8134 | 279.0 | 333.3 | 14,066 | 15,234 |
| Tyre, exhaust and windscreen fitters | 8135 | | | | |
| Sewing machinists | 8137 | 294.5 | 316.1 | 14,866 | 15,905 |
| Assemblers and routine operatives n.e.c. | 8139 | 339.2 | 364.4 | 16,855 | 18,101 |
| Construction operatives | 814 | 380.5 | 422.7 | 20,697 | 21,367 |
| Scaffolders, stagers and riggers | 8141 | | | | |
| Road construction operatives | 8142 | | | | |
| Rail construction and maintenance operatives | 8143 | 625.2 | 709.0 | X | 29,632 |
| Construction operatives n.e.c. | 8149 | 372.9 | 394.3 | 19,007 | 20,091 |
| Transport and mobile machine drivers and operatives | 82 | 376.3 | 453.5 | 19,455 | 23,315 |
| Road transport drivers | 821 | 360.0 | 401.2 | 18,560 | 20,144 |
| Large goods vehicle drivers | 8211 | 479.7 | 478.1 | 21,670 | 23,034 |
| Van drivers | 8212 | 304.6 | 357.0 | X | X |
| Bus and coach drivers | 8213 | 426.0 | 458.2 | 22,698 | 23,468 |
| Taxi and cab drivers and chauffeurs | 8214 | 377.1 | 420.9 | 18,037 | 20,476 |
| Driving instructors | 8215 | | | | |
| Mobile machine drivers and operatives | 822 | 354.1 | 406.2 | X | 21,020 |
| Crane drivers | 8221 | | | | |
| Fork-lift truck drivers | 8222 | 369.4 | 394.1 | 19,676 | 21,565 |
| Agricultural machinery drivers | 8223 | | | | |
| Mobile machine drivers and operatives n.e.c. | 8229 | X | 393.4 | X | 19,503 |
| Other drivers and transport operatives | 823 | 806.1 | 776.3 | 43,938 | 38,991 |
| Train and tram drivers | 8231 | 951.1 | 936.8 | 49,627 | 46,926 |
| Marine and waterways transport operatives | 8232 | | | | |
| Air transport operatives | 8233 | | | | |
| Rail transport operatives | 8234 | X | X | X | X |
| Other drivers and transport operatives n.e.c. | 8239 | X | X | X | X |
| **Elementary occupations** | 9 | 293.4 | 318.0 | 14,973 | 15,903 |
| Elementary trades and related occupations | 91 | 310.9 | 326.7 | 15,886 | 16,740 |
| Elementary agricultural occupations | 911 | 312.1 | 327.6 | 16,534 | 16,623 |
| Farm workers | 9111 | 323.5 | 338.4 | 15,043 | 16,428 |
| Forestry workers | 9112 | | | | |
| Fishing and other elementary agriculture occupations n.e.c. | 9119 | 294.6 | 311.2 | 16,695 | 16,206 |
| Elementary construction occupations | 912 | 278.9 | 304.0 | 15,104 | 16,409 |
| Elementary process plant occupations | 9120 | 278.9 | 304.0 | 15,104 | 16,409 |
| Elementary process plant occupations | 913 | 310.7 | 326.8 | 15,835 | 16,751 |
| Industrial cleaning process occupations | 9130 | 326.9 | 337.7 | 17,452 | 16,839 |
| Packers, bottlers, canners and fillers | 9134 | 312.7 | 326.9 | 15,789 | 16,757 |
| Elementary process plant occupations n.e.c. | 9139 | 300.2 | 324.9 | 15,515 | 16,721 |
| Elementary administration and service occupations | 92 | 290.5 | 316.4 | 14,748 | 15,744 |
| Elementary administration occupations | 921 | 78.3 | 399.9 | 21,066 | 21,003 |
| Postal workers, mail sorters, messengers and couriers | 9211 | 462.7 | 464.6 | 23,346 | 23,872 |
| Elementary administration occupations n.e.c. | 9219 | 281.5 | 297.5 | 14,612 | 15,535 |
| Elementary cleaning occupations | 923 | 274.0 | 293.2 | 13,723 | 14,267 |
| Window cleaners | 9231 | | | | |
| Street cleaners | 9232 | | | | |
| Cleaners and domestics | 9233 | 273.8 | 294.0 | 13,690 | 14,198 |
| Launderers, dry cleaners and pressers | 9234 | 260.0 | 271.1 | 13,571 | 14,055 |
| Refuse and salvage occupations | 9235 | 309.3 | 332.7 | 15,731 | 17,284 |
| Vehicle valeters and cleaners | 9236 | 288.8 | 352.2 | X | 17,586 |
| Elementary cleaning occupations n.e.c. | 9239 | 369.5 | 389.1 | | |

F7: Average Earnings Statistics

**Full-time Females employees on adult rates (where pay was not affected by absence) in UK**

n.e.c. = not elsewhere classified
X = unreliable

| Occupation SOC 2010 | SOC Code | Gross Weekly Pay (in April) 2015 | | Gross Annual Pay in tax year 2015/16 | |
|---|---|---|---|---|---|
| | | Median £ | Mean £ | Median £ | Mean £ |
| Elementary security occupations | 924 | 418.7 | 444.3 | 21,592 | 22,556 |
| Security guards and related occupations | 9241 | 440.7 | 468.4 | 23,030 | 24,009 |
| Parking and civil enforcement occupations | 9242 | 408.0 | 407.7 | 20,460 | 20,953 |
| School midday and crossing patrol occupations | 9244 | 275.4 | 315.9 | 13,442 | 15,284 |
| Elementary security occupations n.e.c. | 9249 | 413.8 | 448.2 | 20,350 | 21,953 |
| Elementary sales occupations | 925 | 296.0 | 312.5 | 15,051 | 15,962 |
| Shelf fillers | 9251 | 295.8 | 311.6 | 14,953 | 15,847 |
| Elementary sales occupations n.e.c. | 9259 | 312.9 | 318.6 | 15,829 | 16,711 |
| Elementary storage occupations | 926 | 323.9 | 349.3 | 16,485 | 17,349 |
| Elementary storage occupations | 9260 | 323.9 | 349.3 | 16,485 | 17,349 |
| Other elementary services occupations | 927 | 271.9 | 284.5 | 13,481 | 13,746 |
| Hospital porters | 9271 | 318.7 | 339.3 | 17,475 | 19,029 |
| Kitchen and catering assistants | 9272 | 273.6 | 285.7 | 13,626 | 13,871 |
| Waiters and waitresses | 9273 | 265.9 | 279.7 | 13,498 | 13,920 |
| Bar staff | 9274 | 267.6 | 279.9 | 12,507 | 12,804 |
| Leisure and theme park attendants | 9275 | 269.2 | 296.7 | X | X |
| Other elementary services occupations n.e.c. | 9279 | 313.7 | 318.0 | 13,946 | 14,169 |
| Not Classified | | | | | |

*Source: Annual Survey of Hours and Earnings, Office for National Statistics*, Tables 14.1a and 14.7a.

# F8: Public sector comparable earnings

In the table below we show gross salary ranges and compare with equivalent gross salaries in the public sector

| Gross salary range From (£) | To (£) | Comparable gross salaries |
|---|---|---|
| 10,000 | 14,999 | National Minimum Wage (adults 21+, 39 hours per week) £14,095; National Living Wage (adults 25+, 39 hours per week) £14,602; Army (new entrants) £14,784 |
| 15,000 | 19,999 | Porter or Cook (NHS, B) £15,251; Porter or Cook (NHS, T) £17,978; Army Private (B) £18,306 |
| 20,000 | 24,999 | Army Private (T) £20,934; Nurse (newly qualified, B) £21,909; Teacher (newly qualified, B) £22,244; Trainee Hospital Doctor (B) £22,862 |
| 25,000 | 29,999 | Nurse Team Leader (B) £26,302; Army Corporal (B) £27,597; Nurse (non-specialist, T) £28,462 |
| 30,000 | 34,999 | Army Sergeant (B) £31,368; NHS Registrar (B) £31,614; Trainee Hospital Doctor (T) £32,066; Teacher (main pay scale, T) £32,831; Dean £34,460; Bishop (B) £34,460; Army Corporal (T) £34,681; Army Staff Sergeant (B) £34,724 |
| 35,000 | 39,999 | Teacher (upper scale, B) £35,218; Nurse Team Leader (T) £35,225; Warrant Officer 2 (B) £37,677; Teacher (upper scale, T) £37,871; Army Sergeant (T) £38,597; Army Captain (B) £39,629 |
| 40,000 | 44,999 | Warrant Officer 1 (B) £40,343; Bishop (T) £42,880; Head Teacher (B) £43,665; Army Staff Sergeant (T) £43,943 |
| 45,000 | 49,999 | Warrant Officer 2 (T) £45,206; Army Captain (T) £47,127; NHS Registrar (T) £47,647; Warrant Officer 1 (T) £48,865; Major (B) £49,918 |
| 50,000 | 59,999 | Teacher (advanced skills, T) £58,677; Major (T) £59,783 |
| 60,000 | 69,999 | Bishop of London £61,120; Archbishop of York £66,680 |
| 70,000 | 79,999 | Lieutenant Colonel (B) £70,059; MP £74,962; NHS Consultant (B) £76,001; Archbishop or Canterbury £77,810 |
| 80,000 | 99,999 | Lieutenant Colonel (T) £81,123; Colonel (B) £84,878; Colonel (T) £93,304; GP (Primary Medical Services contract, A) £99,800 |
| 100,000 | 119,999 | Brigadier (B) £101,147; NHS Consultant (excluding clinical excellence awards, T) £102,465; Brigadier (TS) £105,240; District Judge £106,623; Head Teacher (T) £107,210; Major General (B) £112,683 |
| 120,000 | 139,999 | Major General (T) £124,143; Lieutenant General (B) £131,109; Circuit Judge and Senior District Judge £133,506; Cabinet Minister £135,527 |
| 140,000 | 159,999 | Prime Minister £143,462; Senior Circuit Judge £144,172; Permanent Secretary (B) £152,500; Lieutenant General (T) £158,929 |
| 160,000 | 179,999 | Chief Executive, Health & Safety Executive (M) £162,500; General (B) £171,995; NHS Consultant (including maximum clinical excellence awards, T) £177,247 |
| 180,000 | 199,999 | High Court Judge £183,328; Government Actuary (M) £187,500; Permanent Secretary (T) £187,500; General (T) £192,703 |
| 200,000 | 219,999 | Director of Public Prosecutions (M) £202,500; Lord Justice of Appeal £204,695; Supreme Court Justice & Family Division President £215,256 |
| 220,000 | and over | Master of the Rolls £222,862; Lord Chief Justice £249,583; Chief of Defence Staff (M) £257,500; Chief Executive, Nuclear Decommissioning Authority (M) £277,500; Chief Executive, Civil Aviation Authority (M) £307,500; Chief Executive, Green Investment Bank (M) £327,500 |

Notes: All categories are subject to varying terms and conditions. (A), (B) and (T) indicate average, bottom and top of range or seniority for post or rank. (M) indicates midpoint of published £5,000 pay band, including taxable benefits and allowances

# Group G
*Tax and National Insurance*

G1: Net equivalents to a range of gross annual income figures

G2: Illustrative net earnings calculations

G3: Income tax reliefs and rates

G4: National Insurance contributions

G5: VAT registration thresholds and rates

## G1: Net equivalents to a range of gross annual income figures

| Gross income | 2004/05 Net equivalent income | | 2005/06 Net equivalent income | | 2006/07 Net equivalent income | |
|---|---|---|---|---|---|---|
| | Employed | Self-employed | Employed | Self-employed | Employed | Self-employed |
| £pa | £pa | £pa | £pa | £pa | £pa | £pa |
| 1,000 | 1,000 | 1,000 | 1,000 | 1,000 | 1,000 | 1,000 |
| 2,000 | 2,000 | 2,000 | 2,000 | 2,000 | 2,000 | 2,000 |
| 3,000 | 3,000 | 3,000 | 3,000 | 3,000 | 3,000 | 3,000 |
| 4,000 | 4,000 | 4,000 | 4,000 | 4,000 | 4,000 | 4,000 |
| 5,000 | 4,946 | 4,847 | 4,977 | 4,872 | 5,000 | 4,891 |
| 6,000 | 5,736 | 5,667 | 5,767 | 5,692 | 5,797 | 5,717 |
| 7,000 | 6,498 | 6,459 | 6,556 | 6,511 | 6,587 | 6,537 |
| 8,000 | 7,168 | 7,159 | 7,226 | 7,211 | 7,280 | 7,260 |
| 9,000 | 7,838 | 7,859 | 7,896 | 7,911 | 7,950 | 7,960 |
| 10,000 | 8,508 | 8,559 | 8,566 | 8,611 | 8,620 | 8,660 |
| 11,000 | 9,178 | 9,259 | 9,236 | 9,311 | 9,290 | 9,360 |
| 12,000 | 9,848 | 9,959 | 9,906 | 10,011 | 9,960 | 10,060 |
| 13,000 | 10,518 | 10,659 | 10,576 | 10,711 | 10,630 | 10,760 |
| 14,000 | 11,188 | 11,359 | 11,246 | 11,411 | 11,300 | 11,460 |
| 15,000 | 11,858 | 12,059 | 11,916 | 12,111 | 11,970 | 12,160 |
| 16,000 | 12,528 | 12,759 | 12,586 | 12,811 | 12,640 | 12,860 |
| 17,000 | 13,198 | 13,459 | 13,256 | 13,511 | 13,310 | 13,560 |
| 18,000 | 13,868 | 14,159 | 13,926 | 14,211 | 13,980 | 14,260 |
| 19,000 | 14,538 | 14,859 | 14,596 | 14,911 | 14,650 | 14,960 |
| 20,000 | 15,208 | 15,559 | 15,266 | 15,611 | 15,320 | 15,660 |
| 21,000 | 15,878 | 16,259 | 15,936 | 16,311 | 15,990 | 16,360 |
| 22,000 | 16,548 | 16,959 | 16,606 | 17,011 | 16,660 | 17,060 |
| 23,000 | 17,218 | 17,659 | 17,276 | 17,711 | 17,330 | 17,760 |
| 24,000 | 17,888 | 18,359 | 17,946 | 18,411 | 18,000 | 18,460 |
| 25,000 | 18,558 | 19,059 | 18,616 | 19,111 | 18,670 | 19,160 |
| 26,000 | 19,228 | 19,759 | 19,286 | 19,811 | 19,340 | 19,860 |
| 27,000 | 19,898 | 20,459 | 19,956 | 20,511 | 20,010 | 20,560 |
| 28,000 | 20,568 | 21,159 | 20,626 | 21,211 | 20,680 | 21,260 |
| 29,000 | 21,238 | 21,859 | 21,296 | 21,911 | 21,350 | 21,960 |
| 30,000 | 21,908 | 22,559 | 21,966 | 22,611 | 22,020 | 22,660 |
| 31,000 | 22,578 | 23,259 | 22,636 | 23,311 | 22,690 | 23,360 |
| 32,000 | 23,276 | 23,979 | 23,306 | 24,011 | 23,360 | 24,060 |
| 33,000 | 24,046 | 24,749 | 23,976 | 24,728 | 24,030 | 24,760 |
| 34,000 | 24,816 | 25,519 | 24,646 | 25,498 | 24,746 | 25,492 |
| 35,000 | 25,586 | 26,288 | 25,541 | 26,268 | 25,516 | 26,262 |
| 40,000 | 28,742 | 29,444 | 28,904 | 29,631 | 29,066 | 29,812 |
| 45,000 | 31,692 | 32,394 | 31,854 | 32,581 | 32,016 | 32,762 |
| 50,000 | 34,642 | 35,344 | 34,804 | 35,531 | 34,966 | 35,712 |
| 55,000 | 37,592 | 38,294 | 37,754 | 38,481 | 37,916 | 38,662 |
| 60,000 | 40,542 | 41,244 | 40,704 | 41,431 | 40,866 | 41,612 |
| 65,000 | 43,492 | 44,194 | 43,654 | 44,381 | 43,816 | 44,562 |
| 70,000 | 46,442 | 47,144 | 46,604 | 47,331 | 46,766 | 47,512 |
| 75,000 | 49,392 | 50,094 | 49,554 | 50,281 | 49,716 | 50,462 |
| 80,000 | 52,342 | 53,044 | 52,504 | 53,231 | 52,666 | 53,412 |
| 85,000 | 55,292 | 55,994 | 55,454 | 56,181 | 55,616 | 56,362 |
| 90,000 | 58,242 | 58,944 | 58,404 | 59,131 | 58,566 | 59,312 |
| 95,000 | 61,192 | 61,894 | 61,354 | 62,081 | 61,516 | 62,262 |
| 100,000 | 64,142 | 64,844 | 64,304 | 65,031 | 64,466 | 65,212 |
| 150,000 | 93,642 | 94,344 | 93,804 | 94,531 | 93,966 | 94,712 |
| 200,000 | 123,142 | 123,844 | 123,304 | 124,031 | 123,466 | 124,212 |
| 250,000 | 152,642 | 153,344 | 152,804 | 153,531 | 152,966 | 153,712 |
| 300,000 | 182,142 | 182,844 | 182,304 | 183,031 | 182,466 | 183,212 |

G1: Net equivalents to a range of gross annual income figures

|  | 2007/08 Employed | | | | 2007/08 Self–employed | | |
|---|---|---|---|---|---|---|---|
| Gross income £pa | Net equivalent income £pa | Net per £100 extra £pa | Reason | Gross income £pa | Net equivalent income £pa | Net per £100 extra £pa | Reason |
| 1,000 | 1,000 | 100 | | 1,000 | 1,000 | 100 | |
| 2,000 | 2,000 | 100 | | 2,000 | 2,000 | 100 | |
| 3,000 | 3,000 | 100 | | 4,000 | 4,000 | 100 | |
| 4,000 | 4,000 | 100 | | 4,635 | 4,635 | * | ← £114 NIC Class 2 payable |
| 5,000 | 5,000 | 100 | | 5,000 | 4,886 | * | |
| 5,225 | 5,225 | 79 | ← 10% tax payable and 11% NIC Class 1 payable | 5,225 | 5,111 | 82 | ← 10% tax payable and 8% NIC Class 4 payable |
| 6,000 | 5,837 | 79 | | 6,000 | 5,747 | 82 | |
| 7,000 | 6,627 | 79 | | 7,000 | 6,567 | 82 | |
| 7,455 | 6,986 | 67 | ← 22% tax payable | 7,455 | 6,940 | 70 | ← 22% tax payable |
| 8,000 | 7,352 | 67 | | 8,000 | 7,321 | 70 | |
| 9,000 | 8,022 | 67 | | 9,000 | 8,021 | 70 | |
| 10,000 | 8,692 | 67 | | 10,000 | 8,721 | 70 | *£2.20 x 52 weeks =£114 pa fixed for any level of income in excess of £4,635 pa. So net equivalent of £4,650 gross is £4,536. |
| 11,000 | 9,362 | 67 | | 11,000 | 9,421 | 70 | |
| 12,000 | 10,032 | 67 | | 12,000 | 10,121 | 70 | |
| 13,000 | 10,702 | 67 | | 13,000 | 10,821 | 70 | |
| 14,000 | 11,372 | 67 | | 14,000 | 11,521 | 70 | |
| 15,000 | 12,042 | 67 | | 15,000 | 12,221 | 70 | |
| 16,000 | 12,712 | 67 | | 16,000 | 12,921 | 70 | |
| 17,000 | 13,382 | 67 | | 17,000 | 13,621 | 70 | |
| 18,000 | 14,052 | 67 | | 18,000 | 14,321 | 70 | |
| 19,000 | 14,722 | 67 | | 19,000 | 15,021 | 70 | |
| 20,000 | 15,392 | 67 | | 20,000 | 15,721 | 70 | |
| 21,000 | 16,062 | 67 | | 21,000 | 16,421 | 70 | |
| 22,000 | 16,732 | 67 | | 22,000 | 17,121 | 70 | |
| 23,000 | 17,402 | 67 | | 23,000 | 17,821 | 70 | |
| 24,000 | 18,072 | 67 | | 24,000 | 18,521 | 70 | |
| 25,000 | 18,742 | 67 | | 25,000 | 19,221 | 70 | |
| 26,000 | 19,412 | 67 | | 26,000 | 19,921 | 70 | |
| 27,000 | 20,082 | 67 | | 27,000 | 20,621 | 70 | |
| 28,000 | 20,752 | 67 | | 28,000 | 21,321 | 70 | |
| 29,000 | 21,422 | 67 | | 29,000 | 22,021 | 70 | |
| 30,000 | 22,092 | 67 | | 30,000 | 22,721 | 70 | |
| 31,000 | 22,762 | 67 | | 31,000 | 23,421 | 70 | |
| 32,000 | 23,432 | 67 | | 32,000 | 24,121 | 70 | |
| 33,000 | 24,102 | 67 | | 33,000 | 24,821 | 70 | |
| 34,000 | 24,772 | 67 | | 34,000 | 25,521 | 70 | |
| 34,840 | 25,335 | 77 | ← NIC Class 1 reduced to 1% | 34,840 | 26,109 | 77 | ← NIC Class 4 reduced to 1% |
| 35,000 | 25,458 | 77 | | 35,000 | 26,233 | 77 | |
| 37,500 | 27,382 | 77 | | 37,500 | 28,157 | 77 | |
| 39,825 | 29,172 | 59 | ← 40% tax payable | 39,825 | 29,947 | 59 | ← 40% tax payable |
| 40,000 | 29,276 | 59 | | 40,000 | 30,051 | 59 | |
| 45,000 | 32,226 | 59 | | 45,000 | 33,001 | 59 | |
| 50,000 | 35,176 | 59 | | 50,000 | 35,951 | 59 | |
| 55,000 | 38,126 | 59 | | 55,000 | 38,901 | 59 | |
| 60,000 | 41,076 | 59 | | 60,000 | 41,851 | 59 | |
| 65,000 | 44,026 | 59 | | 65,000 | 44,801 | 59 | |
| 70,000 | 46,976 | 59 | | 70,000 | 47,751 | 59 | |
| 75,000 | 49,926 | 59 | | 75,000 | 50,701 | 59 | |
| 80,000 | 52,876 | 59 | | 80,000 | 53,651 | 59 | |
| 85,000 | 55,826 | 59 | | 85,000 | 56,601 | 59 | |
| 90,000 | 58,776 | 59 | | 90,000 | 59,551 | 59 | |
| 95,000 | 61,726 | 59 | | 95,000 | 62,501 | 59 | |
| 100,000 | 64,676 | 59 | | 100,000 | 65,451 | 59 | |
| 150,000 | 94,176 | 59 | | 150,000 | 94,951 | 59 | |
| 200,000 | 123,676 | 59 | | 200,000 | 124,451 | 59 | |
| 250,000 | 153,176 | 59 | | 250,000 | 153,951 | 59 | |
| 300,000 | 182,676 | 59 | | 300,000 | 183,451 | 59 | |

## G1: Net equivalents to a range of gross annual income figures

| | 2008/09 Employed | | | | 2008/09 Self-employed | | |
|---|---|---|---|---|---|---|---|
| Gross income £pa | Net equivalent income £pa | Net per £100 extra £pa | Reason | Gross income £pa | Net equivalent income £pa | Net per £100 extra £pa | Reason |
| 1,000 | 1,000 | 100 | | 1,000 | 1,000 | 100 | |
| 2,000 | 2,000 | 100 | | 2,000 | 2,000 | 100 | |
| 3,000 | 3,000 | 100 | | 4,000 | 4,000 | 100 | |
| 4,000 | 4,000 | 100 | | 4,825 | 4,825 | * | ← £120 NIC Class 2 payable |
| 5,000 | 5,000 | 100 | | 5,000 | 4,880 | 100 | |
| 5,435 | 5,435 | 89 | ← 11% NIC Class 1 payable | 5,435 | 5,315 | 92 | ← 8% NIC Class 4 payable |
| 6,000 | 5,938 | 89 | | 6,000 | 5,835 | 92 | |
| 6,035 | 5,969 | 69 | ← 20% tax payable | 6,035 | 5,867 | 72 | ← 20% tax payable |
| 7,000 | 6,635 | 69 | | 7,000 | 6,562 | 72 | |
| 8,000 | 7,325 | 69 | | 8,000 | 7,282 | 72 | |
| 9,000 | 8,015 | 69 | | 9,000 | 8,002 | 72 | |
| 10,000 | 8,705 | 69 | | 10,000 | 8,722 | 72 | |
| 11,000 | 9,395 | 69 | | 11,000 | 9,442 | 72 | *£2.30 x 52 weeks =£120 pa fixed for any level of income in excess of £4,825 pa. So net equivalent of £4,850 gross is £4,730. |
| 12,000 | 10,085 | 69 | | 12,000 | 10,162 | 72 | |
| 13,000 | 10,775 | 69 | | 13,000 | 10,882 | 72 | |
| 14,000 | 11,465 | 69 | | 14,000 | 11,602 | 72 | |
| 15,000 | 12,155 | 69 | | 15,000 | 12,322 | 72 | |
| 16,000 | 12,845 | 69 | | 16,000 | 13,042 | 72 | |
| 17,000 | 13,535 | 69 | | 17,000 | 13,762 | 72 | |
| 18,000 | 14,225 | 69 | | 18,000 | 14,482 | 72 | |
| 19,000 | 14,915 | 69 | | 19,000 | 15,202 | 72 | |
| 20,000 | 15,605 | 69 | | 20,000 | 15,922 | 72 | |
| 21,000 | 16,295 | 69 | | 21,000 | 16,642 | 72 | |
| 22,000 | 16,985 | 69 | | 22,000 | 17,362 | 72 | |
| 23,000 | 17,675 | 69 | | 23,000 | 18,082 | 72 | |
| 24,000 | 18,365 | 69 | | 24,000 | 18,802 | 72 | |
| 25,000 | 19,055 | 69 | | 25,000 | 19,522 | 72 | |
| 26,000 | 19,745 | 69 | | 26,000 | 20,242 | 72 | |
| 27,000 | 20,435 | 69 | | 27,000 | 20,962 | 72 | |
| 28,000 | 21,125 | 69 | | 28,000 | 21,682 | 72 | |
| 29,000 | 21,815 | 69 | | 29,000 | 22,402 | 72 | |
| 30,000 | 22,505 | 69 | | 30,000 | 23,122 | 72 | |
| 31,000 | 23,195 | 69 | | 31,000 | 23,842 | 72 | |
| 32,000 | 23,885 | 69 | | 32,000 | 24,562 | 72 | |
| 33,000 | 24,575 | 69 | | 33,000 | 25,282 | 72 | |
| 34,000 | 25,265 | 69 | | 34,000 | 26,002 | 72 | |
| 35,000 | 25,955 | 69 | | 35,000 | 26,722 | 72 | |
| 37,500 | 27,680 | 69 | | 37,500 | 28,522 | 72 | |
| 40,000 | 29,405 | 69 | | 40,000 | 30,322 | 72 | |
| 40,040 | 29,432 | 79 | ← NIC Class 1 reduced to 1% | 40,040 | 30,351 | 79 | ← NIC Class 4 reduced to 1% |
| 40,835 | 30,060 | 59 | ← 40% tax payable | 40,835 | 30,979 | 59 | ← 40% tax payable |
| 45,000 | 32,518 | 59 | | 45,000 | 33,436 | 59 | |
| 50,000 | 35,468 | 59 | | 50,000 | 36,386 | 59 | |
| 55,000 | 38,418 | 59 | | 55,000 | 39,336 | 59 | |
| 60,000 | 41,368 | 59 | | 60,000 | 42,286 | 59 | |
| 65,000 | 44,138 | 59 | | 65,000 | 45,236 | 59 | |
| 70,000 | 47,268 | 59 | | 70,000 | 48,186 | 59 | |
| 75,000 | 50,218 | 59 | | 75,000 | 51,136 | 59 | |
| 80,000 | 53,168 | 59 | | 80,000 | 54,086 | 59 | |
| 85,000 | 56,118 | 59 | | 85,000 | 57,036 | 59 | |
| 90,000 | 59,068 | 59 | | 90,000 | 59,986 | 59 | |
| 95,000 | 62,018 | 59 | | 95,000 | 62,936 | 59 | |
| 100,000 | 64,968 | 59 | | 100,000 | 65,886 | 59 | |
| 150,000 | 94,468 | 59 | | 150,000 | 95,386 | 59 | |
| 200,000 | 123,968 | 59 | | 200,000 | 124,886 | 59 | |
| 250,000 | 153,468 | 59 | | 250,000 | 154,386 | 59 | |
| 300,000 | 182,968 | 59 | | 300,000 | 183,886 | 59 | |

## G1: Net equivalents to a range of gross annual income figures

| | 2009/10 Employed | | | | 2009/10 Self–employed | | |
|---|---|---|---|---|---|---|---|
| | Net equivalent income | Net per £100 extra | Reason | | Net equivalent income | Net per £100 extra | Reason |
| Gross income £pa | £pa | £pa | | Gross income £pa | £pa | £pa | |
| 1,000 | 1,000 | 100 | | 1,000 | 1,000 | 100 | |
| 2,000 | 2,000 | 100 | | 2,000 | 2,000 | 100 | |
| 3,000 | 3,000 | 100 | | 3,000 | 3,000 | 100 | |
| 4,000 | 4,000 | 100 | | 4,000 | 4,000 | 100 | |
| 5,000 | 5,000 | 100 | | 5,075 | 5,075 | * | ← £125 NIC Class 2 payable |
| 5,715 | 5,715 | 89 | ← 11% NIC Class 1 payable | 5,715 | 5,590 | 92 | ← 8% NIC Class 4 payable |
| 6,000 | 5,969 | 89 | | 6,000 | 5,852 | 92 | |
| 6,475 | 6,391 | 69 | ← 20% tax payable | 6,475 | 6,289 | 72 | ← 20% tax payable |
| 7,000 | 6,754 | 69 | | 7,000 | 6,667 | 72 | |
| 8,000 | 7,444 | 69 | | 8,000 | 7,387 | 72 | |
| 9,000 | 8,134 | 69 | | 9,000 | 8,107 | 72 | *£2.40 x 52 weeks =£125 pa fixed for any level of income in excess of £5,075 pa. So net equivalent of £5,100 gross is £4,975. |
| 10,000 | 8,824 | 69 | | 10,000 | 8,827 | 72 | |
| 11,000 | 9,514 | 69 | | 11,000 | 9,547 | 72 | |
| 12,000 | 10,204 | 69 | | 12,000 | 10,267 | 72 | |
| 13,000 | 10,894 | 69 | | 13,000 | 10,987 | 72 | |
| 14,000 | 11,584 | 69 | | 14,000 | 11,707 | 72 | |
| 15,000 | 12,274 | 69 | | 15,000 | 12,427 | 72 | |
| 16,000 | 12,964 | 69 | | 16,000 | 13,147 | 72 | |
| 17,000 | 13,654 | 69 | | 17,000 | 13,867 | 72 | |
| 18,000 | 14,344 | 69 | | 18,000 | 14,587 | 72 | |
| 19,000 | 15,034 | 69 | | 19,000 | 15,307 | 72 | |
| 20,000 | 15,724 | 69 | | 20,000 | 16,027 | 72 | |
| 21,000 | 16,414 | 69 | | 21,000 | 16,747 | 72 | |
| 22,000 | 17,104 | 69 | | 22,000 | 17,467 | 72 | |
| 23,000 | 17,794 | 69 | | 23,000 | 18,187 | 72 | |
| 24,000 | 18,484 | 69 | | 24,000 | 18,907 | 72 | |
| 25,000 | 19,174 | 69 | | 25,000 | 19,627 | 72 | |
| 26,000 | 19,864 | 69 | | 26,000 | 20,347 | 72 | |
| 27,000 | 20,554 | 69 | | 27,000 | 21,067 | 72 | |
| 28,000 | 21,244 | 69 | | 28,000 | 21,787 | 72 | |
| 29,000 | 21,934 | 69 | | 29,000 | 22,507 | 72 | |
| 30,000 | 22,624 | 69 | | 30,000 | 23,227 | 72 | |
| 31,000 | 23,314 | 69 | | 31,000 | 23,947 | 72 | |
| 32,000 | 24,004 | 69 | | 32,000 | 24,667 | 72 | |
| 33,000 | 24,694 | 69 | | 33,000 | 25,387 | 72 | |
| 34,000 | 25,384 | 69 | | 34,000 | 26,107 | 72 | |
| 35,000 | 26,074 | 69 | | 35,000 | 26,827 | 72 | |
| 37,500 | 27,799 | 69 | | 37,500 | 28,627 | 72 | |
| 40,000 | 29,524 | 69 | | 40,000 | 30,427 | 72 | |
| 43,875 | 32,197 | 59 | ← NIC Class 1 reduced to 1% and 40% tax payable | 43,875 | 33,217 | 59 | ← NIC Class 4 reduced to 1% and 40% tax payable |
| 45,000 | 32,861 | 59 | | 45,000 | 33,881 | 59 | |
| 50,000 | 35,811 | 59 | | 50,000 | 36,831 | 59 | |
| 55,000 | 38,761 | 59 | | 55,000 | 39,781 | 59 | |
| 60,000 | 41,711 | 59 | | 60,000 | 42,731 | 59 | |
| 65,000 | 44,661 | 59 | | 65,000 | 45,681 | 59 | |
| 70,000 | 47,611 | 59 | | 70,000 | 48,631 | 59 | |
| 75,000 | 50,561 | 59 | | 75,000 | 51,581 | 59 | |
| 80,000 | 53,511 | 59 | | 80,000 | 54,531 | 59 | |
| 85,000 | 56,461 | 59 | | 85,000 | 57,481 | 59 | |
| 90,000 | 59,411 | 59 | | 90,000 | 60,431 | 59 | |
| 95,000 | 62,361 | 59 | | 95,000 | 63,381 | 59 | |
| 100,000 | 65,311 | 59 | | 100,000 | 66,331 | 59 | |
| 150,000 | 94,811 | 59 | | 150,000 | 95,831 | 59 | |
| 200,000 | 124,311 | 59 | | 200,000 | 125,331 | 59 | |
| 250,000 | 153,811 | 59 | | 250,000 | 154,831 | 59 | |
| 300,000 | 183,311 | 59 | | 300,000 | 184,331 | 59 | |

## G1: Net equivalents to a range of gross annual income figures

| | 2010/11 Employed | | | | 2010/11 Self–employed | | |
|---|---|---|---|---|---|---|---|
| Gross income £pa | Net equivalent income £pa | Net per £100 extra £pa | Reason | Gross income £pa | Net equivalent income £pa | Net per £100 extra £pa | Reason |
| 1,000 | 1,000 | 100 | | 1,000 | 1,000 | 100 | |
| 2,000 | 2,000 | 100 | | 2,000 | 2,000 | 100 | |
| 3,000 | 3,000 | 100 | | 3,000 | 3,000 | 100 | |
| 4,000 | 4,000 | 100 | | 4,000 | 4,000 | 100 | |
| 5,000 | 5,000 | 100 | | 5,075 | 5,075 | * | ← £125 NIC Class 2 payable |
| 5,715 | 5,715 | 89 | ← 11% NIC Class 1 payable | 5,715 | 5,590 | 92 | ← 8% NIC Class 4 payable |
| 6,000 | 5,969 | 89 | | 6,000 | 5,852 | 92 | |
| 6,475 | 6,391 | 69 | ← 20% tax payable | 6,475 | 6,289 | 72 | ← 20% tax payable |
| 7,000 | 6,754 | 69 | | 7,000 | 6,667 | 72 | |
| 8,000 | 7,444 | 69 | | 8,000 | 7,387 | 72 | |
| 9,000 | 8,134 | 69 | | 9,000 | 8,107 | 72 | * £2.40 x 52 weeks |
| 10,000 | 8,824 | 69 | | 10,000 | 8,827 | 72 | = £125 pa fixed for any |
| 11,000 | 9,514 | 69 | | 11,000 | 9,547 | 72 | level of income in excess of |
| 12,000 | 10,204 | 69 | | 12,000 | 10,267 | 72 | £5,075 pa. So net |
| 13,000 | 10,894 | 69 | | 13,000 | 10,987 | 72 | equivalent of £5,100 |
| 14,000 | 11,584 | 69 | | 14,000 | 11,707 | 72 | gross is £4,975. |
| 15,000 | 12,274 | 69 | | 15,000 | 12,427 | 72 | |
| 16,000 | 12,964 | 69 | | 16,000 | 13,147 | 72 | |
| 17,000 | 13,654 | 69 | | 17,000 | 13,867 | 72 | |
| 18,000 | 14,344 | 69 | | 18,000 | 14,587 | 72 | |
| 19,000 | 15,034 | 69 | | 19,000 | 15,307 | 72 | |
| 20,000 | 15,724 | 69 | | 20,000 | 16,027 | 72 | |
| 21,000 | 16,414 | 69 | | 21,000 | 16,747 | 72 | |
| 22,000 | 17,104 | 69 | | 22,000 | 17,467 | 72 | |
| 23,000 | 17,794 | 69 | | 23,000 | 18,187 | 72 | |
| 24,000 | 18,484 | 69 | | 24,000 | 18,907 | 72 | |
| 25,000 | 19,174 | 69 | | 25,000 | 19,627 | 72 | |
| 26,000 | 19,864 | 69 | | 26,000 | 20,347 | 72 | |
| 27,000 | 20,554 | 69 | | 27,000 | 21,067 | 72 | |
| 28,000 | 21,244 | 69 | | 28,000 | 21,787 | 72 | |
| 29,000 | 21,934 | 69 | | 29,000 | 22,507 | 72 | |
| 30,000 | 22,624 | 69 | | 30,000 | 23,227 | 72 | |
| 31,000 | 23,314 | 69 | | 31,000 | 23,947 | 72 | |
| 32,000 | 24,004 | 69 | | 32,000 | 24,667 | 72 | |
| 33,000 | 24,694 | 69 | | 33,000 | 25,387 | 72 | |
| 34,000 | 25,384 | 69 | | 34,000 | 26,107 | 72 | |
| 35,000 | 26,074 | 69 | | 35,000 | 26,827 | 72 | |
| 37,500 | 27,799 | 69 | | 37,500 | 28,627 | 72 | |
| 40,000 | 29,524 | 69 | | 40,000 | 30,427 | 72 | |
| 43,875 | 32,197 | 59 | ← NIC Class 1 reduced to 1% and 40% tax payable | 43,875 | 33,217 | 59 | ← NIC Class 4 reduced to 1% and 40% tax payable |
| 45,000 | 32,861 | 59 | | 45,000 | 33,881 | 59 | |
| 50,000 | 35,811 | 59 | | 50,000 | 36,831 | 59 | |
| 55,000 | 38,761 | 59 | | 55,000 | 39,781 | 59 | |
| 60,000 | 41,711 | 59 | | 60,000 | 42,731 | 59 | |
| 65,000 | 44,661 | 59 | | 65,000 | 45,681 | 59 | |
| 70,000 | 47,611 | 59 | | 70,000 | 48,631 | 59 | |
| 75,000 | 50,561 | 59 | | 75,000 | 51,581 | 59 | |
| 80,000 | 53,511 | 59 | | 80,000 | 54,531 | 59 | |
| 85,000 | 56,461 | 59 | | 85,000 | 57,481 | 59 | |
| 90,000 | 59,411 | 59 | | 90,000 | 60,431 | 59 | |
| 95,000 | 62,361 | 59 | | 95,000 | 63,381 | 59 | |
| 100,000 | 65,311 | 39 | ← PA reduces here | 100,000 | 66,331 | 39 | ← PA reduces here |
| 112,950 | 70,362 | 59 | ← PA reduced to zero | 112,950 | 71,381 | 59 | ← PA reduced to zero |
| 150,000 | 92,221 | 49 | ← 50% tax payable | 150,000 | 93,241 | 49 | ← 50% tax payable |
| 200,000 | 116,721 | 49 | | 200,000 | 117,741 | 49 | |
| 250,000 | 141,221 | 49 | | 250,000 | 142,241 | 49 | |
| 300,000 | 165,721 | 49 | | 300,000 | 166,741 | 49 | |

## G1: Net equivalents to a range of gross annual income figures

| | 2011/12 Employed | | | | 2011/12 Self–employed | | |
|---|---|---|---|---|---|---|---|
| Gross income £pa | Net equivalent income £pa | Net per £100 extra £pa | Reason | Gross income £pa | Net equivalent income £pa | Net per £100 extra £pa | Reason |
| 1,000 | 1,000 | 100 | | 1,000 | 1,000 | 100 | |
| 2,000 | 2,000 | 100 | | 2,000 | 2,000 | 100 | |
| 3,000 | 3,000 | 100 | | 3,000 | 3,000 | 100 | |
| 4,000 | 4,000 | 100 | | 4,000 | 4,000 | 100 | |
| 5,000 | 5,000 | 100 | | 5,315 | 5,315 | * | ← £130 NIC Class 2 payable |
| 6,000 | 6,000 | 100 | | 6,000 | 5,870 | * | |
| 7,000 | 7,000 | 100 | | 7,000 | 6,870 | * | |
| 7,225 | 7,225 | 88 | ← 12% NIC Class 1 payable | 7,225 | 7,095 | 91 | ← 9% NIC Class 4 payable |
| 7,475 | 7,445 | 68 | ← 20% tax payable | 7,475 | 7,322 | 71 | ← 20% tax payable |
| 8,000 | 7,802 | 68 | | 8,000 | 7,695 | 71 | |
| 9,000 | 8,482 | 68 | | 9,000 | 8,405 | 71 | * £2.50 x 52 weeks |
| 10,000 | 9,162 | 68 | | 10,000 | 9,115 | 71 | = £130 pa fixed for any |
| 11,000 | 9,842 | 68 | | 11,000 | 9,825 | 71 | level of income in excess of |
| 12,000 | 10,522 | 68 | | 12,000 | 10,535 | 71 | £5,315 pa. So net |
| 13,000 | 11,202 | 68 | | 13,000 | 11,245 | 71 | equivalent of £5,400 |
| 14,000 | 11,882 | 68 | | 14,000 | 11,955 | 71 | gross is £5,270. |
| 15,000 | 12,562 | 68 | | 15,000 | 12,665 | 71 | |
| 16,000 | 13,242 | 68 | | 16,000 | 13,375 | 71 | |
| 17,000 | 13,922 | 68 | | 17,000 | 14,085 | 71 | |
| 18,000 | 14,602 | 68 | | 18,000 | 14,795 | 71 | |
| 19,000 | 15,282 | 68 | | 19,000 | 15,505 | 71 | |
| 20,000 | 15,962 | 68 | | 20,000 | 16,215 | 71 | |
| 21,000 | 16,642 | 68 | | 21,000 | 16,925 | 71 | |
| 22,000 | 17,322 | 68 | | 22,000 | 17,635 | 71 | |
| 23,000 | 18,002 | 68 | | 23,000 | 18,345 | 71 | |
| 24,000 | 18,682 | 68 | | 24,000 | 19,055 | 71 | |
| 25,000 | 19,362 | 68 | | 25,000 | 19,765 | 71 | |
| 26,000 | 20,042 | 68 | | 26,000 | 20,475 | 71 | |
| 27,000 | 20,722 | 68 | | 27,000 | 21,185 | 71 | |
| 28,000 | 21,402 | 68 | | 28,000 | 21,895 | 71 | |
| 29,000 | 22,082 | 68 | | 29,000 | 22,605 | 71 | |
| 30,000 | 22,762 | 68 | | 30,000 | 23,315 | 71 | |
| 31,000 | 23,442 | 68 | | 31,000 | 24,025 | 71 | |
| 32,000 | 24,122 | 68 | | 32,000 | 24,735 | 71 | |
| 33,000 | 24,802 | 68 | | 33,000 | 25,445 | 71 | |
| 34,000 | 25,482 | 68 | | 34,000 | 26,155 | 71 | |
| 35,000 | 26,162 | 68 | | 35,000 | 26,865 | 71 | |
| 37,500 | 27,862 | 68 | | 37,500 | 28,640 | 71 | |
| 40,000 | 29,562 | 68 | | 40,000 | 30,415 | 71 | |
| 42,475 | 31,245 | 58 | ← NIC Class 1 reduced to 2% and 40% tax payable | 42,475 | 32,172 | 58 | ← NIC Class 4 reduced to 2% and 40% tax payable |
| 45,000 | 32,709 | 58 | | 45,000 | 33,636 | 58 | |
| 50,000 | 35,609 | 58 | | 50,000 | 36,536 | 58 | |
| 55,000 | 38,509 | 58 | | 55,000 | 39,436 | 58 | |
| 60,000 | 41,409 | 58 | | 60,000 | 42,336 | 58 | |
| 65,000 | 44,309 | 58 | | 65,000 | 45,236 | 58 | |
| 70,000 | 47,209 | 58 | | 70,000 | 48,136 | 58 | |
| 75,000 | 50,109 | 58 | | 75,000 | 51,036 | 58 | |
| 80,000 | 53,009 | 58 | | 80,000 | 53,936 | 58 | |
| 85,000 | 55,909 | 58 | | 85,000 | 56,836 | 58 | |
| 90,000 | 58,809 | 58 | | 90,000 | 59,736 | 58 | |
| 95,000 | 61,709 | 58 | | 95,000 | 62,636 | 58 | |
| 100,000 | 64,609 | 38 | ← PA reduces here | 100,000 | 65,536 | 38 | ← PA reduces here |
| 114,950 | 70,290 | 58 | ← PA reduced to zero | 114,950 | 71,217 | 58 | ← PA reduced to zero |
| 150,000 | 90,619 | 48 | ← 50% tax payable | 150,000 | 91,546 | 48 | ← 50% tax payable |
| 200,000 | 114,619 | 48 | | 200,000 | 115,546 | 48 | |
| 250,000 | 138,619 | 48 | | 250,000 | 139,546 | 48 | |
| 300,000 | 162,619 | 48 | | 300,000 | 163,546 | 48 | |

# G1: Net equivalents to a range of gross annual income figures

| | 2012/13 Employed | | | | 2012/13 Self-employed | | | |
|---|---|---|---|---|---|---|---|---|
| | Net equivalent income | Net per £100 extra | Reason | | Net equivalent income | Net per £100 extra | Reason |
| Gross income £pa | £pa | £pa | | Gross income £pa | £pa | £pa | |
| 1,000 | 1,000 | 100 | | 1,000 | 1,000 | | |
| 2,000 | 2,000 | 100 | | 2,000 | 2,000 | | |
| 3,000 | 3,000 | 100 | | 3,000 | 3,000 | | |
| 4,000 | 4,000 | 100 | | 4,000 | 4,000 | | |
| 5,000 | 5,000 | 100 | | 5,595 | 5,595 | * | ← £130 NIC Class 2 payable |
| 6,000 | 6,000 | 100 | | 6,000 | 5,862 | * | |
| 7,000 | 7,000 | 100 | | 7,000 | 6,862 | * | |
| 7,605 | 7,605 | 88 | ← 12% NIC Class 1 payable | 7,605 | 7,467 | 91 | ← 9% NIC Class 4 payable |
| 8,000 | 7,953 | 88 | | 8,000 | 7,826 | 91 | |
| 8,105 | 8,045 | 68 | ← 20% tax payable | 8,105 | 7,922 | 71 | ← 20% tax payable |
| 9,000 | 8,654 | 68 | | 9,000 | 8,557 | 71 | * £2.65 x 52 weeks |
| 10,000 | 9,334 | 68 | | 10,000 | 9,267 | 71 | = £138 pa fixed for any |
| 11,000 | 10,014 | 68 | | 11,000 | 9,977 | 71 | level of income in excess of |
| 12,000 | 10,694 | 68 | | 12,000 | 10,687 | 71 | £5,595 pa. So net |
| 13,000 | 11,374 | 68 | | 13,000 | 11,397 | 71 | equivalent of £5,600 |
| 14,000 | 12,054 | 68 | | 14,000 | 12,107 | 71 | gross is £5,462. |
| 15,000 | 12,734 | 68 | | 15,000 | 12,817 | 71 | |
| 16,000 | 13,414 | 68 | | 16,000 | 13,527 | 71 | |
| 17,000 | 14,094 | 68 | | 17,000 | 14,237 | 71 | |
| 18,000 | 14,774 | 68 | | 18,000 | 14,947 | 71 | |
| 19,000 | 15,454 | 68 | | 19,000 | 15,657 | 71 | |
| 20,000 | 16,134 | 68 | | 20,000 | 16,367 | 71 | |
| 21,000 | 16,814 | 68 | | 21,000 | 17,077 | 71 | |
| 22,000 | 17,494 | 68 | | 22,000 | 17,787 | 71 | |
| 23,000 | 18,174 | 68 | | 23,000 | 18,497 | 71 | |
| 24,000 | 18,854 | 68 | | 24,000 | 19,207 | 71 | |
| 25,000 | 19,534 | 68 | | 25,000 | 19,917 | 71 | |
| 26,000 | 20,214 | 68 | | 26,000 | 20,627 | 71 | |
| 27,000 | 20,894 | 68 | | 27,000 | 21,337 | 71 | |
| 28,000 | 21,574 | 68 | | 28,000 | 22,047 | 71 | |
| 29,000 | 22,254 | 68 | | 29,000 | 22,757 | 71 | |
| 30,000 | 22,934 | 68 | | 30,000 | 23,467 | 71 | |
| 31,000 | 23,614 | 68 | | 31,000 | 24,177 | 71 | |
| 32,000 | 24,294 | 68 | | 32,000 | 24,887 | 71 | |
| 33,000 | 24,974 | 68 | | 33,000 | 25,597 | 71 | |
| 34,000 | 25,654 | 68 | | 34,000 | 26,307 | 71 | |
| 35,000 | 26,334 | 68 | | 35,000 | 27,017 | 71 | |
| 37,500 | 28,034 | 68 | | 37,500 | 28,792 | 71 | |
| 40,000 | 29,734 | 68 | | 40,000 | 30,567 | 71 | |
| 42,475 | 31,417 | 58 | ← NIC Class 1 reduced to 2% and 40% tax payable | 42,475 | 32,325 | 58 | ← NIC Class 4 reduced to 2% and 40% tax payable |
| 45,000 | 32,881 | 58 | | 45,000 | 33,789 | 58 | |
| 50,000 | 35,781 | 58 | | 50,000 | 36,689 | 58 | |
| 55,000 | 38,681 | 58 | | 55,000 | 39,589 | 58 | |
| 60,000 | 41,581 | 58 | | 60,000 | 42,489 | 58 | |
| 65,000 | 44,481 | 58 | | 65,000 | 45,389 | 58 | |
| 70,000 | 47,381 | 58 | | 70,000 | 48,289 | 58 | |
| 75,000 | 50,281 | 58 | | 75,000 | 51,189 | 58 | |
| 80,000 | 53,181 | 58 | | 80,000 | 54,089 | 58 | |
| 85,000 | 56,081 | 58 | | 85,000 | 56,989 | 58 | |
| 90,000 | 58,981 | 58 | | 90,000 | 59,889 | 58 | |
| 95,000 | 61,881 | 58 | | 95,000 | 62,789 | 58 | |
| 100,000 | 64,781 | 38 | ← PA reduces here | 100,000 | 65,689 | 38 | ← PA reduces here |
| 116,210 | 70,941 | 58 | ← PA reduced to zero | 116,210 | 71,849 | 58 | ← PA reduced to zero |
| 150,000 | 90,539 | 48 | ← 50% tax payable | 150,000 | 91,447 | 48 | ← 50% tax payable |
| 200,000 | 114,539 | 48 | | 200,000 | 115,447 | 48 | |
| 250,000 | 138,539 | 48 | | 250,000 | 139,447 | 48 | |
| 300,000 | 162,539 | 48 | | 300,000 | 163,447 | 48 | |

## G1: Net equivalents to a range of gross annual income figures

| | 2013/14 Employed | | | | 2013/14 Self-employed | | |
|---|---|---|---|---|---|---|---|
| Gross income £pa | Net equivalent income £pa | Net per £100 extra £pa | Reason | Gross income £pa | Net equivalent income £pa | Net per £100 extra £pa | Reason |
| 1,000 | 1,000 | 100 | | 1,000 | 1,000 | | |
| 2,000 | 2,000 | 100 | | 2,000 | 2,000 | | |
| 3,000 | 3,000 | 100 | | 3,000 | 3,000 | | |
| 4,000 | 4,000 | 100 | | 4,000 | 4,000 | | |
| 5,000 | 5,000 | 100 | | 5,725 | 5,725 | * | ← £140 NIC Class 2 payable |
| 6,000 | 6,000 | 100 | | 6,000 | 5,860 | * | |
| 7,000 | 7,000 | 100 | | 7,000 | 6,860 | * | |
| 7,755 | 7,755 | 88 | ← 12% NIC Class 1 payable | 7,755 | 7,615 | 91 | ← 9% NIC Class 4 payable |
| 8,000 | 7,971 | 88 | | 8,000 | 7,838 | 91 | |
| 9,000 | 8,851 | 88 | | 9,000 | 8,748 | 91 | |
| 9,440 | 9,238 | 68 | ← 20% tax payable | 9,440 | 9,148 | 71 | ← 20% tax payable |
| 10,000 | 9,619 | 68 | | 10,000 | 9,546 | 71 | * £2.70 x 52 weeks |
| 11,000 | 10,299 | 68 | | 11,000 | 10,256 | 71 | = £140 pa fixed for any |
| 12,000 | 10,979 | 68 | | 12,000 | 10,966 | 71 | level of income in excess of |
| 13,000 | 11,659 | 68 | | 13,000 | 11,676 | 71 | £5,725 pa. So net |
| 14,000 | 12,339 | 68 | | 14,000 | 12,386 | 71 | equivalent of £6,100 |
| 15,000 | 13,019 | 68 | | 15,000 | 13,096 | 71 | gross is £5,960. |
| 16,000 | 13,699 | 68 | | 16,000 | 13,806 | 71 | |
| 17,000 | 14,379 | 68 | | 17,000 | 14,516 | 71 | |
| 18,000 | 15,059 | 68 | | 18,000 | 15,226 | 71 | |
| 19,000 | 15,739 | 68 | | 19,000 | 15,936 | 71 | |
| 20,000 | 16,419 | 68 | | 20,000 | 16,646 | 71 | |
| 21,000 | 17,099 | 68 | | 21,000 | 17,356 | 71 | |
| 22,000 | 17,779 | 68 | | 22,000 | 18,066 | 71 | |
| 23,000 | 18,459 | 68 | | 23,000 | 18,776 | 71 | |
| 24,000 | 19,139 | 68 | | 24,000 | 19,486 | 71 | |
| 25,000 | 19,819 | 68 | | 25,000 | 20,196 | 71 | |
| 26,000 | 20,499 | 68 | | 26,000 | 20,906 | 71 | |
| 27,000 | 21,179 | 68 | | 27,000 | 21,616 | 71 | |
| 28,000 | 21,859 | 68 | | 28,000 | 22,326 | 71 | |
| 29,000 | 22,539 | 68 | | 29,000 | 23,036 | 71 | |
| 30,000 | 23,219 | 68 | | 30,000 | 23,746 | 71 | |
| 31,000 | 23,899 | 68 | | 31,000 | 24,456 | 71 | |
| 32,000 | 24,579 | 68 | | 32,000 | 25,166 | 71 | |
| 33,000 | 25,259 | 68 | | 33,000 | 25,876 | 71 | |
| 34,000 | 25,939 | 68 | | 34,000 | 26,586 | 71 | |
| 35,000 | 26,619 | 68 | | 35,000 | 27,296 | 71 | |
| 37,500 | 28,319 | 68 | | 37,500 | 29,071 | 71 | |
| 40,000 | 30,019 | 68 | | 40,000 | 30,846 | 71 | |
| 41,450 | 31,005 | 58 | ← NIC Class 1 reduced to 2% and 40% tax payable | 41,450 | 31,875 | 58 | ← NIC Class 4 reduced to 2% and 40% tax payable |
| 45,000 | 33,064 | 58 | | 45,000 | 33,934 | 58 | |
| 50,000 | 35,964 | 58 | | 50,000 | 36,834 | 58 | |
| 55,000 | 38,864 | 58 | | 55,000 | 39,734 | 58 | |
| 60,000 | 41,764 | 58 | | 60,000 | 42,634 | 58 | |
| 65,000 | 44,664 | 58 | | 65,000 | 45,534 | 58 | |
| 70,000 | 47,564 | 58 | | 70,000 | 48,434 | 58 | |
| 75,000 | 50,464 | 58 | | 75,000 | 51,334 | 58 | |
| 80,000 | 53,364 | 58 | | 80,000 | 54,234 | 58 | |
| 85,000 | 56,264 | 58 | | 85,000 | 57,134 | 58 | |
| 90,000 | 59,164 | 58 | | 90,000 | 60,034 | 58 | |
| 95,000 | 62,064 | 58 | | 95,000 | 62,934 | 58 | |
| 100,000 | 64,964 | 38 | ← PA reduces here | 100,000 | 65,834 | 38 | ← PA reduces here |
| 118,880 | 72,138 | 58 | ← PA reduced to zero | 118,880 | 73,008 | 58 | ← PA reduced to zero |
| 150,000 | 90,188 | 53 | ← 45% tax payable | 150,000 | 91,058 | 53 | ← 45% tax payable |
| 200,000 | 116,688 | 53 | | 200,000 | 117,558 | 53 | |
| 250,000 | 143,188 | 53 | | 250,000 | 144,058 | 53 | |
| 300,000 | 169,688 | 53 | | 300,000 | 170,558 | 53 | |

## G1: Net equivalents to a range of gross annual income figures

| | 2014/15 Employed | | | | 2014/15 Self-employed | | | |
|---|---|---|---|---|---|---|---|---|
| | Net equivalent income | Net per £100 extra | Reason | | Net equivalent income | Net per £100 extra | Reason |
| Gross income £pa | £pa | £pa | | Gross income £pa | £pa | £pa | |
| 1,000 | 1,000 | 100 | | 1,000 | 1,000 | 100 | |
| 2,000 | 2,000 | 100 | | 2,000 | 2,000 | 100 | |
| 3,000 | 3,000 | 100 | | 3,000 | 3,000 | 100 | |
| 4,000 | 4,000 | 100 | | 4,000 | 4,000 | 100 | |
| 5,000 | 5,000 | 100 | | 5,885 | 5,885 | * | ← £140 NIC Class 2 payable |
| 6,000 | 6,000 | 100 | | 6,000 | 5,857 | * | |
| 7,000 | 7,000 | 100 | | 7,000 | 6,857 | * | |
| 7,956 | 7,956 | 88 | ← 12% NIC Class 1 payable | 7,956 | 7,813 | 91 | ← 9% NIC Class 4 payable |
| 8,000 | 7,995 | 88 | | 8,000 | 7,853 | 91 | |
| 9,000 | 8,875 | 88 | | 9,000 | 8,763 | 91 | |
| 10,000 | 9,755 | 68 | ← 20% tax payable | 10,000 | 9,673 | 71 | ← 20% tax payable |
| 11,000 | 10,435 | 68 | | 11,000 | 10,383 | 71 | |
| 12,000 | 11,115 | 68 | | 12,000 | 11,093 | 71 | *£2.75 x 52 weeks |
| 13,000 | 11,795 | 68 | | 13,000 | 11,803 | 71 | = £143 pa fixed for any |
| 14,000 | 12,475 | 68 | | 14,000 | 12,513 | 71 | level of income in excess of |
| 15,000 | 13,155 | 68 | | 15,000 | 13,223 | 71 | £5,725 pa. So net |
| 16,000 | 13,835 | 68 | | 16,000 | 13,933 | 71 | equivalent of £6,100 |
| 17,000 | 14,515 | 68 | | 17,000 | 14,643 | 71 | gross is £5,957. |
| 18,000 | 15,195 | 68 | | 18,000 | 15,353 | 71 | |
| 19,000 | 15,875 | 68 | | 19,000 | 16,063 | 71 | |
| 20,000 | 16,555 | 68 | | 20,000 | 16,773 | 71 | |
| 21,000 | 17,235 | 68 | | 21,000 | 17,483 | 71 | |
| 22,000 | 17,915 | 68 | | 22,000 | 18,193 | 71 | |
| 23,000 | 18,595 | 68 | | 23,000 | 18,903 | 71 | |
| 24,000 | 19,275 | 68 | | 24,000 | 19,613 | 71 | |
| 25,000 | 19,955 | 68 | | 25,000 | 20,323 | 71 | |
| 26,000 | 20,635 | 68 | | 26,000 | 21,033 | 71 | |
| 27,000 | 21,315 | 68 | | 27,000 | 21,743 | 71 | |
| 28,000 | 21,995 | 68 | | 28,000 | 22,453 | 71 | |
| 29,000 | 22,675 | 68 | | 29,000 | 23,163 | 71 | |
| 30,000 | 23,355 | 68 | | 30,000 | 23,873 | 71 | |
| 31,000 | 24,035 | 68 | | 31,000 | 24,583 | 71 | |
| 32,000 | 24,715 | 68 | | 32,000 | 25,293 | 71 | |
| 33,000 | 25,395 | 68 | | 33,000 | 26,003 | 71 | |
| 34,000 | 26,075 | 68 | | 34,000 | 26,713 | 71 | |
| 35,000 | 26,755 | 68 | | 35,000 | 27,423 | 71 | |
| 37,500 | 28,455 | 68 | | 37,500 | 29,198 | 71 | |
| 40,000 | 30,155 | 68 | | 40,000 | 30,973 | 71 | |
| 41,865 | 31,423 | 58 | ← NIC Class 1 reduced to 2% and 40% tax payable | 41,865 | 32,297 | 58 | ← NIC Class 4 reduced to 2% and 40% tax payable |
| 45,000 | 33,241 | 58 | | 45,000 | 34,115 | 58 | |
| 50,000 | 36,141 | 58 | | 50,000 | 37,015 | 58 | |
| 55,000 | 39,041 | 58 | | 55,000 | 39,915 | 58 | |
| 60,000 | 41,941 | 58 | | 60,000 | 42,815 | 58 | |
| 65,000 | 44,841 | 58 | | 65,000 | 45,715 | 58 | |
| 70,000 | 47,741 | 58 | | 70,000 | 48,615 | 58 | |
| 75,000 | 50,641 | 58 | | 75,000 | 51,515 | 58 | |
| 80,000 | 53,541 | 58 | | 80,000 | 54,415 | 58 | |
| 85,000 | 56,441 | 58 | | 85,000 | 57,315 | 58 | |
| 90,000 | 59,341 | 58 | | 90,000 | 60,215 | 58 | |
| 95,000 | 62,241 | 58 | | 95,000 | 63,115 | 58 | |
| 100,000 | 65,141 | 38 | ← PA reduces here | 100,000 | 66,015 | 38 | ← PA reduces here |
| 120,000 | 72,741 | 58 | ← PA reduced to zero | 120,000 | 73,615 | 58 | ← PA reduced to zero |
| 150,000 | 90,141 | 53 | ← 45% tax payable | 150,000 | 91,015 | 53 | ← 45% tax payable |
| 200,000 | 116,641 | 53 | | 200,000 | 117,515 | 53 | |
| 250,000 | 143,141 | 53 | | 250,000 | 144,015 | 53 | |
| 300,000 | 169,641 | 53 | | 300,000 | 170,515 | 53 | |

## G1: Net equivalents to a range of gross annual income figures

| | 2015/16 Employed | | | | 2015/16 Self-employed | | |
|---|---|---|---|---|---|---|---|
| Gross income £pa | Net equivalent income £pa | Net per £100 extra £pa | Reason | Gross income £pa | Net equivalent income £pa | Net per £100 extra £pa | Reason |
| 1,000 | 1,000 | 100 | | 1,000 | 1,000 | 100 | |
| 2,000 | 2,000 | 100 | | 2,000 | 2,000 | 100 | |
| 3,000 | 3,000 | 100 | | 3,000 | 3,000 | 100 | |
| 4,000 | 4,000 | 100 | | 4,000 | 4,000 | 100 | |
| 5,000 | 5,000 | 100 | | 5,965 | 5,965 | * | ← £146 NIC Class 2 payable |
| 6,000 | 6,000 | 100 | | 6,000 | 5,854 | * | |
| 7,000 | 7,000 | 100 | | 7,000 | 6,854 | * | |
| 8,000 | 8,000 | 100 | | 8,000 | 7,854 | * | |
| 8,060 | 8,060 | 88 | ← 12% NIC Class 1 payable | 8,060 | 7,914 | 91 | ← 9% NIC Class 4 payable |
| 9,000 | 8,887 | 88 | | 9,000 | 8,769 | 91 | |
| 10,000 | 9,767 | 68 | | 10,000 | 9,679 | 91 | |
| 10,600 | 10,295 | 68 | ← 20% tax payable | 10,600 | 10,225 | 71 | ← 20% tax payable |
| 11,000 | 10,567 | 68 | | 11,000 | 10,509 | 71 | |
| 12,000 | 11,247 | 68 | | 12,000 | 11,219 | 71 | *£2.80 x 52 weeks |
| 13,000 | 11,927 | 68 | | 13,000 | 11,929 | 71 | = £146 pa fixed for any |
| 14,000 | 12,607 | 68 | | 14,000 | 12,639 | 71 | level of income in excess of |
| 15,000 | 13,287 | 68 | | 15,000 | 13,349 | 71 | £5,965 pa. So net |
| 16,000 | 13,967 | 68 | | 16,000 | 14,059 | 71 | equivalent of £6,100 |
| 17,000 | 14,647 | 68 | | 17,000 | 14,769 | 71 | gross is £5,954. |
| 18,000 | 15,327 | 68 | | 18,000 | 15,479 | 71 | |
| 19,000 | 16,007 | 68 | | 19,000 | 16,189 | 71 | |
| 20,000 | 16,687 | 68 | | 20,000 | 16,899 | 71 | |
| 21,000 | 17,367 | 68 | | 21,000 | 17,609 | 71 | |
| 22,000 | 18,047 | 68 | | 22,000 | 18,319 | 71 | |
| 23,000 | 18,727 | 68 | | 23,000 | 19,029 | 71 | |
| 24,000 | 19,407 | 68 | | 24,000 | 19,739 | 71 | |
| 25,000 | 20,087 | 68 | | 25,000 | 20,449 | 71 | |
| 26,000 | 20,767 | 68 | | 26,000 | 21,159 | 71 | |
| 27,000 | 21,447 | 68 | | 27,000 | 21,869 | 71 | |
| 28,000 | 22,127 | 68 | | 28,000 | 22,579 | 71 | |
| 29,000 | 22,807 | 68 | | 29,000 | 23,289 | 71 | |
| 30,000 | 23,487 | 68 | | 30,000 | 23,999 | 71 | |
| 31,000 | 24,167 | 68 | | 31,000 | 24,709 | 71 | |
| 32,000 | 24,847 | 68 | | 32,000 | 25,419 | 71 | |
| 33,000 | 25,527 | 68 | | 33,000 | 26,129 | 71 | |
| 34,000 | 26,207 | 68 | | 34,000 | 26,839 | 71 | |
| 35,000 | 26,887 | 68 | | 35,000 | 27,549 | 71 | |
| 37,500 | 28,587 | 68 | | 37,500 | 29,324 | 71 | |
| 40,000 | 30,287 | 68 | | 40,000 | 31,099 | 71 | |
| 42,385 | 31,909 | 58 | ← NIC Class 1 reduced to 2% and 40% tax payable | 42,385 | 32,793 | 58 | ← NIC Class 4 reduced to 2% and 40% tax payable |
| 45,000 | 33,426 | 58 | | 45,000 | 34,310 | 58 | |
| 50,000 | 36,326 | 58 | | 50,000 | 37,210 | 58 | |
| 55,000 | 39,226 | 58 | | 55,000 | 40,110 | 58 | |
| 60,000 | 42,126 | 58 | | 60,000 | 43,010 | 58 | |
| 65,000 | 45,026 | 58 | | 65,000 | 45,910 | 58 | |
| 70,000 | 47,926 | 58 | | 70,000 | 48,810 | 58 | |
| 75,000 | 50,826 | 58 | | 75,000 | 51,710 | 58 | |
| 80,000 | 53,726 | 58 | | 80,000 | 54,610 | 58 | |
| 85,000 | 56,626 | 58 | | 85,000 | 57,510 | 58 | |
| 90,000 | 59,526 | 58 | | 90,000 | 60,410 | 58 | |
| 95,000 | 62,426 | 58 | | 95,000 | 63,310 | 58 | |
| 100,000 | 65,326 | 38 | ← PA reduces here | 100,000 | 66,210 | 38 | ← PA reduces here |
| 121,200 | 73,382 | 53 | ← PA reduced to zero | 121,200 | 74,266 | 58 | ← PA reduced to zero |
| 150,000 | 90,086 | 53 | ← 45% tax payable | 150,000 | 90,970 | 53 | ← 45% tax payable |
| 200,000 | 116,586 | 53 | | 200,000 | 117,470 | 53 | |
| 250,000 | 143,086 | 53 | | 250,000 | 143,970 | 53 | |
| 300,000 | 169,586 | 53 | | 300,000 | 170,470 | 53 | |

## G1: Net equivalents to a range of gross annual income figures

| | 2016/17 Employed | | | | 2016/17 Self-employed | | |
|---|---|---|---|---|---|---|---|
| | Net equivalent income | Net per £100 extra | Reason | | Net equivalent income | Net per £100 extra | Reason |
| Gross income £pa | £pa | £pa | | Gross income £pa | £pa | £pa | |
| 1,000 | 1,000 | 100 | | 1,000 | 1,000 | 100 | |
| 2,000 | 2,000 | 100 | | 2,000 | 2,000 | 100 | |
| 3,000 | 3,000 | 100 | | 3,000 | 3,000 | 100 | |
| 4,000 | 4,000 | 100 | | 4,000 | 4,000 | 100 | |
| 5,000 | 5,000 | 100 | | 5,965 | 5,965 | * | ← £146 NIC Class 2 payable |
| 6,000 | 6,000 | 100 | | 6,000 | 5,854 | * | |
| 7,000 | 7,000 | 100 | | 7,000 | 6,854 | * | |
| 8,000 | 8,000 | 100 | | 8,000 | 7,854 | * | |
| 8,060 | 8,060 | 88 | ← 12% NIC Class 1 payable | 8,060 | 7,914 | 91 | ← 9% NIC Class 4 payable |
| 9,000 | 8,887 | 88 | | 9,000 | 8,769 | 91 | |
| 10,000 | 9,767 | 88 | | 10,000 | 9,679 | 88 | |
| 11,000 | 10,647 | 68 | ← 20% tax payable | 11,000 | 10,589 | 71 | |
| 12,000 | 11,327 | 68 | | 12,000 | 11,299 | 71 | * £2.80 x 52 weeks |
| 13,000 | 12,007 | 68 | | 13,000 | 12,009 | 71 | = £146 pa fixed for any |
| 14,000 | 12,687 | 68 | | 14,000 | 12,719 | 71 | level of income in excess of |
| 15,000 | 13,367 | 68 | | 15,000 | 13,429 | 71 | £5,965 pa. So net |
| 16,000 | 14,047 | 68 | | 16,000 | 14,139 | 71 | equivalent of £6,100 |
| 17,000 | 14,727 | 68 | | 17,000 | 14,849 | 71 | gross is £5,954. |
| 18,000 | 15,407 | 68 | | 18,000 | 15,559 | 71 | |
| 19,000 | 16,087 | 68 | | 19,000 | 16,269 | 71 | |
| 20,000 | 16,767 | 68 | | 20,000 | 16,979 | 71 | |
| 21,000 | 17,447 | 68 | | 21,000 | 17,689 | 71 | |
| 22,000 | 18,127 | 68 | | 22,000 | 18,399 | 71 | |
| 23,000 | 18,807 | 68 | | 23,000 | 19,109 | 71 | |
| 24,000 | 19,487 | 68 | | 24,000 | 19,819 | 71 | |
| 25,000 | 20,167 | 68 | | 25,000 | 20,529 | 71 | |
| 26,000 | 20,847 | 68 | | 26,000 | 21,239 | 71 | |
| 27,000 | 21,527 | 68 | | 27,000 | 21,949 | 71 | |
| 28,000 | 22,207 | 68 | | 28,000 | 22,659 | 71 | |
| 29,000 | 22,887 | 68 | | 29,000 | 23,369 | 71 | |
| 30,000 | 23,567 | 68 | | 30,000 | 24,079 | 71 | |
| 31,000 | 24,247 | 68 | | 31,000 | 24,789 | 71 | |
| 32,000 | 24,927 | 68 | | 32,000 | 25,499 | 71 | |
| 33,000 | 25,607 | 68 | | 33,000 | 26,209 | 71 | |
| 34,000 | 26,287 | 68 | | 34,000 | 26,919 | 71 | |
| 35,000 | 26,967 | 68 | | 35,000 | 27,629 | 71 | |
| 37,500 | 28,667 | 68 | | 37,500 | 29,404 | 71 | |
| 40,000 | 30,367 | 68 | | 40,000 | 31,179 | 71 | |
| 43,000 | 32,407 | 58 | ← NIC Class 1 reduced to 2% and 40% tax payable | 43,000 | 33,309 | 58 | ← NIC Class 4 reduced to 2% and 40% tax payable |
| 45,000 | 33,567 | 58 | | 45,000 | 34,469 | 58 | |
| 50,000 | 36,467 | 58 | | 50,000 | 37,369 | 58 | |
| 55,000 | 39,367 | 58 | | 55,000 | 40,269 | 58 | |
| 60,000 | 42,267 | 58 | | 60,000 | 43,169 | 58 | |
| 65,000 | 45,167 | 58 | | 65,000 | 46,069 | 58 | |
| 70,000 | 48,067 | 58 | | 70,000 | 48,969 | 58 | |
| 75,000 | 50,967 | 58 | | 75,000 | 51,869 | 58 | |
| 80,000 | 53,867 | 58 | | 80,000 | 54,769 | 58 | |
| 85,000 | 56,767 | 58 | | 85,000 | 57,669 | 58 | |
| 90,000 | 59,667 | 58 | | 90,000 | 60,569 | 58 | |
| 95,000 | 62,567 | 58 | | 95,000 | 63,469 | 58 | |
| 100,000 | 65,467 | 38 | ← PA reduces here | 100,000 | 66,369 | 38 | ← PA reduces here |
| 122,000 | 73,827 | 58 | ← PA reduced to zero | 122,000 | 74,729 | 58 | ← PA reduced to zero |
| 150,000 | 90,067 | 53 | ← 45% tax payable | 150,000 | 90,969 | 53 | ← 45% tax payable |
| 200,000 | 116,567 | 53 | | 200,000 | 117,469 | 53 | |
| 250,000 | 143,067 | 53 | | 250,000 | 143,969 | 53 | |
| 300,000 | 169,567 | 53 | | 300,000 | 170,469 | 53 | |

Sweet & Maxwell

# G2: Illustrative net earnings calculations

## Man under 65 at 2016/17 tax rates

| | | Employed person | | | | Self-employed person | | | |
|---|---|---:|---:|---:|---:|---:|---:|---:|---:|
| | | £pa | £pa | £pa | £pa | £pa | £pa | £pa | £pa |
| Gross income | [a] | 15,000 | 35,000 | 50,000 | 110,000 | 160,000 | 35,000 | 50,000 | 110,000 | 160,000 |
| **Income tax** | | | | | | | | | | |
| Gross | | 15,000 | 35,000 | 50,000 | 110,000 | 160,000 | 35,000 | 50,000 | 110,000 | 160,000 |
| Personal allowance (note 1) | | (11,000) | (11,000) | (11,000) | (6,000) | – | (11,000) | (11,000) | (6,000) | – |
| Taxable | | 4,000 | 24,000 | 39,000 | 104,000 | 160,000 | 24,000 | 39,000 | 104,000 | 160,000 |
| Tax payable | | | | | | | | | | |
| – At 20% | | 800 | 4,800 | 6,400 | 6,400 | 6,400 | 4,800 | 6,400 | 6,400 | 6,400 |
| – At 40% | | | | 2,800 | 28,800 | 47,200 | | 2,800 | 28,800 | 47,200 |
| – At 45% | | | | | | 4,500 | | | | 4,500 |
| | [b] | 800 | 4,800 | 9,200 | 35,200 | 58,100 | 4,800 | 9,200 | 35,200 | 58,100 |
| **National insurance** | | | | | | | | | | |
| Class 1 | | | | | | | | | | |
| – At 12% | | 833 | 3,233 | 4,193 | 4,193 | 4,193 | | | | |
| – At 2% | | | | 140 | 1,340 | 2,340 | | | | |
| Class 2 | | | | | | | 146 | 146 | 146 | 146 |
| Class 4 | | | | | | | | | | |
| – At 9% | | | | | | | 2,425 | 3,145 | 3,145 | 3,145 |
| – At 2% | | | | | | | | 140 | 1,340 | 2,340 |
| | [c] | 833 | 3,233 | 4,333 | 5,533 | 6,533 | 2,571 | 3,431 | 4,631 | 5,631 |
| Net income | [a–b–c] | 13,367 | 26,967 | 36,467 | 69,267 | 95,367 | 27,629 | 37,369 | 70,169 | 96,269 |
| Net % of gross | | 89.1% | 77.0% | 72.9% | 63.0% | 59.6% | 78.9% | 74.7% | 63.8% | 60.2% |
| **Note 1: personal allowance** | | | | | | | | | | |
| Personal allowance | | 11,000 | 11,000 | 11,000 | 11,000 | 11,000 | 11,000 | 11,000 | 11,000 | 11,000 |
| Restriction for excess of income over limit* | | – | – | – | (5,000) | (11,000) | – | – | (5,000) | (11,000) |
| Net allowance | | 11,000 | 11,000 | 11,000 | 6,000 | – | 11,000 | 11,000 | 6,000 | – |

*If gross pay does not exceed £100,000, no restriction.
If gross pay does exceed £100,000, restriction is the lower of:
(a) (gross pay–£100,000)/2; and
(b) £11,000

# G3: Income tax reliefs and rates

**Introductory notes**

**Personal allowance**

Every taxpayer resident in the UK (as well as certain non-UK residents) is entitled to a personal allowance.

From 2010/11, the personal allowance has been subject to an income limit of £100,000. Where total income exceeds this limit, the personal allowance is reduced by 50 per cent of the excess. Accordingly, no personal allowance is available on incomes in excess of £122,000 in 2016/17.

**Age-related personal allowance**

The age-related personal allowance has been frozen from 2012/13 onwards and from 2016/17 onwards all individuals will be entitled to the same personal allowance, regardless of the individuals' date of birth.

**Age-related married couple's allowance**

Where a couple was married before 5 December 2005, live together and at least one spouse was born before 6 April 1935, the husband can claim married couple's allowance.

Where a couple married or entered into a civil partnership on or after 5 December 2005, live together and at least one spouse or partner was born before 6 April 1935, the person with the higher income can claim married couple's allowance.

For 2016/17 the allowance is £8,355 and the rate of tax relief is 10 per cent, subject to an income limit—£27,700 for 2016/17.

Where the claimant's income exceeds the income limit, the married couple's allowance is reduced by 50 per cent of the excess less any reduction of the personal allowance (as above), until the allowance is equal to the following amounts:

| | | |
|---|---|---|
| Tax year 2006/07 | Minimum allowance £2,350 | Tax relief £235 |
| Tax year 2007/08 | Minimum allowance £2,440 | Tax relief £244 |
| Tax year 2008/09 | Minimum allowance £2,540 | Tax relief £254 |
| Tax year 2009/10 | Minimum allowance £2,670 | Tax relief £267 |
| Tax year 2010/11 | Minimum allowance £2,670 | Tax relief £267 |
| Tax year 2011/12 | Minimum allowance £2,800 | Tax relief £280 |
| Tax year 2012/13 | Minimum allowance £2,960 | Tax relief £296 |
| Tax year 2013/14 | Minimum allowance £3,040 | Tax relief £304 |
| Tax year 2014/15 | Minimum allowance £3,140 | Tax relief £314 |
| Tax year 2015/16 | Minimum allowance £3,220 | Tax relief £322 |
| Tax year 2016/17 | Minimum allowance £3,220 | Tax relief £322 |

**Child Tax Credit**

Child Tax Credit is a means-tested benefit paid directly into the bank account of the main carer of the child(ren), on a weekly or four-weekly basis.

## G3: Income tax reliefs and rates

Child Tax Credit neither is affected by, nor affects, Child Benefit (see below).

Child Tax Credit is based initially on the income of the previous tax year.

The claim is corrected to actual income basis in due course.

Before April 2012 Child Tax Credit was usually available if income did not exceed a limit of £41,300. From 6 April 2012 this limit is lower for most people and depends on the claimant's individual circumstances. As a rough guide, no Child Tax Credit will be available from 6 April 2012 where the claimant has:

—one child and annual income of more than about £26,000; or

—two children and annual income of more than about £32,200.

### Child Benefit

From January 2013, if an individual's income is more than £50,000 and they, or their partner, choose to carry on getting Child Benefit payments, they will need to declare these payments by registering for Self Assessment and filling in a tax return as they may be liable for a High Income Benefit charge, being one per cent of the Child Benefit for each £100 of income between £50,000 and £60,000.

### Taxation of savings income

Savings income is subdivided into dividends and other savings income, with dividends treated as the top slice of savings income.

Prior to 2016/17 dividends were "grossed up" by the Dividend Tax Credit and tax was payable on dividend income (prior to deducting the Dividend Tax Credit) at the dividend ordinary rate of 10 per cent up to the basic rate limit, and at the dividend upper rate of 32.5 per cent thereafter up to the higher rate limit. From 2010/11 to 2015/16, in addition to these rates, tax is payable on dividend income falling into the additional rate band at the dividend additional rate, as follows:

| | |
|---|---|
| Tax year 2010/11 | 42.5 per cent |
| Tax year 2011/12 | 42.5 per cent |
| Tax year 2012/13 | 42.5 per cent |
| Tax year 2013/14 | 37.5 per cent |
| Tax year 2014/15 | 37.5 per cent |
| Tax year 2015/16 | 37.5 per cent |

From 2016/17 that whole methodology of taxing dividends has been abolished. The Dividend Tax Credit has been replaced by a tax-free Dividend Allowance of £5,000. There is no tax payable on the Dividend Allowance, no matter what non-dividend income is received. Tax is payable on any dividend income in excess of the Dividend Allowance at the following rates:

- 7.5 per cent on dividend income within the basic rate band
- 32.5 per cent on dividend income within the higher rate band
- 38.1 per cent on dividend income within the additional rate band

Tax is payable on other savings income at 10 per cent on income in the starting rate band, at 20 per cent on income in the basic rate band, and at 40 per cent thereafter up to the higher rate limit. From 2010/11, in addition to these rates, tax is payable on other savings income falling into the additional rate band at the following rates:

| | | |
|---|---|---|
| Tax year 2010/11 | 50 per cent | |
| Tax year 2011/12 | 50 per cent | |
| Tax year 2012/13 | 50 per cent | |
| Tax year 2013/14 | 45 per cent | |
| Tax year 2014/15 | 45 per cent | |
| Tax year 2015/16 | 45 per cent | |
| Tax year 2016/17 | 45 per cent | |

Between 2008/09 and 2014/15 there was a 10 per cent starting rate for savings income only. From 2015/16 there is a 0 per cent starting rate for savings only, so the following rates and limits apply:

| | Rate | Limit |
|---|---|---|
| Tax year 2008/09 | 10 per cent | £2,320 |
| Tax year 2009/10 | 10 per cent | £2,440 |
| Tax year 2010/11 | 10 per cent | £2,440 |
| Tax year 2011/12 | 10 per cent | £2,560 |
| Tax year 2012/13 | 10 per cent | £2,710 |
| Tax year 2013/14 | 10 per cent | £2,790 |
| Tax year 2014/15 | 10 per cent | £2,880 |
| Tax year 2015/16 | 0 per cent | £5,000 |
| Tax year 2016/17 | 0 per cent | £5,000 |

If the taxpayer's non-savings income exceeds these limits, the savings rate does not apply.

From 2016/17 a new Personal Savings Allowance was introduced which means that basic rate taxpayers will not have to pay tax on the first £1,000 of savings income they receive and higher rate taxpayers will not have to pay tax on their first £500 of savings income.

## 2008/09 to 2016/17

| Fiscal year: | 2008/09 £ | 2009/10 £ | 2010/11 £ | 2011/12 £ | 2012/13 £ | 2013/14 £ | 2014/15 £ | 2015/16 £ | 2016/17 £ |
|---|---|---|---|---|---|---|---|---|---|
| **Income tax reliefs** | | | | | | | | | |
| Personal allowance | 6,035 | 6,475 | 6,475* | 7,475* | 8,105* | 9,440* | 10,000* | 10,600* | 11,000* |
| **Income tax rates** | | | | | | | | | |
| Basic rate band – Payable at 20% | 34,800 | 37,400 | 37,400 | 35,000 | 34,370 | 32,010 | 31,865 | 31,785 | 32,000 |
| Higher rate band – Payable at 40% | Balance | Balance | 112,600 | 115,000 | 115,630 | 117,990 | 118,135 | 118,215 | 118,000 |
| Additional rate band – Payable at 45% | – | – | – | – | – | Balance | Balance | Balance | Balance |
| Additional rate band – Payable at 50% | – | – | Balance | Balance | Balance | – | – | – | – |

* Please refer to the preceding note on personal allowance for possible restriction.

# G4: National Insurance contributions

**Introductory notes**

1. Married women and widows have been able to elect to pay a reduced contribution as follows:

   - 4.85 per cent on earnings between primary threshold and upper earnings limit, and one per cent on earnings above upper earnings limit from 2003/04 to 2010/11.

   - 5.85 per cent on earnings between primary threshold and upper earnings limit, and two per cent on earnings above upper earnings limit in 2011/12 to 2016/17.

2. Class 1 employee contributions and Class 2 contributions cease to be payable when an individual reaches State pension age.

3. Class 4 contributions are not payable in respect of any fiscal year that starts after State pension age has been reached.

4. Class 3 contributions are voluntary at a flat weekly rate (£14.10pw in 2016/17).

5. From 6 April 2009 an Upper Accrual Point (UAP) was introduced at a frozen rate of £770.00 per week for the calculation of the State Second Pension (S2P) and Class 1 National Insurance rebates under contracted-out schemes. From the same date the Upper Earnings Limit (UEL) previously used for these purposes was aligned with the higher rate threshold for income tax.

6. Employment allowance will reduce employers' Class 1 National Insurance each time the payroll is run until the £3,000 allowance (2016/17 rate) has been fully utilised or the tax year ends (whichever is sooner). Claims are only against employers' Class 1 National Insurance paid, up to a maximum of £3,000 each tax year. The employment allowance was £2,000 in 2014/15 and 2015/16.

   Employment Allowance can be claimed by businesses or charities (including community amateur sports clubs) paying employers' Class 1 National Insurance. Claims can also be made by individuals that employ a care or support worker.

   Claims can not be made if:

   - you are the director and only paid employee in your company;

   - you employ someone for personal, household or domestic work (e.g. a nanny or gardener) —unless they are a care or support worker;

   - you are a public body or business doing more than half your work in the public sector (e.g. local councils and NHS services)—unless you are a charity;

   - you are a service company with only deemed payments of employment income under "IR35 rules".

7. On 6 April 2016 the current basic State pension and S2P were abolished and replaced by a single-tier State pension. The abolition of S2P also meant the end of contracting-out. The measures that implemented the single-tier State pension and abolition of contracting-out are contained in the Pensions Act 2014.

## 2008/09 to 2011/12

| Fiscal year: | 2008/09 £ | 2009/10 £ | 2010/11 £ | 2011/12 £ |
|---|---|---|---|---|
| **Class 1 contributions (Employees)** | | | | |
| Lower earnings limit (LEL) (pa) | 4,680 | 4,940 | 5,044 | 5,304 |
| Primary threshold (PT) (pa) | 5,435 | 5,715 | 5,715 | 7,225 |
| Upper Accrual Point (UAP) (pa) | | 40,040 | 40,040 | 40,040 |
| Upper earnings limit (UEL) (pa) | 40,040 | 43,875 | 43,875 | 42,475 |
| **Standard rate** | | | | |
| If earnings below LEL: | Nil | Nil | Nil | Nil |
| If earnings at or above LEL: | | | | |
| – Contribution rate on earnings up to PT | Nil | Nil | Nil | Nil |
| – Contribution rate on earnings between PT and UEL | 11% | 11% | 11% | 12% |
| – Contribution rate on earnings above UEL | 1% | 1% | 1% | 2% |
| Maximum contribution (pa) | 3,807 +1% of excess over UEL | 4,198 +1% of excess over UEL | 4,198 +1% of excess over UEL | 4,230 +2% of excess over UEL |
| **Contracted-out rate** | | | | |
| As standard rate except | | | | |
| – Contribution rate on earnings between PT and UEL | 9.4% | | | |
| – Contribution rate on earnings between PT and UAP | | 9.4% | 9.4% | 10.4% |
| – Contribution rate on earnings between UAP and UEL | | 11.0% | 11.0% | 12.0% |
| Maximum contribution (pa) | 3,253 +1% of excess over UEL | 3,648 +1% of excess over UEL | 3,648 +1% of excess over UEL | 3,705 +2% of excess over UEL |
| **Class 2 contributions (Self-employed)** | | | | |
| Small earnings exception limit | 4,635 | 4,825 | 5,075 | 5,315 |
| Fixed weekly contributions (pw) | 2.30 | 2.40 | 2.40 | 2.50 |
| **Class 4 contributions (Self-employed)** | | | | |
| Lower profits limit (LPL) (pa) | 5,435 | 5,715 | 5,715 | 7,225 |
| Upper profits limit (UPL) (pa) | 40,040 | 43,875 | 43,875 | 42,475 |
| Contribution rate on profits between LPL and UPL | 8.0% | 8.0% | 8.0% | 9.0% |
| Contribution rate on profits above UPL | 1.0% | 1.0% | 1.0% | 2.0% |
| Maximum contribution (pa) | 2,768 +1% of excess over UPL | 3,053 +1% of excess over UPL | 3,053 +1% of excess over UPL | 3,173 +2% of excess over UPL |

## G4: National Insurance contributions

### 2012/13 to 2015/16

| Fiscal year: | 2012/13 £ | 2013/14 £ | 2014/15 £ | 2015/16 £ |
|---|---|---|---|---|
| **Class 1 contributions (Employees)** | | | | |
| Lower earnings limit (LEL) (pa) | 5,564 | 5,668 | 5,772 | 5,824 |
| Primary threshold (PT) (pa) | 7,605 | 7,755 | 7,956 | 8,060 |
| Upper Accrual Point (UAP) (pa) | 40,040 | 40,040 | 40,040 | 40,040 |
| Upper earnings limit (UEL) (pa) | 42,475 | 41,450 | 41,865 | 42,385 |
| **Standard rate** | | | | |
| If earnings below LEL: | Nil | Nil | Nil | Nil |
| If earnings at or above LEL: – Contribution rate on earnings up to PT | Nil | Nil | Nil | Nil |
| – Contribution rate on earnings between PT and UEL | 12% | 12% | 12% | 12% |
| – Contribution rate on earnings above UEL | 2% | 2% | 2% | 2% |
| Maximum contribution (pa) | 4,184 +2% of excess over UEL | 4,043 +2% of excess over UEL | 4,069 +2% of excess over UEL | 4,119 +2% of excess over UEL |
| **Contracted-out rate** | | | | |
| As standard rate except – Contribution rate on earnings between PT and UEL | | | | |
| – Contribution rate on earnings between PT and UAP | 10.6% | 10.6% | 10.6% | 10.6% |
| – Contribution rate on earnings between UAP and UEL | 12.0% | 12.0% | 12.0% | 12.0% |
| Maximum contribution (pa) | 3,730 +2% of excess over UEL | 3,591 +2% of excess over UEL | 3,620 +2% of excess over UEL | 3,671 +2% of excess over UEL |
| **Class 2 contributions (Self-employed)** | | | | |
| Small earnings exception limit | 5,595 | 5,725 | 5,885 | |
| Small profits threshold | | | | 5,965 |
| Fixed weekly contributions (pw) | 2.65 | 2.70 | 2.75 | 2.80 |
| **Class 4 contributions (Self-employed)** | | | | |
| Lower profits limit (LPL) (pa) | 7,605 | 7,755 | 7,956 | 8,060 |
| Upper profits limit (UPL) (pa) | 42,475 | 41,450 | 41,865 | 42,385 |
| Contribution rate on profits between LPL and UPL | 9.0% | 9.0% | 9.0% | 9.0% |
| Contribution rate on profits above UPL | 2.0% | 2.0% | 2.0% | 2.0% |
| Maximum contribution (pa) | 3,138 +2% of excess over UPL | 3,033 +2% of excess over UPL | 3,052 +2% of excess over UPL | 3,089 +2% of excess over UPL |

## 2016/17

| Fiscal year: | 2016/17 £ |
|---|---|
| **Class 1 contributions (Employees)** | |
| Lower earnings limit (LEL) (pa) | 5,824 |
| Primary threshold (PT) (pa) | 8,060 |
| Upper Accrual Point (UAP) (pa) | 40,040 |
| Upper earnings limit (UEL) (pa) | 43,000 |
| **Standard rate** | |
| If earnings below LEL: | Nil |
| If earnings at or above LEL: – Contribution rate on earnings up to PT | Nil |
| – Contribution rate on earnings between PT and UEL | 12% |
| – Contribution rate on earnings above UEL | 2% |
| Maximum contribution (pa) | 4,193 +2% of excess over UEL |
| **Contracted-out rate** | |
| As standard rate except – Contribution rate on earnings between PT and UEL | |
| – Contribution rate on earnings between PT and UAP | n/a |
| – Contribution rate on earnings between UAP and UEL | n/a |
| Maximum contribution (pa) | n/a |
| **Class 2 contributions (Self-employed)** | |
| Small profits threshold | 5,965 |
| Fixed weekly contributions (pw) | 2.80 |
| **Class 4 contributions (Self-employed)** | |
| Lower profits limit (LPL) (pa) | 8,060 |
| Upper profits limit (UPL) (pa) | 43,000 |
| Contribution rate on profits between LPL and UPL | 9.0% |
| Contribution rate on profits above UPL | 2.0% |
| Maximum contribution (pa) | 3,145 +2% of excess over UPL |

# G5: VAT registration thresholds and rates

Registration is required when a person's turnover (taxable supplies from all the person's businesses) exceeds prescribed limits.

Past and future turnover limits apply (looking one year back and one year forward).

Registration is also required if a turnover limit is to be exceeded in a period of 30 days.

The registration levels are:

|  | Past turnover | | Future turnover |
| --- | --- | --- | --- |
|  | 1 year | Unless turnover for next year will not exceed | 30 days |
|  | £ | £ | £ |
| 1 April 2004 to 31 March 2005 | 58,000 | 56,000 | 58,000 |
| 1 April 2005 to 31 March 2006 | 60,000 | 58,000 | 60,000 |
| 1 April 2006 to 31 March 2007 | 61,000 | 59,000 | 61,000 |
| 1 April 2007 to 31 March 2008 | 64,000 | 62,000 | 64,000 |
| 1 April 2008 to 30 April 2009 | 67,000 | 65,000 | 67,000 |
| 1 May 2009 to 31 March 2010 | 68,000 | 66,000 | 68,000 |
| 1 April 2010 to 31 March 2011 | 70,000 | 68,000 | 70,000 |
| 1 April 2011 to 31 March 2012 | 73,000 | 71,000 | 73,000 |
| 1 April 2012 to 31 March 2013 | 77,000 | 75,000 | 77,000 |
| 1 April 2013 to 31 March 2014 | 79,000 | 77,000 | 79,000 |
| 1 April 2014 to 31 March 2015 | 81,000 | 79,000 | 81,000 |
| 1 April 2015 to 31 March 2016 | 82,000 | 80,000 | 82,000 |
| From 1 April 2016 | 83,000 | 81,000 | 83,000 |

De-registration depends on satisfying HM Revenue & Customs that the future annual limit (being the same as the "unless turnover for next year will not exceed" in the table above, e.g. £81,000 from 1 April 2016) will not be exceeded.

**Note:**

These registration and de-registration limits can be of particular relevance in considering likely turnover levels for businesses such as taxis and driving schools, where VAT registration may render charges uncompetitive (because most such businesses operate below the registration limits).

## VAT Rates

| Date | VAT Rate |
| --- | --- |
| From 1 April 1991 to 30 November 2008 | 17.5% |
| 1 December 2008 to 31 December 2009 | 15.0% |
| 1 January 2010 to 3 January 2011 | 17.5% |
| 4 January 2011 | 20.0% |

# Group H
*Pension*

H1: Net equivalents to a range of gross annual pension figures

H2: Illustrative net pension calculations

H3: Note on pension losses

H4: State pension age timetables

# H1: Net equivalents to a range of gross annual pension figures

**Introductory notes**

1. The following table sets out the net equivalents to a range of annual pension figures in 2016/17, distinguishing between a single person and a married person.

2. The table is followed by illustrative net pension calculations for each marital status and age category, at income levels of £15,000, £20,000, £30,000, £50,000, £110,000 and £160,000 per annum.

3. Since pensions are not subject to National Insurance contributions, the net equivalent figures represent the gross pension less income tax. Given that liability to primary Class 1 National Insurance contributions falls away when the earner has reached State pension age [note 2 of G4], it follows that the net equivalent figures for those of State pension age or over apply equally to earnings from employment and pensions.

    Similarly, given that Class 4 contributions are not payable in respect of any fiscal year that starts after State pension age has been reached [note 3 of G4], it follows that the net equivalent figures for those of State pension age or over apply also to earnings from self-employment where State pension age has been reached in a prior fiscal year.

## H1: Net equivalents to a range of gross annual pension figures

| Gross pension £pa | 2016/17 Net equivalent pension | | | |
|---|---|---|---|---|
| | Single, or married where neither spouse was born before 6.4.35 | | Married, where either spouse was born before 6.4.46 | |
| | £pa | Net per £100 extra | £pa | Net per £100 extra |
| 1,000 | 1,000 | 100 | 1,000 | 100 |
| 2,000 | 2,000 | 100 | 2,000 | 100 |
| 3,000 | 3,000 | 100 | 3,000 | 100 |
| 4,000 | 4,000 | 100 | 4,000 | 100 |
| 5,000 | 5,000 | 100 | 5,000 | 100 |
| 6,000 | 6,000 | 100 | 6,000 | 100 |
| 7,000 | 7,000 | 100 | 7,000 | 100 |
| 8,000 | 8,000 | 100 | 8,000 | 100 |
| 9,000 | 9,000 | 100 | 9,000 | 100 |
| 10,000 | 10,000 | 100 | 10,000 | 100 |
| 11,000 | 11,000 | 80 | 11,000 | 100 |
| 12,000 | 11,800 | 80 | 12,000 | 100 |
| 13,000 | 12,600 | 80 | 13,000 | 100 |
| 14,000 | 13,400 | 80 | 14,000 | 100 |
| 15,000 | 14,200 | 80 | 15,000 | 100 |
| 15,180 | | | 15,180 | 80 |
| 16,000 | 15,000 | 80 | 15,836 | 80 |
| 17,000 | 15,800 | 80 | 16,636 | 80 |
| 18,000 | 16,600 | 80 | 17,436 | 80 |
| 19,000 | 17,400 | 80 | 18,236 | 80 |
| 20,000 | 18,200 | 80 | 19,036 | 80 |
| 21,000 | 19,000 | 80 | 19,836 | 80 |
| 22,000 | 19,800 | 80 | 20,636 | 80 |
| 23,000 | 20,600 | 80 | 21,436 | 80 |
| 24,000 | 21,400 | 80 | 22,236 | 80 |
| 25,000 | 22,200 | 80 | 23,036 | 80 |
| 26,000 | 23,000 | 80 | 23,836 | 80 |
| 27,000 | 23,800 | 80 | 24,636 | 80 |
| 27,700 | | | 25,196 | 75 |
| 28,000 | 24,600 | 80 | 25,421 | 75 |
| 29,000 | 25,400 | 80 | 26,171 | 75 |
| 30,000 | 26,200 | 80 | 26,921 | 75 |
| 31,000 | 27,000 | 80 | 27,671 | 75 |
| 32,000 | 27,800 | 80 | 28,421 | 75 |
| 33,000 | 28,600 | 80 | 29,171 | 75 |
| 34,000 | 29,400 | 80 | 29,921 | 75 |
| 35,000 | 30,200 | 80 | 30,671 | 75 |
| 37,970 | | | 32,898 | 80 |
| 40,000 | 34,200 | 80 | 34,522 | 80 |
| 43,000 | 36,600 | 60 | 36,922 | 60 |
| 45,000 | 37,800 | 60 | 38,122 | 60 |
| 50,000 | 40,800 | 60 | 41,122 | 60 |
| 55,000 | 43,800 | 60 | 44,122 | 60 |
| 60,000 | 46,800 | 60 | 47,122 | 60 |
| 65,000 | 49,800 | 60 | 50,122 | 60 |
| 70,000 | 52,800 | 60 | 53,122 | 60 |
| 75,000 | 55,800 | 60 | 56,122 | 60 |
| 80,000 | 58,800 | 60 | 59,122 | 60 |
| 85,000 | 61,800 | 60 | 62,122 | 60 |
| 90,000 | 64,800 | 60 | 65,122 | 60 |
| 95,000 | 67,800 | 60 | 68,122 | 60 |
| 100,000 | 70,800 | 40 | 71,122 | 40 |
| 122,000 | 79,600 | 60 | 79,922 | 60 |
| 150,000 | 96,400 | 55 | 96,722 | 55 |
| 200,000 | 123,900 | 55 | 124,222 | 55 |
| 250,000 | 151,400 | 55 | 151,722 | 55 |
| 300,000 | 178,900 | 55 | 179,222 | 55 |

# H2: Illustrative net pension calculations

**Single person* at 2016/17 rates**

|  |  | £pa | £pa | £pa | £pa | £pa | £pa |
|---|---|---|---|---|---|---|---|
| **Gross pension** | [a] | 15,000 | 20,000 | 30,000 | 50,000 | 110,000 | 160,000 |
| **Income tax** | | | | | | | |
| Gross | | 15,000 | 20,000 | 30,000 | 50,000 | 110,000 | 160,000 |
| Personal allowance (see note 1 below) | | (11,000) | (11,000) | (11,000) | (11,000) | (6,000) | – |
| Taxable | | 4,000 | 9,000 | 19,000 | 39,000 | 104,000 | 160,000 |
| Tax payable | | | | | | | |
| – At 20% | | 800 | 1,800 | 3,800 | 6,400 | 6,400 | 6,400 |
| – At 40% | | | | | 2,800 | 28,800 | 47,200 |
| – At 45% | | | | | | | 4,500 |
|  | [b] | 800 | 1,800 | 3,800 | 9,200 | 35,200 | 58,100 |
| **Net income** | [a–b] | 14,200 | 18,200 | 26,200 | 40,800 | 74,800 | 101,900 |
| Net % of gross | | 94.7% | 91.0% | 87.3% | 81.6% | 68.0% | 63.7% |
| **Note 1: personal allowance** | | | | | | | |
| Personal allowance | | 11,000 | 11,000 | 11,000 | 11,000 | 11,000 | 11,000 |
| Restriction for excess of income over limit# | | – | – | – | – | (5,000) | (11,000) |
| Net allowance | | 11,000 | 11,000 | 11,000 | 11,000 | 6,000 | – |

#If gross pay does not exceed £100,000, no restriction.
If gross pay does exceed £100,000, restriction is the lower of:
(a) (gross pay–£100,000)/2; and
(b) £11,000.

* = and married persons that do not meet the criteria shown in the married persons' calculations below

# H2: Illustrative net pension calculations

## Married person at 2016/17 rates

(But only applies if at least one spouse born before 6 April 1935 and full married couple's allowance allocated to pensioner in this calculation)*

| | | £pa | £pa | £pa | £pa | £pa | £pa |
|---|---|---|---|---|---|---|---|
| **Gross pension** | [a] | 15,000 | 20,000 | 30,000 | 50,000 | 110,000 | 160,000 |
| **Income tax** | | | | | | | |
| Gross | | 15,000 | 20,000 | 30,000 | 50,000 | 110,000 | 160,000 |
| Personal allowance (see note 1 below) | | (11,000) | (11,000) | (11,000) | (11,000) | (6,000) | – |
| Taxable | | 4,000 | 9,000 | 19,000 | 39,000 | 104,000 | 160,000 |
| Tax payable | | | | | | | |
| – At 20% | | 800 | 1,800 | 3,800 | 6,400 | 6,400 | 6,400 |
| – At 40% | | | | | 2,800 | 28,800 | 47,200 |
| – At 45% | | | | | | | 4,500 |
| | | 800 | 1,800 | 3,800 | 9,200 | 35,200 | 58,100 |
| Relief for married couple's allowance (note 2) | | (836) | (836) | (721) | (322) | (322) | (322) |
| | [b] | – | 964 | 3,079 | 8,878 | 34,878 | 57,778 |
| **Net income** | [a–b] | 15,000 | 19,036 | 26,921 | 41,122 | 75,122 | 102,222 |
| Net % of gross | | 100.0% | 95.2% | 89.7% | 82.2% | 68.3% | 63.9% |
| **Note 1: personal allowance** | | | | | | | |
| Personal allowance | | 11,000 | 11,000 | 11,000 | 11,000 | 11,000 | 11,000 |
| Restriction for excess of income over limits# | | – | – | – | – | (5,000) | (11,000) |
| Net allowance | | 11,000 | 11,000 | 11,000 | 11,000 | 6,000 | – |

#If gross pension does not exceed £100,000, no restriction.
If gross pension does exceed £100,000, restriction is the lower of:
(a) (gross pension–£100,000)/2; and
(b) £11,000

**Note 2: married couple's allowance**

| | £pa | £pa | £pa | £pa | £pa | £pa |
|---|---|---|---|---|---|---|
| Married couple's allowance for age 77 and over | 8,355 | 8,355 | 8,355 | 8,355 | 8,355 | 8,355 |
| Restriction for excess of income over limit^ | – | – | (1,150) | (5,135) | (5,135) | (5,135) |
| Net allowance | 8,355 | 8,355 | 7,205 | 3,220 | 3,220 | 3,220 |
| Relief at 10% | 836 | 836 | 721 | 322 | 322 | 322 |

^ If gross pension does not exceed £27,700, no restriction.
If gross pension does exceed £27,700, restriction is the lower of:
(a) [(gross pension–£27,700)/2] **less** restriction of personal allowance; and
(b) £8,355 – £3,220 = £5,135

* If these criteria are not met, use Single Person calculator shown above

# H3: Note on pension losses

1. **Purpose of note**

   The purpose of this note is to provide some basic guidance to practitioners who need to consider whether a pension loss is likely to arise in any specific case.

2. **"Final Salary" or "Money Purchase" scheme?**

   Ascertain which type of scheme was being contributed to.

   There are two types of Defined Benefit schemes:

   **1) Final Salary schemes**

   - benefits are defined in advance, usually in terms of:
     - final salary,
     - number of years of service,
     - a factor (often 1/60th or 1/80th for each year of service), and
   - the financial risk of ensuring that benefits are paid lies with the employer.

   **2) Career Average Revalued Earnings schemes (also known as CARE schemes)**

   - benefits depend on a combination of:
     - each year's pensionable earnings,
     - annual increases,
     - the scheme's accrual rate, and
   - the financial risk of ensuring that benefits are paid lies with the employer.

   There are also **Money Purchase schemes** (also known as Personal Pensions or Defined Contribution schemes)

   - benefits depend on a combination of:
     - the amounts paid in by the member (if any)
     - the amounts paid in by the employer (if any and if there is one),
     - the investment returns (net of charges) achieved up to retirement,
     - the annuity rates available on retirement if an annuity is selected rather than the drawdown method, and
   - the financial risk lies with the member.

   By definition, a self-employed person will have no employer contributions.

3. **Is there likely to be a loss?**

   Start by assuming that there will be a loss to be evaluated, if:

   - the claimant (and/or the employer) was contributing to a pension scheme,

- there is a claim for loss of earnings, and
- in respect of Money Purchase schemes, annual contributions were greater than £3,600.

## 4. Final salary scheme member

Potential pension:

- Obtain a copy of the members' guide (which will often be in simple terms).

- Obtain a copy of the most recent statement of the individual member's scheme benefits (an estimate of pension at normal retirement age based on current salary).

- With these documents, and the projection of final salary being used for evaluating loss of earnings, it should be possible to calculate the expected pension at retirement date (at its present day value).

Actual pension:

- Establish the actual (reduced) pension that will be payable at normal retirement date (at its present day value).

Proceed by:

- Applying *Wells v Wells*[1] principles. Follow the step-by-step guide at Table B3.

- Calculating loss of annual pension (after tax). Table H1 will assist.

- Applying an appropriate multiplier drawn from the Ogden tables. Tables A1 and A8 refer.

Calculations incorporating a loss of lump sum benefit can be complex and will only be possible if the effect that taking the lump sum has on the annual pension can be ascertained with reasonable certainty. (Public pension schemes usually provide separately for lump sum and annual pension benefits, so the figures are generally straightforward to ascertain.)

## 5. Career Average Revalued Earnings scheme member

Potential pension:

- Obtain a copy of the members' guide (which will often be in simple terms).

- Obtain a copy of the most recent statement of the individual member's scheme benefit (an estimate of pension at normal retirement age based on current salary). Note: this may include estimated future inflation to normal retirement age, which must be ignored.

- With these documents, and the projection of annual salary being used for evaluating loss of earnings, it should be possible to calculate pension at retirement date (at its present day value), by following the step-by-step guide at Table B3.

---

[1] [1999] 1 A.C. 345.

Actual pension:

- Establish the actual (reduced) pension that will be payable at normal retirement date (at its present day value).

Proceed by:

- Applying *Wells v Wells*[2] principles. Follow the step-by-step guide at Table B3.

- Calculating loss of annual pension (after tax). Table H1 will assist.

- Applying an appropriate multiplier drawn from the Ogden Tables. Tables A1 and A8 refer.

Calculations incorporating a loss of lump sum benefit can be complex and will only be possible if the effect that taking the lump sum has on the annual pension can be ascertained with reasonable certainty. (Public pension schemes usually provide separately for lump sum and annual pension benefits, so the figures are generally straightforward to ascertain).

6. **Money purchase scheme member**

A forensic accountant will often approach evaluation of loss along the following lines:

Potential pension:

- Ascertain current value of pension fund.

- Calculate contributions foregone (payable by member and by employer if applicable).

- Calculate value of potential pension fund at retirement, based on contributions foregone and an assumed rate of investment return within the fund.

- Calculate in turn:

    - the lump sum benefit available on retirement (discounted to present day value), and
    - the gross annual pension (based on annuity tables or the drawdown method).

Actual pension:

- Calculate value of actual pension fund at retirement, based on any future contributions to the scheme and the assumed rate of investment return within the fund.

- Calculate in turn:

    - the lump sum benefit available (discounted to present day value), and
    - the gross annual pension.

Proceed by:

- Calculating the loss of lump sum (at present day value).

- Calculating the loss of annual pension (after tax). Table H1 will assist.

[2] [1999] 1 A.C. 345.

- Applying an appropriate multiplier drawn from the Ogden tables.
- Consider whether any further adjustments should be applied for contingencies.

## 7. Important cases

Have regard to:

- *Parry v Cleaver*[1]:

    Briefly: pension loss only runs from anticipated retirement age.

    So that: no credit need be given against earnings losses for an early/ill health pension

- *Longden v British Coal Corporation*[2]:

    Briefly: explains how to apportion an actual tax-free lump sum received ahead of expected retirement age between pre- and post-retirement periods.

    So that: treatment of the actual lump sum is brought into line with *Parry v Cleaver* principles.

- *Aboul-Hosn v Trustees of the Italian Hospital*[3]:

    Briefly: allows for a simple calculation in which pension loss is based on the tax relief foregone on the claimant's potential personal pension contributions.

## 8. Further points

- Do not rely on quotations from pension providers; they invariably incorporate inflation and are not therefore compatible with conventional multipliers.
- Keep in mind the reality of life expectancy. If life expectancy is impaired, pension loss will be reduced.
- That said, do not overlook the possibility of a "lost years" claim in respect of pension losses between the end of the post-accident life expectancy and the end of the pre-accident life expectancy.
- Do not assume that individuals necessarily retire at State pension age.
- Bear in mind that, between April 2010 and November 2018, the State pension age for women will gradually increase from 60 to 65. The State pension age for men and women is then, based on current legislation, increasing from 65 to 68 between December 2018 and April 2046. A table of State pension ages is provided at Table H4 and there is a State pension age calculator at *www.gov.uk/state-pension-age*.
- Claims for loss of State pension may also need to be considered, following the above principles.
- Smaller pension losses may sometimes not be worth pursuing, given the safety net of the State Pension Credit. See Table I2.

[1] [1970] A.C. 1.
[2] [1998] A.C. 653.
[3] (1987) (unreported).

# H4: State pension age timetables

## Introductory notes

The following tables show how the legislated increases in State pension age will be phased in. A State pension age calculator is provided on the Gov.uk website: *www.gov.uk/state-pension-age*. This calculator tells people when they will reach their State pension age, under current legislation, based on their gender and date of birth.

The Pensions Act 2014 provides for a regular review of the State pension age, at least once every five years. The Government is not planning to revise the existing timetables for the equalisation of State pension age to 65 or the rise in the State pension age to 66 or 67. However the timetable for the increase in the State pension age from 67 to 68 could change as a result of a future review. Before any future changes could become law Parliament would need to approve the plans.

**Changes under the Pensions Act 2011**

Under the Pensions Act 2011, women's State pension age will increase more quickly to 65 between April 2016 and November 2018. From December 2018 the State pension age for both men and women will start to increase to reach 66 by October 2020.

**Women's State pension age under the Pensions Act 2011**

| Date of birth | Date State pension age reached |
|---|---|
| 6 April 1953 – 5 May 1953 | 6 July 2016 |
| 6 May 1953 – 5 June 1953 | 6 November 2016 |
| 6 June 1953 – 5 July 1953 | 6 March 2017 |
| 6 July 1953 – 5 August 1953 | 6 July 2017 |
| 6 August 1953 – 5 September 1953 | 6 November 2017 |
| 6 September 1953 – 5 October 1953 | 6 March 2018 |
| 6 October 1953 – 5 November 1953 | 6 July 2018 |
| 6 November 1953 – 5 December 1953 | 6 November 2018 |

**Increase in State pension age from 65 to 66, men and women**

| Date of birth | Date State pension age reached |
|---|---|
| 6 December 1953 – 5 January 1954 | 6 March 2019 |
| 6 January 1954 – 5 February 1954 | 6 May 2019 |
| 6 February 1954 – 5 March 1954 | 6 July 2019 |
| 6 March 1954 – 5 April 1954 | 6 September 2019 |
| 6 April 1954 – 5 May 1954 | 6 November 2019 |
| 6 May 1954 – 5 June 1954 | 6 January 2020 |
| 6 June 1954 – 5 July 1954 | 6 March 2020 |
| 6 July 1954 – 5 August 1954 | 6 May 2020 |
| 6 August 1954 – 5 September 1954 | 6 July 2020 |
| 6 September 1954 – 5 October 1954 | 6 September 2020 |
| 6 October 1954 – 5 April 1960 | 66th birthday |

H4: State pension age timetables

**Increase in State pension age from 66 to 67 under the Pensions Act 2014**

The Pensions Act 2014 brought the increase in the State pension age from 66 to 67 forward by eight years. The State pension age for men and women will now increase to 67 between 2026 and 2028. The Government also changed the way in which the increase in State pension age is phased so that rather than reaching State pension age on a specific date, people born between 6 April 1960 and 5 March 1961 will reach their State pension age at 66 years and the specified number of months.

**Increase in State pension age from 66 to 67, men and women**

| Date of birth | Date State pension age reached |
|---|---|
| 6 April 1960 – 5 May 1960 | 66 years and 1 month |
| 6 May 1960 – 5 June 1960 | 66 years and 2 months |
| 6 June 1960 – 5 July 1960 | 66 years and 3 months |
| 6 July 1960 – 5 August 1960 | 66 years and 4 months* |
| 6 August 1960 – 5 September 1960 | 66 years and 5 months |
| 6 September 1960 – 5 October 1960 | 66 years and 6 months |
| 6 October 1960 – 5 November 1960 | 66 years and 7 months |
| 6 November 1960 – 5 December 1960 | 66 years and 8 months |
| 6 December 1960 – 5 January 1961 | 66 years and 9 months# |
| 6 January 1961 – 5 February 1961 | 66 years and 10 months^ |
| 6 February 1961 – 5 March 1961 | 66 years and 11 months |
| 6 March 1961 – 5 April 1977~ | 67 |

\* = A person born on 31 July 1960 is considered to reach the age of 66 years and 4 months on 30 November 2026.
\# = A person born on 31 December 1960 is considered to reach the age of 66 years and 9 months on 30 September 2027.
^ = A person born on 31 January 1961 is considered to reach the age of 66 years and 10 months on 30 November 2027.
~ = For people born after 5 April 1969 but before 6 April 1977, under the Pensions Act 2007, State pension age was already 67.

**Increase in State pension age from 67 to 68 under the Pensions Act 2007**

Under the Pensions Act 2007 the State pension age for men and women will increase from 67 to 68 between 2044 and 2046.

The Pensions Act 2014 provides for a regular review of the State pension age, at least once every five years. The review will be based around the idea that people should be able to spend a certain proportion of their adult life drawing a State pension. The first review must by completed by May 2017. As well as life expectancy, it will take into account a range of factors relevant to setting the pension age. After the review has reported, the Government may then choose to bring forward changes to the State pension age. Any proposals to do so would, like now, have to go through Parliament before becoming law.

The Government is not planning to revise the existing timetables for the equalisation of State pension age to 65 or the rise in the State pension age to 66 or 67. However the timetable for the increase in the State pension age from 67 to 68 could change as a result of the review.

In the Autumn Statement on 5 December 2013, the Chancellor announced that this Government believes that future generations should spend up to a third of their adult life in retirement. This principle implies that State pension age should rise to 68 by the mid-2030s, and 69 by the late 2040s. However, the Government is not currently legislating for this change—these dates are indicative only, showing a general direction of travel for future State pension age changes.

The information in the table below is based on the current law.

**Increase in State pension age from 67 to 68, men and women**

| Date of birth | Date State pension age reached |
|---|---|
| 6 April 1977 – 5 May 1977 | 6 May 2044 |
| 6 May 1977 – 5 June 1977 | 6 July 2044 |
| 6 June 1977 – 5 July 1977 | 6 September 2044 |
| 6 July 1977 – 5 August 1977 | 6 November 2044 |
| 6 August 1977 – 5 September 1977 | 6 January 2045 |
| 6 September 1977 – 5 October 1977 | 6 March 2045 |
| 6 October 1977 – 5 November 1977 | 6 May 2045 |
| 6 November 1977 – 5 December 1977 | 6 July 2045 |
| 6 December 1977 – 5 January 1978 | 6 September 2045 |
| 6 January 1978 – 5 February 1978 | 6 November 2045 |
| 6 February 1978 – 5 March 1978 | 6 January 2046 |
| 6 March 1978 – 5 April 1978 | 6 March 2046 |
| 6 April 1978 onwards | 68th birthday |

# Group I
*Benefits, Allowances, Charges*

I1: **Social security benefits (non-means-tested)**

I2: **Social security benefits and tax credits (means-tested)**

I3: **Personal injury trusts**

I4: **Claims for loss of earnings and maintenance at public expense**

I5: **Foster care allowances**

# I1: Social security benefits (non-means-tested)

## How they work

Generally, all of these benefits may be claimed independently of each other. However, there are overlapping benefit rules which prevent more than one income replacement benefit being payable. If the claimant is entitled to more than one income replacement benefit, then the amount of the highest will be payable.

Many benefits are contributory, entitlement being dependent on satisfying conditions as to amount of national insurance contributions paid.

Until April 2003, increases were payable for many benefits for dependent children, subject to an earnings limit. The increases have now been replaced by Child Tax Credit (see section I2) but people in receipt of the increases on 5 April 2003 have transitional protection.

Entitlement to non-means-tested benefits is frequently affected if claimants are in hospital or in full-time care.

Claims for all benefits must be made in writing. Claims can be backdated only to a limited extent (varying according to the type of benefit).

## A. Income replacement

### 1. Retirement

| Retirement Pension | 2016–2017 |
|---|---|
| Claimant (Category A) | £119.30 |
| (Category B) | £71.50 |
| Adult dependant | £71.50 |

Either spouse/civil partner may qualify in their own right (Category A) or as a spouse or civil partner (Category B). Special rules apply for parents, carers, divorced people, widows and widowers. Women's State pension age is gradually increasing to 65 by November 2018.

Highly variable rates according to contribution history.

Contributory and taxable.

For information for Form E submit Form BR20 (for valuation of additional State pension); or Form BR19 (for benefit forecast): downloadable at *http://www.direct.gov.uk*

### 2. Ill Health

| i. Statutory Sick Pay | 2016–2017 |
|---|---|
| Standard rate | £88.45 |

Paid by the employer for up to 168 days (28 six-day weeks), to employees earning not less than £112 gross p.w. Taxable.

| ii. Employment and Support Allowance (ESA) | 2016–2017 |
|---|---|
| Single person under 25: | £57.90 |
| Single person 25 or over: | £73.10 |
| Lone parent under 18: | £57.90 |
| Lone parent 18 or over: | £73.10 |
| Couple, both under 18: | £57.90 |
| Couple, both under 18, with a child: | £87.50 |
| Couple, both over 18: | £114.85 |
| Single people with work-related activity component: | £49.05 |
| Single people with the support group component: | £41.90 |
| Single people with no component: | £78.10 |
| Couples in which the claimant gets the work-related activity component: | £86.95 |
| Couples in which the claimant gets the support group component: | £79.80 |
| Couples with no component: | £116.00 |
| Premiums | |
| Severe disability-single: | £61.85 |
| Severe disability-couple: | £123.70 |
| Enhanced disability-single: | £15.75 |
| Enhanced disability-couple: | £22.60 |
| Carer premium: | £34.60 |

Includes both contributory and "income-related" (means-tested) benefit, based on either limited capability for work (placed in "work-related activity group", helped to prepare for suitable work) or limited capability for work-related activity (not expected to work, placed in support group).

Benefit paid at basic rate during 13-week assessment phase. Lower rates for under 25s during assessment period; youth ESA abolished for new claimants from April 2012; existing claimants able to go on claiming, but only for one year from entitlement, disregarding time in support group. Contributory ESA: time-limited to one year for those in work-related activity group; also no age or spouse's additions, and no housing costs allowances. Income related ESA (IRESA): assessment, housing costs and capital rules modelled on IS (Table 29). Child maintenance and up to £20 earnings p.w. disregarded (or 16 hours p.w. earning up to £97.50 p.w. for 52 weeks). Passport to other benefits including full HB and CTB (HB & CTB: Table 29). Contributory ESA taxable: IRESA not.

| iii. Carer's Allowance | 2016–2017 |
|---|---|
| Claimant | £62.10 |

Paid to people over 16 who spend at least 35 hours p.w. caring for recipient of higher or middle rates of

---

Entitlement to contributory benefits depends on payment of National Insurance Contributions. Amounts are per week.

Care Component of Disability Living Allowance, Attendance Allowance, or Constant Attendance Allowance at or above the normal rate with a related pension. Claimant can earn no more than £100 p.w. net and must not be in full-time education; however, entitled to offset against earnings up to half any sums paid to someone else (not close relative) to care for either recipient of allowances or carer's children under 16.

Claimant's benefit and adult dependency increases are taxable; child dependency increases are not.

### 3. Unemployment—Jobseeker's Allowance (JSA)

**i. Contribution-based JSA**  2016–2017
Claimant 18–24  £57.90
25 and over  £73.10

**ii. Income-based JSA (IBJSA)**  2016–2017
Claimant 16–24  £57.90
25 and over  £73.10
Couple Both over 18  £114.85
Dependent children
—(existing claimants only—
others see Child Tax Credit)
till day before 20th birthday  £66.90

Premiums: as for IS (Table 29)

Contributory JSA is age-related flat-rate payment; without dependant allowances: paid for up to 26 weeks. IBJSA is paid with, or from expiry of, contributory JSA, with IS-style rules for income, capital, premiums and mortgage interest.
Personal allowance payments and premiums for children are being phased out (replaced by Child Tax Credit). Child maintenance is disregarded. Claimants must be under State pension age, available for and actively seeking work, and have a current Jobseeker's Agreement: IBJSA is a passport to other benefits including full HB & CTB. Men are eligible for Pension Credit (PC) although those who are not yet 65 may claim PC instead.
Main rates only given. Not usually available for those under 18 or those working 16+ hours p.w. Only main rates shown.
Personal allowance taxable.

### 4. Maternity/paternity/adoption

**i. Statutory Maternity Pay (SMP)**  2016–2017
Payable to employees earning on average at least £112 a week.
Higher rate (first 6 weeks)  90 per cent of average weekly wage
Lower rate (for up to next 33 weeks)  £139.58[2]

Paid by employer for a maximum of 39 weeks. Taxable.

**ii. Statutory Paternity Pay (SPP)**  2016–2017
Rate  £139.58[2]
Payable for up to two weeks. Additional SPP at same rate if upon mother's return to work, baby 20 weeks old and she would otherwise still be entitled to SMP, SAP or MA. Not payable beyond mother's 39-week maternity period. Taxable.

**iii. Maternity Allowance**  2016–2017
Average earnings threshold  £27.00
Standard rate  £139.58[2]

Paid to claimants not entitled to SMP but employed or self-employed for at least 26 weeks in 66 weeks before due date, and average pay over earnings threshold. Maximum 39 weeks (during which may work up to 10 days). Adult dependency increases no longer paid. Non-taxable.

**iv. Statutory Adoption Pay**[1]  2016–2017
Standard rate  £139.58

Paid by employer for a maximum of 39 weeks. Taxable.

**v. Surestart Maternity Grant**  2016–2017
Standard one-off payment  £500.00

Subject to complex conditions. Available only for first child.

### 5. Bereavement

**i. Bereavement Benefit**  2016–2017
Lump sum  £2,000.00

**ii. Bereavement Allowance
(age-related)**  £33.77 to £112.55

Available to bereaved spouses/civil partners over 45 but under State pension age who do not remarry or cohabit and who are not bringing up children. Standard rate £112.55 for those 55 and over.
Payable for up to 52 weeks from date of bereavement.

**iii. Widowed Parent's Allowance**  £112.55

Available to bereaved spouses/civil partners under State pension age and in receipt of child benefit who do not remarry or cohabit.
Widowed Parent's Allowance and Bereavement Allowance cannot be claimed together.
All benefits are contributory and (save lump sum) taxable.

[1] Qualifying conditions based on length of service and average earnings
[2] Or (if less) 90 per cent of the parent's weekly average earnings

Entitlement to contributory benefits depends on payment of National Insurance Contributions. Amounts are per week.

## B. Special needs

1. PERSONAL INDEPENDENCE PAYMENT (PIP)

|  |  | 2016–2017 |
|---|---|---|
| Care Component | Enhanced | £82.30 |
|  | Standard | £55.10 |
| Mobility Component | Enhanced | £57.45 |
|  | Standard | £21.80 |

The claimant must qualify before reaching 65. Available to under-16s too.

2. ATTENDANCE ALLOWANCE

|  | 2016–2017 |
|---|---|
| Higher rate | £82.30 |
| Lower rate | £55.10 |

Paid for care needs of those over 65.
Both allowances are based on need, but there are no restrictions on how they are used. Both allowances are non-contributory, non-means-tested, non-taxable and are ignored as income for means-tested benefits

## C. Children

1. CHILD BENEFIT (CB)

|  | 2016 |
|---|---|
| Only/elder/eldest child | £20.70 |
| Each subsequent child | £13.70 |

A child must be under 16, or under 20 and in full-time secondary education, or under 18 and registered for work or work-based training. Will no longer be available to all high rate tax payers from 2013 onwards. Non-contributory and non-taxable.
Administered by HMRC.

2. GUARDIAN'S ALLOWANCE

|  | 2016–2017 |
|---|---|
| Guardian's allowance | £16.55 |

Payable with child benefit to those raising the children of deceased (or, sometimes, unavailable) parents. Non-contributory, non-taxable. Administered by HMRC.

---

Entitlement to contributory benefits depends on payment of National Insurance Contributions.
Amounts are per week except for the Surestart Maternity Grant payment and Bereavement Benefit lump sum.

# I2: Social security benefits and tax credits (means-tested)

**Income Support (IS) 2016–2017**

For reduced cohort of those under pension age on low income, working less than 16 hrs p.w. (e.g. lone parents of young children, carers, some sick workers and some students). Not for the unemployed (see JSA: Table 28) or new claimants who are sick/disabled (see ESA: Table 28) or most childless people under 18. Children remain dependent while CB (Table 28) is payable, but replacement of allowances by CTC continues.

With some exceptions for existing claimants, new conditions restrict entitlement for lone parents as youngest child reaches threshold age: 5.

Main rates only are shown.

IS brings automatic entitlement on income grounds to other benefits including maximum HB and CTC.

A need level is established from the allowances and Premiums right, plus mortgage interest at Bank of England's published monthly average mortgage rate (currently 3.66 per cent) on loans of up to £200,000 (with restrictions on increases during a claim and a reduction for resident non-dependants; current maximum interest payment is £139 p.w.). IS is then paid to supplement other income to the need level. There are detailed rules on the application of premiums and disregarded income. Payments from a former partner may disqualify, including a lump sum payment of any amount (treated as income) but all child maintenance disregarded. No disregard for childcare costs.

Capital up to £6,000 is disregarded (£10,000 for those in residential/nursing homes; £3,000 for child). Capital between £6,000 and £16,000 is deemed to produce tariff income of £1 for each £250 (or part) over £6,000. There is no entitlement to IS if capital exceeds £16,000, disregarding value of home. Notional capital rules penalise deliberate deprivation of capital to obtain IS.

Non-contributory. Rarely taxable.

**Personal allowances**

|  |  | p.w. | p.a. |
|---|---|---|---|
| Single person | 16–24 | 57.90 | 3,010.80 |
|  | 25 or over | 73.10 | 3,801.20 |
| Lone parent | Under 18 | 57.90 | 3,010.80 |
|  | Over 18 | 73.10 | 3,801.20 |
| Couple | Both over 18 | 114.85 | 5,972.20 |

**Main Premiums**

| | p.w. | p.a. |
|---|---|---|
| Carer | 34.60 | 1,799.20 |
| Enhanced disability | | |
| Single | 15.75 | 819.00 |
| Couple | 22.60 | 1,175.20 |
| Severe disability | | |
| Single (or one of couple) | 61.85 | 3,216.20 |
| Couple (both qualifying) | 123.70 | 6,432.40 |

**Existing claimants only** (others see CTC)

| | p.w. | p.a. |
|---|---|---|
| Family/lone parent family | 17.45 | 907.40 |
| Disabled child | 60.06 | 3,123.12 |
| Enhanced disability (child) | 24.43 | 1,270.36 |

**Pension Credit (PC) 2016–2017**

PC comprises two elements: Guarantee Credit (GC) for those of qualifying age whose income is below the "standard minimum guarantee"; and Savings Credit for those 65 and over with modest savings or income. Either or both are claimable.

Age at which GC available is rising gradually in line with increases in State pension age; this is key date for other benefits and retirement age-related provisions: for current law see Pensions Act 1995 Sch.4.

Means-tested, some income disregarded. No upper capital limit. £10,000 disregarded; thereafter tariff income is £1 for every £500 (or part).

Not a tax credit. State pension is not affected. Administered by the Pension Service. Child maintenance disregarded; other maintenance disregarded only for savings credit. No provision for childcare costs. Housing costs as for IS. Guarantee Credit is a passport to maximum HB and CTB.

Non-contributory. Not taxable.

### Standard Minimum Guarantee

| | p.w. |
|---|---|
| Single | 115.60 |
| Couple | 237.55 |
| Additional amount for severe disability | |
| Single | 61.85 |
| Couple (both qualify) | 123.70 |
| Additional amount for carers | 34.60 |

### Savings Credit

| | | p.w. |
|---|---|---|
| Threshold | Single | 126.50 |
| | Couple | 201.80 |
| Maximum | Single | 13.07 |
| | Couple | 14.75 |

### Working Tax Credit (WTC) 2016–2017

| | p.a. |
|---|---|
| First Income threshold | 6,420.00 |
| Withdrawal rate (41%) | |
| Basic element | 1,960.00 |
| Additional couple's/lone parent element | 2,010.00 |
| 30 hours element | 810.00 |
| Disabled worker element | 2,970.00 |
| Severe disability element | 1,275.00 |

### Childcare element

| | p.w. |
|---|---|
| Percentage of eligible costs covered (70%) | |
| Maximum eligible cost (maximum payable £210 p.w.) | 300.00 |
| Maximum eligible cost for one child (maximum payable £122.50 p.w.) | 175.00 |

Based on gross annual income: in-work support for families with child/children where lone parent over 16 works at least 16 hours p.w., or couple's combined work hours total 24 hours p.w., with one parent working at least 16 hours p.w. Extra payment for working at least 30 hours p.w. Also in-work support for some households without child, including those aged 25 and over working at least 30 hours p.w., and those aged 60 and over or with disability working at least 16 hours p.w. Up to first threshold, claimants receive the maximum. Credit then tapers by 41p per £1 of income as income rises. Above first threshold, claimant loses main element of WTC first, then childcare element, then child element of any CTC.

Elements are cumulative. Complex assessment rules. Maintenance ignored. Assessment on annual income, joint incomes for couples (disregarding £300 of certain types of unearned income).

Awards provisional until end of year notice identifies under/overpayments. Disregard of £2,500 before in-year falls in income affect entitlement; disregard of £10,000 before in-year rises in income affect entitlement. Administered by HMRC.

### Child Tax Credit (CTC) 2016–2017

|  | p.a. |
|---|---|
| First Income threshold for those entitled to CTC only | 16,105.00 |
| Withdrawal rate (41%) | |

### Family elements

| | |
|---|---|
| Family element | 545.00 |

### Child elements

| | |
|---|---|
| Child element (per child) | 2,780.00 |
| Disabled child additional element | 3,140.00 |
| Severely disabled child additional element | 1,275.00 |

Based on gross annual income, support for families with child/children. First the per child element then the family element taper by 41p per £1 of income once income above £16,105.00 (WTC abated first).

One family element per family. The child elements are cumulative, including any disabled child or severely disabled child additional elements. Paid to nominated main carer.

Replaces most benefit additions for children.

Administered by HMRC.

# 13: Personal injury trusts

## Introduction

Following a serious personal injury a client may receive substantial sums of money, be they from a claim for damages, personal accident insurance payouts, charitable gifts, or other sources.

Such clients often have to live for many years, if not the rest of their lives, with the personal, social and financial repercussions that arise because of their injury. They may be left unable to work, their family members may give up jobs to provide care, and they may have expensive ongoing costs to pay for, such as the costs of private care, case management, specialist aids and equipment. They will also continue to have their regular living costs to meet, including the maintenance of any children or dependant relatives.

Therefore, it is important to ensure that each client is provided with proper and complete advice, and practical support where required, to ensure that:

- they get the best possible award from their personal injury claim;
- they are able to claim all of the state benefits they are entitled to and statutory care and support they need, both now and in years to come; and
- they have a suitable structure in place to properly manage and invest their award in the future.

It is, of course, important for any legal advisor to ensure that they have given each and every client the proper advice with regard to each of these matters. To fail to do so has in the past led to a number of personal injury lawyers being found to have been negligent because they have not provided their clients with proper advice about the possible use of personal injury trusts.

## What is a personal injury trust?

A personal injury trust is a formal structure in which to hold and manage any funds which the client has received as a consequence of their personal injury.

A formal trust deed should be put in place, which sets out the rules for the management of the funds. It is important that it is the right kind of trust, that best suits the client's requirements in their particular circumstances.

The trust deed should specify the trustees—two or more people, or a trust corporation, who are then in charge of the trust. The trustees should together make decisions about the management of the trust funds, including any payments made out of those funds, and are under an obligation to exercise their powers for the benefit of those named as beneficiaries. In most cases there will only be one beneficiary, the injured person.

## The benefits of a personal injury trust

There are several benefits of having a personal injury trust in place, which include the following (albeit not an exhaustive list):

## 13: Personal injury trusts

- If held in a personal injury trust, capital derived from a payment made in consequence of any personal injury to the claimant or the claimant's partner is disregarded for the purpose of many means-tested state benefits and services.

    Therefore, a client (and their partner if they claim benefits together) can continue to receive these benefits, despite having funds within the trust which, if held by them personally, would have left them with too much capital to remain entitled.

    These means-tested state benefits include Income Support, Income Related Employment Support Allowance, Income Based Job Seekers Allowance, Universal Credit, Housing Benefit and Council Tax Support. A personal injury trust exempts capital from means testing for a disabled facilities grant. A trust also protects entitlement to Local Authority funding for care.

- The trust structure can help to protect the interests of young, older, disabled or otherwise vulnerable clients.

    Because of the requirement to have trustees in place who must each authorise all transactions within the trust, a client can be protected if their trustees are vigilant to any inappropriate proposals for the use of the funds.

    A steadfast trustee, be they a solicitor, interested family friend or parent, can exercise their effective veto against the use of trust funds to ensure that the funds are only applied in the client's best interests. The balance of power will depend on the type of trust chosen, and clients who fear that they may need extra safeguards should be advised carefully about this.

- A client can benefit from the knowledge, experience and wisdom of their trustees.

    Having appropriate trustees appointed can provide a client with important advice and support when making big decisions. Particularly when dealing with a large lump sum, this can be invaluable to ensure that decisions are appropriate to protect and ensure the long-term interests of the client.

    Some clients prefer to have an appropriately experienced solicitor appointed as one of their trustees, so that they can give advice on matters such as investment decisions, budgeting, and large items of capital expenditure.

- The personal injury trust helps to define and "ring fence" the funds that arise as a consequence of the client's personal injury, keeping them separate from other assets that may belong to the client.

    This can be of help if the client's circumstances change in the future and they suddenly find that they may be eligible for means-tested benefits or care funding; for example, if they have to go in to a care home, or if they separate from a working partner.

    The personal injury trust "wrapper" can also help to define what funds were awarded for their future needs. This can help to differentiate the funds if the client goes through a divorce or any other process where their personal finances are taken into consideration.

### The basic rules for entitlement to means-tested benefits

As you may imagine, the rules for assessing a client's entitlement to means-tested benefits are detailed and complex.

However, when considering how personal injury funds may affect a client's entitlement to means-tested benefits, the key principles for Income Support, Income Related Employment Support Allowance, Income Based Job Seeker's Allowance, Universal Credit, Housing Benefit and Council Tax Support are, broadly speaking, as follows:

- When considering a client's capital, it is important to consider both the personal injury funds that they are due to receive, as well as any savings or investments that they already hold.
- The first payment of any money derived from a personal injury will be ignored for 52 weeks from the date of receipt. An interim payment, or indeed any other payment received as a consequence

of the injury, will qualify as the first payment. The intention of this disregard is that the claimant will have an appropriate period to seek advice and set up the trust.
- If a client has capital below £6,000, then their capital will not affect their entitlement. This lower threshold is £10,000 for those living in a care home or independent hospital.
- If a client has capital between £6,000 and £16,000, then their entitlement will be reduced. For capital between those two thresholds they will be treated as having income of £1 for every £250 or part thereof above £6,000.
- If a client has capital over £16,000 they will be excluded from entitlement altogether.
- A client and their partner (with whom they live) will share a capital allowance, so it is important to look at their capital together. They should ideally have less than £6,000 between them both, if they are to maintain full entitlement.
- Certain assets, such as the value of the home a client lives in and their personal possessions, are disregarded when calculating capital.
- Any income received by the client, including that received by their partner, is deducted from the amount of benefits payable, albeit subject to some personal disregards and allowances.

**The basic rules for entitlement to means-tested benefits for elderly clients**

For Pension Credit (currently available for new claimants after age 62, which age will increase gradually to 65 by 2018), the lower capital threshold is £10,000, and above that amount tariff income from a client's capital is assumed at a rate of £1 for every £500, or part thereof. There is no upper capital threshold. Income derived from a personal injury settlement is ignored, whether paid from a trust or otherwise. Actual capital is ignored, except to the extent that it creates assumed tariff income.

For Housing Benefit and Council Tax Support, if a client is in receipt of Pension Guarantee Credit, all capital, including partner's capital, is ignored. The effect is that personal injury funds are also ignored. If a client is over 60 and not receiving a qualifying benefit (such as Income Support, Income Related Employment Support Allowance, Income Based Job Seekers Allowance), the lower capital threshold is £6,000 and the capital threshold is £16,000. However, personal injury monies are ignored completely, whether in a trust or not, both in respect of capital and income. Due to the vagaries of the rules, there is a concern that growth on capital assets may not be disregarded. In addition, in order to access the disregard for residential care funding a trust will be required and so it is best to advise clients to consider a trust even if it appears their damages will be disregarded at the moment.

**Welfare reform**

Since the implementation of the Welfare Reform Act 2012 in March 2013, Council Tax Benefit was abolished from March 31, 2013 and replaced by a discretionary scheme designed by local authorities. Each local authority has its own scheme although there is a national precedent scheme which local authorities can adopt. Ten per cent less money is available to reduce people's Council Tax than was previously available under the Council Tax Benefit scheme. Local authorities have to protect the position of pensioners. The net result is that in many local authority areas, people of working age are having to pay a proportion of their Council Tax even if they would previously have been entitled to full Council Tax Benefit. A number of people have been caught out by this in the belief that they are entitled to full Council Tax Support and so have not paid a great deal of attention to the Council Tax statement which comes once a year until they receive a summons for non-payment.

The primary income related benefits are being replaced by Universal Credit for new claims. That started with October 2013. There can be no new claims for Income Support, Income Related

Employment Support Allowance and Income Based Job Seeker's Allowance after April 2016. Current claimants for these benefits will be migrated to Universal Credit by 2017.

Readers will be aware that benefits have been a very hot topic in recent years and it is fair to say that we may not yet seen the full effects of the reforms. It also remains to be seen how far this will have a knock-on effect on social care funding, the calculation of which is closely tied to the existing income-related benefits regulations.

**Care funding**

*Adult funding in England*

The Care Act 2014 was implemented on April 1, 2015. It applies in England only.

Part 1 of the Act introduced significant changes to the law on care provision and charging for that provision. Under transitional provisions, Part 1 did not apply to cases where immediately before April 1, 2015, support or services were being provided, or payments towards the cost of support or services were being made by the local authority.

The transitional provisions order required local authorities to complete a reassessment in such cases before April 1, 2016. That reassessment was to be carried out under Part 1 Care Act. If no reassessment was carried out before April 1, 2016, Part 1 Care Act applied after that date in any event. In consequence the means testing provisions under the Care Act also apply. There are some significant differences to the treatment of domiciliary care and in particular the treatment of periodical payments to which disregards now apply in some circumstances. Where no reassessment of means has been carried out under the Care Act, some individuals will be due repayments of charges unlawfully made.

The Care and Support (Charging and Assessment of Resources) Regulations 2014 (CSCAR) now apply to all cases. Capital placed in a personal injury trust is disregarded for means assessment purposes, both for home and residential care. The arguments previously raised by local authorities that they had discretion to take account of the care element of such assets in domiciliary care cases have no arguable basis under the CSCAR.

For the year 2015-6 there is an upper capital limit for assessable capital of £23,250. There is a lower capital limit of £14,250. Between these 2 limits, the resident is treated as having income of £1 for every £250 or part of £250. This is called tariff income.

Investment income paid to a deputy or trustee of a PI trust is disregarded.

Periodical payments placed in a personal injury trust are also disregarded as income but an issue may arise if this was done to avoid care fees.

Payments made out of a trust to the claimant by the trustees are disregarded unless they are to pay for care. But if they accumulate to a sum exceeding the lower capital limit, they will be taken into account. Periodical payments made direct to the claimant should be disregarded if they are awarded for care which the council accepts is a genuine need but does not fit within the new statutory eligibility criteria. There is a further condition that they are actually used for that purpose. The aim is to allow such payments to be used for topping up care.

Payments made by trustees directly to a domiciliary care provider are disregarded. It is possible that regular payments made by trustees to a residential care provider may be treated as the income of the resident.

## Care capping proposals

Section 15 of the Care Act provides that the cost to an adult of their care and support other than for daily living costs may be capped.

A consultation on the detail of the measures to be implemented under this section closed on March 30, 2015.

The proposals were to the effect that:

- Care capping would commence on April 1, 2016.
- The care cap would be nil for adults whose care and support needs began before the commencement of the provision and who were aged under 25 at the commencement of the provision.
- For any other adult, the care cap at commencement would be £72,000.
- The cap relates to costs which the local authority assess as eligible for support under the statutory eligibility criteria and are the amount of the personal budget which the authority allows to meet those needs.

In response to the consultation and in particular representations made by the Local Government Association, the Department of Health decided that care capping will not commence until April 2020. This is just before the next general election which will be held in May 2020. There is a degree of scepticism as to whether these proposals will be introduced or if they are introduced, in what form. Advisors may think it unwise to place much reliance on it at this time.

## Care funding for minors in England

The provision of care support for minors in England continues to be provided under sections 17 & 18 Children Act 1989 and under section 2 Chronically Sick and Disabled Persons Act 1970.

Section 29 sets out that a local authority may charge for these services except where they are for advice, guidance or counselling. There are no regulations made under this section.

The section also states that where the child is under 16, the person to be charged is the "parent". Where the child is over 16, it is the child.

The means testing position is complicated by the fact that section 17(8) states that "Before giving any assistance or imposing any conditions, a local authority shall have regard to the means of the child concerned and of each of his parents." There is no case law on how this relates to section 29. But if the two provisions are to work together in a sensible manner, it suggests that the local authority must have regard generally to the means of the parents and the child when deciding whether they will make a charge under section 29.

## The Social Services and Well-Being (Wales) Act 2014

This Act was implemented on April 5th 2016. A major difference between this Act and the Care Act in England, is that the Welsh Act incorporates care and support provision for minors and so replaces the Children Act 1989 and the Chronically Sick & Disabled Persons Act 1970.

Part 5 of the Act deals with charging and financial assessment. Section 59 permits a local authority to make a charge for providing the service. The Care and Support (Financial Assessment) (Wales) Regulations 2015 and the Care and Support (Charging) (Wales) Regulations 2015 provide a unified scheme for the means testing of domiciliary and residential support. This scheme of charging does not apply to looked after and accommodated children under Part 6.

Paragraph 60 provides that a charge for a service provided to a child may be imposed upon an adult with parental responsibility for that child.

There is an upper capital limit which for the year 2015-6 is £24,000. There is no tariff income scheme in Wales.

The disregards for personal injury trusts, funds paid in consequence of a personal injury and held by a deputy and the first payment of money paid in consequence of a personal injury to the claimant, are all the same as under the National Assistance (Assessment of Resources) Regulations 1992 which applied in Wales before April 5th 2016. They are also the same as those now applying under the Care Act 2014 in England.

Investment income paid to a deputy or trustee of a PI trust is disregarded

Periodical payments paid to a deputy are disregarded.

Payments made out of a trust to the claimant by the trustees are disregarded unless they are to pay for care. Periodical payments made direct to the claimant should be disregarded if they are awarded for care which the council accepts is a genuine need but does not fit within the new statutory eligibility criteria. There is a further condition that they are actually used for that purpose. The aim is to allow such payments to be used for topping up care.

Where it is proposed that periodical payments paid into a personal injury trust, they should be disregarded but an issue may arise if this was done to avoid care fees.

Payments made by trustees directly to a domiciliary care provider are disregarded. It is possible that regular payments made by trustees to a residential care provider may be treated as the income of the resident.

Contributions from income to the cost of domiciliary support are capped and the limit is presently £60 per week. This includes income in the form of periodical payments.

There are no proposals for care capping contained in the Welsh Care Act.

**What funds can go into a personal injury trust?**

The benefits regulations for most benefits take a wide definition, allowing any sums of capital to be disregarded if they are "derived from a payment made in consequence of any personal injury to the claimant or the claimant's partner". However, the Universal Credit regulations refer to "compensation". The effect of that may be to narrow the types of funds which can be protected in a personal injury trust for injured people who are claiming Universal Credit. Some clients may find that they are in a dual system where certain funds within a trust might be disregarded for care purposes for example but not for Universal Credit. For most benefits however the wider definition means that

The use of personal injury trusts are not just limited to awards of damages, and can include:

- A personal injury award, including interim payments received during the course of a claim.
- A Criminal Injuries Compensation Authority award.
- A Motor Insurers' Bureau award.

- Payments from the Armed Forces Compensation Scheme, and similar schemes.
- Payments from various "no fault" schemes, sometimes set up by government bodies both here and abroad, such as payments from the Irish Residential Institutions Redress Board.
- Funds received from a Periodical Payment or Structured Settlement.
- Charitable or public donations following an accident.
- Funds received from accident or travel insurance.
- Funds received from a professional negligence claim paid to compensate for an undervalued or negligently pursued personal injury claim.

It is vitally important to remember that, although the capital disregard is quite wide, the income disregard is rather more restricted. Where a person receives income from, for example, a personal accident policy or an occupational ill health pension, it is unlikely that those funds would be able to be disregarded, even if they are placed in to a personal injury trust.

**When to set up a personal injury trust**

It is important that, if at all possible, a personal injury trust is set up before a client receives their funds.

Lawyers should be aware that any client funds held on their Client Account may be treated as the client's money by the benefits agency and local authority. Therefore, any funds held on Client Account can jeopardise a client's benefit entitlement and consideration should be given to the suitability of a personal injury trust straight away.

Lawyers also run the risk that if funds remain on their client account, and they are aware that the client has not notified the benefits agency, they could find their firm obliged to report the client's non-disclosure as defrauding the benefits agency. Furthermore, they run the risk that they may be construed as aiding and abetting the client in a possible benefits fraud.

While it is usually best advice that a personal injury trust should be set up sooner rather than later, it is possible to set up a trust after the funds have been received and held personally by the client for some time. There is no restriction upon when personal injury funds must be placed into a trust, so funds can be held for months, or years, before a client arranges to place them in a trust. This does not allow the client to claim retrospectively for any benefits that they have missed out on prior to the trust being set up.

However, a client will have to demonstrate to the satisfaction of the benefits agency, or local authority, that the funds placed into the trust are purely those arising from their personal injury. There is a risk that the funds may over time have been mixed up with, or diluted by, other income or capital belonging to the client. Therefore, clients may find that they have some difficulty persuading the authorities that all of the funds should be disregarded.

**Setting up a personal injury trust**

It will be necessary to appoint appropriate trustees. There should be at least two trustees, and no more than four. They must be over 18 years of age and mentally capable of acting as a trustee. It is usually best to avoid trustees whose health and age might make them incapable of fulfilling their obligations in the foreseeable future.

The choice of trustees is an important one, as they will for all intents and purposes have full control over the personal injury trust and the assets held within it. It is important to consider whether they will

13: Personal injury trusts

be able to work well together and continue to act in the best interests of the beneficiaries. For this reason, some caution should be exercised before appointing partners, spouses, or other family members as trustees, if there is a risk of the relationship breaking down in the future.

Some clients may prefer to have an appropriately experienced solicitor appointed as one of their trustees. This allows an impartial and professional person to assist in the trustees' deliberations and decision making. It can help to ensure that the trustees are making decisions together which are appropriate to the needs of the beneficiaries, as well as providing the professional expertise and experience that can be invaluable when making difficult decisions.

It is also important that a client receives the correct advice about the right kind of trust to put in place. Consideration needs to be given to the client's particular circumstances, their potential liability to tax and the provision that they may wish to make for their family in the future. This will in turn affect whether the client is named as the sole beneficiary of the trust, or whether other beneficiaries are named and, if so, whether the trustees have any discretion in how they apply funds for their benefit.

The client being advised about Personal Injury Trusts should be advised about wills at the same time.

Once the advice is given, and the necessary decisions are made, the trust deed will need to be prepared by the instructed lawyer, before being signed in the presence of witnesses, and dated. The personal injury trust will usually have a suitable title, such as the "John Smith Personal Injury Trust."

**Once a personal injury trust is set up**

Once a personal injury trust is set up, the trustees' first act will usually be to open a bank or building society account to hold the trust funds. The account should be suitably named, such as the "Josephine Anne Bloggs Personal Injury Trust". The account should usually require that each and every one of the trustees is required to sign to authorise all transactions on account, including all cheques.

Once the trustees have set up the trust bank account, the personal injury lawyer can confidently arrange for a cheque to be issued for the personal injury funds, ensuring that the cheque is made payable to the trust, i.e. payable to the "Josephine Anne Bloggs Personal Injury Trust", and not to the client personally.

The trustees will need to keep to certain rules in order to be able to use funds from the trust without affecting the client's benefit entitlement, namely:

- Any income arising from the funds in the trust, such as interest or dividends, should be paid into a trust account, and not paid to the client personally.
- The trustees can transfer funds into the client's own personal account, but should take care to ensure that the client's capital (including the capital held by their partner if they are claiming benefits as a couple) stays below £6,000 at all times, which is the lower capital threshold for most means-tested benefits.
- Possibly the simplest way to use funds from the trust is to make direct payments from the trust to third parties. This way the funds go directly from the trust account, to the third party and do not go through the client's hands in any way.
- Any further assets set up to be held by the trustees, be they bank accounts, investments or property, should be set up with the same restrictions as the original trust bank account, namely:
- in the name of the trust, or trustees; and

- with the restriction that each and every one of the trustees is required to sign all transactions with regard to that asset.

### Is a client likely to benefit from a personal injury trust in the future?

For many clients it is easy to determine that they are entitled to means-tested benefits, or care funding, at the time that they receive their funds, and so it makes sense to protect their entitlement straight away by setting up a personal injury trust.

However, some clients may at the time have no entitlement to means-tested benefits, and so a personal injury trust may not seem immediately relevant. In such cases careful consideration should be given to the client's potential to claim means-tested benefits in the future.

A client may become entitled to means-tested benefits in the future if their relevant circumstance change, which may include:

- If they need to move to live in a residential care home.
- If they move out of the family home to live on their own.
- If they leave full or part-time education.
- If they are discharged from hospital or residential care.
- If they and their spouse divorce or separate.
- When they reach a significant age for benefits purposes, such as 16, 18 or 60 years of age or within state pension age, currently 62.
- If they or their partner lose their job, retire or are medically unable to continue to work.
- If they, or their partner, lose their entitlement to another benefit or source of income.
- If they, or their partner, find their health deteriorates and they become entitled to higher rates of disability benefits, which in turn have a knock-on effect for some means-tested benefits.
- If they, or their partner, find that they have used up their pre-existing savings (those which have not arisen from the personal injury claim and which have previously prevented them claiming means-tested benefits) and so find that they would become entitled to means-tested benefits if their personal injury funds were disregarded as capital.

In such cases clients should be advised to use up their pre-existing savings with some caution. The benefits agency or local authority can ask to look at a person's history of expenditure, and any gifts made, to see if the client has in the opinion of the authority, deliberately depleted their estate in order to gain entitlement to means-tested benefits or services. If the authority feels that a client has deliberately depleted their estate in such a manner, they can decide to treat the spent funds as "notional capital", essentially treating the client as if they still have the funds and leaving them with no entitlement to the means-tested benefit or service which they have applied for. Therefore, it is important that clients keep a careful record of their expenditure to demonstrate that their use of funds has been reasonable and not a deliberate attempt to deplete their estate.

### The 52-week rule

Payments received as a consequence of a personal injury are disregarded for the purpose of assessing entitlement to means tested benefits for the first 52 weeks after they are received.

However, that disregard applies only to the first payment received as a consequence of that personal injury, which may often be the client's first interim payment. It is also important to check to see a client has received other earlier payments, which may count as their "first payment", such as payments from an accident insurance policy or even a capital payment from a charity.

Any later payments, including further interim payments, are not protected by this disregard after the expiry of the original 52-week period.

Under the Universal Credit regulations there is a disregard of 52 weeks for every payment. That may be helpful for some clients who receive smaller awards but if they decide not to set up a trust they will need to be extremely careful in monitoring the various 52 week disregard periods. Establishing which funds form part of which interim and when the disregard therefore runs out could be quite tricky and the client would be caught out.

Therefore, when receiving a first payment as a consequence of a personal injury, a client may choose not to set up a trust if they anticipate spending enough of that sum to bring their capital below the relevant threshold by the end of the 52-week period. However, they should be advised to hold that payment in a bank account separate from any other funds. That way, if towards the end of period they find that they unexpectedly have funds remaining, they can still arrange to place them into a personal injury trust safe in the knowledge that the funds have not become mixed up with other capital in any way.

However, in many cases it will be appropriate to set up a personal injury trust as soon as any funds are received, regardless of the 52-week rule. Where the amount of funds due to the client overall are almost certainly going to last longer than that period, there is little if no benefit in delaying the setting up of a personal injury trust which is likely to remain in place to manage the client's funds for many years to come.

## Personal injury trusts for children and protected parties

In most cases the decision as to whether or not to set up a personal injury trust is one for the client to make for themselves, albeit with the benefit of good advice from a lawyer. The matter does not require court approval in any way.

However, if a client is unable to make their own decision it will be necessary to obtain approval from the appropriate court with authority to make a decision on behalf of the client (CPR r.21.11 and supplementary Practice Direction), namely:

- The High Court will need to approve the establishment of a personal injury trust to manage an infant's funds until the infant reaches 18 years of age.
- In cases involving mentally incapable people, the Court of Protection will need to approve the establishment of a personal injury trust, in preference to the appointment of a Deputy for Property and Affairs. Following the case of *Re HM*,[1] the court is likely to approve the establishment of trusts in limited circumstances only.

It is important to note that the disregards which apply for benefits for funds derived from a personal injury are also available for injury derived funds held under the auspices of the Court of Protection.

As regards disregards for care and support under the Care Act 2014, the disregards for deputies and personal injury trusts are very similar.

---

[1] (2011) C.O.P. 11875043 April 11, 2011.

## 14: Claims for loss of earnings and maintenance at public expense

The Administration of Justice Act 1982 s.5 provides that where an injured claimant seeks to recover damages for loss of earnings, the defendant can set off against that claim any saving attributable to maintenance (either wholly or partly) at public expense in a hospital, nursing home or other institution.

This deduction is comparable to (but not the same as) the common law principle that where a claimant is in a private hospital or home (in respect of which damages are claimed from the defendant), credit must be given for the domestic expenses thereby saved. This is the "domestic element" which was discussed in *Fairhurst v St Helens and Knowsley Health Authority*.[1]

## 15: Foster care allowances

**Introductory notes:**

Every April the Fostering Network publishes the cost of bringing up a child in its own home for the next 12 months. Contact Fostering Network Publications, 87 Blackfriars Road, London SE1 8HA (tel: 020 7620 6400; *http://www.fostering.net*).

The Fostering Network publishes Foster Care Finance, with recommended minimum weekly allowances for fostering in the UK and a full survey of allowances paid by each local authority. The Fostering Network's recommended minimum allowance depends on the age of the child and whether or not the placement is in London. The allowances do not include any form of reward for carers themselves. The Fostering Network recommends four extra weeks' payment, to cover the cost of birthdays, holidays and a religious festival. It encourages local authorities to pay allowances to all carers at least in line with its recommended rates. Despite such encouragement the majority of local authorities give foster carers less than the Fostering Network's recommended minimum allowances for spending on the care of fostered children. From a survey published by the Fostering Network in September 2003, 53 per cent of local authorities in England and 87 per cent of local authorities in Wales paid below the Fostering Network's recommended minimum allowance.

**Fostering Network recommended costs of bringing up a child in its own home for the year beginning 6 April 2016**

| Age of child (years) | London (£ per week) | South East (£ per week) | Rest of the UK (£ per week) |
|---|---|---|---|
| 0–4 | 145.00 | 140.00 | 126.00 |
| 5–10 | 163.00 | 156.00 | 139.00 |
| 11–15 | 184.00 | 177.00 | 159.00 |
| 16+ | 216.00 | 208.00 | 185.00 |

In *Spittle v Bunney*[2] it was said that the cost of fostering services is not an appropriate measure for the value of the loss of a (deceased) mother's services, but the case is not uncontroversial.

[1] [1995] P.I.Q.R. Q1, at Q8 and Q9.
[2] [1988] 1 W.L.R. 847.

# Group J
*Court of Protection*

J1: **Note on the Court of Protection**

J2: **The incidence of Deputyship costs over a claimant's life**

J3: **Deputyship costs**

# J1: Note on the Court of Protection

## The Mental Capacity Act 2005 and the Court of Protection

It is important to understand some of the background to, and the purpose of, the legislation. The original bill was known as the Mental Incapacity Bill. This became the Mental Capacity Act (the Act). That change is critical in that the removal of those two letters make all the difference to the tone of the Act. The Act is very much intended to empower incapacitated adults. All of us practitioners in this field need to acknowledge that fact and continually keep the principles as set out in s.1 of the Act in the forefront of our minds at all times:

1. A person must be assumed to have capacity unless it is established that he lacks capacity.
2. A person is not to be treated as unable to make a decision unless all practicable steps to help him to do so have been taken without success.
3. A person is not to be treated as unable to make a decision merely because he makes an unwise decision.
4. An act done, or decision made, under this Act for or on behalf of a person who lacks capacity must be done, or made, in his best interests.
5. Before the act is done, or the decision is made, regard must be had to whether the purpose for which it is needed can be as effectively achieved in a way that is less restrictive of the person's rights and freedom of action.

It is easy to assume that, because the Court of Protection has not changed its name and the Public Guardianship Office has only changed slightly to the Office of the Public Guardian, nothing much occurred on 1 October 2007 when the Act came fully into force. In fact fundamental changes took place.

It is also important to note that there is a complete separation now between the Office of the Public Guardian (OPG) and the Court of Protection.

The old Court of Protection was merely an Office of the Supreme Court, whereas the new court is a superior Court of Record with equal authority to that of the High Court. Indeed certain functions of the High Court concerning termination of life cases have been transferred to the new Court of Protection. However, it is important to remember that an application to the court is the last remedy to consider. The Code of Practice established under the Act sets out clearly that matters should, wherever possible, be reached by negotiation rather than an application to the court.

The PGO was the administrative office of the old court, whereas the new Office of the Public Guardian has no connection with the court. Its role is purely to act on behalf of the Public Guardian and its role so far as this note is concerned is to supervise the conduct of Deputies. It has no part in the administration of cases.

The new court has no administrative arm and has no continuing record of clients, or case workers dealing with their affairs. Its role is purely to make decisions by the issuing of declarations or orders which might or might not involve the appointment of a Deputy.

The new court has wider powers than the old court and can make orders about welfare issues as well as financial matters.

The aim of the court is always to resolve matters in the manner least intrusive into a person's affairs. As a result the process of appointing a Financial Deputy is only to be pursued when it is quite clear, based on medical evidence, that a client lacks capacity to manage his financial affairs. The Mental Capacity Act is an evolving piece of legislation. Since coming fully into force on October 1, 2007 the Act has had significant amendments to it. The Mental Health Act 2008 amended the Act in respect of

Deprivation of Liberty issues and brought in a second Code of Practice on Deprivation of Liberty safeguards. Furthermore, from the outset the OPG announced an intention to review the implementation of the Act 12 months after coming into force in order to review its aims and ambitions, of both empowering and protecting those who lacked capacity, were being met.

This has resulted in a series of consultation papers which have amended from time to time the numerous statutory instruments supporting the principle legislation. The first related to "Forms, supervision and fees". This resulted in two new statutory instruments coming into force on 1 May 2010. One related to Enduring Powers of Attorney. The other made minor amendments to the fees exemption region and the bonding process.

This was followed by a consultation on rule changes. Recommendations were made as a result of that consultation but as yet no changes have been implemented.

A third consultation ended in May 2011 in relation to OPG fees and a new structure of fees came into effect from 1 October 2011.

1. **The scope and authority of the Court of Protection**
   As mentioned above, it is important to remember that the court is a solution of last resort in most respects. However, as far as the personal injury/clinical negligence lawyer is concerned it is the first resort to obtain the appointment of a Deputy to deal with an incapacitated client's financial affairs.

   To make an application it has to be established that a person lacks capacity in accordance with the definition as set out in s.2 of the Act:

   "A person lacks capacity in relation to a matter if at the material time he is unable to make a decision for himself in relation to the matter because of an impairment of, or a disturbance, in the functioning of the mind or brain".

   It is important to remember that there is no general level below which a client lacks capacity and above which he does not. The statement that a person "lacks capacity" in itself is meaningless. When and in connection with what issues does a person lack capacity? Clearly some clients will lack capacity concerning all their financial affairs but most clients retain some capacity and it is for the Deputy to establish the areas and the extent to which the client has capacity and ensure that he does not trespass there. All Deputyship Orders make it absolutely clear that the Deputy has no authority to decide any matters on which the client retains capacity.

   The second part of the test is equally important. One must establish that the lack of capacity is as a result of "an impairment of, or a disturbance in the functioning of the mind or brain". A COP3 Assessment of Capacity form establishing both heads is required in support of the application.

   Section 3 of the Act sets out that for the purposes of establishing the lack of capacity it is necessary to show that the client is unable:

   "(a) to understand the information relevant to the decision;
   (b) to retain that information;
   (c) to use or weigh that information as part of the process of making the decision; or;
   (d) to communicate his decision (whether by talking, using sign language or any other means)."

   In essence failing to meet any one of the first three tests will establish the lack of capacity on a specific decision. However, someone who passes all three tests yet is unable to communicate his decision also is deemed to lack capacity in this context, even though medically he may have full capacity.

Putting all this in the context of personal injury or clinical negligence litigation one of the first occasions where capacity may be an issue, apart from the actual commencement of proceedings, is when the first interim payment is to be made. Can the client manage this? It is quite possible that a head-injured client may have capacity to manage modest funds of, say, a few thousand pounds. However, when a significant interim payment is made, he may not. A Deputy is not needed until you reach the point where the client cannot manage the funds available. However, if a Deputy is appointed knowing a significant settlement is due eventually, then the role of the Deputy in respect of minor interims may be just to stand aside and let the client deal with them.

2. **The appointment of a property and affairs Deputy**
Practitioners need to understand that the role of a Deputy is different to that of the pre-MCA Receiver. The appointment of a Receiver was based on the concept of a one-off assessment of capacity. If it was found that the client "lacked capacity" then the power of the Receiver meant that the Receiver could take over all financial decision-making from the client and there was no need to re-consider the matter again. All Deputyship orders make it quite clear that whilst the Deputy may have wide powers to manage all of a client's financial affairs, under no circumstances can a Deputy make a decision on a matter where the client has the capacity to make his own decision. Furthermore, if the Deputy did do so then that decision would be invalid. A Deputy's authority only extends to matters where it is "established" that the client lacks capacity himself. As a result a lot more time and effort needs to be taken on a decision-by-decision basis for many clients to establish a lack of capacity.

Often there can be conflicting medical evidence as to the question of capacity. If that is the case then all such evidence must be put before the court when making an application. This can be a problem for litigators because there may be contrary evidence in existence which they do not wish to disclose in the litigation. It has to be disclosed in the Court of Protection application.

3. **The timing of an application**
It is important not to apply sooner than necessary. For instance, a client may have capacity to manage small interim payments but not to manage a larger sum.

Applications will usually be dealt with within the terms of the court's service levels of 21 weeks. However, Orders can be issued more quickly in some cases. As from 1 September 2010, Orders are only issued once the surety bond is in place. Previously the Order was issued but did not come into force until one calendar month after issue to allow for the bond to be put in place. This change in procedure means a slight delay in the issuing of Orders but it means the Order is fully effective from the date of its issue.

4. **Professional or lay Deputy**
In cases involving recovery of large amounts of, say, £500,000 or more (excluding Deputyship costs) it is reasonable to apply for the appointment of a professional Deputy and recover the costs of the professional Deputyship as a specific head of future loss. There is no prescribed figure for the application for the appointment of a professional Deputy. A lot will depend on the circumstances of the individual claimant. However, in larger damages cases it is suggested that a professional is preferred as it can often remove family tensions that get in the way when a family member is appointed. Also if no professional costs are claimed at the outset then, if in later life a professional is needed, his costs are a real drain on the funds of the claimant.

5. **Decision making by Deputies**
When a Deputy makes a decision on behalf of a person he needs to make that decision in the person's best interests. There is no definition of "best interests" under the Act; merely guidelines of what to consider in deciding what is in a person's best interests. These guidelines are set out in s.4 of the Act. The overriding rule is that the decision maker must consider all relevant circumstances. In that respect the client has a role to play in the decision making process. The Deputy

*must* consider whether it is likely that the client will have capacity at some time in relation to the decision and if so, when. Also the Deputy "so far as reasonably practicable" *must* permit and encourage the client to be involved as far as possible in the decision making process. He must also "if it is practicable" *and appropriate* consult certain others such as family, and carers, etc. The need to consult these others is often referred to whereas the need to consult and involve the client, which is a stronger obligation, is often forgotten. It may be uncomfortable but it is required.

6. **The role of the financial Deputy**
It is often assumed that the role of the financial Deputy is akin to that of a bank manager or book keeper. This is not so. Whilst there is a high element of routine involved, in high value cases there is a lot of highly technical and complex work to be carried out in connection with such things as house adaptations, carer employment, and investments. It is important to allocate the lowest appropriate grade or fee earner to each piece of work. As a result the Deputy will probably only be able to charge at grade A or B for small amounts of work.

In summary, the routine work of a professional Deputyship includes the following, amongst other things:

(a) liaison with an application to the Court of Protection and the Office of the Public Guardian where necessary;
(b) preparation of annual accounts/reports to the Office of the Public Guardian;
(c) completion of tax returns and payment to HMRC as necessary;
(d) dealing with requests for capital expenditure;
(e) setting appropriate budgets and regular payments as appropriate;
(f) considering and approving investment proposals;
(g) overseeing and arranging the employment and retention of care workers and other employed staff, and liaison as appropriate with the case manager;
(h) overseeing and arranging payment of national insurance contributions and PAYE tax in respect of any employees' wages;
(i) liaising with the person whose affairs are being dealt with and, wherever possible, taking all practical steps to enable them to make their own decisions;
(j) liaising with the person's family, associates, care managers and other parties as appropriate (in accordance with the "best interests" criteria);
(k) ensuring that the person receives the correct state benefits, council tax benefits and exemptions, housing benefit and local authority/public funding for care; and
(l) payment of bills, fees and regular expenses.

Most of these items should be carried out at grade C or D where possible. If there is not such a grade fee earner available then higher grade fee earners will only recover the lower grade hourly rates. The Supreme Court Costs Office is becoming very focused on the proportionality of charges.

7. **Welfare Deputies**
When the Act came into being there was much talk about appointing welfare Deputies in some numbers. However, in reality very few welfare Deputies have been appointed. This is because if you follow through the principles of the Act and in particular the concept of dealing with decisions in a way which is least restrictive of the person's rights and freedoms then the idea of having a welfare Deputy is, in fact, the most restrictive way of dealing with welfare matters. Accordingly, welfare Deputyships are only really for the most severely disabled who require constant welfare decisions made for them. The concept of a professional welfare Deputy is also extremely rare and the payment structure under the court's rules extremely limited as a consequence.

8. **Approval of damages awards by the Court of Protection**
Prior to October 2007 the Master of the Court of Protection would often provide email approval of a personal injury settlement, but this procedure has now ceased as from 1 October 2007. The Civil Procedure (Amendment) Rules 2007 set out amendments to CPR Pt 21 which provides that only a Master, designated Civil Judge or his nominee should normally hear applications for the approval of a settlement or compromise involving a "protected beneficiary" (a person who lacks capacity to manage or control any money recovered by him or on his behalf in the proceedings). Therefore, the approval of the Court of Protection is no longer required.

9. **Charges for the appointment of Deputies and management by professional Deputies.**
The costs of a professional Deputy is a significant item of any large personal injury or clinical negligence claim (including CICA and MIB) involving a head-injured client.

It is important to put together the claim for Deputyship costs extremely carefully as they will be a significant item of any claim. Even if you have the in-house experience to prepare your own costs statement there is a line of argument that an independent expert's statement is to be preferred merely to establish objectivity.

Whilst many elements of a claim will be standard, e.g. court fees and OPG fees, the annual costs of acting as a professional Deputy will vary from case to case. It may well be that a "difficult" client's costs will be significantly higher than those of a very passive head-injured client. Costs will vary between the early and late years of a case. It is impossible to be prescriptive about the costs of a professional Deputy. The role is not like that of a carer or even a case manager where exact numbers of hours are claimed each month. It is therefore prudent in the case of a Deputy to include some contingency for unexpected events. It is very difficult to weigh up accurately how many head-injured clients will behave on a long-term basis. A lot comes down to experience.

The requirements of the MCA and the Code of Practice means in ensuring that a Deputy does not make decisions which the client can make for himself mean a lot more time can be spent on assessing capacity now. When it is established that there is a lack of capacity in respect of a specific decision, it is necessary for the Deputy to assess what will be in the client's best interests. All this takes time.

It is a requirement for the Deputy, or at least someone on his behalf, to visit the client at least once a year at home, but it may be that such visits are necessarily more frequently for some clients. It would be usual for more visits to be required in the early stages, particularly after settlement, owing to the number of decisions which will be required at that time.

Regarding the terms of the Deputyship Order, it should also be borne in mind that a Deputy may need to make further applications from time to time to the court. Orders can be limited as to time and the amount of funds that can be spent in a year. Time-limited Orders are typically given at the outset before a compensation claim has been settled. Financially limited Orders may be given to reduce the surety bond costs or for many other reasons. All Orders are not the same.

10. **Fixed costs in the Court of Protection**
A new Practice Direction lays down categories of fixed costs effective from 1 February 2011. They provide an alternative in low cost cases to having your bills assessed. Court Orders will state whether fixed costs are to apply. Normally Deputyship Orders will give the option to take fixed costs or have detailed assessment.

The Practice Direction deals with the following:

(a) Payments on account—where detailed assessment applies, a professional Deputy may take payments on account for the first three quarters of the year which are proportionate to the work undertaken but which must not exceed 20 per cent of the estimated annual charges. The balance is then recovered following the detailed assessment. The only bill submitted for assessment is at the end of the Deputyship year.

(b) Solicitors' costs in court proceedings:

(i) Work up to and including the making of the Order appointing a Deputy for Property and Affairs—an amount not exceeding £850 plus VAT.
(ii) Annual management fees for the first year of Deputyship—an amount not exceeding £1,500 plus VAT: for the second and subsequent years £1,185 plus VAT.
(iii) Preparation and lodgement of accounts—an amount up to £235 plus VAT.
(iv) Preparation of HMRC Income Tax return—an amount up to £235 plus VAT.

(c) Conveyancing costs—for the first time for many years there are fixed fees for conveyancing. On sales or purchases a value element of 0.15 per cent of the consideration may be charged subject to a minimum of £350 and a maximum of £1,500 plus VAT and disbursements. This is a reduction from previous fixed rates. There are other fixed fees in the Practice Direction—see the details on the HMCS website.

## 11. Court fees in relation to Deputyship

As mentioned previously the OPG's fees are undergoing review in a consultation that ends on May 21, 2011. The new fees are intended to apply from July 1, 2011. The editors do not know what they will be but the proposals are outlined below.

The current fees are:

### OPG fees

1. Deputy Assessment fee £100

A one-off fee for carrying out a risk assessment to decide the level of supervision to apply.

2. Supervision fees:

- Type I supervision (highest) £320 per annum
- Type IIA (intermediate) £320 per annum
- Type II supervision (lower) £320 per annum
- Type III supervision (minimal) £35 per annum

Supervision will vary. Typically on larger cases with a professional Deputy there will be Type 1 Supervision until the case settles and then it will move to II or IIA. Type III applies to small value cases for which the capital threshold is currently £18,000 increasing to £19,500 in April 2013 and then £21,000 in April 2014.

### Court of Protection fees

- Application fee for the appointment of a Deputy £400
- Application fee for any other application, e.g. statutory will £400
- Appeal fee for filing a notice appealing a court decision £400
- Hearing fee—in addition to the application fee £500

### Fee remissions and exemptions

There are fee exemptions and remissions available for both the OPG and Court of Protection fees.

For both OPG and Court of Protection fees a full exemption is available if a person is in receipt of any of the following means-tested benefits:

- Income Support/ESA.
- Income-based Jobseeker's Allowance.
- State Pension Guarantee Credit.
- A combination of Working Tax Credit and either Child Tax Credit, Disability Element or Severe Disability Element.
- Housing Benefit.
- Council Tax Benefit.

AND the person has not been awarded damages of more than £16,000 which were disregarded in calculating chargeability for any of the above benefits.

For Court of Protection fees a person is eligible for the relevant fee remission if their gross annual income falls within the following bands

| | |
|---|---|
| Up to £12,000 | Full remission |
| £12,001–£13,500 | 75 per cent remission |
| £13,501–£15,000 | 50 per cent remission |
| £15,501–£16,500 | 25 per cent remission |
| £16,501 and above | No remission |

For OPG fees a person is eligible for a 50 per cent reduction if their gross annual income is less than £12,000.

## 12. Surety Bonds for Deputies

Initially, there was a great deal of uncertainty about Surety Bonds. Judicial independence meant that there was no set scale and there was clear evidence that different judges had different attitudes to bonding and the amount of surety required. As a result of the case of *Re H*[1] (COP) this has now been resolved. Judge Hazel Marshall laid down clear guidelines to be followed in calculating a suitable level of surety.

Typically, bond premiums for solicitors acting as professional Deputies in high value personal injury/clinical negligence claims are no more than £250–£350 per annum, even where settlement levels are several million pounds. (This takes account of the existence of the solicitors' professional indemnity policy.) Where a large portion of a settlement is met by periodic payments then that will serve to reduce the level of bonding.

## 13. Wills and statutory wills

No one under the age of 18 may make a will. This principle cannot be avoided even by the use of trusts for minors who, it may be thought, will not survive beyond 18.

If a person of 18 or over has testamentary capacity he can make a will for himself and give his own instructions. If not, then it is possible for a statutory will to be made.

In order to give instructions for a will a person must be able to understand the following:

(a) The nature of the document to be executed.
(b) The extent of his property and estate.
(c) The nature of the claims of those he proposes to benefit or exclude from participation in the will.

These are the criteria set down in the case of *Banks v Goodfellow*.[2]

---

[1] [2009] EWHC B31.
[2] (1870) L.R. 5 Q.B.

Many clients whose financial affairs are dealt with by a Deputy have such testamentary capacity. If the Deputy obtains a certificate of testamentary capacity the client can give instructions and execute his will in the usual way. However, if it is established that the client lacks testamentary capacity then an application to the Court of Protection for a statutory will to be executed on his behalf should be made.

Practice Direction F supplemental to Pt 9 of the Court of Protection Rules 2007 sets out the detailed procedure.

The cost of such an application can be significant as the procedure requires the involvement of the Official Solicitor on behalf of the client and the notification of anyone adversely affected by the applications, e.g. those who might lose their entitlement under an intestacy by the terms of the proposed will.

A Medical Certificate will be required. The court fee of £400 will apply to the application and if it goes to a hearing a further £500 court fee will apply. Many applications are dealt with on the papers and no attendance is required. Hearings will normally only be required if there are serious disputes over the proposed will. Costs can amount in the simplest of cases to a few thousand pounds and in the most difficult of cases tens of thousands of pounds. The usual rule about costs is that all parties' costs are paid out of the testator's estate. However, the court has discretion to order costs against any party if it believes he has acted unreasonably. It is important to claim this item properly in the compensation claim.

## 14. Keeping up to date

As from April 2011 the OPG website has closed. Information about the OPG is now found in the DIRECTGOV site and that for the Court of Protection on the HMCS website. Neither is as easy to navigate as the OPG site but hopefully that will change.

# SOME IMPORTANT INFORMATION ABOUT BENEFITS RELEVANT TO DEPUTIES

**Income Support (Amended) Regulations 1987 as amended.**

*52-week disregard*

Under para.12A of Sch.10 to the Regulations (which since 7 April 2008 extend to means-testing for Local Authority funded care or Direct Payments) practitioners have to be careful when receiving interim payments.

In essence there is a period of 52 weeks running from the day of receipt of the first payment (no matter how small) in consequence of a personal injury claim, during which the capital received will be disregarded. However, you do not receive a separate 52-week period on future payments.

e.g.  £10,000 interim received six months ago.
£100,000 final compensation received today.

The 52-week period starts on the date of the first payment, so that the disregard for the £100,000 will actually expire in 26 weeks' time.

In most cases interims are received over a much longer period such that the disregard will run out well before the interim is exhausted. As a result the funds received do have to be disclosed. However, if the funds are held by the Deputy under the Deputyship order then they are disregarded regardless of the 52-week period. There is no need to put funds in a personal injury trust if they are held by a Deputy under a Court of Protection Order.

Payments other than the interim may also trigger the 52-week disregard period if they are paid "in consequence of" a personal injury, e.g. personal accident insurance or a statutory "no fault" scheme.

*Funds held in or out of court*

Under the Regulations, funds received as a consequence of a personal injury are disregarded entirely if they are either held in trust or are under the control of the Court of Protection.

Most practitioners are aware of the trust exception but may not fully understand the Court of Protection exemption. Originally, in order to qualify for the exemption, the funds of a Deputy had to be held in court, i.e. actually be invested through Court Funds Office. However, since 7 April 2008 as a result of SI 593/2008 that restriction no longer applies. Now funds held "to the Order of the Court" are disregarded. As a result funds invested more freely, including in property, remain disregarded as long as they are in the Deputy's name. Accordingly there is no need to contemplate personal injury trusts where there is a Deputyship.

# J2: The incidence of Deputyship costs over a claimant's life

1. The appointment of a Deputy is likely to arise for a personal injury/clinical negligence claimant when he lacks capacity to manage his financial and property affairs, i.e. he is a protected person for the purpose of the Mental Capacity Act 2005 prior to the index injury or insult or as a consequence thereof. In either case Deputyship costs are a recoverable head of loss:

   - where the incapacity preceded the index injury or insult, but it is only in consequence of that injury or insult that the claimant has financial affairs and property of sufficient size and complexity to warrant the appointment of a Deputy, and
   - where the incapacity is a direct consequence of the injury/insult.

2. Minority is not of itself an incapacity for these purposes but it is the Court of Protection's practice to appoint a Deputy for infants where the damages are significant and the probability is that the infant will not acquire legal capacity on attaining his majority.

3. At the latest admission of liability and/or judgment an application should be made without delay. This is in order that a decision maker, i.e. the Deputy, can be put in place as soon as possible to enable interim funds to be applied for the claimant's benefit. An application may be made earlier if the circumstances in which an eventual award is a probability.

4. The process of application for a Deputy will involve the solicitor concerned in undertaking a fact-find with the claimant and his family for preparation and completion of the application; service in person upon the claimant and close members of family of notice of intention to apply; and of the application itself once issued. Fees will arise for the Court of Protection on application; and on appointment with the Office of the Public Guardian. Work may typically be undertaken by the Deputy and/or solicitors acting on his behalf on an interim basis in relation to the management of the claimant's property and affairs either in anticipation of, or with the benefit of, interim authorities provided on application by the court.

5. The order appointing a Deputy is also authority for assessment of costs involved in the application. Cost Draftsman and SCCO assessment fees will arise accordingly to the claimant's account.

6. The court will in addition require the Deputy to enter into a security bond. The extent of the bond appropriate is in the discretion of the judge. Considerations are detailed in the case of *Re H*.[3] They include whether the Deputy is a professional and has the benefit of PII and in a solicitor's case of the compensation fund; the extent of the annual income; and the size of assets generally which are readily accessible by the Deputy without further reference to the court. The figure provided in the accompanying cost breakdown is an estimate in a typical cerebral palsy and/or catastrophic brain injury case.

7. It is important to check the terms in which the first general order is made to ensure that it provides the Deputy with the authorities sought on the application and/or likely to be required, for example to purchase a property and/or to invest. Failing this, short of the court's accepting an error which requires correction, a separate application for amendment will be required and will attract a fee and costs associated with its preparation and conduct. Applications will generally be dealt with on paper without a hearing but nonetheless can take three months to be processed even on that basis. The initial application can be anticipated to take at least six months as will an application for appointment of a new Deputy.

8. The management of the claimant's property and affairs then proceeds in annual stages—Deputyship years. The anniversary of the initial order appointing the Deputy is authority for the Deputy's

---

[3] [2009] EWHC B31.

assessment of his/her costs of the preceding year. The Deputy can take payments on account during the year at quarterly intervals: currently the amount is 20 per cent of the total anticipated annual costs per quarter, for the first three quarters of the Deputyship year, which will be set off against the eventual bill once approved by the SCCO.

9. The security bond will be renewed on an annual basis and in addition an OPG annual supervision fee will be payable. This is charged according to a scale and depends upon the level of supervision deemed appropriate by the OPG. It will generally be higher in the case of a lay, as opposed to a professional, Deputy. Initially a claim is ongoing and in the immediate post-settlement years the level of supervision may also be set at a higher level (probably type 2A intermediate), being reduced once a routine is in place (down to type 2 light touch). All levels of supervision, apart from level three supervision where a client has minimal assets, now carry a fixed fee of £320 per annum.

10. In the initial years of a Deputyship, costs can be anticipated to be higher than they will be in subsequent years. Costs are given in the accompanying breakdown for the "first two Deputyship years" within which it is contemplated that significant structural issues will be addressed including:

    - acquisition and adaptation of accommodation,
    - the major/initial investment decisions, and
    - the establishment, through Case Managers or otherwise, of care and other support regimes.

11. The impact of the litigation should be factored in while this is being undertaken. Litigation will inevitably increase costs because:

    - long-term budgeting even on an annual basis will not generally be possible while the Deputyship is in its infancy and the claimant is dependent upon interim payments,
    - liaison with the litigation team will be required including as to the claimant's requirements for interim funding; the adequacy of offers made in these connections; the provision of evidence in support of applications; the provision of copy financial and other records and their appropriate collation; and the consideration of the eventual form of order and of financial advice in relation thereto, and
    - stresses will occur to the claimant and his family. These can be anticipated to extend beyond settlement of the action/final judgment. It is a commonplace that the first year or two post-litigation are likely to be unsettled.

12. Thus "the first two Deputyship years" may extend over a greater period of time. When the conclusion of the assessment of damages approaches, there are likely to be a number of years that are already "history". When concluding assessment of damages approaches, these are likely to be a number of years for which the bills for Deputyship costs have been assessed and paid. Heightened costs associated with the litigation itself and the major structural adjustments in prospect will extend beyond the end of the litigation. At least one year should be allowed for the major investment decisions and for the claimant and family to settle down (even if relocation to suitable alternative accommodation has already taken place).

13. The general management costs identified for "the first two Deputyship years" are for a case of medium-level complexity. Depending on all the circumstances and needs of the claimant including importantly the interplay and relationship with his/her family, the costs could be greater or less. All is contingent upon the level of activity required of the Deputy and their team. The range might be between £12–13,000 and £30,000 or more for general management costs.

14. Matters usually settle down to a general routine after that period. A range of £8–12,000 for general management costs might be anticipated in a typical cerebral palsy/acquired brain injury claim. Decisions may have to be taken about the claimant and his best interest and those of the family. Previous decisions should be revised.

15. It must be borne in mind that the MCA requires the Deputy to consult on decisions to be made. A claimant will often require face-to-face meetings so that the Deputy is able to provide him with appropriate explanations for decisions. The time and cost of dealing with this appropriately should not be underestimated.

16. "Some claimants will have behavioural problems, these include excessive contact, abusive behaviour, and the claimant working against the Deputy. The claimant may feel the Deputy is intruding into his life and taking his money. The claimant may also be exhibiting these behaviours to other professionals and the care/support team around him. Where these behaviours occur it is often difficult to overcome these and the resultant costs from the Deputy having to deal with these behaviours, or indeed the aftermath in terms of the breakdown of a care team or support regime, are often significant. Careful consideration should be given to the nature of the clients behaviours and additional costs should be included to allow for these where they occur. It is not unusual for such cases to see annual costs well in excess of £30,000.00 plus VAT per annum and these costs should not be underestimated."

17. "As with everyone, issues arise in the clients life periodically which are impossible to foresee. These can be changes in family circumstances for example the death of a close family member. A contingency sum has been allowed in the accompanying schedule, however this should be amended to reflect the clients life expectancy as a longer life expectancy will mean that inevitably as higher contingency sum should be allowed and of course the reverse for clients with a shorter life expectancy."

18. On attaining majority the claimant requires a will. If he has testamentary capacity (as opposed to capacity to manage financial and property affairs), the will can be prepared on his instructions and subject to the court's approval, signed on his behalf by the Deputy. If not, a statutory will must be made by the court on application. The Official Solicitor will be appointed to act on behalf of the claimant. In either case the application will need to be supported by evidence as to those who might be required as having a claim upon the claimant's natural love and affection, and as to the claimant's best interest (*Re P*). In either case a medical report will be required concerning capacity. The costs given in the accompanying breakdown are estimated on the assumption that an attended hearing will be required. Depending upon the degree of contention, the costs may be greater or smaller. All parties that may be affected by any new will must be notified. If the claimant would have been intestate, this will include a natural parent, even if the parent has re-married, and estranged children from former relationships, etc. If the proposed will is contested the cost will increase significantly.

19. The will requires periodic review in the light of changed circumstances and provision is accordingly made for the preparation of a further will every 10 years.

20. The application for a new Deputy amounts to a fresh application, but as much of the information will already be available, the costs incurred are likely to be lower. A medical certificate will be required concerning capacity and the application might be expected to take up to six months, again. The appointment of a new Deputy will give rise to an authority for assessment of the existing/retiring Deputy's costs.

21. The Deputyship will come to an end either on: (a) application by the claimant for discharge on the footing that he or she now has sufficient capacity to manage his or her own finances and affairs; or (b) death. In either case there will be winding-up costs associated with accounting to the protected person or to the representatives of their estate. An application for discharge on the ground of regained capacity of the protected person will generally require to be supported by a medical certificate.

22. No provision has been made in the accompanying breakdown for incidental applications for additional or special authority but each will cost £400 in application fees.

23. A professional Deputy will be required to submit an annual bill of costs to the Senior Court Costs Office (SCCO) on the anniversary of each deputyship year. The bill will need to be prepared by a Costs Draftsman and the costs of the bill being prepared will be around 5.5 per cent of the profit costs claimed. Additionally there is an assessment fee of £225 which is payable to the SCCO on application for the assessment.

## J3: Deputyship costs

### One-off cost of application for a Deputy to be appointed

| 1 | Solicitors' costs | £4,000 | |
|---|---|---|---|
| 2 | *Plus VAT* | £800 | |
| 3 | Disbursements (medical cert/travel) | £400 | |
| 4 | *Plus VAT* | £80 | Total set-up costs: £6,563 |
| 5 | Court of Protection Application fee | £400 | |
| 6 | Office of the Public Deputy Assessment Fee | £100 | |
| 7 | Security Bond Premium | £337.50 | |
| 8 | Cost Draftsman's fees | £220 | |
| 9 | SCCO Assessment Fee | £225 | |

### Estimated annual costs for each of the first two Deputyship years

| 10 | General management costs | £18,000 | |
|---|---|---|---|
| 11 | *Plus VAT* | £3,600 | |
| 12 | Plus Disbursements | £150 | Total annual cost for each of the first two years: £23,653 pa |
| 13 | *Plus VAT* | £30 | |
| 14 | Costs Draftsman's fee | £990 | |
| 15 | SCCO Annual Assessment fee | £225 | |
| 16 | Security Bond Premium | £337.50 | |
| 17 | OPG Annual Supervision fee | £320 | |

### Estimated annual costs for following years

| 18 | General management costs | £10,000 | |
|---|---|---|---|
| 19 | *Plus VAT* | £2,000 | |
| 20 | Plus Disbursements | £150 | |
| 21 | *Plus VAT* | £30 | Total annual cost: £13,613 |
| 22 | Costs Draftsman's fee | £550 | |
| 23 | SCCO Annual Assessment fee | £225 | |
| 24 | Security Bond Premium | £337.50 | |
| 25 | OPG Annual Supervision fee | £320 | |

## Other future costs

| 26 | Solicitors' costs in dealing with a statutory will application (assuming a hearing is required) | £5,500 | |
|---|---|---|---|
| 27 | *Plus VAT* | £1,100 | |
| 28 | Official Solicitor's costs in dealing with statutory will (assuming a hearing is required) | £2,500 | |
| 29 | *Plus VAT* | £500 | Each of these items to be incurred every 10 years = total of £12,720 every 10 years |
| 30 | Court of Protection fee for statutory will | £400 | |
| 31 | Disbursements involved in statutory will | £400 | |
| 32 | *Plus VAT* | £80 | |
| 33 | Solicitors' Costs for appointment of new Deputy/Obtaining new order | £1,200 | |
| 34 | *Plus VAT* | £240 | |
| 35 | Disbursements (Medical Cert) | £250 | |
| 36 | *Plus VAT* | £50 | |
| 37 | CP Application Fee for appointment of a new Deputy | £400 | |
| 38 | OPG Deputy Appointment Fee | £100 | |
| 39 | Winding-up costs | £1,500 | One off |
| 40 | *Plus VAT* | £300 | One off |
| 41 | Contingency sum | £30,000 | One off |
| 42 | *Plus VAT* | £6,000 | One off |

**Notes**

There has been little change in costs from the previous years, the main reason being that the guideline hourly rates have been retained at the 2010 levels. This remains the case this year.

There is a reduction in the Security Bond premiums as, where there is a professional Deputy, the courts have been setting lower bonds, and the premiums have also reduced in the past couple of years as competition has come into the market.

The Senior Court Costs Office assessment fee has risen by £5 to £225 per annum.

The costs of Capacity assessments are rising and it is getting increasingly difficult to get GPs to complete the COP3 forms. In injury cases it is usually the expert who completes the form and they are usually charging higher fees for this now.

A big issue affecting Deputies, who employ care staff on behalf of clients, is the pension auto-enrolment requirements. These requirements are time consuming and will add to the costs. There will be ongoing additional costs to the Deputy of administering the monthly payments and returns for the carers' pensions to comply with the regulations.

# Group K
*Carer Rates and Rehabilitation*

K1: Care and attendance

K2: Nannies, cleaners and school fees

K3: DIY, gardening and housekeeping

K4: Hospital self-pay (uninsured) charges

K5: NHS charges

K6: The 2007 Rehabilitation Code

K7: Rehabilitation: a practitioner's guide

K8: APIL Serious Injury Guide

# K1: Care and attendance

## Introduction

A series of cases since 2005 involving injuries of the utmost severity has led to highly developed claims for care and attendance, including case management.[1] This section aims to be a source of practical assistance to practitioners and courts setting about the task of assessing damages for care and attendance.

## Past non-commercial care

2. Damages awarded in respect of non-commercial care, usually by family members, are governed by the following rules/practical advice.
3. The aim is to award the reasonable value of/proper recompense for gratuitous services rendered—*Hunt v Severs*.[2]
4. Accordingly, a claimant holds the damages on trust for those who provided the care.[3]
5. If a tortfeasor has himself provided the care, there can be no recovery of damages on that score.[4]
6. If a claimant has fallen out with the care provider so that the recovery on trust will not be honoured, again there will be no award in damages.[5]
7. There is no threshold requirement to be satisfied before an award can be made, whether in terms of severity of injury or level of care.[6] Extra domestic services are sufficient.[7]
8. While there is no threshold to satisfy, there must be actual care. So, when a claimant is still in hospital, damages are not to be awarded for mere visiting—only for any periods of care given during the course of the visit.[8]

---

[1] Readers interested in the finer detail of big cases can find it set out in the updated paper by James Rowley QC "Serious PI litigation—a Quantum Update" with the accompanying tables at: *www.byromstreet.com*.

[2] [1994] 2 A.C. 350 at 363A ff. These are special damages. While not referred to expressly in the speeches, the rationale in *Daly v General Steam Navigation Co Ltd* [1981] 1 WLR 120 CA—awarding general damages in respect of past non-commercial domestic services—was overruled by the House of Lords through the result in *Hunt v Severs*.

[3] *Hunt v Severs* above also expressly over-ruled the line of authority derived from *Donnelly v Joyce* [1974] QB 454 in favour of that derived from Lord Denning's judgment in *Cunningham v Harrison* [1973] QB 942. No longer is an award for services considered as a claimant's damages (based on his need for the care) for him then to make a present to the carer. Rather it is recompense to the carer and only held by a claimant on trust.

[4] *Hunt v Severs* at 363D. This is a common occurrence when passengers are suing a member of the family who was the negligent driver. Where liability is split, there is no known authority but no reason in principle why a tortfeasor carer cannot recover to the extent of another tortfeasor's share of the blame.

[5] See *ATH v MS* [2003] PIQR Q1 at [30] as to the principle; but in this case of fatal accident, the court was already ordering damages to be paid into court for investment on behalf of dependent children and felt able to enforce the trust through the investment control of the court. It would be otherwise if the monies were simply to be paid over to a claimant and the court really felt the trust would not be honoured.

[6] The Court of Appeal in *Giambrone v Sunworld Holidays Ltd* [2004] PIQR Q4 at Q36 decided that dicta in *Mills v British Rail Engineering Ltd* [1992] PIQR Q130 to the effect that there was a threshold of devoted care or care well beyond the ordinary call of duty (and similar phrases) were obiter and not to be followed.

[7] The Court of Appeal in *Mills* had overlooked a passage from Lord Denning in *Cunningham v Harrison*—quoted with apparent approval by Lord Bridge in *Hunt v Severs* above at 360E—"Even though she had not been doing paid work but only domestic duties in the house, nevertheless all extra attendance on him certainly calls for compensation." [1973] QB 942 at 952B-C.

[8] *Havenhand v Jeffrey* (unreported, 24 February 1997 CA); *Tagg v Countess of Chester Hospital Foundation NHS Trust* [2007] EWHC 509 (QB) at [85]; *Huntley v Simmons* [2009] EWHC 405 (QB) at [65].

K1: Care and attendance

9. Compensable care must relate to the person—the claimant himself or, under the rule in *Lowe v Guise*[9], another disabled member of the same household, usually cared for by the claimant but who, because of the claimant's injury, is cared for by another. So, where the provision spreads out into non-commercial cover for the claimant in his business, different considerations apply; there is no compensable claim here for the hours provided by analogy with real care.[10]

10. Claims are rarely put on the following footing but where a carer has lost earnings in the provision of services, the value can be assessed as the lost net earnings up to a ceiling of the commercial value of the care provided.[11]

11. In the majority of cases the exercise is to examine the care and make a fair assessment of the number of hours in fact provided. (In doing this, one will in passing register if care has been given at anti-social hours or has been particularly demanding.) The assessment is easy in respect of discrete blocks of care; but calls for more subtle evidence/judgment when care is given in multiple short bursts over the course of day and night or constitutes more general supervision/support in the home while daily life continues.

12. Hourly rates are then applied to the determined number of hours.

13. Many different scales have been used in the past; but now there is uniformity in taking rates derived from Local Authority Spinal Point 8.

14. The suggested starting points are the basic (daytime weekday) rate or the enhanced aggregate rate (which takes into account care in the evenings, at night and at weekends). Both are set out in the table below.

15. The aggregate rate balances all the hours of the week by their relative number and appropriate rate. It is logically entirely apt only when care is spread out evenly through the whole week and the hours of the day and night. The odd hour here and there in the evening will not justify an aggregate rate; but intensive care given only at night and not by day, seven days a week (for example when commercial daytime care has been purchased but a relative left to care at night), would logically justify more than the aggregate rate. Where a spouse has risen early to provide care before going to work and then carried on in the evenings on returning home, no care has been given when the daytime weekday rate is applicable.

16. There is no reason in principle why different rates cannot be used in different periods—the aggregate rate during more intensive care in early convalescence and the basic rate afterwards; or a rate over the whole period averaged somewhere between the two. No doubt the exercise would have to be relatively broad brush but it may be none the worse for that.[12] The overarching aim is to attach a reasonable value to the actual care and award proper recompense.

17. Notwithstanding the logical attraction, however, of choosing a rate close to the circumstances of the actual provision, following *Fairhurst v St Helens & Knowsley Health Authority*[13] the basic rate

---

[9] [2002] QB 1369 at [38]. The ratio of this case (and how widely or narrowly the rule established should be construed) is a fertile area for argument. Is it really confined to care of a disabled member or will care of a baby or child suffice? Is the element of provision being within the same household essential to the legal rule? Is it an important difference if a disabled mother has come to rely on her daughter's care while living in the next street; or in a self-contained granny-flat within the curtilage of the daughter's house; or in the spare room of her house?

[10] *Hardwick v Hudson* [1999] 1 WLR 1770.

[11] *Housecroft v Burnett* [1986] 1 All ER 332 O'Connor LJ at 343e, albeit his view of the *Cunningham v Harrison* and *Donnelly v Joyce* debate was over-ruled in *Hunt v Severs*. The ceiling of the commercial rate has sometimes been criticised on the basis that it would have been enough simply to apply a wider test of reasonableness to the evaluation of the mother's claim for care of her daughter. However, that evaluation was at the very heart of the appeal and it would be difficult to contend that the invocation of the commercial ceiling was not part of the ratio.

[12] Averaging things with a broad brush appealed to Stuart-Smith J in *Ali v Caton & MIB* [2013] EWHC 1730 (QB) at [323b–d] and he effectively reached a rate between the aggregate and basic ones. He took the starting point of the claimant's expert's figures and discounted them by 25 per cent on account of arguments over both rates and the number of hours. " . . . Adoption of a basic rate throughout would lead to under-compensation while adoption of the enhanced rate would have the opposite effect." See below for more about this case.

[13] [1995] PIQR Q.1.

was used for over a decade in reported cases, even those of maximum severity when the care was of an onerous nature and much of it provided at nights and at weekends.[14]

18. Notwithstanding *Wells v Wells*[15] and modernisation of the assessment of damages for personal injuries, it took until *Massey v Tameside*[16] for there to be a reported case at the aggregate rate. Since then there has been a move away from using the basic rate as the universal starting point in very serious cases at least.[17]

19. It is unclear whether, in more routine cases where a significant proportion of the care has been carried out at anti-social times, a rate other than the basic rate is being awarded in unreported decisions[18]; or if the basic rate still rules.

20. It is increasingly common for experts in very valuable cases to break the past down into a large number of periods with minor fluctuations in hours and annual increases in rates. It may be fine in that type of case, albeit use of properly considered averages would surely simplify things considerably at no significant cost in overall accuracy. In cases without experts, practical experience suggests focussing on fewer distinct periods of care and taking into account minor fluctuations through the reasoned choice of an average number of hours or average rate[19] rather than embarking on over-elaborate calculation. Where cases involve gradually diminishing care from a point on hospital discharge to recovery or a plateau of continuing need, looking to the level of care midway through that period has much to commend it as a starting point in picking an overall average.

21. Since personal injury damages are awarded net of tax and NI, there is invariably an appropriate reduction in respect of past non-commercial care.[20] It is now almost always 25 per

---

[14] Many settlements were negotiated with an enhancement for a higher rate, but there was no reported case until *Massey v Tameside* [2007] EWHC 317 (QB).

[15] [1999] 1 AC 345.

[16] [2007] EWHC 317 (QB).

[17] After *Massey* above came *Noble v Owens* [2008] EWHC 359 (QB)—a serious case but not quite of the utmost severity—in which the court retreated to *Fairhurst* and the basic rate. Since then, in *Crofts* (2008) QBD Lawtel, *Smith* [2008] EWHC 2234 (QB) and *Whiten v St George's Healthcare NHS Trust* [2011] EWHC 2066 (QB)—all cases of the utmost severity—the court has awarded the aggregate rate or (*Crofts*) a broad-brush average rate close to it. Recently, in a case of more moderate value (arthritis and pain syndrome—general damages £93,000) Sir David Eady awarded the basic rate at [44]; he had been shown *Noble v Owens* but no other authorities are mentioned.

[18] In the asbestosis case of *Nicholas v MoD* [2013] EWHC 2351 (QB), HHJ Burrell QC (sitting as a High Court Judge) awarded the aggregate rate at [23]. In *Knauer v MOJ* [2014] EWHC 2553 (QB) Bean J (as he then was) awarded the aggregate rate in respect of general household tasks [13]. In neither case does it appear there was any spirited resistance.

[19] See also *Ali v Caton & MIB*, above.

[20] At a time when the basic rate was being used as the universal starting point, a few very serious cases emerged where it was felt that a deduction from such a low rate would leave a carer with inadequate recompense; and some Courts refused to make a deduction. Now that the quality and difficulty of care is beginning to be reflected through higher rates, this method of achieving a fair result is no longer required. Choose the appropriate rate for the quality/intensity of care; but then make the principled deduction for tax and NI. As with any rule, however, there is the odd reasoned departure to be found: in *AC v Farooq & MIB* [2012] EWHC 1484 QB) King J did not make deduction from the £7.11 rate used by one of the nursing experts since it already represented a compromise over what was the appropriate commercial rate [131].

Recently in *Totham v King's College Hospital NHS Foundation Trust* [2015] EWHC 97 (QB), the parties agreed the rate and the hours. Nevertheless, the claimant submitted that Mrs Totham had given up highly paid work and consequently there should be no discount at all for the non-commercial element. The submission was rejected by Laing J at [25]–[28]: the argument in respect of Mrs Totham's work did not go to the correct non-commercial reduction (principally to do with tax and NI), rather it went to the correct rate to be allowed for the hours (which had already been compromised.) The moral of the tale is to take the advice in the earlier part of this footnote to heart and to chose the right rate to start with to provide proper recompense.

cent[21] but the bracket appears historically to have been between 20 per cent and 33 per cent.[22]

22. A sum equivalent to any Carer's Allowance received is to be deducted from an award for non-commercial care.[23]

**Example schedule**[24]

| | | |
|---|---:|---:|
| Care while an in-patient—2 weeks<br>Average of 2 hours actual care at the bedside each evening (including Saturday and Sunday):<br>2 hours × 14 days @ the aggregate rate (£9.44) | 264 | |
| Care during 4 weeks intensive convalescence at home:<br>6 hours provided daily, including weekends and evenings:<br>6 hours × 28 days @ the aggregate rate (£9.44) | 1,586 | |
| Further 6 months of care gradually diminishing from 6 hours a day to nil, more during the evenings and weekends at the beginning than at the end:<br>Average of 3 hours a day care × 365/2 × the average of the basic and aggregate rates (£8.31) | 4,550 | |
| | 6,400 | |
| Non-commercial discount | ×0.75 | |
| | | 4,800 |
| No continuing personal care but assistance still required in respect of heavier DIY, gardening etc. chores<br>Making allowance from £1,500 p.a.[25] for the chores still possible:<br>£750 pa × 10 (discounted lifetime multiplier to say 70): | | |
| | | 7,500 |
| Total | | £12,300 |

---

[21] This was the considered reduction in *Whiten* above from the already chosen aggregate rate—see [144]. It was described by Stuart-Smith J in *Ali v Caton & MIB* above, footnote 12, as the "conventional 25% discount" and he refused to make more adjustment [323c]. 25 per cent has been the reduction in *Loughlin v Singh* [2013] EWHC 1641 (QB); *Farrugia* [2014] EWHC 1036 (QB); *Tate v Ryder Holdings* [2014] EWHC 4256 (QB); *Ellison v University Hospitals of Morecambe Bay NHS Foundation* Trust [2015] EWHC 366 (QB); *Totham* above; *Robshaw v United Lincolnshire Hospitals NHS Trust* [2015] EWHC 923 (QB) and other cases too numerous to specify.

[22] *Evans v Pontypridd Roofing Limited* [2002] PIQR Q5 is the leading general authority on the non-commercial reduction. In *Zambarda v Shipbreaking (Queenborough) Ltd* [2013] EWHC 2263 (QB), John Leighton Williams QC (sitting as a Deputy High Court Judge) made only a 20 per cent discount [64] because the sum was so small that income tax would not be paid. It is a very long time since an argued and reported decision at 33 per cent: *Nash v Southmead Health Authority* [1993] P.I.Q.R. Q.156, decided in late 1992, is the case usually cited.

[23] Teare J in *Massey* above at [52]:
> "To the extent that the carer has received benefits in respect of his or her voluntary care the claimant does not need a sum of money to give proper recompense for that care. It therefore seems to me that the Defendant's contention is right in principle."

Where there has been a discount on liability for litigation risk, carers might well argue that the Carers Allowance should be considered as filling in for that reduction and not taken off their already reduced claims for non-commercial care.

[24] The example will pick up the threads of the "logical" approach as outlined in the text. No doubt a counter schedule, as well as attempting to reduce the number of hours, would take a point that the basic rate only should be allowed in a case beneath that of maximum severity. Readers should report decided cases on the issue of hourly rate applied and kindly inform the writer when a case reference is available via james.rowley@byromstreet.com.

[25] Mackay J in *Fleet v Fleet* [2009] EWHC 3166 (QB):
> "25. This is claimed based on a multiplicand of £1500 p.a. I do not understand the multiplier to be controversial. The defendant contends for between £750 and £1,000 per annum as a 'more conventional sum' than the £1500 sought by the

## Past commercial care

23. Where there has been actual expenditure in the past on commercial care, it should be capable of easy proof (or reasonably accurate estimation if records have not been kept.)
24. It will usually be awarded in full unless the defendant raises issues of unreasonable provision (or elements of separate causation leading to unrelated provision.)[26]

Claimant. The evidence on this issue is that Mr Fleet did all the DIY in the house and had in the past installed a new bathroom according to his wife. He was a skilled man albeit he was busy and worked long days and sometimes long weeks. He also said that he had plans to redecorate the house, and Mrs Fleet said that the living room now needs redecoration; though she could do some of the preparatory work, and did do so when her husband did the work, she could not in my judgement be reasonably expected to fill the gap left by him.

26. Equally, there is considerable garden at the house which Mrs Fleet tends but she cannot manage the trimming of the trees a screen of which separates the house from its neighbours and which has to be kept in order, or cut the grass.

27. I believe I am justified in saying that I can take into account the general level of awards under this head of damage from past experience. It would be dismal if experts had to be called to say how much it costs to mow a lawn or paint a room; after all judges do have some experience of that kind of activity and what it cost to buy it in the market place.

28. I see nothing wrong with the figure of £1,500 per annum claimed by the plaintiff and I think that is the right sum."

John Leighton Williams QC (sitting as a High Court Judge) allowed £1,250 p.a. to age 77 in *Zambarda v Shipbreaking (Queenborough) Ltd* above at [88]. Contrast Stuart-Smith J in *Ali v Caton & MIB* above and below at [337] where he awarded £250 p.a. to a young man with no track record for DIY, decorating and gardening. In *McGinty v Pipe* [2012] EWHC 506 (QB) HHJ Foster QC (sitting as a High Court Judge) awarded a woman of 51 £750 p.a. for gardening and DIY with a multiplier of 16 (to just beyond 70.) Kenneth Parker J in *Tate v Ryder Holdings* above discounted the claim for a 24-year-old man heavily to a lump sum award of £15,000 because of the considerable uncertainty over whether he would have carried out such activities. HHJ McKenna (sitting as a High Court Judge) awarded [96] £900 p.a. between the ages of 25 and 70 in *FM v Ipswich Hospital NHS Trust* [2015] EWHC 775 (QB). Foskett J [421] awarded £1,500 p.a. in *Robshaw* above from age 25 when life expectancy was reduced to 63.

[26] In *O'Brien v Harris* (Transcript 22 February 2001) the BIRT rehabilitation costs (£21,860) significantly exceeded those originally estimated (£13,700) [191]. There was no evidence from BIRT explaining the difference or resiling from the estimate [192]. The case manager was not called to justify the additional case management costs (£10,834 v £6,461) [193]. Some increased costs were allowed based on inferences from the invoices to the effect that a higher quality of support worker had been provided than in the estimate [195]. There had, however, been inadequate management of cost [194] (but by whom?—see below) and Pitchford J made an overall award of £18,500 [196].

In the case of *Loughlin v Singh* above, Kenneth Parker J was invited [62] to disallow the costs of past care and case management on the basis that "the standard of such care and management fell significantly below that which could reasonably be expected to meet the exigencies of the claimant's condition and circumstances". The full submission was rejected as "wholly disproportionate and unjust"; but the claim was reduced by 20 per cent with a broad brush on account of the case manager's failure to address the claimant's need for a specific and effective sleep hygiene regime in timely fashion. Kenneth Parker J made a finding that

"the efforts made on this fundamental aspect of the rehabilitation were simply not adequate [61]. . . . Principle requires that I should take due account of the fact, that I have found, that the standard of the care and case management services did, in an important respect, fall significantly below the standard that could reasonably have been expected. In other words, the objective value of what the Claimant received was less than the amount of the charges made for the relevant services" [62].

There was no finding in *Loughlin* that the claimant through his Financial Deputy had knowingly appointed an incompetent case manager. Kenneth Parker J made no finding of failure to mitigate against the claimant/Financial Deputy in the handling/funding of the case manager (although this may have been an under-current in the case). As long as Kenneth Parker J's findings amounted to *gross* negligence on the part of the case manager, his observations can be squared with wider principles of *novus actus* under *Rahman v Arearose Ltd* [2001] QB 351 and *Webb v Barclays Bank* [2001] EWCA Civ 1141: insofar as the increased costs of failing to implement a sleep hygiene regime were caused by the gross negligence of a third party, they were separately caused. It is difficult to see, however, why a finding of mere as against gross negligence in the past on the part of a case manager should break the chain of causation and lead to the dis-allowance of part of the claim.

In the more recent case of *Ali v Caton & MIB* above and below, Stuart-Smith J awarded the full claim for past support workers, the regime having been set up in accordance with apparently competent third party advice.

"The position of a significantly brain-damaged claimant who acts on the basis of apparently reasonable advice is strong,

25. The primary measure of damage against which to judge the claimed level of provision is one of reasonable care to meet a claimant's needs.[27]
26. If, at first blush, the claim in the past appears to exceed the primary measure of damage, principles of mitigation of loss may yet come to a claimant's aid if some evidence is adduced to explain the apparent over-spend. Once a claimant raises such arguments, the burden of proof lies on a defendant to prove a failure in mitigation; and the standard against which to judge a claimant's actions is not a harsh one.[28]
27. The value of direct payments stands to be deducted.[29] There is no loss to the extent that there is NHS continuing care.

**Future non-commercial care**

28. If non-commercial care is to be carried on long into the future, the potential break down of the package is a contingency to be assessed. Where there is detailed expert evidence, there will often be an alternative package laid out drawing on greater commercial care. It will then be a matter for the judge to reach a fair balanced assumption in monetary terms between two or more packages, weighting the award according to the available evidence.[30]
29. Where the evidence is not so detailed and there is no provision elsewhere in the calculations for a break down in the non-commercial care package, it may well be appropriate to reflect adverse contingencies by refusing to apply the usual non-commercial discount. In this way some allowance is made with a broad brush for the possibility of more expensive commercial care on separation/ill health/death in the family member who is to supply the care.[31]

---

though not always impregnable, when seeking to recover the costs of doing so from a tortfeasor. On this item, the balance of the argument strongly favours the claimant" [323f–h].
This approach is in keeping with the writer's understanding of the real legal issue set out in the previous paragraph.
Laing J in *Totham* above conveniently ignored deciding whether the poor case management had been grossly negligent or merely negligent and awarded the whole claim on the basis that Mrs Totham "had acted reasonably in appointing [the case management company] in the first place, and in continuing to employ, and pay, them until they walked off the job." [39]

[27] The principle was put succinctly by Lord Lloyd in *Wells v Wells* [1999] 1 AC 345 at 377F in just 17 words: "Plaintiffs are entitled to a reasonable standard of care to meet their requirements, but that is all." Stephenson LJ traced in *Rialis v Mitchell* (Court of Appeal transcript, 6 July 1984) how the 100 per cent principle was finessed through a series of Victorian cases involving fatal accidents on the railways to reflect the recovery of reasonable rather than perfect compensation. Reasonable compensation is now 100 per cent compensation since it is the primary measure of damage. Professor Andrews Burrows, writing Chapter 28 of the leading practitioner's textbook *Clerk & Lindsell*, 21st Edition, clearly espouses what this Chapter has considered the orthodox line: see §28-23. For an alternative view, see Dr Harvey McGregor in *McGregor on Damages*, 19th Edition, at 38-056 (but his line ignores *Rialis* and Lord Lloyd in *Wells* above, as well as practice over decades and the other decisions mentioned in footnote 206 within his own section).

Recently, claimants and defendants are jousting, the one using the language of "full compensation" and the other "proportionality". It is far from clear what these ideas add if the primary measure of damage is "reasonable compensation": this test is infinitely flexible and requires no gloss; all the decisions are ultimately explicable applying a simple test of *reasonableness* to the very specific facts. Readers interested in seeing the development of this trend can look to *Whiten* above at [4]-[5]; *Totham* above at [12]; *Ellison* above at [9]; *Robshaw* above at [161]-[167].

[28] The topic is beyond the scope of this chapter; an obvious source of assistance lies in *McGregor on Damages* 19th edition (London: Sweet & Maxwell, 2014) para. 9-074 and in the surrounding paragraphs.

[29] *Crofton v NHS Litigation Authority* [2007] 1WLR 923.

[30] In *C v Dixon* [2009] EWHC 708 (QB) King J assessed damages where the relationship between the claimant and his partner was far from assured in the long run. He took an assumed period of 10 years before break up as a fair reflection of the chances and proceeded to do the arithmetic from that starting point.

[31] See *Willbye v Gibbons* [2004] PIQR P15 at [12] and [16] in which, on a quality of evidence which was insufficient to warrant fine alternative contingency calculations in the event of breakdown in the non-commercial package, Kennedy LJ varied the sum awarded by removing the non-commercial discount allowed by the Recorder.

## Future commercial care

### Care—hourly rates

30. There is no "conventional" hourly rate for future commercial care, whether recruited through direct employment or an agency. All depends on the nature/difficulty of the required care; the level of need for continuity in carers; the prevailing rates local to a claimant's home (probably the biggest factor). Evidence on all three scores is highly desirable.[32] The most recent cases have not always involved argument over the hourly rate. Examples in the biggest cases (direct employment not agency rates) are as follows:

| Case[33] | Weekday—£ | Weekend—£ | Location |
|---|---|---|---|
| *Manna*[34] (determined—July 2015) | 10.50 | 11.50 | Bolton suburbs |
| *Robshaw* (agreed—March 2015) | 10 | 11 | Lincs. |
| *Farrugia*[35] (determined—March 2014) | 11.50 | 14 | Hants. |
| *Streeter*[36] (determined—Sept. 2013) | 9 | 10 | Aylesbury |
| *Whiten* (agreed—mid-2011) | 13 | 15 | "Good" London rates |
| *Sklair* (agreed—late 2009) | 11 | 13 | Beckenham, Kent |
| *C v Dixon* (determined—evidence as at mid-2008) | 10 | 11 | Barnsley |
| *Huntley* (determined—aggregate rate for late 2008) | 9.50 | 9.50 | Portsmouth Cosham/ Hillsea |
| *XXX* (agreed—late 2008) | 12 | 14 | Guildford |
| *Smith* (determined—mid-2008) | 10 | 12 | Herts. |
| *Crofts* (agreed composite rate—summer 2008) | 12 | 12 | Herts. |

---

[32] Jack J bewailed the lack of evidence of decent quality in *XXX* [2008] EWHC 2727 (QB) at [16].
[33] Full case references can be found in the wider text of this Chapter and footnotes if not given explicitly.
[34] *Manna v Central Manchester University Hospitals NHS Foundation Trust* [2015] EWHC 2279 (QB) at [214].
[35] [2014] EWHC 1036 (QB) Jay J at [102].
[36] [2013] EWHC 2841 (QB): the judgment at [209] did not articulate the figures beyond the annual multiplicands but the accepted rates were as set out in Mrs Gough's evidence in the Joint Statement. This was a tetraplegia case and Mrs Gough adduced evidence of actual research into local rates.

K1: Care and attendance

**Case management—hourly rates**

31. As with support worker rates there is no "conventional" hourly rate for case management; but the rate for this (as against the number of hours required) is mostly uncontroversial. The rate has crept up gradually and £90 an hour + travel time (£45 an hour plus mileage) was agreed in *Whiten*. £95 an hour was awarded in *Ali v Caton* [332], *Streeter* [217] (noting the agreement of Mrs Gough's costing) and *Farrugia* at [107], all above. £98 an hour was the rate allowed in *Tait v Gloucestershire Hospitals NHS Foundation Trust*.[37] Despite a claim for £107 an hour actually being paid for case management in *Manna* above, Cox J allowed [217] only £95 an hour, accepting the defendant's evidence that £107 an hour was beyond the normal range. Irwin J [142] awarded £98 an hour in *AB v Royal Devon & Exeter*.[38]
32. The required number of hours varies greatly and will be lower where there is agency care as against direct employment.

**Provision for holidays, sick pay etc.**

33. Where future care is to be provided through direct employment rather than agency provision, it is now customary to take into account i) paid holidays ii) higher hourly rates paid on Bank holidays iii) sick leave and iv) down time in the package for training days by adopting calculations based on a notional 60 weeks in the year.[39] While a few experts continue to use it, the alternative method of taking 52 weeks in the year and a percentage uplift to cover the required extras (which started at around 27 per cent and rose steadily) has fallen out of favour in reported cases. Jay J in *Farrugia* above described [100] taking a 60-week year as "standard practice".

**ERNIC**

34. Calculation of ERNIC on carers' wages was often misunderstood. It is currently (tax year 2016/17, unchanged from 2015/16) payable at 13.8 per cent on wages above the secondary threshold[40] (£156 a week × 52 weeks = £8,112 p.a.) So, to reach the annual sum of ERNIC, calculate the annual wages bill and deduct from it (£8,112 × the likely number of carers in the package) to give the sum on which 13.8 per cent is likely to be paid.

---

[37] [2015] EWHC 848 (QB) at [92].
[38] [2016] EWHC 1024 (QB).
[39] See: *XXX* above at [24] and *Whiten v St George's Healthcare NHS Trust* [2011] EWHC 2066 (QB) at [167]–[168]. For the evolution of the 60-week calculation, see the paper at footnote 1. *Streeter* above is an exception, where the experts both adopted 59.6 weeks but made an additional allowance on Bank holidays—ruled on by Baker J in line with Mrs Gough at £1 an hour uplift.

It is clear that down time for training days, additional pay for bank holidays etc. are included in the 60-week calculation. Those care experts who take 60 weeks and routinely bill for training time and so on in addition might be said to be trying too hard. The taking of 60 weeks, however, might be distinguished up or down for the specific training etc. requirements of any case since it has evolved out of the bigger cases—it might be easier to distinguish down rather than up (or the attempt not worth the effort). See also the discussion below in the main text with regard to liaison and MDT meetings as within the 60-week calculation.

In *HS v Lancashire Teaching Hospitals NHS Trust* [2015] EWHC 1376 (QB), the claimant's care expert asked for a 5% contingency uplift (5% × 60 weeks = 3 more weeks) "in order to cover holidays, sickness and other unexpected and sudden absences on the part of employed carers". William Davis J rejected the argument at [31] on the basis that the 60-week calculation included holidays and sickness. He continued: "Any maternity leave will be funded from the public purse given the number of employees. Any other absences will almost certainly be accommodated with the carers' shift patterns."

[40] There is an upper ceiling; but no carer is ever paid enough to bring it into play.

**NEST pension contributions**

35. The following information comes from the NEST website on 6 May 2016.
36. If enrolled within the scheme, employers pay a percentage of *qualifying earnings*: for tax year 2016/17 this is between £5,824 and £43,000 p.a.
37. Enrolment is compulsory for all workers aged at least 22 but under State retirement age who earn at least £10,000 p.a. from that employer, who work (or normally work) in the UK and who are not already an active member of a qualifying scheme with that employer.
38. Enrolment is at a worker's own option if aged at least 16 and under 75, with the employer having to contribute if they have *qualifying earnings,* i.e. earn over £5,824 p.a.
39. The staged introduction of the duties depending on the size of the employer has begun: all care packages have fewer than 30 employees so stand to be introduced into the scheme between January 2016 and April 2017.
40. Once the duties have bitten on an employer, the full impact of the contributions is also to be phased in: the plan keeps sliding and is still subject to final Parliamentary approval:[41]

|  | Minimum percentage of qualifying earnings that must be paid in total | Minimum percentage of qualifying earnings that **employers** must pay |
| --- | --- | --- |
| To end March 2018 | 2 per cent | **1 per cent** |
| April 2018 to end March 2019 | 5 per cent | **2 per cent** |
| April 2019 onwards | 8 per cent | **3 per cent** |

**Child care as a possibility**

41. The possible costs of caring for children have been claimed recently in *Totham* and *Robshaw*, both above. They were cases of cerebral palsy and the claims were resisted on the basis that neither claimant would realistically have children. The defences succeeded with slightly different formulations in the rationale. In *Totham*, Laing J found [71] that she was "not satisfied that there is a more than fanciful chance that Eva will have children". In *Robshaw*, Foskett J [191] would not go so far as to say the chance was "merely speculative or fanciful" but nevertheless said that the discount for contingencies would have to be so significant that "it would reduce the figure to something that would bear no real relationship to that actual cost if the event itself materialised. An award of such a sum would, in my view, be wholly artificial." And he made no award at all [192].

**Parental contribution to the future care package**

42. The court's attitude to any fair offset from future commercial care of very severely damaged children on account of parental involvement has evolved since 2006. The seeds sown by Sir Rodger Bell in *Iqbal*[42]—to the effect that parents are not to be presumed to take part in the care of grievously injured children requiring onerous care—have grown on strongly via Teare J in *Massey* [64], Lloyd Jones J in *A v Powys* [57] and HHJ Collender QC (sitting as a High Court Judge) in *Crofts* [120]. By the time of *Whiten* (2011) the NHSLA was no longer apparently arguing for any real offset: the only point at which the parents' potential contribution was considered relevant was in allowing for a single night sleeper in the commercial package on the basis that they would be available in an emergency [205]. In *Farrugia* above [96], care was awarded for 14 hours a day x 2 commercial carers except when a family member would take the place of one commercial carer

---

[41] See *http://www.nestpensions.org.uk/schemeweb/NestWeb/public/pensions/contents/auto-enrolment.html*
[42] [2006] EWHC 3111 (QB) [20].

in outings spread over 10 hours each week. This modest adjustment to the rates for family provision covered only 48 weeks in the year up to the claimant's age of 49. While not arguing for any offset in *Robshaw* above (claimant 12 years old), the NHSLA renewed its fight in *HS v Lancs*.[43] (claimant only eight) but were again unsuccessful.

**Pre-existing conditions—a matter of causation or deduction?**

43. In *Huntley*[44] the claimant's pre-accident problems had not led to any prior requirement for care and attendance. In other cases, later negligence increases a pre-existing need for care, accommodation and therapies above those that would have been required anyway. How should the court approach the task? Is it a matter of *causation* so that, when damages are assessed, it is only in respect of the strictly increased elements satisfying the prior test of causation? Or, is it a matter of *quantification of damage* so that the whole of the reasonable needs are taken as the starting point and the pre-existing needs considered only as a matter of potential deduction? If the latter, a claimant can recover damages for the whole of his condition on a commercial basis and, if the pre-existing needs would have been satisfied at essentially no cost to him (family or local authority care), giving little or no credit.

44. In *Sklair v Haycock*,[45] the claimant (49 and looked after informally by his "Bohemian" father) had suffered with Asperger's Syndrome and Obsessive Compulsive Disorder. Edwards-Stuart J found that the claimant's elderly father would have continued to look after him for 5–10 years longer, when his wider family would have looked after him at a financial cost to them of £150–£200 per week for 5–10 years, after which a residential placement in local authority care would have been likely. The accident had turned the claimant's need for this lower level of care (as a matter of fact) into a reasonable need for 24-hour commercial care [80.] The findings of Edwards-Stuart J amounted to deciding the causation issue on the basis that the negligence had caused the whole of the need for care (awarding the full commercial cost) and he then made, as a matter of quantification of the damages, a small deduction only for the short period when modest financial cost would have been incurred.

45. In *Reaney v Various Staffs NHS Trusts*,[46] the claimant's spinal cord condition had been made worse by clinical negligence: she would have needed some more modest care etc. anyway but now needed, on Foskett J's findings, an intensive commercial package. He too decided that the negligence had caused the whole of the need for commercial care etc. and made no real deduction in respect of the prior needs. He went so far as to say that the principle of *material contribution* would have led him to a similar result [71].

46. The defendant appealed in *Reaney* where the Master of the Rolls overturned the reasoning and remitted the case for further consideration. The essential question is one of *causation* not *deduction*. Where negligence increases a claimant's needs *quantitatively* (even if *significantly* or *substantially* so—"more of the same") [21], a defendant's negligence only *causes* the additional need, not the underlying one: *Performance Cars Ltd v Abraham*[47] followed, as applied in *Steel v Joy*.[48] How the need would have been/will now be supplied (whether at commercial cost or free) is irrelevant to the causation question [33].

47. If, however, the negligence makes a *qualitative* difference—the needs are no longer of the same type—it has *caused* the whole of it in its different form. The Master of Rolls agreed with counsel for the appellant that the causation result in *Sklair* might be explained on the basis that the care need before and after the negligence was indeed qualitatively different—the difference between

[43] [2015] EWHC 1376 (QB).
[44] [2009] EWHC 405 (QB).
[45] [2009] EWHC 3328 (QB).
[46] [2014] EWHC 3016 (QB).
[47] [1962] 1 QB 33.
[48] [2004] 1 WLR 3002.

"personal support in a 24-hour care regime and general supervisory care of an essentially independent life" [32]. Nothing was said, in that event, as to the correctness of making even a small deduction at the quantification stage. In *Reaney*, however, despite the findings of Foskett J for very substantially increased needs, they did not go far enough to move the case across the line between the negligence having made merely a *quantitative* as against a *qualitative* difference. It may be, on future reconsideration by Foskett J, that most of the current needs and claimed losses were caused by the negligence of the Trusts but, as the Court of Appeal has found, not all of them.

48. Further he had been wrong to have recourse to ideas of *material contribution* and invocation of the principle (described by the MR as an "accurate distillation of the law") in *Bailey v MoD*.[49] Since there was no doubt as to the claimant's needs before and after the negligence, the principle could have no application. See the discussion at [36].

## Resident carers

49. The old arguments for residential agency care have almost completely fallen away in the most serious cases. There may still be a place for such a provision, however, in cases requiring a lighter touch, as with care of the partial tetraplegic claimant in *Davies*[50] (between the ages of 70 and 75, after which extensive top up for double up hours was added.) The last gasp of the argument for residential care in the most serious cases came when the NHSLA in *Whiten* above tried to run a *Davies*-post-75-style argument in the case of a grievously injured child with mixed spastic-dystonic, severe, quadriplegic cerebral palsy. It suggested the bedrock of a care package through a residential agency carer with extensive hourly top up. Swift J rejected that potential solution without hesitation [204].

50. Nevertheless, in the unusual case of *AB v Devon & Exeter NHS Foundation Trust*[51]—a high paraplegic with severe spasm—a single resident carer was the answer to age 55 and two resident carers, overlapping and doubling up sensibly, from that age onwards.

## Risk/benefit applied to care regimes

51. Davies and *C v Dixon*, both above, have also been interesting in the detailed way in which Wilkie J and King J balanced risk and benefit to the claimant in reaching the appropriate care package. In each case the defendant argued that the package suggested by the claimant's experts amounted to substantial over-provision and would be stifling of the claimant. In *Davies* some risk of falling was found to be acceptable without a resident carer always on hand before the age of 70: a resident carer package before that age did not take into account the contribution which a degree of self-reliance has to a person's sense of worth and well-being [110]. In *C v Dixon* the claimant was not to be wrapped in cotton wool [35] with unnecessary commercial and double-up provision—he could have the required 24-hour care in a looser sense, including some down time in the package as long he had someone to contact in an emergency. Since his partner was assumed to be with him for the next 10 years, there was no need for commercial overnight care during that period.

52. In the moderate (general damages £147,500—July 2013) brain injury case of *Ali v Caton & MIB* above Stuart-Smith J described the scope of the care package there allowing 15 hours a week of support as follows [331ii]:

---

[49] [2007] EWHC 2913 (QB).
[50] [2008] EWHC 740 (QB) Wilkie J.
[51] [2016] EWHC 1024 (QB) Irwin J.

K1: Care and attendance

> "The purpose of the future care regime should be to provide sufficient support to enable [the claimant] to pursue a structured and constructive existence so far as possible, reinforcing constructive routines and being available to assist when he is confronted by the new, the unfamiliar or the complex."

**Two carers throughout the day**

53. Until *Manna* in 2015, whether two carers are required throughout the day had not been litigated for a while to a formal decision—it was common ground in the 2014 case of *Farrugia* above (severe brain injury) that it was necessary and in *Streeter* above in 2013 (C5/6 motor tetraplegia) that it was not. In *A v B*[52] two carers were required throughout waking hours (essentially in respect of transfers for toileting which could not be forecast as to timing) in a case of severe compromise in dystonic athetoid tetraplegic cerebral palsy. A similar result ensued in *XXX*. In both cases the claimants had little or no appreciation of their predicament but swift availability of changing was necessary for their health and comfort. The result was the same in *Massey* for a different reason: here the claimant had substantially retained intellect in a grossly malfunctioning body: for him the availability of two carers was essential for transfers and transport so that he could exercise autonomy and make decisions to act on impulse rather than live in the straightjacket of double-up provision which was less than continuous and at fixed hours of the day.

54. In *Farrugia* above, while awarding care based on two carers in attendance during waking hours, Jay J said this when considering whether two *commercial* carers had to be present throughout:

> "I do not accept . . . that Jack should, in effect, be free to do whatever he wishes at the spur of the moment. I do not consider that Jack's personal autonomy is overridden, or the dictates of spontaneity are unreasonably quelled, by providing for a regime which presupposes a modest degree of pre-planning and organisation. This, after all, reflects the realities of ordinary life."

55. The case for two carers in respect of a sentient adult who can give basic cooperation with hoisted transfers (in the sense of not lashing out or being subject to spasm) has not yet been clearly made out for transfers within the home. While the NHS commonly uses two nurses for such transfers even with a hoist on hospital wards, that appears to be at least partly because two nurses are available in such a setting and the use of two speeds things up.

56. Manna above saw the principal dispute at trial focus on the amount of double up care for an ambulant young man with profound cognitive problems and prone to outbursts: 14+14 hours per day—total daytime double-up—was found to be reasonable because of the unpredictability of outbursts [209]; it would simply be too much for one person alone to provide the required structured care all day [211]; 28 hours of double-up *per week* was rejected.

**Day centre provision**

57. The argument for offset from a commercial care package for down time while an adult claimant attends a local authority day centre was never strong. With its lack of forensic success, coupled with further funding cuts and closure of day centres, the argument is not currently being aired.

**Team leaders**

58. Although the payment of a higher rate to a member of the support worker team did not find favour 10 years ago now in *Crofton* or *Iqbal*, the allowance of a team leader (reducing the amount and

[52] [2006] EWHC 1178 (QB).

cost of case management intervention) has become pretty standard more recently in really serious cases. An extra £2 an hour was conceded in *XXX*. In *Whiten* the principle was disputed; and as a fall back it was suggested by the defendant that any provision could be by reference to a small proportion of the hours worked by the team leader, i.e. only those hours when in fact engaged on team leader duties. Swift J [164] rejected that line and allowed 30 hours a week at a weekday rate enhanced by £3 an hour (London). The whole point was to attract someone to the post with experience and ability: the defendant's suggestion would not achieve the aim. Contrast *Farrugia*, in which Jay J awarded an increase of £5 an hour (Hants.) [104] but over only 22 hours a week [103], commenting that he simply could not accept that a full week's work was required for the combination of tasks required of the team leader. In *Streeter*, Baker J allowed an increment of £2 an hour over 15 hours a week.[53] In *Robshaw*, Foskett J [183]–[184] allowed an enhanced rate of £4 an hour for 30 hours a week to age 19; £5 an hour (the gap being said to grow over time) over 25 hours a week from that age onwards. In *HS v Lancs.* William Davis J awarded 33.5 hours a week at unspecified team leader rates. In *Manna* Cox J awarded £5 an hour uplift but the number of hours is unclear.

59. Much appears to depend on the precise nature of the case, the experts and the judge as to how things are expressed. Perhaps now, however broken down, a team leader incentive of about £100 a week in very serious cases appears to be emerging as a benchmark.

## Hand over meetings

60. Claiming hand over periods of up to half an hour at the conclusion of each shift has never appeared an attractive argument and is not generally being run at the moment unless in unusual circumstances.

## Liaison/team meetings

61. Recently, these were not contended for in *Whiten* or *Farrugia*; allowed as to merely one hour a month in *C v Dixon*, and substantially conceded in *XXX*. There may have been oversight when these allowances have been made or conceded: as the "60 weeks in the year" evolved, it was probably supposed to take into account a routine allowance for training and team meetings—see the discussion of the evidence in the Judgment of Penry-Davey J in *Smith*.[54]
62. The result was more complicated in *Robshaw* above, where Foskett J allowed for the costs of therapists attending multi-disciplinary meetings but decided—in line with the above discussion —that the attendance of the case manager, team leader and support workers should be funded out of the normal working time already awarded within the 60-week year. He allowed five meeting in the first year; four per annum then until age 18; three per annum then to age 25; the claim was limited to one per annum then for life but he would have awarded two per annum. All meetings were said to require two hours allocated to them and should not be rushed. See [474]–[479].

## The status of family choice on behalf of a claimant

63. The issue of the status of a future family choice on behalf of a claimant raised its head in the recent case of *Harman v East Kent Hospitals NHS Foundation Trust*.[55] The claimant, aged 13 and suffering severe autism with significant cognitive impairment, was being cared for in a specialist placement funded by the LEA but spending eight weeks a year at home. The issue was where the claimant

---

[53] See footnote 37.
[54] [2008] EWHC 2234 (QC)—the transcript lacks numbered paragraphs.
[55] [2015] EWHC 1662 (QB).

would live when his education came to an end in 12 years at age 25: the parents wanted him then to come home. Turner J found in favour of that course, following expert evidence that a care package which met with the aspirations of the parents would be more likely to succeed than one which did not [38]. As to the underlying point of law, however, the parents' choice did not trump the view of the court of the primary measure of damage in the future:

> "[36] Care must be taken in cases such as this not to equiparate the preferences of relatives with the regime of care and support the cost of which should be the basis of reasonable compensation. Each case must be looked at on its own facts. There may well be circumstances in which, however strong and genuine the desire of the parents or a spouse or partner may be to have the claimant home, there are good reasons for taking a contrary course. The purpose of damages in a personal injury claim is to compensate the victim and not to accommodate the wishes of his family whatever the extent of the inevitable personal sympathy one might have for those who are left to pick up the pieces and suffer the inevitable and sustained emotional impact of serious injury to someone dear to them."

### Chance contingencies and PPOs for care

64. *Huntley* above illustrates that the essential chance assessment of damages for future loss has survived the new PPO regime, which purports to trace everything back to a claimant's needs. There the claimant, who had suffered a frontal lobe injury and whose rehabilitation had not gone well up to trial, contended for 24 hours of care per day as the long term solution: the defendant submitted for 21 hours per week. Underhill J (as he then was) approached matters by evaluating first of all the hard-core minimum level that he thought was reasonable, which he assessed at six hours a day [109]. This hard-core cost he would have put within a PPO [114] but not the full chance reasonable amount that he went on to evaluate as follows. He uplifted the package by 50 per cent from six hours to nine hours a day with a broad brush for all the possibilities of needing greater care. He then discounted that back by one hour to eight hours a day for the chance that the claimant would not in fact engage all the care that he might reasonably require. There was a real chance that he would reject care (as he would if he entered a stable relationship) and small chances of imprisonment and detention under the Mental Health Act. The resulting additional two hours a day beyond the core six hours Underhill J would have provided within an additional lump sum award; but the whole PPO submission was withdrawn when the claimant did not recover for 24-hour care.
65. For a further example taking contingencies into account, see the decision of Kenneth Parker J in *Tate v Ryder Holdings* above [38]–[42] where he averaged the cost of caring for the claimant in his own and residential accommodation, catering for different times in his life, and adjusted further for the chances of non-compliance by 20 per cent for reasons similar to those set out by Underhill J in *Huntley*. As in *Huntley*, the adjustments led to a lump sum award rather than PPO.

## National Joint Council Payscales – Spinal Column Point 8

| Year | Time of day | Hourly rate £ | Hours pw | Cost pw £ | Divided by hours pw | Aggregate rate |
|---|---|---|---|---|---|---|
| Jul 1992 to Jun 1993 | Basic<br>Evening<br>Weekend | £4.04<br>£5.05<br>£6.06 | 55<br>65<br>48 | £222.20<br>+ £328.25<br>+ £290.88<br>= £841.33 | 168 | £5.01 |
| Jul 1993 to Aug 1994 | Basic<br>Evening<br>Weekend | £4.21<br>£5.26<br>£6.32 | 55<br>65<br>48 | £231.55<br>+ £341.90<br>+ £303.36<br>= £876.81 | 168 | £5.22 |
| Sep 1994 to May 1995 | Basic<br>Evening<br>Saturday<br>Sunday | £4.44<br>£5.55<br>£6.66<br>£8.88 | 55<br>65<br>24<br>24 | £244.20<br>+ £360.75<br>+ £159.84<br>+ £213.12<br>= £977.91 | 168 | £5.82 |
| Jun 1995 to Mar 1996 | Basic<br>Evening<br>Saturday<br>Sunday | £4.56<br>£5.70<br>£6.84<br>£9.12 | 55<br>65<br>24<br>24 | £250.80<br>+ £370.50<br>+ £164.16<br>+ £218.88<br>= £1,004.34 | 168 | £5.98 |
| Apr 1996 to Mar 1997 | Basic<br>Evening<br>Saturday<br>Sunday | £4.69<br>£5.86<br>£7.03<br>£9.38 | 55<br>65<br>24<br>24 | £257.95<br>+ £380.90<br>+ £168.72<br>+ £225.12<br>= £1,032.69 | 168 | £6.15 |
| Apr 1997 to Mar 1998 | Basic<br>Evening<br>Saturday<br>Sunday | £4.84<br>£6.05<br>£7.26<br>£9.68 | 55<br>65<br>24<br>24 | £266.20<br>+ £393.25<br>+ £174.24<br>+ £232.32<br>= £1,066.01 | 168 | £6.35 |
| Apr 1998 to Mar 1999 | Basic<br>Evening<br>Saturday<br>Sunday | £4.98<br>£6.22<br>£7.47<br>£9.96 | 55<br>65<br>24<br>24 | £273.90<br>+ £404.30<br>+ £179.28<br>+ £239.04<br>= £1,096.52 | 168 | £6.53 |
| Apr 1999 to Mar 2000 | Basic<br>Evening<br>Saturday<br>Sunday | £5.13<br>£6.41<br>£7.69<br>£10.26 | 55<br>65<br>24<br>24 | £282.15<br>+ £416.65<br>+ £184.56<br>+ £246.24<br>= £1,129.60 | 168 | £6.72 |
| Apr 2000 to Mar 2001 | Basic<br>Evening<br>Saturday<br>Sunday | £5.29<br>£6.61<br>£7.93<br>£10.58 | 55<br>65<br>24<br>24 | £290.95<br>+ £429.65<br>+ £190.32<br>+ £253.92<br>= £1,164.84 | 168 | £6.93 |
| Apr 2001 to Mar 2002 | Basic<br>Evening<br>Saturday<br>Sunday | £5.49<br>£6.86<br>£8.23<br>£10.97 | 55<br>65<br>24<br>24 | £301.95<br>+ £455.90<br>+ £197.52<br>+ £263.28<br>= £1,208.61 | 168 | £7.19 |
| Apr 2002 to Sep 2002 | Basic<br>Evening<br>Saturday<br>Sunday | £5.65<br>£7.06<br>£8.47<br>£11.30 | 55<br>65<br>24<br>24 | £310.75<br>+ £458.90<br>+ £203.28<br>+ £271.20<br>= £1,244.13 | 168 | £7.41 |
| Oct 2002 to Mar 2003 | Basic<br>Evening<br>Saturday<br>Sunday | £5.71<br>£7.14<br>£8.56<br>£11.42 | 55<br>65<br>24<br>24 | £314.05<br>+ £464.10<br>+ £205.44<br>+ £274.08<br>= £1,257.67 | 168 | £7.49 |

## K1: Care and attendance

| Year | Time of day | Hourly rate £ | Hours pw | Cost pw £ | Divided by hours pw | Aggregate rate |
|---|---|---|---|---|---|---|
| Apr 2003 to Mar 2004 | Basic<br>Evening<br>Saturday<br>Sunday | £5.90<br>£7.37<br>£8.85<br>£11.80 | 55<br>65<br>24<br>24 | £324.50<br>+ £479.05<br>+ £212.40<br>+ £283.20<br>= £1,299.15 | 168 | £7.73 |
| Apr 2004 to Mar 2005 | Basic<br>Evening<br>Saturday<br>Sunday | £6.06<br>£7.57<br>£9.09<br>£12.12 | 55<br>65<br>24<br>24 | £333.30<br>+ £492.05<br>+ £218.16<br>+ £290.88<br>= £1,334.39 | 168 | £7.94 |
| Apr 2005 to Mar 2006 | Basic<br>Evening<br>Saturday<br>Sunday | £6.24<br>£7.80<br>£9.36<br>£12.48 | 55<br>65<br>24<br>24 | £343.20<br>+ £507.00<br>+ £224.64<br>+ £299.52<br>= £1,374.36 | 168 | £8.18 |
| Apr 2006 to Mar 2007 | Basic<br>Evening<br>Saturday<br>Sunday | £6.43<br>£8.04<br>£9.65<br>£12.86 | 55<br>65<br>24<br>24 | £353.65<br>+ £522.60<br>+ £231.60<br>+ £308.64<br>= £1,416.49 | 168 | £8.43 |
| Apr 2007 to Mar 2008 | Basic<br>Evening<br>Saturday<br>Sunday | £6.59<br>£8.24<br>£9.88<br>£13.18 | 55<br>65<br>24<br>24 | £362.45<br>+ £535.60<br>+ £237.12<br>+ £316.32<br>= £1,451.49 | 168 | £8.64 |
| Apr 2008 to Mar 2009 | Basic<br>Evening<br>Saturday<br>Sunday | £6.75<br>£8.44<br>£10.13<br>£13.50 | 55<br>65<br>24<br>24 | £371.25<br>+ £548.60<br>+ £243.12<br>+ £324.00<br>= £1,486.97 | 168 | £8.85 |
| Apr 2009 to Mar 2013 | Basic<br>Evening<br>Saturday<br>Sunday | £6.85<br>£8.56<br>£10.28<br>£13.70 | 55<br>65<br>24<br>24 | £376.75<br>£556.40<br>£246.72<br>£328.80<br>= £1,508.67 | 168 | £8.98 |
| April 2013 to Dec 2014 | Basic<br>Evening<br>Saturday<br>Sunday | £6.90<br>£9.21<br>£10.36<br>£13.81 | 70<br>50<br>24<br>24 | £483.32<br>£460.31<br>£248.57<br>£331.42<br>= £1,523.62 | 168 | £9.07 |
| Jan 2015 to 31 Mar 2016 | Basic<br>Evening<br>Saturday<br>Sunday | £7.19<br>£9.59<br>£10.78<br>£14.38 | 70<br>50<br>24<br>24 | £503.28<br>£479.31<br>£258.83<br>£345.11<br>= £1,586.53 | 168 | £9.44 |
| April 2016 to 31 Mar 2017 | Basic<br>Evening<br>Saturday<br>Sunday | £7.66<br>£10.21<br>£11.48<br>£15.31 | 70<br>50<br>24<br>24 | £535.93<br>£510.41<br>£275.62<br>£367.50<br>= £1,689.46 | 168 | £10.06 |
| April 2017 to 31 Mar 2018 | Basic<br>Evening<br>Saturday<br>Sunday | £7.90<br>£10.54<br>£11.85<br>£15.80 | 70<br>50<br>24<br>24 | £553.17<br>£526.83<br>£284.49<br>£379.32<br>= £1,743.81 | 168 | £10.38 |

**Notes for 2016/17 and 2017/18**

Agreement between the LGA and NJC Trade union side was reached in May 2016 with uplifted rates being applicable from 1 April 2016 and 1 April 2017 respectively, taking into account implementation of the National Living Wage.

Bank holiday pay is not incorporated into the above as the LGA provision is for staff to be paid at the normal rate for the period in question and to take either a half or full day time off in lieu, according to time worked. Specific calculation is therefore difficult and is likely to make minimal difference at 0.03 per cent overall.

**Source for above rates: National Joint Council for Local Government Services Green Book**

# K2: Nannies, cleaners and school fees

The death or incapacity of a spouse frequently involves incurring the costs of a nanny or a housekeeper or of sending a child to boarding school so that the surviving parent can continue working. Also, with some employments, typically when they involve overseas postings or frequent moves, school fees are part of the remuneration and will be lost if the employee dies or is disabled from that particular employment.

## Nannies

|  | Live-out | | Live-in | |
| --- | --- | --- | --- | --- |
|  | Weekly net | Annual gross | Weekly net | Annual gross |
| Central London | £511.36 | £34,649 | £342.01 | £21,664 |
| Outer London/Home Counties | £467.17 | £31,260 | £370.68 | £23,860 |
| Other areas | £390.66 | £25,394 | £337.42 | £21,311 |

The figures are derived from the 2015 survey by *Nannytax*. The total cost to the client will be more than the gross wage as it is necessary to pay for holidays, sickness, employer's national insurance contribution, agency fees and so on. (See the discussion in the notes to Table K1: Care and attendance.)

## Cleaners

The services of cleaners in London are currently (April 2016) advertised at the following rates. These are commonly for three or more hours a week: one-off visits usually cost more.

| Homeclean | £8.73 per hour | (three hours a week) |
| --- | --- | --- |
|  | £9.09 per hour | (two hours a week: the cleaner is paid separately avoiding VAT; and there is an annual agency fee which is greater in the first year) |
| Housekeep | £12.50 per hour | (Minimum visit: two hours) |
| Amy Cleaning | £11.00 per hour | (Varies. The cleaner is paid separately, avoiding VAT; there is also an agency fee). |

## School fees

Annual school fees for a three-term year are as follows.

| Public school | | Independent Schools Council (average) | |
| --- | --- | --- | --- |
| Boarders (Upper school) | £35,058 | Boarder | £30,369 |
| Day pupils (Upper school) | £24,276 | Day pupil (boarding school) | £16,902 |
| Day pupils (Under school or preparatory school) | £17,034 | Day pupil (day school) | £12,522 |

### Notes:

1. Fees for pupils entering in the sixth form may be higher.

2. Fees for weekly as opposed to full-time boarders may be lower.

*The information has been obtained from the websites of Nannytax, Homeclean, Housekeep, Amy Cleaning, Westminster School, and the Independent Schools Council.*

# K3: DIY, gardening and housekeeping

1. The sort of injury which limits one's capacity to earn will often also limit one's capacity to do jobs around the house. Depending on the kind of injury and the claimant's pre-accident talents, these may range from the skilled, such as plumbing or electrical work, to the mundane, such as washing up and putting out the bins.

2. It is well established that these skills have a monetary value[1] and that "the loss of ability to do work in the home is a recoverable head of damages and includes 'services' such as general housekeeping, gardening and maintenance".[2]

3. The Court of Appeal decided in *Daly v General Steam Navigation Co*[3] that *special* damages for past loss must comprise actual expenditure (or presumably the value of gratuitous care actually provided by others). Absent actual expenditure or gratuitous care, loss of capacity before trial is reflected in enhanced *general* damages. With regard to future loss, however, the court held that the claimant need not prove an actual intention to employ replacement services (paid or unpaid). Bridge LJ said:

> " . . . it seems to me that it was entirely reasonable and entirely in accordance with principle in assessing damages, to say that the estimated cost of employing labour for that time, . . . , was the proper measure of her damages under this heading. It is really quite immaterial, in my judgment, whether . . . the plaintiff chooses to alleviate her own housekeeping burden . . . by employing the labour which has been taken as the estimate on which damages have been awarded, or whether she continues to struggle with the housekeeping on her own and to spend the damages which have been awarded to her on other luxuries which she would otherwise be unable to afford."

4. One difficulty is finding an appropriate rate and working out a number of hours per week which these tasks take. People in rented accommodation may do little maintenance, and older people often, though not invariably, find their appetite for such tasks diminishes. The claimant will need evidence that he or she would be carrying out the work personally if it had not been for the injury. The evidence may include (in addition to witness statements) photographs, estimates from those providing such services locally (for labour only), and reports from a local surveyor and/or an independent agency. There are however differences of judicial opinion as to the utility of expert evidence: some judges accept it[4], whilst Mackay J in *Fleet v Fleet*[5] derived his own figure from experience, saying, "It would be dismal if experts had to be called to say how much it costs to mow a lawn or paint a room."

5. The courts have made a range of awards, sometimes using a multiplier/multiplicand approach and sometimes making a global award.[6] Cases in *Kemp & Kemp* show (adjusted for inflation to 2016) multiplicands for DIY and gardening of the order of £1,270–£2,090, and global awards of some £15,500–£21,000.

---

[1] *Phipps v Brooks Dry Cleaning Services* [1996] P.I.Q.R. Q 100.
[2] "Damages for Personal Injury: Medical, Nursing and Other Expenses", Law Commission, Law Com. No.262 (1999), para.2.34.
[3] [1981] W.L.R. 120,127.
[4] e.g. *Smith v East and North Hertfordshire Hospitals NHS Trust* [2008] EWHC 2234 (QB).
[5] [2009] EWHC 3166 (QB).
[6] See the analysis in *Kemp & Kemp* Vol. 1, Ch. 17.

## K3: DIY, gardening and housekeeping

Handyman, gardening and housekeeping services are being advertised in April 2016 at the following rates:

|  | London | Home Counties | Rest of country |
|---|---|---|---|
| **Handymen per hour** | £48 per hour | £25 per hour | £25 per hour |
| **Handymen half-day** | £183 per half-day | £90 per half-day | £75 per half-day |
| **Handymen day rates** | £276 per day | £170 per day | £130 per day |
| **Gardening— small one-man type business** | £15 per hour | £13.50 per hour | £12.50 per hour |
| **Gardening— medium–large business (for team of two)** | £47.50 per hour | £40 per hour | £37.50 per hour |
| **Cleaning and housekeeping** | £11 per hour | £12.95 per hour | £10 per hour |

**Notes to the table:**

- The figure in the table is generally the median.
- Charges for handymen and gardeners vary with the type of work. Plumbing and electrical work is usually dearer than decorating and putting up shelves. Garden design and planting may cost more than garden maintenance such as mowing the lawn and trimming the hedge.
- There is often a minimum period or a supplemental charge for the first hour.
- Charges are generally higher in the evenings and at weekends.
- Some firms prefer to quote for a specified job and do not advertise an hourly rate.
- Some firms provide services at a reduced rate for pensioners and those on a low income. These are not reflected in the table.

# K4: Hospital self-pay (uninsured) charges

The following figures are inclusive of hospital charges and surgeons' and anaesthetists' fees. The charges are approximate, as certain factors affecting cost, such as length of stay or prosthesis used, vary from patient to patient.

|  | Cost | | |
| --- | --- | --- | --- |
| **Treatment** | **Lowest** | **Average** | **Highest** |
| breast lump removal | £585 | £1,500 | £2,139 |
| carpal tunnel release | £900 | £2,000 | £2,866 |
| cataract removal | £1,200 | £2,415 | £3,537 |
| circumcision | £967 | £1,947 | £2,205 |
| colonoscopy | £1,213 | £1,887 | £2,700 |
| coronary artery bypass | £17,500 | £17,500 | £17,500 |
| cruciate knee ligament repair | £3,950 | £6,142 | £8,695 |
| cystoscopy | £800 | £1,550 | £4,495 |
| epidural injection | £695 | £1,452 | £2,490 |
| gall bladder removal | £4,173 | £5,313 | £6,932 |
| facet joint injection under x-ray and anaesthetic | £400 | £2,003 | £3,369 |
| gastric banding | £2,200 | £6,995 | £11,760 |
| gastric balloon insertion | £1,995 | £4,040 | £5,500 |
| gastric bypass | £7,900 | £10,925 | £12,180 |
| gastroscopy | £750 | £1,570 | £2,779 |
| grommets insertion | £1,200 | £2,032 | £3,130 |
| haemorrhoids removal | £290 | £2,665 | £3,495 |
| hernia repair (inguinal) | £1,800 | £2,520 | £3,695 |
| hip replacement | £8,400 | £11,079 | £14,981 |
| hysterectomy | £4,500 | £6,134 | £8,667 |
| hysteroscopy | £1,500 | £2,405 | £4,688 |
| knee arthroscopy | £1,666 | £3,375 | £8,530 |
| knee replacement | £8,816 | £11,130 | £14,365 |
| laparoscopy | £1,800 | £2,711 | £4,350 |
| prostate removal | £4,720 | £10,157 | £14,595 |
| sigmoidoscopy | £375 | £1,705 | £3,825 |
| termination of pregnancy | £625 | £1,103 | £1,580 |
| vaginal repair | £2,615 | £4,870 | £7,296 |
| varicose vein surgery (one leg) | £1,475 | £2,565 | £4,250 |
| varicose vein surgery (both legs) | £1,625 | £3,102 | £5,124 |
| varicose vein laser treatment EVLT (one leg) | £2,180 | £2,857 | £4,895 |
| varicose vein laser treatment EVLT (both legs) | £2,825 | £2,875 | £6,935 |
| vasectomy | £275 | £920 | £1,600 |
| vasectomy reversal | £2,125 | £2,818 | £4,200 |

*These figures are drawn from around the country. Charges vary from hospital to hospital and between different areas of the country. They are generally higher in London than elsewhere.*
*All figures have been sourced from www.privatehealth.co.uk and are correct as of June 2016.*

# K5: NHS charges

## NHS prescriptions (from 1 April 2016)

| Charge per prescribed item | | £8.40 |
|---|---|---|
| Prescription prepayment certificate: | three months | £29.10 |
| | 12 months | £104.00 |

For items dispensed in combination (duo) packs, there is a charge for each different drug in the pack.

## NHS dental treatment (from 1 April 2016)

If a patient is not exempt from charges, he should pay one of the following rates for each course of treatment he receives:

| Course of treatment | Cost | Scope |
|---|---|---|
| Band 1 | £19.70 | This covers an examination, diagnosis (e.g. x-rays), advice on how to prevent future problems, and a scale and polish if needed. |
| Band 2 | £53.90 | This covers everything listed in Band 1, plus any further treatment such as fillings, root canal work or extractions. |
| Band 3 | £233.70 | This covers everything listed in Bands 1 and 2 above, plus crowns, dentures or bridges. |

Notes

1. These are the only charges for NHS dental treatment.
2. A patient only has to pay one charge for each course of treatment, even if it takes more than one visit to the dentist to finish it.
3. If the patient needs more treatment within the same or lower charge band (e.g. an additional filling), within two months of completing a course of treatment, there is no extra charge.
4. There is no charge for repairing dentures or for having stitches removed.
5. Children under 18, and many adults, do not have to pay NHS charges. (See form HC11, "Help with Health Costs", which can be found on the Department of Health website: *http://www.dh.gov.uk*.)

## NHS wigs and fabric supports (from 1 April 2016)

| Stock modacrylic wig | £68.90 |
|---|---|
| Partial wig—human hair | £182.50 |
| Full bespoke wig—human hair | £266.90 |
| Abdominal support | £42.20 |
| Spinal support | £42.20 |
| Surgical brassière | £27.90 |

# K6: The 2007 Rehabilitation Code

### (Code of Best Practice on Rehabilitation, Early Intervention and Medical Treatment in Personal Injury Claims)

The aim of this code is to promote the use of rehabilitation and early intervention in the compensation process so that the injured person makes the best and quickest possible medical, social and psychological recovery. This objective applies whatever the severity of the injuries sustained by the claimant. The Code is designed to ensure that the claimant's need for rehabilitation is assessed and addressed as a priority, and that the process of so doing is pursued on a collaborative basis by the claimant's lawyer and the compensator.

Therefore, in every case, where rehabilitation is likely to be of benefit, the earliest possible notification to the compensator of the claim and of the need for rehabilitation will be expected.

## 1. INTRODUCTION

1.1 The purpose of the personal injury claims process is to put the individual back into the same position as he or she would have been in had the accident not occurred, insofar as money can achieve that objective. The purpose of the rehabilitation code is to provide a framework within which the claimant's health, quality of life and ability to work are restored as far as possible before, or simultaneously with, the process of assessing compensation.

1.2 Although the Code is recognised by the Personal Injury Pre-Action Protocol, its provisions are not mandatory. It is recognised that the aims of the Code can be achieved without strict adherence to the terms of the Code, and therefore it is open to the parties to agree an alternative framework to achieve the early rehabilitation of the claimant.

1.3 However, the Code provides a useful framework within which claimant's lawyers and the compensator can work together to ensure that the needs of injured claimants are assessed at an early stage.

1.4 In any case where agreement on liability is not reached it is open to the parties to agree that the Code will in any event operate, and the question of delay pending resolution of liability should be balanced with the interests of the injured party. However, unless so agreed, the Code does not apply in the absence of liability or prior to agreement on liability being reached.

1.5 In this code the expression "the compensator" shall include any loss adjuster, solicitor or other person acting on behalf of the compensator.

## 2. THE CLAIMANT'S SOLICITOR

2.1 It should be the duty of every claimant's solicitor to consider, from the earliest practicable stage, and in consultation with the claimant, the claimant's family, and where appropriate the claimant's treating physician(s), whether it is likely or possible that early intervention, rehabilitation or medical treatment would improve their present and/or long-term physical and mental well being. This duty is ongoing throughout the life of the case but is of most importance in the early stages.

2.2 The claimant's solicitors will in any event be aware of their responsibilities under section 4 of the Pre-Action Protocol for Personal Injury Claims.

2.3 It shall be the duty of a claimant's solicitor to consider, with the claimant and/or the claimant's family, whether there is an immediate need for aids, adaptations, adjustments to employment to enable the claimant to keep his/her existing job, obtain suitable alternative employment with the same employer or retrain for new employment, or other matters that would seek to alleviate problems caused by disability, and then to communicate with the compensators as soon as practicable about any such rehabilitation needs, with a view to putting this Code into effect.

2.4 It shall not be the responsibility of the solicitor to decide on the need for treatment or rehabilitation or to arrange such matters without appropriate medical or professional advice.

2.5 It is the intention of this Code that the claimant's solicitor will work with the compensator to address these rehabilitation needs and that the assessment and delivery of rehabilitation needs shall be a collaborative process.

2.6 It must be recognised that the compensator will need to receive from the claimant's solicitors sufficient information for the compensator to make a proper decision about the need for intervention, rehabilitation or treatment. To this extent the claimant's solicitor must comply with the requirements of the Pre-Action Protocol to provide the compensator with full and adequate details of the injuries sustained by the claimant, the nature and extent of any or any likely continuing disability and any suggestions that may have already have been made concerning the rehabilitation and/or early intervention.

2.7 There is no requirement under the Pre-Action Protocol, or under this code, for the claimant's solicitor to have obtained a full medical report. It is recognised that many cases will be identified for consideration under this code before medical evidence has actually been commissioned or obtained.

## 3. THE COMPENSATOR

3.1 It shall be the duty of the compensator, from the earliest practicable stage in any appropriate case, to consider whether it is likely that the claimant will benefit in the immediate, medium or longer-term from further medical treatment, rehabilitation or early intervention. This duty is ongoing throughout the life of the case but is most important in the early stages.

3.2 If the compensator considers that a particular claim might be suitable for intervention, rehabilitation or treatment, the compensator will communicate this to the claimant's solicitor as soon as practicable.

3.3 On receipt of such communication, the claimant's solicitor will immediately discuss these issues with the claimant and/or the claimant's family pursuant to his duty set out above.

3.4 Where a request to consider rehabilitation has been communicated by the claimant's solicitor to the compensator, it will usually be expected that the compensator will respond to such request within 21 days.

3.5 Nothing in this or any other code of practice shall in any way modify the obligations of the compensator under the Protocol to investigate claims rapidly and in any event within three months (except where time is extended by the claimant's solicitor) from the date of the formal claim letter. It is recognised that, although the rehabilitation assessment can be done even where liability investigations are outstanding, it is essential that such investigations proceed with the appropriate speed.

## 4. ASSESSMENT

4.1 Unless the need for intervention, rehabilitation or treatment has already been identified by medical reports obtained and disclosed by either side, the need for and extent of such intervention, rehabilitation or treatment will be considered by means of an assessment by an appropriately qualified person.

4.2 An assessment of rehabilitation needs may be carried out by any person or organisation suitably qualified, experienced and skilled to carry out the task. The claimant's solicitor and the compensator should endeavour to agree on the person or organisation to be chosen.

4.3 No solicitor or compensator may insist on the assessment being carried out by a particular person or organisation if (on reasonable grounds) the other party objects, such objection to be raised within 21 days from the date of notification of the suggested assessor.

4.4 The assessment may be carried out by a person or organisation which has a direct business connection with the solicitor or compensator, only if the other party agrees. The solicitor or compensator will be expected to reveal to the other party the existence of and nature of such a business connection.

## 5. THE ASSESSMENT PROCESS

5.1 Where possible, the agency to be instructed to provide the assessment should be agreed between the claimant's solicitor and the compensator. The method of providing instructions to that agency will be agreed between the solicitor and the compensator.

5.2 The assessment agency will be asked to carry out the assessment in a way that is appropriate to the needs of the case and, in a simple case, may include, by prior appointment, a telephone interview but in more serious cases will probably involve a face-to-face discussion with the claimant. The report will normally cover the following headings:

1. The injuries sustained by the claimant.
2. The current disability/incapacity arising from those injuries. Where relevant to the overall picture of the claimant's needs, any other medical conditions not arising from the accident should also be separately annotated.
3. The claimant's domestic circumstances (including mobility accommodation and employment) where relevant.
4. The injuries/disability in respect of which early intervention or early rehabilitation is suggested.
5. The type of intervention or treatment envisaged.
6. The likely cost.
7. The likely outcome of such intervention or treatment.

5.3 The report should not deal with issues relating to legal liability and should therefore not contain a detailed account of the accident's circumstances.

5.4 In most cases it will be expected that the assessment will take place within 14 days from the date of the letter of referral to the assessment agency.

5.5 It must be remembered that the compensator will usually only consider such rehabilitation to deal with the effects of the injuries that have been caused in the relevant accident and will normally not be expected to fund treatment for conditions which do not directly relate to the accident unless the effect of such conditions has been exacerbated by the injuries sustained in the accident.

## 6. THE ASSESSMENT REPORT

6.1 The report agency will, on completion of the report, send copies on to both the claimant's solicitor and compensator simultaneously. Both parties will have the right to raise questions on the report, disclosing such correspondence to the other party.

6.2 It is recognised that for this assessment report to be of benefit to the parties, it should be prepared and used wholly outside the litigation process. Neither side can therefore, unless they agree in writing, rely on its contents in any subsequent litigation.

6.3 The report, any correspondence related to it and any notes created by the assessing agency to prepare it, will be covered by legal privilege and will not be disclosed in any legal proceedings unless the parties agree. Any notes or documents created in connection with the assessment process will not be disclosed in any litigation, and any person involved in the preparation of the report or involved in the assessment process, shall not be a compellable witness at court. This principle is also set out in para.4.4, above, of the Pre-Action Protocol.

6.4 The provision in para.6.3, above as to treating the report, etc. as outside the litigation process is limited to the assessment report and any notes relating to it. Any notes and reports created during the subsequent case management process will be covered by the usual principle in relation to disclosure of documents and medical records relating to the claimant.

6.5 The compensator will pay for the report within 28 days of receipt.

6.6 This code intends that the parties will continue to work together to ensure that the rehabilitation which has been recommended proceeds smoothly and that any further rehabilitation needs are also assessed.

## 7. RECOMMENDATIONS

7.1 When the assessment report is disclosed to the compensator, the compensator will be under a duty to consider the recommendations made and the extent to which funds will be made available to implement all or some of the recommendations. The compensator will not be required to pay for intervention treatment that is unreasonable in nature, content or cost or where adequate and timely provision is otherwise available. The claimant will be under no obligation to undergo intervention, medical or investigation treatment that is unreasonable in all the circumstances of the case.

7.2 The compensator will normally be expected to respond to the claimant's solicitor within 21 days from the date upon which the assessment report is disclosed as to the extent to which the recommendations have been accepted and rehabilitation treatment would be funded and will be expected to justify, within that same timescale, any refusal to meet the cost of recommended rehabilitation.

7.3 If funds are provided by the compensator to the claimant to enable specific intervention, rehabilitation or treatment to occur, the compensator warrants that they will not, in any legal proceedings connected with the claim, dispute the reasonableness of that treatment, nor the agreed costs, provided of course that the claimant has had the recommended treatment. The compensator will not, should the claim fail or be later discontinued, or any element of contributory negligence be assessed or agreed, seek to recover from the claimant any funds that they have made available pursuant to this Code.

# K7: Rehabilitation: a practitioner's guide

## Compiled by the Bodily Injury Claims Management Association

Norman W. Cottington, The Injury Care Clinics (President)
David Blofeld, past Claims Manager, Hart Re
Christopher Crook, Solicitor, Edwards Duthie
Tony Goff, Solicitor, George Ide Phillips
Graham Plumb, Claims Manager, AXA Insurance
Keith O. Popperwell, Solicitor Silverbeck Rymer
Bernard Rowe, Solicitor, Lyons Davidson (Treasurer)
Martin Saunders, Allianz Cornhill Insurance
Martin Staples, Solicitor, Vizards
Janet Tilley, Solicitor, Colemans CTTS (Secretary)
Ian Walker, Solicitor, Russell Jones and Walker (Vice President)

## CONTENTS

1. Case Management
2. Immediate Needs Assessment
3. Emotional and Psychological Care
4. Physiotherapy, Osteopathy and Chiropractic
5. Accommodation
6. Nursing, Care and Equipment
7. Social Services
8. Social Security Benefits
9. Mobility
10. Vocational

## 1. CASE MANAGEMENT

One of the first decisions to make is who will manage the rehabilitative process. The various specialist disciplines are outlined below. The task of organising so many disciplines may seem daunting, but help can be found.

One way is to use a case manager to act as case co-ordinator.

The appointment of a case manager at an early stage in the claim will need to be discussed and preferably agreed with the claimant and the insurer. A case manager must have close contact with the claimant and his/her family.

A case manager must have the time available to deal with the claimant and preferably be based close to the claimant.

Case managers can come from a variety of disciplines, but look for someone trained and committed to the standards laid down by the Case Management Society of the UK (CMSUK).

There are a number of specialist case management organisations in the UK, although the number of claimants is likely to outweigh the availability of specialists for some time to come.

A case manager will co-ordinate all of the available services and should be required as appropriate to:

- assess the personal circumstances and needs of the claimant and his/her family;
- monitor medical rehabilitation and, if necessary, provide for multi-disciplinary assessment;
- liaise with the DSS and claim appropriate benefits;
- liaise with the local authority for interim support prior to a statutory assessment (currently Community Care Act 1990); review such assessment and negotiate the provision of services and financial assistance from the local authority;
- arrange for therapies;
- monitor the needs of the claimant's family and arrange for respite care, if necessary;
- assist the claimant in obtaining training and monitoring carers;
- facilitate employment rehabilitation;
- arrange appropriate accommodation;
- review personal transport arrangements;
- consider mobility issues; and
- consider funding arrangements for rehabilitation.

**Cost**

Following an initial assessment, case management will normally be charged on an hourly basis (expect to pay between £65 and £85 per hour). Input by a case manager should reduce once rehabilitation needs have been addressed.

## 2. IMMEDIATE NEEDS ASSESSMENT

**Why?**
Rehabilitation in the long-term will be difficult, if not impossible, if short-term needs are overlooked. "First Aid" support is essential to overcome the immediate aftermath of an injury and to provide a platform on which to build long-term rehabilitation.

**At what level?**
As a rule of thumb, an immediate needs assessment is applicable to claimants who have sustained injuries likely to cause incapacity for several months or longer.

**When?**
The assessment should be done as soon as possible, even before discharge from hospital, with a view to ensuring the home environment to which the claimant will be discharged is suitable at least for the basic needs of the claimant and his/her family. However, an assessment undertaken years after the event of the injury can still help.

**What to expect**
The report should provide preliminary background information about the claimant's circumstances, including the following:

a. the nature and extent of the injury;
b. any relevant medical background;
c. family circumstances;
d. immediate home adaptation needs;

e. steps to improve the claimant's quality of life and support for family carers; and
f. how, and at what cost, recommendations can be implemented.

Relatively simple and inexpensive measures can make a big difference, for example, stair handrails, ramps for wheelchair access, raised toilet seats, widened doorways, and lowered light switches or doorknobs.

Recommendations should be capable of being put into immediate effect and at proportionate, reasonable cost.

Do not confuse an immediate needs assessment with long-term care needs and costs, which will be addressed by appropriate experts in the claim.

### By whom?
A case manager trained and committed to the standards laid down by the Case Management Society of the UK (CMSUK) is the most obvious choice.

An occupational therapist or anyone with a social care background, for example, a community care nurse, a social worker or a general practitioner, may similarly be able to conduct the assessment.

### Cost
The Code requires that the insurer be responsible for the cost.

The charge will depend upon the complexity of the report and travel expenses, but expect to pay between £750 and £1,750.

The defendant's insurer should usually fund reasonable recommendations by way of an interim payment (see section 7 of the Code).

### Liability
Only a complete denial of liability should prevent a defendant's insurer from considering an immediate needs assessment (but also consider an assessment via Social Services).

If the dispute is confined to contributory negligence, the comparatively low cost of an assessment will be justified.

## 3. EMOTIONAL AND PSYCHOLOGICAL CARE

### Why?
Anyone who has suffered a serious injury has experienced a major life event. The injured person, his/her family and close friends will be totally unprepared for either the injury or what follows.

Those who have suffered a serious injury will need to come to terms with what has happened to them. There may also be psychological disorders triggered by the accident, which must be recognised and dealt with. Failure to do so may prevent other treatments from being effective and may hinder a return to work.

Emotional, and in many cases psychological support needs to be given to help the claimant and those upon whom he/she depends.

### When?
Support should be offered as soon as possible. Often this will be determined by the willingness of the injured claimant and/or his/her family to accept outside help. Many people are frightened by their feelings or by the idea of sharing them with someone. Proper counselling can also be of great assistance to relatives acting as carers.

An early assessment can in itself help identify problems or potential problems in time to prevent prolonged post-traumatic stress disorder.

An assessment and, where needed, counselling or psychological treatment are best considered soon after the injury and/or return home from hospital (i.e. within the first three months of injury). The need for emotional and psychological support may last much longer than the medical treatment.

### By whom?
Clinical psychologists should normally carry out an initial assessment. If there is any suggestion of brain injury, then a neuropsychologist should be used.

It is useful to check first whether the claimant's hospital team has already involved a psychologist to help with rehabilitation or whether there is a facility within the GP's practice.

Arrangements should be made with a clinical psychologist close to the claimant's home. Where necessary, appointments can be arranged at the claimant's home, which is important if the claimant is distressed by travel.

There are a number of agencies that have panels of psychologists available or you can contact the British Psychological Society at St. Andrew's House, 48 Princess Road East, Leicester LE1 7DR or by telephone on 0116 254 9568.

### What to expect
Most assessments involve some psychological testing. This is necessary to determine what help is needed. Better insight and understanding by the claimant and/or his/her family of what to expect of themselves and their feelings will help to achieve maximum recovery.

### Cost
A clinical psychologist's assessment and recommendations will cost between £200 and £500.

A neuropsychologist's assessment will cost between £750 and £1,750.

Psychological therapy costs between £75 and £150 per session.

## 4. PHYSIOTHERAPY, OSTEOPATHY AND CHIROPRACTIC

### Why?
Early mobilisation following injury is now widely recognised as an important part of treatment and needs to be encouraged, provided that it is consistent with medical advice. Damaged tissue needs careful handling. Injury victims need to be shown how to regain movement and function as soon as possible. Whilst treatment methods vary amongst the different professions, these all work towards maximising useful function and can help prevent an injury from becoming a permanent disability.

## When?
In the case of serious injuries, this type of treatment is normally determined by the hospital medical team. After discharge from hospital, it is all too easy to overlook the benefit to be gained from continuing physiotherapy and other treatments. Treatment is not just about relieving pain, but equally about achieving the best possible recovery of movement, strength and function. In the case of soft tissue injuries, treatment should be assessed as soon as possible, i.e. within a few weeks, not months, of the injury. In more serious cases, initial treatment should be considered as part of the overall medical management of the patient. After discharge, treatment should be considered as part of the overall nursing plan or by direct referral to a practitioner.

## By whom?
This type of treatment is provided by chartered physiotherapists, osteopaths or chiropractors. Increasingly, it is possible to find that two or more of these disciplines are offered at the same clinic. There are a number of specialist agencies that will provide and co-ordinate treatment. Details of local practitioners can also be found in the Yellow Pages. Alternatively, information is available from:

- Chartered Society of Physiotherapists: 0207 306 6666
- General Council of Osteopaths: 0207 357 6655
- British Chiropractic Association: 0118 950 5950

## What to expect
Make sure the practitioner is a member of a relevant professional body and that there are well-equipped treatment rooms. All practitioners will want to assess the patient before offering treatment. The assessment may involve x-rays as well as a physical examination.

If treatment is offered, a treatment plan should be prepared that identifies the number of treatments and when they are to be given. Often a patient will be taught exercises to help speed up the recovery process.

## Cost
The cost will vary from clinic to clinic. Average costs for an assessment will be in the order of £40–£60. Treatment is likely to cost in the order of £30–£45 per session depending upon locality.

## 5. ACCOMMODATION

### Why?
A secure, comfortable and accessible home is likely to be a pre-requisite for any home-based rehabilitation plan. Accommodation that was suitable for a claimant before an injury may be unsuitable after injury.

### When?
Assessment of accommodation needs should be undertaken as soon as possible. For many patients, the only obstacle to being discharged from hospital is their inability to access their own home.

The need for substantial adaptations to accommodation or even a purpose-built property is normally a long-term consideration. Permanent arrangements are best dealt with when it is reasonably clear what the long-term requirements will be.

Physical needs will be identified in medical, occupational therapist and nursing reports.

Short-term needs are as important a consideration as long-term needs. Short-term may, in fact, mean several months or even longer. Immediate needs may have been dealt with under an immediate needs report, but this will need to be updated.

### By whom?
A case manager or occupational therapist may be able to advise upon minor alterations that are needed until permanent needs become clear. Once these needs have been identified, a good local builder will be able to carry out minor works such as installing rails, ramps and widening doorways.

If major alterations are needed, a report will be required from an accommodation expert, usually a surveyor or architect, and preferably one with experience of designing accommodation for use by people with disabilities. Whoever carries out the assessment should be familiar with and liaise with the local authority, from which grants may be available. This is particularly relevant in cases where damages may be reduced as a result of an apportionment of liability.

### What to expect
A visit to the claimant's home or proposed home, after consideration of the medical and other reports. This will lead to a report detailing the physical requirements of the property that are necessary in order for the claimant to maximise his/her potential for independent living. In addition, it will take into account the possibility that a carer might need accommodation.

The report should detail the work needed, together with costs, including likely maintenance and/or replacement costs.

### Cost
The cost of this report will vary from case to case. Hourly charge-out rates will be in the order of £100–£150 per hour. A detailed report is likely to cost £1,000 or more.

## 6. NURSING, CARE AND EQUIPMENT

### Why?
The objective will be to establish the most beneficial regime, aimed at ensuring the health and welfare of the injured person, and optimising independence and self-esteem by the most cost-effective means.

### When?
It is important to establish in advance what arrangements will be beneficial at each stage of the recovery process, and not address each stage as it occurs. At each stage, it is vital that the case manager, or those reporting, are fully aware of the current medical prognosis, including any anticipated changes.

### By whom?
The appointed case manager is likely to be the best choice, as they often possess all of the relevant experience. The person chosen must have an understanding of the medical and physical needs of the claimant, and how to provide for them. Not all nursing/care experts may deal with aids and equipment. Separate advice may be needed from an occupational therapist.

**What to expect**
The expert will need to see all existing reports and it may be beneficial for the different disciplines to confer.

The expert will need to speak to the claimant and his/her family and carers as well as those responsible for medical treatment. The report should address:

- the injured person's capacity for coping with the challenges of his/her injury and impairment;
- existing care, by whom and in what environment;
- external features impacting on the situation, e.g. accommodation, social contact, locality and family dynamics;
- the level of nursing care required;
- vulnerabilities—health and safety issues for the claimant and his/her carers at present and in the future;
- the need for an enabler;
- the need for domestic assistance;
- details of equipment needed;
- detailed cost of recommendations and suggested providers; and
- objectives and their timescales.

**Cost**
This will depend upon the circumstances and the complexity of each case. Reports will cost from £1,000. Hourly charging rates are likely to range from £65–£90 per hour, but could possibly be higher.

## 7. SOCIAL SERVICES

Social services are provided pursuant to the National Health Service Community Care Act 1990 by local authorities' Social Services departments, which are entitled to call upon:

- Health Authorities.
- Housing Departments.

The trigger for support is an assessment by the local authority pursuant to s.47 of the NHS and Community Care Act 1990. The right to an assessment is absolute.

Once an assessment has been carried out, a written copy must be provided to the Social Services department. A complaints and review procedure is available if the assessment is considered unsatisfactory.

Following assessment, the local authority will make a decision about whether to provide services and the type of services to be provided.

Social services available include:

- home helps or carers;
- respite breaks for carers;
- laundry service;
- therapies;
- odd job scheme;
- rehabilitation;

- carer support;
- residential care;
- transport;
- housing adaptation; and
- provision of accommodation suitable to the claimant's needs.

The provision of services may be dependent upon the resources of the local authority. Each local authority publishes eligibility criteria. Certain services must be provided under a legal duty. Other services may be provided on a discretionary basis, but there is no duty to do so.

Section 2 of the Chronically Sick and Disabled Persons Act sets out services that must be supplied as a legal duty:

- home help;
- provision of radio, television, library or residential services;
- home adaptations for greater safety, comfort or convenience;
- holidays;
- meals; and
- telephone.

The local authority will formulate a case plan, which will be administered by a case manager. This will specify all needs, including those that cannot be met due to budget restraints.

Local authorities are empowered to make direct cash payments to disabled persons so that they can purchase care services for themselves (Community Care (Direct Payments) Act 1996). In addition, cash payments are available from Independent Living Funds and from the DWP.

If the claimant needs suitable accommodation, the local authority has a duty to provide this pursuant to s.21 of the National Assistance Act.

Residential care can be arranged by both local authorities and health authorities. Provision of residential care by a health authority is free, but DWP benefits are treated as if the claimant were in hospital. Local authority residential care is subject to means testing. Residential care includes the provision of basic accommodation.

A claimant can choose his/her preferred accommodation and can ask a third party (e.g. an insurer or tortfeasor) to meet any shortfall if the cost is more than the local authority would normally pay.

If a local authority provides services free of charge, a claimant cannot make a claim against the insurer in respect of such services.

A local authority has discretion to charge for services other than residential care.

The right to charge for services is subject to a two-stage test:

1. whether it is reasonable in all the circumstances; and
2. whether the claimant has sufficient means to pay for the services.

Where residential accommodation is provided by a local authority, there is a duty to charge, subject to means testing.

However, such charges can be avoided by the creation of a trust or if the damages are administered by the court (see Preservation of Benefits, below).

## 8. SOCIAL SECURITY BENEFITS

**Aim**
To maximise benefits and to preserve the right to means-tested benefits.

**Non-means-tested benefits**
There are four main groups of non-means-tested benefits that are payable as a consequence of disability:

1. <u>Incapacity for Work</u>
   Incapacity Benefit
   Severe Disablement Allowance

2. <u>Care and Supervision</u>
   Disability Living Allowance
   Care Component
   Constant Attendance Allowance

3. <u>Mobility</u>
   DLA Mobility Component

4. <u>Degree of Disablement</u>
   Severe Disablement Allowance
   Industrial Disablement Benefit

**Income Support**
This is paid to the claimant if he/she is incapable of working, and to a carer if regularly and substantially engaged in caring for another person.

If the claimant has capital in excess of £8,000 (or £16,000 if in residential care), he/she does not qualify for income support.

**Disability Working Allowance**
This is intended to encourage people with disabilities to return to work. It is paid to people who work 16 hours or more per week. If a claimant (or his/her partner) has capital of more than £16,000, the claimant does not qualify for this allowance.

**Disability Living Allowance**
The DLA is not means-tested.

This allowance comprises a care component and a mobility component. The care component is for personal care needs and is paid at three different rates. The mobility component is paid at two different rates.

Tests are administered by an Adjudication Officer.

Receipt of the DLA acts as a gateway to the following benefits:

- Disability Premium.

- Severe Disability Premium.
- Independent Living Funds.
- Motability Scheme.

**Industrial Injuries Benefit**
This benefit is paid to those who are disabled by a loss of physical and mental capacity caused by an industrial accident or disease.

It is paid in addition to any other non means-tested benefit.

**Incapacity Benefit**
This is paid to those who are unable to work due to disability. It is non-means-tested, but it is only payable if sufficient national insurance contributions (NIC) have been made.

**Severe Disablement Allowance**
This allowance is paid for 28 weeks to those who are incapable of working but have made insufficient NIC to qualify for the incapacity benefit.

**How to claim**
Benefit is generally paid from the date that a claim is received by a DWP Office.

There is discretion to accept anything in writing "as sufficient" in the circumstances of a particular case.

The DLA is paid from the date a claim form is requested, so long as the claim form is returned within six weeks.

Income support is paid from the date of notifying the DWP, so long as the claim form is returned within one month. There is discretion to extend time limits in some cases.

Claims should be made to a local DWP Office or by telephoning the Benefit Enquiry Line on 0800 882200.

Appeals are made to the local DWP Office. An appeal can be made within three months of any decision. There is some discretion to extend the time limit up to six years, but it is difficult to make a late appeal.

**The effect of receipt of damages on income-related benefits**
Lump sum payments of compensation are treated as capital and are added to any other capital that the claimant may have. The effect is that:

- a claimant or partner may have up to £8,000 (£16,000 if in residential care) in capital and benefit will not be affected;
- deductions are made on a sliding scale in Income Support, DLA, Housing Benefit and Council Tax Benefit, depending on the amount of capital;
- income support is not payable where there is capital in excess of £8,000 (or £16,000 if in residential care); and
- no Housing Benefit, Council Tax Benefit or DLA is payable if capital exceeds £16,000.

**Preservation of benefits**
Benefits paid to a claimant can be managed by creating a trust or ensuring the damages fund is administered by the court.

**Trusts**
The trust may be set up by the claimant or someone acting on behalf of the claimant. If a trust is created:

- the capital value of the trust fund is wholly disregarded;
- payments from the trust fund to the claimant or on his/her behalf will be treated as income or capital, depending on frequency of payment and the terms of the trust; and
- regular discretionary payments will be disregarded, provided they are used for needs other than those intended to be covered by benefits.[1]

**Funds administered by the court**
A decision of the Social Security Commissioner[2] makes it clear that money in the Court of Protection should not be taken into account for entitlement to Income Support under the terms of para.12 to Sch.120 to the Income Support (General) Regulations (as amended).

### 9. MOBILITY

**Why?**
Restricted mobility emphasises impairment and threatens independence. Mobility contributes toward independence.

**When?**
Immediate thought should be given to mobility within the home, which is often effectively achieved by simple steps such as providing ramps and widening doorways for wheelchair users.

Longer-term projects, such as specialised wheelchairs or appropriate motor vehicles, may have to await medical recovery.

**What to expect?**
A driving assessment can identify and address any barriers to independent driving ability, and can identify aids, adaptations or controls required to overcome those barriers.

The Disability Living centres identify and cost aids and equipment for mobility and dexterity.

**By whom?**
Personal mobility can be assessed by an occupational therapist.

Disability Living centres exhibit and assist in identifying appropriate aids, including wheelchairs, vehicles and prosthetic appliances.

---

[1] This is no longer so. It was changed by the 2006 Regulations. See H4.
[2] (1996) 3 J.S.S.L.D. 136.

Driving Assessment centres can assist in determining the right choice of vehicle and wheelchair.

The claimant or his/her family can apply to the DWP for a Mobility Allowance and/or payment under the Motability Scheme to defray the cost of a vehicle.

Disabled living experts, usually architects, can advise on property alterations to ensure ease of access.

**Cost**
A driving assessment is unlikely to cost £50–£100 or more, at a mobility centre.

The Disability Living centres provide their services at no cost, although the equipment they recommend can cost anything from a few pounds for a wide-handled toothbrush to more than £1,000 for a suitable wheelchair.

## 10. VOCATIONAL

**Why?**
A return to work is more likely to raise a claimant's self-esteem than anything else. It provides independence and self-respect.

**When?**
A claimant should be helped to return to work, if appropriate, as soon as possible.

It is vital to:

- take early steps to consider, with the involvement of the employer, the preservation of the claimant's pre-accident job, by adapting the workplace or duties in accordance with the Equality Act 2010; and
- if remaining with the pre-accident employer is not possible, then consider all alternative avenues.

Insurers may be willing to fund the necessary steps to achieve these goals.

**By whom?**
A vocational or employment rehabilitation expert should assess the claimant's suitability to return to work and his/her requirements.

A vocational report should not be confused with the reports commonly commissioned from employment consultants. The latter are generally designed to assist in the quantification of loss, whereas the former is intended to identify the injured person's potential and motivation for employment, and to recommend how to achieve a return to suitable work. The expert should know the local area and sympathetic employers, whilst having a good working relationship with the Disability Employment Advisor.

**What to expect**
A detailed interview should be undertaken to identify the claimant's former work experience abilities and qualifications, his/her aspirations, and a general assessment of his/her current physical and mental ability.

The next stage should, ideally, be a meeting between the vocational assessor and the previous employer with a view to identifying whether re-employment is possible, either in full or reduced capacity; whether other placements may be available; and/or whether adaptations to the work place may be necessary to facilitate such employment.

If employment with the pre-accident employer is not possible for whatever reason, then consideration will be given to other suitable local job opportunities.

If no such opportunities exist, a more detailed vocational assessment, carried out over a period of one week, may be recommended.

There are numerous facilities nationwide where such assessments can take place either on a day or residential basis. Assessments take place in a working environment and measure dexterity, co-ordination, ability, communication skills, confidence, and motivation. Speed, ability and quality of work is recorded, assessed and reported upon.

Following assessment, recommendations may include finding a work placement properly suited to the claimant's skills and abilities or sending the claimant on a training scheme to learn new skills. Another possibility is for the claimant to be supported by a trainer or friend, who would work alongside him/her in a work placement until confidence is gained in employment skills.

A return to some form of remunerative employment is the most effective way an injured person can regain his/her self-esteem and achieve an improved quality of life.

**Cost**
This will vary depending upon the type of assessment and the time it takes. Expect charges of £750–£1,500 for a vocational interview and report. More detailed assessments will cost more. A residential five-day assessment is likely to cost £2,000 or more.

**Case management—the early days**
As health care options, delivery methods and financing mechanisms became more complex, with inconsistent incentives and accountability, the need for assistance in obtaining timely and appropriate care to achieve recovery and optimal functioning has become increasingly evident.

The first Case Management Society was established in America in 1990 (CMSA) after recognition of the need for a supportive body for this rapidly expanding profession. In 1996, the Case Management Society International was established to provide an umbrella for global affiliation. Canada, Australia, South Africa and a number of European countries already have their own case management societies.

In response to this growth in case management, an informal group of care professionals involved in case management practice started meeting during 2000 to explore the possibility of a national, non-profit, professional membership association for case managers.

**About CMSUK**
The overall goals and ambitions are to:

- advise on the development of a professional case management qualification;
- develop and encourage consistent professional standards of best practice, competence, service and conduct of case managers;

- provide comprehensive continuing education programmes;
- provide support for its members;
- instil confidence for purchasers when employing the services of a CMSUK member;
- development of case managers within existing public/private health and social environment; and
- one of our main aims is to be affiliated with and accredited by the main professional bodies that currently register practising case managers.

With evolving care structures, CMSUK will play an integral part in setting and upholding standards to ensure that cost-effective and timely outcomes are achieved.

If you would like to know more about CMSUK, please write to: CMSUK, 100 Fetter Lane, London, EC4A 1BN. Email: cmsukltd@yahoo.co.uk

# K8: APIL Serious Injury Guide

**The APIL Serious Injury Guide is published by APIL and FOIL**

## INTRODUCTION

This best practice Guide is designed to assist with the conduct of personal injury cases involving complex injuries, specifically cases with a potential value on a full liability basis of £250,000 and above and that are likely to involve a claim for an element of future continuing loss. The parties may well agree to operate the Guide in relation to lower value multi track cases. The Guide excludes clinical negligence and asbestos related disease cases.

The Guide is intended to help parties involved in these multi track claims resolve any/all issues whilst putting the claimant at the centre of the process. It puts in place a system that meets the reasonable needs of the injured claimant whilst ensuring the parties work together towards resolving the case by cooperating and narrowing the issues.

This Guide creates an environment that encourages positive collaborative behaviour from both sides, and will work in parallel with the Civil Procedure Rules.

Nothing within this document affects a solicitor's duty to act in the best interests of the client and upon their instructions.

**It is recognised that there will be occasions when the defendant[1] insurer and or agent cannot commit a commercial client for whom they are handling agents to comply with the Guide. The claimant representative will be notified of this issue immediately.**

**It is recognised that there will be occasions where either the claimant or the defendant insurer /and or the claims handling agent are unable to comply with the Guide. Where this occurs it is expected that notification of this fact to the opposing party should be made immediately.**

This Guide comprises the following:

- Objectives
- Guidance
- Collaboration
- Early notification
- First contact
- Rehabilitation
- Ongoing review and case planning
- Dispute resolution and escalation
- Costs

## OBJECTIVES

The principal aims are as follows:

- to resolve liability as quickly as possible;

---

[1] Any reference to defendant or defendant insurer can be taken to be singular or pleural when more than one defendant or insurer is involved or potentially involved.

- where beneficial to the claimant to provide early access to rehabilitation to maximise their recovery;
- to resolve claims in a cost appropriate and proportionate manner;
- to resolve claims within an appropriate agreed time frame;
- resolution through an environment of mutual trust, transparency and collaboration;

To achieve the above the parties agree to work collaboratively bringing tangible benefits to all parties.

The key objectives are:

### i. Notification

Early notification of claims to defendants and their insurers when known, with a view to achieving resolution of the case as quickly as possible and where liability is admitted or established, providing compensation.

### ii. Case planning

Collaboration and dialogue are a central objective to achieve efficient case progression through an agreed action plan, dealing with but not limited to liability resolution, rehabilitation, quantum evidence and overall settlement.

### iii. Liability

In all cases handled under the Guide a commitment to resolve liability by agreement, with a view to this being finalised within a maximum period of six months from the date of first notification. Where this is not possible, to identify the barriers that are stopping liability being resolved and to agree an action plan to conclude the issue at the earliest opportunity. The plan can include trial or alternative dispute resolution as appropriate.

For cases handled in accordance with this Guide the withdrawal of an admission would only be in exceptional circumstances and an admission made by any party may well be binding on that party in the litigation. The rules concerning admissions at CPR 14.1A continue to apply.

### iv. Considerations on resolution of liability

A commitment to an early interim payment of disbursements (the subject matter of which has been disclosed) in addition to base costs related to liability once resolved. If the parties are unable to agree the amount of contribution an action plan will be developed to conclude the issue at the earliest opportunity.

The objectives and processes set within the Guide do not prevent the parties agreeing to additional items such as payment of interest on general damages, stay of proceedings or on any other issue in the course of the claim, all such discussions being in the spirit of the Guide.

### v. Rehabilitation

Discussion at the earliest opportunity by all parties to consider effective rehabilitation where reasonably required.

Appointment, where necessary, of an independent clinical case manager instructed by the claimant, or subject to the claimant's agreement, on a joint basis.

vi. **Interim damages**

A willingness to make early and continuing interim payments where appropriate.

vii. **Part 36/Calderbank offers**

No Part 36/Calderbank offers unless or until the parties have tried to agree an issue through dialogue and negotiation but cannot do so.

viii. **Documents**

Commitment by all parties to obtain and disclose promptly all relevant documents, such as

    a. liability documents
    b. police reports in road accident cases
    c. accident report documentation
    d. medical notes and records
    e. documents relating to past loss
    f. case manager records
    g. other relevant non-privileged material

Where possible, all parties are to obtain evidence in such a way as to avoid duplication of effort and cost.

## GUIDANCE: ACHIEVING THE OBJECTIVES

### 1. COLLABORATION AND CASE PLANNING

**1.1.** The aims and objectives of this Guide will be achieved through the parties working together, allocating tasks where appropriate, narrowing the issues throughout the claim, leading to resolution at the earliest time.

**1.2.** Collaboration begins with a commitment to early notification of a claim to the potential defendant.

Collaborative working between the parties should continue throughout the life of the claim with the objective of achieving:

- early liability resolution
- maximising rehabilitation opportunities
- making provision for early interim payments
- emphasising restitution and redress, (rather than just compensation)
- early identification of issues not in dispute
- flexible approaches to resolution of issues in dispute

**1.3.** The parties should aim to agree a framework/timetable for engaging on a regular basis in order to bring the case to conclusion.

### 2. EARLY NOTIFICATION

**2.1.** The claimant's solicitor should ensure that the defendant and their insurers / handling agents are given early notification of the claim. The recommended contents of the early notification letter are set out below.

**2.2.** A full formal detailed letter of claim is not expected (in the first instance). The aim is to alert the proposed defendant and insurer / handling agent to the potential claim, applicability of this Guide and to enable:

- an initial view for the purpose of understanding the nature of the claim and severity of injuries
- allocation of the case to an appropriate level of file handler within their organisation
- liability to be resolved promptly without further investigation by the proposed claimant.

**2.3.** The claimant's solicitors should aim to send a written notification within 7 calendar days of instruction. This should include where available but not be limited to:

- Name, address, date of birth and NI number of claimant (Such personal data should not be sent in one letter because of the risk of fraud.)
- Date, time and place of accident or date of onset of condition giving rise to the claim
- Factual outline of accident and injury if available
- Who is said to be responsible and relationship to claimant
- Any other party approached
- Occupation and approximate income
- Name and address of employer if there is one
- Current medical status in summary form (e.g. inpatient or discharged)
- Any immediate medical or rehabilitation needs if known
- The identity of the firms' escalation point of contact (see escalation section) and email address
- Protected party status on a without prejudice basis.

**2.4.** In the notification letter, the name of file hander with conduct at the claimant's solicitor's firm and immediate line manager/supervisor should be identified. Relevant e-mail addresses and telephone numbers should also be included.

**2.5.** The solicitors representing the claimant should take all reasonable steps to locate and notify the appropriate insurer / handling agent. Where known the letter should be sent to an established address to enable the file to be allocated at the correct handling level within the insurance company / handling agents.

**2.6.** If an insurer or handling agent is unknown, a short notification letter should be sent to the proposed defendant with a request to pass it on to any relevant insurer. In RTA cases, the MIB should be approached in the absence of an alternative insurer.

**2.7.** In the event that more than one potential defendant is identified details should be communicated to all other defendants (see section 4 below).

**2.8.** The reasonable costs of the solicitor in complying with this section will not be challenged for the lack of a retainer at this point in time.

## 3. FIRST CONTACT

**3.1.** At the earliest opportunity but no later than:

> **3.1.1.** 14 calendar days of receipt of the notification letter, the defendant insurer / handling agent must acknowledge the correspondence in writing and confirm it is with the correct handler,

confirming the name of the file handler, escalation contact point, as well as e-mail addresses and telephone numbers of the same.

**3.1.2.** 28 calendar days of receipt of the notification letter, the defendant insurer shall make contact with the claimant solicitor. The purpose of this first contact is to establish lines of communication between the parties, to include but not limited to:

- the parties' views on liability
- update on injuries
- any rehabilitation needs identified
- other potential defendants
- agreement as to when to hold further discussions.

## 4. CLAIMS INVOLVING MULTIPLE DEFENDANTS

**4.1.** The claimant solicitor must be kept informed in the event that additional defendants are identified.

**4.2.** In the event that there is more than one potential defendant it is expected that one defendant will coordinate correspondence with the claimant representatives. The identity of the coordinating party in such cases ought to be communicated within 28 calendar days of the last letter of claim where more than one is sent.

**4.3.** Where a coordinating contact point is offered the claimant representative shall restrict communication to that party, save that in the event that they consider there is a failure to make satisfactory progress in accordance with this Guide, all other known defendants should be alerted to the concern(s) raised. It is expected that this step will not be taken unless the escalation procedure has been tried first.

**4.4.** The defendants should confer within a maximum of 28 days in order to agree a response or to appoint a replacement coordinating defendant.

**4.5.** It may be that a coordinating defendant cannot be agreed between the defendants. In such cases the claimant must be notified of the fact immediately. However there is a continuing expectation that the defendants will, as soon as possible, agree a coordinating defendant.

## 5. ONGOING REVIEW AND FORWARD PLANNING

**5.1** Regular on-going dialogue should take place between the parties with a view to agreeing the next steps required to progress the case. Material changes in circumstances should be communicated immediately (e.g. death of the claimant, loss of capacity, significant medical deterioration, material change in care regime costs, risk of loss of employment etc).

**5.2** The claimant solicitor should give reasonable access for medical facilities when requested by the defence insurer. The parties should liaise on the issue of selection of any expert and the status thereof as part of the planning process.

## 6. REHABILITATION

**6.1.** One of the overriding aims of the Guide is to help claimants to access rehabilitation when appropriate. At the earliest practical stage the parties should, in consultations with the claimant and/or the claimant's family, consider whether early intervention, rehabilitation or medical treatment would improve the present or long term situation. Defendants should reply promptly to any request to rehabilitation, and in any event within 21 days.

**6.2.** Further guidance can be found in the following material:

**6.2.1.** APIL's **Think Rehab! Best Practice Guide** on rehabilitation and the parties http://www.apil.org.uk/files/pdf/rehabiliation-guide-to-best-practice.pdf

**6.2.2.** The **Guide to Best Practice at the Interface Between Rehabilitation and the Medico-legal Process** endorsed by BSRM, APIL and the Royal College of Physicians published November 2006, http://www.bsrm.co.uk/publications/Guide2BestPracticeIntRehabMedLegal.pdf

**6.2.3.** The Rehabilitation Code 2015 (official implementation 1 December 2015) http://iual.informz.ca/IUAL/data/images/2015%20Circular%20Attachments/067%20REHAB%20CODE.pdf

**6.2.4.** The Guide to Case Managers 2015 (official implementation 1 December 2015) http://iual.informz.ca/IUAL/data/images/2015%20Circular%20Attachments/067%20CM%20GUIDE%20MASTER2.pdf

**6.3.** The parties are encouraged to try to agree the selection of an appropriately qualified case manager best suited to the claimant's needs.

**6.4.** The insurer and/or appointed solicitor will be kept up to date with rehabilitation progress as part of the case planning process, by whatever means is agreed between the parties or generally.

**6.5.** Rehabilitation reports and case management material should be provided to the insurer on a regular basis.

**6.6.** The parties should seek to agree the frequency with which records and documents should be disclosed.

**6.7.** The parties should seek to agree the frequency of meetings or conference calls with the case manager (if such meetings or calls are appropriate).

## 7. ESCALATION PROCEDURE

**7.1.** In the event that either party feels that the opposing handler is not acting in accordance with the spirit of the Guide the first step must always be to exhaust attempts to resolve the point of concern by dialogue or a meeting.

**7.2.** If such dialogue still fails to allay the concerns, contact should be made with the nominated contact point at the firm/insurer/handling agent (see notification stage above) in order to try to deal with the issue.

**7.3.** In circumstances where a defendant solicitor has been instructed, the signatory insurer escalation point will remain the nominated contact point for the purposes of the Serious Injury Guide. The claimant solicitor should contact the signatory insurer escalation point directly with any escalation procedure issues, and in doing so, there will be no issue raised in relation to the Code of Conduct. The defendant solicitor should be notified of the intention to escalate, and should be copied into the correspondence sent to the insurer escalation contact point.

**7.4.** All parties are expected to adhere to the objectives set out above.

## 8. DISPUTE RESOLUTION

**8.1.** Ongoing dialogue is fundamental to the process. The parties will continue to discuss the case on a regular basis and at the times agreed. There may be occasions when issues arise that cannot be resolved through discussion.

**8.2.** On those occasions the parties should consider and agree if possible how they will approach such disputes. Such an approach should be adopted when any dispute emerges in the case, whether it relates to a discrete issue or resolution of the dispute generally.

**8.3.** All methods of dispute resolution should be considered. Including:

- Stocktake/cooling off period before the parties re-engage
- Early Neutral Evaluation
- Joint Settlement Meeting
- Mediation
- Arbitration

**8.4.** Considering other methods of dispute resolution does not prevent the parties from starting legal proceedings including Detailed Assessment if needed.

## 9. COSTS

**9.1.** Following resolution of liability, the Guide recognises an early commitment to pay an interim payment towards disbursements and a contribution towards base costs. See objective (iv) above.

**Signatories:**

**The following general insurers and claimant firms and professional organisations have agreed to follow this Guide. See www.seriousinjuryguide.co.uk for a full and up-to-date list. All named firms commit that all handlers within their organisations will follow the Guide in all respects including the escalation process.**

Acromas
Admiral
Allianz
Aviva
AXA
Direct Line Group
Esure
Hastings
LV/Highway
MIB
QBE
RSA
Ashton KCJ Solicitors
Atherton Godfrey
Barlow Robbins LLP
Blakeley Solicitors
Beardsells Solicitors
Beecham Peacock LLP

K8: APIL Serious Injury Guide

Bolt Burdon Kemp
Boys and Maughan
Brethertons LLP
Carpenters
CFG Law
Coles Miller Solicitors
Field Fisher
Ford Simey LLP
Freeths LLP
George Ide LLP
Healys
Higgs and Sons Solicitors
Irwin Mitchell
Liddys Solicitors
Mason Baggott and Garton
Morrish Solicitors
Novum Law
Osbornes
Pattinson & Brewer
Patrick Blackmore
Peace Legal
Pierre Thomas and Partners
Potter Rees Dolan
Serious Law
Shoosmiths (Access Legal)
Simpkins and Co Solicitors
Slater & Gordon
Smith Jones Solicitors
Stewarts
Stones Solicitors
Thomas Dunton Solicitors
Thompsons

# Group L
*Motoring and Allied Material*

**L1:** **Motoring costs**

**L2:** **Taxation of car and fuel benefits**

**L3:** **The Motability Scheme**

**L4:** **The costs of buying and replacing cars**

**L5:** **Time, speed and distance**

# L1: Motoring costs

## AA motoring costs

**Petrol cars**

| | Cost New (£) | | | | |
|---|---|---|---|---|---|
| | Up to £13,000 | £13,000 to £18,000 | £18,000 to £25,000 | £25,000 to £32,000 | Over £32,000 |
| **Standing charges per annum (£s)** | | | | | |
| Vehicle Excise Duty (Road tax) | 110.00 | 145.00 | 180.00 | 283.00 | 609.00 |
| Insurance | 360.00 | 409.00 | 481.00 | 571.00 | 762.00 |
| Cost of capital | 203.00 | 251.00 | 355.00 | 494.00 | 877.00 |
| Depreciation | 1190.00 | 2156.00 | 2611.00 | 3672.00 | 6974.00 |
| (at 10,000 miles/annum) | | | | | |
| Breakdown cover | 50.00 | 50.00 | 50.00 | 50.00 | 50.00 |
| Total, standing charges only (£s) | 1913.00 | 3011.00 | 3678.00 | 5070.00 | 9271.00 |
| **Standing charges per mile (pence)** | | | | | |
| at 5,000 miles per year | 37.78 | 59.36 | 72.51 | 99.93 | 182.64 |
| 10,000 | 19.13 | 30.11 | 36.78 | 50.70 | 92.71 |
| 15,000 | 13.07 | 20.65 | 25.21 | 34.78 | 63.67 |
| 20,000 | 10.16 | 16.13 | 19.69 | 27.18 | 49.84 |
| 25,000 | 8.22 | 13.08 | 15.96 | 22.04 | 40.43 |
| 30,000 | 6.89 | 10.97 | 13.39 | 18.49 | 33.93 |
| **Running costs per mile (pence)** | | | | | |
| Petrol* | 10.84 | 13.12 | 14.55 | 16.22 | 18.04 |
| Tyres | 1.37 | 1.57 | 1.94 | 2.32 | 3.35 |
| Service labour costs | 2.10 | 2.07 | 2.09 | 2.04 | 2.34 |
| Replacement parts | 2.24 | 2.39 | 2.25 | 2.73 | 3.34 |
| Parking and tolls | 2.00 | 2.00 | 2.00 | 2.00 | 2.00 |
| Total, running costs only (pence) | 18.56 | 21.14 | 22.83 | 25.31 | 29.06 |
| * Petrol @ 129.0 p/litre. | | | | | |
| For every penny more or less, add or subtract | 0.08 | 0.10 | 0.11 | 0.13 | 0.14 |

**Total of standing charges and running costs (in pence) based on annual mileage:**

| | | | | | |
|---|---|---|---|---|---|
| at 5,000 miles per year | 56.34 | 80.51 | 95.34 | 125.24 | 211.70 |
| 10,000 miles | 37.68 | 51.26 | 59.60 | 76.01 | 121.78 |
| 15,000 miles | 31.63 | 41.79 | 48.04 | 60.09 | 92.73 |
| 20,000 miles | 28.72 | 37.28 | 42.52 | 52.49 | 78.91 |
| 25,000 miles | 26.78 | 34.22 | 38.79 | 47.35 | 69.50 |
| 30,000 miles | 25.45 | 32.12 | 36.22 | 43.80 | 62.99 |

Please see the associated notes for more detail. These figures are typical but do not represent all types of vehicle and conditions of use. The figures change from time to time.

## L1: Motoring costs

### Diesel cars

| | Cost New (£) | | | | |
|---|---|---|---|---|---|
| | Up to £16,000 | £16,000 to £22,000 | £22,000 to £26,000 | £26,000 to £36,000 | Over £36,000 |
| **Standing charges per annum (£s)** | | | | | |
| Vehicle Excise Duty (Road tax) | 30.00 | 110.00 | 180.00 | 180.00 | 361.00 |
| Insurance | 424.00 | 499.00 | 511.00 | 601.00 | 771.00 |
| Cost of capital | 245.00 | 325.00 | 429.00 | 541.00 | 823.00 |
| Depreciation (at 10,000 miles/annum) | 1705.00 | 2426.00 | 2618.00 | 3373.00 | 5197.00 |
| Breakdown cover | 50.00 | 50.00 | 50.00 | 50.00 | 50.00 |
| Total, standing charges only (£s) | 2454.00 | 3411.00 | 3788.00 | 4745.00 | 7203.00 |
| **Standing charges per mile (pence)** | | | | | |
| at 5,000 miles per year | 48.40 | 67.24 | 74.71 | 93.55 | 141.98 |
| 10,000 | 24.54 | 34.11 | 37.88 | 47.45 | 72.03 |
| 15,000 | 16.81 | 23.38 | 25.95 | 32.53 | 49.40 |
| 20,000 | 13.12 | 18.27 | 20.25 | 25.41 | 38.61 |
| 25,000 | 10.63 | 14.81 | 16.41 | 20.60 | 31.31 |
| 30,000 | 8.92 | 12.42 | 13.76 | 17.28 | 26.26 |
| **Running costs per mile (pence)** | | | | | |
| Diesel fuel* | 9.28 | 10.20 | 12.65 | 12.88 | 16.79 |
| Tyres | 1.15 | 1.49 | 2.06 | 2.02 | 2.87 |
| Service labour costs | 2.10 | 2.14 | 2.29 | 2.24 | 2.76 |
| Replacement parts | 2.73 | 2.43 | 2.53 | 2.99 | 3.44 |
| Parking and tolls | 2.00 | 2.00 | 2.00 | 2.00 | 2.00 |
| Total, running costs only (pence) | 17.26 | 18.25 | 21.54 | 22.14 | 27.85 |
| * Diesel fuel @ 137.0 p/litre. For every penny more or less, add or subtract | 0.07 | 0.07 | 0.09 | 0.09 | 0.12 |

**Total of standing charges and running costs (in pence) based on annual mileage:**

| | | | | | |
|---|---|---|---|---|---|
| at 5,000 miles per year | 65.66 | 85.49 | 96.25 | 115.69 | 169.83 |
| 10,000 miles | 41.80 | 52.35 | 59.41 | 69.59 | 99.88 |
| 15,000 miles | 34.08 | 41.64 | 47.49 | 54.67 | 77.26 |
| 20,000 miles | 30.39 | 36.52 | 41.79 | 47.55 | 66.47 |
| 25,000 miles | 27.90 | 33.06 | 37.94 | 42.74 | 59.16 |
| 30,000 miles | 26.18 | 30.67 | 35.30 | 39.42 | 54.11 |

## Notes to the AA tables

*The AA tables are published annually as a guide to the likely cost to the average private user to run a car. (In previous years tables were also produced for motorcycles and scooters.) The figures given can only be a guide, as individual vehicles will vary: for instance fuel consumption will depend on traffic conditions and the type of journey, and repairs can be very unpredictable. The aim is to show a representative cost that reflects all the important items, so that the motorist can see how it all adds up. This should help make the most suitable choice of economical and environmentally less damaging transport.*

**Standing Charges** The basic costs which you have to pay whether you use the car or not. They include the Road Tax (annual VED), insurance, the cost of the capital used for the vehicle, the loss of value of the vehicle or depreciation, and AA breakdown cover. Depreciation is affected by mileage.

**Running Costs** The actual costs of using the car include petrol, oil, tyres, routine servicing, repairs and parking.

**Vehicle Groups** Cars are put into groups depending on the new car price, as this is a better guide to what they cost to run than for instance the engine size. Take the new car list price when it was first registered (including the main options such as automatic gearbox, air conditioning etc supplied with the car), not the current list price. If in doubt, used-car price guides will give the original list prices.

**Claiming Mileage** How much an employer pays for mileage is a matter for negotiation between them and the employees, as circumstances will vary. HMRC operates the Approved Mileage Allowance Payment (AMAP) system (in our Table L2)—further details from your local tax office or:

*http://www.hmrc.gov.uk/mileage/index.htm*, and
*http://www.hmrc.gov.uk/cars/fuel_company_cars.htm*.

The figures given in our tables are VAT inclusive.

**The AA Website** The Motoring Costs tables are also on the AA website at *http://www.theaa.com* Here some of the data will be updated throughout the year, and there is an interactive version that can tailor the costs to an individual car model and, for instance, the actual insurance premium paid.

**Road Tax** There are three regimes for Vehicle Tax according to the date of registration of the vehicle. They take into account engine size, fuel type, carbon dioxide emissions and list price. For details see the separate Vehicle Tax tables on a later page.

**Insurance** The UK average cost for a comprehensive policy with a 60 per cent no-claims discount.

**Cost of capital** This represents the loss of income from the owner's having money tied up in a vehicle, which could otherwise be earning interest in a deposit account, calculated at 2.2 per cent (the AA's online saving rate) of the average value for the car cost group. If the money is borrowed, the cost of capital will instead consist of the charges for loans or hire-purchase finance.

**Depreciation** Cars lose value at different rates, depending on make, age, mileage, condition and even colour. Older cars will in general depreciate at a slower rate. The tables assume that depreciation costs are averaged over four years from purchase, and include typical adjustments for the different annual mileage in that period. Different rates are used for mileages differing from 10,000 miles per annum.

**AA breakdown cover** For AA "Roadside" annual vehicle based cover.

## L1: Motoring costs

**Fuel cost**  Based on the average UK price, but can be adjusted for price changes using the factors given. The fuel consumption figures taken are typical for each of the car bands listed.

**Tyres**  Based on using six tyres in a four-year period. Actual tyre life will vary with individual driving style. The prices in each car category are based on prices from high street retailers for a well-known brand: they include valve, balance, and the disposal charge for the old tyre. The prices at main dealers will be higher.

**Service and labour costs**  Average cost for each car cost group for normal servicing and parts replacement at a dealer, taking average UK labour rates. Actual labour rates vary between different parts of the country and different brands.

**Replacement parts**  The replacement parts included cover those likely to be needed under normal driving conditions, such as brake materials, oils, filters, bulbs, wipers, and hoses, plus the cost of one MOT.

**Parking and tolls**  The allowance for parking and road tolls is based on a national average for an urban driver. You may pay more or less depending on patterns of use.

**Editors' note:**

1. The AA notes have been re-arranged by us, with the AA's permission, in the interests of space.
2. Figures for the taxation of car and fuel benefits are at Table L2.

### Vehicle Tax

**Vehicles registered before March 2001**

If the engine capacity is 1,549 cc or less the duty is £145; if it is over 1,549 cc the duty is £235. (Vehicles registered more than 40 years before 1 January in the current year are entitled to exemption from Vehicle Tax.)

**Vehicles registered between 1 March 2001 and 31 March 2017**

The tax depends on the fuel type and the emissions of carbon dioxide in the legislated Type Approval tests. In the tables, averages for the price groups are used for the tax rate. There is a first year rate (for new car purchases only) and a standard rate for all subsequent years.

| Bands | $CO_2$ Emission | Petrol or Diesel Car | |
|---|---|---|---|
| | | First year rate (new cars only) | Standard rate |
| | (g/km) | £ | £ |
| Band A | Up to 100 | 0 | 0 |
| Band B | 101–110 | 0 | 20 |
| Band C | 111–120 | 0 | 30 |
| Band D | 121–130 | 0 | 110 |

| Bands | $CO_2$ Emission | Petrol or Diesel Car | |
|---|---|---|---|
| | | First year rate (new cars only) | Standard rate |
| | (g/km) | £ | £ |
| Band E | 131–140 | 130 | 130 |
| Band F | 141–150 | 145 | 145 |
| Band G | 151–165 | 185 | 185 |
| Band H | 166–175 | 300 | 210 |
| Band I | 176–185 | 355 | 230 |
| Band J | 186–200 | 500 | 270 |
| Band K | 201–225 | 650 | 295 |
| Band L | 226–255 | 885 | 500 |
| Band M | Over 255 | 1,120 | 515 |

Band K includes cars with a $CO_2$ figure over 225 g/km which were registered before 23 March 2006.

An alternative fuel car has a discount of £10 for all bands.

The $CO_2$ emission of a particular vehicle can be found at a website provided by the Vehicle Certification Agency (VCA): *www.carfueldata.direct.gov.uk*. It is also on the V5 registration document.

**Vehicles registered on or after 1 April 2017**

Only vehicles with zero emissions will benefit from zero tax.

There is a premium of £310 in years 2–6 on all cars costing over £40,000, even if they have zero emissions; the premium depends on *list price*, not the actual purchase price.

| $CO_2$ Emission | First year rate (new cars only) >£40k | Petrol or Diesel Car Standard rate Year 2 onwards— cars not >£40k Year 7 onwards— cars >£40k | Premium rate Years 2–6— cars >£40k |
|---|---|---|---|
| (g/km) | £ | £ | £ |
| Zero | 0 | 0 | 310 |
| 1–50 | 10 | 140 | 450 |
| 51–75 | 25 | 140 | 450 |
| 91–100 | 120 | 140 | 450 |
| 101–110 | 140 | 140 | 450 |
| 111–130 | 160 | 140 | 450 |
| 131–150 | 200 | 140 | 450 |
| 151–170 | 500 | 140 | 450 |
| 171–190 | 800 | 140 | 450 |
| 191–225 | 1,200 | 140 | 450 |
| 226–255 | 1,700 | 140 | 450 |
| Over 255 | 2,000 | 140 | 450 |

## Illustrative motorcycle running costs

RAC Motoring Services, in conjunction with Emmerson Hill Associates (Vehicle Management Consultants), have compiled the following illustrative motorcycle running costs. The figures represent a guide to the cost of running a privately-owned motorcycle for a period of three years with an annual mileage of 6,000 miles.

| Engine size (cc) | 100cc | 125cc | 250 | up to 400cc | 600cc | 750cc | 1000cc | over 1000cc |
|---|---|---|---|---|---|---|---|---|
| Assumed fuel consumption | 80 | 68 | 56 | 48 | 45 | 43 | 37 | 33 |
| Average cost new | 1,950 | 2,150 | 2,950 | 4,250 | 4,500 | 4,950 | 5,950 | 7,500 |
| Average value @ 3 years | 950 | 1,250 | 1,850 | 2,150 | 2,650 | 3,100 | 3,500 | 4,450 |
| Projected depreciation | 1,000 | 900 | 1,100 | 2,100 | 1,850 | 1,850 | 2,450 | 3,050 |
| Finance charge @ 4.8% APR | 144 | 159 | 218 | 315 | 333 | 366 | 440 | 555 |
| Fuel cost @ £1.10/litre | 1,125 | 1,324 | 1,607 | 1,875 | 2,000 | 2,093 | 2,432 | 2,727 |
| Insurance & repairs | 650 | 825 | 975 | 1,050 | 1,325 | 1,325 | 1,550 | 1,550 |
| Servicing & maintenance | 250 | 295 | 525 | 550 | 600 | 725 | 795 | 825 |
| Tyres & replacement parts | 350 | 450 | 650 | 690 | 740 | 820 | 820 | 900 |
| Excise licences 3 years | 51 | 51 | 114 | 114 | 174 | 240 | 240 | 240 |
| RAC Membership | 150 | 150 | 150 | 150 | 150 | 150 | 150 | 150 |
| Protective clothing/helmet | 425 | 425 | 525 | 525 | 525 | 525 | 525 | 525 |
| Total cost | 4,145 | 4,579 | 5,864 | 7,369 | 7,697 | 8,094 | 9,403 | 10,522 |
| Annual cost | 1,382 | 1,526 | 1,955 | 2,456 | 2,566 | 2,698 | 3,134 | 3,507 |
| **Cost per mile in pence** | 23.0 | 25.4 | 32.6 | 40.9 | 42.9 | 45.0 | 52.2 | 58.5 |
| **Standing costs per mile** | 13.4 | 13.9 | 17.1 | 23.6 | 24.2 | 24.8 | 29.7 | 33.8 |
| **Running costs per mile** | 9.6 | 11.5 | 15.5 | 17.3 | 18.6 | 20.2 | 22.5 | 24.7 |
| **Adjustment for change in fuel price of 1p +/-** | 0.06 | 0.07 | 0.08 | 0.09 | 0.10 | 0.10 | 0.12 | 0.14 |

**Note to the RAC motorcycle figures above:**

The standing and running costs per mile and the adjustment for changes in fuel price have been calculated by the editors from the RAC figures.

**Standing costs** include Vehicle Tax, insurance and repairs, finance charges, depreciation, protective clothing and RAC membership.

**Running costs** include fuel, tyres and replacement parts, service and maintenance.

# L2: Taxation of car and fuel benefits

## Car benefit 2007/08 to 2016/17

| CO$_2$ emissions (g/km) | | | | | | | | | | Percentage of car's price taxed if car does not run solely on diesel (%) | Percentage of car's price taxed if car does run solely on diesel (%) |
|---|---|---|---|---|---|---|---|---|---|---|---|
| 2007/08 | 2008/09 | 2009/10 | 2010/11 | 2011/12 | 2012/13 | 2013/14 | 2014/15 | 2015/16 | 2016/17 | | |
| N/A | N/A | N/A | 1-75 | 1-75 | 1-75 | 1-75 | 1-75 | 0-50 | N/A | 5 | 8 |
| N/A | N/A | N/A | N/A | N/A | N/A | N/A | N/A | N/A | 0-50 | 7 | 10 |
| N/A | N/A | N/A | N/A | N/A | N/A | N/A | N/A | 51-75 | N/A | 9 | 12 |
| N/A | 0-120 | 0-120 | 76-120 | 76-120 | 76-99 | 76-94 | N/A | N/A | N/A | 10 | 13 |
| N/A | N/A | N/A | N/A | N/A | 100-104 | 95-99 | 76-94 | N/A | 51-75 | 11 | 14 |
| N/A | N/A | N/A | N/A | N/A | 105-109 | 100-104 | 95-99 | N/A | N/A | 12 | 15 |
| N/A | N/A | N/A | N/A | N/A | 110-114 | 105-109 | 100-104 | 76-94 | N/A | 13 | 16 |
| N/A | N/A | N/A | N/A | N/A | 115-119 | 110-114 | 105-109 | 95-99 | N/A | 14 | 17 |
| 0-144 | 121-139 | 121-139 | 121-134 | 121-129 | 120-124 | 115-119 | 110-114 | 100-104 | 76-94 | 15 | 18 |
| 145-149 | 140-144 | 140-144 | 135-139 | 130-134 | 125-129 | 120-124 | 115-119 | 105-109 | 95-99 | 16 | 19 |
| 150-154 | 145-149 | 145-149 | 140-144 | 135-139 | 130-134 | 125-129 | 120-124 | 110-114 | 100-104 | 17 | 20 |
| 155-159 | 150-154 | 150-154 | 145-149 | 140-144 | 135-139 | 130-134 | 125-129 | 115-119 | 105-109 | 18 | 21 |
| 160-164 | 155-159 | 155-159 | 150-154 | 145-149 | 140-144 | 135-139 | 130-134 | 120-124 | 110-114 | 19 | 22 |
| 165-169 | 160-164 | 160-164 | 155-159 | 150-154 | 145-149 | 140-144 | 135-139 | 125-129 | 115-119 | 20 | 23 |
| 170-174 | 165-169 | 165-169 | 160-164 | 155-159 | 150-154 | 145-149 | 140-144 | 130-134 | 120-124 | 21 | 24 |
| 175-179 | 170-174 | 170-174 | 165-169 | 160-164 | 155-159 | 150-154 | 145-149 | 135-139 | 125-129 | 22 | 25 |
| 180-184 | 175-179 | 175-179 | 170-174 | 165-169 | 160-164 | 155-159 | 150-154 | 140-144 | 130-134 | 23 | 26 |
| 185-189 | 180-184 | 180-184 | 175-179 | 170-174 | 165-169 | 160-164 | 155-159 | 145-149 | 135-139 | 24 | 27 |
| 190-194 | 185-189 | 185-189 | 180-184 | 175-179 | 170-174 | 165-169 | 160-164 | 150-154 | 140-144 | 25 | 28 |
| 195-199 | 190-194 | 190-194 | 185-189 | 180-184 | 175-179 | 170-174 | 165-169 | 155-159 | 145-149 | 26 | 29 |
| 200-204 | 195-199 | 195-199 | 190-194 | 185-189 | 180-184 | 175-179 | 170-174 | 160-164 | 150-154 | 27 | 30 |
| 205-209 | 200-204 | 200-204 | 195-199 | 190-194 | 185-189 | 180-184 | 175-179 | 165-169 | 155-159 | 28 | 31 |
| 210-214 | 205-209 | 205-209 | 200-204 | 195-199 | 190-194 | 185-189 | 180-184 | 170-174 | 160-164 | 29 | 32 |
| 215-119 | 210-214 | 210-214 | 205-209 | 200-204 | 195-199 | 190-194 | 185-189 | 175-179 | 165-169 | 30 | 33 |
| 220-224 | 215-119 | 215-119 | 210-214 | 205-209 | 200-204 | 195-199 | 190-194 | 180-184 | 170-174 | 31 | 34 |
| 225-229 | 220-224 | 220-224 | 215-119 | 210-214 | 205-209 | 200-204 | 195-199 | 185-189 | 175-179 | 32 | 35 |
| 230-234 | 225-229 | 225-229 | 220-224 | 215-119 | 210-214 | 205-209 | 200-204 | 190-194 | 180-184 | 33 | 36 |
| 235-239 | 230-234 | 230-234 | 225-229 | 220-224 | 215-119 | 210-214 | 205-109 | 195-199 | 185-189 | 34 | 37 |
| 240+ | 235+ | 235+ | 230+ | 225+ | 220+ | 215+ | 210+ | 200-204 | 190-194 | 35 | 37 |
| N/A | N/A | N/A | N/A | N/A | N/A | N/A | N/A | 205-209 | 195-199 | 36 | 37 |
| N/A | N/A | N/A | N/A | N/A | N/A | N/A | N/A | 210+ | 200+ | 37 | 37 |

**Notes**

1. From 6 April 2002, although the benefit of a company car is still to be calculated as a percentage of the price of the car (normally list price), the percentage is graduated according to carbon dioxide ($CO_2$) emissions and adjustments for business mileage and older cars no longer apply.
2. There are discounts for certain cleaner alternatively-propelled cars, which may reduce the minimum charge to that shown in the table.
3. The diesel supplement and the discounts for cleaner alternatives apply only to cars first registered on 1 January 1998 or later.
4. Cars without an approved $CO_2$ emissions figure are taxed according to engine size. This includes all cars registered before 1998 but only a tiny proportion of those registered 1998 and later.
5. Except where otherwise indicated, the exact $CO_2$ figure is rounded down to the nearest five grams per kilometre when using the above table.
6. From 6 April 2008 there was a new lower rate of 10 per cent (13 per cent for diesel) for cars with $CO_2$ emissions of 120 grams per kilometre or less.

## L2: Taxation of car and fuel benefits

7. From 6 April 2010 cars and vans with zero $CO_2$ emissions were exempt from company car tax for five tax years.
8. From 6 April 2010 an ultra low carbon cars band was introduced for five years.

### Car fuel benefit — petrol and diesel — cash equivalent 2003/04 to 2016/17

**Notes**

1. From 6 April 2003, the car fuel benefit is, like the car benefit, linked directly to the $CO_2$ emissions of the company car.
2. There are the same diesel supplement and discounts for cleaner alternatively-propelled cars as there are in calculating the car benefit.
3. To calculate the car fuel benefit the percentage in the table used for calculating car benefit is multiplied against a set figure for the year:

    | | |
    |---|---|
    | 2003/04 to 2007/08 | £14,400 |
    | 2008/09 to 2009/10 | £16,900 |
    | 2010/11 | £18,000 |
    | 2011/12 | £18,800 |
    | 2012/13 | £20,200 |
    | 2013/14 | £21,100 |
    | 2014/15 | £21,700 |
    | 2015/16 | £22,100 |
    | 2016/17 | £22,200 |

    Thus, if the car benefit percentage for 2016/17 is 23 per cent, the fuel benefit would be £22,200 × 23% = £5,106.
4. For cars registered before 1 January 1998 and cars with no approved $CO_2$ emissions figure, the percentage to be applied is the same as that used to calculate the car benefit.

### Authorised Mileage Allowance Payments — tax-free rates in pence per mile 2002/03 to 2016/17

| | Annual mileage | Pence per mile |
|---|---|---|
| Cars and vans | Up to 10,000 | 45p* |
| | 10,001 + | 25p |
| Motorcycles | | 24p |
| Bicycles | | 20p |
| Business Passengers | | 5p |

* For 2002/03 to 2010/11 (inclusive) this rate was 40 pence per mile

# L3: The Motability Scheme

Disabled people who need a motor vehicle may obtain one by utilising most if not all of the Higher Rate component of the Disability Living Allowance, the War Pensioner's Mobility Supplement or the Armed Forces Independence Payment. Motability is only available to those in receipt of any of these benefits who assign all or some of them to the scheme for the duration of the contract. Because of the very wide range of physical and mental disabilities of those in receipt of them the scheme does not require the person seeking to use it to be a driver: anyone in receipt of one of these allowances who is over three is entitled to use it. Under the Scheme there are three available options:

1. A new car can be obtained on a three-year hire lease contract.
2. A wheelchair accessible vehicle (WAV) can be obtained on a five-year lease hire contract or three-year for a secondhand one.
3. A powered wheelchair or scooter may be taken on a three-year contract hire.

A national network of some 4,500 dealers provides a wide range of suitably adapted new and used cars. In the case of any option, the scheme requires a capital sum and a monthly payment which is provided for by the assignment of the relevant state benefit to the scheme. As well as the adapted vehicle, all maintenance is provided to include the cost of tyres, as is insurance for two named drivers who are over 25, annual road fund disc and roadside recovery. Fuel, oil and other incidentals are the responsibility of the driver. There is a 60,000-mile limit on use over the three years of the contract for Option 1 or 100,000 miles for a WAV, with an annual limit of 20,000 miles in the case of Option 2. Any mileage over that limit attracts a penalty of 5p per mile. At the end of the contract period the car reverts to the scheme. Hire purchase is no longer available under the scheme.

When costing, care must be taken to distinguish between the three elements of any claim:

(i) the capital cost of both purchase and adaptation which recur every three years;
(ii) the monthly running costs covered by the Motability Scheme; and
(iii) the running costs not covered by the scheme such as oil, petrol and car washes.

Not all cars are available and advice must be obtained as to whether what is available adequately meets the needs of the disabled person. When experts have recommended that a car be obtained under the scheme practitioners should ensure that they are clear which option is being recommended and ensure that they compare like for like.

The condition precedent for using the Motability Scheme is that the beneficiary is in receipt of a state benefit which falls within the Second Schedule of the Social Security (Recovery of Benefits) Act 1997. It is now clear, following *Eagle v Chambers (No.2)*[1], that s.17 of the Act precludes a court from insisting that the mobility component of the Disabled Living Allowance should be used by any recipient to mitigate her loss. Henceforth no defendant can insist that a claimant use the mobility allowance to participate in the Motability Scheme.

DLA, hitherto the gateway into Motability, is over the next 3 years being replaced by the Personal Independence Payment (PIP). When this is fully implemented only those receiving the enhanced rate of the mobility component of PIP will be eligible to use the Motability Scheme. During the transitional period those with the higher rate of the mobility component of DLA continue to be eligible. PIP is assessed in a less generous way than DLA and it is likely that as the shift occurs to PIP some will cease to be eligible for Motability.

Further reading and assistance in specific cases can be obtained at:
http://www.motabilitycarscheme.co.uk and Customer Services (0300) 456 4566.

[1] [2004] EWCA Civ 1033.

# L4: The costs of buying and replacing cars

There are a number of commonly encountered calculations involving the cost of cars. This section contains tables and examples of calculations dealing with the following and should be read along with the table of Motoring costs in section L1:

1. New car prices.
2. Cost of future replacements.
3. Cost of more frequent replacement.
4. Cost of automatic cars.
5. Cost of additional mileage.
6. Cost of professional servicing.
7. Cost of Assessment.

We have classified cars as follows:

| | |
|---|---|
| Mini: | Most cars of 1.1 litre or under, such as Toyota Aygo 1.0, Vauxhall Corsa 1.0 |
| Super mini: | Similar cars between 1.1 and 1.4, Ford Fiesta 1.25, Suzuki Swift 1.2 |
| Small: | Cars of the smaller Ford Focus, VW Golf type, mostly 1.3–1.6 litre |
| Medium: | The Ford Mondeo, VW Passat type, mostly cars from 1.6–1.9 litre |
| Executive: | The larger Passat, Volvo S60 type, mostly 2.0–2.8 litre |
| Prestige: | The BMW 330d, Jaguar 3.0, mostly up to 3.5 litre |
| Luxury: | The Jaguar XJ, Audi A8 4.2, mostly over 3.5 litre and expensive |
| Estate etc: | Self-explanatory |

**Notes:**

1. The first table is intended to convey in broad terms the purchase costs of cars across a range of models. The material is taken from *Parker's Car Price Guide* and *What Car?* with the kind permission of the publishers.

    The *New Price* is the recommended retail price (including VAT) according to the latest manufacturer's price list: all prices stated are "on the road" and include delivery charges, 12 months' road fund licence, number plates and £25 registration tax. *Tax band* is the vehicle tax band.

2. Depreciation: Different cars, even produced by the same manufacturer, depreciate at different rates. As a model of car may change after a few years even if the same name is retained, losses over a long period cannot be calculated for individual models but only by reference to the general position.

3. Automatics: The comparison of manual and automatic cars is similarly a generalisation. The calculation for depreciation assumes that the new price of the automatic is *higher* than for the manual model. There is considerable variation, even among cars of similar type with similar new prices, in the rate at which the premium for the automatic version is eroded. With some cars the gap disappears very quickly: with some the premium for the automatic version is actually greater for used cars than for new ones.

4. Where the current new price of the manual and automatic versions is the same, which is often the case with expensive cars, the used automatic tends to retain its value *better* than the manual model. It may nevertheless have higher fuel consumption but whether it will be more expensive overall may depend on the mileage.

## 1. New Car Prices

|  | New Price (£) | Tax band |
|---|---|---|
| **Mini** | | |
| Citroën C1 1.0i VT 68 Touch 3d | 8,345 | A |
| Toyota Aygo 1.0 3d | 8,845 | A |
| Vauxhall Corsa 1.0 Design 3d | 13,065 | B |
| **Super Mini** | | |
| Citroën DS3 1.2 82 Dsign 3d | 13,295 | B |
| Ford Fiesta 1.25 82 Style 3d | 12,495 | D |
| Suzuki Swift 1.2 SZ2 3d | 8,999 | C |
| Vauxhall Corsa 1.4 SE 3d | 14,510 | E |
| Volkswagen Polo 1.2 TSi 3d | 16,425 | B |
| **Small** | | |
| Citroën C4 1.6 Touch 5d | 16,745 | A |
| Ford Focus 1.6 Style 5d | 16,965 | E |
| Honda Civic 1.4 i VTEC 5d | 16,470 | D |
| Renault Megane 1.5 110 Expr 5d | 18,245 | A |
| Toyota Auris 1.6 Icon 5d | 17,895 | D |
| Vauxhall Astra 1.6i SRi 5d | 19,580 | F |
| Volkswagen Golf 1.4 125 S 5d | 20,020 | C |
| **Medium** | | |
| BMW 318i SE 4d | 25,160 | D |
| Ford Mondeo 2.0 Style 5d | 22,145 | B |
| Toyota Avensis 1.8 Active 4d | 17,955 | E |
| Vauxhall Insignia 1.8 SRi 5d | 18,689 | H |
| Volkswagen Passat TDI 2.0 S 4d | 23,775 | B |
| Volvo V40 2.0 D3 SE 5d | 23,920 | A |
| **Executive** | | |
| BMW 320i SE 4d | 27,310 | E |
| Ford Focus 2.0 TDCi 185 ST3 5d | 26,545 | B |
| Toyota Avensis 2.0 Excel 4d | 26,795 | D |
| Volkswagen Passat 2.0 TDi 150 GT 4d | 26,875 | B |
| Volvo S60 2.0 D4 SE 4d | 29,845 | B |

L4: The costs of buying and replacing cars

|  | New Price (£) | Tax band |
|---|---|---|
| **Prestige** Audi Quattro A4 3.0 S line 4d | 37,180 | C |
| BMW 330d SE Buss 5d | 37,725 | E |
| Jaguar XF 3.0 V6 Luxury 4d | 49,645 | G |
| Mercedes-Benz E220 SE 4d | 34,270 | C |
| Volvo S80 2.0 D4 SE Lux 4d | 33,920 | B |
| **Luxury** Audi Quattro A8 4.2 SE Exec 4d | 72,995 | J |
| BMW 550i Lux 5d | 58,875 | K |
| Jaguar XJ 3.0 V6 Prem Lux 4d | 62,545 | F |
| Mercedes-Benz S400 SE 4d | 71,850 | G |
| **Estate** Citroën C5 2.0 VTR 5d | 25,515 | B |
| Ford Mondeo Estate 2.0 Zetec (Nav) 5d | 24,345 | C |
| Mercedes-Benz E220 CDI SE 5d | 34,540 | E |
| Seat Leon 1.4 TSi SE 5d | 19,295 | C |
| Volkswagen Passat 2.0 TDi 150 S 5d | 25,325 | B |
| Volvo V60 2.0 T3 SE 5d | 27,325 | E |
| **4 x 4** Honda CR-V 2.0 i-VTEC S 5d | 22,475 | H |
| Nissan 1.6 X-Trail DIC-T Tekna 5d | 28,300 | F |
| Suzuki Vitara 1.6 SZ4 5d | 13,999 | D |
| Volkswagen Touareg 3.0 SE TDi 205 5d | 43,605 | H |
| Volvo XC90 2.0 D5 Momentum 5d | 46,106 | F |
| **People carriers** Citroën C4 Grand Picasso 1.6 Excl 5d | 24,035 | B |
| Ford Galaxy 2.0 Zetec 5d | 27,845 | D |
| Renault Grand Scenic 1.6 dCi 130 Dyn 5d | 24,285 | C |
| Toyota Verso 1.6 D-4D Icon 5d | 21,995 | C |
| Vauxhall Zafira 2.0 Design 5d | 20,725 | D |
| Volkswagen Touran 1.6 110 S 5d | 22,840 | C |

## 2. Cost of future replacements

Table 1 below has representative trade-in values of used *manual* cars expressed as a proportion of the *current* new price (calculated from material in *Parker's Car Price Guide*). Automatic cars may depreciate faster. Where the new price of an automatic car is *higher* than that of the corresponding manual car, there is a tendency for the automatic to depreciate by about one per cent more (altogether, not per year).

### Table 1 Trade-in values of used manual cars

| Age of car | Residual value | Loss of value | Equivalent annual depreciation |
|---|---|---|---|
| 1 | 0.64 | 0.36 | 0.360 |
| 2 | 0.50 | 0.50 | 0.256 |
| 3 | 0.41 | 0.59 | 0.204 |
| 4 | 0.36 | 0.64 | 0.168 |
| 5 | 0.33 | 0.67 | 0.143 |
| Adjustment for automatics | −0.01 | +0.01 | |

The table can be used to calculate the future net costs of replacements where the replacements will be second hand as well as where they will be new.

Example 1: The claimant is 54 and needs a people carrier such as a Chrysler Grand Voyager 3.3 LE Auto 5d, automatic version. He will need to replace it every four years, the final replacement being when he is 70. He would not otherwise have had a car (or the car is additional to whatever vehicle would have been bought in any event).

| | | |
|---|---|---|
| Initial price of people carrier, say | | £32,995.00 |
| Proportion of price lost at each replacement (Table 1 above, + 0.01) | 0.65 | |
| Cost of each replacement | 0.65 × 32,995 = 21,446.75 | |
| Multiplier for 16 years (Table A5, 2.5%, four-yearly) | 3.14 | |
| Cost of future replacements | 3.14 × 21,446.75 = | £67,342.80 |
| Total | | £100,337.80 |

Example 2: The same claimant currently runs a manual Volvo S80 2.4 SE and will replace it with the Chrysler people carrier. The additional cost is the future cost of the Chryslers *minus* the corresponding figure saved on Volvos. (If either both cars are manual or both automatic the calculation is simpler.)

| | | |
|---|---|---|
| Initial price of Volvo saved, say | | £28,245.00 |
| Proportion of price saved at each replacement (Table 1 above, manual) | 0.64 | |
| Cost of each replacement | 0.64 × 28,245.00 = 18,076.80 | |
| Multiplier for 16 years (Table A5, 2.5%, four-yearly) | 3.14 | |
| Cost of future replacements saved | 3.14 × 18,076.80 = | £56,761.15 |
| Total saved | | £85,006.15 |
| Net future cost of Chryslers instead of Volvos (100,337.80 − 85,006.15) | = | £15,331.65 |

## 3. Cost of more frequent replacement

Claimants are sometimes advised that because of their condition they need a more reliable car and should therefore replace it more often than they needed to do before the injury. Table 2, which is derived from Table 1, shows the additional annual cost, expressed as a proportion of the new price. Find the row corresponding to the new interval in years and the column corresponding to the old interval.

Note that the table expresses the multiplier as an *annual* cost, not the cost *on each exchange*. Thus in row 2, column 4, the figure 0.088 means that the additional expense of replacing a car every two years, instead of every four years, is 8.8 per cent of the price of the car per year for however long the claimant continues to drive.

**Table 2 Multipliers for additional annual cost of replacing car more frequently**

|  |  | Old interval in years | | | | |
|---|---|---|---|---|---|---|
|  |  | 1 | 2 | 3 | 4 | 5 |
|  | 1 | 0 | 0.104 | 0.156 | 0.192 | 0.217 |
| New | 2 |  | 0 | 0.052 | 0.088 | 0.113 |
| interval | 3 |  |  | 0 | 0.036 | 0.061 |
| in | 4 |  |  |  | 0 | 0.025 |
| years | 5 |  |  |  |  | 0 |

Example: The claimant is 40 and drives a car currently costing £11,995 new. She has just bought one. She can continue to drive a similar car, with modifications. She has been advised that because of her disability she should now change it every three years rather than every five as she has until now. She should stop driving at about 73, so the last change will be at about age 70.

| | | |
|---|---|---|
| Multiplier for additional annual cost from table above – new frequency three years, old frequency five years | 0.061 | |
| Multiplier for woman of 40 until age 70 (Table A1) | 20.65 | |
| Multiplier for additional cost of more frequent replacement | 0.061 × 20.65 | = 1.26 |
| Current cost of car | | £11,995.00 |
| Additional cost of replacing car more frequently until age 70 | | £15,113.70 |

## 4. Cost of automatic cars

Claimants' injuries sometimes make it necessary for them to have an automatic car which they would not otherwise have needed. Generally this involves additional costs in three respects: the automatic car is more expensive to buy, is more expensive to run and tends to depreciate faster than the corresponding manual model (but see the notes in the introduction).

**Table 3 Added cost of automatic cars**

|  |  | Mini and Super Mini | Small | Medium and Executive | Prestige and Luxury | Estate, 4×4 and MPV |
|---|---|---|---|---|---|---|
| Added cost of new car in £ | | 850 | 1,075 | 1,145 | 1,275 | 1,245 |
| **Petrol** at 129.0p per litre | Added cost in pence per mile | 3.42 | 1.73 | 1.42 | 0.41 | – |
| | For every penny more/less, add/subtract | 0.030 | 0.015 | 0.012 | 0.004 | – |

**Greater depreciation**

Where the new price of an automatic model of a car is *higher* than that of the corresponding manual car, there is a tendency for the automatic to depreciate by about one per cent more (altogether, not per year)—see Table 1 above. Thus:

| | | | |
|---|---|---|---|
| New manual model | £11,000 | three-year-old manual | 11,000 × 0.41 = £4,510 |
| New automatic | £12,000 | three-year-old automatic | 12,000 × 0.40 = £4,800 |

Example: The claimant is 48. He drives a manual car of medium type whose price new is about £16,000. He drives about 10,000 miles a year and changes his car every three years. Because of his injury he now needs an automatic at a cost of £17,145. He is likely to stop driving in about 30 years.

Extra cost of automatic car:
On first purchase (from Table 3, column 3 above):                                                                 £1,145.00

Cost at each replacement of automatic (Table 1, row 3): 17,145 × 0.60 =   10,287.00
*less* cost at each replacement of manual                        16,000 × 0.59 =    9,440.00
Additional cost at each replacement                                                      £   847.00
Crude multiplier for replacements (Table A5, 27 years, three-yearly) 6.33
Multiplier for 27 years certain (Table A5, cont's loss)          19.71
Multiplier for man of 48 until age 75 (Table A1)                 18.42
Multiplier discounted for mortality        (6.33 × 18.42/19.71) =              5.92    £5,014.24

Extra cost per mile, petrol at 135.7 p/litre (Table 3, column 3) =
    1.42 + (6.7 × 0.012) = 1.50 pence
Extra running cost 10,000 miles pa                                                 £150.00
Crude multiplier (table A5, 30 years, cont's loss)          21.19
Multiplier discounted for mortality (21.19 × 18.42/19.71) =              19.80    £2,970.00

Total extra cost:                                                                                                       £9,129.24

L4: The costs of buying and replacing cars

## 5. Cost of additional mileage

The AA figures for *running* costs at Table L1 do not include depreciation. Mileage reduces the value of a car by a factor which varies with the type of car and its age on resale. Age on resale is not necessarily the length of time the claimant had the car. The categories A, B, C, etc. are derived from *Parker's Price Guide*.

The table may not be appropriate for mileages below 1,000 miles a year or above 30,000 miles a year.

### Table 4   Adjustment for depreciation for extra mileage

| Age on resale | Depreciation in pence per mile | | | | | | | |
|---|---|---|---|---|---|---|---|---|
| | A | B | C | D | E | F | G | H |
| 1 | 3.00 | 4.00 | 5.00 | 6.00 | 7.00 | 8.50 | 10.50 | 13.50 |
| 2 | 2.50 | 3.50 | 4.50 | 5.50 | 6.50 | 7.50 | 9.00 | 11.00 |
| 3 | 2.00 | 3.00 | 3.50 | 4.50 | 5.00 | 6.00 | 7.50 | 10.00 |
| 4 | 1.20 | 2.00 | 2.50 | 3.50 | 4.00 | 5.00 | 6.00 | 8.00 |
| 5 | 1.00 | 1.50 | 2.00 | 2.50 | 3.00 | 4.00 | 5.00 | 7.00 |
| 6 | 0.70 | 1.20 | 1.50 | 2.00 | 2.50 | 3.00 | 4.00 | 6.00 |
| 7 | 0.50 | 0.90 | 1.00 | 1.50 | 2.00 | 2.50 | 3.50 | 5.00 |
| 8 | 0.40 | 0.60 | 0.90 | 1.00 | 1.50 | 2.00 | 2.50 | 4.00 |

Example: The claimant would have had a car anyway. His mileage is increased by 4,000 miles a year because of his injury. He buys a one-year-old car and changes it after four years costing about £14,500 in category C in the mileage adjustment table. Petrol costs 135.7 pence per litre.

| | |
|---|---|
| Running cost per mile from AA figures (Table L1) | 21.14 pence |
| Adjustment for petrol price (from Table L1) (6.7p × 0.10) | 0.67 |
| Adjustment for mileage (category C, Four years old) | 2.50 |
| Total per mile | 24.31 pence |
| Total annual cost (4,000 × 24.31) | £972.40 |

## 6. Cost of professional servicing

Some claimants will have carried out the routine servicing of their cars themselves, but their injury may make that impracticable and they will in future need to have the car serviced professionally.

The resulting increased cost consists essentially in the labour element in the cost of servicing. Costs such as the cost of the Ministry of Transport test itself will remain the same and will not form an element of the loss. There will be *some* increase in the cost of materials such as replacement parts and oil, as these may be less expensive online or at a supermarket rather than at a garage. On the other hand, particularly with newer models, the more complex servicing tasks may not be feasible without specialised equipment, and so even mechanically minded car owners may be unable to do these jobs themselves. This section therefore takes the loss as equivalent to the cost of labour and treats these other factors as neutral overall.

Labour costs vary between main dealers and independent garages, and between different parts of the country. They are generally cheaper in the north and away from London, but do not conform to any clear pattern. In a 2011 survey Gwynedd was one of the most expensive areas, but Clwyd, not far away, was one of the cheapest. Also, as will be seen from the figures in Table L1: Motoring Costs, the most expensive cars involve higher labour costs but the cheapest cars to buy are not the cheapest to service. For those reasons it is not straightforward to try to produce figures independently on the basis of time estimates and hourly labour charges, and the editors recommend using the following figures derived from Table L1.

### Table 5 Additional cost of professional servicing

| | Additional cost in pence per mile | | | | |
|---|---|---|---|---|---|
| Cost of car new | Up to £13,000 | £13–18,000 | £18–25,000 | £25–32,000 | over £32,000 |
| Petrol cars | 2.10 | 2.07 | 2.09 | 2.04 | 2.34 |
| Cost of car new | Up to £16,000 | £16–22,000 | £22–26,000 | £26–36,000 | over £36,000 |
| Diesel cars | 2.10 | 2.14 | 2.29 | 2.24 | 2.76 |

Example: The same claimant as in section 5 used to do his own servicing and because of his injury is now unable to do so. His car cost £14,500 new. Before the accident he drove 12,000 miles a year, but because of the accident he must now drive a further 4,000 miles, making 16,000 miles in all. He incurs the additional cost of professional servicing, as well as the additional cost of extra mileage.

| | |
|---|---|
| Extra cost of professional servicing per mile | 2.07 pence |
| Annual cost (for *12,000* miles)    12,000 × 2.07 pence | £   241.40 |
| Cost of additional 4,000 mileage (from section 5 example) | £   972.40 |
| Total annual cost | £1,213.80 |

Note that the figure for running costs used to calculate the cost of additional mileage already includes service labour costs. The extra cost of servicing must therefore be based on the pre-accident 12,000 miles: there will be double counting if it is calculated on the basis of the post-accident 16,000 miles.

### 7. Cost of assessment

At the Banstead Mobility Centre in Surrey, the Queen Elizabeth Foundation for Disabled People conducts a variety of driving assessments, such as car adaptation assessments, for people with disabilities, and will provide a report. (See section M7 for address etc.) The centre also provides advice and training but does not provide costings or carry out adaptations itself.

The cost of an assessment for litigation purposes is £1,200 (including VAT).

There is a lower, subsidised, rate for individuals not requiring the report for litigation, but the Centre will then deal only with the client personally, and not with others such as solicitors or case managers.

Sections 2–5 are based on figures in *Parker's Car Price Guide* and from the websites of the Vehicle Certification Agency and the United States Department of Transportation.

## L5: Time, speed and distance

### Table of speeds and distances

| Speeds | | | Distances in yards | | | | | | | | | | | | | | | |
|---|---|---|---|---|---|---|---|---|---|---|---|---|---|---|---|---|---|---|
| mph | km/h | yd/sec | m/sec | 5 | 10 | 15 | 20 | 25 | 30 | 40 | 50 | 60 | 75 | 100 | 125 | 150 | 175 | 200 | 225 | 250 | 300 | 400 | 500 |
| 5 | 8.0 | 2.44 | 2.24 | 2.0 | 4.1 | 6.1 | 8.2 | 10.2 | 12.3 | 16.4 | 20.5 | 24.5 | 30.7 | 40.9 | 51.1 | 61.4 | 71.6 | 81.8 | 92.0 | 102.3 | 122.7 | 163.6 | 204.5 |
| 10 | 16.1 | 4.89 | 4.47 | 1.0 | 2.0 | 3.1 | 4.1 | 5.1 | 6.1 | 8.2 | 10.2 | 12.3 | 15.3 | 20.5 | 25.6 | 30.7 | 35.8 | 40.9 | 46.0 | 51.1 | 61.4 | 81.8 | 102.3 |
| 15 | 24.1 | 7.33 | 6.71 | 0.7 | 1.4 | 2.0 | 2.7 | 3.4 | 4.1 | 5.5 | 6.8 | 8.2 | 10.2 | 13.6 | 17.0 | 20.5 | 23.9 | 27.3 | 30.7 | 34.1 | 40.9 | 54.5 | 68.2 |
| 20 | 32.2 | 9.78 | 8.94 | 0.5 | 1.0 | 1.5 | 2.0 | 2.6 | 3.1 | 4.1 | 5.1 | 6.1 | 7.7 | 10.2 | 12.8 | 15.3 | 17.9 | 20.5 | 23.0 | 25.6 | 30.7 | 40.9 | 51.1 |
| 25 | 40.2 | 12.22 | 11.18 | 0.4 | 0.8 | 1.2 | 1.6 | 2.0 | 2.5 | 3.3 | 4.1 | 4.9 | 6.1 | 8.2 | 10.2 | 12.3 | 14.3 | 16.4 | 18.4 | 20.5 | 24.5 | 32.7 | 40.9 |
| 30 | 48.3 | 14.67 | 13.41 | 0.3 | 0.7 | 1.0 | 1.4 | 1.7 | 2.0 | 2.7 | 3.4 | 4.1 | 5.1 | 6.8 | 8.5 | 10.2 | 11.9 | 13.6 | 15.3 | 17.0 | 20.5 | 27.3 | 34.1 |
| 35 | 56.3 | 17.11 | 15.65 | 0.3 | 0.6 | 0.9 | 1.2 | 1.5 | 1.8 | 2.3 | 2.9 | 3.5 | 4.4 | 5.8 | 7.3 | 8.8 | 10.2 | 11.7 | 13.1 | 14.6 | 17.5 | 23.4 | 29.2 |
| 40 | 64.4 | 19.56 | 17.88 | 0.3 | 0.5 | 0.8 | 1.0 | 1.3 | 1.5 | 2.0 | 2.6 | 3.1 | 3.8 | 5.1 | 6.4 | 7.7 | 8.9 | 10.2 | 11.5 | 12.8 | 15.3 | 20.5 | 25.6 |
| 45 | 72.4 | 22.00 | 20.12 | 0.2 | 0.5 | 0.7 | 0.9 | 1.1 | 1.4 | 1.8 | 2.3 | 2.7 | 3.4 | 4.5 | 5.7 | 6.8 | 8.0 | 9.1 | 10.2 | 11.4 | 13.6 | 18.2 | 22.7 |
| 50 | 80.5 | 24.44 | 22.35 | 0.2 | 0.4 | 0.6 | 0.8 | 1.0 | 1.2 | 1.6 | 2.0 | 2.5 | 3.1 | 4.1 | 5.1 | 6.1 | 7.2 | 8.2 | 9.2 | 10.2 | 12.3 | 16.4 | 20.5 |
| 60 | 96.6 | 29.33 | 26.82 | 0.2 | 0.3 | 0.5 | 0.7 | 0.9 | 1.0 | 1.4 | 1.7 | 2.0 | 2.6 | 3.4 | 4.3 | 5.1 | 6.0 | 6.8 | 7.7 | 8.5 | 10.2 | 13.6 | 17.0 |
| 70 | 112.7 | 34.22 | 31.29 | 0.1 | 0.3 | 0.4 | 0.6 | 0.7 | 0.9 | 1.2 | 1.5 | 1.8 | 2.2 | 2.9 | 3.7 | 4.4 | 5.1 | 5.8 | 6.6 | 7.3 | 8.8 | 11.7 | 14.6 |
| 80 | 128.7 | 39.11 | 35.76 | 0.1 | 0.3 | 0.4 | 0.5 | 0.6 | 0.8 | 1.0 | 1.3 | 1.5 | 1.9 | 2.6 | 3.2 | 3.8 | 4.5 | 5.1 | 5.8 | 6.4 | 7.7 | 10.2 | 12.8 |
| 90 | 144.8 | 44.00 | 40.23 | 0.1 | 0.2 | 0.3 | 0.5 | 0.6 | 0.7 | 0.9 | 1.1 | 1.4 | 1.7 | 2.3 | 2.8 | 3.4 | 4.0 | 4.5 | 5.1 | 5.7 | 6.8 | 9.1 | 11.4 |
| 100 | 160.9 | 48.89 | 44.70 | 0.1 | 0.2 | 0.3 | 0.4 | 0.5 | 0.6 | 0.8 | 1.0 | 1.2 | 1.5 | 2.0 | 2.6 | 3.1 | 3.6 | 4.1 | 4.6 | 5.1 | 6.1 | 8.2 | 10.2 |

Seconds

# L5: Time, speed and distance

**Notes:**

1. The table shows the time taken to cover a given distance at a given speed, to the nearest $\frac{1}{10}$ second.

2. The table can also be used to ascertain the approximate speed of a vehicle, if the time and distance are known.

3. As an example, to find how long it would take to cover 125 yards at 35 mph, follow the vertical column down from the figure 125 and follow the horizontal row across from the figure 35: they meet at the figure 7.3, which is the number of seconds taken to cover the distance.

4. A speed of z miles per hour approximately equals [0.5z] yards per second.

5. The general formula for the number of seconds to cover a given distance at a given speed is approximately:

$$\frac{\text{distance in yards} \times 2.04545}{\text{speed in miles per hour}}$$

**Typical Stopping Distances (average car length = 4 metres)**

| Speed (mph) | Thinking Distance (metres) | Braking Distance (metres) | Total Stopping Distance (metres) | (car lengths) |
|---|---|---|---|---|
| 20 | 6 | 6 | 12 | 3 |
| 30 | 9 | 14 | 23 | 6 |
| 40 | 12 | 24 | 36 | 9 |
| 50 | 15 | 38 | 53 | 13 |
| 60 | 18 | 55 | 73 | 18 |
| 70 | 21 | 75 | 96 | 24 |

Extracted from *The Highway Code*, published by The Stationery Office.

# Group M
*Other Information*

M1: **Senior Court Costs Office Guideline Rates for Summary Assessment**

M2: **Conversion formulae**

M3: **Perpetual calendar**

M4: **Religious festivals**

M5: **Medical reference intervals and scales**

M6: **Websites**

M7: **Useful organisations**

# M1: Senior Court Costs Office Guideline Rates for Summary Assessment

| Band One | A | B | C | D |
|---|---|---|---|---|
| 2011–present | 217 | 192 | 161 | 118 |
| 2010 | 217 | 192 | 161 | 118 |
| 2009 | 213 | 189 | 158 | 116 |
| 2008 | 203 | 180 | 151 | 110 |
| 2007 | 195 | 173 | 145 | 106 |

Aldershot, Farnham, Bournemouth (including Poole), Birmingham Inner, Bristol, Cambridge City, Harlow, Canterbury, Maidstone, Medway and Tunbridge Wells, Cardiff (Inner), Chelmsford South, Essex and East Suffolk, Chester, Fareham, Winchester, Hampshire, Dorset, Wiltshire, Isle of Wight, Kingston, Guildford, Reigate, Epsom, Leeds Inner (within two-kilometres radius of the City Art Gallery), Lewes, Liverpool, Birkenhead, Manchester Central, Newcastle—City Centre (within a two-mile radius of St Nicholas Cathedral), Norwich City, Nottingham City, Oxford, Thames Valley, Southampton, Portsmouth, Swindon, Basingstoke, Watford.

| Band Two | A | B | C | D |
|---|---|---|---|---|
| 2011–present | 201 | 177 | 146 | 111 |
| 2010 | 201 | 177 | 146 | 111 |
| 2009 | 198 | 174 | 144 | 109 |
| 2008 | 191 | 168 | 139 | 105 |
| 2007 | 183 | 161 | 133 | 101 |

Bath, Cheltenham and Gloucester, Taunton, Yeovil, Bury, Chelmsford North, Cambridge County, Peterborough, Bury St E, Norfolk, Lowestoft, Cheshire and North Wales, Coventry, Rugby, Nuneaton, Stratford and Warwick, Exeter, Plymouth, Hull (City), Leeds Outer, Wakefield and Pontefract, Leigh, Lincoln, Luton, Bedford, St Albans, Hitchin, Hertford, Manchester Outer, Oldham, Bolton, Tameside, Newcastle (other than City Centre), Nottingham and Derbyshire, Sheffield, Doncaster and South Yorkshire, Southport, St Helens, Stockport, Altrincham, Salford, Swansea, Newport, Cardiff (Outer), Wigan, Wolverhampton, Walsall, Dudley and Stourbridge, York, Harrogate.

| Band Three | A | B | C | D |
|---|---|---|---|---|
| 2011–present | 201 | 177 | 146 | 111 |
| 2010 | 201 | 177 | 146 | 111 |
| 2009 | 198 | 174 | 144 | 109 |
| 2008 | 174 | 156 | 133 | 99 |
| 2007 | 167 | 150 | 128 | 95 |

Birmingham Outer, Bradford (Dewsbury, Halifax, Huddersfield, Keighley and Skipton), Cumbria, Devon, Cornwall, Grimsby, Skegness, Hull Outer, Kidderminster, Northampton and Leicester, Preston, Lancaster, Blackpool, Chorley, Accrington, Burnley, Blackburn, Rawenstall and Nelson, Scarborough and Ripon, Stafford, Stoke, Tamworth, Teesside, Worcester, Hereford, Evesham and Redditch, Shrewsbury, Telford, Ludlow, Oswestry, South and West Wales.

| London City [EC1–4] | A | B | C | D |
|---|---|---|---|---|
| 2011–present | 409 | 296 | 226 | 138 |
| 2010 | 409 | 296 | 226 | 138 |
| 2009 | 402 | 291 | 222 | 136 |
| 2008 | 396 | 285 | 219 | 134 |
| 2007 | 380 | 274 | 210 | 129 |

M1: Senior Court Costs Office Guideline Rates for Summary Assessment

| London Central [W1, WC1, WC2, SW1] | A | B | C | D |
|---|---|---|---|---|
| 2011–present | 317 | 242 | 196 | 126 |
| 2010 | 317 | 242 | 196 | 126 |
| 2009 | 312 | 238 | 193 | 124 |
| 2008 | 304 | 231 | 189 | 121 |
| 2007 | 292 | 222 | 181 | 116 |
| London Outer [N, E, SE, W, SW, NW, Bromley, Croydon, Dartford, Gravesend and Uxbridge] | A | B | C | D |
| 2011–present | 229–267 | 172–229 | 165 | 121 |
| 2010 | 229–267 | 172–229 | 165 | 121 |
| 2009 | 263–225 | 225–169 | 162 | 119 |
| 2008 | 256–219 | 219–165 | 158 | 116 |
| 2007 | 246–210 | 210–158 | 152 | 111 |

A – Solicitors and Fellows of CILEx with over eight years' post-qualification experience including at least eight years' litigation experience.
B – Solicitors, legal executives and costs lawyers with over four years' post-qualification experience including at least four years' litigation experience.
C – Other solicitors and legal executives, costs lawyers and fee earners of equivalent experience.
D – Trainee solicitors, paralegals and fee earners of equivalent experience.
Note: "Legal Executive" means a Fellow of the Institute of Legal Executives.

**Entitlement to VAT on Costs**

| DATE | VAT RATE |
|---|---|
| 1 April 1991–30 November 2008 | 17.5% |
| 1 December 2008–31 December 2009 | 15% |
| 1 January 2010–3 January 2011 | 17.5% |
| 4 January 2011 to date | 20% |

**Costs PD 44 para.2.3** deals with entitlement to VAT on Costs. It provides:

"VAT should not be included in a claim for costs if the receiving party is able to recover the VAT as input tax. Where the receiving party is able to obtain credit from HM Revenue and Customs for a proportion of the VAT as input tax, only that proportion which is not eligible for credit should be included in the claim for costs."

**Costs PD 44 para.2.7** deals with the form of a Bill of Costs where the VAT Rate changes. It provides:

"Where there is a change in the rate of VAT, suppliers of goods and services are entitled by ss.88(1) and 88(2) of the VAT Act 1994 in most circumstances to elect whether the new or the old rate of VAT should apply to a supply where the basic and actual tax points span a period during which there has been a change in VAT rates."

**Costs PD 44 para.2.8** provides:

"It will be assumed, unless a contrary indication is given in writing, that an election to take advantage of the provisions mentioned in paragraph 2.7 and to charge VAT at the lower rate has been made. In any case in which an election to charge at the lower rate is not made, such a decision must be justified to the court assessing the costs."

**Costs PD 44 para.2.9** deals with apportionment. It provides:

"Subject to 2.7 & 2.8 all bills of costs, fees and disbursements on which VAT is included must be divided into separate parts so as to show work done before, on and after the date or dates from which any change in the rate of VAT takes effect. Where, however, a lump sum charge is made for work which spans a period during which there has been a change in VAT rates, and paragraphs 2.7 and 2.8 above do not apply, reference should be made to paragraphs 30.7 or 30.8 of the VAT Guide (Notice 700) (or any revised edition of that notice) published by HMRC. If necessary, the lump sum should be apportioned. The totals of profit costs and disbursements in each part must be carried separately to the summary."

## M2: Conversion formulae

|  | To convert | Multiply by |
|---|---|---|
| Area | square inches to square centimetres | 6.452 |
|  | square centimetres to square inches | 0.1555 |
|  | square metres to square feet | 10.7638 |
|  | square feet to square metres | 0.0929 |
|  | square yards to square metres | 0.8361 |
|  | square metres to square yards | 1.196 |
|  | square miles to square kilometres | 2.590 |
|  | square kilometres to square miles | 0.3861 |
|  | acres to hectares | 0.4047 |
|  | hectares to acres | 2.471 |
| Length | inches to centimetres | 2.540 |
|  | centimetres to inches | 0.3937 |
|  | feet to metres | 0.3048 |
|  | metres to feet | 3.281 |
|  | yards to metres | 0.9144 |
|  | metres to yards | 1.094 |
|  | miles to kilometres | 1.609 |
|  | kilometres to miles | 0.6214 |
| Temperature | Centigrade to Fahrenheit | $\times 9 \div 5 + 32$ |
|  | Fahrenheit to Centigrade | $-32 \times 5 \div 9$ |
| Volume | cubic inches to cubic centimetres | 16.39 |
|  | cubic centimetres to cubic inches | 0.06102 |
|  | cubic feet to cubic metres | 0.02832 |
|  | cubic metres to cubic feet | 35.31 |
|  | cubic yards to cubic metres | 0.7646 |
|  | cubic metres to cubic yards | 1.308 |
|  | cubic inches to litres | 0.01639 |
|  | litres to cubic inches | 61.024 |

# M2: Conversion formulae

|  | To convert | Multiply by |
|---|---|---|
| Weight | gallon to litres | 4.545 |
|  | litres to gallons | 0.22 |
|  | grains to grams | 0.0647 |
|  | grams to grains | 15.43 |
|  | ounces to grams | 28.35 |
|  | grams to ounces | 0.03527 |
|  | pounds to grams | 453.592 |
|  | grams to pounds | 0.0022 |
|  | pounds to kilograms | 0.4536 |
|  | kilograms to pounds | 2.2046 |
|  | tons to kilograms | 1016.05 |
|  | kilograms to tons | 0.0009842 |
| Speed | miles per hour to kilometres per hour | 1.6093 |
|  | kilometres per hour to miles per hour | 0.6214 |
| Fuel cost | pence per litre to pounds per gallon | 0.045 |
|  | pounds per gallon to pence per litre | 22.00 |
| USA measures | Dry USA pint to UK pint | 0.9689 |
|  | UK pint to USA pint | 1.1032 |
|  | USA pint to litres | 0.5506 |
|  | litres to USA pint | 1.816 |
|  | USA bushel to UK bushel | 0.9689 |
|  | UK bushel to USA bushel | 1.032 |
|  | USA bushel to litres | 35.238 |
|  | litres to USA bushel | 0.0283 |
|  | Liquid USA pint (16 fl oz) to UK pint | 0.8327 |
|  | UK pint to USA pint | 1.2 |
|  | USA pint to litres | 0.4732 |
|  | litres to USA pint | 2.113 |
|  | USA gallon to UK gallon | 0.8327 |
|  | UK gallon to USA gallon | 1.2 |
|  | USA gallon to litres | 3.7853 |
|  | litres to USA gallons | 0.2641 |

# M2: Conversion formulae

## Clothing

### Shirts

| UK/USA | 14 | 14½ | 15 | 15½ | 16 | 16½ | 17 | 17½ |
|---|---|---|---|---|---|---|---|---|
| Europe | 36 | 37 | 38 | 39 | 40 | 41 | 42 | 43 |

### Ladies clothes

| UK | | | | | | | |
|---|---|---|---|---|---|---|---|
| Size code | 10 | 12 | 14 | 16 | 18 | 20 | 22 |
| Bust/hip inches | 32/34 | 34/36 | 36/38 | 38/40 | 40/42 | 42/44 | 44/46 |
| Bust/hip cm | 84/89 | 88/93 | 92/97 | 97/102 | 102/107 | 107/112 | 112/117 |
| **USA** | | | | | | | |
| Size code | 6 | 8 | 10 | 12 | 14 | 16 | 18 |
| Bust/hip inches | 34½/36½ | 35½/37½ | 36½/38½ | 37½/39½ | 38/40 | 39½/41½ | 41/43 |

*European sizes vary from country to country*

### Footwear—Men

| British | 6 | 7 | 8 | 9 | 10 | 11 | 12 |
|---|---|---|---|---|---|---|---|
| American | 6½ | 7½ | 8½ | 9½ | 10½ | 11½ | 12½ |
| Continental | 40 | 41 | 42 | 43 | 44 | 45 | 46 |

### Footwear—Women

| British | 3 | 4 | 5 | 6 | 7 | 8 | 9 |
|---|---|---|---|---|---|---|---|
| American | 4½ | 5½ | 6½ | 7½ | 8½ | 9½ | 10½ |
| Continental | 36 | 37 | 38 | 39 | 40 | 42 | 43 |

### Children's clothes

| UK | | | | | | | | | | | | |
|---|---|---|---|---|---|---|---|---|---|---|---|---|
| Age | 1 | 2 | 3 | 4 | 5 | 6 | 7 | 8 | 9 | 10 | 11 | 12 |
| Height/inches | 32 | 36 | 38 | 40 | 43 | 45 | 48 | 50 | 53 | 55 | 58 | 60 |
| Height/cm | 80 | 92 | 98 | 104 | 110 | 116 | 122 | 128 | 134 | 140 | 146 | 152 |
| **USA** | | | | | | | | | | | | |
| Boys' size code | 1 | 2 | 3 | 4 | 5 | 6 | 8 | | 10 | | 12 | |
| Girls' size code | 2 | 3 | 4 | 5 | 6 | 6x | 7 | 8 | 10 | | 12 | |
| **Europe** | | | | | | | | | | | | |
| Height/cm | 80 | 92 | 98 | 104 | 110 | 116 | 122 | 128 | 134 | 140 | 146 | 152 |

# M3: Perpetual calendar

The number opposite each of the years in the list below indicates which of the calendars on the following pages is the one for that year. Thus the number opposite 2000 is 14, so calendar 14 can be used as a 2000 calendar.

## Leap years

Years divisible by four without remainder are leap years with 366 days instead of 365 (29 days in February instead of 28). However, the first year of the century is not a leap year except when divisible by 400.

| Year | Calendar | Year | Calendar | Year | Calendar | Year | Calendar | Year | Calendar | Year | Calendar |
|---|---|---|---|---|---|---|---|---|---|---|---|
| 1980 | 10 | 1992 | 11 | 2004 | 12 | 2016 | 13 | 2028 | 14 | 2040 | 8 |
| 1981 | 5 | 1993 | 6 | 2005 | 7 | 2017 | 1 | 2029 | 2 | 2041 | 3 |
| 1982 | 6 | 1994 | 7 | 2006 | 1 | 2018 | 2 | 2030 | 3 | 2042 | 4 |
| 1983 | 7 | 1995 | 1 | 2007 | 2 | 2019 | 3 | 2031 | 4 | 2043 | 5 |
| 1984 | 8 | 1996 | 9 | 2008 | 10 | 2020 | 11 | 2032 | 12 | 2044 | 13 |
| 1985 | 3 | 1997 | 4 | 2009 | 5 | 2021 | 6 | 2033 | 7 | 2045 | 1 |
| 1986 | 4 | 1998 | 5 | 2010 | 6 | 2022 | 7 | 2034 | 1 | 2046 | 2 |
| 1987 | 5 | 1999 | 6 | 2011 | 7 | 2023 | 1 | 2035 | 2 | 2047 | 3 |
| 1988 | 13 | 2000 | 14 | 2012 | 8 | 2024 | 9 | 2036 | 10 | 2048 | 11 |
| 1989 | 1 | 2001 | 2 | 2013 | 3 | 2025 | 4 | 2037 | 5 | 2049 | 6 |
| 1990 | 2 | 2002 | 3 | 2014 | 4 | 2026 | 5 | 2038 | 6 | 2050 | 7 |
| 1991 | 3 | 2003 | 4 | 2015 | 5 | 2027 | 6 | 2039 | 7 | 2051 | 1 |

## 1

### January
- M: 2 9 16 23 30
- T: 3 10 17 24 31
- W: 4 11 18 25
- T: 5 12 19 26
- F: 6 13 20 27
- S: 7 14 21 28
- S: 1 8 15 22 29

### February
- M: 6 13 20 27
- T: 7 14 21 28
- W: 1 8 15 22
- T: 2 9 16 23
- F: 3 10 17 24
- S: 4 11 18 25
- S: 5 12 19 26

### March
- M: 6 13 20 27
- T: 7 14 21 28
- W: 1 8 15 22 29
- T: 2 9 16 23 30
- F: 3 10 17 24 31
- S: 4 11 18 25
- S: 5 12 19 26

### April
- M: 3 10 17 24
- T: 4 11 18 25
- W: 5 12 19 26
- T: 6 13 20 27
- F: 7 14 21 28
- S: 1 8 15 22 29
- S: 2 9 16 23 30

### May
- M: 1 8 15 22 29
- T: 2 9 16 23 30
- W: 3 10 17 24 31
- T: 4 11 18 25
- F: 5 12 19 26
- S: 6 13 20 27
- S: 7 14 21 28

### June
- M: 5 12 19 26
- T: 6 13 20 27
- W: 7 14 21 28
- T: 1 8 15 22 29
- F: 2 9 16 23 30
- S: 3 10 17 24
- S: 4 11 18 25

### July
- M: 3 10 17 24 31
- T: 4 11 18 25
- W: 5 12 19 26
- T: 6 13 20 27
- F: 7 14 21 28
- S: 1 8 15 22 29
- S: 2 9 16 23 30

### August
- M: 7 14 21 28
- T: 1 8 15 22 29
- W: 2 9 16 23 30
- T: 3 10 17 24 31
- F: 4 11 18 25
- S: 5 12 19 26
- S: 6 13 20 27

### September
- M: 4 11 18 25
- T: 5 12 19 26
- W: 6 13 20 27
- T: 7 14 21 28
- F: 1 8 15 22 29
- S: 2 9 16 23 30
- S: 3 10 17 24

### October
- M: 2 9 16 23 30
- T: 3 10 17 24 31
- W: 4 11 18 25
- T: 5 12 19 26
- F: 6 13 20 27
- S: 7 14 21 28
- S: 1 8 15 22 29

### November
- M: 6 13 20 27
- T: 7 14 21 28
- W: 1 8 15 22 29
- T: 2 9 16 23 30
- F: 3 10 17 24
- S: 4 11 18 25
- S: 5 12 19 26

### December
- M: 4 11 18 25
- T: 5 12 19 26
- W: 6 13 20 27
- T: 7 14 21 28
- F: 1 8 15 22 29
- S: 2 9 16 23 30
- S: 3 10 17 24 31

## 2

### January
- M: 1 8 15 22 29
- T: 2 9 16 23 30
- W: 3 10 17 24 31
- T: 4 11 18 25
- F: 5 12 19 26
- S: 6 13 20 27
- S: 7 14 21 28

### February
- M: 5 12 19 26
- T: 6 13 20 27
- W: 7 14 21 28
- T: 1 8 15 22
- F: 2 9 16 23
- S: 3 10 17 24
- S: 4 11 18 25

### March
- M: 5 12 19 26
- T: 6 13 20 27
- W: 7 14 21 28
- T: 1 8 15 22 29
- F: 2 9 16 23 30
- S: 3 10 17 24 31
- S: 4 11 18 25

### April
- M: 2 9 16 23 30
- T: 3 10 17 24
- W: 4 11 18 25
- T: 5 12 19 26
- F: 6 13 20 27
- S: 7 14 21 28
- S: 1 8 15 22 29

### May
- M: 7 14 21 28
- T: 1 8 15 22 29
- W: 2 9 16 23 30
- T: 3 10 17 24 31
- F: 4 11 18 25
- S: 5 12 19 26
- S: 6 13 20 27

### June
- M: 4 11 18 25
- T: 5 12 19 26
- W: 6 13 20 27
- T: 7 14 21 28
- F: 1 8 15 22 29
- S: 2 9 16 23 30
- S: 3 10 17 24

### July
- M: 2 9 16 23 30
- T: 3 10 17 24 31
- W: 4 11 18 25
- T: 5 12 19 26
- F: 6 13 20 27
- S: 7 14 21 28
- S: 1 8 15 22 29

### August
- M: 6 13 20 27
- T: 7 14 21 28
- W: 1 8 15 22 29
- T: 2 9 16 23 30
- F: 3 10 17 24 31
- S: 4 11 18 25
- S: 5 12 19 26

### September
- M: 3 10 17 24
- T: 4 11 18 25
- W: 5 12 19 26
- T: 6 13 20 27
- F: 7 14 21 28
- S: 1 8 15 22 29
- S: 2 9 16 23 30

### October
- M: 1 8 15 22 29
- T: 2 9 16 23 30
- W: 3 10 17 24 31
- T: 4 11 18 25
- F: 5 12 19 26
- S: 6 13 20 27
- S: 7 14 21 28

### November
- M: 5 12 19 26
- T: 6 13 20 27
- W: 7 14 21 28
- T: 1 8 15 22 29
- F: 2 9 16 23 30
- S: 3 10 17 24
- S: 4 11 18 25

### December
- M: 3 10 17 24 31
- T: 4 11 18 25
- W: 5 12 19 26
- T: 6 13 20 27
- F: 7 14 21 28
- S: 1 8 15 22 29
- S: 2 9 16 23 30

# M3: Perpetual calendar

## 3

|   | January | February | March | April |
|---|---|---|---|---|
| M |   7 14 21 28 |   4 11 18 25 |   4 11 18 25 | 1  8 15 22 29 |
| T | 1  8 15 22 29 | 5 12 19 26 | 5 12 19 26 | 2  9 16 23 30 |
| W | 2  9 16 23 30 | 6 13 20 27 | 6 13 20 27 | 3 10 17 24 |
| T | 3 10 17 24 31 | 7 14 21 28 | 7 14 21 28 | 4 11 18 25 |
| F | 4 11 18 25 | 1  8 15 22 | 1  8 15 22 29 | 5 12 19 26 |
| S | 5 12 19 26 | 2  9 16 23 | 2  9 16 23 30 | 6 13 20 27 |
| S | 6 13 20 27 | 3 10 17 24 | 3 10 17 24 31 | 7 14 21 28 |

|   | May | June | July | August |
|---|---|---|---|---|
| M |   6 13 20 27 |   3 10 17 24 | 1  8 15 22 29 | 5 12 19 26 |
| T |   7 14 21 28 | 4 11 18 25 | 2  9 16 23 30 | 6 13 20 27 |
| W | 1  8 15 22 29 | 5 12 19 26 | 3 10 17 24 31 | 7 14 21 28 |
| T | 2  9 16 23 30 | 6 13 20 27 | 4 11 18 25 | 1  8 15 22 29 |
| F | 3 10 17 24 31 | 7 14 21 28 | 5 12 19 26 | 2  9 16 23 30 |
| S | 4 11 18 25 | 1  8 15 22 29 | 6 13 20 27 | 3 10 17 24 31 |
| S | 5 12 19 26 | 2  9 16 23 30 | 7 14 21 28 | 4 11 18 25 |

|   | September | October | November | December |
|---|---|---|---|---|
| M |   2  9 16 23 30 |   7 14 21 28 |   4 11 18 25 | 2  9 16 23 30 |
| T | 3 10 17 24 | 1  8 15 22 29 | 5 12 19 26 | 3 10 17 24 31 |
| W | 4 11 18 25 | 2  9 16 23 30 | 6 13 20 27 | 4 11 18 25 |
| T | 5 12 19 26 | 3 10 17 24 31 | 7 14 21 28 | 5 12 19 26 |
| F | 6 13 20 27 | 4 11 18 25 | 1  8 15 22 29 | 6 13 20 27 |
| S | 7 14 21 28 | 5 12 19 26 | 2  9 16 23 30 | 7 14 21 28 |
| S | 1  8 15 22 29 | 6 13 20 27 | 3 10 17 24 | 1  8 15 22 29 |

## 4

|   | January | February | March | April |
|---|---|---|---|---|
| M |   6 13 20 27 |   3 10 17 24 |   3 10 17 24 31 |   7 14 21 28 |
| T |   7 14 21 28 | 4 11 18 25 | 4 11 18 25 | 1  8 15 22 29 |
| W | 1  8 15 22 29 | 5 12 19 26 | 5 12 19 26 | 2  9 16 23 30 |
| T | 2  9 16 23 | 6 13 20 27 | 6 13 20 27 | 3 10 17 24 |
| F | 3 10 17 24 31 | 7 14 21 28 | 7 14 21 28 | 4 11 18 25 |
| S | 4 11 18 25 | 1  8 15 22 | 1  8 15 22 29 | 5 12 19 26 |
| S | 5 12 19 26 | 2  9 16 23 | 2  9 16 23 30 | 6 13 20 27 |

|   | May | June | July | August |
|---|---|---|---|---|
| M |   5 12 19 26 | 2  9 16 23 30 |   7 14 21 28 | 4 11 18 25 |
| T |   6 13 20 27 | 3 10 17 24 | 1  8 15 22 29 | 5 12 19 26 |
| W |   7 14 21 28 | 4 11 18 25 | 2  9 16 23 30 | 6 13 20 27 |
| T | 1  8 15 22 29 | 5 12 19 26 | 3 10 17 24 31 | 7 14 21 28 |
| F | 2  9 16 23 30 | 6 13 20 27 | 4 11 18 25 | 1  8 15 22 29 |
| S | 3 10 17 24 31 | 7 14 21 28 | 5 12 19 26 | 2  9 16 23 30 |
| S | 4 11 18 25 | 1  8 15 22 29 | 6 13 20 27 | 3 10 17 24 31 |

|   | September | October | November | December |
|---|---|---|---|---|
| M | 1  8 15 22 29 |   6 13 20 27 |   3 10 17 24 | 1  8 15 22 29 |
| T | 2  9 16 23 30 |   7 14 21 28 | 4 11 18 25 | 2  9 16 23 30 |
| W | 3 10 17 24 | 1  8 15 22 29 | 5 12 19 26 | 3 10 17 24 31 |
| T | 4 11 18 25 | 2  9 16 23 30 | 6 13 20 27 | 4 11 18 25 |
| F | 5 12 19 26 | 3 10 17 24 31 | 7 14 21 28 | 5 12 19 26 |
| S | 6 13 20 27 | 4 11 18 25 | 1  8 15 22 29 | 6 13 20 27 |
| S | 7 14 21 28 | 5 12 19 26 | 2  9 16 23 30 | 7 14 21 28 |

## 5

|   | January | February | March | April |
|---|---|---|---|---|
| M |   5 12 19 26 |   2  9 16 23 |   2  9 16 23 30 | 6 13 20 27 |
| T |   6 13 20 27 | 3 10 17 24 | 3 10 17 24 31 | 7 14 21 28 |
| W |   7 14 21 28 | 4 11 18 25 | 4 11 18 25 | 1  8 15 22 29 |
| T | 1  8 15 22 29 | 5 12 19 26 | 5 12 19 26 | 2  9 16 23 30 |
| F | 2  9 16 23 30 | 6 13 20 27 | 6 13 20 27 | 3 10 17 24 |
| S | 3 10 17 24 31 | 7 14 21 28 | 7 14 21 28 | 4 11 18 25 |
| S | 4 11 18 25 | 1  8 15 22 | 1  8 15 22 29 | 5 12 19 26 |

|   | May | June | July | August |
|---|---|---|---|---|
| M |   4 11 18 25 | 1  8 15 22 29 |   6 13 20 27 | 3 10 17 24 31 |
| T |   5 12 19 26 | 2  9 16 23 30 |   7 14 21 28 | 4 11 18 25 |
| W |   6 13 20 27 | 3 10 17 24 | 1  8 15 22 29 | 5 12 19 26 |
| T |   7 14 21 28 | 4 11 18 25 | 2  9 16 23 30 | 6 13 20 27 |
| F | 1  8 15 22 29 | 5 12 19 26 | 3 10 17 24 31 | 7 14 21 28 |
| S | 2  9 16 23 30 | 6 13 20 27 | 4 11 18 25 | 1  8 15 22 29 |
| S | 3 10 17 24 31 | 7 14 21 28 | 5 12 19 26 | 2  9 16 23 30 |

|   | September | October | November | December |
|---|---|---|---|---|
| M |   7 14 21 28 |   5 12 19 26 | 2  9 16 23 30 |   7 14 21 28 |
| T | 1  8 15 22 29 |   6 13 20 27 | 3 10 17 24 | 1  8 15 22 29 |
| W | 2  9 16 23 30 |   7 14 21 28 | 4 11 18 25 | 2  9 16 23 30 |
| T | 3 10 17 24 | 1  8 15 22 29 | 5 12 19 26 | 3 10 17 24 31 |
| F | 4 11 18 25 | 2  9 16 23 30 | 6 13 20 27 | 4 11 18 25 |
| S | 5 12 19 26 | 3 10 17 24 31 | 7 14 21 28 | 5 12 19 26 |
| S | 6 13 20 27 | 4 11 18 25 | 1  8 15 22 29 | 6 13 20 27 |

## 6

|   | January | February | March | April |
|---|---|---|---|---|
| M |   4 11 18 25 | 1  8 15 22 | 1  8 15 22 29 | 5 12 19 26 |
| T |   5 12 19 26 | 2  9 16 23 | 2  9 16 23 30 | 6 13 20 27 |
| W |   6 13 20 27 | 3 10 17 24 | 3 10 17 24 31 | 7 14 21 28 |
| T |   7 14 21 28 | 4 11 18 25 | 4 11 18 25 | 1  8 15 22 29 |
| F | 1  8 15 22 29 | 5 12 19 26 | 5 12 19 26 | 2  9 16 23 30 |
| S | 2  9 16 23 30 | 6 13 20 27 | 6 13 20 27 | 3 10 17 24 |
| S | 3 10 17 24 31 | 7 14 21 28 | 7 14 21 28 | 4 11 18 25 |

|   | May | June | July | August |
|---|---|---|---|---|
| M |   3 10 17 24 31 |   7 14 21 28 |   5 12 19 26 | 2  9 16 23 30 |
| T |   4 11 18 25 | 1  8 15 22 29 |   6 13 20 27 | 3 10 17 24 31 |
| W |   5 12 19 26 | 2  9 16 23 30 |   7 14 21 28 | 4 11 18 25 |
| T |   6 13 20 27 | 3 10 17 24 | 1  8 15 22 29 | 5 12 19 26 |
| F |   7 14 21 28 | 4 11 18 25 | 2  9 16 23 30 | 6 13 20 27 |
| S | 1  8 15 22 29 | 5 12 19 26 | 3 10 17 24 31 | 7 14 21 28 |
| S | 2  9 16 23 30 | 6 13 20 27 | 4 11 18 25 | 1  8 15 22 29 |

|   | September | October | November | December |
|---|---|---|---|---|
| M |   6 13 20 27 |   4 11 18 25 | 1  8 15 22 29 |   6 13 20 27 |
| T |   7 14 21 28 |   5 12 19 26 | 2  9 16 23 30 |   7 14 21 28 |
| W | 1  8 15 22 29 |   6 13 20 27 | 3 10 17 24 | 1  8 15 22 29 |
| T | 2  9 16 23 30 |   7 14 21 28 | 4 11 18 25 | 2  9 16 23 30 |
| F | 3 10 17 24 | 1  8 15 22 29 | 5 12 19 26 | 3 10 17 24 31 |
| S | 4 11 18 25 | 2  9 16 23 30 | 6 13 20 27 | 4 11 18 25 |
| S | 5 12 19 26 | 3 10 17 24 31 | 7 14 21 28 | 5 12 19 26 |

## 7

|   | January | February | March | April |
|---|---|---|---|---|
| M |   3 10 17 24 31 |   7 14 21 28 |   7 14 21 28 | 4 11 18 25 |
| T |   4 11 18 25 | 1  8 15 22 | 1  8 15 22 29 | 5 12 19 26 |
| W |   5 12 19 26 | 2  9 16 23 | 2  9 16 23 30 | 6 13 20 27 |
| T |   6 13 20 27 | 3 10 17 24 | 3 10 17 24 31 | 7 14 21 28 |
| F |   7 14 21 28 | 4 11 18 25 | 4 11 18 25 | 1  8 15 22 29 |
| S | 1  8 15 22 29 | 5 12 19 26 | 5 12 19 26 | 2  9 16 23 30 |
| S | 2  9 16 23 30 | 6 13 20 27 | 6 13 20 27 | 3 10 17 24 |

|   | May | June | July | August |
|---|---|---|---|---|
| M |   2  9 16 23 30 |   6 13 20 27 |   4 11 18 25 | 1  8 15 22 29 |
| T |   3 10 17 24 31 |   7 14 21 28 |   5 12 19 26 | 2  9 16 23 30 |
| W |   4 11 18 25 | 1  8 15 22 29 |   6 13 20 27 | 3 10 17 24 31 |
| T |   5 12 19 26 | 2  9 16 23 30 |   7 14 21 28 | 4 11 18 25 |
| F |   6 13 20 27 | 3 10 17 24 | 1  8 15 22 29 | 5 12 19 26 |
| S |   7 14 21 28 | 4 11 18 25 | 2  9 16 23 30 | 6 13 20 27 |
| S | 1  8 15 22 29 | 5 12 19 26 | 3 10 17 24 31 | 7 14 21 28 |

|   | September | October | November | December |
|---|---|---|---|---|
| M |   5 12 19 26 |   3 10 17 24 31 |   7 14 21 28 |   5 12 19 26 |
| T |   6 13 20 27 |   4 11 18 25 | 1  8 15 22 29 |   6 13 20 27 |
| W |   7 14 21 28 |   5 12 19 26 | 2  9 16 23 30 |   7 14 21 28 |
| T | 1  8 15 22 29 |   6 13 20 27 | 3 10 17 24 | 1  8 15 22 29 |
| F | 2  9 16 23 30 |   7 14 21 28 | 4 11 18 25 | 2  9 16 23 30 |
| S | 3 10 17 24 | 1  8 15 22 29 | 5 12 19 26 | 3 10 17 24 31 |
| S | 4 11 18 25 | 2  9 16 23 30 | 6 13 20 27 | 4 11 18 25 |

## 8

|   | January | February | March | April |
|---|---|---|---|---|
| M |   2  9 16 23 30 |   6 13 20 27 |   5 12 19 26 | 2  9 16 23 30 |
| T |   3 10 17 24 31 |   7 14 21 28 |   6 13 20 27 | 3 10 17 24 |
| W |   4 11 18 25 | 1  8 15 22 29 |   7 14 21 28 | 4 11 18 25 |
| T |   5 12 19 26 | 2  9 16 23 | 1  8 15 22 29 | 5 12 19 26 |
| F |   6 13 20 27 | 3 10 17 24 | 2  9 16 23 30 | 6 13 20 27 |
| S |   7 14 21 28 | 4 11 18 25 | 3 10 17 24 31 | 7 14 21 28 |
| S | 1  8 15 22 29 | 5 12 19 26 | 4 11 18 25 | 1  8 15 22 29 |

|   | May | June | July | August |
|---|---|---|---|---|
| M |   7 14 21 28 |   4 11 18 25 | 2  9 16 23 30 |   6 13 20 27 |
| T | 1  8 15 22 29 |   5 12 19 26 | 3 10 17 24 31 |   7 14 21 28 |
| W | 2  9 16 23 30 |   6 13 20 27 | 4 11 18 25 | 1  8 15 22 29 |
| T | 3 10 17 24 31 |   7 14 21 28 | 5 12 19 26 | 2  9 16 23 30 |
| F | 4 11 18 25 | 1  8 15 22 29 | 6 13 20 27 | 3 10 17 24 31 |
| S | 5 12 19 26 | 2  9 16 23 30 | 7 14 21 28 | 4 11 18 25 |
| S | 6 13 20 27 | 3 10 17 24 | 1  8 15 22 29 | 5 12 19 26 |

|   | September | October | November | December |
|---|---|---|---|---|
| M |   3 10 17 24 | 1  8 15 22 29 |   5 12 19 26 | 3 10 17 24 31 |
| T |   4 11 18 25 | 2  9 16 23 30 |   6 13 20 27 | 4 11 18 25 |
| W |   5 12 19 26 | 3 10 17 24 31 |   7 14 21 28 | 5 12 19 26 |
| T |   6 13 20 27 | 4 11 18 25 | 1  8 15 22 29 | 6 13 20 27 |
| F |   7 14 21 28 | 5 12 19 26 | 2  9 16 23 30 | 7 14 21 28 |
| S | 1  8 15 22 29 | 6 13 20 27 | 3 10 17 24 | 1  8 15 22 29 |
| S | 2  9 16 23 30 | 7 14 21 28 | 4 11 18 25 | 2  9 16 23 30 |

# M3: Perpetual calendar

## 9

|   | January | February | March | April |
|---|---|---|---|---|
| M | 1 8 15 22 29 | 5 12 19 26 | 4 11 18 25 | 1 8 15 22 29 |
| T | 2 9 16 23 30 | 6 13 20 27 | 5 12 19 26 | 2 9 16 23 30 |
| W | 3 10 17 24 31 | 7 14 21 28 | 6 13 20 27 | 3 10 17 24 |
| T | 4 11 18 25 | 1 8 15 22 29 | 7 14 21 28 | 4 11 18 25 |
| F | 5 12 19 26 | 2 9 16 23 | 1 8 15 22 29 | 5 12 19 26 |
| S | 6 13 20 27 | 3 10 17 24 | 2 9 16 23 30 | 6 13 20 27 |
| S | 7 14 21 28 | 4 11 18 25 | 3 10 17 24 31 | 7 14 21 28 |

|   | May | June | July | August |
|---|---|---|---|---|
| M | 6 13 20 27 | 3 10 17 24 | 1 8 15 22 29 | 5 12 19 26 |
| T | 7 14 21 28 | 4 11 18 25 | 2 9 16 23 30 | 6 13 20 27 |
| W | 1 8 15 22 29 | 5 12 19 26 | 3 10 17 24 31 | 7 14 21 28 |
| T | 2 9 16 23 30 | 6 13 20 27 | 4 11 18 25 | 1 8 15 22 29 |
| F | 3 10 17 24 31 | 7 14 21 28 | 5 12 19 26 | 2 9 16 23 30 |
| S | 4 11 18 25 | 1 8 15 22 29 | 6 13 20 27 | 3 10 17 24 31 |
| S | 5 12 19 26 | 2 9 16 23 30 | 7 14 21 28 | 4 11 18 25 |

|   | September | October | November | December |
|---|---|---|---|---|
| M | 2 9 16 23 30 | 7 14 21 28 | 4 11 18 25 | 2 9 16 23 30 |
| T | 3 10 17 24 | 1 8 15 22 29 | 5 12 19 26 | 3 10 17 24 31 |
| W | 4 11 18 25 | 2 9 16 23 30 | 6 13 20 27 | 4 11 18 25 |
| T | 5 12 19 26 | 3 10 17 24 31 | 7 14 21 28 | 5 12 19 26 |
| F | 6 13 20 27 | 4 11 18 25 | 1 8 15 22 29 | 6 13 20 27 |
| S | 7 14 21 28 | 5 12 19 26 | 2 9 16 23 30 | 7 14 21 28 |
| S | 1 8 15 22 29 | 6 13 20 27 | 3 10 17 24 | 1 8 15 22 29 |

## 10

|   | January | February | March | April |
|---|---|---|---|---|
| M | 7 14 21 28 | 4 11 18 25 | 3 10 17 24 31 | 7 14 21 28 |
| T | 1 8 15 22 29 | 5 12 19 26 | 4 11 18 25 | 1 8 15 22 29 |
| W | 2 9 16 23 30 | 6 13 20 27 | 5 12 19 26 | 2 9 16 23 30 |
| T | 3 10 17 24 31 | 7 14 21 28 | 6 13 20 27 | 3 10 17 24 |
| F | 4 11 18 25 | 1 8 15 22 29 | 7 14 21 28 | 4 11 18 25 |
| S | 5 12 19 26 | 2 9 16 23 | 1 8 15 22 29 | 5 12 19 26 |
| S | 6 13 20 27 | 3 10 17 24 | 2 9 16 23 30 | 6 13 20 27 |

|   | May | June | July | August |
|---|---|---|---|---|
| M | 5 12 19 26 | 2 9 16 23 30 | 7 14 21 28 | 4 11 18 25 |
| T | 6 13 20 27 | 3 10 17 24 | 1 8 15 22 29 | 5 12 19 26 |
| W | 7 14 21 28 | 4 11 18 25 | 2 9 16 23 30 | 6 13 20 27 |
| T | 1 8 15 22 29 | 5 12 19 26 | 3 10 17 24 31 | 7 14 21 28 |
| F | 2 9 16 23 30 | 6 13 20 27 | 4 11 18 25 | 1 8 15 22 29 |
| S | 3 10 17 24 31 | 7 14 21 28 | 5 12 19 26 | 2 9 16 23 30 |
| S | 4 11 18 25 | 1 8 15 22 29 | 6 13 20 27 | 3 10 17 24 31 |

|   | September | October | November | December |
|---|---|---|---|---|
| M | 1 8 15 22 29 | 6 13 20 27 | 3 10 17 24 | 1 8 15 22 29 |
| T | 2 9 16 23 30 | 7 14 21 28 | 4 11 18 25 | 2 9 16 23 30 |
| W | 3 10 17 24 | 1 8 15 22 29 | 5 12 19 26 | 3 10 17 24 31 |
| T | 4 11 18 25 | 2 9 16 23 30 | 6 13 20 27 | 4 11 18 25 |
| F | 5 12 19 26 | 3 10 17 24 31 | 7 14 21 28 | 5 12 19 26 |
| S | 6 13 20 27 | 4 11 18 25 | 1 8 15 22 29 | 6 13 20 27 |
| S | 7 14 21 28 | 5 12 19 26 | 2 9 16 23 30 | 7 14 21 28 |

## 11

|   | January | February | March | April |
|---|---|---|---|---|
| M | 6 13 20 27 | 3 10 17 24 | 2 9 16 23 30 | 6 13 20 27 |
| T | 7 14 21 28 | 4 11 18 25 | 3 10 17 24 31 | 7 14 21 28 |
| W | 1 8 15 22 29 | 5 12 19 26 | 4 11 18 25 | 1 8 15 22 29 |
| T | 2 9 16 23 30 | 6 13 20 27 | 5 12 19 26 | 2 9 16 23 30 |
| F | 3 10 17 24 31 | 7 14 21 28 | 6 13 20 27 | 3 10 17 24 |
| S | 4 11 18 25 | 1 8 15 22 29 | 7 14 21 28 | 4 11 18 25 |
| S | 5 12 19 26 | 2 9 16 23 | 1 8 15 22 29 | 5 12 19 26 |

|   | May | June | July | August |
|---|---|---|---|---|
| M | 4 11 18 25 | 1 8 15 22 29 | 6 13 20 27 | 3 10 17 24 31 |
| T | 5 12 19 26 | 2 9 16 23 30 | 7 14 21 28 | 4 11 18 25 |
| W | 6 13 20 27 | 3 10 17 24 | 1 8 15 22 29 | 5 12 19 26 |
| T | 7 14 21 28 | 4 11 18 25 | 2 9 16 23 30 | 6 13 20 27 |
| F | 1 8 15 22 29 | 5 12 19 26 | 3 10 17 24 31 | 7 14 21 28 |
| S | 2 9 16 23 30 | 6 13 20 27 | 4 11 18 25 | 1 8 15 22 29 |
| S | 3 10 17 24 31 | 7 14 21 28 | 5 12 19 26 | 2 9 16 23 30 |

|   | September | October | November | December |
|---|---|---|---|---|
| M | 7 14 21 28 | 5 12 19 26 | 2 9 16 23 30 | 7 14 21 28 |
| T | 1 8 15 22 29 | 6 13 20 27 | 3 10 17 24 | 1 8 15 22 29 |
| W | 2 9 16 23 30 | 7 14 21 28 | 4 11 18 25 | 2 9 16 23 30 |
| T | 3 10 17 24 | 1 8 15 22 29 | 5 12 19 26 | 3 10 17 24 31 |
| F | 4 11 18 25 | 2 9 16 23 30 | 6 13 20 27 | 4 11 18 25 |
| S | 5 12 19 26 | 3 10 17 24 31 | 7 14 21 28 | 5 12 19 26 |
| S | 6 13 20 27 | 4 11 18 25 | 1 8 15 22 29 | 6 13 20 27 |

## 12

|   | January | February | March | April |
|---|---|---|---|---|
| M | 5 12 19 26 | 2 9 16 23 | 1 8 15 22 29 | 5 12 19 26 |
| T | 6 13 20 27 | 3 10 17 24 | 2 9 16 23 30 | 6 13 20 27 |
| W | 7 14 21 28 | 4 11 18 25 | 3 10 17 24 31 | 7 14 21 28 |
| T | 1 8 15 22 29 | 5 12 19 26 | 4 11 18 25 | 1 8 15 22 29 |
| F | 2 9 16 23 30 | 6 13 20 27 | 5 12 19 26 | 2 9 16 23 30 |
| S | 3 10 17 24 31 | 7 14 21 28 | 6 13 20 27 | 3 10 17 24 |
| S | 4 11 18 25 | 1 8 15 22 29 | 7 14 21 28 | 4 11 18 25 |

|   | May | June | July | August |
|---|---|---|---|---|
| M | 3 10 17 24 31 | 7 14 21 28 | 5 12 19 26 | 2 9 16 23 30 |
| T | 4 11 18 25 | 1 8 15 22 29 | 6 13 20 27 | 3 10 17 24 31 |
| W | 5 12 19 26 | 2 9 16 23 30 | 7 14 21 28 | 4 11 18 25 |
| T | 6 13 20 27 | 3 10 17 24 | 1 8 15 22 29 | 5 12 19 26 |
| F | 7 14 21 28 | 4 11 18 25 | 2 9 16 23 30 | 6 13 20 27 |
| S | 1 8 15 22 29 | 5 12 19 26 | 3 10 17 24 31 | 7 14 21 28 |
| S | 2 9 16 23 30 | 6 13 20 27 | 4 11 18 25 | 1 8 15 22 29 |

|   | September | October | November | December |
|---|---|---|---|---|
| M | 6 13 20 27 | 4 11 18 25 | 1 8 15 22 29 | 6 13 20 27 |
| T | 7 14 21 28 | 5 12 19 26 | 2 9 16 23 30 | 7 14 21 28 |
| W | 1 8 15 22 29 | 6 13 20 27 | 3 10 17 24 | 1 8 15 22 29 |
| T | 2 9 16 23 30 | 7 14 21 28 | 4 11 18 25 | 2 9 16 23 30 |
| F | 3 10 17 24 | 1 8 15 22 29 | 5 12 19 26 | 3 10 17 24 31 |
| S | 4 11 18 25 | 2 9 16 23 30 | 6 13 20 27 | 4 11 18 25 |
| S | 5 12 19 26 | 3 10 17 24 31 | 7 14 21 28 | 5 12 19 26 |

## 13

|   | January | February | March | April |
|---|---|---|---|---|
| M | 4 11 18 25 | 1 8 15 22 29 | 7 14 21 28 | 4 11 18 25 |
| T | 5 12 19 26 | 2 9 16 23 | 1 8 15 22 29 | 5 12 19 26 |
| W | 6 13 20 27 | 3 10 17 24 | 2 9 16 23 30 | 6 13 20 27 |
| T | 7 14 21 28 | 4 11 18 25 | 3 10 17 24 31 | 7 14 21 28 |
| F | 1 8 15 22 29 | 5 12 19 26 | 4 11 18 25 | 1 8 15 22 29 |
| S | 2 9 16 23 30 | 6 13 20 27 | 5 12 19 26 | 2 9 16 23 30 |
| S | 3 10 17 24 31 | 7 14 21 28 | 6 13 20 27 | 3 10 17 24 |

|   | May | June | July | August |
|---|---|---|---|---|
| M | 2 9 16 23 30 | 6 13 20 27 | 4 11 18 25 | 1 8 15 22 29 |
| T | 3 10 17 24 31 | 7 14 21 28 | 5 12 19 26 | 2 9 16 23 30 |
| W | 4 11 18 25 | 1 8 15 22 29 | 6 13 20 27 | 3 10 17 24 31 |
| T | 5 12 19 26 | 2 9 16 23 30 | 7 14 21 28 | 4 11 18 25 |
| F | 6 13 20 27 | 3 10 17 24 | 1 8 15 22 29 | 5 12 19 26 |
| S | 7 14 21 28 | 4 11 18 25 | 2 9 16 23 30 | 6 13 20 27 |
| S | 1 8 15 22 29 | 5 12 19 26 | 3 10 17 24 31 | 7 14 21 28 |

|   | September | October | November | December |
|---|---|---|---|---|
| M | 5 12 19 26 | 3 10 17 24 31 | 7 14 21 28 | 5 12 19 26 |
| T | 6 13 20 27 | 4 11 18 25 | 1 8 15 22 29 | 6 13 20 27 |
| W | 7 14 21 28 | 5 12 19 26 | 2 9 16 23 30 | 7 14 21 28 |
| T | 1 8 15 22 29 | 6 13 20 27 | 3 10 17 24 | 1 8 15 22 29 |
| F | 2 9 16 23 30 | 7 14 21 28 | 4 11 18 25 | 2 9 16 23 30 |
| S | 3 10 17 24 | 1 8 15 22 29 | 5 12 19 26 | 3 10 17 24 31 |
| S | 4 11 18 25 | 2 9 16 23 30 | 6 13 20 27 | 4 11 18 25 |

## 14

|   | January | February | March | April |
|---|---|---|---|---|
| M | 3 10 17 24 31 | 7 14 21 28 | 6 13 20 27 | 3 10 17 24 |
| T | 4 11 18 25 | 1 8 15 22 29 | 7 14 21 28 | 4 11 18 25 |
| W | 5 12 19 26 | 2 9 16 23 | 1 8 15 22 29 | 5 12 19 26 |
| T | 6 13 20 27 | 3 10 17 24 | 2 9 16 23 30 | 6 13 20 27 |
| F | 7 14 21 28 | 4 11 18 25 | 3 10 17 24 31 | 7 14 21 28 |
| S | 1 8 15 22 29 | 5 12 19 26 | 4 11 18 25 | 1 8 15 22 29 |
| S | 2 9 16 23 30 | 6 13 20 27 | 5 12 19 26 | 2 9 16 23 30 |

|   | May | June | July | August |
|---|---|---|---|---|
| M | 1 8 15 22 29 | 5 12 19 26 | 3 10 17 24 31 | 7 14 21 28 |
| T | 2 9 16 23 30 | 6 13 20 27 | 4 11 18 25 | 1 8 15 22 29 |
| W | 3 10 17 24 31 | 7 14 21 28 | 5 12 19 26 | 2 9 16 23 30 |
| T | 4 11 18 25 | 1 8 15 22 29 | 6 13 20 27 | 3 10 17 24 31 |
| F | 5 12 19 26 | 2 9 16 23 30 | 7 14 21 28 | 4 11 18 25 |
| S | 6 13 20 27 | 3 10 17 24 | 1 8 15 22 29 | 5 12 19 26 |
| S | 7 14 21 28 | 4 11 18 25 | 2 9 16 23 30 | 6 13 20 27 |

|   | September | October | November | December |
|---|---|---|---|---|
| M | 4 11 18 25 | 2 9 16 23 30 | 6 13 20 27 | 4 11 18 25 |
| T | 5 12 19 26 | 3 10 1 24 31 | 7 14 21 28 | 5 12 19 26 |
| W | 6 13 20 27 | 4 11 18 25 | 1 8 15 22 29 | 6 13 20 27 |
| T | 7 14 21 28 | 5 12 19 26 | 2 9 16 23 30 | 7 14 21 28 |
| F | 1 8 15 22 29 | 6 13 20 27 | 3 10 17 24 | 1 8 15 22 29 |
| S | 2 9 16 23 30 | 7 14 21 28 | 4 11 18 25 | 2 9 16 23 30 |
| S | 3 10 17 24 | 1 8 15 22 29 | 5 12 19 26 | 3 10 17 24 31 |

# M4: Religious festivals

| 2015 | | |
|---|---|---|
| ☬ | Birthday of Guru Gobind Singh | 5 January |
| ✝ | Ash Wednesday | 25 February |
| ✡ | Purim | 6 March |
| ॐ | Holi | 6 March |
| ☬ | Hola Mohalla | 6 March |
| ✝ | Good Friday | 3 April |
| ✡ | Passover | 4 April |
| ✝ | Easter Sunday | 5 April |
| ✝ | Easter Monday | 6 April |
| ☬ | Baisakhi Day | 14 April |
| ✝ | Ascension Day | 2 May |
| ✝ | Pentecost | 24 May |
| ✡ | Shavuot | 24 May |
| ☪ | Ramadan begins | 18 June |
| ☪ | Eid al-Fitr | 18 July |
| ✡ | Rosh Hashanah | 4 September |
| ✡ | Yom Kippur | 23 September |
| ☪ | Eid al-Adha | 23 September |
| ✡ | Succot | 28 September |
| ☪ | Hijra – New year | 14 October |
| ॐ | Dasarah | 22 October |
| ☪ | Ashurah | 23 October |
| ॐ | Diwali | 11 November |
| ☬ | Birthday of Guru Nanak | 25 November |
| ✡ | Chanukah | 7 December |
| ☪ | Mawlid-al-Nabi | 23 December |
| ✝ | Christmas Day | 25 December |

| 2016 | | |
|---|---|---|
| ☬ | Birthday of Guru Gobind Singh | 5 January |
| ✝ | Ash Wednesday | 10 February |
| ॐ | Holi | 23 March |
| ✡ | Purim | 24 March |
| ☬ | Hola Mohalla | 24 March |
| ✝ | Good Friday | 25 March |
| ✝ | Easter Sunday | 27 March |
| ✝ | Easter Monday | 28 March |
| ☬ | Baisakhi Day | 14 April |
| ✡ | Passover | 23 April |
| ✝ | Ascension Day | 5 May |
| ✝ | Pentecost | 15 May |
| ☪ | Ramadan begins | 6 June |
| ✡ | Shavuot | 12 June |
| ☪ | Eid al-Fitr | 7 July |
| ☪ | Eid al-Adha | 11 September |
| ☪ | Muharram – New year | 2 October |
| ✡ | Rosh Hashanah | 3 October |
| ☪ | Dasarah | 11 October |
| ☪ | Ashurah | 12 October |
| ✡ | Yom Kippur | 12 October |
| ✡ | Succot | 17 October |
| ॐ | Diwali | 30 October |
| ☬ | Birthday of Guru Nanak | 14 November |
| ☪ | Mawlid-al-Nabi | 12 December |
| ✡ | Chanukah | 25 December |
| ✝ | Christmas Day | 25 December |

| 2017 | | |
|---|---|---|
| ☬ | Birthday of Guru Gobind Singh | 5 January |
| ✝ | Ash Wednesday | 1 March |
| ✡ | Purim | 12 March |
| ॐ | Holi | 12 March |
| ☬ | Hola Mohalla | 13 March |
| ✡ | Passover | 11 April |
| ☬ | Baisakhi Day | 14 April |
| ✝ | Good Friday | 14 April |
| ✝ | Easter Sunday | 16 April |
| ✝ | Easter Monday | 17 April |
| ✝ | Ascension Day | 25 May |
| ☪ | Ramadan begins | 27 May |
| ✡ | Shavuot | 31 May |
| ✝ | Pentecost | 4 June |
| ☪ | Eid al-Fitr | 26 June |
| ☪ | Eid al-Adha | 1 September |
| ✡ | Rosh Hashanah | 21 September |
| ☪ | Hijra – New Year | 21 September |
| ✡ | Yom Kippur | 30 September |
| ॐ | Dasarah | 30 September |
| ☪ | Ashurah | 1 October |
| ✡ | Succot | 5 October |
| ॐ | Diwali | 19 October |
| ☬ | Birthday of Guru Nanak | 4 November |
| ☪ | Mawlid-al-Nabi | 1 December |
| ✡ | Chanukah | 13 December |
| ✝ | Christmas Day | 25 December |

✝ Christian  
ॐ Hindu  
✡ Jewish  
☪ Muslim  
☬ Sikh

Note: all Islamic and Jewish holidays begin at sundown on the preceding day.

# M5: Medical reference intervals and scales

## Haematology—reference intervals

| Measurement | Reference interval |
|---|---|
| White cell count | $4.0–11.0 \times 10^9/l$ |
| Red cell count – Male: | $4.5–6.5 \times 10^{12}/l$ |
| Female: | $3.9–5.6 \times 10^{12}/l$ |
| Haemoglobin – Male: | 13.5–18.0g/dl |
| Female: | 11.5–16.0g/dl |
| Platelet count | $150.0–400.0 \times 10^9/l$ |
| Erthrocyte sedimentation rate (ESR) – Male: | Up to age in years divided by two. |
| Female: | Up to (age in years plus 10) divided by two. |
| Prothrombin time (factors II, VII, X) | 10–14 seconds |
| Activated partial thromboplastic time (VIII, IX, XI, XII) | 35–45 seconds |

## Proposed therapeutic ranges for prothrombin time (British Society for Haematology guidelines on oral anticoagulants, 1984)

| British ratio (NR) | Clinical state |
|---|---|
| 2.0–2.5 | Prophylaxis of deep vein thrombosis including high risk surgery (e.g. for fractured femur). |
| 2.5–3.0 | Treatment of deep vein thrombosis, pulmonary embolism, transient ischaemic attacks. |
| 3.0–4.5 | Recurrent deep vein thrombosis an pulmonary embolism, arterial disease including myocardial infarction, arterial grafts, cardiac prosthetic valves and grafts. |

## Cerebrospinal fluid—reference intervals

| | |
|---|---|
| Opening pressure (mmCSF) | Infants: < 80; children: < 90; adults: < 210 |

| Substance | Reference interval |
|---|---|
| Glucose | 3.3–4.4 mmol/l or ≥ 2/3 of plasma glucose |
| Chloride | 122–128 mmol/l |
| Lactate | < 2.8 mmol/l |

## Biochemistry—reference intervals

| Substance | Specimen | Reference Interval |
|---|---|---|
| Albumin | P | *35–50 g/l |
| a-amylase | P | 0–180 Somogyi U/dl |
| Bicarbonate | P | *24–30 mmol/l |
| C reactive protein (CRP) | P | < 6 mg/l |
| Calcium (ionised) | P | 1.0–1.25 mmol/l |
| Calcium (total) | P | *2.12–2.65 mmol/l |
| Chloride | P | 98–107 mmol/l |
| Cholesterol | P | 3.3–6.2 mmol/l |
| Creatinine | P | *58–110 mmol/l |
| Glucose (fasting) | P | 3.5–5.5 mmol/l |
| Glycosylated haemoglobin | B | 5–8% |
| Phosphate | P | 0.8–1.45 mmol/l |
| Potassium | P | 3.6–5.0 mmol/l |
| Protein (total) | P | 60–80 g/l |
| Sodium | P | *137–145 mmol/l |
| Urea | P | *2.5–7.5 mmol/l |

**Key:** P = plasma; B = whole blood

* Reference intervals for these substances differ in pregnancy. Reference intervals in pregnancy are not reproduced here.

### Arterial blood gases—reference intervals

| pH: | 7.35–7.45 |
|---|---|
| $PaO_2$: | >10.6 kPa |
| $PaCO_2$: | 4.7–6.0 kPa |
| Base excess | ±2 mmol/l |
| NB: 7.6 mmHg = 1 kPa  (atmospheric pressure = 100 kPa) ||

### Apgar scoring chart

A baby's condition is assessed at one and five minutes after birth by means of the Apgar score. This system observes five signs. A score of nought, one or two is awarded for each sign.

| Sign | 0 | 1 | 2 |
|---|---|---|---|
| Heart rate | absent | slow (below 100) | over 100 |
| Respiratory effect | absent | weak cry, hypoventilation | good cry |
| Muscle tone | limp | some flexion of extremities | well flexed |
| Reflex irritability | no response | some motion | cry |
| Colour | blue, pale | body pink, extremities blue | completely pink |

NB: An Apgar score of 10 represents optimal condition. A score of three or less indicates a markedly asphyxiated infant.

### Glasgow coma scale

Three types of response are assessed:

| | Score | |
|---|---|---|
| Best motor response | 6 | Obeys commands |
| | 5 | Localises to pain |
| | 4 | Flexion/withdrawal to pain |
| | 3 | Abnormal flexion |
| | 2 | Abnormal extension |
| | 1 | None |
| Best verbal response | 5 | Oriented |
| | 4 | Confused |
| | 3 | Inappropriate words |
| | 2 | Incomprehensible sounds |
| | 1 | None |
| Eye opening | 4 | Spontaneously |
| | 3 | To speech |
| | 2 | To pain |
| | 1 | None |

## M5: Medical reference intervals and scales

The overall score is the sum of the scores in each area, e.g. no response to pain + no verbal response + no eye opening = three.

In severe injury the score is eight or under.
In moderate injury the score is nine–12.
In minor injury the score is 13–15.

### PULHHEEMS rating

This is a system of physical and mental grading used by all three branches of the British Armed Forces. It is taken from the joint Services publication JSP 346 which is issued to all Service and Civilian medical practitioners required to examine applicants for entry to the Armed Forces. It is carried out on new recruits, and repeated at five-yearly intervals after the age of 30. After the age of 50, it is performed at two-yearly intervals.

PULHHEEMS is an abbreviation for the factors to be tested. These include:

| P | Physique |
|---|---|
| U | Upper limbs |
| L | Locomotion—i.e. lower limbs and back |
| H | Hearing in the left ear |
| H | Hearing in the right ear |
| E | Visual acuity—left eye |
| E | Visual acuity—right eye |
| M | Mental function |
| S | Stability (emotional) |

The maximum score is eight (excellent) and the minimum one (unfit for service). In the form this appears in a table as follows (Lord Nelson taken as an example):

| P | U | L | H | H | E | E | M | S |
|---|---|---|---|---|---|---|---|---|
| 8 | 4 | 8 | 8 | 8 | 8 | 1 | 8 | 5 |

## FDI World Dental Federation notation

FDI Two-Digit Notation

### Permanent Teeth

| upper right | | | | | | | | upper left | | | | | | |
|---|---|---|---|---|---|---|---|---|---|---|---|---|---|---|
| 18 | 17 | 16 | 15 | 14 | 13 | 12 | 11 | 21 | 22 | 23 | 24 | 25 | 26 | 27 | 28 |
| 48 | 47 | 46 | 45 | 44 | 43 | 43 | 41 | 31 | 32 | 33 | 34 | 35 | 36 | 37 | 38 |
| lower right | | | | | | | | lower left | | | | | | |

### Deciduous teeth (baby teeth)

| upper right | | | | | | upper left | | | | |
|---|---|---|---|---|---|---|---|---|---|
| | 55 | 54 | 53 | 52 | 51 | 61 | 62 | 63 | 64 | 65 |
| | 85 | 84 | 83 | 82 | 81 | 71 | 72 | 73 | 74 | 75 |
| lower right | | | | | | lower left | | | | |

Codes, names and usual number of roots

| Codes | | Names | Usual number of roots |
|---|---|---|---|
| 11 | 21 | maxillary central incisor | 1 |
| 41 | 31 | mandibular central incisor | 1 |
| 12 | 22 | maxillary lateral incisor | 1 |
| 42 | 32 | mandibular lateral incisor | 1 |
| 13 | 23 | maxillary canine | 1 |
| 43 | 33 | mandibular canine | 1 |
| 14 | 24 | maxillary first premolar | 2 |
| 44 | 34 | mandibular first premolar | 1 |
| 15 | 25 | maxillary second premolar | 1 |
| 45 | 35 | mandibular second premolar | 1 |
| 16 | 26 | maxillary first molar | 3 |
| 46 | 36 | mandibular first molar | 2 |
| 17 | 27 | maxillary second molar | 3 |
| 47 | 37 | mandibular second molar | 2 |
| 18 | 28 | maxillary third premolar | 3 |
| 48 | 38 | mandibular third premolar | 2 |

How the codes are constructed

Syntax: <quadrant code><tooth code>

**Quadrant codes**

| 1 | upper right |
| 2 | upper left |
| 3 | lower left |
| 4 | lower right |

**Tooth codes**

| 1 | central incisors |
| 2 | lateral incisors |
| 3 | canines |
| 4 | 1st premolars |
| 5 | 2nd premolars |
| 6 | 1st molars |
| 7 | 2nd molars |
| 8 | 3rd molars |

# M6: Websites

**Useful web sites**

| Site | Address |
|---|---|
| Acts of Parliament | http://www.legislation.gov.uk |
| Australasian Legal Information Institute | http://www.austlii.edu.au |
| Bank of England | http://www.bankofengland.co.uk |
| Bar Council | http://www.barcouncil.org.uk |
| British and Irish Legal Information Institute | http://www.bailii.org |
| Child Support Agency | https://www.gov.uk/child-maintenance/overview |
| Social Security and Child Support Commissioners' Decisions | www.osscsc.gov.uk |
| Companies House | https://www.gov.uk/government/organisations/companies-house |
| Court of Justice of the European Union | http://europa.eu/about-eu/institutions-bodies/court-justice/index_en.htm |
| Her Majesty's Court and Tribunals Service | https://www.gov.uk/government/organisations/hm-courts-and-tribunals-service |
| Carers Trust | https://www.carers.org |
| Delia Venables Legal Resources | http://www.venables.co.uk |
| DCA Human Rights site | http://www.dca.gov.uk/peoples-rights/human-rights/index.htm |
| Department of Health | https://www.gov.uk/government/organisations/department-of-health |
| Electronic Share Information (iii) | http://www.iii.co.uk |
| European Court of Human Rights | http://www.echr.coe.int |
| Financial Times | http://www.ft.com |
| Government Actuary's Department | https://www.gov.uk/government/organisations/government-actuarys-department |
| Government Information Service | https://www.gov.uk/ |
| Hague Conference on Private International Law | http://www.hcch.net/index_en.php |
| Hague Convention on Child Abduction | http://www.hcch.net/index_en.php?act=text.display&tid=21 |
| Hansard: House of Commons Debates | http://www.parliament.uk/business/publications/hansard/commons |
| House of Lords Debates | http://www.parliament.uk/business/publications/hansard/lords |
| Land Registry | https://www.gov.uk/government/organisations/land-registry |
| Legislation.gov.uk | http://www.legislation.gov.uk |
| House of Commons | http://www.parliament.uk/business/commons/ |
| House of Lords | http://www.parliament.uk/business/lords/ |
| House Price Indices (Halifax) | http://www.lloydsbankinggroup.com/media/economic-insight/halifax-house-price-index/ |
| Information for Lawyers | http://www.infolaw.co.uk |
| HM Revenue & Customs | https://www.gov.uk/government/organisations/hm-revenue-customs |
| Judicial Committee of the Privy Council | http://www.jcpc.gov.uk |
| Laurie West-Knights' homepage | http://www.lawonline.cc |
| Law Society | http://www.lawsociety.org.uk |
| Legal Services Commission | https://www.gov.uk/government/organisations/legal-services-commission |
| Ministry of Justice | http://www.justice.gov.uk |
| National Savings & Investments | http://www.nsandi.com/ |
| Official Solicitor and Public Trustee Office | https://www.gov.uk/government/organisations/official-solicitor-and-public-trustee |
| ONS–Consumer Price Index and Retail Price Index | http://www.ONS.gov.uk/ons/guide-method/user-guidance/prices/cpi-and-rpi/index.html |

| | |
|---|---|
| RPI (full table) | *http://www.ons.gov.uk/ons/datasets-and-tables/data-selector.html?cdid=CHAW&dataset=mm23&table-id=2.1* |
| Statutory Instruments | *http://www.legislation.gov.uk/uksi* |
| Sweet & Maxwell | *http://www.sweetandmaxwell.co.uk* |
| The Stationery Office | *http://www.tso.co.uk* |
| The Supreme Court | *http://www.supremecourt.uk* |
| The Times | *http://www.thetimes.co.uk* |
| UK Parliament | *http://www.parliament.uk* |
| Zoopla | *http://www.zoopla.co.uk* |

# M7: Useful organisations

## Part 1—Medical

**British Medical Association**

*www.bma.org.uk*

**General Dental Council**

Email: information@gdc-uk.org
*www.gdc-uk.org*

**British Association for Accident and Emergency Medicine—merged with the College of Emergency Medicine**

Email: communications@rceng.ac.uk

**The Royal College of Emergency Medicine**

*www.rcem.ac.uk/*

**General Medical Council**

Email: gmc@gmc-uk.org
*www.gmc-uk.org*

**General Optical Council**

Email: goc@optical.org
*www.optical.org*

**Nursing and Midwifery Council**

Email: UKenquiries@nmc-uk.org
*www.nmc.org.uk/*

### Accidents

Royal Society for the Prevention of Accidents (RoSPA)
Email: help@rospa.co.uk
*www.rospa.com*

### Alcoholism

Medical Council on Alcohol
Email: info@m-c-a.org.uk
*www.m-c-a.org.uk*

### Alzheimer's disease

Email: enquiries@alzheimers.org.uk
*www.alzheimers.org.uk*

### Anaesthetics

Obstetric Anaesthetists' Association
Email: secretariat@oaa-anaes.ac.uk
*www.oaa-anaes.ac.uk/home*

### Asthma

Asthma UK
Email: info@asthma.org.uk
*www.asthma.org.uk*

### Bereavement

Child Bereavement Charity
Email: enquiries@childbereavement.org.uk
*www.childbereavementuk.org*

The Compassionate Friends
(counselling for bereaved parents)
Email: info@tcf.org.uk
*www.tcf.org.uk*

### Biochemistry

Biochemical Society
Email: genadmin@biochemistry.org
*www.biochemistry.org*

### Blindness

Royal National Institute of the Blind
Email: helpline@rnib.org.uk
*www.rnib.org.uk*

### Brain

Brain Research Trust
Email: info@brt.org.uk
*www.brt.org.uk*

British Association of Brain Injury Case Managers
*www.babicm.org*

Centre for Brain Injury, Rehabilitation and Development (BIRD)
*www.birdcharity.org.uk*

**Brittle bone disease**

Brittle Bone Society
Email: bbs@brittlebone.org
*www.brittlebone.org*

**Cancer**

British Association of Cancer United Patients (BACUP)
Email: info@cancerbacup.org.uk

The Association for Cancer Surgery
Email: admin@baso.org.uk
*www.baso.org.uk*

Macmillan Cancer Relief
Email: cancerline@macmillan.org.uk
*www.macmillan.org.uk*

Cancer Research UK
*www.cancerresearchuk.org*

Marie Curie Cancer Care
Email: supporter.services@mariecurie.org.uk
*www.mariecurie.org.uk*

**Cardiology**

British Cardiovascular Society
Email: enquiries@bcs.com
*www.bcs.com/pages/default.asp*

British Heart Foundation
*www.bhf.org.uk*

Society of Cardiothoracic Surgeons in Great Britain & Ireland
Email: sctsadmin@scts.org
*www.scts.org*

**Childbirth**

The Association for Post-Natal Illness
Email: info@apni.org
*www.apni.org*

The National Childbirth Trust
Email: enquiries@nct.org.uk
*www.nct.org.uk*

Royal College of Midwives
Email: info@rcm.org.uk
*www.rcm.org.uk*

Stillbirth and Neonatal Death Society (SANDS)
Email: helpline@uk-sands.org
*www.uk-sands.org*

**Children**

The National Association for Children with Lower Limb Abnormalities (STEPS)
Email: info@steps-charity.org.uk
*www.steps-charity.org.uk*

Barnardo's
*www.barnardos.org.uk*

Baby Life Support Systems (Bliss)
*www.bliss.org.uk*

Child Accident Prevention Trust
Email: safe@capt.org.uk
*www.capt.org.uk*

Child Poverty Action Group (CPAG)
Email: info@cpag.org.uk
*www.cpag.org.uk*

(see also **Paediatric**)

**Chiropody**

Institute of Chiropodists & Podiatrists
Email: secretary@iocp.org.uk
*www.iocp.org.uk*

Society of Chiropodists & Podiatrists
Email: reception@scpod.org
*www.scpod.org*

**Colostomy**

Colostomy Association
Email: cass@colostomyassociation.org.uk
*www.colostomyassociation.org.uk*

**Counselling**

British Association for Counselling and Psychotherapy
Email: bacp@bacp.co.uk
*www.bacp.co.uk*

**Cystic fibrosis**

Cystic Fibrosis Trust
Email: enquiries@cysticfibrosis.org.uk
*www.cysticfibrosis.org.uk*

**Day surgery**

British Association of Day Surgery
Email: bads@bads.co.uk
*www.daysurgeryuk.net/en/home*

# M7: Useful organisations

**Deafness**

Royal Association for Deaf People
Email: info@royaldeaf.org.uk
www.royaldeaf.org.uk

Royal National Institute for Deaf People
Email: informationline@hearingloss.org.uk
www.actiononhearingloss.org.uk

**Dentists**

British Dental Association
Email: enquiries@bda.org
www.bda.org

**Dermatology**

British Association of Dermatologists
Email: admin@bad.org.uk
www.bad.org.uk

**Diabetes**

Diabetes UK Central Office
Email: info@diabetes.org.uk
www.diabetes.org.uk

**Diagnostics**

Cellmark Diagnostics
Email: info@cellmark.co.uk
www.cellmark.co.uk

**Dietetics**

British Dietetic Association
Email: info@bda.uk.com
www.bda.uk.com

British Nutrition Foundation
www.nutrition.org.uk

**Digestion**

Digestive Disorders CORE Foundation
Email: info@corecharity.org.uk
www.corecharity.org.uk

**Disability**

Disabled Living Foundation
Email: info@dlf.org.uk
www.dlf.org.uk

Royal Association for Disability and Rehabilitation (RADAR)
Email: radar@radar.org.uk
www.disabilityrightsuk.org

**Disfigurement**

Changing Faces
(Charity for Facially Disfigured People)
Email: info@changingfaces.org.uk
www.changingfaces.org.uk/Home

**Down's Syndrome**

Down's Syndrome Association (DSA)
Email: info@downs-syndrome.org.uk
www.downs-syndrome.org.uk

**Drugs**

Committee on Safety of Medicines (for adverse reaction reports)
Email: info@mhra.gsi.gov.uk

**Dyslexia**

Dyslexia Action
Email: info@dyslexiaaction.org.uk
www.dyslexiaaction.org.uk

**Ear, nose and throat**

British Association of Otorhinolaryngologists
ENT UK at The Royal College of Surgeons
Email: entuk@entuk.org
www.entuk.org

(see also **Deafness**)

**Elderly**

British Geriatrics Society
Email: general.information@bgs.org.uk
www.bgs.org.uk

British Association for Service to the Elderly (BASE)
Email: basenul@intonet.co.uk

**Endocrinology**

Society for Endocrinology
Email: info@endocrinology.org
www.endocrinology.org

**Epilepsy**

Epilepsy Action
Email: epilepsy@epilepsy.org.uk
www.epilepsy.org.uk

**Forensic science**

British Academy of Forensic Sciences
Tel: 020 7377 9201

## Gastroenterology

British Society of Gastroenterology
Email: j.rother@bsg.org.uk
*www.bsg.org.uk*

## Glaucoma

International Glaucoma Association
Email: info@iga.org.uk
*www.glaucoma-association.com*

## General information

Health Information (will provide a wide range of health information for both doctors and their patients)
Tel: 0800 665 544

## Haematology

British Society for Haematology
Email: info@b-s-h.org.uk
*www.b-s-h.org.uk*

## Haemophilia

The Haemophilia Society
Email: info@haemophilia.org.uk
*www.haemophilia.org.uk*

## Hand surgery

British Society of Surgery of the Hand
Email: secretariat@bssh.ac.uk
*www.bssh.ac.uk*

## Head injuries

Headway (The Brain Injuries Association)
Email: enquiries@headway.org.uk
*www.headway.org.uk*

## Health visitors

Community Practitioners' and Health Visitors Association (Amicus/CPHVA)—Unite
*www.unitetheunion.org*

## Hysterectomy

Hysterectomy Association
*www.hysterectomy-association.org.uk*

## Injury

(See **Rehabilitation**)

## Kidneys

National Kidney Federation
Email: nfk@kidney.org.uk
*www.kidney.org.uk*

Kidney Research UK (previously The National Kidney Research Fund)
Email: enquiries@kidneyresearchuk.org
*www.kidneyresearchuk.org*

## Lungs

(See **Thoracic**)

## Lupus

Lupus UK
Email: headoffice@lupusuk.org.uk
*www.lupusuk.org.uk*

## Maxillofacial surgery

(See **Oral**)

## M.E.

Myalgic Encephalomyelitis Association
Email: enquiries@meassociation.org.uk
*www.meassociation.org.uk*

## Medicine

Committee on Safety of Medicines
Email: info@mhra.gsi.gov.uk

Medical Society of London
*www.medsoclondon.org*

Medicines Commission
Email: info@mhra.gsi.gov.uk

The Royal Society of Medicine
*www.rsm.ac.uk*

## Meningitis

The National Meningitis Trust
Email: info@meningitis-trust.org.uk
*www.meningitisnow.org*

## Menopause (premature)

The Menopause Amarant Trust
*www.amarantmenopausetrust.org.uk*

## Mental health

National Association for Mental Health (MIND)
Email: contact@mind.org.uk
*www.mind.org.uk*

Royal Society for Mentally Handicapped Children and Adults (MENCAP)
Email: information@mencap.org.uk
*www.mencap.org.uk*

## M7: Useful organisations

**Midwives**

(See **Childbirth**)

**Migraine**

Migraine Trust
Email: info@migrainenetrust.org
www.migrainetrust.org

**Mobility**

Banstead Mobility Centre
www.qef.org.uk

**Motor Neurone Disease**

Motor Neurone Disease Association
Email: enquiries@mndassociation.org
www.mndassociation.org

**Multiple Sclerosis**

MS Society
Email: info@mssociety.org.uk
www.mssociety.org.uk

**Muscular Dystrophy**

Muscular Dystrophy Campaign
Email: info@muscular-dystrophy.org
www.musculardystrophyuk.org

**Narcolepsy**

Narcolepsy UK
Email: nicola.rule@narcolepsy.org.uk
www.narcolepsy.org.uk

**Neurology**

Association of British Neurologists
Email: info@theabn.org
www.theabn.org

**Neurosurgery**

Society of British Neurological Surgeons
Email: admin@sbns.org.uk
www.sbns.org.uk

**Nursing**

Royal College of Nursing of the United Kingdom
Email: membership@rcn.org.uk //
web.enquiries@rcn.org.uk
www.rcn.org.uk

BNA Care Assessment Services
Email: info@bna.co.uk
www.bna.co.uk/index.php?option=com_content&view=frontpage&Itemid=184

Carers Trust
Email: info@carers.org
www.carers.org

**Occupational medicine**

Society of Occupational Medicine
Email: admin@som.org.uk
www.som.org.uk

**Occupational therapy**

British Association of Occupational Therapists/
College of Occupational Therapists
Email: reception@cot.co.uk
www.cot.co.uk

**Oncology**

(See **Cancer**)

**Oral**

British Association of Oral & Maxillofacial Surgeons
Email: office@baoms.org.uk
www.baoms.org.uk

**Orthopaedic**

British Orthopaedic Association
Email: secretary@boa.ac.uk
www.boa.ac.uk

**Osteoporosis**

National Osteoporosis Society
Email: info@nos.org.uk
www.nos.org.uk

**Pain**

The British Pain Society
Email: info@britishpainsociety.org
www.britishpainsociety.org

National Back Pain Association
Email: info@backcare.org.uk
www.backcare.org.uk

**Parkinson's disease**

Parkinson's UK
Email: hello@parkinsons.org.uk
www.parkinsons.org.uk

**Pathology**

Pathological Society of Great Britain & Ireland
Email: admin@pathsoc.org.uk
www.pathsoc.org

Royal College of Pathologists
Email: info@rcpath.org
www.rcpath.org

## Patients

Patients Association
Email: mailbox@patients-association.com
ww.patients-association.org.uk

## Physiotherapy

Chartered Society of Physiotherapy
Email: csp@csphysio.org.uk
www.csp.org.uk

## Plastic surgery

British Association of Plastic Surgeons
Email: info@baaps.org.uk
www.baaps.org.uk

## Polio

British Polio Fellowship
Email: info@britishpolio.org
www.britishpolio.org.uk

## Post-natal illness

(See **Childbirth**)

## Psoriasis

Psoriasis Association
Email: mail@psoriasis-association.org.uk
www.psoriasis-association.org.uk

## Psychiatry

Royal College of Psychiatrists
Email: reception@rcpsych.ac.uk
www.rcpsych.ac.uk

## Psychology

British Psychological Society
Email: enquiries@bps.org.uk
www.bps.org.uk

David McGlown
Clinical Psychologist Public Trust Office
Tel: 020 7269 7085

## Psychotherapy

British Association of Psychotherapists
Email: mail@bap-psychotherapy.org
www.britishpsychotherapyfoundation.org.uk

## Radiography and Radiology

Society and College of Radiographers
Email: info@sor.org
www.sor.org

Royal College of Radiologists
Email: enquiries@rcr.ac.uk
www.rcr.ac.uk

## Rehabilitation

British Society of Rehabilitation Medicine
Email: admin@bsrm.co.uk
www.bsrm.co.uk

REMEDI (Rehabilitation and Medical Research Trust for Relief of Disability)
Email: info@remedies.org.uk
www.remedi.org.uk

The Injury Care Clinics Ltd
www.ticcs.co.uk

## Research

Medical Research Society
www.amrc.org.uk

## Rheumatology

British Society for Rheumatology
Email: bsr@rheumatology.org.uk
www.rheumatology.org.uk

## Schizophrenia

Rethink
Email: info@rethink.org
www.rethink.org

## SCOPE

Scope
www.scope.org.uk

## Speech

Royal College of Speech & Language Therapists
Email: info@rcslt.org
www.rcslt.org

Association for all Speech-Impaired Children (AFASIC)
Email: info@afasic.org.uk
www.afasicengland.org.uk

## Spinal injuries

Spinal Injuries Association
Email: sia@spinal.co.uk
www.spinal.co.uk

(See also **Back pain** under **Pain**)

## Stroke

The Stroke Association
Email: info@stroke.org.uk
www.stroke.org.uk

## Torture

Freedom from Torture
www.freedomfromtorture.org

## M7: Useful organisations

### Thoracic

British Thoracic Society
Email: bts@brit-thoracic.org.uk
www.brit-thoracic.org.uk

British Lung Foundation
Email: enquiries@blf.org.uk
www.blf.org.uk

Society of Cardiothoracic Surgeons of Great Britain & Ireland
Email: sctsadmin@scts.org

(See also **Asthma**)

### Transplants

NHS Blood and Transplant Organ Donation and Transplantation Directorate
Email: enquiries@nhsbt.nhs.uk
www.nhsbt.nhs.uk

### Tropical Medicine

Liverpool School of Tropical Medicine
Email: info@lstmed.ac.uk
www.liv.ac.uk/lstm

London School of Hygiene and Tropical Medicine
Email: registry@lshtm.ac.uk
www.lshtm.ac.uk

HPA Malaria Reference Laboratory (for advice on prophylaxis)
Tel: 020 7636 7921
Email: red.team@hPa.org.uk
www.malaria.lshtm.ac.uk/facilities/malaria-reference-laboratory-mrl

### Urology

British Association of Urological Surgeons
Email: admin@baus.org.uk
www.baus.org.uk

## Part 2—Litigation

### Action Against Medical Accidents (AvMA)

Lawyers service: ls@avma.org.uk
Email: advice@avma.org.uk
www.avma.org.uk

### Association of Personal Injury Lawyers (APIL)

Email: mail@apil.org.uk
www.apil.org.uk

### Association of Trial Lawyers of America

Email: help@justice.org
www.justice.org

### Clinical Disputes Forum

Email: margaret.dangoor@blueyonder.co.uk
www.clinical-disputes-forum.org.uk

### Compensation Recovery Unit (CRU)

Email: cru-info-management@dwp.gsi.gov.uk
www.gov.uk/government/collections/cru

### Disability Law Service

Email: aqdvice@dls.org.uk
www.dls.org.uk

### General Council of the Bar (Bar Council)

Email: ContactUs@BarCouncil.org.uk
www.barcouncil.org.uk

### Incorporated Council of Law Reporting for England and Wales

Email: enquiries@iclr.co.uk
www.lawreports.co.uk

### Inquest

Email: inquest@inquest.org.uk
www.inquest.org.uk

### Law Society

www.lawsociety.org.uk

### Legal Services Commission

**Legal Aid Agency**
Email: contactcivil@legalaid.gsi.gov.uk
www.gov.uk/government/organisations/legal-aid-agency

**Ministry of Justice**
Email: general.queries@justice.gsi.gov.uk
www.gov.uk/government/organisations/ministry-of-justice

Legal Services Commission London/South Exchange Tower (Area No. 1)
Tel: 020 7718 8466
Email: london@legalservices.gov.uk

# M7: Useful organisations

Legal Services Commission (Area No. 2)
Tel: 01273 878 800

Legal Services Commission (Area No. 3)
Tel: 020 7715 3991

Legal Services Commission Wales and the West Group Area Offices (Area No. 4)
Tel: 0117 302 3000

Legal Services Commission (Area No. 5)
Tel: 0300 200 2020
Email: Cardiff@legalservices.gsi.co.uk

Legal Services Commission Midlands Group Area Offices (Area No. 6)
Tel: 0121 232 5500
Email: Birmingham@legalservices.gsi.co.uk

Legal Services Commission (Area No. 7)
Tel: 0300 200 2020
Email: manchester@legalservices.gsi.co.uk

Legal Services Commission (Area No. 9)
Tel: 0113 390 7300
Email: leeds@legalservices.gsi.co.uk

Legal Services Commission (Area No. 10)
Tel: 0115 908 4200

Legal Services Commission (Area No. 11)
Tel: 0300 200 2020
Email: legal-enquiries@legalservices.gsi.co.uk

Legal Services Commission North Western Group Area Offices (Area No. 12)
Tel: 01244 404 500
Email: Chester@legalservices.gsi.gov.uk

Legal Services Commission (Area No. 15)
Tel: 0151 242 5200
Email: liverpool@legalservices.gsi.gov.uk

**Medical Defence Union**
Email: advisory@themdu.com
www.themdu.com

**The Medical Protection Society Ltd**
Email: info@medicalprotection.org
www.medicalprotection.org/uk/home

**Medico-Legal Society**
Email: caron.heyes@bllaw.co.uk or
www.medico-legalsociety.org.uk

**Motor Insurers Bureau**
Linford Wood House
Email: enquiries@mib.org.uk
www.mib.org.uk

**National Association of Guardians ad Litem and Reporting Officers (NAGALRO)**
Email: nagalro@globalnet.co.uk
www.nagalro.com

**Official Solicitor to the Supreme Court**
Email: enquiries@offsol.gsi.gov.uk
www.gov.uk/government/organisations/official-solicitor-and-public-trustee

**The Patients' Association**
Email: mailbox@patients-association.com
www.patients-association.org.uk

**Personal Injury Bar Association (PIBA)**
Email: admin@piba.org.uk
www.piba.org.uk

**Professional Negligence Bar Association (PNBA)**
Email: woodbridge@crownofficechambers.com
www.pnba.co.uk

**Witnesses Against Abuse by Health and Care Workers**

**Smith Bernal Reporting Ltd**
Email: London@merrillcorp.com
www.mls.merrillcorp.com

## Part 3—Government

**Commission for Local Administration in England**
(Local Government Ombudsman)
Email: training@lgo.org.uk
www.lgo.org.uk

**Department of Health**
www.gov.uk/government/organisations/department-of-health

**Department of Work and Pensions**
Email: ministers@dwp.gsi.gov.uk
www.dwp.gov.uk

**Department of Health Social Care Group**
Tel: 020 7210 4850

**Health & Safety Executive**
www.hse.gov.uk

## M7: Useful organisations

**Health and Safety Executive—Health Policy Division**

www.hse.gov.uk

**Home Office**

Direct communications unit
www.gov.uk/government/organisations/home-office

**HM Inspector of Anatomy**

Department of Health
www.gov.uk/government/organisations/department-of-health

**Lord Chancellor's Department**

Tel: 020 7210 8614

**Care Quality Commission**

Email: enquiries@cqc.org.uk
www.cqc.org.uk

**Mental Welfare Commission for Scotland**

Email: enquiries@mwcscot.org.uk
www.mwcscot.org.uk

**National Blood Authority**

NHS Blood and Transplant
Email: enquiries@nhsbt.nhs.uk
www.nhsbt.nhs.uk

**Scottish Office Home and Health Department**

Email: ceu@scotland.gsi.gov.uk
www.gov.scot/Home
London Office:
Email: scottish.secretary@scotland.gsi.gov.uk
www.gov.uk/government/organisations/scotland-office

**Scottish National Blood Transfusion Service**

www.scotblood.co.uk

### Part 4—Courts and Tribunals

**The Supreme Court**

Email: Enquiries@supremecourt.gsi.gov.uk
www.supremecourt.gov.uk

**Court of Appeal**

www.justice.gov.uk/courts/rcj-rolls-building/court-of-appeal/civil-division

**High Court of Justice**

www.justice.gov.uk

**Court of Protection**

Email: courtofprotectionenquiries@hmcts.gsi.gov.uk
www.justice.gov.uk/courts/rcj-rolls-building/court-of-protection

**Criminal Injuries Compensation Authority (CICA)**

Email: enquiries@criminal-injuries.co.uk
www.criminal-injuries.co.uk

### Part 5—Other

**Child Poverty Action Group**

Email: info@cpag.org.uk

**Fostering Network**

Email: info@fostering.net
www.fostering.net

**Leonard Cheshire Disability**

Email: info@LCDisability.org
www.leonardcheshire.org

**The Bank of England**

Email: enquiries@bankofengland.co.uk
www.bankofengland.co.uk/Pages/home.aspx